NETWORK-CENTRIC COLLABORATION AND SUPPORTING FRAMEWORKS

IFIP – The International Federation for Information Processing

IFIP was founded in 1960 under the auspices of UNESCO, following the First World Computer Congress held in Paris the previous year. An umbrella organization for societies working in information processing, IFIP's aim is two-fold: to support information processing within its member countries and to encourage technology transfer to developing nations. As its mission statement clearly states,

> *IFIP's mission is to be the leading, truly international, apolitical organization which encourages and assists in the development, exploitation and application of information technology for the benefit of all people.*

IFIP is a non-profitmaking organization, run almost solely by 2500 volunteers. It operates through a number of technical committees, which organize events and publications. IFIP's events range from an international congress to local seminars, but the most important are:

• The IFIP World Computer Congress, held every second year;
• Open conferences;
• Working conferences.

The flagship event is the IFIP World Computer Congress, at which both invited and contributed papers are presented. Contributed papers are rigorously refereed and the rejection rate is high.

As with the Congress, participation in the open conferences is open to all and papers may be invited or submitted. Again, submitted papers are stringently refereed.

The working conferences are structured differently. They are usually run by a working group and attendance is small and by invitation only. Their purpose is to create an atmosphere conducive to innovation and development. Refereeing is less rigorous and papers are subjected to extensive group discussion.

Publications arising from IFIP events vary. The papers presented at the IFIP World Computer Congress and at open conferences are published as conference proceedings, while the results of the working conferences are often published as collections of selected and edited papers.

Any national society whose primary activity is in information may apply to become a full member of IFIP, although full membership is restricted to one society per country. Full members are entitled to vote at the annual General Assembly, National societies preferring a less committed involvement may apply for associate or corresponding membership. Associate members enjoy the same benefits as full members, but without voting rights. Corresponding members are not represented in IFIP bodies. Affiliated membership is open to non-national societies, and individual and honorary membership schemes are also offered.

NETWORK-CENTRIC COLLABORATION AND SUPPORTING FRAMEWORKS

IFIP TC5 WG 5.5 Seventh IFIP Working Conference on Virtual Enterprises, 25-27 September 2006, Helsinki, Finland

Edited by

Luis M. Camarinha-Matos
New University of Lisbon, Portugal

Hamideh Afsarmanesh
University of Amsterdam, The Netherlands

Martin Ollus
VTT Industrial Systems, Finland

 Springer

Network-Centric Collaboration and Supporting Frameworks

Edited by L. M. Camarinha-Matos, H. Afsarmanesh and M. Ollus

p. cm. (IFIP International Federation for Information Processing, a Springer Series in Computer Science)

ISSN: 1571-5736 / 1861-2288 (Internet)

eISBN: 10: 0-387-38269-0

ISBN: 13: 978-1-4419-4257-9

eISBN: 13: 978-0-387-38269-2

Printed on acid-free paper

9 8 7 6 5 4 3 2 1
springer.com

TABLE OF CONTENTS

x

TECHNICAL SPONSORS:

IFIP WG 5.5 COVE
Co-Operation infrastructure for Virtual Enterprises and
electronic business

ECOLEAD
European Collaborative Networked Organizations
Leadership Initiative
IST IP 506958 project

Society of Collaborative Networks

ORGANIZATIONAL CO-SPONSORS

New University of Lisbon

PRO-VE'06 – 7th IFIP Working Conference on VIRTUAL ENTERPRISES
Helsinki, Finland, 25-27 September 2006

Program Chair - Prof. Luis M. Camarinha-Matos (PT)

Program track co-chairs:
- CNO coordination and management - Dr. Alexandra Klen (BR)
- ICT Infrastructures & interoperability - Rama Akkiraju (US), Prof. Ricardo Rabelo (BR)
- Modeling, ontologies and theoretical issues - Prof. Tomasz Janowski (MO)
- Value systems and business perspectives -Prof. Dimitris Assimakopoulos (FR)
- Virtual Communities and Social Networks – Hans Schaffers (NL)
- Virtual Organizations Breeding Environments - Dr. Hamideh Afsarmanesh (NL)

Organization Chair - Chief research scientist Martin Ollus (FI)

Associated events chairs:
- Panel organization - Sergio Gusmeroli (IT)
- Session on SME networks case studies - Iris Karvonen (FI)
- Birds of a feather session - Wico Mulder (NL), Sobah Abbas Petersen (NO)

REFEREES FROM THE PROGRAMME COMMITTEE

Chima Adiele (CA)
Hamideh Afsarmanesh (NL)
Rama Akkiraju (US)
Dimitris Assimakopoulos (FR)
Américo Azevedo (PT)
Eoin Banahan (UK)
José Barata (PT)
Peter Bernus (AU)
Peter Bertok (AU)
Kirsimarja Blomqvist (FI)
Luis M. Camarinha-Matos (PT)
Wojciech Cellary (PL)
Heiko Dirlenbach (DE)
Eero Eloranta (FI)
Jens Eschenbaecher (DE)
Elsa Estevez (AR)
João Pinto Ferreira (PT)
Joaquim Filipe (PT)
Myrna Flores (CH)
Cesar Garita (CR)
Ted Goranson (US)
Fernando Guerrero (ES)
Angappa Gunasekaran (US)
Sergio Gusmeroli (IT)

Jairo Gutierrez (NZ)
Tarek Hassan (UK)
Raimo Hyötyläinen (FI)
Tomasz Janowski (MO)
Toshiya Kaihara (JP)
Alexandra Klen (BR)
Bernhard Koelmel (DE)
Adamantios Koumpis (GR)
George Kovacs (HU)
Jarmo Laitinen (FI)
Nada Lavrac (SI)
Celson Lima (FR)
Vladimir Marik (CZ)
José M. Mendonça (PT)
Karsten Menzel (DE)
Arturo Molina (MX)
Ugo Negretto (DE)
Laszlo Nemes (AU)
José M. Neves (PT)
Shimon Y Nof (US)
Ovidiu Noran (AU)
Adegboyega Ojo (MO)
Eugénio Oliveira (PT)
Gus Olling (US)
Martin Ollus (FI)
Angel Ortiz (ES)

Luis Osório (PT)
Kulwant Pawar (UK)
Willy Picard (PL)
Sofia Pinto (PT)
Michel Pouly (CH)
Kenneth Preiss (IL)
Goran Putnik (PT)
Ricardo Rabelo (BR)
Heri Ramampiaro (US)
Jukka Ranta (FI)
Bob Roberts (UK)
Rainer Ruggaber (DE)
Hans Schaffers (NL)
Weiming Shen (CA)
Waleed W. Smari (US)
Riitta Smeds (FI)
António L. Soares (PT)
Jorge P. Sousa (PT)
Volker Stich (DE)
Klaus-Dieter Thoben (DE)
Peter Weiß (DE)

FOREWORD

Collaborative networks in action

Collaborative Networks (CN) is a fast developing area, as shown by the already large number of diverse real-world implemented cases and the dynamism of its related involved research community. Benefiting from contributions of multiple areas, namely computer science, computer engineering, communications and networking, management, economy, social sciences, law and ethics, etc., the area of Collaborative Networks is being consolidated as a **new scientific discipline** of its own.. On one hand significant steps towards a stronger **theoretical foundation** for this new discipline are being taken. On the other hand, a growing number of **application cases** are being developed and applied in industry and services. A good collection of active and emerging VO Breeding Environments and Professional Virtual Communities can be found in various regions of the world. This phenomenon is particularly evident in Europe where considerable investments in collaborative networks have been made in many of its regions.

Based on the experiences and lessons learned in many research projects and pilot cases developed during the last decade, a new emphasis is now being put on the development of holistic frameworks, combining business models, conceptual models, governance principles and methods, as well as supporting infrastructures and services. In fact, reaching the phase in which the computer and networking technologies provide a good starting basis for the establishment of collaborative platforms, the emphasis is now turning to the understanding of the collaboration promotion mechanisms and CN governance principles. Therefore, issues such as the value systems, trust, performance, and benefits distribution are gaining more importance.. Encompassing all these developments, the efforts to develop reference models for collaborative networks represent a major challenge in order to provide the foundation for further developments of the CN.

PRO-VE represents a good synthesis of the work in this area, and plays an active role in the promotion of these activities. Being recognized as the most focused scientific and technical conference on Collaborative Networks, PRO-VE continues to offer the opportunity for presentation and discussion of both the latest research developments as well as the practical application case studies. Following the vision of **IFIP** and **SOCOLNET**, the PRO-VE conference offers a forum for collaboration and knowledge exchange among experts from different regions of the world.

This book includes a number of selected papers from the PRO-VE'06 conference, representing a comprehensive overview of recent advances in various domains and lines *of research and development on collaborative networks. Of particular relevance are the topics of modeling frameworks, value systems and competency management, trust building and risk, performance indicators and network management, collaboration platforms and tools, VO creation and negotiation, and applications in industry and services.*

The PRO-VE'06 held in Helsinki, Finland, is the 7th event in a series of successful conferences including PRO-VE'99 (held in Porto, Portugal), PRO-VE 2000 (held in Florianopolis, Brazil), PRO-VE'02 (held in Sesimbra, Portugal), PRO-VE'03 (held in Lugano, Switzerland), PRO-VE'04 (held in Toulouse, France), and PRO-VE'05 (held in Valencia, Spain).

We would like to thank all the authors both from academia/research and industry for their contributions. We appreciate the dedication of the PRO-VE program committee members and other reviewers who helped both with the selection of articles and contributed with valuable comments to improve their quality.. As a result of this cooperative and highly distributed work we hope that the PRO-VE'06 book constitutes a valuable tool for all those interested in the emerging applications, research advances, and challenges of the collaborative networks.

The editors,

Luís M. Camarinha-Matos
Faculty of Science and Technology
New University of Lisbon, Portugal

Hamideh Afsarmanesh
Faculty of Science
University of Amsterdam, The Netherlands

Martin Ollus
VTT Industrial Systems, Finland

PART 1

MODELING FRAMEWORKS

A MODELING FRAMEWORK FOR COLLABORATIVE NETWORKED ORGANIZATIONS

Luis M. Camarinha-Matos [1]; Hamideh Afsarmanesh [2]
[1] *New University of Lisbon, PORTUGAL, cam@uninova.pt*
[2] *University of Amsterdam, THE NETHERLANDS, hamideh@science.uva.nl*

Collaborative networked organizations are complex entities whose proper understanding, design, implementation, and management require the integration of different modeling perspectives. A comprehensive modeling framework is therefore proposed as a first step towards the elaboration of a reference model for collaborative networks. Modeling tools and theories developed in other disciplines are also analyzed in terms of their potential applicability in this domain.

1. INTRODUCTION

Modeling is one of the key activities in understanding, designing, implementing, and operating systems. Modeling is at the very heart of any scientific and engineering activity. When a team of researchers or system designers develop a new system, the output of the design phase is a model or set of models of the system to be implemented. A model, as an abstract representation of the intended system, will then be used to guide the implementation. Due to a number of practical contingencies, the implemented system might show some (minor) differences regarding the original model (usually the case). Furthermore, a model is also very useful in order to supervise (manage) the operation of the developed system during its life cycle. Complementarily, a model can also be used to predict the behavior of the system being developed or managed.

As in any other scientific discipline or engineering branch, collaborative networked organizations (CNOs) require the development of models, not only as a help to better understand the area, but also as the basis for the development of methods and tools for better decision-making. In fact proper decision-making in all phases of the CNO life cycle needs to be based on well argued and verified models and methodologies. These models and methodologies constitute the basis for the ICT-based support for business and organizational development and operation, as well as the base for education, training, and effective operation of CNOs.

Please use the following format when citing this chapter:

Camarinha-Matos, L. M., Afsarmanesh, H., 2006, in IFIP International Federation for Information Processing, Volume 224, Network-Centric Collaboration and Supporting Fireworks, eds. Camarinha-Matos, L., Afsarmanesh, H., Ollus, M., (Boston: Springer), pp. 3–14.

CNOs are complex systems, emerging in many forms in different application domains, and consist of many facets whose proper understanding requires the contribution from multiple disciplines. However, an analysis of past modeling efforts indicates that practitioners and researchers are not fully aware of a comprehensive spectrum of suitable modeling processes, tools, and methodologies. For instance, very often modeling is restricted to a "processes view" (e.g. SCOR type of models for traditional supply chains). Or they stick with one approach such as using UML even though it might not the most appropriate approach for all or a part of the modeling effort.

This situation is however improving and lately some theories and paradigms defined elsewhere have been suggested by several research groups as promising tools to help understand and characterize emerging collaborative organizational forms [1], [2], [3]. Nevertheless, it is unlikely that any of these theories and modeling methods will cover all needs of CNO; they can be used as a starting point but extensions or adaptations are needed. There is no single formal modeling tool / approach that adequately covers all perspectives – no "universal language" for all problems. And yet existing knowledge on diverse manifestations of "traditional" collaborative networks is quite fragmented, being urgent to proceed with an integration and formalization effort. Nevertheless, purely formal methods in addition to being hard to apply are also difficult to follow by those not familiar with such methods.

Dissemination and communication is one important purpose for modeling CNOs. As such, we must acknowledge that this area is addressed by a large variety of people with different backgrounds; not all of them possess a strong formal background, and even many of the ICT practitioners do not have a formal education on computer engineering or computer science. This might suggest, in some cases, the appropriateness of semi-formal methods. On the other hand, new forms of collaborative networks and new patterns of behavior are being invented and explored, for which it is not feasible to develop fully consistent formal models at start. In these cases, semi-formal models, or even informal analogies as represented by metaphors, can provide valuable insights towards a preliminary level of understanding of new collaborative forms.

This paper analyses a set of relevant modeling needs for CNOs, considers a collection of tools and theories developed elsewhere that might be useful here, and suggests a modeling framework for CNOs integrating multiple perspectives.

2. MODELING NEEDS IN CNO

In the context of a complex system like a CNO, modeling is fundamental for understanding, managing, simulating / predicting the behavior of CNOs, and certainly also for software development. For instance, in the VOSTER project [4], several purposes for modeling in this domain were also considered. In ECOLEAD a large number, though incomplete, of modeling purposes were identified for various kinds of CNOs. Based on those examples, Figure 1 illustrates some of the important questions a modeler may pose when attempting to model a virtual organizations breeding environment (VBE).

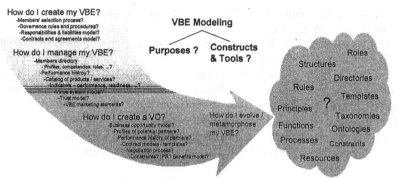

Figure 1 – Examples of modeling purposes in VBE

Certainly many other relevant questions may be asked in relation to a VBE. Similarly, for VO management a large number of modeling purposes are typically considered (Figure 2).

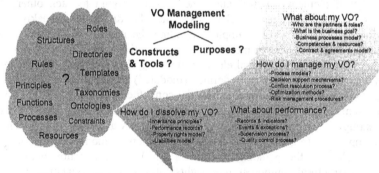

Figure 2 – Examples of modeling purposes in VO management

In the same way many purposes are identifiable for Professional Virtual Communities (PVCs) and other forms of CNOs. Given this large diversity of modeling purposes, which also leads to different types of models, it is important to establish a framework for modeling that structures and guides the modeling process.

3. CNO MODELING DIMENSIONS

As a first attempt to reach a comprehensive modeling framework for CNO modeling, four dimensions are proposed as follows:

- **Structural dimension.** This perspective addresses the structure or composition of the CNO in terms of its constituting elements (participants and their relationships) as well as the roles performed by those elements and other characteristics of the network nodes such as the location, time, etc. This perspective is used in many disciplines (e.g. systems engineering, software engineering, economy, politics, cognitive sciences, manufacturing), although with different "wording" and diversified tools.

- **Componential dimension.** This dimension focuses on the individual tangible/intangible elements in the CNO's network, e.g. the resource composition such as human elements, software and hardware resources, information and knowledge. Not all these elements are "physical" in a strict sense but rather represent the "things" of which the network is built of. Furthermore, the componential dimension also consists of ontology and the description of the information/knowledge repositories that pertain to the CNO.
- **Functional dimension.** This perspective addresses the "base operations" available at the network and the execution of time-sequenced flows of operations (processes and procedures) related to the "operational phase" of the CNO's life cycle.
- **Behavioral dimension.** This dimension addresses the principles, policies, and governance rules that drive or constrain the behavior of the CNO and its members over time. Included here are elements such as principles of collaboration and rules of conduct, contracts, conflict resolution policies, etc.

These specific dimensions are chosen for the reason of their "near-orthogonality" in the sense that if elements in different dimension are bound to each other, then changes in one dimension affect the elements of the other dimensions, weakly across some region of relevance. For example, extending the number of workers in one organization (a physical element modeling an organization) may change the options in a process workflow (a functional element modeling that organization). As such, every CNO can be comprehensively defined (modeled) by the collection of its four models, as well as a set of bindings across the constituents of those models. Every model represents specific (and orthogonal) aspects/perspective/dimension of a CNO.

Two examples for bindings follow: 1- Dependencies and bounds between the physical components (e.g. the personnel) and the structural model counterpart (e.g. the role and skill of the personnel) within a CNO. 2- Connection between an organization's structural component (e.g. rights/duties of the organization in a VO) and the behavioral model counterpart (e.g. the contract component in the VO).

The suggested dimensions are still very general and it is important to consider a finer level of granularity; in other words, to consider a set of sub-dimensions for each dimension. Therefore the following set of sub-dimensions is initially proposed for a CNO modeling framework:

1. Structural dimension
a) *Actors / relationships* – identifying all the participating actors (nodes) in the network as well as their inter-relationships (arcs). The actors can be enterprises, other types of organizations, or people. Two (or more) actors can be linked through a number of different types of relationships, e.g. client-supplier, sharing, co-authoring, etc.
b) *Roles* – describing and characterizing the roles that can be performed by the actors in the network. A role defines an expected behavior for an actor in a given context. Examples of roles include member, coordinator, broker, planner, etc.

2) Componential dimension
a) *Hardware / software resources* – characterizing the equipment, software, and infrastructures used / shared in the network. In terms of ICT equipment this model can include the architecture of the computer network supporting the collaboration. In

the case of manufacturing networks it can include the layout of the shared facilities as well as the logistics networks.

b) *Human resources* – a characterization of the human resources available in the network, namely in terms of their competencies, profile, potential roles they can perform, etc.

c) *Information / knowledge resources* – under this sub-dimension we can include the repositories of information and knowledge that are shared by the network members or that support the collaboration processes and the networked organization.

d) *Ontology resources* – representing the main (common) ontologies used in the network and that facilitate the mutual understanding among the network members. One example can be the ontology of competencies available in the network.

3) Functional dimension

a) *Processes* – this sub-dimension is concerned with the processes involved in the main line of activities of the collaboration. Processes represent the main structured part of the operational activities of the network. An example is the distributed business processes in a business oriented CNO.

b) *Auxiliary processes* – including those processes that are designed to assist the CNO in terms of its maintenance and improvement of operations. Examples include performance monitoring processes, competencies management processes, etc.

c) *Methodologies* – typically less formalized than processes, represent the body of practices, procedures, and rules used mainly by human actors in a CNO. They are frequently represented as a semi-structure set of steps (informal enumeration of activities) combined with some structured representation of input / output information. An example can be the methodology to be followed by a broker to announce a business opportunity to the CNO members.

4) Behavioral dimension

a) *Prescriptive behavior* – capturing the elements that lie down or *prescribe* normative guidelines or rules for the proper behavior of the CNO such as (general) principles, strategies, and protocols. An example is a recommendation for CNO members to give preference to network peers when searching for partners for a business opportunity. Another example could be the recommended protocol when negotiating a contract.

b) *Obligatory behavior* – describing those rules and principles that are mandatory to be followed inside the network. This includes policies, governance values and associated rules, and enforcement steps. An example can be the internal rules used for distribution of benefits or for sharing the operational costs of the network.

c) *Constraints and conditions* – representing those "environmental features" that limit the context of operation of the CNO and its members. An example is a set of restrictions on the use of intellectual property of one member by other members of the network.

d) *Contracts and cooperation agreements* – covering both the contracts between the CNO and external customers and the internal contracts and cooperation agreements among the network members. These models may include both representations understandable to humans and to software systems.

Nevertheless it shall be noted that these sub-dimensions are not exhaustive. They are shown mainly to better characterize, by illustration, the scope of each dimension.

4. MAP OF POTENTIAL APPROACHES

A large number of theories and tools, developed elsewhere, are potentially useful in modeling CNOs or in giving insights to better understand these networks. It would be a matter of practical convenience for the CNO community to have a kind of map or "shopping list" relating such tools and theories to the CNO modeling needs or modeling dimensions. In this direction, Table 1 illustrates the potential applicability of the various theories with respect to the four modeling dimensions introduced in chapter 3. In this table the letters **[SD]**, **[CD]**, **[FD]**, **[BD]** stand for Structural, Componential, Functional, and Behavioral dimension, respectively.

Table 1 – Some theories and their potential applicability in CNOs

Theory / Tool	Potential contribution to CNO modeling
Benchmarking	[FD] Assessment of performance in comparison with a reference (benchmark), including assessment of processes, trustworthiness, and suggestion of best practices.
Complexity theories	[FD] Methods for forecasting emergent behavior, trustworthiness, etc. [BD] Modeling of emergent behavior in advanced networks. Qualitative (macro) understanding of CNO's life cycle.
Decision support	[FD] Give a basis for developing methods to assist humans in decision making.
Deontic logic	[BD] Represent in a formal way aspects such as "it is obligatory that ...", "it is forbidden that ...", "it is permitted that ...", which can be useful in the governance of behavior.
Distributed group dynamics	[SD] Focus on inter-group relationships such as power, leadership, etc, [BD] Analysis of leadership behavior, hostility, compliancy, etc.
Diversity in work teams	[SD] Characterization of the diversity of individuals and cultures found in CNOs and analysis of the potential induced by this diversity.
Evolving ontologies	[CD] To capture the evolution of mutual understanding among members of the network, but still is offering limited results.
Federated systems	[SD] Providing a vision of the CNO as a federation of autonomous, heterogeneous, and distributed sources of resources (data / information, services). Relate roles with authorized access to and visibility of resources. [CD] Distributed data / information repositories.
Formal engineering methods	[SD] [CD] [FD] [BD] Rigorous specifications (mathematical-based) with potential application in verification and synthesis of systems. Very hard to apply.
Formal theories	[SD] [CD] [FD] [BD] Solve design problems (architecture, protocols, verification of specifications according to correctness and completeness), but very hard to develop. If developed for specific perspectives / subsystems, can contribute to reduce ambiguities and provide a sound basis for further developments.
Game theory	[FD] Can provide concepts for decision-making, e.g.: - Cooperative game theory: distribution of responsibility and resources. - Non-cooperative game theory: selection of partners, sustaining cooperation and trust building. [BD] Model interactions with formalized incentive structures.
Graph theory	[SD] Representation of the structure of the network – topology, routing, activity, flow. [FD] Methods to perform computations on flows and optimization.
Knowledge mapping	[CD] Providing visual representations of knowledge which can facilitate analysis of the CNO and its resources.
Memetics	[BD] Help understanding some aspects of the dynamics of evolutionary processes (cognitive and business) in multi-cultural contexts.

Metaphors	[SD] [CD] [FD] [BD] Quick description for human communication namely a possible help in expressing complex ill-defined concepts. Can be used in early stages (conceptual design) as long as they are not taken too literally.
ML/ Bayesian networks	[FD] Use of probabilistic inference to update and revise belief values. Can support complex inference modeling including rational decision making systems, value of information and sensitivity analysis. Causality analysis and support a form of automated learning (parametric discovery, network discovery, and causal relationships discovery).
Multi-agent systems	[FD] [BD] Model societies of autonomous, distributed and heterogeneous entities, giving insights on how these societies can be organized and their behavior regulated through norms and institutions. [FD] Brokering, coalition formation and negotiation. [BD] Simulation of self-organizing behavior.
Multi-agent dependency theory	[FD] [SD] Representation of social interactions among agents – dependency relations, power relations.
Network analysis	[SD] [FD] Specialized graph theory-based algorithms for application in network management systems (mostly applied in telecommunication networks).
Portfolio theory	[FD] Decision making such as in VO creation (to select the optimal VO from a VBE)
Real options theory	[FD] Decision making, e.g. decision to create a VO for a business opportunity, evaluation of the minimum profitable bid in a call for tenders, etc.
Scopos theory	[FD] Understand transformation of information or knowledge from one cultural and language environment to others in such a way that the understanding and conception of the source information or knowledge would be the same for all.
Self-organizing systems	[BD] Understanding and simulation of self-organizing behavior. [FD] Help in predicting evolution.
Semiotics	[BD] Model responsibility relationships and commitments. Prescribe norms and roles – epistemic, deontic and axiologic.
Social network analysis	[SD] Analysis of social and organizational structure of CNOs, including provision of a number of metrics. Ongoing research may lead to useful results on the inclusion of soft-modeling aspects.
Soft computing	[FD] [BD] Represent and exploit the tolerance for imprecision, uncertainty, partial truth, and approximation. Particularly important to model human and social aspects.
Synergetics	[BD] Help understanding emerging behavior and emerging values.
Temporal and modal logic	[FD] [BD] Focus on the representation of temporal information within a logical framework. Can be used to model temporal aspects of processes and some aspects of behavior.
Transactions cost theory	[FD] Understand and analyze governance structures based on transaction costs.
Trust building models	[FD] Organize and systematize the trust building and trust management processes.
Web & text mining	[FD] Analysis and knowledge discovery from unstructured data: documents in free text form, web documents. Potential applications include evolution of ontologies, finding business opportunities, etc.

In addition to these theories and associated tools, there are other modeling tools that have a generic applicability or have been already widely used in the CNO's community and therefore were not studied in this work. Nevertheless they shall be considered as important candidates to some or all of the modeling dimensions. These generic tools include:

Table 2 - Additional tools and their potential applicability in CNOs

Ontology	[SD] [CD] [FD] [BD] Representation of the main CNO concepts and their relationships.
Petri nets	[FD] Modeling or processes and auxiliary processes.
Workflow	[FD] Modeling or processes and auxiliary processes.
UML	[SD] [CD] [FD] [BD] Generic object-oriented modeling tool (graphical language) with potential application to all dimensions of CNO. However, being a generic tool, it does not properly capture all specificities of each dimension.

Figure 3 represents a simplified attempt to establish a map relating theories / tools to the modeling dimensions. This map is not exhaustive and certainly not fully accurate, but just a contribution to give a rough idea of the many possibilities that can be considered.

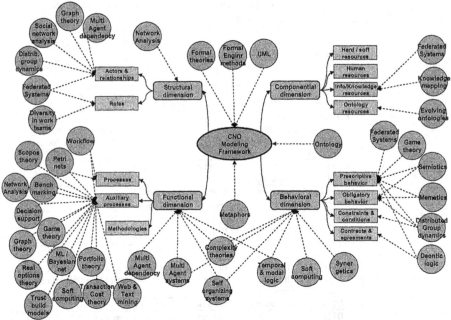

Figure 3 – An attempt to map modeling theories applicable to CNOs

Some theories and tools have a generic nature, others are very specific. For instance, UML or formal engineering methods are quite general and thus potentially applicable to all modeling dimensions; on the other hand, deontic logic is quite specific and potentially useful in the modeling of some aspects of behavior.

As also shown in Figure 3, there are some sub-dimensions for which there is no specialized theory that is particularly suited (e.g. hard/soft resources). Nevertheless there are some generic theories / tools (associated to CNO modeling framework in the center) that are "good for everything", like UML, ontology, etc. Another aspect to consider is that some theories might cover, in part, more than one dimension or sub-dimension. For instance, complexity theories can be linked to the functional and behavioral dimensions. Not all these possibilities are represented in Figure 3.

The suitability of a theory / tool to be applied to a particular modeling perspective also depends on the experience of the modeler with that theory / tool. There are in fact several "gray areas" of applicability. For instance, self-organizing systems could, in a limited way, also relate to the structure of the network. Therefore, and in order to not make the map too complex, only what currently seems to be the most important and obvious links are represented.

5. TOWARDS A HOLISTIC MODELING FRAMEWORK

When modeling a CNO, it is important to consider both its internal and external aspects (Fig. 4) i.e. how to see the network from inside and from outside.

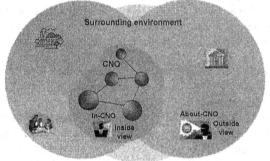

Figure 4 – Two modeling perspectives

We can therefore consider two modeling perspectives or sub-spaces: In-CNO and About-CNO:

In-CNO sub-space. This perspective aims at providing an abstract representation of the CNO *from inside*, namely the identification of a set of characteristic properties that can together capture the elements constituting CNOs. As discussed in chapter 3, building In-CNO abstract representation is challenging due to the large number of distinct and varied entities, concepts, functionality, rules and regulations, etc. inside the CNOs. In addition to a variety of tangible elements and resources inside the CNO, there are always networks of organizations, in which each node plays a specific role and has heterogeneous relationships with other nodes. Furthermore, there are certain rules of behavior that either constitute the norms, or shall be obeyed by the CNO participants, and needless to say that in every CNO there are a set of activities and functionalities that also need to be abstracted. The four dimensions introduced previously are adequate to model the CNO from the inside perspective.

About-CNO sub-space. This perspective aims at reaching an abstract representation of the CNO as seen from the outside, i.e. which characteristic properties the CNO reveals in its interaction with its "logical" surrounding environment. A CNO as a whole might interact with, influence, and be influenced by a number of "interlocutors", e.g. customers, competitors, external institutions, potential new partners. The interactions between the CNO and these external entities are quite different, the same as the way each of these entity groups looks at the CNO.

In order to better characterize these differences, the following additional modeling dimensions are proposed for the external or About-CNO perspective:

- **Market dimension.** This dimension covers both the issues related to the interactions with "customers" (or potential beneficiaries) and "competitors". The customers' facet involves elements such as the transactions and established commitments (contracts), marketing and branding, etc. On the competitors' side issues such as market positioning, market strategy, policies, etc. can be considered. The purpose / mission of the CNO, its value proposition, joint identity, etc. are also part of this dimension.

- **Support dimension.** Under this dimension the issues related to support services provided by third party institutions are to be considered. Examples include certification services, insurance services, training, external coaching, etc.
- **Societal dimension.** This dimension captures the issues related to the interactions between the CNO and the society in general. Although this perspective can have a very broad scope, the idea is to model the impacts the CNO has or potentially can have on the society (e.g. impact on employment, economic sustainability of a given region, potential for attraction of new investments) as well as the constraints and facilitating elements (e.g. legal issues, public body decisions, education level) the society provides to the CNO development.
- **Constituency dimension.** This perspective focuses on the interaction with the universe of potential new members of the CNO, i.e. the interactions with those organizations that are not part of the CNO but that the CNO might be interested in attracting. Therefore, general issues like sustainability of the network, attraction factors, what builds / provides a sense of community, or specific aspects such as rules of adhesion and specific "marketing" policies for members, are considered here.

In addition to these perspectives, a CNO model can be defined at multiple levels of abstraction (**model intent perspective**). Currently three levels are being considered in our framework:

- **General concepts level** – that includes the most general concepts and related relationships, common to all CNOs independently of the application domain.
- **Specific modeling level** – an intermediate level that includes more detailed models focused on different classes of CNOs.
- **Implementation modeling level** – that represents models of concrete CNOs.

CNO-Life-Cycle perspective. In a typical (long-term) organization, usually its operation stage constitutes its entire livelihood. In other words most successful organizations spend only a negligible fraction of their life time in their setting up and dissolution. Therefore, earlier research on reference modeling for enterprises did not need to elaborate much on the life cycle perspective. But unlike typical organizations, for a wide variety of classes of CNOs their creation stage (as well as their dissolution or metamorphosis) is complex and takes up considerable effort. This is certainly not a negligible fraction of time, and due to the involved complexity, it requires receiving proper attention during the build up of the reference model. Our earlier study of the life cycle stages for CNOs has revealed 4 main stages for the CNO life cycle – **Creation**, **Operation**, **Evolution**, and **Metamorphosis / Dissolution**.

The ongoing plan for this work is to define "A Reference model for COllaborative Networks" (ARCON). The elaboration of a comprehensive modeling framework, integrating all the above perspectives, is the first step of this initiative.

Figures 5 and 6 combine the life-cycle perspective with the In-CNO and About-

CNO perspectives respectively.

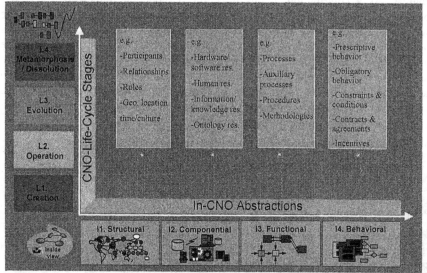

Figure 5 – Crossing CNO life cycle and In-CNO abstractions

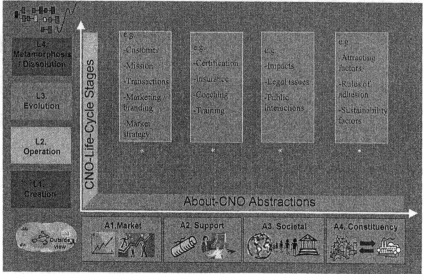

Figure 6 – Crossing CNO life cycle and About-CNO abstractions

Fig. 7 combines the addressed perspectives into a single diagram that summarizes the various perspectives considered in the proposed modeling framework.

6. CONCLUSIONS

The establishment of a comprehensive modeling framework for CNOs is a very important basis for the elaboration of a reference model, a base element in the consolidation of existing knowledge in this area, and a basis for its consistent further progress. As a contribution in this direction, a modeling framework for CNOs considering multiple perspectives was proposed. Nevertheless it is clear that the establishment of a reference model, able to capture the variety of CNOs and their complexity, is a long term endeavor that needs to start with a careful analysis of the current baseline and definition of related reference modeling frameworks. Current work is focused on the identification of the general modeling elements according to the proposed framework. This analysis is based on different classes of CNOs, namely VO breeding environments, virtual organizations, professional virtual communities, and virtual learning communities.

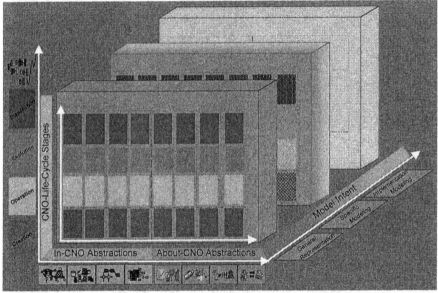

Figure 7 – A modeling framework for CNOs

Acknowledgements. This work was funded in part by the European Commission through the ECOLEAD project. The authors thank the contributions of their partners in this project.

6. REFERENCES

1. Camarinha-Matos, L. M.; Abreu, A. - Towards a foundation for virtual organizations, in Proceedings of Business Excellence 2003 –Int. Conf. Performance measures, Bench-marking, and Best Practices in New Economy, Guimarães, Portugal, 10-13 Jun 2003.
2. Camarinha-Matos, L. M.; Afsarmanesh, H. - Formal modeling methods for collaborative networks, in *Collaborative Networked Organizations – A research agenda for emerging business models*, cap. 6.3, Springer, 2004.
3. Eschenbaecher, J.; Ellmann, S. – Foundation for networking: A theoretical view on the virtual organization, in Processes and Foundations for Virtual Organizations, Kluwer, 2003.
4. Löh, H.; Zhang, C.; Katzy, B. – Modeling for virtual organizations, in Virtual Organizations – Systems and Practices, Springer, 2005.

A CONCEPTUAL FRAMEWORK FOR MODELING COMPLEX ADAPTATION OF COLLABORATIVE NETWORKS

Dmitry Ivanov[1], Joachim Kaeschel[1], Boris Sokolov[2],
Alexander Arkhipov[3]

[1]*Chemnitz University of Technology, GERMANY*
*dmitri.ivanov@mail.ru**
j.kaeschel@wirtschaft.tu-chemnitz.de

[2]*Russian Academy of Science,*
Saint Petersburg Institute of Informatics and Automation (SPIIRAS), RUSSIA
sokol@iias.spb.su

[3]*Saint Petersburg State University of Technology and Design, RUSSIA*
A_arkhipov@sutd.ru

The paper elaborates methodological basis of collaborative networks (CN) complex adaptation. We consider challenges and underlying principles of the CN complex adaptation. Subsequently, the DIMA-methodology of the integrated CN modeling is considered. The paper ends with the presentation of the five-level CN complex adaptation concept and summarizing DIMA-methodology application in the CN complex adaptation settings.

1. INTRODUCTION

On the modern global markets, collaborative networks (CN) emerge in a decentralized and dynamical way instead of former static hierarchical cooperation and value chains (Camarihna-Matos et al., 2005). The CN modeling and optimization issues are cross-linked and multi-disciplinary. They differ from those in the classical control theory and operations research by highly specific features of the CN complexity and uncertainty. Thus, specific modeling and optimization methodologies and techniques are required.

The CN execution is accomplished by permanent changes of internal network properties and external environment. It requires dynamic CN adaptation to the current execution environment and the goals and decisions of the configuration phase. Although the problem of the CN configuration was presented in details in a number of recent papers, the research on CN execution is still very limited.

Please use the following format when citing this chapter:

Ivanov, D., Kaschel, J., Sokolov, B., Arkhipov, A., 2006, in IFIP International Federation for Information Processing, Volume 224, Network-Centric Collaboration and Supporting Fireworks, eds. Camarinha-Matos, L., Afsarmanesh, H., Ollus, M., (Boston: Springer), pp. 15–22.

2. CHALLENGES OF COLLABORATIVE NETWORKS ADAPTATION

Some recent research papers (Camarihna-Matos, 2005, Ivanov et al., 2004, 2005, 2006) have dealt with forming of CN management methodology. According to these works and the system theory basics, the large variety of the issues can be classified into the subclasses of CN analysis and synthesis (Figure 1).

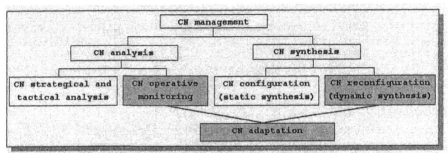

Figure 1. General classification of CN management issues

The most of the CN management issues are multi-disciplinary and cross-linked. In this paper, we pay particular attention to the CN execution. The elaboration of the CN operative adjustment methodology can be based on the conceptual framework of adaptive systems (Bellmann 1972, Casti, 1979). Generally, the adaptation is considered as operative adjustment according to the changing execution environment. However, the CN have particular features, which distinguish them from the technical systems being considered in the classical systems and control theories.

In terms of systems theory, *a complex system* is characterized by uncertain interactions of the elements, distributed goals, and is described by a number of different model classes (Mesarovic and Takahara, 1975, Casti, 1979, Sterman, 2000, Sokolov and Yusupov, 2004). The particular features of CN are mostly caused by their *complexity and uncertainty,* the main sources of which are the following (Ivanov, 2006):

Table 1 - Complexity and uncertainty of CN

	Sources of CN complexity and uncertainty
1	uncertain interactions of partners
2	considerable environmental uncertainty while CN functioning
3	activity of network elements and their free-will interactions
4	high structure and process dynamics
5	combination of centralized and decentralized management resulted in conflicting nondescript multi-criteria objectives of global and local nature,
6	a large number of uncontrolled internal and external factors,
7	considerable cross-linking of various CN management models.

The *uncertain interactions* of partners are the primary cause of the CN complexity and uncertainty. Moreover, additional complexity and uncertainty arise from the *activity of network elements* and their free-will interactions. Besides, operation of the CN is accompanied by perturbation impacts (*disturbances*), which influence the plan execution and the network environment.

A collaborative network can be *defined as a complex open decentralized system with active independent elements*. The classic adaptation approaches do not consider such types of systems, so that they can be used only as conceptual framework. The usage of their formalizing and modeling techniques requires more detailed analysis.

The elaborated methodological basis of the CN complex adaptation contains the following main parts:
- conceptual model of the CN design and execution (Ivanov et al., 2006),
- conceptual framework of CN complexity and uncertainty analysis (Ivanov, 2006),
- system of categories and figures of CN analysis and synthesis under the terms of uncertainty,
- methodological framework of decision making under integrated risk modelling in CN,
- methodological framework for the embedding of risk factors into the CN modelling,
- methodological framework of the the CN complex adaptation
- mathematical models and algorithms of CN adaptation.

In this paper, we consider the methodological basis of CN complex adaptation. Section 3 considers the underlying principles of CN complex adaptation methodology. In section 4, the principles of the DIMA (Decentralized Integrated Modeling Approach)-methodology are discussed. The paper ends with the presentation of the concept of five-level CN complex adaptation and short description summarizing DIMA-methodology application in CN complex adaptation settings.

3. THE CN COMPLEX ADAPTATION UNDERLYING PRINCIPLES

Based on the conceptual framework of the CN complexity and uncertainty analysis, the following underlying principles of the CN complex adaptation can be defined.
- Not only original objects, but also *dynamics of their interactions, environment, and models* are subjects of planning. Planning process is interpreted as *continuous control of system dynamics under the terms of uncertainty*,
- Results of planning are not only ideal operations model, but also a set of the *CN execution scenarios, models, algorithms*, intended for system functioning support in case of disturbances and deviations,
- There is a certain period of time between the decision making about the CN, adjustment and the launch of the execution. Practically it leads to the parallel existing of the "old" CN and the new (reconfigured) one. It requires the *simultaneous synthesis of both new CN and the programs of the CN adjustment* based on the adaptation principles with the forecasting models for describing the CN functioning in the adjustment period,
- All the CN management phases (planning, monitoring, analysis, and adjustment) must be considered as a whole based on the unified methodological basis. This basis should ensure the *CN models cross-linking and inter-corresponding* as well as the adaptation of the processes and models to the *current execution environment*,
- The CN management problems differ from those in classical control theory and operation research by highly specific complexity and uncertainty features. That is

why the classical modeling techniques of the systems theory, control theory and operations research do not suit to the CN modeling because of insufficient complexity and uncertainty consideration. They must be enhanced by combining with the multi-agent paradigm, fuzzy-logic and evolutionary algorithms.

The presented challenges of the CN modelling let to draw a conclusion that a *multi-disciplinary integrated modelling framework* is needed (Camarinha-Matos and Afsarmanesh, 2004, Ivanov et al., 2005, 2006). The widespread agent-based frameworks can be considered only from the simulation point of view. The agents are implemented as a result of some partial heuristics. They do not have any grounded theoretical background, which would cover all the CN modelling aspects. The control theory frameworks have well-elaborated theoretical backgrounds, but they were developed for the technical systems and do not take into account the *goal-oriented (active) behaviour* of enterprises. The analytical frameworks of the operation research are not flexible enough and unsuitable for the large-scale problems. So these frameworks must be enhanced by the advantages of each other.

4. DIMA – AN INTEGRATED APPROACH OF THE CN MODELING

In the DIMA-methodology, various modeling approaches are not set off with each other, but considered as a united modelling framework. The multi-agent ideology is considered as a basis for the *active elements modelling*. The control theory serves as a *theoretical background* of systems analysis and synthesis. The general scheme of the DIMA-methodology is shown in Figure 2.

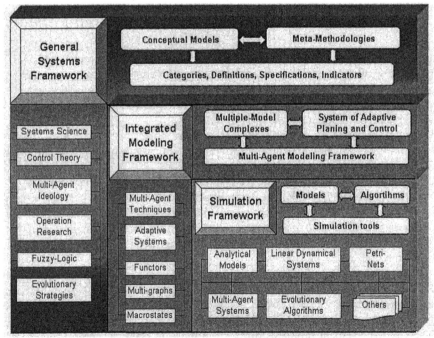

Figure 2. The general scheme of the DIMA-methodology

The main parts of the DIMA-methodology are: the general systems framework, the integrated modelling framework, and the simulation framework (Ivanov, 2006). *The general systems framework* defines conceptual models, meta-methodologies, and set of categories, definitions, specifications, indicators, etc., which are developed as combination of various theoretical frameworks (Ivanov et al., 2005, 2006). The advantage is that the conceptual basics of the CN modelling posses the elaborated in the systems science theoretical background and also takes into account particular features of the CN such as *emergent enterprise behaviour* by the MAS-ideology (*but not the MAS as software!*) using.

The integrated modelling framework defines the rules of the integrated multi-disciplinary mathematical models building. It proposes some constructive methods and techniques of (i) how to combine various model classes and (ii) how to model interconnected the partial CN problems. The main parts of the proposed integrated modelling framework are: *multi-agent conceptual modeling framework, multiple-model complexes system of adaptive planning and control* (Ivanov et al, 2005, 2006).

The simulation framework integrates building of mathematical models and algorithms, and their implementation as software. Based on the integrated modelling framework, there are built multi-disciplinary models, algorithms, and simulation tools, which allow problem examining and solution in different classes of models, and result representation in the desired class of models (concept of *"virtual" modeling*). As examples of the models and algorithms the problems of the CN design, monitoring, adaptation were considered (Ivanov et al., 2004, 2005, 2006).

The DIMA-methodology represents a multi-disciplinary modeling framework, which meets the CN modeling particular features. The approach creates a unified methodological basis of the CN integrated modeling, from the conceptual level, mathematical modeling up to algorithms and simulation tools. One of the frameworks elaborated on the DIMA basis is CN five-level complex adaptation framework that will be discussed in the next section.

5. THE CN FIVE-LEVEL COMPLEX ADAPTATION

Conventional tools (such as APS and SCEM systems) evince considerable deficiencies (Stadtler, 2004). Their hierarchical functioning principle is not applicable in non-hierarchical approaches based on decentralized management. Their optimization cycle is slow and does not let appropriate taking into account operative oscillations in demand, material availability, lead times, production charges etc. Besides the *parametrical oscillations*, the structural and goal oscillations are to be considered. Various *structures changes*, such as organizational, technological, informational, financial, might let to the situation when initial CN *models* would be no more *representative and adequate*. The clients and network participants' goal changing also cause the models changing (adaptation) necessity. Such model changing is very cost-intensive and must be linked to the other aspects of the CN adaptation. The elaborated concept of the complex CN adaptation is built as a five-level structure. Each level characterizes certain control loop in accordance with the oscillations and deviations appeared (see Figure 3).

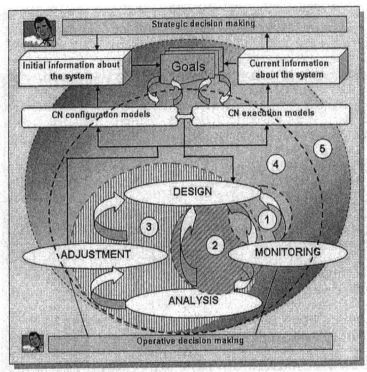

Figure 3. The five-level CN complex adaptation

Table 3 provides a systematical view on the levels of complex adaptation concept.

Table 3 - levels of complex adaptation concept

	Adaptation level	What is adopted?	How can be adopted?	Management horizon
1	Parametric adaptation	CN parameters	Capacities reconfiguration, rush orders, etc.	Operative
2	Structural-functional adaptation	CN structures	Operations reallocation, supplier changing, etc.	Operative-tactical
3	Goal adaptation I	CN goal	Project goal adaptation, e.g. delivery delay	Tactical
4	Model adaptation	CN models	Introduction of new parameters, structures, restrictions and goals	Tactical-strategic
5	Goal adaptation II	CN models and plans	Management goal adaptation (mission adaptation)	Strategic

Particular features of the concept are the control loops 4 and 5 intended for the CN model adaptation and the CN strategic management perspectives adaptation.

6. RESULTS AND IMPLEMENTATION

On the basis of the DIMA-methodology the methodological basis of the CN complex adaptation is elaborated. The main aspects of the CN complex adaptation and the ways of their solution are shown in the table 4.

Table 4 - The main aspects of the CN complex adaptation and the ways of their solution in the DIMA-methodology

The main aspects of the CN complex adaptation	The ways of problems solution in the DIMA-methodology
Interconnection of static and dynamical models	Categorical-functoral conception Structural-mathematical approach
Elements' activity and decentralized management; Personal (subjective) uncertainty	Multi-agent systems Evolutionary algorithms
CN structure dynamics; Simultaneous multi-criteria synthesis of the CN design and the CN execution programs; Simultaneous synthesis of both new (reconfigured) CN and the programs of the CN adjustment	Dynamical alternative multi-graph; Macro-structural macro states; Multiple-model complexes; Theory of structure dynamics control;
Cross-linking and interrelations of all CN life cycle models	Dynamical alternative multi-graph; Multiple-model complexes
Multi-criteria problems definition	General selection multi-criteria structure
Embedding of the uncertainty factors into the CN models	Conceptual frameworks of the risk management and adjustment in the CN

On the basis of the proposed CN complex adaptation framework the methodological framework of decision making under integrated risk modelling in the CN, the methodological framework for the embedding of risk factors into the CN modelling, and a number of mathematical models and algorithms of the CN adaptation were elaborated. Some of the obtained theoretical results are implemented as software SNDC (Supply Network Dynamic Control) and EVCM (Extended Value Chain Management) (Teich, 2003, Ivanov et al., 2004).

7. CONCLUSIONS

The paper presented methodological basis of the CN complex adaptation. We considered the challenges of the CN adaptation and the underlying principles of the CN complex adaptation methodology. The CN adaptation must be based on the *integrated multi-disciplinary methodologies and information systems*. We described the principles of the *decentralized integrated modeling approach (DIMA)*. Subsequently, the concept of five-level CN complex adaptation was presented. The paper ended with the summarizing of the DIMA-methodology application in the CN complex adaptation. The practical relevance of this research lies in the development of the new generation of information technologies for the CN management support, which would make up the deficiencies of conventional APS, SCEM, LES and SCMo systems. The scientific relevance of the work lies in the area of generic model constructions development for the CN design and control, and contribution to advancing of the CN theoretical foundations.

8. ACKNOLEDMENTS

The research described in this paper is partially supported by grants from Russian Foundation for Basic Research (grant №05-07-90088), Institute for System Analysis RAS (Project 2.5), CRDF Project #: Rum2-1554-ST-05, and the Alexander von Humboldt Foundation. The authors thank also Collaborative Research Centre 457 at the Chemnitz University of Technology, which is financed from the Deutsche Forschungsgemeinschaft (German Research Foundation). The authors thank the contribution from their partners in such projects.

9. REFERENCES

1. Bellmann R. (1972) *Adaptive Control Processes: A Guided Tour*, Princeton Univ. Press, Princeton, New Jersey.
2. Camarinha-Matos, L. (ed.) (2004). *Virtual Enterprises and Collaborative Networks*, Kluwer Academic Publishers.
3. Camarinha-Matos LM, Afsarmanesh H. The emerging discipline of collaborative networks. In: Virtual Enterprises and Collaborative Networks, edited by L.Camarihna-Matos, Kluwer Academic Publishers, 2004: 3-16.
4. Camarinha-Matos, L., Afsarmanesh, H. and A. Ortiz (eds.) (2005). *Collaborative Networks and Their Breeding Environments*, Springer.
5. Casti JL. Connectivity, Complexity and Catastrophe in Large-Scale Systems. Wiley-Intersc., 1979.
6. Ivanov D., Arkhipov A., Sokolov B.: Intelligent Supply Chain Planning in Virtual Enterprises. In: Virtual Enterprises and Collaborative Networks, edited by L.Camarihna-Matos, Kluwer Academic Publishers, 2004: 215-223.
7. Ivanov, D., Käschel, J., Arkhipov, A., Sokolov, B., and Zschorn L. (2005): *Quantitative Models of Collaborative Networks*, In: Collaborative Networks and Their Breeding Environments, edited by L.Camarihna-Matos, H. Afsarmanesh, A. Ortiz, Springer, 2005, pp. 387-394.
8. Ivanov, D.A., Arkhipov, A.V., and Sokolov, B.V. (2006): *Intelligent planning and control of manufacturing supply chains in virtual enterprises*, in: International Journal of Manufacturing Technology and Management, in print.
9. Ivanov, D.A. (2006). DIMA - Decentralized Integrated Modeling Approach for supply chain management and virtual enterprises, *Proceedings of the German-Russian Logistik-Workshop, Saint-Petersburg, Russia, 20-21 April, 2006*, pp. 23-46.
10. Mesarovic MD, Takahara Y. General Systems Theory: Mathematical Foundations. Academic Press, New York, Can Francisco, London, 1975.
11. Sokolov BV, Yusupov RM. Conceptual Foundations of Quality Estimation and Analysis for Models and Multiple-Model Systems. Int. Journal of Computer and System Sciences, 6(2004): 5-16.
12. Stadtler, H., Kilger, C. *Supply Chain Management and Advanced Planning*, 3. Auflage, Springer, Berlin, 2004
13. Sterman JD. Business dynamics: systems thinking and modeling. McGraw-Hill, 2000.
14. Teich, Tobias. Extended Value Chain Management (EVCM). GUC-Verlag, 2003.

3 — UEML: COHERENT LANGUAGES AND ELEMENTARY CONSTRUCTS DETERMINATION

Matthieu Roque[1], Bruno Vallespir[1], Guy Doumeingts[1, 2]

*(1) LAPS/GRAI, UMR CNRS 5131, University Bordeaux 1 - ENSEIRB
351, Cours de la Libération, 33405 Talence FRANCE
matthieu.roque@laps.u-bordeaux1.fr
bruno.vallespir@laps.u-bordeaux1.fr
(2) ADELIOR / Itrec gestion 62bis, Avenue André Morizet
92100Boulogne-BillancourtFrance
doumeingts@itrec.com*

Nowadays, one of the important subjects of research in the enterprise modelling domain is the development of a unified language, often called UEML (Unified Enterprise Modelling Language). This paper is focused on one of the more illustrating points about UEML: the comparison of the constructs of the enterprise modelleling language. In previous work we have put in evidence few situations which can occur when we want to compare some modelling constructs belonging to different languages. We investigate more in detail this problem of comparison, in using a formal approach based on the set theory.This paper propses some concepts and guidelines in order to develop UEML.

1. INTRODUCTION

Since the first development in the area of enterprise modelling started in the US in the years of 70's (ex. SADT, SSAD, IDEF0, Data Flow Diagram,...), a lot of enterprise modelling languages have been elaborated world-wide. We can mention for example, Entity Relationship model, MERISE, GRAI grid and nets, CIMOSA constructs and building blocks, OMT, IEM, ARIS method, IDEFx,...(Petit, 1997), (Vallespir, 2003), (Vallespir *et al.*, 2003), (Vernadat, 1996). It is generally recognised that there are too many heterogeneous modelling languages available in the "Market" and it is difficult for business users to understand and choose a suitable one. Main problems related to this situation have already presented in (Chen *et al.*, 2002) and will not explain in this paper. However, it seems that the elements behind these various languages are similar or slightly differ in details. Thus, it is natural to think about the development of a Unified Enterprise Modelling Language. One of the principal benefits to have a Unified Enterprise Modelling Language is to be able to translate a model of an enterprise built in a language in another one (Chen *et al.*, 2002), (Doumeingts *et al.*, 1999), (Vallespir, 2003), (Vallespir *et al.*, 2003*)*, (Vernadat, 2001), (Vernadat, 1999). Moreover, requirements about UEML have been stated during the UEML project (IST-2001-4229) (Knothe, 2003). The third

Please use the following format when citing this chapter:

Roque, M., Vallespir, B., Doumeingts, G., 2006, in IFIP International Federation for Information Processing, Volume 224, Network-Centric Collaboration and Supporting Fireworks, eds. Camarinha-Matos, L., Afsarmanesh, H., Ollus, M., (Boston: Springer), pp. 23–30.

most important requirement stated was the expectation for an "invariant and unique behavioural semantic" language. Thus, the language UEML is used like a "pivot" language and thus it allows to avoid the one-to-one translation (Chen *et al.*, 2002), (Berio, 2003). Several approaches can be considered for elaborating our unified language like the bottom-up approach which starts with an analysis and then synthesis of existing enterprise modelling languages. Indeed, for the moment, it seems to be more efficient to use the principle which consists in integrating existing languages (Chen *et al.*, 2002), (Vallespir *et al.*, 2003).

In this paper, we only focus on the determination of the common constructs in order to find the elementary constructs. The comparisons of the links between the constructs are not taking into account in these works.

2. DEFINITION OF THE ELEMENTARY CONSTUCTS

In previous works, the concept of elementary construct has been introduced and we highlighted that its determination is not easy (Roque *et al.*, 2005). The objective, of this paper is to propose a formal approach in order to facilitate the determination of the elementary constructs. The definition of the elementary construct is recalled below.

A construct is an elementary construct, if it exists completely or not at all for each considered languages.

For instance, in Figure1, we can see that all the constructs are elementary constructs except the construct C2. This construct belongs completely to the language A but only a part of this construct belongs to the language B. Thus, it is not an elementary construct.

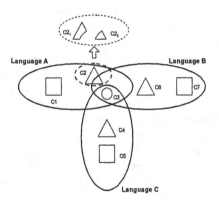

Figure 1 – Elementary constructs

3. CONSTRUCTS COMPARISON

In our approach, we consider the meta-modelling in optics to define a unified enterprise modelling language. Some approaches like XML (DTDs and Schemas), MOF, Telos, can be used as meta-modelling language (Panetto *et al.*, 2004). The meta-modelling language that we use is the UML (Unified Modelling Language) class diagram (OMG, 2003) because it seems sufficient to deal with our problem which is, in first time, to describe the syntactical aspects of the languages. Indeed, for each language, a meta-model[1] is built with the class diagram, in order to represent the constructs of each language. With these meta-models we can compare the constructs of the different languages. Thus, to elaborate the UEML meta-model we have to compare a number N_c of constructs corresponding to all the constructs of the languages. Our objective is to provide a systematic approach in order to determinate which constructs we have to integrate in the UEML language and which are the correspondences rules between them and the constructs of the considered languages. The UEML language is composed by all the elementary constructs which are possible to identify among the N_c conctructs. In order to define these elementary constructs we use an approach based on the set theory approach where each construct is represented by a set.

3.1 Definition of the elementary constructs

Each constructs can be easily represented by a set. Thus, we can write some equations in order to determine the elementary constructs in the case of a number "N_c" of constructs and how the constructs of each language can be recomposed. We can define in the first time the set **E** corresponding to the union of the N_c constructs. Thus, we can define N_{EC} elementary constructs (EC_i) corresponding to all the sub-sets which is possible to create with the intersections of all constructs (1). To determine the elementary constructs, it is useful to use a truth table (as in Boolean algebra) with all constructs. In this table, each "0" corresponds to the complementary[2] of the set in the set E and each "1" corresponds to the set. Thus, each combination of the truth table defines an elementary constructs excepted the first one because $^cC1 \cap {}^cC_2 \cap {}^cC_3 = \varnothing$. Thus, in the case of three constructs, we can write the equations below in order to find the elementary constructs and the correspondences rules (see Table 1).

Table 1 – Determination of the elementary constructs

Elementary constructs		Correspondances rules
$CE_1 = C_1 \cap C_2 \cap C_3$	$CE_5 = {}^cC_1 \cap C_2 \cap C_3$	$C_1 = CE_1 \cup CE_2 \cup CE_3 \cup CE_4$
$CE_2 = C_1 \cap C_2 \cap {}^cC_3$	$CE_6 = {}^cC_1 \cap C_2 \cap {}^cC_3$	$C_2 = CE_1 \cup CE_2 \cup CE_5 \cup CE_6$
$CE_3 = C_1 \cap {}^cC_2 \cap C_3$	$CE_7 = {}^cC_1 \cap {}^cC_2 \cap C_3$	$C_3 = CE_1 \cup CE_3 \cup CE_5 \cup CE_7$
$CE_4 = C_1 \cap {}^cC_2 \cap {}^cC_3$		

---

[1] However, meta-modelling is not an easy step for several reasons: first because given a language it is possible to build different meta-models (as in the case of modelling the same situation) and because there is the need of some guidelines which are not explained in this paper.

[2] equal to [E - (C_k)] noted $^c(C_k)$

The number of the elementary constructs, in the case of N_c constructs, is given by the equation (1)

$$N_{EC} = 2^{N_c} - 1 \qquad (1)$$

3.2 Coherent languages and elementary constructs

The equation (1) does not assume that the intersections between the constructs of a same language are equals to the empty set. Indeed, some languages can have some redundancies or overlapping between their constructs. For the reason, we define the concept of **coherent language**.

> *A coherent language is a language whose all the intersections between its constructs are equals to the empty set.*

Thus, for a coherent language there is no redundancy and no overlapping between its constructs. In the case of the considered languages for elaborating UEML are coherent languages, the number of the elementary constructs can be reduced. Indeed, in this case this number is not equals to (1) but to the equation (2) in removing all the elementary constructs resulting of the comparison of two constructs of same languages.

$$N_{EC} = \left[2^{\sum_{i=1}^{N_L} N_C(L_i)} - 1 \right] - \left[\sum_{i=1}^{N_L} 2^{N_C(L_i)} - 1 \right] \qquad (2)$$

Where:
> N_L is the number of the considered languages,
> $N_c(L_i)$ is the number of the constructs of the language L_i.

4. APPROACH FOR DEFINGING THE ELEMENTARY CONSTRUCTS

Finally, we can define three different steps in order to determinate the elementary constructs.

1. Write the equations to define all the elementary constructs for the considered number of constructs.

However, the concept of coherent language of the section 3.2 is very important. In our approach, the definition of UEML is based on the union of constructs of existing languages. For this reason, the problem of redundancy and overlapping constructs of these languages has to be solved before, in order to have simpler and more coherent UEML. In this case, the correspondences rules will be less complicated. Consequently, it seems to be more efficient to apply our approach for defining the elementary constructs (before the first step), to each language in order to have coherent languages. Moreover, there is no interest to define a unified enterprise modelling language in using languages whose their constructs or part of constructs are not unique in a same language.

2. Interview the providers of the languages in order to identify the intersections between the constructs of the languages.

This step is really not obvious. Indeed, most of the languages have not a formal definition of their constructs. In this case, the comparison is mainly based on informal comparisons where each construct is only defined by a textual description. In the UEML project (Berio, 2003) which provided UEML 1.0, this comparison had been performed by using a scenario. This scenario had been modelled in each considered enterprise modelling language. The study of the intersections between the constructs had been done on the bases of this scenario. Even if, this approach do not provide a formal approach in order to compare the constructs, the lack of formal definition of the constructs, do not permit to use a formal and automatic method. The UEML 2.0 (Berio, 2005) undertakes a very different, eventually complementary approach. Indeed, it requires to fully model the languages in their three conceptual components: abstract syntax, semantic domain and semantics. These three components are organised according to a meta-meta-model: any language is represented by constructs, in turn associated to some meaning provided by a semantic domain. However, the subject of the paper is not to discuss on the way to get the different equations which represent the intersections between the constructs.

3. Resolve the equations according to the results of the preceding step.

5. ILLUSTRATION EXAMPLE

Let us assume that we want to deal with only two pieces of languages: the SADT and the GRAI activities (Roque *et al.*, 2005) as shown in Figure 2.

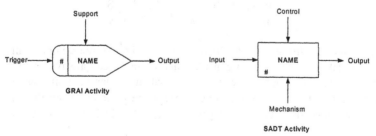

Figure 2 – GRAI and SADT activities

The two simplified meta-models (the links between the constructs of the languages are not represented) of our example are represented in UML class diagrams in the Figure 3. In this paper we focus only on the constructs comparison. In a first comparison, we can identify three elementary constructs which are the Name, the Number and the Output. In the two languages, these concepts are used for representing the same things. For simplify, these three constructs can be grouped into only one elementary constructs which is called Activity.min (3).

$$Activity.min = \{Name, Number, Output\} \tag{3}$$

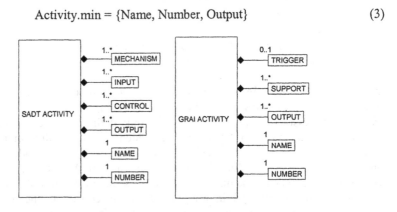

Figure 3 – GRAI and SADT simplified meta-models

5.1 Definition of the elementary constructs and the correspondences rules

5.1.1 First step: Write the equations

Now, we have to consider only five constructs (Support, Trigger, Control, Mechanism and Input) because we have created the Activity.min elementary construct. Thus, with the equation (1) we can define 31 elementary constructs. However, if we use the equations (2) we can reduce this number to 11 elementary constructs. For this example, it is possible to add another assumption in order to reduce again the number of elementary constructs. Indeed, if we take the case of the control, we can see that this constructs is decomposed in three elementary constructs[3]:

$$EC_9 = C \cap {}^C M \cap {}^C I \cap {}^C T \cap {}^C S$$
$$EC_{10} = C \cap {}^C M \cap {}^C I \cap {}^C T \cap S$$
$$EC_{11} = C \cap {}^C M \cap {}^C I \cap T \cap {}^C S$$

EC_9 represents a control in SADT which is neither a Trigger nor a Support in SADT. For transformation issue, we can consider that a control can always be linked to a Trigger or a Support. Thus, we can assume that the generalization relationship is complete and that $EC_9 = \varnothing$. We can apply the same principle of all the constructs and finally we have also $EC_1 = \varnothing$, $EC_2 = \varnothing$, $EC_3 = \varnothing$ and $EC_6 = \varnothing$.

$$N_{EC} = \left[2^{\sum_{i=1}^{N_L} N_C(L_i)} - 1 \right] - \left[\sum_{i=1}^{N_L} 2^{N_C(L_i)} - 1 \right] - \left[\sum_{i=1}^{N_L} N_c(L_i) \right] \tag{4}$$

---

[3] Support → S ; Trigger → T ; Control → C ; Mechanism → M ; Input → I ; Not Triggering Control → NTC

The equations (2) can be modified in order to take into account this remark, like is illustrated by the equation (4). With this equation the number of elementary constructs is reduced to 6.

5.1.2 Second step: Interview the providers of the languages

For the five constructs of the two activities, we can write the six relationships below, which will be used to define all the elementary constructs.

1. Trigger $\subset$ Control
2. Trigger $\cap$ Input
3. Trigger $\cap$ Mechanism $= \varnothing$
4. Support $\cap$ Control $\neq \varnothing$
5. Input $\subset$ Support
6. Mechanism $\subset$ Support

5.1.3 Third step: Resolve the equations

In conclusion, we have only 6 elementary constructs. These elementary constructs and the correspondences rules are in Table 2.

Table 2 – Elementary constructs and correspondences rules.

Elementary constructs	Correspondences rules
$EC_4 = {}^{C}C \cap {}^{C}M \cap I \cap {}^{C}T \cap S = I_{UEML}$	$S = I_{UEML} \cup M_{UEML} \cup NTC$
$EC_5 = {}^{C}C \cap {}^{C}M \cap I \cap T \cap {}^{C}S = \varnothing$	$I = I_{UEML}$
$EC_7 = {}^{C}C \cap M \cap {}^{C}I \cap {}^{C}T \cap S = M_{UEML}$	$M = M_{UEML}$
$EC_8 = {}^{C}C \cap M \cap {}^{C}I \cap T \cap {}^{C}S = \varnothing$	$C = NTC \cup T_{UEML}$
$EC_{10} = C \cap {}^{C}M \cap {}^{C}I \cap {}^{C}T \cap S = NTC$	$T = T_{UEML}$
$EC_{11} = C \cap {}^{C}M \cap {}^{C}I \cap T \cap {}^{C}S = T_{UEML}$	

5.2 UEML meta-model and correspondences rules

Finally, we can build the UEML meta-model of this example in UML class diagram (see Figure 4).

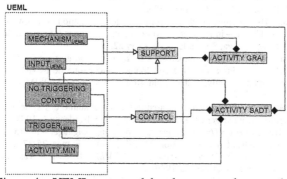

Figure 4 – UEML meta-model and correspondences rules

This class diagram illustrates the UEML meta-model and the correspondences rules between the UEML constructs and the constructs of the GRAI and the SADT activities. Practically, this rule leads to get elementary constructs belonging to UEML that enable to rebuild constructs of languages (so-called local constructs) by generalization. Since these local constructs are obtained, they can be composed to get the whole language.

6. CONCLUSION

In this paper, we have wanted to put in evidence some difficulties concerning the comparison of constructs of enterprise modelling languages. We have presented a systematic approach which provides some help for the determination of the core constructs of the UEML language and the correspondences rules. However, an important question not addressed is the applicability of the methodology for a real case due to the algorithm complexity. Indeed, the number of elementary constructs is of the exponential order and the automatic determination will be difficult without a software support which has to be developed.

7. REFERENCES

1. Berio G., *Requirements analysis: initial core constructs and architecture*, UEML Thematic Network - Contract n°: IST – 2001 – 34229, Work Package 3 Deliverable 3.1, May 2003.
2. Berio G., *UEML 2.0. Deliverable 5.1.* INTEROP project UE-IST-508011 (www.interop-noe.org). 2005
3. Chen D., Vallespir B., Doumeingts G. *Developing an unified enterprise modelling language (UEML) – Roadmap and requirements.* – in Proc. of 3rd IFIP Working conference on infrastructures for virtual enterprise, PROVE, Sesimbra, Portugal, 1st-3 May 2002 – Collaborative Business Ecosystems and Virtual Enterprises, Kluwer Academic Publishers.
4. Doumeingts G., Vallespir B. UEML : *Position du LAP/GRAI.* – Seminar of Groupement pour la Recherche en Productique, GRP, Nancy, France, 25 November 1999.
5. Knotte T., Busselt C. and Böll D. – *Report on UEML (needs and requirements).* - UEML Thematic Network - Contract n°: IST – 2001 – 34229, Work Package 1 Report, April 2003.
6. OMG. *Unified Modeling Language Specification.* – Version 1.5, formal / 03-03-0, 2003.
7. Panetto H., Berio G., Benali K., Boudjlida N., Petit M. (2004). *A Unified Enterprise Modelling Language for enhanced interoperability of Enterprise Models.* Proceedings of the 11th IFAC INCOM Symposium, Bahia, Brazil, April 5-7, 2004.
8. Petit M. *Enterprise Modelling State of the Art*, UEML Thematic Network - Contract n°: IST – 2001 – 34229 – Work Package 1 Report, October 2002.
9. Roque M., Vallespir B. and Doumeingts G. From a models translation case towards identification of some issues about UEML – in Proc. of the workshop on Entreprise Integration, Interoperability and Networking (EI2N), Geneva, Switzerland, February 22, 2005.
10. Vallespir B., Braesch C., Chapurlat V., Crestani D. *L'intégration en modélisation d'entreprise : les chemins d'UEML.* – in Proc. of 4ème conférence francophone de Modélisation et Simulation, Organisation et conduite d'activités dans l'industrie et les services, MOSIM, Toulouse, France, 23-25 April 2003.
11. Vallespir B. - Modélisation d'entreprise et architecture de conduite des systèmes de production. – Thesis for Habilitation à Diriger des Recherches, University Bordeaux 1, 19 December 2003.
12. Vernadat F. UEML: *Towards a Unified Enterprise Modelling Language.* – in Proc. of 3rd Conférence Francophone de Modélisation et Simulation, MOSIM, Troyes, France, 25-27 April 2001.
13. Vernadat F. *Unified Enterprise Modelling Language (UEML).* – IFAC-IFIP Task force Interest group on UEML, Paris, France, 16 December 1999.
14. Vernadat F.B. Enterprise modelling and integration: principles and applications. Chapman & Hall, 1996.

PART 2

COLLABORATIVE NETWORKS MODELS

4

SELF-ORGANIZING VIRTUAL ENTERPRISES

H T Goranson
Sirius-Beta
1976 Munden Point Road
Virginia Beach, Virginia, 23457-1227, USA
tedg@sirius-beta.com

We reintroduce a model of virtual enterprises that is based on features, from customer needs to delivered product. The features in this case correspond to agents that exhibit self-organizing, emergent behavior. The most innovative notion is that features have all the mechanisms necessary to evolve an optimized virtual enterprise. The notion of "narrative urge" is introduced.

The first part is some history of the discovery of types of virtual enterprises, placing the reintroduced concept in perspective. Then we define the notion of a functional agent, feature-driven domain intuitively, indicating some challenges.

Then follows an overview of a general theory of emergence. The virtual enterprise case is mapped to that. A scenario is indicated. Due to space limits, only an overview is given.

1. INTRODUCTION

Two decades ago, the US military performed some large classified studies of the state of the manufacturing enterprise. The impetus was a by now well known problem: doing complex work in large enterprises is so heavily burdened by the machinery of running the enterprise that things cost too much (typically twice), they evolve too slowly in terms of technology and some things just cannot be done at all.

Three radically different models of the future enterprise emerged. One seemed most natural to power brokers at the time, the "integrated enterprise." In this model, large relatively stable enterprises became more "frictionless" with information flowing along designated lines of command and control. The enterprise can be and often is "virtual" in the sense that many companies are "linked" in a supply chain. A characteristic is that the integrating strategy and management is integrated with the management of production and capital at the top, with a prime contractor or leader.

A second vision was rather radical. It attempted to decouple the three (production, capital, integration). The integrating technologies and methods would be provided from the surrounding environment, perhaps as standards, best practices

Please use the following format when citing this chapter:

Goranson, H. T., 2006, in IFIP International Federation for Information Processing, Volume 224, Network-Centric Collaboration and Supporting Fireworks, eds. Camarinha-Matos, L., Afsarmanesh, H., Ollus, M., (Boston: Springer), pp. 33–44.

and distributed facilitating agents. This was termed the "virtual enterprise," with a trivial version consisting of prequalified partners that could easily "plug and play." In this vision, the prequalification would be performed by a sort of virtual prime.

A more advanced virtual enterprise notion depended on more flexible, federating technologies and methods, allowing companies that had never met to aggregate to perform work that they may have never done before. Still, in this vision, one needed agents to support some management of production, capital and integration. The goal was that these three functions need not be linked, but in practice so far, they always have been and performed by a partner in the virtual enterprise.

US research became overtaken by political forces, and the sponsorship there stuck at integrating technologies to help (politically powerful) large enterprises become more so. Research into the virtual enterprise case has been to a degree carried by the European Community, but has similarly stuck on the trivial case of relatively small pools of pre-integrated potential partners.

It is unlikely that either of those business models will advance much beyond the rut that they are in, technology not-withstanding. There just is not the government will, and the academic research communities have dug into existing power centers, an unfortunate byproduct of the way research is funded, dominantly through political and market forces.

It is time, in our opinion, to revisit the third business model, the so-called "self-organizing virtual enterprise." The reason for trying to run before we walk should be obvious. If we can propose a model — however radical — that has sufficient financial benefits, perhaps a kind of discontinuous, beneficial change can occur, the type of change that characterizes the best of technology and provides the stuff for societal optimists.

In simple form this model considers all the components of the potential enterprise as active agents. The level of granularity is presumably fine, so we are not talking about companies, but small workgroups or even individuals within them. Each of these has some sort of independent agency.

This model is not so hard to envision. The system would be triggered by some enterprise goal, presumably a product design and the many, many agents would go to work, negotiating with and informing each other to produce and continue to refine the virtual enterprise. The research challenge here is how to manage multilevel optimization.

Agent systems usually work best when one goal is desired and that goal provides a consistent narrative. The problem is that product designs have little to directly indicate enterprise goals (like profitability and stock value), so need to be translated. Also, there need to be selfish organizing imperatives at many levels, the agent (whatever the granularity), and on up through several layers including the containing small firms then further up to the overarching enterprise.

At the same time, there are "vertical layers," the enterprise-wide functional flows of quality and financial measurement and control, for instance. There seem to be eleven of these, each of which has its own emergent behaviors to optimize, as different in ontology as many of the horizontal organizational layers.

We've made detailed examination of the technical problems associated with this multi-level emergent behavior when you are presented with product models or features. There are profound difficulties with this because there is no way at present to formally harmonize the parallel emergence. A tentative consensus is that until we have a better way of managing "semantic distance" as a federation metric, this vision will not be supported.

We believe that a better approach is to look at the more "advanced" concept of self-organizing virtual enterprises. This vision of the enterprise is much harder to describe. (There are some in the business world who just cannot "get" it with any effort.) Though this enterprise notion is more arcane in some ways, the technical problems in emergent systems design become more tenable and possibly completely solvable with existing conceptual tools and methods.

2. A MODEL OF EMERGENT BEHAVIOR

2.1 Features

In management schools, you'll often hear talk of a customer-centric enterprise or "value chain," one in which there is tight coupling to the customer's needs. If it were a virtual enterprise, the customer might be considered one of the partners.

If the old model is that the customer is there to sell stuff to so as to benefit the enterprise, a new model might be that the enterprise is there to benefit the customer. In the former, the customer incidentally benefits (or is convinced so) while in the latter it is the enterprise that incidentally benefits.

Our model, the one we explore in this paper, differs from either of these. It is a matter of who has the primary agency. The first, normal model is that the enterprise forms around a product. The enterprise components have the agency. In the second model, the customer enters the virtual enterprise and serves many of the roles of the prime contractor, the organizing agent.

What if the product model itself (instead of any group of people) had the agency? But a product is just one instance of a collection of customer needs instanced according to certain constraints. What if the features of the model themselves had the agency? That's precisely what we have been investigating and report on here.

In fact, we'll go a bit further toward the unusual but workable — quite a bit further — and apply some newly maturing ideas on emergent systems theory.

The basic idea here is to model the enterprise not in terms of entities that have functions and take actions, which is the usual way. Instead, to model the world of the enterprise as consisting of "urges" or desires. Perhaps even the term "seductions" could work. In this model, the elements with agency are the urges themselves and they assemble entities into virtual enterprises as a way of expressing those selves.

In the conventional model, components of the virtual enterprise exhibit emergent behavior (that is, they have agency) and the product model (with other models like metrics of success) provides the map, concept or "story" around which these elements form structure. In the new model, the elements of the product model are a collection of urges that have agency and they arrange the elements of the virtual enterprise.

There are precedents for this sort of shifting of the frame of reference. The most familiar to engineers will be shifting from the time to the frequency domain. In software, there is a better known and more widely debated schism between those that model code procedurally (like Java) and those that break the problem down as functions that transform, so-called "functional programming."

Other metaphors concern the shift from a noun-oriented breakdown to one based on verbs. Also of interest is the change in genetics from thinking about genes as a collection of molecules that act, to a model of information packets that "act selfishly" and in the process incidentally create their own type of enterprises: humans and societies. In logic, the analogy is to shift between a set-theoretic foundation and one based on category theory, the theory of functions.

As it happens, all of these: logical, genetic, programming, linguistic... they together provide a coherent, rigorous theoretical basis for supporting our new way of looking at emergent behavior of all kinds. We appropriate that in our model of emergent behavior in virtual enterprises.

(It should be remarked that this notion is quite different than incubated in the "complexity theory" domain. The difference is one of whether the semantics are geometric or algebraic, a discussion of which is beyond this paper.)

3. THE FEATURE-BASED ENTERPRISE

3.1 General

Without the notions of agency and emergent behavior, the idea of looking at features is very intuitive. Features in this context can easily be seen the way they commonly are in the Computer Aided Design modeling world: the constituents of a product model.

It is easy to think of a model of customer needs that transmutes to a product model, or many successors, each of which lead in concert to a production and management model with thousands of associated process models. And it is relatively easy to think of these as composed of features which collaboratively deal with each other, transforming each other, forming societies from which the next level emerges and shaping elements of its surrounding to incidentally produce a healthy, profitable virtual enterprise.

Seen this way, it is not so unintuitive to think of the world in terms of selfish features, each of which has agency, all of which can be modeled functionally. These functional models are more than ordinary models that represent; they can be executable code that can simulate or control the emergent behavior.

So, our model of the self-organizing (virtual) enterprise is based on the notion of seeing the world as a collection of urges, expressed as features that have agency and act as functions, exhibiting emergent behavior.

3.2 The "Layer" Problem

We still have the layer problem, but it is more tenable.

The layer problem is simple to describe. In the general emergent systems world, it is often explained thus: we have a good theory of chemical interactions and we have another quite different theory of biological interactions. Each is in their own "layer." But clearly there are actions in one layer that affect behavior in the others, and in fundamental ways. How does the language that molecules "speak" to one another relate to the different language cells use?

Now shift the problem into a more difficult context by introducing the self-organizing notion. Chemical elements in this world clearly self-organize with one result that cells come into being. And throughout the life of the cell there is information conveyed "up" and down that layer boundary, non-trivial information related to organizational urges and scripts.

The similarity to the virtual enterprise case is obvious. If not, the reader needs to be reminded that individual reward systems are radically different than those of work cells and plants and small companies, on up to the enterprise and beyond to healthy societies. The ontological differences in these layers are of the same significant order in the enterprise case as in the layers of physics, chemistry, biology, organisms and societies. (The top layer: "societies" is the same in both cases, virtual enterprise and general science.)

This layer problem is well known, an open problem in science. Interim solutions involve either transporting a mechanism from the top or the bottom. The "bottom" here means physics and the concept is entropy, the degree of organization of a physical system, characterized statistically. Clever thinkers have figured out jury-rigs to apply a "negentropy" principle to organizing tendencies at higher levels, on up to economics.

Transporting down from the top is equally popular. A prevailing theory of information and language in humans is semiotics. Similarly clever thinkers have applied this very human-oriented principle of representative meaning to the lower levels and "biosemiotics" is an active field. Both of these approaches work well enough in limited cases to survive. But both lack the formal depth a solid solution to this layer problem needs.

What makes the layer problem so much easier now that we move to a categoric feature space for the enterprise is that we build an equivalence between features and transforms in the form of functional agents. Features in one layer can act on each other or aggregate with each other to form features of completely different types (according to strict rules) at higher or lower levels. The problem of transforming and shifting levels of abstraction are "built in" to the space, as it were. Our only problem is in defining the functional transforms. We approach this below by ordinary group operators.

3.3 The Problem of "Scripts"

All of the familiar enterprise models have agents and scripts. We've made the agent problem go away, but what about the script problem? By script, we mean the rules by which an enterprise is organized. Each agent in the ordinary models has access to its part of the script, even if it that script is somehow built in. To simplify this in the enterprise case, these scripts are based on vertical domains with relatively orthogonal, stable and mature concepts. Thus, we have financial infrastructure, product design, sales, human resources and so on, each with a set of rules, abstractions, metrics and information flows.

If we do away with agents reading scripts, we need to be able to have our functions reinvent them on the fly them to a meaningful degree. After all, what kills enterprise engineering the way we do it now is that we have to figure out the scripts (process plans, best management practices, performance metrics and so on) and maintain them in parallel with building and maintaining the enterprise. The main advantage of self-organizing systems is that they should be able to figure most of that out without human guidance — and possibly do it more cleverly.

So we have the script problem. We had it before, partially managed by cleanly dividing the enterprise and separating it, only to have to integrate the pieces. Now we have it in a different, possibly more tenable way.

What makes it more tenable is that instead of dealing with constraints and normal forms, we can reinvent approaches on the fly based on goals. And isn't that the point of self-organization, to come up with optimized structures that work in unfamiliar ways that we never would have thought of?

Naturally we still need all sorts of constraints, legal, ethical and so on, to have as external references, boundary conditions.

3.4 The Problem of "Memory"

The final problem is termed "memory" which we will show below is a key concept. But the problem definition is larger, one of introspection of the enterprise, pattern matching to prior situations and prediction based on history.

This problem comes from the plain fact that we can reinvent how enterprises form and operate, but we cannot reinvent what surrounds them. Among other things that will remain (like customer infrastructure and legal constraints), we have the problem of finance. Finance is based on explanations and predictions and despite the common use of the term "management science," it is an inductive science where repeatability is the rule.

You cannot understand something in business unless you have seen something like it before. And if you cannot understand it, you cannot finance it. A huge collection of monitoring and reporting tasks usually support this notion in the ordinary enterprise. But if we have no scripts and we don't even know who the actors are until they announce themselves — if we have no idea what the enterprise will look like or even what it will make, how can we fuel it with capital?

In theory, this new model takes us much closer to a market force driven economy, but in some respects further away from capitalism. To mitigate this, we have to introduce "apparent determinism." The self-organizing system doesn't have to be deterministic, it just has to look that way to the financial linkages from the outside.

The problem of memory and scripts we solve with a system of concepts, formal and intuitively informal, that we term "narrative." Each of our elements is a feature based on an urge. Each urge is a tendency to want to make a story. Different stories compete, some fitting the constraints better than others, some singing more eloquently.

Formally, each feature is a function with transformative possibilities toward certain complex situations, the situations specified by a situation logic. These "situations" capture the "what" we'll call narrative. but we get ahead of ourselves.

4. A THEORY OF EMERGENT BEHAVIOR

4.1 General

In this section, we provide some overview of work being done in new theoretical foundations for emergent systems. The idea is to apply this larger science to the virtual enterprise domain we've been discussing.

As noted, the problem of a coherent theory of emergent behavior is a vexing one. A few pockets of suboptimal solutions exist. We do not explore here why complexity theory, biosemiotics and quantum statistics are inadequate for a general theory of emergence.

Our requirements are for a system that can both describe how a system works and be used by that system internally. In other words, it should work if you are inside and part of the system and/or outside the system watching or perhaps engineering it.

The domains of application will include human systems (like virtual enterprises) and non-human (like molecules and the features or urges we've noted). The types of system will be mixed between natural systems (like the behavior of molecules) and engineered (like the behavior of programs that schedule work according to business rules).

The idea is not to just describe but to create and not in any one domain but in mixed domains. The special case is where one domain like an enterprise or human body can emerge from components of lower levels like features/urges and molecules.

We've found three principles that seem promising, both in the case of general emergent systems and the self-organizing virtual enterprise as we've described. Each has formal mechanics and a human-specific metaphor.

4.2 Identity

Instead of particles, fields and forces, we look at things in terms of urges and narrative fragments. Urges have and generate associated particles in a complement to the generally accepted notion of particles and their associated fields.

From the normal representations we abstract three new functions associated with identity, introspection and equivalence. These can be seen as urges themselves and have identity as functions in their own spaces and types in each other's space. Categories collect each type and relationships among them and functors build groups used below,

Essentially what's happening is that we have an ordered space to talk about what something is, what it wants to be and how it "thinks" about that. This ordered space also contains the relationships among these abstractions as first class abstractions in the space. The point is to give us a well ordered concept space so that we can reason among and operate on elements in the space; where all the abstractions have a metaphoric equivalent, namely "urge" toward "narrative," as intuitive and no more arbitrary than "particle" and "field;" and where the relationships among the different citizens are functors.

That's the most esoteric part, creating the abstractions. The intuitive metaphor of narrative is easy, but settling on the categories needs specific mapping from each domain. We expect associates to assist with the hardest domains: physics and chemistry. The enterprise case is tricky as well. Actually it is easy in a generic, test case where we can arbitrarily model processes using anything that works.

But real enterprises have what we've called vertical layers, independent domains that do accounting and management of different types. Human resources and production for instance, also finance and strategic planning. Industries have their own peculiar frameworks in this regard. Doing the categoric mapping is relatively easy to do but requires lengthy refinement and validation to be trustworthy for the "apparent determinism" we mentioned.

This notion of throwing everything into category space is common in functional programming and follows a suggestion made by Saunders Mac Lane and fleshed out by Jon Barwise.

4.3 Aggregation and Transformation

Where the first set of formalisms deal with how the representations of the concept space are determined, this second set deal with how they interact. It is the rough equivalent to the operation of the enterprise. It is how things interact with each other, exhibiting emergent behavior that structures systems and operate those systems.

In this, we follow the dominant tendency and employ group theory. It will appear that we are different than most applications because the abstractions are a bit unfamiliar, but we simply apply the wreath product to two interacting collections to discover potential higher level groups derived from, but still linked.

It is the formalism we use to link layers and was inspired by mechanisms described by Michael Leyton that manage the two most important characteristics: "precedence" and "history." We have to explicitly provide for these because normal notions of time and causality are lost in our new identity domain. That domain is inherently stateless, so memory is captured as a new, persistent, higher level.

The group operators predict and generate the new layers.

4.4 Logic

We are indebted to Jon Barwise and others for this component of the approach as well.

We need a logic to apply in reasoning about all this. It has to be "soft" and deeply introspective for the humans reasoning about everything, including the above. It has to have a different sort of softness for humans reasoning about systems they are parts of.

The soft (meaning unknown or unrepresentable) facts in this new logic are explicitly captured as "situations" or components of situations, and the extended logic is known as "situation theory." There is a corresponding situation semantics and logic. It is hairy compared to good old first order logic, and costly to employ, but the world is a hairy place.

We've adapted it slightly to accommodate the soft urges that non-human speech acts would convey or follow in the urge-based agents.

At the time of his death, Barwise was harmonizing the first and last of these theories (category and situation theories) in something he called "channel theory" as a basis for a general theory of information flow.

To summarize: we represent the world in terms of verbs or functions and to do so, employ category theory to make our concept space well ordered, better ordered than what we inherited as an accident of history. This is truly a world model, a general abstract semantics for every domain and tendency. The metaphor is urges toward global, multilevel (or folded) narrative.

Once that is done, the functions apply to each other in the normal way, some of which transform elements from one domain of reality to another, "higher" one. The topological transforms of group theory are used in those functions, with different topologies corresponding to different functional groups.

That's the internal machinery of how the functions trigger and cluster. But we need a logic for elements to reason about other elements. It has to be more flexible and accommodating than first order logic, so we employ a slightly extended situation semantics.

4.5 The Virtual Enterprise Domain

Our group got into looking at the general problem of emergent systems because of the self-organizing virtual enterprise case. Now we are working primarily on that general case and mapping back to the virtual enterprise domain (and one other).

The virtual enterprise case is more difficult in that at least nominally it is 100% a human system. Although the laws of natural science constrain processes, they are all in the context of human goals. What makes the virtual enterprise case simpler is that we know those goals; they are explicitly expressed and generally simple. Moreover, we can assume that though there are many dimensions, all the players get rewarded in much the same way, measured by similar metrics.

The case in chemistry, for instance, is different. It makes little sense to infer how molecules "think" about rewards. It is quite a bit easier to infer how urges function at that level because anticipation is built into the metaphor. But the notion of successful organizations is still elusive, say for biochemical systems, unless you have a desired outcome in mind.

This idea of engineered systems sits a bit uneasily in the container of self-organizing ones unless we limit ourselves to engineering by setting boundary conditions only. So that is what we must do for systems in which we cannot directly participate, like chemical ones. Human systems differ in that reward systems and new metrics can appear as part of the innate tendencies in the system. In this way the virtual enterprise case is simpler.

In our experience, the business case is much more difficult in getting the basic abstractions right. As noted, the layers aren't as coherent as one finds in chemical systems. They have all these parallel infrastructures, each of which has its own ontology and requires a unique mapping. And different industries have their own semantic peculiarities as well.

To mitigate this effect, we expect to rely on a single normal set of semantics and federate what we find using the formal ontological methods of the Process Specification Language, which we believe can be used to federate function semantics from one functional expression to another. (But this does not help with the problem we encounter when the stuff of representations is incorrect as we find sometimes, or deliberately cloaked, as we often find in criminal or military enterprises.)

4.6 A Scenario

We are working with four test scenarios. Three are only of passing interest here.

One involves a study of narrative itself and specifically introspective, folded narrative as it moves through the popular culture, meme-like and exhibits in film. Another concerns the detailed mechanisms of stem cells and the biochemical urges involved in branching. A third is for self-organized concept mining in large data libraries.

Our virtual enterprise scenario is a refinement of one we have been using for a few years now in workshops.

The customer base in this is initially civilian war injured who lack a limb, a depressingly large group of concern to all in the developed world. Prosthetic limbs are notoriously unfriendly to mass production; each would ideally be fitted or even engineered and manufactured in lots of one.

We have allowed this test scenario to be more complex than supposed in as many dimensions as we could envision. For instance, we posit a virtual enterprise of virtual enterprises, some forming in villages in the developing world, some forming around innovative design resources and non-governmental organizations (which themselves in this scenario might be virtual), and others from components of large established enterprises in the west, all linked in dynamic constellations, emerging and fading.

Moreover, we assume that the features would not only reach as deeply as the design and fitting of personal prosthetics, but their actual composition and control systems as well. That means that some of the features may be creating software or polymers in a self-organizing way within their respective domains. We do limit the emergent behavior to devices rather than services because we want to understand how project model features relate to the feature clouds involved in such a manifold system. Product features are a well understood beast and a necessary link to the apparent determinism strategy used. Ultimately, we wish to extend this to agile self-organizing drug design and manufacture, which is why we are looking at stem cell mechanisms.

5. RESEARCH CHALLENGES

This paper is a research note on a new project rather than the usual report on research completed. It is too early to provide exportable details from the work here. But we do hope to indicate some research challenges.

Concerning the definition of active features: as it happens, the Computer Aided Design community is well suited to address this issue, with research focused on extensions to ISO standard 10303 and existing tools that express similar features. Alas, the process modeling and enterprise integration community has really slipped a decade behind in this. There is no serious effort I know to look at process features outside of the interoperability community.

We need to address this inadequacy fast, as the product data management community is growing in power at the expense of the traditional enterprise integration base. We believe this is why.

ISO 18629 is the Process Specification Language that is the most robust formal ontological approach for general semantic federation of the type needed to federate across domains in the enterprise and among different enterprises. Little work has been accomplished toward this use.

There has been an unfortunate confluence of process modeling for the enterprise and modeling for software, with the unhappy result that research in enterprise dynamics is nearly all object oriented. Yet functional programming is growing as its comparative successes pile up. We need a robust basis in functional thinking in the enterprise, and pedagogical examples in the programming language Haskell.

Though entirely appropriate for this type of reasoning whether function-centric or not, situation theory is cumbersome and difficult to work with for non-specialists. We need a "situation theory light" for relatively unsophisticated users.

The biomedical community has some familiarity with these methods. A better relationship between the pharmaceutical enterprise and the virtual enterprise community would benefit both.

Studies in folded narrative need to be more robust.

6. REFERENCES

1. Barwise J, "Constraints, Channels and the Flow of Information". In Situation Theory and its Applications, Aczel P, Isreal D, Katagiri Y, Peters S eds. Palo Alto: Stanford University, 1990.

2. Collier J, "Order from Rhythmic Entrainment and the Origins of Levels through Dissipation". in Symmetry: Culture and Science. 1998; 9:2: 165-178.

3. Gass WH, Finding a Form. Ithica: Cornell University Press, 1996.

4. Goranson HT, The Agile Virtual Enterprise. Westport CT: Quorum Books, 1999.

5. Goranson HT, Cost Analyses and Survey of Meta=abstraction for Modeling. Norfolk: Classified DOD report, 2002.

6. Goranson HT, Chu B, Gruninger M, Ivezic N, Kulvantanyou S, Larbrou Y, Masouka R, Peng Y, Sheth A, Shorter D, "Ontologies as a New Cost Factor in Enterprise Integration". In Enterprise Inter and Intra 7. Organizational Integration, Kosanke K, Jochem R, Nell JG, Bas AO, eds. Berlin: Kluwer, 2003.

8. Hilbert D, Cohn-Vossen S, Geometry and the Imagination. New York: Chelsea, 1952.

9. Hilfinger PN, Abstraction Mechanisms and Language Design, Cambridge MA: MIT Press, 1982.

10. Leyton M, Symmetry Causality Mind. Cambridge MA: MIT Press, 1992.

11. Kauffmann S, Distinguishing Features. Baltimore: Johns Hopkins University Press, 1994.

12. MacLaine S, Categories for the Working Mathematician. New York: Springer-Verlag, 1971

13. Myers K, Konolige K, "Reasoning with Analogical Representations". In Diagrammatic Reasoning, 14. Glasgow J, Narayanan NH, Chandrasekaran B eds. Cambridge MA: MIT Press, 1995.

15. National Research Council, Visionary Manufacturing Challenges. Washington: National Academy Press, 1998.

16. Rosen R, "On Psychomimesis". In Essays on Life Itself. New York: Comulbia University Press, 2000.

17. Stilman B, Linguistic Geometry. Boston: Kluwer, 2002.
18. Vernadat FB, Enterprise Modeling and Integration. New York: Chapman & Hall, 1996.

5

A CONTRIBUTION TO A PRODUCTION NETWORK (PN) THEORY

Hermann Kuehnle

Institute for Ergonomics, Manufacturing Systems and Automation, Otto-von-Guericke-University Magdeburg, Universitaetsplatz 2, D 39196 Magdeburg, Germany, Centre for Extended Enterprises CE2
E-mail: CE2@mb.uni-magdeburg.de
E-mail: hermann.kuehnle@mb.uni-magdeburg.de
Internet: http://www.uni-magdeburg.de/iaf

In Production Networks' planning and control innovative concepts and solutions may result from exploiting network properties and simultaneous application of selected models. Model systems may generate very efficient solution procedures for PN planning and control as proven by several examples. Such Model systems may be interpreted as part of a theory conjecture for PN, based on a topological core. All models appear as embedded structures of network units and connections, carrying fold/unfold properties of graphs and systems. Interoperability requirements induce standardisations for the models. The theory approach proposed intends helping to explain network phenomena and provide solution approaches for PN problems.

1. INTRODUCTION

In recent years, Production Network (PN) concepts, typologies and software supports etc. have been developed generating mostly singular problem solutions. Incoherent approaches for different problem aspects often lead to heterogeneous and non consistent model fragments. Therefore large portions of the acquired knowledge about PN are cast into rather singular models or solution procedures uniquely based on case experiences and anecdotal verifications that need to be further validated. Moreover, most of the methodologies applied have been outcomes of systems theories and the resulting procedures still show characteristics of one-time static interventions not apt to dynamic network configurations.

Since PNs are complex, optimisation of interlinked agents/units is often reduced to ordinary (data) interface handling. A more promising approach for PN Planning and Control seems to be the optimisation of agents/units interrelations, cross impacts and collaborations, engaging distributed and concurrent procedures that continuously and progressively generate "evolutive" solutions, (Bennett & Dekkers, 2005).

Please use the following format when citing this chapter:

Kuehnle, H., 2006, in IFIP International Federation for Information Processing, Volume 224, Network-Centric Collaboration and Supporting Fireworks, eds. Camarinha-Matos, L., Afsarmanesh, H., Ollus, M., (Boston: Springer), pp. 45–54.

Analysing such solution procedures for PN planning reveals that good results have been achieved by synthesising selected models of PNs and PN units. These approaches can be generalised by putting a number production network models upon a common base. The interpretation of PNs as specific topological structures enables to propose a PN theory design, which allows quicker and better problem solutions.

The approach is motivated by complexity theory, topology and fractal organisation experiences and intends to contribute to specific network sciences as called for by increasing numbers of researchers (Barbasi, 2002; Camarinha-Matos & Afsarmanesh, 2005).

2. MODELS AND PRODUCTION NETWORKS

2.1 Models in Production Networks

Networks are obviously controlled/attracted by directives and objectives. Re-configurable dynamic set ups are interrelated, inter-linking/detaching units, establishing and optimising varying and changing process chains. Global order structures may "emerge" as results of local interactions if networks will self-organise towards attractors. Business opportunities may represent "attractors" that orientate and reconfigure production networks. Therefore we may understand a PN as consisting of self-organising, self-optimising units with own processes and structures not developing in a linear way, not exactly predictable, moving towards such configurations. It appears that a few configurations are 'more favourable' than others in some way.

Planning and control does not regard the units themselves but various models and attributes of these units that are manipulated and put into relations. Each PN planning step makes use of a number of such models raising the question of how the dependencies and simultaneous planning actions influence choices, attributes and levels of detail of the models involved. Therefore the network units' interaction structure must be envisioned as a model system's interrelation structure. As an example for this principle the arrangement of equipment within a factory layout may be given.

2.2 Interrelated Models for Planning

Generally it is assumed, that the site of a unit in the layout plan depends on the material flow, the process sequences, the overall layout and technological influences. Traditionally there is outlined, that any conception of production systems is to be executed by top-down-procedures, assuming proportional relations between length of planning horizon and planning object detail. Inevitably the construct will supply correspondent views of planning horizon lengths and details of planning object levels. Long range decisions are envisioned in direct link with rough sketches and low precision, whereas short planning horizons are associated to details in alternatives and variants for processes and factory layouts. It is well known and widely tolerated that the resulting "one time" solutions are sub optimal, not able to cope with volatile market demands.

Variety and unpredictability call for versatile productions. Therefore there is the permanent need for planning, using all model attributes required concurrently. Such concurrent procedures assume a "pool of models", which is permanently available and may be instantly activated at the requested attribute and detail level. Models of the mentioned unit attributes as flows and restrictions and geometrical attributes and impact relations (noise, vibration) contribute to decisions about layout arrangements could be put into a planning impact diagram, and are activated for decision making (Figure 1).

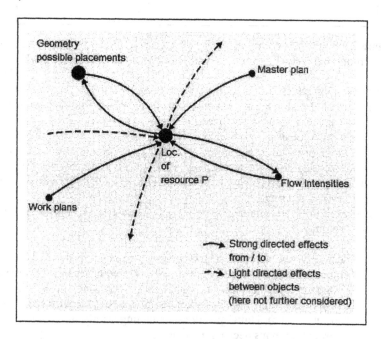

Figure 1 – Planning Impact Diagram - Impacts and relations
between units' attributes for a planning issue: Determine optimum
location of machine P in layout plan

Production re-configurability requirements evidently turn hierarchical planning into a concurrent planning process engaging interrelated models, attached to the network units.

2.3 Production Network (PN) Control

This procedure may be transferred. For Planning and Control of PN, Decision Support models may be attached to the units. Spaces of Activity, SoAs, (Figure 2), viewing state variables which describe the units' activities and success may be introduced.

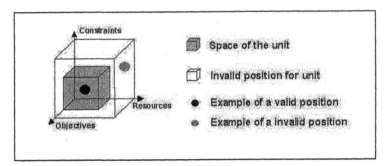

Figure 2 – Space of Activity (SoA) by Mappings for Planning and Control of
Production Network units - viewing positions (Klostermeyer, 2002)

The units' objectives are output of the network strategy, the resources and
constraints affect the structures. In consequence, the SoA volume represents the
unit's decision space, which may be used for self-organisation.

The unit's SoA position gives input for decisions on maintaining the self-
organisation mode or reducing autonomy and calling for PN interference. Dependant
on the unit's inability to cope with changes in the environment, network "order
parameters" may gain influence on units' activities ((self) reproduction, (self)
destruction, (self) structuring).

The PN result must be achieved by commitments on overall objectives (Kühnle,
2005). Each unit may

(I)   decide on the appropriate methods, tools, etc. in order to achieve the
        objectives negotiated and agreed upon. Prerequisites are resources, e.g.
        budgets, competencies, technical and personnel availability and
        constraints (a unit may have to face may be e.g.. legal restrictions and
        capacity limits). Units' positions remaining within the predefined SoA
        allow autonomous decision making.

(II)   loose it's autonomy, if positions within the unit's SoA are not achieved.
        Mechanisms must be activated that prevent the deviations and provide
        PN plan fulfilment.

The PN reacts on any increase of complexity (diversity, uncertainty and
unpredictability) by expansion of the SoAs affected (if affordable). More foreseeable
steady conditions allow to shrink the SoAs' volumes.

2.4 Self similarity and folding of SoA

All objectives, broken down onto the units and subunits, must be negotiated and
harmonised with the over all PN objectives and consistency checks for the
networked organisation on all levels have to be applied (Vasiliu & Brown, 2003). If
there is no consistency on the network level u, the procedure has to be lifted up to
the next network level u+1, where the PN SoA appears as aggregated model. The
iteration has to be continued as long as either highest network level is reached or all
objective figures are achieved.

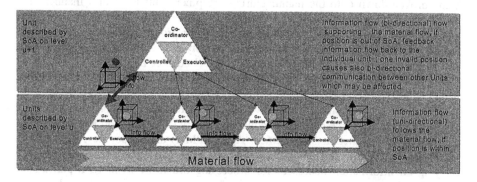

Figure 3 – Information flows for harmonising goal settings of SoAs,
caused by invalid position of the higher u+1 level SoA

Figure 3 illustrates the communication within the meshed control loops
established by SoA interferences for PN control. Higher levels of the network are
represented by SoAs, carrying all SoAs of lower network levels as (self-similar)
folded structures. The configuration is optimised progressively for a short term
horizon. Splitting, removal or re-linking of units are possible decisions to be taken,
if the deviation can not be avoided by the unit's very own efforts (self optimisation).
For medium and long term control of the network, lifecycle procedures may be
applied, as described by GERAM, (GERAM, 1999).

The control mode described is different from traditional planning and control of
company networks, where elaborate plans are calculated for each unit, covering
discrete planning rhythms and horizons. Central control functions (as ERP, MES,..)
are applied to accomplish plan fulfilment by time and load shift on the base of fixed,
quasi - static order – resource prescriptions. Well aware that these plans are incorrect
right after its set ups, the units' staffs are fully occupied with correcting, adapting
and improvising, basically trying to fight PN reactions as bottlenecks, inventory
oscillations, exceeded lead times, bull whip effects or similar so called "chaotic"
behaviour.

Producing much better results (e-Volution II, 2004), the proposed planning and
control procedure is continuous, distributed and concurrent, generating solutions
progressively. Simple procedures, like the SoA logic, are locally applied. Plans,
assignments, units, responsibilities etc. are continuously rearranged, processes newly
established or reconfigured. Again, effective control procedures turn out to be
communication intensive, objective driven adaptation and configuration processes,
using interrelated models.

2.5 Distributed control by Agents

The SoA logic described has also proven to be a useful instrument for Distributed
Automation, the SoA and embedded structures may be unfolded to any network
structure's level, also to the networks Manufacturing Execution level (Kühnle et al.,
2001).

For factory automation, the objective and resource axes may be "rescaled" after being broken down onto the manufacturing equipment unit level in a manner that loads and resource consumptions can be mapped. After the transformation, the SoA visualises and evaluates unit states and objectives for process steps and order loads. Details of objectives, resources and constraints may easily be checked, determined and negotiated by the use of agent technology (Lüder et al., 2004). One generic concept for distributed order control, based this approach is PABADIS (Plant Automation BAsed on DIstributed Systems, (Bratoukhine & al., 2003). In order to execute decision and control in the navigation logic described in 2.4, three types of supporting agents can be defined: Product Agent (PA) for Common Manufacturing Units (CMU), Production Management Agent (PMA) and Resource Agent (RA), (McFarlane & Bussmann, 2000); Sauter & Massotte, 2001). PA is a mobile agent, carrying all information necessary for processing orders between ERP and units. Main decision tasks are the assignments of orders to units as well as the ERP communication, covered by the Look Up Service (LUS) and the assigned SoA. RAs carry unit profiles and information about units' states mapped to the SoAs (rescaled). PABADIS aims at creating an architecture for distributed plant automation as a standard ensuring flexibility, scalability features and plug-and-participate properties for distributed control of PN.

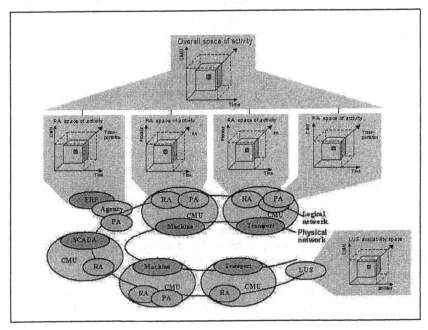

Figure 4 – Example of the PABADIS architecture implementation, involving SoAs and Agents

By splitting up the MES level of the so called "automation control pyramid" into a network of intelligent nodes, adaptable structures are generated (Figure 4). The resulting control solution appears as a structure of interlinked models, detached (virtual) from the manufacturing units, as PABADIS is based on emulated controls, the Java Virtual Machines (JVMs), for all units (Klostermeyer & Klemm, 2005).

Consequently the SoA network of JVMs represents the same degree of complexity as the network of units to be controlled. This rule, generally referred to as "Ashby's Law of Requisite Variety" (Malik, 1993) was the guideline for the pilot "navigation in manufacturing networks" approaches with agents, that later resulted in the architecture (Klostermeyer, 2002) described. Another finding can be stated: Production Planning and Production Simulation can now based on one and the same model system, a requirement, frequently cited for traditional planning, which is -for intrinsic contradictions- unachievable within systems set-ups.

3. THEORY DESIGN APPROACH

The findings outlined above can be generalised. The PN Planning and control examples explicitly deal with phenomena as unpredictability, self-organisation, fractal structures (edge of chaos), diversity and self-similarity (pattern recognition). These are important Complexity Principles (Watts, 2003; Webb et al., 2004). Other findings as the focus on the model world or synergies by adding network units may be seen as specifications of the New Economy Rules: "From places to spaces" and "Increasing Return", (Kelly, 1999).

Productions facing volatility, speed and unpredictability, reach their limits (Kühnle & Schmelzer, 1995) and the pressure by new phenomena calls for explanation, (Kuhn, 1962). For PN, phenomena as diversity and edge of chaos (Stacey, 1996; McKelvey, 2004) are still waiting to be covered by adequate theories (Dekkers et al., 2004). The examples discussed demonstrate the important role of interlinked models for PN description. Rules and laws could be cited where the approach improves congruence of PN observation and model behaviour.

Such elements may (Thagard, 1988) constitute a theory on the field discussed. In the conjecture proposed, the PN nodes are reduced structures, able to unfold many attributes and properties within model the world assigned.. Envisioning the network nodes as elements, a PN may be seen as a specific Hausdorff Space, carrying attached models of attributes, relations and perspectives as tangent spaces. The PN appears as the Quotient Space of surrounding Kolmogoroff Spaces (in topology terms, Boto von Querenburg, 1979), which may arbitrarily "forget" or "remember" attached models (Figure 5).

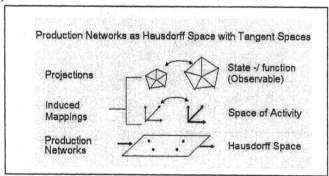

Figure 5 – Production Network as Hausdorff Space with attached the Space of Activity (Tangent Space) model as used above including derived state/function observable

The entire conjecture may be depicted as an orbital/shell set up (Figure 6), with
- Centred formal theoretical core, (Hausdorff Space)
- a shell of phenomenological laws
- a models shell and
- an orbit of real world examples.

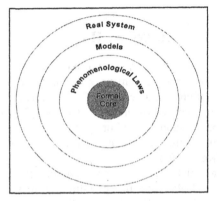

Figure 6 – Production Network Theory set up design: Models derived from Real
Systems find a Formal Core Base and follow Phenomenological Laws

Since interlinked models play a key role in the approach, a prepared pool of PN
specific models is the precondition for successful theory application. A first set has
been proposed by Massotte (Figure 7). This list is open for additional PN models.
Some of the models have been applied in the examples outlined.

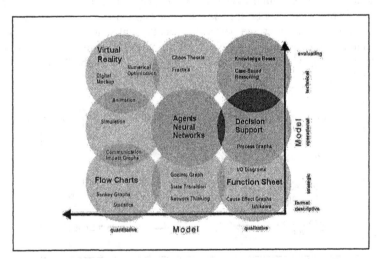

Figure 7 – Portfolio of models frequently used for production according
to Massotte, (Massotte, 1995) to be attached to the network units
(subset in bold letters is applied for the examples outlined)

As Barbasi (Barbasi, 2005) states already, excellent solutions may be generated by applying/synthesizing rather simple models decentralised and interlinked. For PN, units' interoperability requirements might enforce general standardization needs concerning all models involved.

4. CONCLUSIONS

In the search of competitive excellence in production, PNs have received much attention in the last years. Understanding network characteristics in production gives competitive advantages. However concepts, typologies and software supports etc. have been developed so far mostly as singular not general problem solutions, where PNs are simply seen as structures, which link production units.

This outline could point out, that linking the models of PNs and models of units may generate good results. Therefore a selection of models is proposed for better PN planning and control problems solving. Moreover it may facilitate to integrate other findings; the list of models is open, the collection of laws and rules is just started. Exploiting PN advantages is successful in every day operation. Instead of trying to ignore or even eliminate structural behaviour of network nature, network properties may successfully be used to establish solution procedures.

5. ACKNOWLEDGMENTS

This work has been partly funded by the European Commission. The author wishes to acknowledge the Commission and the Ministry for Cultural Affairs Saxony-Anhalt for their support. We wish to acknowledge our gratitude and appreciation to all project partners involved for their contributions.

6. REFERENCES

Barbasi, A-L.(2002) Linked. The New Science of Networks, Cambridge MA
Barbasi, A-L.(2005), Network Theory—the Emergence of the Creative Enterprise- SCIENCE VOL 308, pp 639-641
Bennett, D., Dekkers, R. (2005), Industrial Networks of the future – a critical commentary on research and practice, 12th International EurOMA Conference on Operational and Global Competitiveness, Budapest Proceedings pp. 677-686
Boto von Querenburg (1979), Mengentheoretische Topologie. Heidelberg
Bratoukhine, A., Sauter, T. Peschke, J.,Lüder, A. Klostermeyer, A. (2003), Distributed Automation: PABADIS vs. HMS, 1st IEEE Conference on Industrial Informatics, INDIN 03, Banff, Canada, September 2003, Proceedings, pp. 294-300
Camarinha-Matos, L. M. and Afsarmanesh, H. (2005). "Collaborative Networks: a new scientific discipline", Journal of Intelligent Manufacturing, Vol. 16, No. pp. 439-452
Dekkers, R.; Sauer, A.; Schönung, M.; Schuh, G.: Collaborations as Complex Systems, In: Proceedings of the IMNet 2004 9th Annual Cambridge International Manufacturing Symposium, pp. 60-77.
e-Volution II (2004),- Road map for e-business implementation in Extended Enterprises G1RD-CT-2002-00698,. (http://www.e-vol.net/public/index.cfm)
GERAM (1999): Generalised Enterprise Reference Architecture and Methodology, Version 1.6.3. IFIP–IFAC Task Force on Architectures for Enterprise Integration.

Kelly, K. (1999). "New Rules for the New Economy: 10 Ways the Network Economy is Changing Everything", London

Klostermeyer, A. (2002). „Agentengestützte Navigation wandlungsfähiger Produktionssysteme", PhD Thesis, University of Magdeburg

Klostermeyer, A., Klemm, E. (2005) Multi Agent based Architecture for Plant Automation, The Industrial Information Technology Handbook, Editor R. Zurawski, CRC Press, Industrial Electronics Series, 2005, pp. 108/1-108/19.

Kuhn, Th. S (1962): The Structure of Scientific Revolutions, Chicago

Kühnle, H. (2005), Fractal Extended Enterprise: Framework and Examples for multi-party supply chains, in: Shuping, Yl (Ed.) ; Xiaohui, Chen (Ed.) ; Yu, Yang (Ed.): Modern industrial engineering and innovation in enterprise management, IEEM 2005 (12th international conference on industrial engineering and engineering management, Chongqing, China, proceedings. Vol. 1. pp. 211-217

Kühnle, H.; Schmelzer, S.F, (1995), A NEW PARADIGM - THE FRACTAL VIEW OF THE FACTORY, The Individual in the Focus of the Factory. In: British Academy of Management - Annual Conference 1995 (Sheffield, UK September 11th –13th 1995) - Proceedings, pp. 278-282

Kühnle, H.; Klostermeyer, A.; Lorentz, K.(2001), A Paradigm Shift to Distributed Systems in Plant Automation. In: Fares Sebaaly, M. (Ed.), Proceedings of The International NAISO Congress on Information Science Innovations ISI' 2001, March 17 – 2,1 2001, pp. 463 - 469.

Lüder, A., Peschke, J., Sauter, T., Deter, S., Diep, D. (2004), "Distributed intelligence for plant automation based on multi-agent systems – the PABADIS approach", Special Issue on Application of Multiagent Systems to PP&C, Journal of Production Planning and Control, Vol. 15 (2004), Nr. 2, pp. 201 – 212.

Malik, F. (1993), „Systemisches Management, Evolution, Selbstorganisation", Bern

Massotte, Pierre., Evolution des technologies de l'information et optimation des processus. Habilitation (HDR) 1995, Université de Savoie

McFarlane, D.C., Bussmann, S.(2000), Developments in Holonic Production Planning and Control, International Journal of Production Planning and Control, Vol. 11, No. 6, 2000, pp. 522-536.

McKelvey, B. (2004), "'Simple rules' for improving corporate IQ: basic lessons from complexity science." in: P. Abdriani and G. Passiante (Eds.), in Complexity Theory and the Management of Networks, University of Lecce, Italy: Imperial College Press, pp. 39-52.

Sauter, T.; Massotte, P., Enhancement of Distributed Production Systems through Software Agents, in ETFA 2001, in Emerging Technologies and Factory Automation, IEEE International Conference on, pp. 267-272

Stacey, R D (1996) Complexity and Creativity in Organizations, San Fransisco

Thagard, P. (1998) Computational Philosophy of Science, Cambridge MA

Vasiliu, L., Browne, J. (2003); An integrated modelling approach of extended enterprise using Fractals, Game theory and Neural Networks structures. In F. Weber et al. (eds.), Proceedings of the 9th International Conference on Concurrent Enterprising, Espoo, Finland, University of Nottingham, 275-286.

Watts, D., (2003), Six Degrees: The Science of a Connected Age. Norton

Webb, C., Wohlfahrt, L., Wunram, M. Ziv, A, (2004), The Secrets of the Six Princilpes: A Guide to Robust Development of Organisations, Israel: Innovation Ecology

6

TOWARDS A TAXONOMY FOR NETWORKING MODELS FOR INNOVATION

Myrna Flores
University of Applied Sciences of Southern Switzerland (SUPSI)
Department of Technology and Innovation (DTI)
CIM Institute of Southern Switzerland (iCIMSI), SWITZERLAND
myrna.flores@supsi.ch

In the last decades innovation has been regarded by many policy makers, economists, engineers and business managers as a key element to obtain competitive advantage. Developed countries target innovation to maintain their competitiveness and high standard of living. On the other hand, catching up countries look for innovation as a main source to alleviate poverty and provide new value added jobs and new products to the global markets. But innovation requires knowledge and continuous learning, which in many occasions for companies, specially for SME's (both in developed and catching-up countries) are difficult to achieve by themselves in a systematic way. One very important trend to enable new knowledge creation and transfer in and to SME's is the development of collaborative environments and networks to increase their innovation capabilities as a single unit but also the capabilities of the network as a whole through collective learning. As a consequence, different models have emerged from different disciplines to satisfy the need to understand, promote, enable, measure and improve the networking and learning processes among different entities to spur innovation. The objective of this paper is twofold: 1) present and classify ten identified networking models proposed by different disciplines into two main types and analyse their main strengths and weaknesses and 2) to propose a taxonomy to classify them identifying their main differences and similarities.

1. INTRODUCTION

A large variety of organisational forms of collaboration have emerged during the last years as a result of the many socio-economic challenges faced by the society and enabled by the new ICT developments (Camarinha and Afsarmanesh, 2004). For some authors (Camagni, 1991) creativity and continuous innovation are seen as a collective learning process, where different actors interact either in a formal or informal way for the transfer of know-how and for the imitation of successful managerial practices. As in the case of the innovation process, different disciplines have tried to analyse the collaboration and networking processes; having as a result, the emergence of different models targeting different objectives.

Please use the following format when citing this chapter:

Flores, M., 2006, in IFIP International Federation for Information Processing, Volume 224, Network-Centric Collaboration and Supporting Fireworks, eds. Camarinha-Matos, L., Afsarmanesh, H., Ollus, M., (Boston: Springer), pp. 55–66.

Such collaboration models can be classified in mainly two groups (table 1):

Type 1: Inter and intra firm collaboration

Type 2: Networks as part of a spatial context where not only firms collaborate, but also other local agents, such as universities, research centres, associations and governmental institutions.

Table 1. Classification of Networking Models

Type 1 Intra-Inter Company Networking Models The Firm as an individual entity or part of a network (not linked to a specific territory)	Type 2 National/Regional Networking Models Collaboration as part of a spatial context, innovation for regional/national competitiveness
1. Simultaneous Engineering 2. Supply Chain Management 3. Extended Enterprise 4. Value Chain 5. Virtual Enterprises 6. Breeding Environment	7. Industrial Clusters 8. Innovative Milieu 9. Innovation Systems: National, Regional, Metropolitan, Local 10. Triple Helix

2. TYPE 1 NETWORKING MODELS: THE FIRM AS AN INDIVIDUAL ENTITY AND PART OF A NETWORK

The first six models look forward for the networking of companies but less attention is paid to integrate local institutions (for instance Universities, Research Centres or the Government) as nodes of knowledge and technology transfer. Most of the times, these type 1 models target collaboration for innovation or operational optimisation as they have been proposed to optimise the operational processes inside the single company or the network and/or to reduce innovation costs and lead times. These models apply different Engineering methods and technologies and propose the development of new tools to reduce transactional costs and to orchestrate the innovation processes among different distributed partners in the best efficient way. The unit of analysis is "the company" of the "group of companies" that are part of the network which is formed in most occasions by partners locates in distributed locations.

One key objective proposed by these models, is the production of a new product or service from the idea to its launching into the market. Knowledge is considered as an intangible asset to be applied to develop, produce and market the innovation. Partners in the network are selected due to their competences which will be applied in terms of available skills in the new product development. Researchers in this field are usually from different Engineering schools (Manufacturing, Industrial, Mechanical and Computer Science). Business scientists and lawyers are also linked to these models, specially to understand how to obtain the best economic results of the network, define the network strategy, the business model and the legal framework. These models, contrary to the economists view "outside the black box", look for solutions that can enable better and more efficient ways of working in the network "inside the black box". Many basic and applied research projects have focused on different aspects such as:

1) The development of Information and Communication Technologies (ICT), tools and platforms to enable the entities collaboration and information sharing
2) The analysis and design of new business models that can support the configuration and lean operation of these networks,
3) The assessment methods to select the best possible partners for the network
4) The search for new governance models
5) Readiness assessment tools to identify the readiness of partners to be part of a new or existing network
6) The legal infrastructure
7) The definition and study of the new product development and network life cycles
8) The development of roadmaps in order to enable the formation of future collaborative environments.

One important element of these models is that the innovation output targets the market or final customer needs. In other words, innovations do not remain at the inventors' backyard but target a market to serve. Engineers and business scientists realised the importance of the different functions inside the company to accomplish innovations. A multidisciplinary approach was needed to be successful in launching new products and managing daily operations. Initial networking models targeted the collaboration from different departments "inside" the organisation. Later on, with the advent of the ICT technologies and the globalisation processes both the new product development process and the overall companies' operations were interlinked with more suppliers and clients. Therefore, with time, the networking concept started to consider also suppliers and customers. The six identified type 1 models are:

Simultaneous Engineering (SE) refers to the cross-departmental/cross-company cooperation involved in engineering and marketing tasks. The specific activities are achieved individually, with the goal of parallel execution so that processes that have no dependency on other processes may be carried out at the same time. It is expected that the effectiveness of the Simultaneous Engineering within a company will impact the overall new product development lead times and costs (Ribbens J, 2002).

Supply Chain Management (SCM) is the total manage of a network of facilities and distribution options in a partnership between a consumer, distributor and manufacturer with the purpose of transfer and exchange information and physical goods for the supplier's suppliers to their customer's customers ensuring the right goods in the most efficient manner, reached accurately wherever they are required in a company and beyond (SCOR, 1995). This collaboration model looks mainly for operational processes optimisation to reduce costs and lead times. Less attention is paid to the new product development (NPD) or product innovation.

The Extended Enterprise (EE) regards a new kind of enterprise which is represented by all those organisations or parts of organisations, customers, suppliers and subcontractors and is engaged collaboratively in the design, development, production and delivery of a product to the end user (Brown, 1997). In this collaboration model, both product and process innovations are targeted.

The idea of the **Value Chain (VC)** is based on the process view of organisations, the idea of seeing a manufacturing (or service) organisation as a system, made up of subsystems each with inputs, transformation processes and outputs. But the concept moved beyond the boundaries of the firm as in the real world to deliver the finished product into the market linkages with suppliers, distributors and clients within and without the same sector are required. Within value chains trust is critical to enhance inter-firm cooperation and new forms of work organisation (Porter, 1985).

The **Virtual Enterprise (VE)** approach is based on the ability to create temporary cooperation and to realise the value of a short business opportunity that the partners cannot (or can, but only to lesser extent) capture on their own. (Katzy & Schuch, 1998). The purpose of the virtual enterprise is to provide a new solution for an unpredicted opportunity. Innovation is then an "intrinsic" element of this collaboration model. The concept behind the Virtual Enterprise is that it can accomplish tasks that could not be done by each of the competitors working sequentially or even in tandem, because is formed by integrating core competencies, resources and opportunities (Goldman, Nagel and Preiss, 1995).

The **Breeding Environment (BE)** approach emerged due to the success of several FP5 and FP6 EU funded research projects, which follow EU policies that stress the need of companies to collaborate in networks. A Breeding environment represents an association or pool of organizations and their related supporting institutions that have both the potential and the will to cooperate with each other through the establishment of a "base" long-term cooperation agreement and interoperable infrastructure Camarinha-Matos and Afsarmanesh (2004). In the BE when a business opportunity is identified by one member, a subset of these organisations can be selected and thus forming a Virtual Enterprise. One important point of this model is that its authors argue that a Breeding Environment represents a group of organisational entities that have developed a preparedness for collaboration in case a specific opportunity arises, which could be considered a "pre-condition" to form Virtual Enterprises.

In contrast with the previous type 1 collaboration models, the Breeding Environment also considers the different institutions and industrial associations as part of the breeding environment; but on the contrary, this latter does not refer to the active collaboration of partners to develop an innovative solution, rather it targets the development of a pre-condition for future collaborations to arise. It is important to mention that none of these type 1 models are related to networks linked to a territory, but on the contrary, in all of them, partners could also be located in distant locations where Information and Communication Technologies (ICT's) together with new enterprise business models will enable the collaboration and innovation (specially of SME's). One important aspect is that type 1 models look forward for the competitiveness of the single company and the partners of the network. These models are linked to the resource-based theory (Barney, 1986, 1991), where the approach to strategic management focuses on costly-to-copy attributes of the firm as sources of economic rents and, therefore, as the fundamental drivers for competitive advantage. These models do not analyse the positive or negative spillovers in the territory where partners are located. Table 2 shows the actors involved, strengths and weaknesses and the disciplines related to each one of these six type 1 models.

Table 2. Type 1 Networking Models

	ACTOR(S)	STRENGTHS & WEAKNESSES	DISCIPLINE(S)
1.1 SE	• The firm intends to increase collaboration among its departments and also with its suppliers and customers for the new product development (NPD) process	**STRENGTHS** • New product development lead time reduction • Integration of the different functions inside the firm enhancing information sharing **WEAKNESSES** • Doesn't consider the creation of new knowledge • Doesn't study the knowledge transfer process among entities, specially external • Collaboration with local institutions such as associations, universities and government is not considered	• Industrial Engineering • Mechanical Engineering • Manufacturing Engineering • Business Management
1.2 SCM	• The firm that considers its suppliers and customers to improve its operational processes	**STRENGTHS** • Reduction of operational costs and lead times • Integration of the different functions inside and outside the firm enhancing information sharing • Collaboration increases with the usage of new Information and Communication Technologies (ICT), specially Enterprise Resource Planning systems that focus on sharing operational information **WEAKNESSES** • The development of new products is most of the times not considered (innovation is not the main target) • Collaboration with local institutions such as associations, universities and government is not considered	• Business Management • Industrial Engineering • Computer Science/ Engineering
1.3 EE	• Mainly an Original Equipment Manufacturer (OEM) which tends to develop closer relationships with clients and customers both for NPD and to reduce costs	**STRENGTHS** • The collaboration of partners maximises the combined competencies of partners to achieve each partner's strategic goals and to provide solutions to meet customers needs • Collaboration increases with the usage of new Information and Communication Technologies (ICT), specially Enterprise Resource Planning softwares (ERPs) **WEAKNESSES** • Usually the OEM orchestrates the New Product Development (NPD) process, SME's have very little decisional power • Collaboration with local institutions such as associations, universities and government is not considered	• Industrial Engineering • Mechanical Engineering • Manufacturing Engineering • Computer Engineering • Business Management
1.4 VC	• Mainly companies considering suppliers and customers in the networks	**STRENGTHS** • The idea of seeing a manufacturing (or service) organisation as a system, made up of subsystems each with inputs, transformation processes and outputs. • Divides internal business as primary and secondary to concentrate on activities that add value • The initial concept moved beyond the boundaries of the firm as in the real world to deliver the finished product	• Business Management and Strategy • Development Studies

		into the market linkages with suppliers, distributors and clients within and without the same sector are required. • By some researchers in development studies, the formation and growth of clusters can be a possibility for developing countries to compete in global markets **WEAKNESSES** Many times analysis are realised by economists looking only at the "outside the box" results. The model doesn't: • Analyse deeply the new product development process • Focus to improve the collaboration process among partners with new technologies, procedures and tools.	
1.5 VE	• Mainly companies • Special attention to develop and integrate core competences of Small and Medium Size companies in the temporal alliance (SME's)	**STRENGTHS** • Partners of the VE should be able to share their core-competences (technology, business process or resources) to develop a new product or service with non-reproducible characteristics in the market. • The network has a short life, because it usually satisfies a specific need, usually an specific project is realised, and then the Virtual Enterprise dissolves • Partners in a Virtual Enterprise model can be geographically distributed and the model provides a way for SME's to collaborate in global networks. **WEAKNESSES** • Depends strongly on the availability of Information and Communication Technologies. If a company doesn't count with ICT is very difficult for it to join a VE • The set-up of the network for a temporal alliance is not an easy task. General speaking a business opportunity should be first identified and an external entity mainly called "a broker" that will also orchestrate the new VE. • National and/or regional policies that enable or reduce the innovation capabilities of companies are not considered in the analysis	• Computer Engineering • Manufacturing Engineering • Mechanical Engineering • Industrial Engineering • Business Management • Law Schools
1.6 BE	• Companies and their related supporting institutions (such as associations)	**STRENGTHS** • The approach proposes a network of organisations that are "prepared" to collaborate. Once a new business opportunity is identified a new Virtual Enterprise will be formed. **WEAKNESSES** • The breeding environment (BE) will need a strong leadership and a common objective to hold together the members which will be ready to collaborate. If these elements don't exist, the BE will hardly show results. • As members of the BE are not all located in the same territory/region they will depend strongly on the ability of a Information and Communication Technologies (ICT) to enable this network approach to hold on together while the business opportunity appears or is identified by the broker. • New models are needed to incorporate Universities in the Virtual Enterprises to be formed out of the BE. • National and/or regional policies that enable or reduce the innovation capabilities of companies are not considered in the analysis.	• Industrial Engineering • Mechanical Engineering • Manufacturing Engineering • Computer Engineering • Business Management • Law Schools

3. TYPE 2 NETWORK MODELS: COLLABORATION AS PART OF A SPATIAL CONTEXT FOR REGIONAL / NATIONAL DEVELOPMENT

On the other hand, type 2 models have developed and applied mainly by Economists, Sociologists and Policy Makers to understand how the collaboration and collective learning processes impact and increase the innovation capabilities of regions and nations and to identify and define the different policies that could be implemented to increase competitiveness. These models do not usually focus on the interaction processes or technologies used among individual firms or the single network or how to improve their operation, but on the aggregation mechanisms of companies located in a specific location and the macro innovation outputs such the region/nation per capita income, number of new high tech companies or the number of new patents. The infrastructure provided to these networks to collaborate and innovate in terms of policies, tax incentives, available and skilled workforce, venture capital, university laboratories and public/private R&D are some of the input variables usually analysed to understand why some regions/nations are more innovative than others.

In these type 2 models, regional and national economic performance depends upon the progressive introduction over time of innovations in products and processes to enhance the competitiveness of the regional and national economic base in an increasingly competitive world. Mainly, these models have emerged to analyse the importance and impact of the different actors, the knowledge and learning collective processes and policies that are present at the national, regional, local and metropolitan levels that support innovation in a spatial context. Special attention is paid to the interaction and collective learning of the different agents in the territory such as Firms, Universities and Governments. In this case, the unit of analysis is the " network(s) of entities inside a specific location or territory".

In contrast with the type 1 collaboration models where both basic and applied research are performed to improve the efficiency of the firm or network by providing new tools and methods (typical of an engineering perspective), type 2 models are studied under an economist perspective, in other words the innovation process is not studied inside the "black box". Economics has traditionally primarily dealt with the allocation of resources to innovation (in competition with other ends) and its economic effects, while the innovation process itself has been more or less treated as a "black box". What happens within this "box" has been left to scholars from other disciplines (Fagerberg, 2003).

The first type 2 collaboration model is the **Industrial Cluster (IC)**. It is defined as a concentration of 'interdependent' firms within the same or adjacent industrial sectors in a small geographical area (Observatory of European SMEs, 2002). Porter (1990) defines a cluster as a set of industries related through buyer-supplier and supplier-buyer relationships, or by common technologies, common buyers or distribution channels, or common labour pools. In the last years, there has been an explosion of interest in cluster development across North America, Europe and newly industrialized countries. This interest has been prompted, in part, by fascination with the success of Silicon Valley at reinventing itself through successive waves of new technology; and, in part, by the efforts of other regions to emulate the Silicon Valley model. Saxenian's case study of Silicon Valley undertaken in the early 1990s and the comparison she provided with Route 128 in Massachusetts was one of the initial case studies analysing Silicon Valley success (Wolfe, 2003).

The second model within the type 2 is the **Innovative Milieu (IM)**. It is based on the hypothesis (Aydalot, 1986) that "Local environments play a determinant role as innovation incubators, they act like a prism through which innovations are catalysed and which give the area its particular complexion. A firm is not an isolated innovator, it is part of an area which makes it act and react. The history of an area, it's organisation, it's collective behaviour and it's internal structure of unanimity are the principal components of innovation". This hypothesis justifies an analysis which goes beyond the permissive conditions which enhance the creation and establishment in a particular locality of innovative firm. According to the GREMI (Group de Recherche Européen sur les Milieux Innovateurs) an innovative milieu is the set of relationships that occur within a given geographical area that bring unity to a production system, economic actors, and an industrial culture, that generate a localised dynamic process of collective learning and that act as an uncertainty-reducing mechanism in the innovation process (Camagni, 1995). Many of the studies developed under the innovative milieu approach analyse the learning process for innovation; in fact, the GREMI Group argues that a territory with weak interactions and no learning can't be considered an innovative milieu.

On the other hand, the **Innovation Systems (IS)** model takes into consideration the network of institutions in the public and private sectors, whose activities and interactions initiate, import, modify and diffuse new technologies (Freeman, 1987). This approach considers that the elements and relationships which interact in the production, diffusion and use of new and economically useful knowledge are either located within or rooted inside the boarders of a nation or region. The characteristics of an innovation system can be summarized as (Lundvall, 1992):

- Firms are part of a network of public and private sector institutions whose activities and interactions initiate, import, modify and diffuse new technologies
- An IS consists of linkages (both formal and informal) between institutions
- An IS includes flows of intellectual resources between institutions
- Analysis of IS emphasizes learning as a key economic resource and that geography and location still matter.

The fourth and last type 2 identified model is the **Triple Helix (TH)**. It has been proposed by Henry Etzkowitz and Loet Leydesdorff (2000) and states that Universities play an enhanced role in innovation in increasingly knowledge-based societies. This approach proposes a new level of interaction: University-Industry-Government promoting a "third revolution" in the academic system, where Universities will target a "third mission" of economic development in addition to research and teaching; "The heart of the Triple Helix thesis is an expansion of the role of knowledge in society and of the university in the economy". The Triple Helix Model opens up a new perspective; universities can benefit economically from their innovations, by creating "spin-offs", selling their patents to industry offering consulting services by transferring technology to local companies enabling a sustainable economic development of their regions.

Table 3. Type 2 Networking Approaches

	ACTOR(S)	STRENGTHS & WEAKNESSES	DISCIPLI-NE(S)
2.1 IC	• Companies localised in a specific region • Strong emphasis on SME's	**STRENGTHS** • Proximity facilitates the transfer of knowledge an information • A skilled pool of workers facilitates innovation • Universities such as Stanford in Silicon Valley and Cambridge in Cambridge have played a key role by transferring knowledge and by increasing the innovate capabilities generating hi-tech clusters **WEAKNESSES** • Clusters have also been approached by their capacity to generate knowledge and their learning capabilities, nevertheless in a cluster not all companies collaborate and share information • There is not a unique strategy to develop clusters and make them successful as each country and region relies on different cultures and policies.	• Business Management • Economists • Sociologists • Political • Science
2.2 IM	• Enterprises, regional socio-professional associations, local and regional authorities, universities and laboratories, schools and individuals.	**STRENGTHS** • Proximity facilitates the transfer of knowledge an information • Focuses on the collective learning process to enable innovation **WEAKNESSES** • This approach doesn't study the learning process at the company level but in a "macro" regional perspective which is not easy to measure and replicate • It doesn't take into consideration the possible technologies that can facilitate the collective learning process	• Regional Economists
2.3 IS	• Companies • Research Institutes • Universities • Government	**STRENGTHS** • Takes into consideration the policies that can enable or hinder collaboration at national and regional levels. • The knowledge transfer process among companies and universities is analysed • Considers different units of analysis: national, regional, metropolitan and local. • The MIT developed the Local Innovation Systems (LIS) where successful locations are studied **WEAKNESSES** • In most cases, the analysis of the innovation process is performed "out of the box" under an economist perspective. • Non-successful case studies of new products developed under this model are rarely described	• Business Management • Economists • Sociologists • Development Studies • Policy Studies
2.4 TH	• Companies • Research Institutes • Universities • Government	**STRENGTHS** • The entrepreneurial university takes a proactive stance in putting knowledge to use and in broadening the input into the creation of academic knowledge. **WEAKNESSES** • Non-successful case studies of new products developed under this approach are rarely described • The collaboration between Universities and Local industries is rarely studied in detail by researchers	• Policy Studies • Sociologists • Economists

4. A PROPOSED TAXONOMY TO ANALYSE NETWORKING MODELS

As observed, each networking model targets different objectives and goals, therefore is not an easy task to classify them and analyse their similarities and main differences. In order to realise this comparison a taxonomy has been developed. The proposed taxonomy analyses each model under four major areas: 1) Geography, 2) Collaborating Entities, 3) Scope and 4) Collaboration Enabling Factors. For each identified element under the previous four major areas of the proposed taxonomy a value of "0" (not considered), "1" (low), "2" (medium) or "3" (high) was given taking into consideration its importance for each specific networking model (Table 5). Table 4 shows which are the most important elements for type 1 and type 2 under the four taxonomy elements.

Table 4. Type 1 and Type 2 key elements

TAXONOMY ELEMENTS	TYPES OF NETWORKING MODELS	
	Type 1 **Intra-Inter Company**	Type 2 **National/Regional**
1 Geography	• Intra-Inter Company Networks **not linked** to a territory, partners are geographically distributed	• National or Regional Territorial Networks
2 Collaborating Entities	• Departments' functional collaboration inside the company • Network of Companies (usually in distributed locations)	Network of local/national: • Companies • Companies and Associations • Companies and Universities • Companies, Universities and Government
3 Scope	• Operational Costs and Transaction Costs Reduction • New Product Development and Innovation	• New Product Development and Innovation for regional/national competitiveness • Collective Learning • Knowledge Transfer • Sustainable National/Regional Economic Development • New national/regional policies definition
4 Collaboration Enabling Factors	• Information and Communication Technologies (ICT) • Reduction of costs and lead times as a main goal • Common goal to develop new product(s) • Trust	• Proximity • Development and sharing of Human Capital • New Knowledge Creation • National/Regional culture for Innovation and Collaboration • Governmental Policies • Trust

Table 5. Analysis of Networking Approaches using the proposed Taxonomy

Level of Importance: Non (0), Low (1), Medium (medium), High (3)	Type 1 — Intra-Inter Company Network Models (The Firm as an individual entity or part of a network, not linked to a specific territory)							Type 2 — National/Regional Network Models Collaboration as part of a spatial context, innovation for regional/national competitiveness				
	1.1 Simultaneous Engineering	1.2 Supply Chain Management	1.3 Extended Enterprise	1.4 Value Chain	1.5 Virtual Enterprises	1.6 Breeding Environment	AVERAGE	2.1 Industrial Clusters	2.2 Innovative Milieu	2.3 Innovation Systems	2.4 Triple Helix	AVERAGE
GEOGRAPHY												
Intra-Inter Company Networks not linked to a territory	3	3	3	3	3	3	3.00	2	0	0	0	0.50
Territorial: National/Regional	0	0	0	0	0	0	0.00	3	3	3	3	3.00
COLLABORATING ENTITIES												
Collaboration inside the Company	3	2	2	3	1	1	2.00	0	0	0	0	0.00
Collaboration in a Network of Companies	0	3	3	3	3	3	2.50	3	3	2	2	2.50
Companies and Associations	0	0	0	0	0	2	0.33	3	1	2	2	2.00
Companies-Universities-Government	0	0	0	0	0	0	0.00	1	2	3	3	2.25
SCOPE												
New Product Development / Innovation	2	0	3	3	3	3	2.33	2	3	3	3	2.75
Operational Costs and Transaction Costs Reduction	1	3	1	3	3	3	2.33	3	1	1	1	1.50
Temporal Alliance for Innovation	0	0	0	0	3	3	1.00	0	0	0	3	0.75
Collective Learning	1	0	2	2	3	3	1.83	2	3	3	3	2.75
Knowledge Transfer	1	0	1	1	3	3	1.50	2	3	3	3	2.75
Sustainable National/Regional Economic Development	0	0	0	0	0	0	0.00	3	2	3	3	3.00
COLLABORATION ENABLING FACTORS												
Information and Communication Technologies	3	3	3	3	3	3	3.00	2	0	0	0	0.50
Proximity	0	1	0	0	0	0	0.17	3	3	3	3	3.00
Reduction of costs and lead times as a main goal	2	3	3	2	3	3	2.83	2	1	1	1	1.50
Sharing of resources and core competences	2	0	2	2	3	3	2.00	2	3	2	2	2.00
Informal Relationships	0	0	0	0	0	2	0.33	3	3	3	3	3.00
Trust	3	3	3	3	3	3	3.00	3	3	3	3	3.00
Human Capital	1	1	1	1	3	3	1.67	3	3	3	3	3.00
New Knowledge Creation	1	0	1	1	3	3	1.50	2	3	3	3	2.75
Culture for Innovation and Collaboration	1	1	1	1	3	3	1.67	3	3	3	3	3.00
Legal Infrastructure	0	0	0	0	3	3	1.00	1	0	2	2	1.25
Collaboration readiness	1	1	1	1	3	3	1.67	3	2	2	2	2.00
Governmental Policies	0	0	0	0	0	0	0.00	3	3	3	3	3.00

5. CONCLUSIONS

Several disciplines are targeting in one way or the other to study the networking process of different entities to carry out innovations proposing different models to understand their interactions. As observed, there is not a unique model to cover all the needs and angles. This paper proposed a classification of ten different networking models into Type 1) firm-global network oriented and Type 2) local, regional, national network oriented. A taxonomy has been presented to analyse their main differences and similarities taking into consideration four main elements: 1) Geography, 2) Collaborating Entities, 3)Scope and 4) Collaboration Enabling Factors. The most amazing learning lesson during this research was that even if the different disciplines work in parallel in the same topic, there is very little interaction among them to share concepts and ideas that could enable to cover the different needs in a engineering oriented, economical, political and social perspective; additionally, a common ontology is required to have a common set of definitions.

6. REFERENCES

1. Afsarmanesh H, Camarinha-Matos L., A Framework for Management of VO Breeding Environments, In Collaborative Networks and Their Breeding Environments Eds. Camarinha-Matos, Luis M.; Afsarmanesh, Hamideh; Ortiz, Angel, Springer 2005.
2. Aydalot P., "Milieux innovateurs en Europe", Paris, GREMI, C3E, 1986
3. Barney, J., "Strategic factor markets: expectations, luck, and business strategy", Management Science, 1986, Vol. 32, No. 10, 1231-1241.
4. Barney, J., "Firm Resources and Sustained Competitive Advantage", Journal of Management, 1991, Vol. 17, No. 1, 99-120.
5. Browne J., I. Hunt and J.Zhang, The Extended Enterprise, Handbook of Life Cycle Engineering: Concepts, Models and Technologies, edited by Molina, Sanchez & Kusiak, Kluwer, 1998,
6. Camagni R, Innovation Networks, The GREMI Approach, British Library Cataloguing in Publication Data, 1991
7. Camarinha-Matos L. and Afsarmanesh H., Collaborative Networked Organizations, A research agenda for emerging business models, 2004
8. Etzkowitz H. Leydesdorff L. The dynamics of innovation: from National Systems and "Mode 2" to a Triple Helix of university–industry–government relations, Research Policy 29, 2000 109–123.
9. Fagerberg J., Innovation: A Guide to the Literature, Paper presented at the Workshop "The Many Guises of Innovation: What we have learnt and where we are heading", Ottawa, October 23-24.2003, organized by Statistics Canada.
10. Freeman, C., Technology Policy and Economic Performance: Lessons from Japan. Pinter, London.
11. Goldman, Nagel and Preiss, 1995, Agile Competitors and Virtual Organisations-Strategies for enriching the customer, Van Nostrand Reinhold, 1987.
12. Katzy B., and Schuh, The Virtual Enterprise, Handbook of Life Cycle Engineering: Concepts, Models and Technologies, edited by Molina, Sanchez & Kisiak, 1998.
13. Lundvall B.A., Natinal Systems of Innovation, Towards a Theory of Innovation and Interactive Learning, 1992
14. Observatory of European SMEs, Regional clusters in Europe, European Community, http://europa.eu.int/comm/enterprise, (2002)
15. Porter, M. Competitive advantage: Creating and sustaining superior performance. New York: The Free Press, 1985
16. Porter M., The Competitive Advantage of Nations. Free Press, New York, 1990.
17. Ribbens J., Simultaneous Engineering for New Product Development: Manufacturing Applications, Wiley, 2000
18. SCOR, Suppy Chain Operations Reference Model, www.supply-chain.org 1995
19. Wolf D.A. Clusters from the Inside and Out: Lessons from the Canadian Study of Cluster Development, Paper to be presented at the DRUID Summer Conference 2003 on Creating, Sharing and Transferring Knowledge, the role of Geography, Institutions and Organizations, 2003.

PART 3

NETWORKING AND INNOVATION

7

TOWARDS A CULTURE OF SHARING AND EXCHANGE: INVESTING IN THE INTANGIBLE ASSETS AND INTELLECTUAL CAPITAL FOR THE LEVERAGING OF COLLABORATIVE NETWORKS

Bob Roberts
School of Computing & Information Systems, Kingston University, UK
R.Roberts@kingston.ac.uk
Adamantios Koumpis
Research Programmes Division ALTEC S.A., GREECE
akou@altec.gr

An important challenge in establishing lasting changes of culture and values in an organisation involves ensuring that organized learning processes are anchored within the organisation. Our experience from several projects shows that good intentions are not sufficient for ensuring the operation of a CN. Many of the existing patterns reflect an earlier situation when research was not as strictly monitored for its short-term results and its financial (contributions to) outcomes. The central point of the paper is that collaborative networks (CN) do not need to 'live with' and experience all the deficiencies faced in regard to the introduction of virtual forms of organisation in the corporate world, as these have been introduced in several national or application contexts in Europe.

1. INTRODUCTION

The central point of the paper is that collaborative networks (CN) do not need to 'live with' and experience all the deficiencies faced in regard to the introduction of virtual forms of organisation in the corporate world, as these have been introduced in several national or application contexts in Europe. We have been accumulating lessons learnt in Europe and are in a position today to report on our personal experiences, thus possibly helping provide useful advice and recommendations to the development of some genuine breeding environments for such networks.

The shadow capital on which we argue that we should build such infrastructures are the mistakes that have been made (and to a great extend continue to make) in the addressed area. There has been a repetition of the same old mistakes. These include tendencies for:

*   Overdoses of formalisms and structurally rigorous platforms that only partially work and provide useful solutions to existing problems

Please use the following format when citing this chapter:

Roberts, B., Koumpis, A., 2006, in IFIP International Federation for Information Processing, Volume 224, Network-Centric Collaboration and Supporting Fireworks, eds. Camarinha-Matos, L., Afsarmanesh, H., Ollus, M., (Boston: Springer), pp. 69–76.

- Lack of investment in the human aspects both from the side of the CN provider and the user,
- Focusing only on short-term (and therefore short-sighted) results and deliverables
- Undervaluing the efficacies created through the learning dimension as a medium to increase any organisational as well as individual intellectual assets.

In our paper we make an analysis of two failure stories and focus on the soft aspects related to the introduction of a CN infrastructure and make explicit references to the common mistakes when building or purchasing a ready-for-use system or application. The overall aim is to come up with a set of representative cases that may provide food for thought and radical ideas for avoiding pitfalls related to the suboptimal introduction of the concept of CN.

In contrast to tangible products and services, it is difficult for a CN to import its soft assets from elsewhere. It can 'import' technological infrastructures and capitalize on technological innovations, however, it still remains a question for the people that constitute its grid how they can make best use of concepts selectively and on a need to do basis. Even in the case of non collaborative networks, innovations cannot be copied or lent by other networks - in the same way that the future of a CN and its potential cannot be mortgaged under the procurement of some monolithic and silo infrastructures which have rarely worked.

2. THE ADDRESSED AREA

2.1 European research projects as instances of CN

European Framework research projects are carried out by partners operating as an extended enterprise, whose different Intellectual Assets (IAs) and the value thereof need to be recognised in order to successfully prepare the ground for the completion of the project. Taking this into account, there is a need to manage the project as a 'business' (even if this involves adopting a business attitude), in the sense that it must be approached as a specific endeavour to achieve certain defined goals.

Based on the experience established from our involvement in nine projects that have been implemented over a period of 6 years (1999 – 2004), there is clear empirical evidence that a considerable majority of projects fail because they do not succeed in identifying their individual purpose in terms of the knowledge produced and excellence achieved. One can attribute this shortcoming as project management failure, technical failure, requirements failure, or market definition failure. Like medicine that is not considered as an exact science, as is the case with mathematics, one can rely only on empirical data *and* the relevance that can be validated with certain hypotheses. From our side, the evaluation criteria related to the following success indicators:

- Creation of a jointly recognized and co-owned intellectual asset, and establishment of some elementary structure for its management [C_1];
- Continuation of the collaboration into at least one subset of the initial partnership for a period of at least two years [C_2], and last but not least;

- Organization of processes that are exhibiting at least one of the following (a) recognition of the exact contributions to be made at scientific or techological/technical level, (b) agreement on the qualitative criteria that shall be used for validating the success of the project work, and (c) delineation of information related to the positioning of the project with respect to other research approaches, the market and competition at large. For this last subcriterion, we relied on different techniques, spanning from the traditional SWOT analysis of strengths, weaknesses, opportunities and threats, to more sophisticated ones relying on roadmaps and benchmarking $[C_3]$.

The aforementioned suboptimality derives mainly as a result of a reluctance to develop a common culture and a team spirit which shall facilitate the creation of an open environment, supporting the sharing of knowledge communication, experiences and ideas, and most importantly their sharing. To avoid this, an obvious remedy for any company and therefore any project is to know at each distinct moment: its assets (both tangible and intangible – especially the latter), its competitors, and (of course) the market; how to express them with the most accurate figures possible, and how to increase them by means of opening the various types of corporate information and knowledge resources to the other members of the CN.

It is not uncommon to find projects which fail to have a realistic estimation of the global situation regarding the application of the project's intended outputs in the real world and the related market conditions. Methods for the valuation or measurement of Intellectual Assets can be characterized as 'solutions in search of a problem', and although there seems to be confusion about the distinction between valuation and measurement, the distinction is fundamental yet not fully recognized in the field (Andriessen, 2003). The aim and the motivation of our approach is rather simple and straightforward: to come to a quantitative overview of the monetary value of all types of intangible assets that are to be created by the project in order to be able to exploit these assets, on two levels:

- For the entire CN; and
- For each individual CN member separately.

From the plethora of methodologies and practices which have been built variously on the schools of thought or 'communities' of – amongst others - Intellectual Capital management, Accounting, Performance measurement, and Valuation, we built our approach on an adapted version of the Weightless Wealth Toolkit by Andriessen (Andriessen, 2004).

2.2 The need to invest in intangibles

An important challenge in establishing lasting changes of culture and values in an organisation involves ensuring that organized learning processes are anchored within the organisation. Traditional courses and training are considered efficient, but it often seems as if the long-term effect is missing. Furthermore, traditional courses are often used by organisations to train their employees so they can perform better, but in the same ways as they always have done.

There are several positive aspects to both tactics, but if the goal of the learning is to gain new knowledge and to establish changes in behaviour as well as further learning in the organisation, it is important to use a strategy based on pedagogical theories and methods that take individual as well as organizational learning into consideration. There is a saying: 'Those that have hammers, will see only nails'. In the greater scheme of things, corporate decision-making includes more than scientific approaches and methods.

Our own experience working with decision-making processes dates back to the beginning of 1990. We have been closely involved with a wide range of different organisations in the research, the business software and the IT industry in general, and different types and levels of decision-making styles and cultures. In all these settings, we have been exposed to different learning strategies based on problem-based and project-organised approaches, and our experience is that they provided quite another learning outcome. We consider this Situation-Room learning approach an effective and motivating way to organise the kind of learning situations needed when working with changes in behaviour, strategies, and innovative processes in companies and organizations, as it is for the case of product development.

Authors like (Nonaka, 1991; Nonaka and Tageuchi, 1995), (Leonard-Barton, 1995), (Sveiby, 1997), (Sveiby and Lloyd, 1988), and many more, claim that knowledge is the most important resource. "In an economy where the only certainty is uncertainty, the sure source of lasting competitive advantage is knowledge" (Nonaka, 1995). However, this does not mean that the knowledge-based view is a synonym for the resource-based view. The most important and fundamental difference is that the resource-based view only implicitly refers to knowledge, whereas the knowledge-based view gives extensive elaboration on the nature and definition of knowledge and the way it should be managed (Thompson Klein, 1996). Knowledge management literature can be seen as a further specification or extension (Bontis, 2002) of the resource-based view into a 'knowledge-based theory of the firm'.

In parallel a closely related and more holistic perspective on the value creating resources of the organisation emerged. This intangible-based view of the firm is based on the work of authors like (Sveiby, 1997), (Stewart, 1997) and (Edvinsson, 1997). This so-called Intellectual Capital movement uses knowledge and intellectual capital interchangeably. Although closely related, the meaning of knowledge in this movement fundamentally differs from the definition of knowledge in the knowledge-based view of the firm. Intellectual capital, intellectual assets, intangible assets, intangibles, knowledge assets, knowledge capital or whatever term is used within this movement, refers to the traditional hidden sources of value creation (of which knowledge is just one). Hidden in the sense that existing management techniques do not have the methods or instruments to reveal them.

This intangible-based view of the firm inspired the intellectual capital movement to further elaborate on the nature of intangible resources and the way they should be measured and managed. This view serves as a starting point for application within the corporate environment.

(Weick, 1995) presents a detailed theory of sensemaking in organizational contexts, particularly those characterized by novelty or other forms of description. He suggests that individual and group activities are inextricably intertwined. Weick's work is compatible with constructivist perspectives of knowledge, in that situations become 'real' only through the interpretive processes of sensemaking which reveal how different parties construe the situation. (Choo, 1999) summarizes three-step processes that are central to sensemaking: *Enactment:* the process by which individuals in an organization actively create the environment which they face; *Selection:* the process by which people in an organization generate an enacted environment that provides a cause-and-effect explanation of what is taking place; *Retention:* enacted or meaningful environments are stored for future retrieval upon occurrence of new equivocal situations.

According to Weick, people engage in sensemaking in two main ways. Belief driven sensemaking takes place through arguing (creating meaning by comparing dissimilar ideas) or expecting/confirming (creating meaning by connecting similar ideas). Action-driven sensemaking involves people committing (engaging in highly visible actions to which they have commitment) or manipulating (acting to create an environment that people can comprehend).

Weick addresses the social dimensions of knowledge sharing by drawing on Wiley's work (Wiley, 1988) which suggests that there are three levels of sensemaking above that of the individual: *Intersubjective:* synthesis of self from I to We; *Generic subjective:* interaction to create meaning at the group or organizational level; *Extrasubjective:* meaning attains the strength of culture –'pure meanings'.

Bringing these concepts together, therefore, Weick sees organizational sensemaking as the drive to develop generic subjectivity through arguing, expecting, committing and manipulating. These social dimensions converge with Nonaka and Takeuchi's (Nonaka, 1995) view on the role of socialization in transforming tacit to explicit knowledge. Companies provide many different types of services to their employees and stakeholders; the interactions between the abstract entity of a corporation and its people are mostly process-based and can be categorised as follows (Lenk, 1999): structured procedures or routines, semi-structured decision processes and negotiation-based case-solving.

(Capurro, 2004) furthermore states that what can be managed is information or explicit knowledge and that implicit knowledge can only be "enabled". In this context, explicit means that it can be clearly observed and expressed (and also digitalised), as opposed to implicit knowledge that can not be directly formulated (skills, experiences, insight, intuition, judgement, etc.) When knowledge is explicit, it can be represented as declarative or procedural knowledge. We are aware that in the domain of cognitive sciences, the distinction between procedural and declarative models is related to the brain memory system - see for example (Ullman, 2001), but here we used these terms here in a limited sense, as defined in computer science: *Declarative knowledge components* represent facts and events in terms of concepts and relations; *Procedural knowledge components* describe actions to be taken in order to solve a problem step by step.

For cases where knowledge is implicit and cannot be formalized, we introduced the concept of distribution: knowledge can be individual or collective, and in both cases components identify who has this knowledge or where it can be found. Finally we added a set of metadata (know-where, know-when, know-who, etc.) that describe these knowledge-components and that make it possible to manage them.

3. THE CORPORATE REALITY

3.1 General

- *"An institution able to show a record of efficient involvement in projects and research activities in a specific area in the past is able to set up a similarly adequately skilled research team in any new project".*

- *"A company active in the area addressed by a research project with a successful record of sales (products or services) will be similarly willing to sell the products or services, resulting from the research project it participates in".*

- *"A company or institution participates in a research project in order to develop know-how necessary for its future operations, to cope with future challenges and to establish strategic alliances".*

In many cases, regarding the above, there is a huge discrepancy between what is put forward in a proposal or a review and the daily routine of a project. In certain other cases, intentions need to be supported by actions. In all cases, the everyday financial pressure – in periods of economic uncertainties in particular – affect the initial commitment to a project, under the surging demand for cash-flow and better economic indices of the organization.

A research institution might truly wish to enter a new research area, but has to operate under the tremendous pressure to bring in money – which makes researchers grasp at any opportunity that appears on the street corner. In the event of a proposal being successful, they will lose time and momentum because they will have to organize an ad hoc team – either by asking people who might be interested, or by hiring new people to get on board. This kills the potential of a good head start to a project.

Participation in an RTD project allows an organization to gain additional cashflow, national matching funds (for public research or academic institutes), opportunities for press releases and company promotion (research is always fashionable, to get funded for it is trendy, but to actually conduct it might be considered nerdy!). Sometimes organizations join research consortia just because they cannot stay out of them. Organizations tend to look for ready made consortia to join. In very few cases a proposal is written by more than three people, with most partners limiting their contribution to CVs and lists of previous project participations.

On the project supply-side, there is often ambivalence towards speculative opportunism (yesterday we were selling information brokerage systems – today we sell Semantic Web – tomorrow Grids and Grid computing). It is not uncommon to have such concept drift taking place continuously; this happens in the economy and in the market. As the above may seem apocryphal, here are some examples:

- In a recently completed project, we had taken the responsibility to prepare a business plan. We collaborated closely with the manager. From the very start we had expressed our commitment to support this plan even after the completion of the project. We organized a set of communications and contacts with external consultants and spent much time on it – most of which did not come from the project budget as it involved several people from other departments of our institutions. The result was not positive as the manager's interest faded after the 'successful' completion of the project. To our regret, what we know is that they keep on investing in the platform they developed in that project and they do have a longer-term research plan for their work.

- In another recently completed project, we had taken the responsibility to prepare a business plan. We developed a fully developed draft which we circulated to the consortium, but there was no response or reaction to this. As this project has again terminated "successfully" by submitting also its e-TIP, why bother with such things like a business plan? It is obvious that the completion of the project meant the termination of partners' interest to the subject.

The lesson learned from the above stories from the front line is that there is an urgent need to examine our Value Chains – those that we have and which we need to improve, and those that we don't have and therefore need to create from scratch. Perhaps there is arrogance and a resting on our laurels that exists in our continent in contrast to North America, Asia and Japan that hinders the creation of such Value Chains in the research and innovation fields.

Looking at the intangible assets (in terms of knowledge) won and lost during the projects, as well as to the same assets before these started and after they ended, i.e. considering the particular life cycle of the projects, the picture is not bad for the individual participants of the CN, but it is devastatingly discouraging for the commonly owned assets. To the latter, there is a clear failure in capitalising even at the level of lessons jointly learned. Furthermore,,there is an unequivocal tendency for each party to draw its own conclusions, in the same way as its party forms its own policy and negotiates with the other parties in a very basic and non value added way.

3.2 Concluding remarks

Our experience from several projects shows that good intentions are not sufficient for ensuring the operation of a CN. Many of the existing patterns reflect an earlier situation when research was not as strictly monitored for its short-term results and its financial (contributions to) outcomes.

Furthermore, it seems that the central challenge faced by a CN is the implementation of flexible, time-variant co-operation models. As a result, our view on posing more importance to aspects related to the soft skills of a CN is of direct utility; it is essential nowadays for the created CN structures to be able to dynamically modify their formation (i.e. to evolve continuously) and to have the necessary knowledge to do so appropriately in relation to the intangible assets which they are using.

Having several first and second hand experiences in the success or failures faced from the more demanding and relatively complicated projects or tasks, to less complex and simple ones, the story has to do usually with the same ingredients:
- People, and
- How these interact to each other or with each other, and
- How they perceive and analyse the world they live in, the events that are taking place and to which they have or need to respond to, and
- How they document their knowledge, their wants, their goals, their history of what they did or they aimed to do, and,
- How they access and make use of the documented knowledge – be it theirs or someone else's , and finally,
- How they manage to improve their behavior either at the individual level or at the collective one, or – sometimes – at both through learning processes or other optimization processes.

However, to manage a coordinated behavior of individuals is a difficult, if not unachievable, task. Even if people are working together for the same goal, and have all unanimously agreed to the same objective and target, it is human nature that they shall develop differentiations in regard to the means that each individual shall employ for meeting any specified end. Or, even in the case that there is agreement regarding the means, there will be different opinions on the instrumentations of these very specific means, the orchestration of all individuals around them, etc. This helps us come to the conclusion that the main difficulty concerns the synthesis of all these different 'resources'.

Though the starting point for us has been problems that appear in the corporate world, any type of 'problem' that involves most of the above components can be regarded as subject to the same need for being approached with a preferably simple and consistent method for modeling the problem.

4. REFERENCES

1. Andriessen D., IC Valuation & Measurement: Why and how? PMA IC Research Symposium, October 1-3, 2003, Cranfield School of Management
2. Andriessen D., Making Sense of Intellectual Capital: Designing a method for the valuation of Intangibles, Butterworth – Heinemann, 2004
3. Bontis, N. (2002) 'Managing organizational knowledge by diagnosing intellectual capital. Framing and advancing the state of the field', in N. Bontis and C.W. Choo (Eds.) The Strategic Management of Intellectual Capital and Organizational Knowledge, Oxford, New York: Oxford University Press, pp.621–642.
4. Capurro, R. (2004). Skeptical Knowledge Management. In Hobohm, H.-C., Knowledge Management: Libraries and Librarians Taking Up The Challenge (IFLA Publication, 108, 47-57). Munich: Saur.
5. Choo C. W. (1999) The Knowing Organization: How Organizations Use Information to Construct Meaning, Create Knowledge, and Make Decisions, Oxford, Oxford University Press.
6. Edvinsson, L. and Malone, M.S. (1997) 'Intellectual capital', The proven Way to Establish Your Company's Real Value by Measuring its Hidden Brainpower, London: HarperBusiness.
7. Lenk, K. and Traunmueller, R. (1999) Perspektiven einer radikalen Neugestaltung der oeffentlichen Verwaltung mit Informationstechnik, in: Oeffentliche Verwaltung und Informationstechnik. Schriftenreihe Verwaltungsinformatik, Heidelberg: Decker's Verlag.
8. Leonard-Barton, D. (1995) Wellsprings of Knowledge, Building and Sustaining the Sources of Innovation, Boston, MA: Harvard Business School Press.
9. Nonaka, I. (1991) 'The knowledge creating company', Harvard Business Review, November–December, Vol.69, No.6, pp.96–104.
10. Nonaka, I., Takeuchi,, H. (1995) The knowledge creating company, Oxford: Oxford University Press.
11. Stewart, T.A. (1997) Intellectual Capital, The New Wealth of Organizations, New York: Doubleday.
12. Sveiby, K.E. and Lloyd, T. (1988) Managing Knowhow. Increase Profits by Harnessing the Creativity in Your Company, Bloomsbury, London.
13. Sveiby, K.E. (1997) The New Organizational Wealth. Managing and Measuring Knowledge-Based Assets, San Fransisco: Berret-Koehler Publishers Inc.
14. Thompson Klein J. (1996) Crossing Boundaries: Knowledge, Disciplinarities, and Interdisciplinarities, Charlottesville VA: University Press of Virginia 1996.
15. Ullman, M. T. (2001) A Neurocognitive Perspective on Language: The Declarative/Procedural Model. Nature Reviews - Neuroscience, 2(10), 717-26.
16. Weick, K. E. (1995) Sensemaking in Organizations, Thousand Oaks, Calif., Sage Publications.
17. Wiley, N. (1988) 'The Micro-Macro Problem in Social Theory', Sociological Theory, Vol. 6, pp. 254–61.

8

ORGANIZATIONAL SURVIVAL IN COOPERATION NETWORKS: THE CASE OF AUTOMOBILE MANUFACTURING

Pedro Campos
pcampos@fep.up.pt
Pavel Brazdil
pbrazdil@liacc.up.pt
Paula Brito
mpbrito@fep.up.pt
LIACC-NIAAD and
Faculty of Economics – University of Porto, PORTUGAL

We propose a Multi-Agent framework to analyze the dynamics of organizational survival in cooperation networks. Firms can decide to cooperate horizontally (in the same market) or vertically with other firms that belong to the supply chain. Cooperation decisions are based on economic variables. We have defined a variant of the density dependence model to set up the dynamics of the survival in the simulation. To validate our model, we have used empirical outputs obtained in previous studies from the automobile manufacturing sector. We have observed that firms and networks proliferate in the regions with lower marginal costs, but new networks keep appearing and disappearing in regions with higher marginal costs.

1. INTRODUCTION

According to economic evolutionary theories, firms innovate in order to increase their survival rates. We propose to analyze the dynamics of collective innovation, using a Multi-Agent framework, where firms (the agents) can cooperate for innovation purposes. To explore the impact of cooperation on the survival of organizations, we have used a variation of *density dependence model* (Campos and Brazdil, 2005b). We examined the empirical evidences from automobile manufacturing to improve our Multi-Agent model. Our main conclusion is that there are more networks in regions with lower marginal costs, but nevertheless there are some firms and networks in richer regions, showing that the firms clustering helps to avoid negative results and abandon of the activity. In the following we provide details concerning this study: in section 2 we provide an economic perspective of cooperation models and introduce some important concepts, as *technological distance* and *density dependence*. In section 3, we present some concepts that are useful for the development of the model and in section 4 describe the Multi-Agent Simulation. Section 5 is devoted to the presentation of the results. We end this paper with conclusions and future work.

Please use the following format when citing this chapter:

Campos, P., Bradzil, P., Brito, P., 2006, in IFIP International Federation for Information Processing, Volume 224, Network-Centric Collaboration and Supporting Fireworks, eds. Camarinha-Matos, L., Afsarmanesh, H., Ollus, M., (Boston: Springer), pp. 77–84.

2. A NETWORK MODEL OF COOPERATION

Because innovation is a strategic factor of the regional development, regional theory proposes that "new activity motivate power". Particularly and according to evolutionary theories, firms innovate in order to increase their survival rates. Some authors have related the process of innovation with the creation of networks of firms: Carayol and Roux (2003) consider innovation as a collective and interactive process that generates the formation of networks of organizations. Moreover, innovation and cooperation networks, and, generally, the topic of firms' dynamics have been recently studied with the help of Multi-Agent Simulation models (Zhang, (2003), Gilbert et al., (2001), Cowan et al, (2004), Cortés, (2004)).

One of the most important aspects related with cooperation networks and innovation is the *distance* between firms. Although the geographical distance is an important measure in literature from regional science, empirical evidence has shown that a non-physical distance between firms can also be useful. Some authors (Agata, 2003) call it *cognitive* or *technological distance* and it plays a major role in the effectiveness of knowledge diffusion that can be generated from inter-firm networks. This technological distance measures the distance between firm's know-how and will be crucial for the definition of networks, as we will see.

3. AUTOMOBILE INDUSTRY: SOME EMPIRICAL EVIDENCES

To investigate how this model applies to reality, we have chosen to study the automobile manufacturing industry. In the following we present some concepts that are useful for the development of the model: (1) In automobile manufacturing, as car makers seek to cut costs, they outsource certain activities to the supply industry. (2) Outsourcing also allows greater economies due to specialization, since suppliers are more experienced in certain functions and can supply several carmakers, achieving higher efficiency or productivity. (3) Constructors promoted both the concentration process of component suppliers and room for creating important collaborations and alliances among suppliers and among suppliers and constructors (Rolo, 1998). (4) At the same time, we are facing the migration of OEM to emergent markets of Asia and South America as a way to rationalize production, and capacity reduction. In addition, previous studies of Campos and Brazdil (2005b) have confirmed the existence of factors affecting organizational survival, the number of organizations that existed at the time of birth and at the time of death (referred to as *contemporaneous density* and *density at founding*): (5) *contemporaneous density* has a negative impact on the mortality of organizations, while (6) *density at founding* has a positive impact on the mortality of organizations.

In the next section, we will introduce the model and discuss the components and the decision making process.

4. MODEL DESCRIPTION

A Multi-Agent model has been used, because agents can be configured to be autonomous, and these seem to capture the dynamics (and the survival) in network formation.

4.1 Model components

The agents, knowledge creation and diffusion
We have developed a Multi Agent Model, *NetOrg*, where we have considered, for each market y, n *firms* (i=1, ..., n_y) and m *consumers* (j=1, ..., m_y). There are three different *markets* defined by the products (or production process levels) Y=1, 2 and 3. Car makers, Carburetor suppliers and Clutches suppliers can be defined as examples of these types of markets or industries (as in Swaminathan, 2002).
For every product or production process level (Y=1, 2, 3), we consider a different kind of knowledge (or *stock of capital*) represented by $k^t_{i,Y}$ (the *stock of capital* or knowledge owned by firm *i* in instant *t* that is necessary to produce the product *Y*). In every step there will be an accumulation of knowledge k given by:

$$K_{i,Y}^t = K_{i,Y}^{t-1} + \Delta K_{i,Y}^t$$

$$\text{with, } A_{i,Y}^t = \Delta K_{i,Y}^t = w_{i,Y}^t + \sum_{j \in N\backslash i} \partial^{d^t(i,j)} w_{j,Y}^t$$

where δ is the transferability factor, (i.e., the parameter that measures the share of new knowledge which is effectively transmitted through each link); $w^t_{i,,Y}$ represents the *innovation* of firm i that is related with product Y at moment t and it is defined by a Normal distribution; we have considered, (as in Carayol, 2003) that there is no knowledge diffusion (also known as knowledge *spillover*) between firms that do not share a network connection. Although each firm owns a value of the stock of capital for its particular level y, firms can also detain values for the stock of capital for other levels (Y=1,2,3) because they can manufacture more than one product or interfere in more than one production process.

Technology space / geographical space
As stated before, we followed literature and have considered two types of distances that have been combined into one only weighted distance: (i) $d^{geo}(i,j)$ represents the geographical distance measured by a Euclidean metric. We defined two different regions with different marginal costs associated: region 1 has higher marginal costs than region 2; (ii) $d_Y^{tec,\ t}(i,j)$ represents the technological (or cognitive) distance in instant t for the product Y and takes values in [0,1]. The final weighted distance was obtained by the formula: $d_Y^t(i,j) = [1- d_Y^{tec,\ t}(i,j)] \cdot d_Y^{tec,\ t}(i,j) \cdot [1- d^{geo}(i,j)]$, which gives more importance to the technological distance. Considering, for instance, that two firms (1 and 2) have technological distance of 0.5 and if the geographical distance beween them is, say, 0.1 (geographical distances are normalized to 1), then

$$d_Y^t(1,2) = [1- 0.5] \cdot 0.5 \cdot [1- 0.1] = 0.225$$

Cooperation and Market demand
Some firms are assumed to produce in different markets or work in several levels of the production process (as in the example of carmakers, carburettors and clutches). Therefore, for two firms to cooperate in two or more levels of the production process they must first meet, through a *preferential meeting process* that will be described later. For the definition of the Market demand, we have considered three types of industries (as stated before), where, for each of the markets, consumers are assumed to have love-for-variety preferences (as in Wersching, 2005). Dealing with

heterogeneity from demand side (different consumers), we can formulate the following *utility function* for each consumer in the market:

$$u_j^t(x_{1,j}^t, \ldots, x_{n,j}^t) = \left[\sum_{l=1}^{n} A_i^t . x_{l,j}^t \right]^{1/b_j}$$ The constant b_j is an indicator of the association

of the products in the market: b_j=1, indicates that products are perfect substitutes.

The *quantities* for the demand of product i by consumer j at time t are represented by $X_{i,j}^t$. Consumer j wants to maximize u_j^t, under a budget constraint:

$$\max u_j^t(X_1^t, \ldots, X_n^t) \text{ such that: } \sum_{i=1}^{n} p_{j,i}^t . x_{i,j}^t \leq R_j^t \text{ where } R_t^j \text{ is the income of consumer j}$$

in time t and $p_{j,i}^t$ is the price that consumer j pays for product i at time t. The *demand function* (price) for the market of the good i, is defined by:

$$P_i^t = \frac{(A_i^t)^{b_j}}{(X_{i\bullet}^t)^{1-b_j}} \cdot \frac{R_{average}^t}{\sum_{l=1}^{n} (A_l^t . X_{l\bullet}^t)^{b_j}}$$

Production costs

The profit of a firm is obtained multiplying the quantity sold by the difference between unitary price and unitary cost. $g(w_i^t)$ is the function of the effort needed to create knowledge. We have assumed that $g(w_i^t)$= 0.5 $(w_i^t)^2$ and that c_i^t is the cost function of firm i at time t and will be modelled as: $c_i^t = c - \Delta k_i^t$, where c is the marginal cost and c_i^t is a function of the ith firms' cost at time t; c_i^t integrates the effects of both innovation and absorption which are reduction production costs. From this, we can obtain a final form of the profit function for firm i (considering a particular product Y): $\pi_i^t = (P_i^t - c + \Delta k_{iY}^t) \cdot X_i^t - 0.5 (w_i^t)^2$

4.2 Decision making

Entry/Exit and Production quantities

The entry and exit in the market (birth and death processes) were defined by a variant of the density dependence model (Campos and Brazdil, 2005): if the number of organizations in the neighbourhood of a specific firm belongs to the survival interval $[DS_l ; DS_u]$, then the organization will have higher probability to stay alive. Otherwise it will have higher probability to die by the effect of "overcrowding" or "solitude", depending on whether the number is greater than DS_u or lower than DS_l (where DS_l and DS_u are respectively the lower and upper bounds of the density survival interval). The same idea applies to the process of founding where DB_l and DB_u respectively are the lower and upper bounds of the density founding interval.

Every firm i must also decide about the quantities X_i^t that will produce at instant t, having in mind the maximization of the profit. We have used a heuristic assuming that in the first step there is market equilibrium. In the following steps, we admit that when the profit of firm *i* is positive the quantities will be increased by a factor α greater than 1, otherwise, they will decrease: $\pi_i^{t-1} > 0 \Rightarrow \alpha > 1 ; \pi_i^{t-1} \leq 0 \Rightarrow \alpha < 1$.

Investment in R&D/innovation and Cooperation

As stated before, innovation at instant t (ω_i^t,y) depends on the accumulated knowledge by the firm. In each iteration, we consider that, if $\pi_i^t > 0$, then the innovation ω_i^t must be not null. We have considered three Normal distributions for the innovations in each of the three markets. For the cooperation between two firms, we have defined the following steps: (i) *preferential meeting process*, where we have defined a meeting rate, $m_{i,j}^t$, between two firms where firm i chooses the firm j that maximizes the value $m_{i,j}^t = [1 - d^t(i,j)]$. (ii) *Negotiation:* a simple process was defined, in which two firms cooperate if they are able to reciprocally compensate some lack of profitability in the stock of capital (measured by $\pi_i^t / K_{i,Y}^t$) in some different phases of the production process. For example, if firm *i* has higher profitability in the stock of capital than firm j, considering the product Y=1, but firm *j* has higher profitability in the stock of capital than firm *i* considering the product Y=2, than they can cooperate to invent a new kind of process that may increase the quantities they both produce. This process can be defined by the following condition: if $(\pi_i^t / K_{i,Y=1}^t) > (\pi_j^t / K_{i,Y=1}^t)$ and $(\pi_i^t / K_{i,Y=2}^t) < (\pi_j^t / K_{i,Y=2}^t)$ then => cooperation (see example in table 1).

5. RESULTS FROM *NetOrg*

5.1 Setting up initial parameters

The results presented in this paper are the outcome of more than 100 different runs of the simulation (different runs of 10, 15 and 20 generations were experienced). The following sections present one representative run of 15 generations from where we have taken one representative output. We have defined a set of initial parameters considering that industry 1 could represent an OEM manufacturer and industries 2 and 3 could be its suppliers. The price of the capital (P_k) was set to the same value in all of the industries. The marginal cost was defined differently for the 3 types of industries, and marginal costs in region 2 were half of the corresponding values in the region 1. We maintained the same parameters of the density dependence model in all the experiments ($DS_u=5$; $DS_l=1$; $DB_u=3$; $DB_l=1$). Knowing that R is the average income of the consumers of each market, the number of initial firms was defined by:

$$n = \frac{R}{P_k \times K_{i,Y}^t}.$$

5.2 The emergence of networks

A different n was computed for the three different markets (in average $n_1=3$, $n_2=20$, and $n_3=20$). In all combinations of parameters, firms started cooperating with other firms in order to increase their profit. Firms (and networks) proliferate in region 2 (region with lower marginal costs). Some of the risky firms that migrate (from region 1 to region 2) were able to overcome negative profits. Some of them increased considerably their profits and became top success firms. Although it seems that firms with higher values of risk are in general more profitable, it appears that there is no direct association between the profit of the firm and its level of risk

(Pearson correlation coefficient revealed a weak value of -0.067). Table 1 shows the negotiation results for the cooperation between the first 2 pairs of firms in the simulation, based on the indicator $\pi^t_i / K^t_{i,Y}$. Figure 1 shows the geographical space and the representation of the networks in the 15th generation.

Table 1: First two cooperations (over 98 in total) from one of the runs of NetOrg.

	Cooperating firms		Production process		Profit / Knowledge Stock				Region	
	Firm		Firm							
#	1	Firm2	1	Firm2	$\pi^t_i / K^t_{i,Y=1}$	$\pi^t_j / K^t_{i,Y=1}$	$\pi^t_i / K^t_{i,Y=2}$	$\pi^t_j / K^t_{i,Y=2}$	Firm1	Firm2
1	1	24	1	3	25,73	40,56	44,83	35,62	2	1
2	2	24	1	3	16,31	22,32	28,05	19,56	2	1

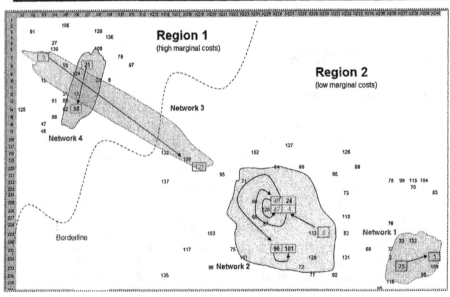

Figure 1 – Representation of the networks in the 15th generation

5.3 Validation of the Model

To explore the strength of the model, we have considered, in section 3, some affirmations made in relation to the Automobile Industry: *(3) Constructors promoted a concentration process of component suppliers (...);.* (4) *OEMs migrate to emergent markets of Asia and South America as a way to rationalize production; (5) Contemporaneous density has a negative impact on the mortality of organizations; (6) Density at founding has a positive impact on the mortality of organizations*
Statistical measures can be used to evaluate the pertinence of these affirmations based on simulated data, but facts (1) and (2) are easy to confirm. In fact, in all iterations, *NetOrg* has produced tens of networks, most of them concentrated in one

ore more OEM, (i.e., industries of type 1) and firms keep migrating to markets with lower marginal costs to increase their profits. To confirm the affirmations (3) and (4), we have analyzed the Regression coefficients from a Cox proportional Hazard Model, to estimate the impact of the covariates *Contemporaneous density* and *Density at founding* on the survival of organizations.

Table 2: Coefficients of some covariates obtained from Cox Regression.

Covariate	Predicted Sign	Coef	se(coef)	p-value
Contemporaneous Density	-	-0.046	0.00992	0.0033
Density at Founding	+	213.77	0.0567	0.0000
Size	-	-0.021	0.0013	0.0022

We have compared the sign of the coefficients with those obtained in other works (Mata, Portugal and Guimarães, 1995; Carroll and Hannan 1989; Carroll and Hannan, 1992). The second column in Table 2 shows the predicted signs (obtained from literature; the same signs have been predicted in all studies) of the association between firm survival and the covariates. All the variables have a significant impact on the survival of firms, which can be seen from the p-values in last column (the standard error of the coefficients are represented as se(coef)). Carroll and Hannan (1989) explain that the density at founding has substantive implications on the survival of organizations. As we can see in Table 2, density at the time of a firm founding has a positive impact on the mortality of organizations while contemporaneous density (the number of firms existing at the moment of the death) has a corresponding negative effect. As expected, the effect of the size on firm survival is also negative, confirming what was said before and helping to validate the simulation model.

5.4 Evolution of Networks

We have also analyzed the evolution of networks to understand their behavior and change. Therefore, we have performed a Multiple Factorial Analysis (Dazy, 2001), which is suitable for evolutionary data, followed by a clustering step to group networks with similar behavior. Input data matrix contains some variables that describe the networks (profit, marginal cost, stock of capital and form of the network). Each observation in this matrix corresponds to a network in a total of 57 networks found in 20 runs of the simulation. Groups of variables have been considered (one for each period of time). In the global analysis of the Multiple Factorial Analysis (MFA), we kept 7 factors that represent more than 80% of the total model variance. In the cluster analysis, if we choose to accept a partition, say, in 2 classes, we must get a clear characterization of the clusters found. In this partition we find a first group composed by 32 individuals and another group of 25. Looking to the networks (observations) that belong to each one of those classes, we may conclude that the clustering method has separated the networks with lower levels of the Stock of capital from those with higher values for the same variables.

We observe that the networks are clustered considering the dimension of their *stock of capital*, a variable that is determinant for the growth of networks.

6. CONCLUSIONS AND FUTURE WORK

We have analysed the networks that have emerged from a process driven by agglomeration and collective innovation, using a Multi-Agent framework. We have concluded that there are more networks in regions with lower marginal costs. However, there are some firms and networks in richer regions, showing that the creation of networks helps to avoid negative results and abandon of the activity. This is related to the phenomenon of firm relocation that is apparent nowadays in the era of globalization. Although it seems that firms with higher values of risk are in general more profitable, it appears that there is no direct association between the profit of the firm and its level of risk. Clustering methods have found two different groups in the evolution of networks: networks with lower values of stock of capital and networks with higher values. There seems to be no association between the size of the networks and geographical location.

In the future, our goal is to continue endowing agents with the capacity of learning and trust and introducing strategies of cooperation. We will also analyze the stochastic stability of the model.

7. REFERENCES

1. Agata A, Santangelo GD. "Cognitive Distance, Kowledge Spillovers and Localisation in a Duopolistic Game 2003. mimeo, Catania
2. Campos, P., Brazdil, P. Density dependence and the survival of firms: a multi-agent approach, ABS'05: Workshop on Agent-Based Simulation, Erlangen, Germany, 2005b
3. Carayol N, Roux P. Self-Organizing Networks: when do small worlds emerge? 4th EMEE
4. Carroll G, Hannan M. Density Delay in the Evolution of Organizational Populations: A model and Five Empirical Tests, Admnistrative Science Quaterly, 1989; 34: 411-430.
5. Carroll G, Hannan, M. The Demography of Corporations and Industries. Princeton University Press, Pinceton, New Jersey, 1992.
6. Dazy F, Le Barzic, J-F, L'Analyse des Données Evolutives, ed. Technip, Paris, 1996,
7. Cortés JCR, Sheremetov, LB. Model of Cooperation in Multi Agent Systems with Fuzzy Coalitions
8. Cowan R, Jonard N, Zimmernmann J-B. Networks as Emergent Structures from Bilateral Collaboration, MERIT, 2004-17
9. Gilbert N, Pyka, A, Ahrweiller. Innovation Networks – A Simulation Approach. Journal of Artificial Societies and Social Simulation 2001; 4, 3
10. Mata, J. Portugal, P. and Guimarães, P., The Survival of New plants: start-up conditions and post-entry evolution, in International Journal of Industrial Organization, 13 ,459-481, 1995
11. Rolo T. Contributo para análise dos factores de sucesso para a dinamização da cooperação inter-empresarial, Dissertation for Master of Sciences in Engineering Policy and Management of Technology, Instituto Superior Técnico – Universidade Técnica de Lisboa, Lisboa, 1998
12. Swaminathan A, Hoetker G, Mitchell W. Network Structure and Business Survival: The Case of U.S. Automobile Component Suppliers. Working Paper from the University of Illinois at Urbana Champagne, 2002
13. Wersching Klaus. Agglomeration in an Innovative and Differentiated Industry with Heterogeneous Knowledge Spillovers 2005; Workshop on Regional Agglomeration, Growth and Multilevel Governance: the E.U. in a comparative perspective, Ghent
14. Zhang, Jungfu. Growing Silicon Valley on a Landscape: an agent-based approach to high-tech industrial clusters. Journal of Evolutionary Economics 2003; 13: 529-548.

9

ISSUES OF PARTICIPANT ABSORPTIVE CAPACITY IN ESTABLISHING VIRTUAL ENTERPRISE OPERATIONS

Ronald C. Beckett

The Reinvention Network & University of Western Sydney, rcb@reinvent.net.au
AUSTRALIA

The author is involved in a multi-year program to establish a number of large-scale SME collaboration projects. It was anticipated that some web-based tools used previously could be adapted, but limits in the participant firm capabilities and the emergence of a different business model led to a change in approach. In this paper an adaptation of the notion of absorptive capacity where both a firm's resource base and its knowledge base are considered is used as a framework to better understand participant requirements in building a web-based Virtual Enterprise support system.

1. INTRODUCTION

The author is involved in a multi-year program (called RELINK [9]) to establish a large-scale (20 – 100 SME manufacturing firms) Virtual Enterprise capability that enhances the market positioning of the participants. The intention is to draw together small firms who have been dislinked from their traditional supply chains and market access pathways due to some effects of globalization so they can access new, broader markets. This paper reports on some observations made over a period of two years where an action research style of interaction was the norm - trying out ideas from previous work, and using outcomes to frame new ideas.

Some management researchers see markets as intersecting networks of actors, activities and resources [www.impgroup.org]. In previous work [2] we have explored the business benefits arising from collaborative inter-firm transactions and compared a number of different instances using an activity theory framework [1]. Activity theory [7, 13] evolved from studies of learning by doing, and suggests a subject will undertake an activity with an objective in mind, and how this is achieved is governed by the distribution of work, tools available, rules associated with the activity and broader community norms. In this paper, we consider one particular aspect of a VE resource network – the uptake of ICT tools that facilitate VE task management, data management and communications. Within that resource network context however, we also have embedded networks of actors, activities and resources that support its operation. In this paper, the focus is on the capabilities of the VE partner enterprise as an actor within the resource network, where we observe that two things influence the style of participation:

- Some limitations on resources available to acquire new ICT tools.

Please use the following format when citing this chapter:

Beckett, R. C., 2006, in IFIP International Federation for Information Processing, Volume 224, Network-Centric Collaboration and Supporting Fireworks, eds. Camarinha-Matos, L., Afsarmanesh, H., Ollus, M., (Boston: Springer), pp. 85–92.

- Some limits on a firms' accessible knowledge to help use ICT tools, effectively

In an activity theory context, these two factors will influence what kinds of tools can be used in practice, but the framework provided by this theory does not help clarify the issues involved.

One objective of the RELINK program was to adapt research findings and system concepts from previous projects involving larger firms [15, 16] relating to the use of enabling Information Technology tools. A number of difficulties were experienced. One related to available infrastructure, and this has been discussed in a previous paper [8]. Another related to the ability of an individual firm to participate. In this paper we adapt the notion of absorptive capacity attributed to Cohen and Levinthal [3] to provide a framework for clarifying the issues to be addressed, and discuss subsequent actions in the RELINK project.

2. SYSTEM CONCEPT

The intended system model is illustrated in Figure 1. It is comprised of a number of reusable components (broadly identified under the headings of contingency factors, modeling, applications and infrastructure and methodology) and some components, models and knowledge specific to a particular VE (VE models and operational ICT environment). The system also embraced the notion of characterizing the establishment and operation of a VE using a life-cycle view (VERAM [15])

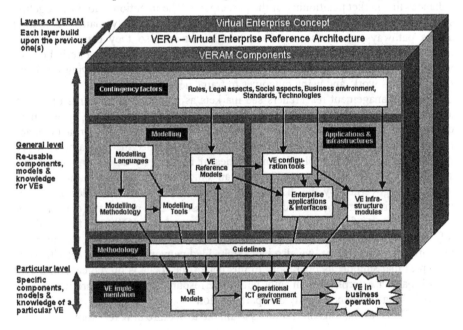

Figure 1 A technology enabled VE capability model

This model can help us understand the position of each potential participant in respect of a number of required capabilities, with a view to building bridges to effective participation as required. It was observed however that embracing these ideas which appeared effective in previous work with large firms was too big a step for most small firms. The participating firms were not comfortable with complex models, even though they might help understand the range of matters to be dealt with in establishing a large-scale collaboration. A different way of packaging the same logical concept was pursued.

3. ICT SUPPORT FOR SMALL COLLABORATING FIRMS AND SOME DIFFICULTIES EXPERIENCED

Whilst IT tools are available to support large scale collaboration, there are issues of scale to be addressed. An example is Teamcenter [11] which is used to support product life-cycle management, but which is typically used by firms 100 times the size of the RELINK project target firms. The RELINK project participant firm size varied from many with less than 10 employees to a few firms having around 100 employees. Most of the firms were involved with the manufacture of production tooling, with each project commonly taking three to nine months to complete. IT capability varied widely between firms. Some firms have a website for advertising purposes, and a few use a password-accessible website facility to provide customers with job progress information. A few firms use ERP systems to manage the flow of work and to collect realistic cost data. Most customer product data is obtained in electronic form (CAD/CAM), and transformed into machine instructions for computer controlled machines to manufacture tooling and components. Microsoft Project software is commonly used by the larger firms for scheduling work and as a progress monitoring tool for customer reporting. Most firms will not have a resident IT specialist, and are not knowledgeable about communications technology. They are not knowledgeable about IT based collaboration technologies, although most use e-mail. The size of the participating firm's means that they do not have access lo a large amount of capital to buy IT equipment that is not central to money-making activities.

4. ISSUES OF ABSORPTIVE CAPACITY

The notion of absorptive capacity was introduced by Cohen and Levinthal [4] who defined it as 'the ability of an organisation to recognise the value of new, external information, assimilate it, and apply it to commercial ends'. They saw the acquisition of this capacity as linked to the R&D capabilities of the organization.

In this paper we extend the theory in two ways. Firstly we take the view that the notion of absorptive capacity can be applied to a variety of capability acquisition situations and secondly we add consideration of resources that facilitate knowledge assimilation and application.

DalZotto [5] has applied the notion of absorptive capacity to a venture capital situation, and Tsai [12] has utilized the idea in better understanding intraorganizational knowledge transfer. Zahra and George [14] and Daghfous [5] extended the theory by specifying four distinct evolutionary stages of absorptive capacity development: knowledge acquisition, assimilation, transformation and exploitation that emerge chronologically in that order. Similar progressive stages were previously noted by Szulanski [10] in the transfer of best practice between different parts of a large enterprise. Szulanski observed 122 best practice transfers in eight companies, and noted a number of barriers to effective transfer. Three dominant factors were a lack of absorptive capacity, causal ambiguity (lack of understanding why something will work in one place but not another) and an arduous relationship between the source and the recipient (too many handovers distort the content or a source in the chain is not trusted). In connection with causal ambiguity, Cohen and Levinthal observe [4,p136] "To integrate certain classes of complex and sophisticated technological knowledge into the firms activities, the firm requires an existing internal staff of technologists and scientists who are both competent in their fields and are familiar with the firm's idiosyncratic needs, organizational procedures, routines, complementary capabilities and extramural relationships". In connection with arduous relationships, Cohen and Levinthal observe the potential value of gate keeping or boundary spanning roles for the identification and translation of technical information that is difficult for internal staff to assimilate.

In our extension of the theory we consider the physical capacity to introduce something new. This has dimensions of capital -- being able to invest in new technology or to buy additional capacity, and of time -- organization members making time available to engage with the new thing being introduced (seeing time as a resource), being able to introduce the new thing in a timely way (seeing timing as a strategic variable). For a period of time during the introduction of something new, old products or practices may coexist with the new, requiring additional resources during the transition period. In addition, there may be a period of some disruption and a firm's ability to accommodate that disruption without impacting on the provision of its normal goods and services can be a factor in deciding whether or not to proceed. Some aspects of time were discussed in Cohen and Levinthal's [4] foundation paper – spending time in repetitively using new knowledge will embed it more deeply in the corporate memory.The second component considered is the knowledge needed to understand the significance of this new thing and to understand how to derive value from it. It is this authors view, based on many years of transferring best practice in industry, that the assimilation and transformation stages described by Daghfous [5] are intertwined – becoming competent in the use of the new capability in the current organization context, and that the exploitation stage involves obtaining leverage from the new capabilities in new organizational contexts.

5. APPLYING THE EXTENDED ABSORPTIVE CAPACITY THEORY

The question we wish to explore here is does the target RELINK participant firm have the resources and the knowledge to effectively participate in technology-enabled large scale collaboration? We argued that there are two primary components of absorptive capacity – available resources and accessible knowledge. Previous studies seem to assume that suitable physical infrastructure exists and have focused on the knowledge component. In the RELINK project, we see that this is not a valid assumption for some of the participants.

In the context of the *applications* aspect of the reference collaboration support model presented in Figure 1, we aspire to have RELINK project participants access and use a business capability for distributed project management and a technological capability to exchange complex technical data and models between distributed partners. Components of the absorptive capacity project participants would need to acquire are illustrated in Table 1. Using the entries in Table 1 to frame a series of questions can reveal the current position of a particular firm.

Component of Requisite Absorptive Capacity		Capability Acquisition Action	
		Business Capability	Technological Capability
Resources (To access new technology)	**Investment capacity** (e.g. borrowing power)	- Invest in distributed project management tools	- Invest in technical data exchange capability - Invest in product and process modeling tools
	Time – Current resource commitment (e.g. people too busy)	- System acquisition and implementation time - Application knowledge acquisition time - Potential disruption time	- System acquisition and implementation time - Application knowledge acquisition time - Potential disruption time
Knowledge (To effectively apply new technology)	**Language** (jargon) and sensemaking	- Familiarity with advanced project management systems terminology and practices	- Familiarity with technical data exchange and modeling tool systems terminology and practices
	Learning process skills and Experimentation capability	- Understanding how to operate advanced project management practices in the context of the current business	- Understanding how to operate data exchange and modeling systems in the context of the current business
	Background competency & experience to **obtain leverage from new knowledge**	- Being able to leverage project management knowledge to operate in an extended enterprise and to tackle projects with significant uncertainties in what to and how to do it.	- Being able to leverage technical data systems knowledge to operate in an extended enterprise and to develop new internal business capabilities.

Table 1: Requisite Absorptive Capacity

Decisions can be made as to whether to (a) integrate with the firm's current position by managing an external interface (a gatekeeper strategy), or (b) whether to enhance the firms ability to interface with more sophisticated systems (acquire absorptive capacity) or some combination of these two things. What emerged in the RELINK project was an information systems strategy where relatively simple IT tools were combined with some agreed practices about how they were to be used as follows: firstly, a decision was made to **not** invest is special purpose project management tools, but to work out how existing tools (e.g. Microsoft Project or Microsoft Outlook) could be utilized within an overarching task definition model. Secondly, data of any kind was to be treated and controlled as a document made available in a password accessible webspace. And finally, project issues could be logged and discussed using a kind of password accessible chat-space

6. DISCUSSION

In broad terms, matters that arose in promoting IT support for virtual enterprise operations in the RELINK project were: low levels of acceptance of a broadly descriptive model, with differing perceptions of value of this model (figure 1), and a limited capability to implement such a concept. Two steps were taken to deal with these issues. The first step was to focus on some very specific application (project management and technical data systems) and infrastructure matters, and secondly to use an absorptive capacity view (table 1) to cluster issues so they could be dealt with in the most appropriate way.

Table 1 helps us understand the enormity of the task confronting small firms if they were to all acquire hardware, software and knowledge currently used by some large corporations to implement the requisite functions. By way of example, a single user version of Microsoft Project may be inexpensive, but understanding it is another matter. A reference text called the Microsoft Office Project 2003 Bible contains about 900 pages. The server version of this software that has more collaboration capability also requires other complementary software and hardware, and requires specialist IT skills to support it, all of which becomes quite expensive. The most practical approach was to target a lower level of ICT usage and simpler applications software, achieving total information system requirements (Figure 1 plus Table1) through manual interfaces.

In the context of figure I, it was found that, regardless of the ICT/manual mix in implementation, that some of the suggested reusable components had to be significantly modified. Two areas of figure 1 will be discussed in this regard. A *contingency* (see figure 1) factor in the RELINK project that differed from past projects was that it attempted to get groups of traditional competitors to collaborate. This influenced some of the roles and social aspects to be managed, and the extent to which knowledge was freely shared, introducing some implicit rules. Some *modeling* (see figure 1) considerations were that whilst a life-cycle VE model was accepted informally; assumptions about the practicality of a substantial peer network business model were not well founded. Rather than all firms participating in the marketing and bidding processes using IT tools to help draw things together, it was found that a few focal firms had to work face-to-face with the customer. Instead of getting prices and technical inputs from all participants, focal firms had to negotiate the best deal they could, then work out how to manage within the price and schedule requirements agreed. This influenced the nature of project management arrangements and who managed technical data.

Overall we saw that some combination of the business models that made sense and the absorptive capacity of the participants influenced the nature of acceptable

ICT tools. By way of example, it was anticipated at the start of the RELINK project that some bid development workbench (previously used in other projects) would be helpful in collaboratively developing customer proposals for large projects. This was not the case because of the way bids had to be put to the customer, and because there were concerns about data confidentiality. In the RELINK project, a collection of hub and spoke arrangements was the most commonly observed network configuration, with the hub firms tending to be the larger ones. Some examples of small regional networks were also observed.

The observed cast of generic actors is similar to that observed by Camarinha-Matos and Afsarmanesh [3], characterized as:

- **Focal firms** that have demonstrated project management skills and can muster useful financial resources
- **Technology providers** that supply tools and methodologies to the participating firms
- **Regional networks** that may choose to operate outside their region as a single group
- **Communities of Practice** that operate across firms to identify collective capabilities and facilitate interaction between firms
- **Supporting firms** that add capacity by providing access to some of their resources on a flexible basis

In this context, the information systems solution trialed was intended to be usable by the supporting firms, but managed by the focal firms, consistent with Cohen and Levinthal's observation [4 p133]- "At the most basic level, the relevant knowledge that permits effective communication within and across subunits consists of shared language and symbols". Adding consideration of resources into Cohen and Levinthal's [4] theory of absorptive capacity helped direct the technology providers towards open source, freeware based solutions. It was observed that whilst the focal firms had more IT knowledge than most of the supporting firms, both groups had problems assigning time as a resource to system integration or in deciding the most appropriate time to upgrade IT capabilities.

As mentioned in the introduction to this paper, we have previously used activity theory [7, 13] to better understand the operation of collaborative ventures by considering the subject that will undertake an activity with an objective in mind, and how this is achieved as governed by the distribution of work, tools available, rules associated with the activity and broader community norms. All of these factors can certainly be identified in the previous discussion – the distribution of work between focal and supporting firms, rules associated with collaboration between competitors, an intention to use ICT tools in some way, and the norms (e.g. firm size) of a particular professional community. In this authors view, consideration of absorptive capacity adds is a consistent way of establishing a firm's ability to participate in a large scale collaboration, which in turn influences the way a collaboration works.

6. CONCLUDING REMARKS

In this paper we focus on collaboration technologies, and have considered experience gained in a particular case where a number of difficulties were experienced in implementing ideas that had been used elsewhere. The paper draws on the notion of absorptive capacity originally introduced by Cohen and Levinthal [4], which had a focus on a firm's knowledge base facilitating the introduction of new technologies into a firm. We have extended the theory, adding capital and time as key resources in the assimilation of new technology, and also consider the status of a firms knowledge base in terms of three levels of maturity: being able to understand the jargon of something new and make sense of it; being able to effectively use something new in the context of the firm; and obtaining leverage from newly acquired capabilities in an extended context. Some of the SME firms participating in a case study project had a low absorptive capacity that precluded adoption of ICT tools that have been used by large firms. It was also noted that the dominant collaboration business model also influenced the nature of appropriate IT support. The extended notion of absorptive capacity provided a good vehicle for matching information system implementations strategies with user capabilities to meet functional needs.

7. REFERENCES

1. Beckett, R.C (2004) "Exploring Virtual Enterprises using Activity Theory". Australian Journal of Information Systems, Vol 12, No 1, pp103 – 110
2. Beckett, R.C. (2004), "Exploring Sustainable Virtual Enterprises". In "Virtual Enterprises and Collaborative Networks"(Ed L.M. Camarinha-Matos) Kwuhler Academic Publishers, the Netherlands, ISBN 1-4020-8138-3. pp 491-498
3. Camarinha-Matos, L.M, and Afsarmanesh, H (2004) "The Emerging Discipline of Collaborative Networks" in "Virtual Enterprises and Collaborative Networks"(Ed L.M. Camarinha-Matos) Kwuhler Academic Publishers, the Netherlands. ISBN 1-4020-8138-3, pp 3-16
4. Cohen, W.M and Levinthal, D.A. (1990) Absorptive Capacity: A New Perspective on Learning and Innovation. Administrative Science Quarterly, Vol 35 pp 128-152
5. Daghfous, A 2004, 'Absorptive capacity and the implementation of knowledge- intensive   best practices' *S.A.M. Advance Management Journal* , vol. 69, no. 2, pp. 21-27.
6. Dal Zotto, C (2003) "Absorptive Capacity and Knowledge Transfer between Venture Capital Firms and their Portfolio Companies" Druid Summer Conference on Creating, Sharing and Transferring Knowledge, Copenhagen, June 12 – 14
7. Engestrom, Y. (1987) "Learning by expanding: an activity-theoretical approach to developmental research" Helsinki: Orienta-Konsultant
8. Mo, J, Beckett, R, and Nemes, L (2005) "Technology Infrastructure for a Virtual Organization of Toolmakers" in Camarinha-Matos, L.M, Afsarmanesh, H and Ortiz, A (Eds) "Collaborative Networks and their Breeding Environments", Springer, New York (ISBN 10 (HB) 0-387-28259-9) pp 493 - 500
9. RELINK (2004) http://relink.agileserve.com
10. Szulanski, G (1996) "Exploring Internal Stickiness: Impediment to the Transfer of Best Practices Within the Firm" Strategic Management Journal, Vol 17, No 10, pp27-43
11. Teamcenter (2006) "Teamcenter overview: powering innovation with knowledge" www.ugs.com (last accessed May 2006)
12. Tsai, W (2001) "Knowledge transfer in intraorganizational networks: Effects of network position and absorptive capacity on business unit innovation and performance" Academy of Management Journal, Vol 44, pp996 – 1004
13. Vygotsky, L.S. (1978) "Mind and Society" Harvard University Press.
14. Zahra, S.A and George, G (2002) "Absorptive Capacity: A Review, Reconceptualizaton and Extension" Academy of Management Review, Vol 27, No 2, pp 185-203
15. Zwegers A., Tolle M., Vesterager J., (2003). "Virtual Enterprise Reference Architecture and Methodology", *Global Engineering and Manufacturing in Enterprise Networks*, VTT Symposium 224, 9-10 December, Helsinki, pp.17-
16. Zhou, M, Zheng, J, Williams, A and Alexander, B (2001) "A Web-based Bidding Workbench for Global Manufacturing" in Mo, J.P.T and Nemes, L (Eds) Global engineering, manufacturing and enterprise networks" Kluwer Academic Publishers, Massachusetts (ISBN 0-7923-7358-8) pp 206-211

10

CONTRIBUTION OF PERVASIVE INTELLIGENCE TO COLLABORATIVE INNOVATION PROCESSES

Veronica Serrano, Thomas Fischer
WHU Otto Beisheim School of Management
veronica.serrano@whu.edu, fischer@whu.edu

Considering the fact that pervasive intelligence will be in foreseeable time a reality, we analyze its influence on collaborative innovation processes and propose a possible innovation system structure. Some ideas about potential ubiquitous systems that could enhance the stages of the innovation process are also presented.

1. INTRODUCTION

In a global and technology-oriented world the requirements on products and services increase continuously. In order to face these challenges in R&D, different abilities and competencies need to be brought together, e.g., through collaboration with suppliers, customers, external service providers and research institutions, with the objective of achieving high-quality innovations. Innovation processes comprise basically multidisciplinary activities that require disperse teams combining expertise and experience in various fields. Advances in ICT are supporting and making virtual collaboration for innovation feasible. One of the latest paradigms in ICT describes ubiquity of information-processing, communication-technology and computer-performance through embedding sensors, actuators and processors in the environment. It is to expect that this new paradigm will change the organization, the management and even the conception of collaborative innovation processes.

The paper begins describing the new IT paradigm in section 2. Section 3 defines the conceptual structures of pervasive intelligence and the properties of ubiquity that characterize ubiquitous systems. Section 4 presents the possible contributions of pervasive intelligence for enhancing collaborative distributed innovation processes. Finally, section 5 concludes this paper and addresses some potential future trends.

2. VISIONS OF UBIQUITY

Three representative conceptions ubiquitous computing, ubiquitous networking and ambient intelligence embody the most important aspects of the vision.

The term ubiquitous computing appeared chronologically at first just before the

Please use the following format when citing this chapter:

Serrano, V., Fischer, T., 2006, in IFIP International Federation for Information Processing, Volume 224, Network-Centric Collaboration and Supporting Fireworks, eds. Camarinha-Matos, L., Afsarmanesh, H., Ollus, M., (Boston: Springer), pp. 93–100.

internet boom and the propagation of the computer use (many computers per person) (Weiser, 1993, 1999). Fundamental issues are, e.g. affording ubiquitous operations of everyday artefacts in terms of computation performance and ICT-capabilities. Ubiquitous computing deals with the creation and/or the augmentation of everyday objects to guarantee ubiquitous provision of operation and service for users.

Ubiquitous network refers to the environment for ICT utilization where "a network is connected at any place, at any time and with any object" (Murakami, 2004). Ubiquitous networking (Murakami, Fujinuma, 2000) emphasizes the possibility of building networks of persons and objects for sending and receiving information of all kinds and thus providing the users with services anytime and at any place. This implies to consider: technological aspects, content-based aspects, and organizational aspects by coordinating the formation and development of (often locally dispersed) groups.

Ambient intelligence is the first term that describes the vision as a whole. It concentrates on the arrangement of the architecture, the organization and the coordination of the components (especially ubiquitous, embedded, networked, adaptive applications) of the intelligent environment (ISTAG, 2001). Ambient intelligence aims building structures for an optimal self-organisation of the environment with the objective of enhancing human communication, creating confidence and providing knowledge and skills for a better quality of life (Philips, 2006).

3. PERVASIVE INTELLIGENCE

Our conception of pervasive intelligence derives from the integration of ubiquitous computing, ubiquitous networking and ambient intelligence. Etymologically, pervasive intelligence means intelligence that can penetrate everything or is present everywhere. Constitutive characteristics are adaptivity and autonomy. Adaptivity describes the capacity for or tendency toward adaptation, which is the adjustment to environmental conditions or the modification of an organism or its parts that makes it more fit for existence under (externally) emerging conditions. Autonomy represents the quality of self-direction, acting independently of other factors. As constitutive characteristics of pervasive intelligence they describe actions as well as structures.

Adaptivity involves reactive actions to predefined conditions of the environment, to the necessities of other objects as well as to the perceived necessities of specified users in determinate situations Adaptivity also implies changing structures because only they enable the reactivity of the environment as a whole.

Autonomy implicates proactive actions, which take place anticipating future problems, needs of users or possible changes in the environment. Self-configuration and self-organisation are two characteristics of structures to guarantee autonomous behaviour. The configuration, i.e. time, location, activation, varies due to the dynamic incorporation or removal of components or due to changes in the way how persons use or interact with them. Self organising structures are those in which components automatically configure their interaction in a way that is compatible with the remaining interactions in the system (Georgiadis et al., 2002).

Pervasive intelligence manifests itself in form of ubiquitous systems. Ubiquitous systems are such systems whose components possess properties like context-awareness, embedding and miniaturization as well as availability, reachability and connectivity of sensors, operators and actuators anytime/anywhere and to anything or anybody, invisibility in terms of calm computing, augmented reality and interactivity. A context-aware system is "the system that uses context to provide relevant information and/or services to the user, where relevancy depends on the user's task" (Dey et al., 1999). Miniaturization of sensors, operators and actuators and embedding them into the physical world afford the integration of intelligence (perception, interpretation and reaction-capabilities) into the environments.

One of the greatest challenges of the ubiquitous vision is calm computing that implies supporting human beings in a way that they do not feel disturbed by thousands of different applications and devices that try to guess their needs (Weiser, Brown, 1996). Augmented reality illustrates the integration of the digital and the real world for enhancing the conditions of the environment. Interactivity is another important property of ubiquitous systems. Actions of users and objects actively influence the reactions of the applications and of the environment (two way interaction). This allows the provision of personalized services for the users.

4. CONTRIBUTION TO COLLABORATIVE INNOVATION

The potential contribution of pervasive intelligence to collaborative innovation comprises different fields of investigation like the creation of conceptual structures of collaborative innovation processes, the study of already existing and the development of new methodologies as well as the analysis of technological requisites. We concentrate here on the first one: the formulation of innovation system structures considering thereby the information flows of the product lifecycle, the organization and the coordination of innovation processes and the creation and management of knowledge.

4.1 Innovation System Structure

Cyclic models represent dynamics and flexibility of innovation processes in a better way than traditional linear ones. Moreover, considering the characteristics of pervasive intelligence, the properties of ubiquitous systems and the interactivity of innovation processes, innovation system structures should be modelled in a cyclical form as outlined in Figure 1.

Three different levels of innovation, i.e. (A) radical, (B) regular or (C) incremental innovations are represented through three cycles.

(A) Radical innovation begins with the stage (1) Identification and Selection, in which the strategic innovation goals are identified and new ideas are screened and generated based on various knowledge resources or basic research. New ideas often result from the iterative collaboration of the design and development team, customers, suppliers and research institutions. Then, the design- and development team structures the ideas and usually supported by customers and suppliers evaluate and select the most feasible, while the useless ones are discarded. Subsequently, the selected ideas are passed to the second stage (2) Concept Definition and Project Planning.

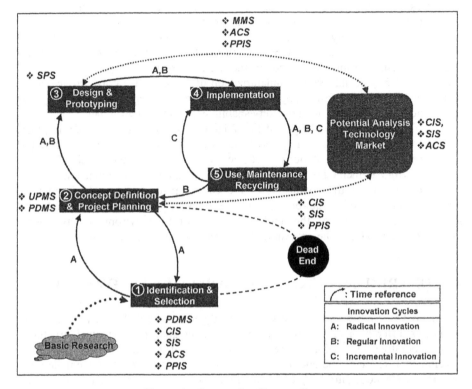

Figure 1 – Innovation System Structure

Combining the selected ideas with the knowledge and the experience of the participants, new concepts are created, e.g., through visualization enabled by augmented reality tools. This also ensures the originality of the transmitted concepts independently of the actual locations of the participants (ubiquity). The validation occurs in form of an analysis of the potential of the new concepts considering their technical feasibility and their market opportunities. The information is between the first and the second stage, rotating from the one to the other until a mature concept is conceived.

Considering the results of the potential analysis, the concept is enhanced and a project plan is set up. Both are sent to the next stage (3) Design and Prototyping where a possible product or process is outlined. This draft serves as basis for the prototype, which is evaluated by customers and technology experts before passing to the next stage. Thus information on possible improvements and especially ideas on new services, which complement the product, are generated

The knowledge and the information generated during the (4) Implementation of the product (service/process) provide a basis for the optimization of the production process. During (5)Use, Maintenance and Recycling the behaviour of the customers is observed applying market studies, surveys or through embedded sensors and (web) interfaces in existing products if they have agreed to send their personal use-data. After-market services like maintenance or recycling contribute to continuously discover improvement potential. Information stored in recycled products, brought back to the company, inspires possible changes or new concepts for modification of products, creation of new services or combinations of services and products.

Beyond radical innovation it is possible to differentiate regular and incremental innovation (cycles B and C). Regular innovation (B) takes place when market feedback is remitted to the stage (2) Concept Definition and Project Planning. From there, cycle B starts aiming at the creation of the next generation of products/services passing (3), (4) and (5). Incremental innovation (C), also called continuous improvement, results when the internal and external data are directly transmitted to the stage (4) Implementation in which the noticed recommendations are immediately realized into products or services of the next series.

4.2 Ubiquitous Innovation Systems

As indicated in the Figure 1, seven potential ubiquitous systems[i] can significantly support the stages of the innovation process.

The first stage can be assisted by Pervasive Design Management System (PDMS), Customer Integration System (CIS), Supplier Involvement System (SIS), Ambient Collaboration System (ACS) and Product and Process Information System (PPIS).

PDMS aims at improving efficiency and target orientation avoiding designs that are never used, delivered or completed. The system affords the association of surging ideas with already completed designs in order to prevent possible repetitions of designs. Multimodal interfaces (voice or handwriting recognition) embedded in the physical design environment and interfaces in portable devices (computer, PDA, cell-phone) recognize future possible design purposes during meetings and present similar and useful designs. Thus creativity is stimulated and an efficient selection of ideas is afforded, which contributes to save time and material resources (design rationalisation).

Properties of ubiquity manifested in this system are (in relevance order) context-awareness, embedding and miniaturization, calm computing, interactivity and ubiquitous communication and reachability.

Context-awareness serves for detecting the "design context", i.e. the logical context of the ideas, e.g. using association techniques. Embedded interfaces in the physical environment collect design information on user's demand (calm computing). Interactivity evinces the possibility of communication of the designers with the system. Different features can be selected to conduct various operations. Augmented reality upgrades the quality of information of already designed ideas and projects, e.g., multimedia files explaining the designs or additional information onto the working surface. Ubiquitous communication and reachability play an important role in distributed design meetings, particularly because it is necessary to recognize the context of design in order to localize and contact the necessary expertise or experts. PDMS can be considered an extension of Product Data Management systems that administer all information around products: CAD models, drawings, their associated documents, product visualizations. PDMS includes additionally designs even if they did not result in products and enhances the support to the design team incorporating ubiquitous features.

CIS intends integrating customers in the innovation process in a more intuitive way. Three different situations of integration are mentioned here: incorporating customers in an artificial environment (living labs), addressing customers directly in the place of consumption or in communal places and forming communities that share similar problems or interests. Real-time communication between the participants of the innovation process facilitates discovering errors and malfunctions as well as solving common problems during operation and application. Recycled products with embedded technology could even gather information about customers' behaviour during the whole period of use.

In CIS the following features are active: context-awareness is necessary for recognizing contexts of use of different customers, embedding and miniaturizing enable the integration of sensing platforms in the environment and in products; calm computing is responsible for not disturbing the customer and not altering the real conditions of use and augmented reality for supporting users by revolving problems during the operation of products. CIS can be understood as specific Customer Relationship Management being a part of a PLM system that integrates various systems along the life cycle (Swink, 2006). Nevertheless, CIS is more specialized because it tries to filter and manages only data that are directly involved in innovation activities.

SIS strives for integrating suppliers early in the innovation process so that real cross-functional team-work is facilitated. Context awareness allows finding adequate suppliers depending on the actual context of the design-task, the design-object, or conditions. Embedded technology and ubiquitous connectivity are responsible for tagging and reaching all the potential (dispersed) suppliers so that even if they are en-route they can be localized or involved through applications in their mobile personal devices. A mixture of context-awareness with ubiquitous connectivity makes possible an intensive but adequate information exchange between suppliers and the rest of participants in the innovation process. The probability of forming open innovation groups as well as unstructured spontaneous meetings could also be increased through context-awareness and ubiquity. All these process should take place in a calm-technology atmosphere so that the suppliers do not feel invaded in their privacy. Augmented reality can enhance the quality of exchanged information. SIS could be part of Supply Chain Management being integrated in a PLM system and concentrating on the collaboration with the supplier in the new product development.

ACS is in charge of the organization and technical realization of successful collaboration in all its forms (co-located and dispersed groups, synchronous or asynchronous, symmetric or asymmetric), which is possible through the coordination of tasks like collecting and exchanging knowledge, distributing experience and skills of multiple team members, etc. Ubiquity permits contacting and localizing the collaborators of the innovation process independent of where they are and respecting what they are doing. Embedded and miniaturized software and hardware augment the capabilities of already used devices and enhance the communication of experts. Context-awareness is responsible for detecting the actual context of the participants so that on the move and without interrupting their main tasks, suppliers, manufacturers, distributors can exchange information at the time that this information surges or when they are available. Ad-hoc collaboration and communication of expertise and experience of extern collaborators (synchronously or asynchronously) enrich the work of the innovation team. Augmented reality contributes by exchange of information so that the transmitted ideas or concepts conserve the meaning given by their originators. ACS is a collaborative development system that facilitates the joint work by the development of a product/service representing an enriched version with properties of ubiquity.

PPIS controls the information flows through the product life cycle especially during operations. Sensing and tracking capabilities afford the acquisition of necessary knowledge and information to evaluate production processes. Seamless information flow allows supervising the product life cycle and acquiring ideas of how the manufacturing processes should be improved or innovated. Embedded technology in the machinery, resources and surroundings enables fast diagnostics of errors, which serves as basis for efficient discovery of enhancement potential, and an efficient allocation of resources. Here, the properties embedding and miniaturizing as well as invisibility in terms of calm computing predominate. Through embedded devices the product life cycle can be better monitored but they should remain invisible in order to avoid disturbing the normal operations in manufacturing. The contribution of the system is acquiring knowledge about the product life cycle which is currently very time-consuming and cost- intensive.

The stage (2) Concept Definition & Project Planning can benefit from the Ubiquitous Project Management System (UPMS) and the PDMS. UPMS like other Project Management Systems is responsible for the organization and management of design projects using information provided by other systems (Material Management Systems (MMS), ACS). Availability of materials can be enquired from any location and an immediate response will be sent to allow dynamic resource allocation and resource mapping (Gajos et al., 2001). Successful project management results from providing easy access to common used services and information. Coordination of appointment calendars that run in different devices and interaction of users for sharing common goods and services represent important goals of this system where ubiquity, interactivity and embedding and miniaturizing predominate. Ubiquity serves to localize the different participants for building distributed virtual organisations in order to provide information about available resources or services. Interactivity is reflected on the constant updating of information about realized tasks, used resources and their interrelations; embedding and miniaturizing of technology enable the collection of lifecycle 's information.

(3)Design and Prototyping can profit from the Smart Prototyping System (SPS), which through embedded sensors, displays or multimodal interfaces in prototypes allows reaching a better quality of the interaction with testers. More transparency, less failure rate and efficiency in the communication among suppliers, marketing staff, manufacturers, partners and in the transmission of opinion, ideas, preferences can be afforded because the prototype transports this information by itself. Experiences with a prototype in specified situations could be recorded and analyzed.

The properties of ubiquitous systems accentuated in SPS are in particular invisibility (through multimodal interfaces) and interactivity to elicit reaction and feedback of the test persons while using prototypes. In addition, context-awareness allows recognizing different behaviours of test-persons according to their actual contexts and embedding and miniaturizing of devices (cameras, sensors) make new forms of obtaining information about the users and their environment more feasible.

The stage (4) Implementation of a new product or a new product-service combination is influenced by the Material Management System (MMS), the ACS and the PPIS. Supported by, e.g. Auto-ID and RFID technologies physical goods can be localized; information about their state can be provided and understood by machines and this in real time. MMS will enrich and complement Enterprise Resource Planning with properties of ubiquity. Before the new concept is realized as a final product, the feasibility and availability of the crude materials, preliminary products, etc. is controlled for an efficient management of resources.

5. CONCLUSIONS

Pervasive intelligence enables a new quality of information sharing, joint planning, joint problem solving, integration of operations, etc. These factors will positively influence collaborative innovation processes. Ubiquitous innovation systems will increase the performance of the whole innovation cycle.

In a near future it is even conceivably that autonomy and adaptivity develop in such a way that a system could even open up unexpected knowledge-sources independently in order to satisfy the needs of actors in the innovation environment. This will be the next step and is what we call "Emergent Intelligence".

6. REFERENCES [ii]

1. Dey A, Salber D, Abowd G. "The Conference Assistant Combining Context-awareness with Wearable Computing". GCU Center, Georgia Institute of Technology, Atlanta, 1999.
2. Gajos K, Weisman L, Shrobe H. "Design principles for Resource Management Systems for Intelligent Spaces". Draft for the Workshop on Self-Adaptive Software, Budapest, Hungary, 2001.
3. Georgiadis I, Magee J, Kramer J. "Self-Organising Software Architectures for Distributed Systems". WOSS 02 in ACM, 2002.
4. ISTAG, "Scenarios for Ambient Intelligence in 2010". http://www.cordis.lu/ist/istag.htm, 2001.
5. Murakami T, Fujinuma A. "Ubiquitous Networking: Towards a New Paradigm". Nomura Research Institute Papers No. 2, 2000.
6. Murakami, Teruyasu. "Ubiquitous Networking: Business Opportunities and Strategic Issues". Nomura Research Institute Papers No. 79, 2004.
7. Philips Research Webpage stand: January 2006.
   http:/www.research.philips.com/technologies/syst_softw/ami/vision.html .
8. Swink, Morgan. "Building collaborative innovation capability". In Research-Technology Management, Volume 49, Number 2, March-April 2006, pp. 37-47(11).
9. Weiser, Mark "Some Computer Science Issues in Ubiquitous Computing". In Communications of ACM, Vol. 36, No. 7, 1993.
10. Weiser M, Brown J. "The Coming Age of Calm Technology". Xerox PARC, 1996.
11. Weiser, Mark. "The computer of the 21st century". In ACM SIGMOBILE, Vol. 3, Issue 3, 1999.

---

[i] In the following the features of ubiquity and in particular pervasive intelligence are addressed in a very compressed form due to the restricted space of the paper. These systems are under current research of the authors.

[ii] The presented ideas are based on a number of papers that cannot be referred in detail due to the restricted space.

VALUE SYSTEMS

11

TOWARDS THE DEFINITION OF BUSINESS MODELS AND GOVERNANCE RULES FOR VIRTUAL BREEDING ENVIRONMENTS

David Romero[1], Nathalie Galeano[1], Jorge Giraldo[1], Arturo Molina[2]

[1]*CYDIT - ITESM Campus Monterrey, Monterrey, MEXICO*
david.romero.diaz@gmail.com, ngaleano@itesm.mx, giraldodiaz@gmail.com
[2]*DIA - ITESM Campus Monterrey, Monterrey, Mexico armolina@itesm.mx*

Virtual Organisation Breeding Environments (VBEs) represent an emerging valued added strategy for small and medium enterprises (SMEs), to respond in a competitive way to changing market conditions, through the integration of their capabilities in the configuration of Virtual Organizations. The creation of sustainable VBEs is a challenge that requires new business models based on collaborative and trustable environments. Since the VBE include several types of organisations its business model must consider a multi-value system definition and a multi-stakeholder perspective; that will also call for a new governing approach. This paper presents first attempts in the definition of guidelines for develop Business Models and Governance Rules in VBEs.

1. INTRODUCTION

A Virtual Organisational Breeding Environment (VBE) represents an association or pool of organisations and their supporting institutions that have both potential and interest to cooperate with each other, through the establishment of a "base" long-term cooperation agreement. When one of the members (acting as a broker) identifies a business/collaborative opportunity, a subset of these organisations can be selected to form a Virtual Organization (VO) [1]. VOs are temporally alliances of organisations that come together to share skills or core competences and resources in order to better respond to business/collaboration opportunities and produce value-added products and services, and whose cooperation is supported by computers [1]. The aim of the VBE is to establish the base trust for organisations to collaborate in VOs, reducing the cost/time to find suitable partners for the VO, and the developing new capabilities by the composition of individual organisations' capabilities [1].

For VBE creation is important to identify sustainable Business Models that support its daily operation and value generation. According to Osterwalder [6] a business model is a conceptual tool containing the set of objects, concepts and their relationships with the objective to express the business concept. It is a simplified

Please use the following format when citing this chapter:

Romero, D., Galeano, N., Giraldo, J., Molina, A., 2006, in IFIP International Federation for Information Processing, Volume 224, Network-Centric Collaboration and Supporting Fireworks, eds. Camarinha-Matos, L., Afsarmanesh, H., Ollus, M., (Boston: Springer), pp. 103–110.

description and representation of the business idea – how it will make money and how it will be sustainable. In short, a VBE business model should define its organisational structure and describes how this VBE delivers products and/or services to create tangible and intangible values all its stakeholders.

Together with the definition of a VBE business model, the identification and clarification of its governance model is also important, it is required to define the operational rules, bylaws and principles that will govern the behaviour of the members of the VBE during its lifecycle. The challenge is the global acceptance of those rules and bylaws by all the members in the VBE. This paper presents some guidelines for develop VBE business model and VBE governance rules.

2. GUIDELINES FOR DEFINE A VBE BUSINESS MODEL

Considering the VBE context, two important characteristics are identified to define its business model: 1) a multi-value system, including the identification of different values: economic, social and knowledge; 2) a multi-stakeholder approach, identifying each stakeholder participation in value generation process.

The guidelines for define a VBE Business Model presented in this paper are based on the Methodology for Business Model Definition of Collaborative Networked Organizations [5], which uses Osterwalder's business model ontology [6]. This ontology is based on four pillars and nine building blocks (see Table 1). These pillars were adapted considering the main characteristics of a VBE: the multi-value proposition and the multi-stakeholder approach. The definition of each element in the VBE business model will allow the description of the business concept and will help to identify critical variables to observe in a particular VBE.

Table 1 – Definition of Business Model Pillars based on Osterwalder Ontology [7]

Pillar	Building Block	Definition
Product	Multi-value Proposition	Value offered to the stakeholder/customer (What).
Multi-Stakeholder Interface	Target Stakeholders	Target stakeholder/customer and target market (Who).
	Distribution Channel	Channels to reach the market and the customer/stakeholder.
	Stakeholders Relationship	Links and strategies to maintain customer/stakeholder relationship.
VBE Infrastructure Management	Multi-Value Configuration	Activities and resources arrangement necessary to create value for the customer (Value Configuration - How).
	VBE Capabilities	Capabilities will be integrated to underpin the VBE value proposition.
	Partnership	Strategic alliances, joint-ventures and long-term partnerships.
Financial Aspects	Cost Structure	Costs incurred in the creation, marketing and delivering of value.
	Revenue Model	Definition of the business model economic sustainability.

2.1 Product Pillar Definition for a VBE

VBE Multi-value proposition: The multi-value proposition of the VBE should be unveiled by the same primary questions used to define the nature and opportunity of any business: What are the needs to be satisfied? What are the main benefits for the stakeholders? Which are the offering and the advantages for the VBE stakeholders?

In the VBE business model the central value proposition for its stakeholders is the creation of a supporting environment based on ICTs, which provides common grounds for interaction/collaboration, and facilitation of VO establishment. The VBE will offer, as part of it central value proposition, a bundle of services for: establish a base of trust for organisations to collaborate in VOs; reduce the cost/time to find sustainable partners for VO configuration; assist with the dynamic VOs reconfiguration; provide some commonality for interaction; and an accepted business culture that includes cooperative business rules. Next table shows a generic value propositions for the main stakeholders involved in a VBE business ecosystem.

Table 2 – Multi-Value Proposition Definition for a VBE

Stakeholder	Value Proposition
VBE Member	A VBE offer to its members a set of services for collaboration and integration that support the creation and operation of VOs. These services can be grouped in: • Core competencies identification services (tools, methodologies, guidelines for proper identification of VBE members' core competencies). • VO support services (services that support the VO creation and operation). • Trust building services (services related to enhance the collaboration among its members). • Commercialization/Marketing related services (marketing VBE member's competencies and assets). • Business process improvement services (derived from best practice implementation). • Support institution's related services (services that can be offered through the support institutions, such as financial, consulting or IT services).
VO Brokerage Team	A VBE offer to the brokerage team a set of services for collaboration and integration that support the VO lifecycle. These services can be grouped in: • VO creation services (information about VBE members profiles, competencies and performance history; negotiation and contracting tools; tools for identifying new business/collaborative opportunities; market monitoring tools; planning tools). • VO management services (project management tools; performance measurement and monitoring tools; decision support tools). • VO quality assurance services (good metrics for quality assurance in product/service delivery of VBE members should be accomplished).
Support Institutions	• A VBE offer to the support institutions access to new customers (members of VBE), opportunities to develop collaborative projects, and opportunities to increase its knowledge base.

2.2 VBE Multi-Stakeholder Interface Pillar Definition

VBE Target Stakeholders: This building block focus on identifying the target stakeholders/customers with all their characteristics. Main questions to be answered are: Who are the target stakeholders? Who are the potential VBE members and support institutions? What are their needs?

The VBE potentially addresses all organisations (essentially SMEs) with the potential and the interest to cooperate with each other, through the establishment of a "base" long-term cooperation agreement [1]. Table 3 presents main VBE stakeholders with their main characteristics and needs.

Table 3 – VBE Target Stakeholders

Stakeholders	Examples of stakeholders	Characteristics to be identified
VBE Member	• Large, Medium and Small Enterprises • VO Broker • VO Planner or Integrator • VO Coordinator • Support Institutions	• Identify its competencies and capabilities (products/services, human resources, physical resources, ICT, process, practices). • Identify their specific needs. • Identify its location.
VO Brokerage Team	• VO Broker • VO Planner or Integrator • VO Coordinator	• Identify its brokerage capabilities. • Identify their specific needs related with the brokerage process.
Support Institutions	• VBE Advisor, VBE Service provider and VBE Ontology provider • Industrial Associations, Chambers of Commerce, Regional Development Agencies • Universities, Government Entities and Financial Institutions	• Identify its offer of products and services. • Identify its competencies and capabilities. • Identify their specific needs.

VBE Distribution Channel: Distribution channels are the mean of getting in touch and interact with VBE stakeholders. Main questions that should be answered are: Which communication channel is established among the VBE and its stakeholders?

Does the VBE offer its services/products through other companies that offer complementary products or services? In a VBE the main media to interact with stakeholders is the collaborative ICT platform (environment for virtual collaboration and cooperation); usually this platform is web-based. The internet is then, the main delivery and communication channel. The VBE can also use viral marketing and co-brand strategies to offer its products and services. Traditional distribution channels such as, television, radio, newspapers, among others can be used.

VBE Stakeholders Relationship: The relationship describes the kind of links that a VBE establishes with its stakeholders. Main issues that should be addressed are: Which are the types of relationships that a VBE should establish with and among its members, brokerage team and support institutions? How are these relationships achieved? The VBE must develop trust-based relationships among its stakeholders and especially among its members. Sometimes members that can participate in a VO do not necessarily know each other, the VBE should provide confidence and trust supporting the collaboration process. There are certain number of mechanisms to build trust in the VBE, such as, performance records, mediation services, third party verification and privacy policies [2]. The ICT collaborative platform supports the stakeholders' relationships offering the right information at the right time and trust-related services.

2.3 VBE Infrastructure Management Pillar Definition

VBE Multi-Value Configuration: A multi-value configuration describes the arrangement of activities and resources that are necessary for the creation of value. Main VBE business processes that support the multi-value configuration in a VBE are: 1) Marketing and commercialization, in two directions: promote capabilities of VBE members, and increase VBE members' base; 2) VO service provisioning, including services that support VO lifecycle, cooperation and collaboration; 3) Enhancement of trust and loyalty; and 4) Business process improvement derived from best practice implementation. One way to evaluate the multi-value configuration is through the identification of the value balance for each stakeholder. Table 4 present one general balance for the VBE member value proposition which should be achieved with the deployment of the VBE business processes.

VBE Capabilities: A capability is the ability to execute a pattern of actions [9] necessary in order to create value. Questions to be answered in this building block are: Which resources should the VBE have? How can the services of the VBE be expanded? Main VBE capabilities are: 1) Offer services to its members, such as brokering, legal, marketing, insurance services; 2) Offer common base ICT infrastructure; 3) Support cooperative business rules; 4) Offer a VBE bag of assets that will be shared by its members; 5) Offer services that support VO creation process; 6) Evaluation, qualification and certification of VBE members; and 7) Manage the VBE organization and its infrastructure.

VBE Partnership: A partnership is a voluntarily initiated cooperative agreement between external organisations to the VBE in order to create value for all the stakeholders, especially VBE members. Main questions to address are: Which are the partnerships developed? What is the reason for the partnership? How is achieved the involvement of partners? VBE support institutions are the main partnerships developed. Support Institutions complements VBE service offer (Table 3 presents main support institutions). Partnerships can be also developed with any organization with the capabilities to eliminate the competencies gap that VBE may have; the VBE should consider these new partners as potential members according to the governance rules defined.

Table 4 – Example of Multi-Value Configuration Definition for VBE Members

Value Type	Receive	Offer
Financial	▪ Opportunity to increase incomes as result of the participation in business/collaborative opportunities. ▪ Access to VBE services at a low cost. ▪ International marketing. ▪ Possible financial support or funding from government and financial institutions. ▪ Reduce project costs and R&D costs by splitting the investment with several VBE members.	▪ Competencies in terms of resources, processes, practices, products/services and associated partners. ▪ Joint purchases to increase negotiation power. ▪ Branding transfer. ▪ VBE membership payment.
Technological	▪ ICT resources that support collaborative work. ▪ Use of a Profile and Competence Management System. ▪ Technical support from different institutions. ▪ VBE bag of assets (technological shared assets)	▪ Provide information to create a VBE member profile with its competencies. ▪ Professional advice to other VBE members. ▪ Technological assets that could be shared.
Knowledge	▪ Opportunity to receive training. ▪ Help in the definition of best practices during the evaluation in VBE recruitment process. ▪ Knowledge transfer between VBE members.	▪ Contribute to the body of knowledge of the VBE. ▪ Share best practices and lessons learned.
Social	▪ Development of relationships between VBE members and support institutions. ▪ Development of collaborative culture. ▪ Reduction of risk in project collaboration.	▪ Openness to start relationships between VBE members and support institutions. ▪ Individual social and cultural values.

2.4 Financial Aspects Pillar Definition for a VBE

This pillar includes two building blocks: cost structure and revenue model, referring to the definition of the VBE business model sustainability (financial performance and growth potential). Four activities should be performed in the creation of a VBE related to financial aspects: 1) identification of the investment required; 2) definition of mechanism to assure cost-effectiveness; 3) definition of: membership/ pricing policy, tariff structure, expenses policy, and analysis of the revenue stream; and 4) conceptualization of the accounting/financial system, and determination of the financial and growth indicators [5]. Questions to be answered in this pillar are: Which are the revenue model, the cost structure and the business model's sustainability of the VBE?

VBE Cost Structure: The cost structure is the representation in money of all the means employed in the business model. General VBE cost structure may include: ICT cost, staffing costs, billing costs, marketing costs (promotion/communication), general and administrative costs and operational cost. It is important to mention that the cost structure depends on each VBE type.

VBE Revenue Model: The revenue model should describe the way a VBE makes money and achieve its sustainability through a variety of revenue flows. Different types of revenue model can be used according to the type of VBE: membership fee,

VO commissions over business opportunity, external funding (government, research funds, banks etc.) and service transaction-based fee. In order to clarify the financial aspects of the VBE and the situations that may occur, Figure 1 shows through a value map a general VBE value transfer. The money flow is represented with the symbol "$", and can be analyzed in more detail if specific amount of money are evaluated in a total balance (what is received vs. what is paid) per each organization. This value map was developed using Gordijn e^3value tool [4] and gives a practical idea of all the actors involved in the VBE and its value transfer.

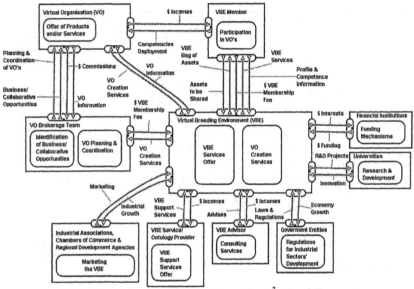

Figure 1 – VBE Value Map using e^3value [4]

3. GUIDELINES FOR DEFINE VBE GOVERNANCE RULES

The governance word suggests the notion of steering, and in the most of the cases refers to the use of structures of authority and even collaboration, to allocate resources and coordinate or control activities in organisations. The governance term in VBE context is specifically aimed to describe the approaching process for facilitating and improving business/collaborative opportunities, as well as guaranteeing the sustainability and correct performance of all stakeholders involved. VBE Governance includes the definition of: principles, Bylaws, Functional Rules and Behavioural Rules.

Principles: values that govern a person or organisation behaviour, they constitute personal guidelines for stakeholders to behave within a VBE. They are referred to the social attitudes which will obviously impact VBE operational performance, such as honesty, trust and integrity, openness, performance orientation, responsibility, accountability, mutual respect and commitment to the organisation.

Bylaws: formally declare rules of operation which will regulate stakeholders' behaviour. VBE bylaws will define the regulations concern with the definition of stakeholders' roles, memberships, incentive and sanctions, ethical code, security principles, ICT use, conflict resolution policy, and establishment of financial policies. VBE principles and bylaws represent a global schema under which a VBE will control and monitor the performed activities of its stakeholders along the VBE lifecycle. Other important elements to bear in mind, when defining VBE principles and bylaws are: representation of those global and common activities for any VBE lifecycle stage, administration processes (accountability), management roles nomination and renewal processes, contract enforcement policy, and purchasing and management of outsourced services.

Rules: divided in two groups related to: stakeholders' behaviour and VBE functions.

VBE Behavioural Rules refers to the rules for good acting and conducting, including the ethical behaviour (ethical code) and culture. The ethical code will support trust building process in order to guarantee the social and operational sustainability of VBE. VBE culture comprises all organisation's beliefs, knowledge, attitudes, customs and socio-organizational aspects. The primary requirements for a proper collaboration culture in a VBE can be associated to: commitment, leadership, trust, self-learning, long-term and global vision, effective communication, innovation, sharing attitude, awareness for win-win development of business/collaborative opportunities, no discrimination, preparedness for collaboration, and recognition of merits for self-organizing leadership. It is important to mention that the VBE culture may result in part from managers' beliefs, but it also can result from VBE members' beliefs (opinions/approaches).

VBE functional rules support both operational and administrative processes along all VBE lifecycle stages (creation, operation, evolution, metamorphosis and dissolution). A general guide to establish the most important operational rules for VBE lifecycle supporting right activities execution is: general management and support process, business process management, membership management and knowledge management. Most of these tasks for defining VBE governance model are given to VBE manager and/or VBE advisor (for instance a specialized professional in laws, or an experienced support institution as consulter in network managing). The VBE manager will be in charge of administrating all tasks for the right daily performance of the VBE (assignment/reassignment of responsibilities, conflict resolution, making common VBE policies, etc), mean while the VBE advisor can serve as specialist consultant in some of these tasks [8]. Finally, the definition of specific governance rules will depend on many criteria as type of VBE, amount of members, past performance records, among others.

4. CONCLUSIONS AND FURTHER RESEARCH

This paper provides the guidelines to define a VBE business model considering a multi-value system characterization and a multi-stakeholder perspective, proposing at the same time the main elements to be concerned in approaching a VBE governance model. Furthermore the VBE governance model is based on the principles of collaborative business and resulting of a first approach through definition of rules and bylaws to achieve a good VBE governing. All this guidelines can be easily instantiated in different VBEs according to the industrial sector of its members, and the market characteristics and constraints.

The visualization of the VBE business model with a value network representation using the e3value tool gives a practical idea of all the actors involved in the VBE business and the value transfer among them (including money transfer).

The VBE business model guidelines proposed represent a contribution towards the definition of business models and eventually business processes for Collaborative Networked Organizations (CNOs).

Guidelines above described related to the VBE governance, represent a general approach to conduct the process of defining the principles, rules and bylaws in order to govern internal and external structure and functioning issues of a VBE, depending on the specific sector where it will perform its activities.

6. ACKNOWLEDGEMENT

The research presented in this document is a contribution for the ECOLEAD Project, funded by the European Community, FP6 IP 506958. The authors wish to acknowledge the support of the Innovation Center in Design and Technology from ITESM - Campus Monterrey.

7. REFERENCES

1. Camarinha-Matos, L., Afsarmanesh, H. and Ollus M. (2005). "ECOLEAD: A Holistic Approach to Creation and Management of Dynamic Virtual Organisations". Collaborative Networks and Their Breeding Environments. IFIP Working Conference on Virtual Enterprises. Springer. pp 3-16.
2. ECOLEAD D21.4b (2006). "Creating and Supporting Trust Culture in Virtual Breeding Environments". Editors: Afsarmanesh, H.; Msanjila, S.; Hodík, J. and Rehák, M. ECOLEAD Project: Internal Document Deliverable.
3. Fensel, D. (2001). "Ontologies: Silver Bullet for Knowledge Management and Electronic Commerce". Heidelberg, Springer-Verlag, 2001.
4. J. Gordijn and J.M. Akkermans, "e3-Value: A Conceptual Value Modeling Approach for e-Business Development", PDF document, Proceedings of K-CAP 2001, First International Conference on Knowledge Capture, Workshop Knowledge in e-Business, pg 29-36.
5. Jimenez, Guillermo, Galeano Nathalie; Nájera, Teresa; Aguirre, José Manuel; Rodríguez Ciprian, and Molina, Arturo (2005). "Methodology for Business Model definition of Collaborative Networked Organizations". Collaborative Networks and Their Breeding Environments. IFIP TC5 WG Sixth IFIP Working Conference on Virtual Enterprises, 26-28 September, 2005, Valencia Spain. Springer.
6. Osterwalder, A. (2004). "The Business Model Ontology a proposition in a design science approach (PhD-thesis)". Lausanne University, Switzerland. http://www.hec.unil.ch/aosterwa/PhD/ pp. 42-102.
7. Osterwalder A.; Ben, Lagha S. and Pigneur, Y. (2002). "An Ontology for Developing e-Business Models". DSIage. http://www.hec.unil.ch/yp/Pub/02-DsiAge.pdf
8. Plüss, Adrian and Huber, Charles (2005). "VirtuelleFabrik.ch – A Source Network for VBE in Mechatronics". Virtual Organizations Systems and Practices. Edited by Luis M. Camarinha-Matos, Hamideh Afsarmanesh and Martin Ollus. Ed. Springer. pp. 255-264.
9. Wallin J. (2000). "Operationalizing Competencies". 5th Annual International Conference on Competence-Based Management, Helsinki, June 10-14.

12

DISTINCT APPROACHES TO VALUE SYSTEM IN COLLABORATIVE NETWORKS ENVIRONMENTS

Patrícia Macedo, Claudio Sapateiro, Joaquim Filipe
Escola Superior de Tecnologia de Setúbal
Instituto Politécnico de Setúbal,PORTUGAL
[1]pmacedo@est.ips.pt,[2] csapateiro@est.ips.pt,[3]jfilipe@est.ips.pt

For several years, Value Systems have been studied by two distinct scientific disciplines: economy and psycho-sociology. Each discipline developed a different concept of Value System, based on distinct assumptions about value. On one hand, economists assume that value means how much (usually money) a product or service is worth to someone, relative to other things; on the other hand socio-psychologists define value as shared beliefs on moral/ethical principles of the organizational unit.

This paper presents a contribution in the study of Value Systems in the context of collaborative network organizations (CNO). The work based on M. Porter's approach applied to CNO is analyzed and related modeling techniques to represent an economic Value System are presented. A similar analysis is presented regarding the axiological perspective from socio-psychology, including the description of possible modeling techniques, in a CNO context. The aim of this paper is to compare these two approaches to Value Systems in the CNO context and to conclude about their relevance in the setup and management of this kind of organization.

1. INTRODUCTION

In the last years, studies conducted in collaborative networks area have shown that some requirements are needed to create collaborative coalition: share goals between members, have some level of mutual trust, had create some common infrastructures and had agreed totally or partially in some practices and values (Afsarmanesh, 2005). In order to be able to create a dynamic collaborative network, mechanisms to make both the selection of partners and the set-up of the network more agile must be developed. The definition and representation of the Value System of each member of the network can be an important tool to network management through its life-cycle.

For several years, Value Systems have been studied by two distinct scientific disciplines: economy and psycho-sociology. Each discipline developed a different concept of Value System, based on distinct assumptions about value. On one hand, economists assume that value means how much (usually money) a product or service is worth to someone, relative to other things; on the other hand socio-

Please use the following format when citing this chapter:

Macedo, P., Sapateiro, C., Filipe, J., 2006, in IFIP International Federation for Information Processing, Volume 224, Network-Centric Collaboration and Supporting Fireworks, eds. Camarinha-Matos, L., Afsarmanesh, H., Ollus, M., (Boston: Springer), pp. 111–120.

psychologists define value as shared beliefs on moral/ethical principles of the organizational unit.

Social sciences consider Value Systems as the ordering and prioritization of the ethical and ideological values that an individual or society holds. Values can be classified in communal and individual. Communal Value Systems are applied to a community or society, and may be supported by a legal set of laws and norms.

Economists defend that a Value System describes the activity links between the firm and its suppliers, other businesses within the firm's corporate family, distribution channels and the firm's end-user customers (Porter, 1985). Nowadays the Porter's system-value concept is generally used by managers and economists in enterprise strategic and operational management. Several informatics applications have been developed to address this issue, where supply chain managements systems (SCM) are well known.

Axiology is a general theory/science of human values, their origins, interrelations and dynamics The philosopher Robert Hartman (Hartman, 1973) is the father of formal axiology, which is a branch of axiology that attempts to use mathematical formalism to define values and Value Systems. There are diverse application studies of Psycho-socio Value System in several scientific areas, as: Education (Cooley, 1977), Organizational Management (Krishnan, 2005) and Information System Design (Shneiderman, 1998) (Goguen, 2004)

Several authors have referenced the Value System topic in their collaborative network studies. Some authors use Value System in its economic perspective (Katzy, 1998) (Liu, 2005) (Tan, 2004) (M.Jamieson, 1986) (Camarinha-Matos, 2005) (Gordijn, 2000) others in a more sociological and ethical approach (Filipe, 2003) (Afsarmanesh, 2005) (Rezgui, 2004).

This paper presents a contribution to the study of Value Systems in the context of collaborative network organizations (CNO). The aim of this paper is to compare the two approaches to Value Systems in the CNO context and to conclude about their relevance in the setup and management of this kind of organizations. The next section presents the economic approach to Value System where the work based on M. Porter's is analyzed and related modeling techniques to represent this Value System are presented. A similar analysis is presented on section three regarding the axiological perspective from socio-psychology, including the description of possible modeling techniques. In section four the application of these concepts of Value System in a CNO context is discussed. Conclusions and future work are present on section five.

2. ECONOMIC APPROACH TO VALUE SYSTEM

2.1 Overview of Porter approach for Value System

To understand Porter's Value System concept, two other related concepts are required: *Value Chain* and *Value Activity*.

- The **value chain** categorizes the generic value-adding activities of an organization. The value chain shows total value and consists of value activities and margin. Company activities can be represented in a value chain that should draw at the business-unit level (Porter, 1985)

- The **value activity** is an activity performed by the organization which is technologically and strategically distinct from any other. Activities are classified in primary activities and support activities. Primary Activities includes: Inbound Logistics; Operations; Outbound Logistics; Sales and Marketing; and Customer Service. Support Activities include: Firm Infrastructure; Human Resource Development; Technology Development; and Procurement. (Porter, 1985)

In Porter perspective a Value System can be used as a tool to analyze how a company positions itself relatively to other companies. A Value System shows the role of a company in the overall activity of providing a product to a customer. The Value System makes explicit who are the suppliers and what are the channels of the given company. It allows understanding if all the companies involved in the sale process are truly collaborating or if they have conflicts of interests. It also allows comparing a company with its competitors. (See Figure 1 for the illustration of the relationship between value chain and Value System).

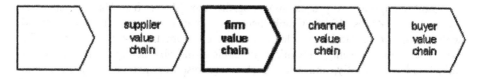

Figure 1 - Value System (Porter, 1985)

2.2   Extended Porter Value System Concept

The concept of value added activity can be applied not just to an economic value. The mission of some Organizations is not to win economic value, but other kinds of rewards, as: reputation, power and influence; belonging and membership; quality improvement, knowledge.

When the goal of an organization is not to increase economic value, it is necessary to define a way to measure value, in order to evaluate the value added. To each kind of value a unit of measure needs to be associated.

Gordijn ,Yao-Huan Tan and Kartseva in his work (Gordijn, 2000) (Tan, 2004) (Kartseva, 2004) about Value Systems has introduced the concepts, of *value object*, and *value activity*. A value activity is performed by an actor to produce objects of value by adding value to other objects of value. They define an actor as an independent entity that adds value to the system doing value activities. An actor can be an economic or and legal entity that engage in business transactions. Actors and value activities exchange value objects. A value object is a service, thing, or consumer experience that is of value to one or more actors. A value object has one or more valuation properties. Such a property has a name and a unit that indicates the scale in which the object is evaluated.

2.3   Modeling Value Systems (economic approach)

Modeling a Value System as describe above implies to be able to describe the sequence of activities that support the Value System, the value object and the actor.

To this purpose we analyze some known techniques commonly applied to process modeling. In a Value System model, resources and activities that not add value are not represented; just value activities and value object are shown. With respect to modeling processes or activities concerning the Value System we can use/adapt several of the existing proposes is processes modeling. One of the most popular is UML. UML diagrams had the advantage of visual/graphics orientation which is easily to adopt/understand and promotes the communication between interested parties without the need of in depth technical skills. However the consistency of the model across all its diagrams and the correctness achieved when transposing from modeling to design is still worth some attention because UML provides only a semi formal approach without sound semantics.

Another approach in process modeling that could be used in Value Systems is graph theory (Krebs, 1998). Graph theory is a branch of mathematics concerned with how networks can be encoded and how their properties can be measured. The main goal is to represent a network in symbolic terms, abstracting reality as a set of linked nodes. Typically, nodes represent objects/resources/people/technologies and the links the connections needed to achieve some goal. In the Value Systems context this network can represent activities flows and ones can have different nets, concerning different perspectives of the system. We can also associate costs to the links between nodes allowing the evaluation of a cost function to some flow. An extension of graph theory respecting to social relationships is the Social Actors Network theory (SAN). SAN are a way to highlight the structural relationships among social actors providing a conceptualization of their interactions in a systematic way. SAN had available metrics that allow interpretation of the kind/depth of connections presents in the net. (Soares, 2005)

Yet other approach that could contribute to model Value Systems are those based in Petri Nets (Aalst, 2001). The Petri nets based approaches have been used with success in modeling dynamic systems of discrete events characterized by parallelism and synchronization needs. If ones consider the Value Systems described in the previous section ones can establish the parallelism with the Petri nets mechanism: an activity takes place in the presence of some pre-conditions and/or inputs and will produce some post-condition and/or outputs. The usual main motivations to the use of this approaches is due to the fact they are based in a strong mathematics foundation and so they had available several analysis tools. These tools permit the inspection of several behavioral and structural net properties. Some of these tools/properties may be used to verification of the net (context independent ones) and others are used to net validation (context dependent ones). Also they had a visual/graphical orientation which has the advantages already pointed to UML but unlike UML in the Petri nets case we create precise formal models. There are some extensions like colored Petri nets which may assign several attributes to each node in the net, or Petri nets with costs parameters in order to evaluate some cost function.

3. SOCIO-PSYCHOLOGY APPROACH TO VALUE SYSTEMS

3.1 Axiological systems

Socio-Psychology in general considers a Value System as a set of principles and values common to a group of people. According to social theory, principles, laws and values are types of norms. Norms can be classified as perceptual ,evaluative, cognitive, behavioral (Stamper, 1996). The different types of norms reflect the different aspects that a social system can share, as perception, interpretation, cognition and behavior.

- Perceptual norms are associated to the attitude of acknowledge the existence of something - Ontological attitude.
- Evaluative norms are associated to the attitude of being disposed in favor or against something in value terms - Axiological attitude.
- Cognitive norms are associated to the attitude of adopting a degree of believe or disbelieve - Epistemic attitude
- Behavioral norms are associated to the attitude of being disposed to act in some way – Deontic attitude.

The philosopher Robert Hartman developed formal Axiology, that is a branch of axiology (axiology is a general theory/science of human values, their origins, interrelations and dynamics) that attempt to use mathematical formalism to define values and Value Systems. Hartman (Hartman, 1973) first defined the concept of value in terms of a logic-based axiom. This axiom is that value can be objectively determined according to a one-to-one correspondence between the properties of a given object and the meaning specifications contained in its concept. An object has value to the degree it fulfils its concept. (Mefford, 1997) Hartman introduced also the concept of Dimension of Value and developed the basic axioms through this concept. He defines three dimensions for value: Systematic Value, Extrinsic Value and Intrinsic Value.

- **Systematic Dimension** - The dimension of formal concepts. Ideas of how things should be. This dimension is the one of definitions or ideals, goals, structured thinking, policies, procedures, rules and laws.
- **Extrinsic Value** - The dimension of abstracting properties, comparing things to each other. This is the dimension of comparisons, relative and practical thinking
- **Intrinsic Value** - The dimension of uniqueness and singularity. This is the dimension of uniqueness, of person or things as they exist in themselves. There is no comparing.

Hartman defends that the foundation concepts of axiology provides the framework for understanding an object's value and valuations of it, in precise terms of the three dimensions and their relation to each other.

Goguen et Linde have developed since 1978 several studies about value and Value System in organizations (Goguen, 1994, Goguen, 1997, Goguen, 2004).They have developed a method for using discourse analysis to determine a Value System for an organization from a collection of stories told by members of the organization among themselves on informal occasions. The evaluative material collected from the stories is classified and represented using a formal structure called a Value System tree. A Value System tree (Goguen, 1994) serves as a formal summary of the interpretation that the analysts had made from the data that has been collected.

Another contribution to the study of values systems came from Distributed Artificial Intelligence discipline. This discipline has developed some theories about Value Systems using agents. (Filipe, 2003) proposed an approach based on organizational agents where is assumed an agent is responsible for its values. The agent's preferences with respect to norms are defined in its Value System. In this approach an agent can represent a member of an organization or an organization itself.

3.2 Modeling Value Systems (socio-psychological approach)

Value System trees, proposed by Goguen (1994), can be modeled and represented using the UML standard, through a class diagram. Another possible approach to model Value System tree it's Prioritized Modal Default Logic (Brewka, 1994), that allows defining the order of values. Modal logic is an extension of ordinary logic and is concerned with logical facts that involve qualifications of propositions.

Formal methods have the advantage of making the conversion to computer programs easy, when compared to languages with graphical notation, such as UML. For the purpose of communication and analysis these kind of languages are more suitable.

Hartman in its works on Formal Axiology have proposed a formal representation for value and for Value Systems based on algebraic mathematic. Some semiotic studies also introduce a formal way to represent the Value Systems based on algebraic theory (Goguen, 1999)

The approach based on agents suggested by (Filipe, 2000), where attempt to model the Value System of an agent (its axiological component) propose the use of default modal logic (Reiter, 1980).

The approaches to modeling socio-psychological Value Systems describe above apply essentially formal methods developed in Computer Science. Formal modeling approaches, as formal axiology, modal default logic and algebraic semiotics are used in order to specify the order and prioritization of the ethical and ideological values

4. POTENTIAL APPLICATION IN CNO CONTEXT

In the last two sections distinct approaches to Value System were presented. In this section it is discussed the applicability of each in the CNO context.

The original purpose of a value chain was to identify the fundamental value-creating processes involved in producing a product or service within a firm, the concept has since been used to describe an entire network (Bouwman, 2003).

Evans (Evans, 2004) classifies collaboration in networks as:

- *Goal-driven* – where the objective is to deliver something (product or service) within stated time, cost and quality goals.

- **Capability-driven** – where the objective are improve personal capability, or knowledge sharing. (examples: Linux community and IEEE)

It's relevant to understand which activities add value to the network and which member contributes with it. The values considered in a goal-driven network type are different from capability-driven networks. (Afsarmanesh, 2005)In order to evaluate the values added by one activity to the network, it have to be defined how the specifics values could be measure. Tom Gilb developed methods and techniques to measure Software quality attributes (Gilb, 1989). His work contributes to the development of measurement technique of social issues. Directly related to Virtual Organizations, (Camarinha-Matos, 2005) exemplify a way to combine values with different scales in order to evaluate the benefit of a collaboration.

Table 1 – potential application of Value System for management through life-cycle

Life-Cycle Phase	Economic Approach of Value System	Socio-Psychologist Approach of Value System
CNO Creation	-Simulate several scenario of Value System in order to decide for the best scenario. -Select partner that can contribute to the Value System.	-Partner selection - helps to select partner with Value Systems that not collide, helps to select partner that best fit in the network.
CNO Configuration	-Define the exact contribution of each partner to the Value System	-Definition of norms to operate the CNO. Value System will provide tools to define norms and to detect possible conflicts between member norms and CNO norms.
CNO Operation	-The Value System model it's the base tool for planning activity. -Value System model can be used to monitories performance.	-Solving conflicts between CNO members. Detecting easily which set of norm it's causing the conflict. -Improve relationship between members. Permit to identify the set of priorities values of each member and act according it.
CNO Dissolution/ Reconfigure.	-To plan reconfiguration, allow the study several Value Systems scenarios	-Select new partners adjust some norms of operation.

The definition and representation of the Value System (economic approach) in a collaborative network have a set of distinct applications in network life-cycle management. It can contribute to the selection of partners that can increase the value of the network. It permits the calculation of the value contribution of each partner.

Value System model can also be used to monitories performance and to plan operational activities.

Values are the essence of what holds communities together (Goguen, 2004), so to choose partners its very important to analyze their core competencies and their coherence with the network strategy .Another important criterion is the amount of effort needed to coordinate and integrate them (Wiendalh, 2002). The definition of Value Systems (socio-psychological approach) will help to understand if Value System of a partner will fit the Value System of the CNO. In order to avoid conflicts, it is important to identify candidate's conflicts points and determine the possible collision between member's internal norms. Another potential of application for Value System is on the member's relationship improvement, by the identification of the set of priorities values in order to act according it.

The potential application of each concept for Value Systems in CNO was analyzed. This analysis is resumed on table 1, where the distinct contributions of each approach for Value System are shown.

5. CONCLUSIONS

Both perspectives of Value Systems (economic and socio-psychological) are relevant to performance management in collaborative networks, as was shown in section above. The analysis presented on table 1 allows us to conclude that these two perspectives of Value Systems are complementary. In essence the Economic perspective provides a transaction mechanism between partners, and the psychosocial perspective provides a regulation mechanism to ensure social cohesion, to avoid and solve conflicts and to build performance indicators.

The definition, representation and application of Value Systems to Collaborative Networks it is a challenging area of research. The main questions that were identified to drive research in this field are:
- How to create a conceptual model that integrates these two approaches of Value System?
  - o   Are there different types of values? Which types?
  - o   A value can be represented as an object? In this case which are the attributes that characterize an object value?
  - o   A system is a set of elements and the relation between them. How to define the functions of relation between elements? Can we apply system theory and classify the relation structural, hierarchical (composition and specialization) and behavioral relations? How to define value priorities inside the system?
- What is the relation between Value System and system of incentives? Can we derive system incentives to CNO from value systems of each CNO member?
- How can we derive CNO performance indicators definition from CNO Value System?
- How can Value Systems contribute to an efficient trust management?

6. REFERENCES

1. W. M. P. v. d. Aalst, " Making Work Flow: On the Application of Petri nets to Business Process Management," 2001.
2. H. Afsarmanesh, "A framework for Management of Virtual Organization Breeding environments," in *PRO-VE*. Valencia, Spain, 2005.
3. H. Bouwman, "State Of the Art on Business Models," 2003.
4. G. Brewka, "Reasoning about Priorities in Default Logic Proceedings of the " presented at AAAI National Conference on Artificial Intelligence, 1994.
5. L. Camarinha-Matos and A. Abreu, "Performance indicatores based on collaboration beneficts," in *PRO-VE 2005 - Collaborative Networks and Value Creation,* Valencia, Spain, 2005.
6. C. R. Cooley, "Cultural Effects in Indian Education:AN APPLICATION OF SOCIAL LEARNING THEORY " *Journal of American Indian Education*, vol. 17, 1977.
7. Evans, "Performance Measurment and added value of networks," in *Collaborative Networked Organizations, Collaborative Networked Organizations* L. Camarinha-Matos, Ed. London: Kluwe Academics Publishers, 2004, pp. (147-152).
8. J. Filipe, "The organisational semeiotics normativa paradigma " in *Collaborative Networked Organizations*, vol. 1, *Collaborative networked organizations. A reasearch agenda for emerging business models* London: Springer, 2003, pp. 261-272.
9. J. Filipe and K.Liu, " The EDA Model: An Organizational Semiotics Perspective To Norm-Based Agent Design," presented at Agents'2000 Workshop on Norms and Institutions in Multi-Agent Systems, Barcelona, Spain, 2000.
10. T. Gilb, *Principies of Software Engineering Management*: Addisson-Wesley, 1989.
11. J. Goguen, "Requirements Engineering as the Reconciliation of Technical and Social Issues," in *Requirements engineering: social and technical issues*, 1994, pp. 162-199.
12. J. Goguen, "Towards a Social, Ethical Theory of Information," in *In Social Science Research, Technical Systems and Cooperative Work: Beyond the Great Divide*, Georey Bowker, Les Gasser, LeighStar, and W. Turner, Eds.: Erlbaum, 1997, pp. 27-56.
13. J. Goguen, "An Introduction to Algebraic Semiotics with Application to User Interface Design," in *Lecture Notes in Artificial Intelligence, Computation for Metaphor, Analogy and Agents*, I. C. Nehaniv, Ed.: Springer Verlag, Berlin (DE), 1999, pp. 242--291.
14. J. Goguen, "Semiotics, compassion and value-centered design," 2004.
15. Gordijn, "Business Modelling is not Process Modelling," in *ECOMO 200*. Salt Lake City, USA: LNCS 1921, 2000.
16. J. Gordijn, J.M. Akkermans, and J. C. v. Vliet, "Value based requirements creation for electronic commerce applications.," presented at In Proceedings of the 33rd Hawaii International Conference On System Sciences, 2000.
17. R. Hartman, "The Measurment of Value," 1973.
18. V. Kartseva, J. Gordijn, H. Akkermans, and "A Design Perspective on Networked Business Models: A Study of Distributed Generation in the Power Industry Sector," presented at 12th European Conference on Information Systems, 2004.
19. B. Katzy, "Value System Redesign," *ACM SIGGROUP Bulletin archive,*, vol. 19, pp. 48-50, 1998.
20. V. Krebs, "Mapping and Measuring Knowledge Creation, Re-Use and Flow," 1998.
21. V. R. Krishnan, "Leader-Member Exchange, Transformational Leadership, and Value System," *EJBO Electronic Journal of Business Ethics and Organization Studies*, vol. 10, 2005.
22. P.-Y. Liu, "A study based on the Value System for the interaction of the multi-tiered supply chain under the trend of e-business," presented at The 7th international conference on Electronic Commerce, 2005.
23. M.Jamieson, T. A., and a. T. A. . "Refocusing collaboration technologies in the construction Value System," 1986.
24. D. Mefford and V. Meffortd, "Values Usage Exercise (VUE) A Tool For Raising Values Awareness ConcerningThe Professional - Personal Values Interface " in *Conference on Professional Ethics*. WASHINGTON, 1997.
25. M. Porter, *Competitive Advantage*. : New York: The Free Press, 1985.
26. R. Reiter, "A logic for default reasoning.," *Artif. Int.*, vol. 13, pp. 81-132, 1980.
27. Y. Rezgui, I. Wilson, W. Olphert, and L. Damodaran, "Socio-Organizational issues," presented at PRO-VE, 2004.
28. B. Shneiderman, *Designing the User Interface: Strategies for Effective User Interface Interaction*, 3rd ed: Addison Wesley Longman, 1998.

29. L. Soares and S. Pereira, "Tecnologias de colaboração em organizações de I&D: Uma abordagem por redes sociais.," in *Conferencia da Associação Portuguesa de Sistemas de Informação.* Bragança, Portugal, 2005.
30. R. Stamper, "Signs, Information, Norms and Systems.," in *Signs of Work, Semiosis and Information Processing in Organizations,* : In Holmqvist et al. (Eds.)Walter de Gruyter Berlin, New York., 1996.
31. Y.-H. Tan, W. Thoen, and J. Gordijn, "Modeling Controls for Dynamic Value Exchange in Virtual Organizations," 2004.
32. Wiendalh, "Production Networks," presented at Anual Conference of CIRP, 2002.

13

A NEW MODEL FOR ACHIEVING VALUE ADDED GOALS IN A COLLABORATIVE INDUSTRIAL SCENARIO

Giuseppe Confessore[1], Giacomo Liotta[1,2], Silvia Rismondo[1]

[1] Istituto di Tecnologie Industriali e Automazione
Consiglio Nazionale delle Ricerche
Area della Ricerca Roma Tor Vergata, Via Fosso del Cavaliere, 100
00133 Roma – ITALY
g.confessore@itia.cnr.it, g.liotta@itia.cnr.it, s.rismondo@itia.cnr.it

[2] Dipartimento di Ingegneria dell'Impresa
Università di Roma "Tor Vergata"
Via del Politecnico 1 – 00133 Roma – ITALY.

Nowadays, at industrial research level, seems to be recognised that the collaboration among firms is becoming a relevant and effective way of operating. For the enterprises rather than compete on costs it could be necessary increase the product/service value added; this goal could be effectively achieved by collaborating with other firms in the value chain.

In this preliminary work, we provide a model formulation for supporting the potential decision of getting new business opportunities through the exploitation of a competence-based collaborative advantage.

We propose a model formulation for maximising the potential value added generated by the convergence of complementary competences in the inter-firm collaboration. For this purpose we assume as given a codified set of competences and for each one of them a codified benchmark value.

1. INTRODUCTION

Nowadays, at industrial research level, seems to be recognised that the collaboration among firms is becoming a relevant and effective way of operating (e.g., see for instance Camarinha-Matos (1999) and Kaihara and Fujii (2002)). In particular, the strong need of new forms of collaboration is necessary consequence of the increasing competition in the industrial scenario mainly due to the emergent markets, such as the Asiatic one, and the new plants' locations, that force the enterprises worldwide to adopt, for instance, new procurement, production or distribution strategies. In this scenario, for the enterprises rather than compete on costs it could be necessary increase the product/service value added; this goal could be effectively achieved by collaborating with other firms in the value chain. In fact, the latest research literature concerning the inter-organizational network field, demonstrates the relevance of knowledge-based (Conner and Prahalad, 1996) and

Please use the following format when citing this chapter:

Confessore, G., Liotta, G., Rismondo, S., 2006, in IFIP International Federation for Information Processing, Volume 224, Network-Centric Collaboration and Supporting Fireworks, eds. Camarinha-Matos, L., Afsarmanesh, H., Ollus, M., (Boston: Springer), pp. 121–128.

dynamic capability (Teece, Pisano and Shuen, 1997) theories, both based on the enterprises competence concept.

Despite the increasing interest on this research field, still a lack can be noticed in terms of models describing the collaboration and thus considering the relevance of competence as a way to achieve the value added goal. On the other hand, the definition of a model could be useful for understanding which could be, in practice, the potential business opportunities generated by the collaboration.

In fact, this preliminary work aims at defining a model formulation for understanding whether a network of collaborative enterprises has the competences for realizing and sustaining a new emerging business process.

The paper is organized as follows. Section 2 refers to related works supporting the adopted approach. Section 3 describes a business process in terms of the activities to be done; secondly, it considers a set of competences and describes the map linking the competences, the activities, and the actors of the collaboration. Finally, Section 4 provides a mathematical formulation and a short example.

2. RELATED WORKS

The presented model introduces the competence concept, that Chung, Yam, and Chan (2004) define as one of the four main drivers for collaboration (e.g., the collaborative advantage, the regional advanced, the innovation capacity -knowledge resource- and the competences). Moreover, it assumes a business process consisting of a set of (interdependent) activities, and through the paper it has been considered as a competence the company's capability in executing, for instance, the process planning, the product/service design and implementation, the distribution, or the company's productive and elaborative capacity, then it considers both quantitative and qualitative aspects.

In this setting, the presented paper proposes an approach for assigning the activities that cover an entire inter-organisational business process to the collaborative enterprises and, concurrently, for maximising the potential value added generated by the convergence of complementary competences in the inter-firm collaboration.

For this purpose, through the paper is assumed as given a codified set of competences and for each one of them a codified benchmark value. Thus, the actors could establish in a consistent way their ability w.r.t. a codified competence. Given these (assumed) codes, a map which links the activities and the competences required to perform them is exploited. In fact, it can be assumed that, for achieving the product/service value added goals, it is necessary to concentrate on the company's capabilities while providing the most promising combination of available competences. A similar approach for codifying the level of expertise into a generic competence frame is presented in Hammami, Burlat, and Champagne (2003). When the authors define a technological map underlying a product, they introduce (*i*) a product attainment graph (i.e. logical sequence of production and administrative activities), and (*ii*) an activities/competencies map. They then present a competencies map for each enterprise of the network for the standardization of the skills' description. Therefore, this paper also defines a map linking the activities and the competences required.

Concerning the data and knowledge sharing within the network, privacy and autonomy needs of participants can impact on the full effectiveness of the collaboration. These relevant factors are in practice possible barriers to the inter-organisational cooperation when the degree of process complexity and the number of transactions increase. Models and technology solutions have been designed for meeting cooperative process management, coordination, integration, privacy needs in inter-organisational business processes, as explained in Perrin and Godart (2004) where the authors provide a model and an architecture for supporting the realization of a collaborative scenario for multi-enterprise business processes.

Interesting case studies concerning corporate collaborative networks are presented in Danilovic and Winroth (2005). Noticeable findings of the reported projects' experiences, among others, concern the increasing level of competences of participating partners, important prerequisites (e.g. openness, trust, and enabling IT resources), investments in time and resource, form of collaboration (influenced by the collaboration objectives), legal aspects. The authors point out the relevance of identifying and analysing the pre-requisites for inter-organisational integration in network settings; they also provide a tentative framework for this purpose.

Also in Carbonara, Giannoccaro, and Potrandolfo (2002), the authors underline the relevant role of the complementary competences (technical and organisational) for very interesting forms of collaboration that take place in the Industrial Districts (i.e. SMEs located and integrated in a geographical area and specialised in complementary production processes or services) when a strategy of external growth is addressed.

3. PROBLEM AND STATEMENT DEFINITION

Given a set of enterprises joining the network, the goal is to allocate among the actors the necessary activities for fulfilling a new emerging business process while maximising the product/service value added. We assume that the value added increases by considering the concept of actors competence (or capability) in carrying out the activities of a business process.

In this setting, (*i*) an industrial scenario involving a set E of z enterprises, $E = \{e_1, ..., e_z\}$ and (*ii*) a business process P consisting of a set A of k activities $A = \{a_1, ..., a_k\}$ have been considered; technological constraints are given forcing each activity to start its execution after the completion time of its predecessors. In the operations research literature, considering a centralized decision-maker, the problem of computing the starting time of the activities respecting the precedence constraints, and minimizing the completion time of all them, is a well known scheduling problem [6]. The computational complexity of this problem increases when a set R of h finite capacity resources is given (i.e., $R = \{r_1, ..., r_h\}$), and for each activity a_i a specific resource requirement v_{iw} is defined (i.e., for all a_i, $w \in R$, and $0 \le v_{iw} \le r_w$). Under this assumption the scheduling problem is characterized by both technological and resource constraints. Classical models and resolution approaches are based on the strong assumption that a centralized decision-making process is given and all the information about resource requirements and technological constraints are known.

Since this work considers an inter-organizational framework, that is a set of (independent) enterprises involved in the execution of a specific collaborative business process is given (that, clearly, could not be modelled as a centralized decision maker), more probably it is known which competence is required to perform the activities rather than the exact set of resources for executing them.

This is one of the main issue of this paper; in fact, in the collaborative perspective, since the information sharing is a crucial issue, in this work the enterprises have not to share their internal data or specialized knowledge (e.g., trust and privacy issues could arise). Companies have to declare what are able to perform and which is their corresponding capability. Actors' capabilities are codified and classified through common benchmark values (assumed as given and accepted within the network).

Nevertheless, the presented preliminary model, that is formalized in the following Section, could be useful for determining commitments and responsibilities among members of a collaborative network when a new business opportunity arise. For this purpose it relies on a competence-based analytical approach for identifying the complementary competences that allow to consider an high value added objective to be pursued through the collaboration.

4. THE MODEL DEFINITION

This work addresses the problem of assigning the activities of a business process to collaborative enterprises while maximising the competence value, thus, in the current perspective, maximising the product/service value added. It assumes that the actors always have the availability to carry out the assigned activities, and it assigns each activity to at most one of the enterprises (e.g., the activities cannot be done simultaneously by two or more actors).

The following sets and parameters can be introduced:

- The set C of w competences $C = \{c_1, ..., c_w\}$ globally accepted between the collaborative enterprises.
- The k sub-sets $C_1, ..., C_k$ representing the set of competences required for the execution of each activity in A (i.e., at each $a_i \in A$ is associated a sub-set $C_i \subseteq C$).
- The z sub-sets $\tilde{C}_j \subseteq C$ representing the set of competences declared by each enterprise e_j according to the standard codes.
- The parameters ε_{jh} providing the degree of capability of enterprise e_j respect to a specific competence c_h. ε_{jh} is a positive value in $[0, 1]$, where 0 means e_j has not the competence h, and $\varepsilon_{jh} = 1$ means e_j has the competence h; the value ε_{jh} is defined by using a common scale of values (accepted by the collaborative actors).

4.1 Model hypothesis and assumptions

The following hypothesis can be formulated:

- Each sub-set C_i can be modelled as a binary vector $u(a_i)$ composed of w elements, where the h-th element (i.e., $u_h(a_i)$) is equal to 0 if activity a_i does not require the competence c_h for being executed, and is equal to 1 otherwise.

- Each sub-set $\widetilde{C}_j$ can be modelled as a vector $v(e_j)$ composed of w elements, where the h-th element (i.e., $v_h(e_j)$) is equal to 0 if the enterprise e_j has not the competence c_h, and is equal to a positive value ε_{jh} otherwise. In particular, ε_{jh} represents the capability of e_j w.r.t. a specific competence framework as mentioned in Section 2.

It can be emphasized that the two vectors are consistent since $u(a_i)$ represents exactly the competences required for executing a_i while assuming the capability respect each competence $c_h \in C$ equal to 1 or 0, that is considering the same scale of values of ε_{jh} (where c_h equal to 1 is exactly the maximum (desired) value).

Furthermore, the definition of the two vectors $u(a_i)$, and $v(e_j)$ is required since this work mainly focuses on two relevant aspects: (1) which enterprise has the competences for carrying out one activity; (2) which level of performance each enterprise could deploy in executing a specific activity. Therefore, it is indispensable to measure how much an enterprise fits the competences required for executing, and then performing as best, a specific activity, thus it is required to measure which is the 'distance' between the vectors. In order to calculate this distance value, it is necessary to introduce the vector $g(a_i, e_j)$ of w elements where the h-th element is computed as follows: $g_h(a_i, e_j) = \min\{u_h(a_i), v_h(e_j)\}$. Vector $g(a_i, e_j)$ extracts from vector $v(e_j)$ exactly those elements that match the corresponding elements of $u(a_i)$ being equal to 1. In other words, it catches the competences of e_j respect to those ones required by a given activity a_i.

Given the activity a_i, it is possible to compute for each $e_j \in E$ the vectors $g(a_i, e_j)$, and calculate the Euclidean distance between $g(a_i, e_j)$, and $u(a_i)$. Below is the standard Euclidean distance formula between vectors $g(a_i, e_j)$ and $u(a_i)$.

$$euc(g(a_i,e_j),u(a_i)) = \left(\sum_{h=1}^{k} (g_h(a_i,e_j) - u_h(a_i))^2 \right)^{\frac{1}{2}}$$

Due to the distance function, the following parameters are introduced:

$$\omega_{ij} = euc(g(a_i, e_j), u(a_i))$$

Each ω_{ij} represents the capability of e_j w.r.t. the execution of the activity a_i.

4.2 The optimization model

The model considers the binary variable x_{ij} equal to 1, if it assigns the activity a_i to the enterprise e_j and 0 otherwise, for all $e_j \in E$, $a_i \in A$, and the problem can be formalized as follows:

$$\min \sum_{i \in A} \sum_{j \in E} \omega_{ij} x_{ij}$$

$s.t.$

$$\sum_{j \in E} x_{ij} = 1 \qquad \forall i \in A \qquad (1)$$

$$x_{ij} \in \{0, 1\} \qquad \forall j \in E, \forall i \in A \qquad (2)$$

Then the model aims at assigning each activity to exactly one enterprise (constraints 1), while minimising the distance among vectors that is obtaining the solution maximising the value added (e.g., competences value).

This is an assignment problem that can be referable to a matching problem; in fact, some enterprises can perform more than one activity. Such multiple assignments can be modeled by simply replicating the enterprises vertices, of the classical bipartite graph, as many times as the number of activities they can handle.

Clearly, this model considers a centralized-decision maker, that is able to collect the enterprises' degree of competence w.r.t. each activity, and to find the best solution. In this setting, it can be remarked that the enterprises have not to share their proper data (that is one of the main motivation of this preliminary work), but they only provide, and then share, the aggregate values ε_{jh}.

4.3 A model example

In the next, a short example is given in order to describe some potentialities of the presented model. In fact, although big enterprises could easily demonstrate which is their core business and their competences in performing specific activities, this could not be so easy, in practice, for the SMEs. A SME could not have the same responsiveness to a specific market request/requirement, but two collaborating SMEs could have it. Due to this fact, this paper provides answers to several questions such as, for instance, how the SMEs can work together for achieving common goals, and how they could be competitive in doing that. For this purpose, a very simple example is given, even if future works will concern the application of the given model to real case-studies.

Suppose there is a set of $z = 2$ SMEs operating in the high-tech sector, and aiming at collaborating for commercial goals; the first one manufactures silicon base for hardware-oriented customers while cutting and preparing the silicon base for molding. It is focused on front-end processes as wafer fabrication and probe. The second one is specialized in data circuit molding thus it is focused on back-end processes as assembly and final test. Clearly, they are on the value chain but they have never collaborated since each one of them has its own specific customers.

Suppose they observe a new market request consisting in producing a new data circuit based on a new silicon base shape. Then, the new business process consists in procuring the row materials for the silicon base production and then in providing the data circuit molding. In particular, four main macro-activities can be defined for fulfilling the emerging business opportunity: (1) procurement; (2) production; (3) assembly and test; (4) delivery.

The specific SMEs core businesses do not allow to meet directly the market needs. They only could address the market being suppliers of big enterprises that work as a market leader. On the other hand, if they collaborate they could exploit both complementary and concurrent competences.

For the sake of simplicity, suppose the activities execution requires eight main competences: (1) bargaining power w.r.t. suppliers; (2) negotiation capability; (3) production planning; (4) production capacity; (5) assembly; (6) test tools; (7) delivery planning; (8) transportation capacity. In this example, the SMEs' plants are supposed to be close to each other (i.e., so doing no transport activities have to be considered).

Therefore, the business process P is composed of four activities a_1, a_2, a_3, a_4 (i.e., $k = 4$), and is given a global accepted code of w competences, $C = (c_1, c_2, c_3, c_4, c_5,$

c_6, c_7, c_8) (i.e., $w = 8$). Each enterprise expresses its degree of competence w.r.t. the scale of values, thus previous information, in synthesis, can be modelled as follows:

1. $u(a_1) = [1, 1, 0, 0, 0, 0, 0, 0]$, $u(a_2) = [0, 0, 1, 1, 0, 0, 0, 0]$, $u(a_3) = [0, 0, 0, 0, 1, 1, 0, 0]$, and $u(a_4) = [0, 0, 0, 0, 0, 0, 1, 1]$ represent the vectors of competences required for a_1, a_2, a_3, and a_4, respectively.

2. $v(e_1) = [0.3, 0.8, 0.1, 0.8, 0.3, 0.4, 0.6, 0.6]$, and $v(e_2) = [0.6, 0.1, 0.5, 0.7, 0.8, 0.9, 0.4, 0.9]$ represent the competence vectors of e_1, and e_2, respectively.

Given the vectors mapping the competences, for each e_j, and for each a_i, the vectors $g(a_i, e_j)$ can be computed.

$g(a_1, e_1) = [0.3, 0.8, 0, 0, 0, 0, 0, 0]$ $g(a_3, e_1) = [0, 0, 0, 0, 0.3, 0.4, 0, 0]$

$g(a_1, e_2) = [0.6, 0.1, 0, 0, 0, 0, 0, 0]$ $g(a_3, e_2) = [0, 0, 0, 0, 0.8, 0.9, 0, 0]$

$g(a_2, e_1) = [0, 0, 0.1, 0.8, 0, 0, 0, 0]$ $g(a_4, e_1) = [0, 0, 0, 0, 0, 0, 0.6, 0.6]$

$g(a_2, e_2) = [0, 0, 0.5, 0.7, 0, 0, 0, 0]$ $g(a_4, e_2) = [0, 0, 0, 0, 0, 0, 0.4, 0.9]$

Then, the Euclidean distance is calculated, as follows:

$euc\ (g(a_1, e_1), u(a_1)) = \omega_{11} = 0.73$ $euc\ (g(a_3, e_1), u(a_3)) = \omega_{31} = 0.92$

$euc\ (g(a_1, e_2), u(a_1)) = \omega_{12} = 0.98$ $euc\ (g(a_3, e_2), u(a_3)) = \omega_{32} = 0.22$

$euc\ (g(a_2, e_1), u(a_2)) = \omega_{21} = 0.92$ $euc\ (g(a_4, e_1), u(a_4)) = \omega_{41} = 0.57$

$euc\ (g(a_2, e_2), u(a_2)) = \omega_{22} = 0.58$ $euc\ (g(a_4, e_2), u(a_4)) = \omega_{42} = 0.61$

Therefore, the model is as follows:

$$\min 0.73x_{11} + 0.98\ x_{12} + 0.92\ x_{21} + 0.58\ x_{22} + 0.92\ x_{31} + 0.22\ x_{32} + 0.57\ x_{41} + 0.61\ x_{42}$$

s.t.

$x_{11} + x_{12} = 1$ $x_{31} + x_{32} = 1$

$x_{21} + x_{22} = 1$ $x_{41} + x_{42} = 1$

$x_{ij} \in \{0,1\}\ \ \forall\ i \in A,\ \forall\ j \in E$

The solution is: $x_{11} = 1, x_{12} = 0, x_{21} = 0, x_{22} = 1, x_{31} = 0, x_{32} = 1, x_{41} = 1, x_{42} = 0$ and corresponds in the assignment of the activity a_1 to e_1, a_2 to e_2, a_3 to e_2, and a_4 to e_1. The objective function value is 2.1.

Although this example can not be exhaustive, it shows how, by preliminary competence evaluation (the distance measuring the enterprises capability w.r.t. the activities), the model could suggest the activities allocation for assuring the best outcome in terms of competences maximization. Clearly, the model will be useful for the collaborative enterprises that aim at fulfilling emerging business processes where, probably, a predefined allocation does not exist. Furthermore, the model could be especially useful when increase either the activities detail, the competence detail, and, obviously, the number of enterprises potentially involved in the business process.

5. CONCLUSIONS

This paper assumes that a way for achieving value added goals in delivering products and services worldwide, the enterprises have to concentrate on their competences.

It proposes a competence-based analytical model for allocating tasks among the actors of a collaborative network in order to potentially fulfil the processes related to high value added products or services. The complementary competences exploitable by the network are maximised while taking into account assignment constraints. So doing the model establishes a direct connection between the competences required for executing the tasks referred to an entire business process and the value added that can be generated by the proper allocation of activities.

Through the preliminary model only possible commitments and responsibilities throughout a complete business process can be determined without generating privacy and autonomy problems among the network's participants. Hence, the proposed approach could be useful for supporting the decision of getting new business opportunities through the collaboration.

The model relevance could increase when it is necessary to consider additional model constraints such as the enterprise temporal availability in carrying out the assigned activity. Due to this fact, future works will enhance the model while taking into account for instance costs, time, and product/service quality. Further, the model will be tested on real industrial settings.

4. REFERENCES

1. Camarinha-Matos, L.M., and H. Afsarmanesh.. The virtual enterprise concept, in Infrastructures for Virtual Enterprises. In: Luis, Afsarmanesh H (eds.): Kluwer Academic Publisher; 3-14, 1999.
2. Carbonara, N., Giannoccaro, I., Potrandolfo, P. Supply Chain within industrial districts: A theoretical framework.. In International Journal of Production Economics; 76 : 159-176, 2002.
3. Chung, W.C., Yam, A.Y.K., Chan M.F.S.. Networked enterprise: a new business model for global sourcing. In International Journal of Production Economics; 87 : 267-280, 2004.
4. Conner, K.R., and C.K. Prahalad, A Resource-Based Theory of the Firm: Knowledge vs. Opportunism, In Organization Science 7, 1996.
5. Danilovic, M., Winroth, M.. A tentative framework for analysing integration in a manufacturing network settings: a case study. In Journal of Engineering and Technology Management; 22 : 141-158, 2005.
6. Demeulemeester, E.L., W.S. Herroelen. Project Scheduling: A Research Handbook. Kluwer 2002.
7. Hammami, A., P. Burlat, and J.P. Champagne. Evaluating orders allocation within networks of firms. In International Journal of Production Economics; 86 : 233-249, 2003.
8. Kaihara, T., Fujii S... A proposal on negotiation methodology in VE, Collaborative Business Ecosystems and Virtual Enterprises, Kluwer Academic Publishers, Boston; pp. 125-132, 2002.
9. Perrin, O., Godart, C., A model to support collaborative work in virtual enterprise. In Data & Knowledge Engineering; 50 : 63-86, 2004.
10. Teece, D.J., G. Pisano and A. Shuen, Dynamic Capabilities and Strategic Management, In Strategic Management Journal; 18(7), 1997.

COMPETENCY MANAGEMENT

14

COMPETENCY AND PROFILING MANAGEMENT IN VIRTUAL ORGANIZATION BREEDING ENVIRONMENTS

Ekaterina Ermilova [1], Hamideh Afsarmanesh [2]
University of Amsterdam, THE NETHERLANDS
[1] *ermilova@science.uva.nl*
[2] *hamideh@science.uva.nl*

A main characteristic of a Virtual organization Breeding Environment (VBE) is the set of competencies that it can offer to the market and society. The VBE competencies are defined in this paper through the competencies of three main VBE information components, such as the VBE member, the Virtual Organization (VO) formed in the VBE, and the VBE itself. Typically competencies appear as a part of the VBE members' profiles. VO's competencies need to be obtained through the VOs' profiles, during the operating stage of the VBE. The competencies of the VBE itself need to be carefully defined at each VBE and are contained in the VBE profile. These three kinds of profiles are addressed in this paper. The management of profiles and competencies within a VBE shall be supported by a special subsystem of the VBE Management System (VMS) – Profiling and Competency Management System (PCMS) specified in this paper.

1. INTRODUCTION

An effective creation of dynamic Virtual Organizations (VOs) requires pre-existence of a suitable Breeding Environment (VBE). *VBE* is currently defined as *"an association of organizations (members) and their related supporting institutions, adhering to a base long term cooperation agreement, and adoption of Common operating principles and infrastructures, with the main goal of increasing their preparedness towards collaboration in potential Virtual Organizations"* (Afsarmanesh, Camarinha-Matos, 2005).

The competencies in VBE need to be defined through the competencies of its three main components, including the VBE member, the VO, and the VBE as a whole. Therefore, competencies in VBEs can be classified as follows:

- *VBE's (self) competencies* address the abilities of the VBE to manage networks of organization towards VO formation;
- *VBE member's competencies* constitute capabilities and capacities of a VBE member which it can offer to the VBE in order to form a VO;
- *VO's competencies* are the result of clustering VBE members in a VO.

The competencies of VBE members and VOs in a VBE can be arranged into the *VBE competency catalogue.*

Please use the following format when citing this chapter:

Ermilova, E., Afsarmanesh, H., 2006, in IFIP International Federation for Information Processing, Volume 224, Network-Centric Collaboration and Supporting Fireworks, eds. Camarinha-Matos, L., Afsarmanesh, H., Ollus, M., (Boston: Springer), pp. 131–142.

Originally competencies are a part of the profiles. In general, an organizational *profile* can be defined as a set of structured information about the organization. VBE has three types of profiles including *VBE member's profile, VO's profile, and VBE's (self) profile*.

This paper specifies *common models for competencies and profiles*, and addresses a *Profiling and Competency Management System* (PCMS) which constitutes an important part of the VBE Management System (VMS).

Chapter 2 of this paper addresses the studied *state of the art* including, *first* the literature study on competency models, *second* the study of existing systems for organization profiling, *third* the study of profiling and competency management in existing VBEs, and *fourth* the experts' requirements to the PCMS.

Chapter 3 addresses the *specification of the PCMS's components and functions*.

This work on this paper was supported in part by the FP6 IP project, called ECOLEAD, funded by the European Commission.

2. STATE OF THE ART

In order to define the elements of the competencies and profiles of the VBE (self), the VBE member, and the VO, as well as to model the PCMS for VBEs, the state-of-the-art related to profiling and competency of organizations is studied.

In this chapter, a summary of some of the state of art work in this area as well as the results of some case studies that we have performed to identify the main requirements for the PCMS, as expressed by the field experts and academic experts, are presented.

2.1 Literature study of competency models

In the literature, different authors propose different definitions for competencies of organizations (companies), with some commonality (Galeano, Ermilova at al, 2006). Two of these definitions closer to our definition of competency are addressed below.

Javidan (Javidan, 1998) defines the competency hierarchy as depicted in Figure 1. According to Javidan, *resources* are the inputs into the organization's value chain. Javidan categorizes resources into three groups of *physical* resources (e.g. equipment, location and assets), *human* resources (e.g. manpower, management team, training and experience) and *organizational* resources (e.g. culture and reputation). *Capabilities* refer to the organization's ability to exploit its resources; they consist of a series of *business processes* that manage the interaction among its resources. Capabilities (e.g. marketing capabilities, production capabilities, distribution capabilities and logistics capabilities) are functionally based. *Competencies* represent a cross-functional integration and coordination of capabilities. In a multi-business corporation, competencies are a set of skills and know-how housed in a SBU (Strategic Business Unit). *Core competencies* are skills and areas of knowledge that are shared across business units and result from integration and harmonization of SBUs' competencies.

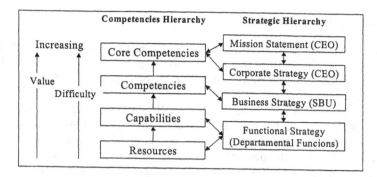

Figure 1 – Competency hierarchy and strategic hierarchy by Javidan

Molina et al (Molina at al, 1997) defines competences as the match between fulfilling the tasks defined by the VO broker with the constituent skills provided by the cluster. In their scenario there is a representation of competency which is describing the capability to make products, perform process or use technologies (humans, practices, resources). Following this argument, competencies can be described using the information entities as illustrated in Figure 2.

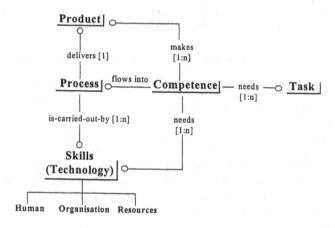

Figure 2 - Representation of competences by Molina et al

Products addressed in Figure 2 are the products of the organization or the VBE, which are attractive from the perspective of the customer, and which make a substantial contribution to organization's or VBE's success. *(Business) processes* are all the processes of the organization, e.g. product development, order generation and fulfillment, integrated logistics, etc. *Skills (Technology)* are theoretical and practical knowledge, human skills and abilities that can be used to develop products and services. According to Molina el al, a representation of competence, which satisfies its definition, can be achieved by combining the information entities of products, business processes and technologies.

Several elements introduced in the above two models are used as the base for specification of the common competency model of the VBEs.

2.2 Study of existing organizational profiling systems

In our study, two de-facto standard profiling information systems, one Dutch and one European, which organize regional centralized profiling, are considered. These systems, addressed below, specify and classify a wide variety of information about organizations.

The Dutch Chamber of Commerce (DCC_URL) has a trade register consisting of a large number of companies' profiles. Each company/organization is presented with the following data: contact information, information on the roles and functions, organization's legal form, date of establishment, number of employees, actual activities, the size of the company, summary of figures, annual accounts, etc. This register provides a very good example of categorizing organization's information for profiles in VBEs.

An example of arranging profiles of non-commercial organizations is the *EU register of organizations involved in proposal submission* (ProposalForms_URL). Organizations' information includes the following categories: organization legal name, short name, department, postal address, legal national registration number (e.g. the Chambers of Commerce register), activity type, legal status, NACE (NACE_URL) business area, annual turnover, annual balance sheet total, number of employees, independence, owners, affiliation, etc.

The profile elements introduced by the two above systems are further used to specify the common profile model for VBEs in ECOLEAD.

2.3 Study of profiling and competency management in existing VBEs

The main aim of analyzing the existing profiling and competency management in running networks of SMEs is to design a more advanced and generic PCMS which can fit most VBE domains and applications.

A questionnaire called Q1, is prepared for collecting information from the running VBEs. We have purposely chosen VBEs from different countries for this study. Five VBEs in Europe and Latina America, including IECOS (Mexico), Virtuelle Fabrik (Switzerland), Toolmaker Cluster of Slovenia (Slovenia), GIZ ACS (Slovenia), and VIRFEBRAS (Brazil).

From the analysis of the answers to Q1, the following conclusions have drawn among others.

- Only four of the VBEs collect profiles of their member organizations. Two of the VBEs address VBE (self) profiles. One VBE collects VO profiles. Three of the VBEs collect competencies of their member organization.
- *Competencies in the VBEs* are in most cases replaced by the combination of member's products/services, business processes and resources.
- *Some elements of profiles common among these* VBEs include information on products/services, customers/suppliers, business processes, performance indicators/benchmark, competencies, strategy and goals of a company, and ICT/human/physical resources.
- *Some functionality of the VBEs in relation to profiling* includes profile creation, search for members to form a VO, assessment of members performance, analysis of the VBE, defining new VO's resources, competencies, etc.

The model designed for the PCMS supports and further extends the above competency and profile structures and the required system functionality.

2.4 Requirements to the PCMS from academic and industry experts

The main aim for analyzing the requirements form experts was to specify the components and functionality of an advanced "future" PCMS for VBEs. In order to identify the requirements for the PCMS, we decided to study by collecting these requirements from the experts both in academia and industry. Therefore two questionnaires were developed, a questionnaire for academic experts, called Q2, and a similar questionnaire for industry experts called Q3.

The study with **academic experts** included more than twenty experts involved in ECOLEAD consortium. Some conclusions from the analysis of Q2 follow.
- *Competency* is defined by most researchers as an ability to perform tasks, business processes, job, core business, activities, practices applying human/physical/ ICT resources (e.g. personnel knowledge, skills, attitude, as well as organization machinery) aimed at offering products and/or services in the market.
- *The common elements of profiles* for VBEs should include contact information, business process, human / physical / ICT resources, products / services, best practices, partner organization (e.g., customer, supplier, as well as filial and corporation).
- *VBE member' profile should also provide* availability of member's competency or free capacity with a high level of detail.
- *VO's profile* should include the VO type, a list of organizations involved, and the information on VBE member components that constitute the VO partners.
- *The arrangement of the profiles catalogue* should be formed as a tree or a network, which may be arranged in several different ways depending on different criteria, and it should have a user-friendly interface and be flexible.
- *PCMS functionality* needs to support indicating what VBE provide in order to promote itself towards new members and customers. The PCMS functions shall support profile creation, profile modification, profile construction, analysis of VBE's evolution, analysis of profile catalogue changes, assessment of VBE members and search for members' competencies to form a VO. The features necessary for the search for VO partners include: classification of organization profile information regarding different criteria (e.g. city, competency, product, etc.), including combination of criteria, several levels of approximation to the result as well as some optimization of the results. Obtaining member's profile information can be either directly performed through structured questionnaires, or indirectly through text-mining of member's documents (e.g. web-sites, brochures).

The above requirements are applied to the further modeling of the PCMS.

A group of **business experts**, involved in our study, responded to Q3 questionnaire. These consisted experts from seven different companies involved in the IECOS network. In summary, the following suggestions were proposed by the contacted organizations to improve PCMS functionality.

- *Customers' letters of recommendation* should appear in VBEs as well as the contact information about the person signed this letter (information of the customer).
- The PCMS could also have information of the VBE members' *network of suppliers*. This will help to find other companies recommended by the VBE members, e.g. to invite them into the VBE to both increase the competency of the VBE, and to be involved in VOs.
- *Letters of confidentiality* should appear in the VBE to make sure that the people that are going to use the PCMS tool will not use the information out of the necessary context.
- A very strict *system of members' data evaluation* is required.

The above requirements are considered for modeling the profile component. Namely, Associated partner, as well as Evidence of validity of profile information are introduced

3. SPECIFICATION OF PCMS

Based on the state of the art addressed in chapter 2, the model of the PCMS is specified. The PCMS mainly consists of: **profiles** of VBE member, VO, and VBE itself as the main information components; **ontology** for profiles and competency; and **functionalities** to access and analyze information.

This chapter provides the common models for profile and competency in VBEs. It introduces the ontology for profiles and competency as a supporting component. It also provides the minimal necessary set of functionalities for the PCMS.

3.1 Common models for profile and competency in VBEs

Profile of an organization (e.g. VBE member, VO, and VBE itself) is defined as a set of structured information that describes the organization. Since the focus of this paper is on competency as the most significant element of profile, the organization's profile information is divided into two main groups – the general organization's information, and is competency-related information, as described below.
- *General information* of an organization contains the basic information about the organization (see section 2.2) including the organization's name, its general description, coordinates, industry sector, legal status, strategy, total sales, financial information, etc.
- *Competency-related information* (see sections 2.3 and 2.4) includes description of: competencies themselves, (business) processes, products/services, resources, practices and associated partners (e.g. customers) available for the organization. These six types of the organization's elements are defined further below as six classes. We have also identified a number of attributes for these classes, which are validated by representatives of the IECOS, a running network of manufacturing organizations (IECOS_URL). The model of the competency-related profile information is presented in Figure 3. In the text below we further define these six classes.

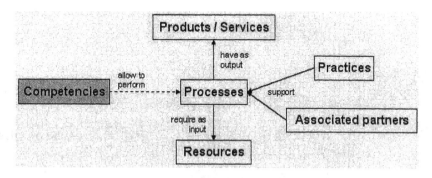

Figure 3 – Competency-related organization information

Process of an organization is a structured and measured, managed and controlled set of interrelated and interacting activities that uses resources to transform inputs into specified outputs (Davenport, 1993), (ISO9004:2000, 2000). The attributes of the process class include Name, Description, and Type.

Product/service of an organization is an output of a process which can be offered to the market/society and which consists of a bundle of tangible or intangible benefits that satisfy customer needs. Product/service class attributes include Name, Description, Strategy, Contribution to sales, and Type.

Resource represents an element applied to a process that performs a number of operations which can transform some tangible/intangible inputs into some outputs. Organization can have three types of resources, including human resources, ICT resources (e.g. software) and physical resources (e.g. buildings, machines, equipment, transport, and knowledge assets). The resource class attributes include, for human resource: Job function, Educational level, Professional field, Degree obtained, Years of experience, and Number of employees; for ICT resource: Name, Description, and Type (e.g. software); for physical resource: Name, Type (e.g. buildings), Description, Number, and Functionality.

Practices are the techniques, methodologies, and procedures that are used in the organizations to perform a job. Practices are used in order to improve business processes in the organization (Stuhlman_URL). Practice class attributes include Name, Description, Implementation time, Introduction date, and Reason for introduction.

Associated partner is an organization which has some (business) relations with the organization. This class appears through the answers for questionnaire Q3. The supposed minimal set of the attributes for this class includes: Name, Type (e.g. suppliers, customers, filial, or corporation), General textual description, and Contact information.

We define **competency** *as the organization's capability to perform (business) processes (in collaboration with partners such as suppliers), having the necessary resources (human, technological, physical) available, and applying certain practices, with the final aim to offer certain products and/or services to the customers.*

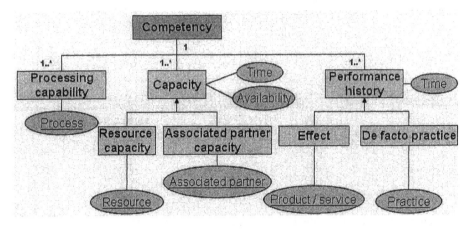

Figure 3 – Competency model

The earlier definition of organization's competency as "capability + capacity" (Afsarmanesh, Camarinha-Matos, 2005) addresses *(processing) capability* as a potential ability to perform a *process,* and the *capacity* as the *availability* of *resources or associated partners.*

As represented in Figure 3, this definition is further extended by including another important descriptor for competency – the *performance history,* that itself includes *effects,* including products/services (Enterprise project_URL) and *practices* of an organization. The ECOLEAD model of an organization competency is illustrated in Figure 3.

3.2 Main information components of the PCMS

Based on the ECOLEAD common models of profile and competency, we define below the VBE member's profile, VO's profile and VBE's (self) profile as components of the PCMS.

The **member's profile** is completely based on the common profile model.

The **VO's profile**, in addition to the common profile elements, includes: a List of VO partners, Type of partnership, Collaborative opportunity description and other general VO-related information. *Competencies of a VO* can be of two types, including, first the VO partners' competencies, and second the new emerging competencies, which are the result of VO partners' collaboration.

The **VBE's (self) profile**, in addition to the common profile elements, includes: a List of members, List of actors, List of roles, List of rules and other general VBE-related information. The examples of VBE's *processes* include network management, VO formation, VO creation, marketing/branding of products/services (to be sold through the VBE), innovation promotion, etc. The examples of *VBE's competencies* include its ability related to VBE management, VO formation and creation, innovation promotion, etc.

Two important catalogues are necessary to be presented and managed inside the VBE, one catalogue for VBE members' profiles, another for VO's profiles catalogue. The **VBE members' profiles catalogue** can be accessed as a collection of members' profiles sorted by different types of organization information. In this catalogue all the competencies, resources, product/services, etc., available in a VBE through its members, as well as the *new emerged competencies* appearing as the result of a possible assembly of VBE members' competencies, can be presented. **VO's profiles catalogue** can be accessed as a collection of VOs' profiles sorted by different types of VOs' information. These two catalogues are combined in a single VBE profiles catalogue system.

3.3 Main functionalities of PCMS

The summary of the PCMS functionalities can be found in Table 1. Please notice that inside the table some details are provided about these functionalities and how they will be achieved, e.g. manually, semi-automatically, etc.

The proposed set of PCMS functionalities is divided into five groups, including **creation, updating, structuring, search & retrieval**, and **analysis**. Each group is addressed by the three PCMS's profile components for VBE member, VO and VBE (itself), as well as by the *catalogue of the VBE members' profiles and VOs' profiles*.

	Member's profile	VO's profile	VBE's profile	VBE members and VOs' profiles catalogue
Creation	Manual / Semi-automatic: – Obtaining the profile data – Creation of the profile – Updating the ontology			
Updating	Manual / Semi-automatic: – Obtaining the profile data – Updating the profile – Updating the ontology			
Structuring	Automatic ontology-based structuring of the profile (e.g. structuring competencies in the profile according to the competency classification)			Automatic ontology-based sorting of the catalogue: – by individual (e.g. city) or combined (e.g. city + competency) elements of the profile – by ratings (e.g. financial rating)
Search & Retrieval				– Specification of values for any set of the profile elements – Value of each element field can be given in different ways and using different types of restrictions, including restrictions on object relations or object attributes – Representation of the search results as a profiles catalogue, as well as graphical visualization – Several levels of approximation to the search results (i.e. search can have several iterations)
Analysis	– Evaluation of a member by different criteria –Suggestion of new competency directions			– Ontology based Gaps identification – Supporting retreat or adding new VBE members for gap elimination – Ontology based "building" of new competencies in VBE, out of the existing ones

Table 1 – Main functionalities of PCMS

3.4 Ontology for profiles and competencies

The ontology for profiles and competencies is a support component for the PCMS that aims at the following: **(1)** providing the *common understanding* of the concepts related to profiles and competencies in VBEs, **(2)** *classification of knowledge* (e.g. competencies) and support of interoperability of knowledge inside the VBE and among the VBEs, and **(3)** *supporting the PCMS functionalities* (see Table 1).

The current PCMS ontology is constructed *top-down* and *manually*, based on both the definitions of the competency-related classes of the generic organization's profile (see section 3.1) and the NACE classification system (NACE_URL) that indirectly addresses the classification of competencies. One snapshot of PCMS ontology developed in Protégé is presented in Figure 4.

The use of ontology for the PCMS functionalities is addressed in Table 1.

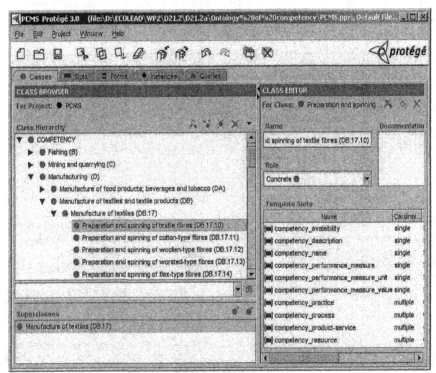

Figure 4 – Ontology for profiles and competencies

3.5 Adaptation/instantiation of the PCMS ontology

To adapt/instantiate the ontology for a specific VBE application (e.g. to add competencies of a specific VBE to the ontology), a *bottom-up* approach is required and suggested in ECOLEAD. The bottom-up approach aims at semi-automatic extraction of information / knowledge from VBE members and VOs for the ontology using online text corpora. Semi-automatic adaptation of the ontology to the VBE application makes the PCMS *replicable*.

Figure 5 illustrates the high level approach for semi-automatic adaptation/instantiation of the PCMS ontology to a specific VBE application. The approach consists of several stages involving a feedback from the organizations side, thus involving the VBE members themselves, the VOs representative organizations, as well as VBE actors such as the VBE administrator, the VBE competency expert and the VBE ontology provider. This approach is mostly based on the results of Metis project devoted to semi-automatic construction of domain and task ontologies (Anjewierden at al, 2003).

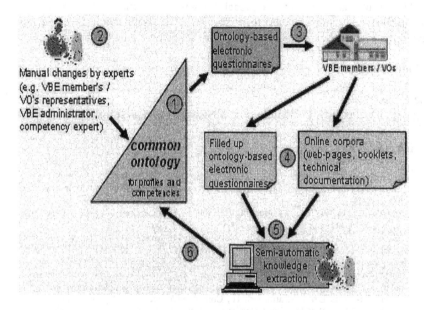

Figure 5– Adaptation of the PCMS ontology to a specific VBE application: (1) the top-down constructed ontology, (2) manual adaptation of the ontology by experts, (3) preparation of questionnaires for organizations, (4) receiving online information from organizations, (5) semi-automatic knowledge extraction through text mining, (6) semi-automatic bottom-up extension of the ontology

4. CONCLUSIONS

The PCMS is a subsystem of the VBE management system, supporting the competency orientation of a VBE which is fundamental for its role of breeding and creation of VOs, and focused on the aim of replicability and coverage of the varied competencies in VBEs.

The specific *innovative contributions* of this research are three-fold. *First*, the specification / modeling of all VBE related profiles / competencies, consists of: (a) specification of the VO's profile and the VBE's profile in addition to proper modeling of the VBE member's profile, (b) extended modeling of organization competencies for VBEs. *Second*, a core common ontology for profiles and competency in VBEs is provided. *Third*, a semi-automatic (bottom-up) approach is suggested for making the PCMS replicable.

The PCMS in ECOLEAD is specified in a generic replicable way, therefore it can fit diverse VBEs from all sectors. Namely, the PCMS can be applied to any industrial sector or other domains, and its generic model can be customized and adjusted to specific application needs according to the VBE type. This process, also called an instantiation, supports that general model is extended and converted into a specific model. This instantiation processes will be realized by following a methodology with necessary steps to adapt general information into specific information, and creating a catalogue of organization profiles and competencies to be supported by the VBE Management System of ECOLEAD.

At present, the work on the approach for semi-automatic adaptation of ontology for profiles and competencies to a specific VBE application is being further developed and will be the subject of the following paper.

Acknowledgments

The author thanks the valuable contributions from their partners in the ECOLEAD consortium, especially the contribution of Nathalie Galeano from ITESM, Mexico.

5. REFERENCES

1.   Afsarmanesh H., Camarinha-Matos L., A framework for management of virtual organization breeding environments, in Collaorative Networks and their Breeding Environments, Springer, 2005, pp. 35-49.
2.   Anjewierden A., Wielinga B.J., Hoog R. de, Kabel S., Task and domain ontologies for knowledge mapping in operational processes, Metis Deliverable 4.2, 2003
3.   Galeano N., Ermilova E., Giraldo J., Afsarmanesh H., Molina A., Definition of Competency Concept in Virtual organization Breeding Environments (VBEs), in Encyclopedia of Networked and Virtual Organizations, 2006
4.   Dutch Chamber of Commerce, http://www.kvk.nl
5.   Enterprise Project, http://www.aiai.ed.ac.uk/project/enterprise/enterprise/ontology.html
6.   Camarinha-Matos L.M., Afsarmanesh H., Collaborative networks: A new scientific discipline, International Journal of Intelligent Manufacturing, vol. 16, N? 4-5, pp439-452, ISSN: 0956-5515, 2005.
7.   Camarinha-Matos L.M., Afsarmanesh H., Ollus M. - ECOLEAD: A holistic approach to creation and management of dynamic virtual organizations, in Collaborative Networks and their Breeding Environments, Springer, 2005, pp. 3-16
8.   Camarinha-Matos, L. M., Silveri, I., Afsarmanesh, H., & Oliveira, A. I.,. Towards a Framework for Creation of Dynamic Virtual Organizations, in Collaborative Networks and their Breeding Environments, Springer, 2005, pp. 69-81.
9.   IECOS, www.iecos.com
10.   ISO/TC 176/SC2 (2000) ISO9004:2000 Quality management system – guidelines for performance improvements
11.   Javidan M., Core Competence: What does it mean in practice? Long Range Planning, Vol. 31, No. 1, 1998, pp 60 to 71. Published by Elsevier Science Ltd. Great Britain.
12.   Molina A. et al. Information Model to represent the Core Competencies of Virtual Industry Clusters. 1997 Technical Note.
13.   NACE, http://europa.eu.int/comm/competition/mergers/cases/index/nace_all.html
14.   Proposal submission forms for financial support from the EC for research projects, ftp://ftp.cordis.lu/pub/fp5/docs/rtdp_guide_en.pdf
15.   Stuhlman management consultants : http://home.earthlink.net/~ddstuhlman/defin1.htm
16.   Verdin, P. and Williamson, P., Successful Strategy: Stargazing or Self-Examination, European Management Journal, 12(1), 1994, pp. 10-18.

COMPETENCE PROFILING IN VIRTUAL COMPANIES

Barbara Odenthal
Chair and Institute of Industrial Engineering and Ergonomics (IAW)
at University of Technology Aachen (RWTH Aachen University), GERMANY
e-mail: B.Odenthal@iaw.rwth-aachen.de

Meikel Peters
Chair and Institute of Industrial Engineering and Ergonomics (IAW)
at University of Technology Aachen (RWTH Aachen University), GERMANY
e-mail: M.Peters@iaw.rwth-aachen.de

The reorganization of the supply chain in the aerospace industry has led to a new situation for small and medium-sized enterprises (SME). In order to react to the changed requirements, one possible solution is the project-oriented and temporary cooperation of SME by building a Virtual Company. This again presents the employees with new challenges regarding the work requirements. Within the research project AerViCo - Aerospace Virtual Company - special tools and instruments considering the effects on employee performance behavior are being developed in order to increase labor productivity and to support the employees within the cooperation.

1. INTRODUCTION

During the past years the development of the corporate strategy of manufacturers in the aerospace industry has led to a new situation for small and medium-sized enterprises (SME). In order to lower their costs, European consolidated companies in the aerospace industry (Airbus, EADS, astrium, Lagardere, ...) have re-organized their supplier network. The number of direct suppliers, that have to be audited and certified, was reduced from several hundred to less than ten, which leads to a significant decrease of administrative work for the large enterprises (figure 1).

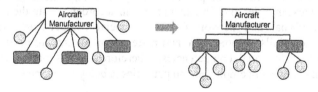

Fig. 1: Re-organization of the supplier network

In consequence, the strategic suppliers are commissioned to deliver completed systems instead of components and assemblies.

Please use the following format when citing this chapter:

Odenthal, B., Peters, M., 2006, in IFIP International Federation for Information Processing, Volume 224, Network-Centric Collaboration and Supporting Fireworks, eds. Camarinha-Matos, L., Afsarmanesh, H., Ollus, M., (Boston: Springer), pp. 143–150.

In addition to the order processing, the first level suppliers are now also responsible for the monitoring and the compliance of second and third level suppliers with the quality standards. Consequently the above mentioned requirements are handed on to the second and the third level suppliers which are mainly SME. In order to respond to the new situation, one possible solution is the creation of a virtual network of SME which join forces in the case of an order processing and adjust flexibly to the requirements at hand (Peters/Bernhard, 2004). Because the success of interorganizational and knowledge-intensive cooperation in a virtual context depends to a large extent on the efficient and effective interaction of employees, the employees of the SME are confronted with new challenges. In order to make work more efficient and to support the employees within the cooperation, it is necessary to provide special tools and instruments considering the effects on employee performance behavior.

In order to ensure compliance of employee behavior while working and acting in cooperation with the Virtual Companies' (VC) goals three aspects are of importance (Killich/Peters, 2003): commitment (motivation), capability (competencies) and conditions (influence of organization, leadership and culture), see figure 2.

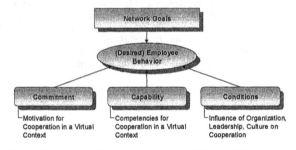

Fig. 2: Employee-Related Aspects of Virtual Companies

In order to support the SME with the operation of a VC, the research project AerViCo - Aerospace Virtual Company – was initiated. The objective of the project is to develop a cooperation network of SME which is the basis for forming project consortiums to process a certain order. One of the achievements of the project is the development of a method to support the employees' competencies for cooperation in a virtual context in order to enable them to act in accordance with the network goals. Even in a virtual and networked context social competencies, language and communication skills become more and more important and are needed in addition to excellent professional competencies. Therefore, in this project a method for profiling and enhancing employee competencies is being developed.

2. CURRENT STATE

In order to acquire a survey of the current state of cooperation within the aerospace industry, interviews (face-to-face and via questionnaires) were carried out (Odenthal/Peters, 2005), in which different fields of interest regarding the job design could be identified. On closer examination the role of the employees in a Virtual

Company must be differentiated into the employees who are directly involved in the cooperation and those who are not. In the context of the project AerViCo the companies concerned mainly offer development, construction and testing services. In these knowledge-intensive services the employees are directly involved in the cooperation. That means that there are points of contact between the company (project leader and member of the project team) and the client. Because of this type of work, special job requirements for the employees involved directly in the cooperation occur. Professional and linguistic competencies, high flexibility in terms of the processing of different tasks and social competencies are necessary in order to successfully operate in interorganizational projects. Furthermore, different types of organizational culture in the virtual context lead to specific characteristics in respect to the job conditions: different ways of working, decision structures, authorities of the contact persons, different remuneration and differences concerning the influence of the workers' council hold the danger of conflicts.

On the one hand companies expect their employees to fulfill these requirements, but on the other hand SME so far hardly provide systematical and methodical support and development of the employees' competencies. Often the companies employ staff members which develop "on-the-job" adapting to the postulated requirements. This procedure holds the danger of not making use of the full potentials concerning employee competencies.

3. TARGET COMPETENCE PROFILES IN VIRTUAL COMPANIES

In order to identify, support and develop the competencies of the employees involved in the cooperation, it is crucial to identify the target competence profile for the concerned roles within a VC which can be consulted in order to compare the target competence profile with the actual competence profile of the employee. This comparison of the two profiles offers the possibility of systematically implementing measures of competence development.

One of the achievements of the AerViCo-project is the development of a method which generates target competence profiles for workplaces and activity fields of employees in SME while considering the special requirements in a VC.

3.1 A method for generating target competence profiles

The method for generating target competence profiles follows a synthetic approach. The basic idea behind the method is that the work tasks and work situation of a role in a virtual company can be described by a set of activities and activity features. Furthermore, activities and activity features require corresponding competencies of the acting person in order to successfully carry out the work tasks.

Following this idea, a classification of activities and activity features was developed on the basis of existing models of activities (Stahl 1998; Kabel 2001) and an analysis of existing methods of psychological job evaluation (Richter 2001). This classification allows the description of work contents and work situations in a virtual context. Furthermore, the described method is based on an existing classification of competencies (Erpenbeck et al. 2002). Erpenbeck defines competencies as dispositions of self-organization, which can be divided in four parts (see figure 3):

- **personal competence**: Disposition to act reflexive self-organized
- **activity and acting competence**: Disposition to act holistic self-organized
- **professional and methodical competence**: Disposition to act theoretical-methodical self-organized
- **social-communicative competence**: Disposition to act communicative and cooperative self-organized

While the classification of competencies is universally valid and not tailored for inter-organizational cooperation, the classification of activities and activity features allows for the specific aspects of work in a virtual context. For instance, concerning activities and activity features, working in VCs includes cooperation processes on a personal level and a high flexibility of the working situation in terms of working time, working place and information flows. These characteristics were taken into account for the development of the classification of the activities and activity features (see figure 3). In order to prove the completeness of this classification – consisting of 29 activities and 21 activity features - the classification was used to represent several existing work processes and work task descriptions with a cooperative character.

Fig. 3: General allocation of competencies to activities and activity features

Using the described classifications, the basis of the method is formed by a weighted allocation of competencies to activities and activity features which was developed in workshops with experts from the field of cooperation in the aerospace industry. However, the goal is to establish a connection between the work tasks of a role in the VC and the required competencies. This happens by describing specific work tasks and situations using the defined activities and activity features. With the predefined allocation of competencies to activities and activity features this leads directly to the respective target competence profile of the considered role. To briefly

Competence profiling in virtual companies

explain this train of thought, the Prime Contractor of the network is taken as an example. By working in a VC, "cooperative problem solving" (activity) gains in importance. Moreover, the job of a Prime Contractor involves frequent travelling (activity feature). Both aspects lead to a higher importance of social-communicative competencies and stress capacity.

3.2 Application of the method considering as example the role of the Broker

In the following, the application of the procedure of generating a target competence profile will be shown using the role of the Broker of the VC as example.

The tasks of a broker are characterized as follows. He/she is responsible for coordination and administrative activities on the platform of the cooperation network independent of the concrete order processing. This includes on the one hand tasks of configuring a cooperation network, e.g. legal agreements between the network partners and the development of the IT-infrastructure for the network. On the other hand, the broker must ensure the smooth flow and operation of the cooperation network by taking over the task of the administration of the partners, conflict management and the controlling of the platform. Additionally, he/she is responsible for the marketing of the cooperation network. The broker acts as a mediator between the customer and the network by marketing the products or services of the network and by forwarding costumers inquiries to the network partners.

Fig. 4: Example of a target competence profile of the broker of a VC (extract: social-communicative competence)

Using the developed method, it is now possible to realise a target competence profile of a broker by allocating and weighting activities and activity features to the job tasks. This step is carried out by the user e.g. the project leader in order to fill a vacancy. The allocation of required competencies to the activities and features is implicitly given by the method. Figure 4 shows an extract of an example for a target competence profile of a broker of a VC. From the point of view of the enterprises, this method for creating target profiles facilitates the process of selection of personnel by means of comparing the target profile of the work field and the current state profile of the (potential) employee. From the point of view of the employee, the comparison of the target profile and the current state profile establishes and provides a basis for initiating measures for personnel development in order to increase the competencies and thus his/her capability continuously.

3.3 Current state profiles and competence development measures

In order to complete the competence profiling, it is necessary to measure the existing competencies of the employees involved in the cooperation (current state competence profile). Because of the wide range of existing competence measuring instruments the application of existing instruments is planned within the research project. A further project objective is the development of a catalogue of measures for competence development on the one hand classified according to the type of measure (e.g. on-the-job, off-the-job) and on the other hand according to the competence which should be developed. It is planned not to limit the catalogue of measure to organized learning situations but also to support the informal development of competencies, e.g. by providing design recommendations for a work organization which supports learning. By comparing the existing competencies (current state profile) of the employee with the required competencies (target profile) of the role, a prediction concerning the selection of competence development measures will be possible in the case of significant differences between the target and the current state profiles.

4. EVALUATION PROJECT

The method which is presented is being evaluated within a concrete engineering project which serves as an evaluation project within the AerViCo-consortium.

The processing of the evaluation project takes place on 3 levels which are: project level, VC level and evaluation level (see figure 5).

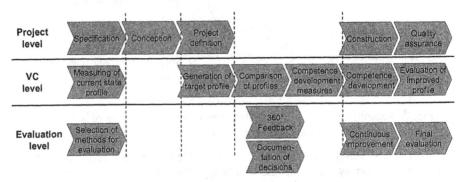

Fig. 5: Process model of the evaluation project

The project level is the conception and construction of one part of the mentioned engineering project - the development of a playground and entertainment area for children.

Competence profiling in virtual companies

On VC level the developed methods for competence profiling will come into operation in order to support the personnel placement within the consortium. In an early stage of the project the current state competence profiles of potential project team members will be measured using a commercial method of competence measurement. After the definition of the project, the presented method will be applied to generate the target competence profiles of the roles required within the project. By comparing the current state profiles with the target profiles the team members suited best for the requirements of the project will be chosen. If necessary measures for competence development will be derived from the comparison of profiles in order to further qualify the project team on the job.

The verification and evaluation of the target profiling instrument takes place on the evaluation level. By using special questionnaires and interview guidelines the effectiveness of the method for supporting the selection of team members and team qualification will be evaluated. The results of the evaluation (on the evaluation level) will be incorporated in a continuous and iterative further development.

5. DISCUSSION AND OUTLOOK

In this article a procedure to generate target competence profiles for roles and positions in a Virtual Company was presented which is based on the one hand on an allocation of competencies to activities and activity features and on the other hand on an allocation of activities and activity features to tasks (regarding a role or position). In order to measure the existing competencies of the employees involved in the cooperation (current state competence profile), existing tools of competence measurement will be used.

Currently the developed method is being applied in an engineering project in order to evaluate the practicability and, if necessary, to further improve the method. One of the next steps in the project progression will be the development and application of a catalogue of measures for competence development.

6. ACKNOWLEDGMENTS

The Project „AerViCo – Aerospace Virtual Company" is funded by the German Federal Ministry of Education and Research (grant number: 01HU0160 – 01HU0169). The other partners are: AIDA Development GmbH, Schwaebisch Hall, ALROUND e.V., Bonn, ANSYS Germany GmbH, Otterfing, Fraunhofer – Institut für Materialfluss und Logistik (IML), Dortmund, HEGGEMANN Aerospace AG, Büren, HTS GmbH, Coswig, IMA Materialforschung und Anwendungstechnik GmbH, Dresden, MST Aerospace GmbH, Köln, ProTec-Recycling, Werne.

7. REFERENCES

1. Erpenbeck, J. & von Rosenstiel, L. 2002, Handbuch der Kompetenzmessung. Stuttgart: Schäffer-Poeschel.
2. Kabel, D. 2001, Entwicklung eines prozeßbasierten Effizienzmodells für Concurrent Engineering Teams. Dissertation RWTH Aachen, Aachen: Shaker-Verlag.
3. Killich, S., Peters, M.: The Interest of employees in Knowledge Sharing: A Theoretical Framework for the Integration of Motivation, Qualification and Organization for Knowledge Management in Networks. In: Luczak, H. ; Zink, K.J. (eds.): Human Factors in Organizational Design and Management - VII. Proceedings of the Seventh International Symposium on Human Factors in Organizational Design and Management held in Aachen, October 1-2, IEA Press, Santa Monica, CA, USA 2003, 373-378.
4. Odenthal, B. & Peters, M. 2005, Specification Model for the Development and Operation of a Virtual Company in the Aerospace Industry, Proceedings of the PRO-VE'05 - 6th IFIP Working Conference on Virtual Enterprises held in Valencia (Spain). New York: Springer, 2005, 371-378.
5. Peters, M., Bernhard, J.: Virtuelle Zulieferkooperationen in der Luftfahrtindustrie – Entwicklung eines Konzeptes zum Aufbau und Betrieb Virtueller Unternehmen unter Berücksichtigung organisatorischer, technischer und personeller Faktoren. In: Unternehmen der Zukunft, Aachen, 5, 2004, 4; 3-4.
6. Richter, G. 2001, Psychologische Bewertung von Arbeitsbedingungen. Bremerhaven: Wirtschaftsverl. NW, Verl. für neue Wiss.
7. Stahl, J. : Entwicklung einer Methode zur Integrierten Arbeitsgestaltung und Personalplanung im Rahmen von Concurrent Engineering. Dissertation RWTH Aachen, Aachen: Shaker-Verlag.

16

COLLABORATIVE PLANNING IN COMPETENCE-CELL BASED NETWORKS

Egon Müller, Jörg Ackermann, Sebastian Horbach
Chemnitz University of Technology, GERMANY
joerg.ackermann@mb.tu-chemnitz.de

Autonomous, elementary units of production, co-operating in temporary networks, are considered as a key organisational form of enterprises in the 21st century. A scientific approach is provided by networks based on customer-oriented, directly linked, smallest autonomous business units called Competence Cells. This approach leads to new requirements for the planning of production systems of such networks. To meet them a framework called 'PlaNet – Planning Concept for Networks' has been developed and is outlined. PlaNet provides the means for Competence Cells to solve their planning problems. The implementation of PlaNet is the Net Planning Assistant as a modular toolset.

1. INTRODUCTION

Autonomous, elementary units of production, co-operating in temporary networks, are viewed as a key organisational form of enterprises in the 21st century. A scientific approach is provided by Non-hierarchical Regional Networks based on customer-oriented, directly linked, smallest autonomous service units called Competence Cells. Simultaneously this concept points out perspectives for present-day small and medium-sized enterprises (SME) to face ever-changing economic conditions.

The approach results in new requirements on the planning of logistics structures and production plants. Therefore the Planning Concept for Networks 'PlaNet' has been developed. PlaNet assists the Competence Cells in tackling their planning problems. The methodical concept of PlaNet is based on the Systems Engineering Methodology.

The implementation of PlaNet is the Net Planning Assistant (NPA). NPA can be configured according to the requirements of the particular planning process by choosing the appropriate tools. These commercially available and proprietary tools are cross-linked through a Production Database. A special emphasis is placed on tools for participative planning.

The approach of Competence-cell based Networks is introduced in section 2. PlaNet is introduced in section 3. NPA is then presented in section 4.

Please use the following format when citing this chapter:

Müller, E., Ackermann, J., Horbach, S., 2006, in IFIP International Federation for Information Processing, Volume 224, Network-Centric Collaboration and Supporting Fireworks, eds. Camarinha-Matos, L., Afsarmanesh, H., Ollus, M., (Boston: Springer), pp. 151–158.

2. COMPETENCE-CELL BASED NETWORKS

2.1 Motivation

There are currently two extreme cases regarding the development of enterprises.

Firstly, there are mergers and acquisitions leading to the development of large-scale enterprises, who usually act as 'global players', concentrating more and more capital.

The other extreme is characterised by an increasing 'atomisation' of enterprises, which concentrate exclusively on their core competences. The economical impact of SMEs is undisputed. With their high share of gross value added they form the backbone of most economies in terms of employment and innovation. For example in Germany the SMEs earn about 50 percent of the gross value added and employ two thirds of the workers. (BMWi, 1998)

Furthermore since the start of the 21st century empirical evidence suggests that the economical impact of micro-enterprises will increase (European Commission, 2004). The bottom line is that

the typical European enterprise is a micro-enterprise.

In this context a key scientific question is how small performance units can become while still remaining capable of competing in the market place independently? Another relevant question is how these smallest-scale enterprises need to act in order to optimally exploit existing potential? This potential is lying in an increase of the competitiveness compared to large-scale enterprises as well as in the increase of the share of exports in the revenues.

Small enterprises have apart from their specific core competences only limited resources. Due to this they can realise only sub-sequences of process chains. Missing competences must be obtained or be supplemented by co-operation and cross-linking. That way the ability for a holistic customer-oriented provision of complex products respectively services can be acquired.

Present forms of co-operation are mainly based on hierarchical structures within and between enterprises. These co-operations are often dominated by a single large-scale enterprise. Dependencies are mandatory. The achieved advantage of relative stability conflicts with the disadvantage of unilateral dominance. These dependencies work as restrictions for regionally established enterprises. They lead to significant market entrance barriers for small- and smallest-scale enterprises and in particular for business start-ups. As a result some regional competences are not completely utilised and an economically desirable dynamic in establishing and developing small enterprises is obstructed.

To overcome these disadvantages it is necessary to aim future efforts at the development of non-hierarchical production structures. This is supported by studies that consider autonomous, elementary business units (Laubacher et al., 1997), co-operating in temporary networks (Malone and Laubacher, 1998) also called 'nanocorps' (Salmons and Babitsky, 2001), as the form of enterprise organisation of the future.

Clusters of SMEs have gained considerable importance in a number of other European countries besides Germany such as Italy (UNIDO, 2006) and France (Villarreal Lizárraga et al., 2005).

There is a need to lay a scientific foundation to the so far rather empirical exploration of collaborative networks. (Camarinha-Matos and Afsarmanesh, 2005)

2.2 Vision and Concept

Due to this development in manufacturing organisation, which in recent years has been lastingly influenced by phenomena of elementarisation and specialisation of competences as well as customer-oriented networking, a specific vision aimed at small and medium-sized business (Figure 1) has been developed (SFB457 1999).

Elementary business units – called Competence Cells – are co-operating in Non-hierarchical Regional Production Networks in a customer-oriented manner and thus capable of facing global competition.

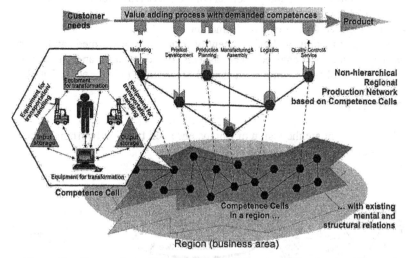

Figure 1 – Conception of Non-hierarchical Regional Production Networks (SFB457 1999)

It is the long-term goal to investigate this vision in its entirety from a scientific perspective. Theories and models will be formulated in order to describe standards of Non-hierarchical Regional Production Networks and to subsequently develop concepts, methods and instruments for generating and operating such networks.

Such structures of the value adding process will contribute to the development of micro firms and furthermore sustainable regional production profiles.

Initially objects of research will be determined by the customer-oriented single piece and small-batch production conducted by mechatronical engineering companies and regional profiles. (SFB457 1999)

In recent years an increasing attention has been paid to 'Virtual Organizations' (Camarinha-Matos et al., 2005), 'Collaborative Business Networks' (COBTEC, 2005) and 'Virtual Organization Breeding Environment' (ECOLEAD, 2005). Often similar assumptions to those of the vision of Competence-cell based Networks have been made. All these research projects are striving for new forms of organisation which meet the new opportunities provided by working together in networks of production. However the central features of the Competence-cell based Networking

Approach – elementarity and autonomy of the performance units as well as the lack of hierarchies and the regionality of the networking – are not explicitly investigated. The focus of these projects is rather on supra-regional, hierarchical value adding organisations with special emphasis on certain aspects of information and communication technology.

2.3 Competence Cell

A Competence Cell is considered as the smallest autonomous indivisible performance unit of value adding, able to exist independently.
The model of the Competence Cell (Figure 2) consists of:
- the human with his competences, arranged according to professional, methodical, social and personnel competences (Erpenbeck, 1998)
- available resources as well as
- the fulfilled task or executed function.

With this function a business entity can be transformed and a certain performance can be achieved. The aspects of dimension and structure were supplemented to obtain a complete technical description. (Müller et al., 2004)

2.4 Networking

In order to substantiate the vision of Competence-cell based networking a Procedure Model has been developed (Figure 2).

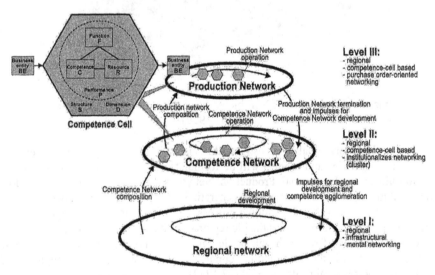

Figure 2 – Model of the Competence Cell and Procedure Model of Competence-cell based networking (revised from Müller et al., 2004)

The model comprises three levels and seven phases.
From loose infrastructural and mental relations present in a regional network (Level I) there initially emerges an institutionalized Competence Network, based on Competence Cells (Level II). Institutionalisation takes place via the coordination of

behaviour (e.g. agreements on offer generation, agreements on cost allocation) and via the pooling of capacity (e.g. common servers and data bases). These facilitate an efficient acting towards the customer and avoid internal discrepancies. Institutionalisation thereby creates the basis on which autonomous Competence Cells join to find to a collective creation of value. In order to hold fixed expenses down, the institutionalisation is to be limited to the necessary amount.

The actual creation of value takes place in a Production Network (Level III), i.e. a temporary linking of selected Competence Cells, initiated by customer request. In order to select and cross-link Competence Cells and to operate the network, co-ordinated ways of behaviour and pre-installed structures are available in the Competence Network. (Müller et al., 2004)

3. PLANET – A PLANNING CONCEPT FOR NETWORKS

3.1 Requirements on Planning of Logistics Structures and Production Plants in Competence-cell based Networks

The Competence-cell based Networking Approach puts special requirements on the planning of logistics structures and production plants. Among them are the extended domain of planned objects, the greater responsibility of the autonomous units which on the other hand might lack planning competence and the participative way in which planning needs to be done due to the lack of hierarchies. Those requirements are only partly met by existing planning approaches.

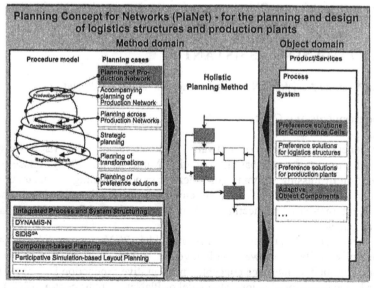

Figure 3 – Planning concept with Holistic Planning Method (Müller et al., 2004)

Therefore a new framework for planning in networks of competence is needed. Such a framework has been developed with the Planning Concept for Networks.

3.2 Contents of PlaNet

PlaNet is intended to enable and support Competence Cells in solving different planning problems in the field of logistics structures and production plants in Competence-cell based production systems, so that they can plan networks in case of need as well as in advance.

PlaNet was designed as a framework, which embraces suitable theories, models, concepts, methods and preference solutions for logistics structures of Competence Cells linked to production systems as well as the planning of network-able production plants (Figure 3).

Both Competence Cells with special planning competences and Competence Cells without such competences are addressed by PlaNet, also for working together in a collaborative way.

3.3 The Methodical Concept

After detailed assessments of existing problem solution and planning approaches the universal, domain-neutral, flexible and adaptable Systems Engineering Methodology (SE) (Daenzer and Huber, 1994) proved to be a suitable basis for the methodical concept. If the components of SE are considered as framework for PlaNet, the respective specific components of PlaNet can be classified in this framework.

With the methodical concept adapted design solutions for logistics structures and production plants can be generated as depicted in Figure 3. Procedures to solve planning cases are formed with the Holistic Planning Method as a template. Methods like Integrated Process and System Structuring and pre-configured object solutions such as Adaptive Object Components are integrated. (Müller et al., 2004)

4. NET PLANNING ASSISTANT

The Net Planning Assistant (NPA) is the implementation of PlaNet.

4.1 Requirements and Concept

Besides general requirements on software, additional requirements rise from special aspects of Competence-cell based Networks (Müller et al., 2004). Those are the consideration of missing planning competences in non-planning Competence Cells, small funds and heterogeneous software environments. On the other hand a holistic approach, internet-based connecting of Competence Cells and Participative Planning should be pursued.

To meet these requirements NPA has like PlaNet a modular structure. Commercially available software tools together with proprietary developments are interlinked through an interface concept. An integrative Production Database (PDB), which is based on the production data model of PlaNet, is in the centre of NPA.

Due to the modular structure the planning instance is able to configurate NPA to its special needs. Those needs are determined by the procedures in which this instance is involved and there especially the underlying methods. Thus the configuration of NPA should contain the appropriate tools for the methods that a particular planning instance has to employ.

NPA is not depending on particular software solutions. It should be rather seen as a general concept for linking together different software solutions which are necessary in the process of planning logistics structures and production plants.

4.2 Components

Potential components of NPA are shown in Figure 4.

A user interface called DataMan supports the management of the Production Database. The usage of a web-based application which can be accessed through an internet browser is suggested for this interface. NPA also contains tools for modelling, planning of logistics structures and production plants, participation and visualisation, simulation and knowledge management.

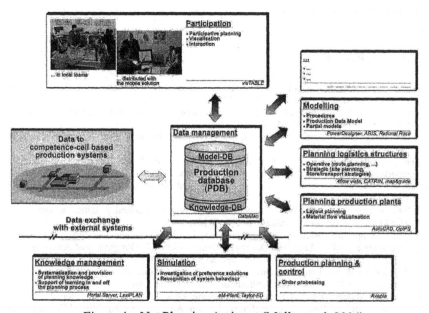

Figure 4 – Net Planning Assistant (Müller et al. 2004)

Planning in Competence-cell based Networks has to be done in a collaborative/ participative way. This does not necessarily take place in one location where all involved parties meet. In fact the participants can stay at different places while the planning is done jointly through the internet. Both ways of participative planning are supported by the planning and visualisation tool visTABLE. Layouts are displayed on a two-dimensional drawing which can be manipulated with a touch screen and also in a three dimensional view which shows the spatial implications of the developed layout. The large size of the screen allows a group of people to work on the layout together as can be seen in Figure 4. Alternatively the underlying software can be used for a distributed planning, accompanied by a chat application to discuss the suggestions of the different planners. For the distributed scenario especially the mobile version of visTABLE (Figure 4) is suitable. (Müller et al., 2004)

5. CONCLUSIONS

Competence-cell based Networks provide a promising approach for future forms of value adding organisations. The approach also points out perspectives for present small and medium-sized enterprises to face ever-changing economic conditions. The Planning Concept for Networks PlaNet serves the special requirements on planning of logistics structures and production plants in such networks. Suitable tools are provided through the Net Planning Assistant as the implementation of PlaNet.

6. ACKNOWLEDGMENTS

Collaborative Research Centre 457 'Non-hierarchical Regional Production Networks' has been supported by German Research Foundation (Deutsche Forschungsgemeinschaft – DFG).

7. REFERENCES

Bundesministerium für Wirtschaft (BMWi), Kleine und mittlere Unternehmen. Früherkennung von Chancen und Risiken. Arbeitsheft, Berlin, 1998.
Camarinha-Matos LM, Afsarmanesh H, "Collaborative networks: a scientific discipline". In Journal of Intelligent Manufacturing, 2005, 16: 439-452.
Camarinha-Matos LM, Afsarmanesh H, Ollus M, Virtual Organizations – Systems and Practises. New York: Springer, 2005.
COBTEC – Collaborative Business Networks and Technology Platforms, Research and development program 2003-2007. http://www.vtt.fi/cobtec/files/cobtec_brochure_web.pdf, 12 July 2005.
Daenzer WF, Huber F, Systems Engineering: Methodik und Praxis. Zürich: Industrielle Organisation, 1994.
ECOLEAD – European Collaborative Networked Organisations Leadership Initiative, Our mission. http://www.ve-forum.org/default.asp?P=284, 05 May 2005.
Erpenbeck J, Kompetenzentwicklung als Forschungsaufgabe. QUEM Bulletin 2/3, 1998.
European Commission (EC), Enterprise Directorate-General of the EC, Observatory of European SMEs – SMEs in Europe. Report 7/2003, KPMG Special Services and EIM Business & Policy Research in the Netherlands in co-operation with European Network for SME Research (ENSR) and Intomart. Luxembourg: Office for Official Publications of the European Communities, 2004.
Laubacher RJ, Malone TW, MIT Scenario Working Group, Two Scenarios for 21st Century Organizations – Shifting Networks of Small Firms or All-Encompassing 'Virtual Countries'? MIT Initiative on Inventing the Organizations of the 21st Century, Working Paper 21C WP #001, 1997.
Malone TW, Laubacher RJ, "The dawn of the e-lance economy". In Harvard Business Review, Sept.-Oct. 1998: 145-152.
Müller E, Horbach S, Ackermann J, Näser P, "Production Management in Competence-cell-based Networks". In Proceedings of APE'2004 IIIrd International Conference on Advances in Production Engineering, Part I, Warsaw, Poland, 17-19 June 2004: 53-62.
Salmons J, Babitsky T, Shamrocks and Nanocorps – Business Model and Technology. Innovation to Bridge the Digital Divide. Net Impact Conference, Chapel Hill, North Carolina, 2001.
SFB457, Sonderforschungsbereich 457 Hierarchielose regionale Produktionsnetze, Finanzierungsantrag 2000, 2001, 2002, TU Chemnitz, 1999.
UNIDO – UNITED NATIONS INDUSTRIAL DEVELOPMENT ORGANIZATION, The UNIDO Cluster/Network Development Programme: The Italian Experience of Industrial Districts. http://www.unido.org/en/doc/4310, 20 February 2006.
Villarreal Lizárraga CL, Dupont L, Gourc D, Pingaud H, "Contributing to Management of shared Projects in SMEs Clusters". In Proceedings (CD-ROM) of the 18th International Conference on Production Research – ICPR, University of Salerno, Italy, 31 July-04 August 2005.

TRUST BUILDING

Simon Samwel Msanjila, Hamideh Afsarmanesh
University of Amsterdam, THE NETHERLANDS
msanjila@science.uva.nl, hamideh@science.uva.nl

To smooth the cooperation within a VBE, and to facilitate the partner selection for VOs configured in VBEs, the VBE member organizations need to trust each other. Among others, lack of trust relationships among organizations, negatively affects their information exchange and resources sharing. In small-size VBEs, organizations have the chance to get to know each, and thus can individually make their judgment on trustworthiness level of others. For large-size VBEs however, new approaches and mechanisms are required to be designed for measuring/assessing the trustworthiness level of other organizations. This paper first addresses this problem area and its challenges and then classifies it into three focus areas. It then introduces an approach for measuring the trustworthiness level of other organizations, based on both the trust criteria defined by the trustor and the past performance of the trustee. Three trust perspectives pentagon, square, and triangle, are then defined addressing the three problem focus areas.

1. INTRODUCTION

Stability and success of a strategic alliance among organizations, such as the Virtual organizations Breeding Environment (VBE), require the right balance of trust among its members. Thus, once in a network or alliance such as a VBE, organizations need suitable approaches and mechanisms to identify and measure trustworthiness of other organizations for the purpose of information exchange, resources sharing, and fruitful collaboration in VOs [Dillon, T. S. et al 2004].

A VBE refers to an association of organizations and their related supporting institutions, adhering to a base long term cooperation agreement, and adoption of common operating principles, and infrastructures, with the main goal of increasing both their chances and their preparedness towards collaboration in potential Virtual Organizations (VO) [Afsarmanesh, 2005]. In larger VBEs, members meet and need to cooperate or collaborate with little known or even unknown other members. Members collaborate in order to achieve common goals. Entering in collaboration requires a member to make decision about the trustworthiness of others.

Trust is a key concept addressed by research in many disciplines and it is gaining more importance in the new emerging information societies. In sociology, trust is related to reputation and previous interactions among individuals. The ways in which reputation for trustworthiness is established or destroyed are important in social trust relationships. According to Good [Good, D., 1988], not only will the perceivers of reputation have access to information which the reputation holder does not control, but also the manner in which both types of information are interpreted is not straightforward. Therefore, individuals wish to have complete information about the people they wish to deal with, before they deal with them [Dasgupta, P., 1988].

Please use the following format when citing this chapter:

Msanjila, S. S., Afsarmanesh, H., 2006, in IFIP International Federation for Information Processing, Volume 224, Network-Centric Collaboration and Supporting Fireworks, eds. Camarinha-Matos, L., Afsarmanesh, H., Ollus, M., (Boston: Springer), pp. 161–172.

In economics, decisions about trust are similar to decisions about taking risky choices. Individuals are presumed to be motivated to establish trust relationship with others in order to either maximize the expected gains, or minimize expected losses from their transactions [Williamson, O. E., 1985, Josang, A. et al 2004]. The critical factor in economic studies about trust is the risk management in trust relationships.

Trust in psychology is related to beliefs [Marsh, S. P. 1994]. A trusting behaviour occurs when an individual believe that there is an ambiguous path; the result of which could be good or bad [Deutsch, M. 1962, Morgan, R. M, et al 1994]. The occurrence of the good or bad result is contingent on the actions of another person. If the individual chooses to go down that path, he makes a trusting choice.

In politics and digital governments, trust is related to truth-telling. It is important for digital government, to maintain high standards of truth-telling, to avoid being associated with the poor reputation and losing trust [Sztompka, P. 1999]. Trust in governments and politics is very important to keep governments and related political parties continuing in power. However, several factors are identified to be influencing the trustworthiness level of governments towards citizens, such as reputation, performance, accountability, commitment, etc. [Sztompka, P. 1999].

In computer science, trust is related to security, reputation, and privacy. Generally, when an environment is secure it is easier to establish trust relationships among systems users, and equally, if a users respect the privacy of others personal data and sensible information, he can be seen as trustworthy [Seigneur, J.M. 2004].

Trust studies as addressed in the above disciplines shows that trustworthiness has been perceived as a probability and thus, measured as a unit less probability value. Moreover, in some studies, trust is mainly related to reputation. Trust in most disciplines also has been studied at the level of individuals and not at the level of organizations. In our approach, we address trust among "organizations" being involved in collaborative environments and specifically, within VBE environments. We have observed and pointed out that trust is multi-criteria and thus trustworthiness cannot be measured with a single value. As presented later in section 3, trustworthiness is measured for different objectives, from different perspectives, and in terms of the values of a set of trust criteria. Thus we address trust as a multi-objective and multi-actor subject, considering all necessary factors that can influence the changes of trustworthiness. More challenges will rise due to the fact that VBEs are new scientific discipline and are characterized with heterogeneity among the interests, goals, disciplines, autonomies, cultures, etc., of their members [Camarinha-matos, 2005, Shao, J. et al 2004]. Trust assessment and creation is among the important subjects that need innovative approach and mechanisms. This paper addresses the assessment and creation of trust in VBEs.

2. TRUST IN VBEs

In this section we address the question of who needs trust and the challenges that must be addressed to realize trust in VBEs. We first start with the base definitions.

2.1 Base definitions

In this section we provide definition for the following terms: trust actors, trust criteria, trustworthiness, and trust relationship.

Trust actors: refer to the two organization parties involved in a specific trust relationship. The first party is the organization that needs to assess the trustworthiness of another party and is referred to as the *trustor*. The second party is the one that needs to be trusted, and thus it will need its trustworthiness to be assessed. This party is referred to as the *trustee*.

Trust criteria: refer to the measurable elements that can establish a judgment about a given trust requirement. For example for the requirement of ICT infrastructure, the measurable trust criteria can include the storage capacity, the computing capacity, frequency of the system's security violation, network speed, etc. Every trust criteria have two attributes for its values, namely: *Trust value metrics,* which refer to the scales that identify the meaning of the measured values for the criterion, (e.g. for computing capacity can be megabyte MB/s), and *Trust value constraints, which* refer to the limits for values that separate the acceptable from unacceptable range of values (e.g. for computing capacity can be >300GB/s).

Trustworthiness: Is the trait of deserving trust and confidence. In this paper, we use the term trustworthiness to refer to the level (intensity) of trust for a trustee in a trust relationship, based on the assessment of the necessary criteria. Clearly enough, the criteria for organizations' trust assessment are varied and wide in spectrum. In our research we focus on those criteria that can be measured, and we have systematically categorized and identified these measurable items as described in section 3.2 and table 1. Trustworthiness cannot be measured directly (by a single value) rather it needs to be measured indirectly through values for a set of criteria. Namely, the level that the constraints for a given set of criteria are met determines the level of trustworthiness.

Trust relationship: A relationship is a state of connectedness among people or organizations or is a state involving mutual dealing among people or parties. The trust relationship refers to the state of connectedness between a trustor and a trustee whose intensity is characterized and based on the trustworthiness level.

2.2 Who needs trust in VBEs?

Three kinds of focus areas (FA) were identified for trust needs in VBE:

FA1- Trust among VBE members: The main aim of establishing and maintaining trust relationships among VBE members is to enhance the efficiency and success of both their cooperation within the VBE as well as their potential collaboration in VOs that will be configured within the VBE. Further to the individual member's achievements, the main criteria that influence the trustworthiness among VBE members include their roles, reputations, and membership level at the VBE as well as their past performance on activities related to the VBE. FA1 is further addressed in **section 3**.

FA2- Trust of a VBE member to the VBE and to the VBE administration: Trust of VBE members to the VBE and VBE's administration enhances the chance of members remaining loyal to the VBE, increases their willingness for active involvement in VBE, and encourages VBE members to invite and bring other valuable organizations into VBE. Among the main issues that influence the trustworthiness of the VBE and the VBE's administration, we can mention: successes in managing the VBE environments, VBE's successes in external markets and recognitions achieved through VBE's marketing and branding,, transparency of the administration procedures and rules, transparency and efficiency of members performance measurement, frequency of opportunities brokerage, and fair possibility for all VBE members to get involved in potential VOs. FA2 is further addressed in **section 4**.

FA3- Trust of a customer to the VBE: VBEs must be trusted by its customers. Customers that create opportunities in the market (to which VBE can respond by creation of VOs) must recognize and trust the VBE to accept its proposed bid. Consumers (end users of VBE results) also need to trust a VBE in order to decide positively on purchasing or accepting VBE's products and services. FA3 is further addressed in **section 5**.

2.3 Trust challenges in VBEs

In relation to trust studies in VBEs, we identified three challenges that must be well addressed in order for the identified trust needs (section 2.2) to be realized.

Challenge 1:- Causality: A main challenge in trust study is its causality. The future trustworthiness of a VBE member is "causally" related to its role and behavior at present, and actions it has performed and events it has caused in the past. Therefore, a part of trust engineering in VBEs is intended to support the decision-making about future trustworthiness of a member, while the information needed for this estimation mostly belongs to the past.

Challenge 2:- Transparency and fairness: One more challenge in assessment of trustworthiness of VBE members is its transparency and fairness to its stakeholders. Each step taken for entire trust assessment process must be clear and transparent to all involved VBE members. For fairness, the steps taken and the approach used for trust assessment must accompany some (formal) reasoning, and also the information used for the assessment must be accredited/certified to avoid personal (subjective) judgment and biases.

Challenge 3:- Complexity: Another challenge in trust study is to handle the complexity of multi-objective, multi-perspective, and multi-criteria nature of trust and trustworthiness in VBEs. Trust is not a single concept [Castelfranchi, 2000] that can be applied to all cases, for trust-based decision making, and its measurements are subjected to both the purpose of the trust relationship, and the specific actors involved. Every case is different and consists of its own specific set of criteria to be considered for estimating trustworthiness.

3. ASSESSING AND CREATING TRUST AMONG MEMBERS

In this section we address the question on how VBE members can trust each other and how their trustworthiness can be assessed. Thus, as described in section 2.2, FA1 is further addressed here.

3.1 Trust perspective pentagon for FA1

There are five possible trust perspectives [[Ratnasingam, 2005]] that a trustor can assume as primary aspects when assessing trustworthiness of the trustee. In addition to providing mechanisms for assessing the trustworthiness, information about every perspective based on generated/specified criteria must also be provided. When a

VBE member needs to trust another VBE member, support for acquiring the needed information and mechanisms to acquire the information in every preferred element must be provided as indicated in trust perspective pentagon (Figure 1).

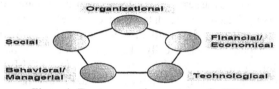

Figure 1: Trust perspective pentagon for FA1.

3.2 "BASE" and "SPECIFIC" trust criteria for FA1

A VBE member will need to be trusted in two different cases: when applying to become a VBE member (base), and when it has to apply (or to be selected) to take a specific task in cooperation in VBE (e.g. to become an administrator) or in collaboration in VO (e.g. to become a VO partner or VO planner). In each case, there might be different trust criteria for assessing the trustworthiness (Table 1).

Perspective	Requirements	BASE Criteria
1. Organizational	Organizational strength	Size of an organization
		Organization coverage
		Competences
		Personnel expertise
2. Social	Community participation	Activities participated
		Community service contribution
	Community compliance	Community standards complied
3. Financial / Economical	Capital	Cash
		Physical capital
		Operational capital
	Financial stability	Cash in
		Cash out
		Profit/Loss
		Operational costs
	VO -Collaboration based financial stability	Cash in
		Cash out
		Profit/Loss
	Financial standards	Auditing standards
		Auditing frequency
4. Technological	ICT- Infrastructure	Network speed (Broadband)
		Interoperability
		Availability
	Technology standards	Protocol supported
		Software standards
		Hardware standards
		Security standards
	Platforms	Operating systems
		Programming languages
	Platform experience	Applied in VOs
		External project applied
		Duration held
5. Managerial / Behavioural	Stable management	Years in power
		Management structure
		Frequency of power change
	VO-Collaborative behaviour	VO opportunistic behaviour occurred
		VO successful collaborations
		VO participation as organizer/leader
	Reliability	Quality
		Adherence to delivery dates

Table 1: Examples of base trust criteria.

BASE trust criteria refer to those criteria that must be complied (at least at the minimum acceptable level) by all members in the VBE. These criteria are identified by trust experts, a-prior to the establishment of the VBE, but can be updated when needed. The trustworthiness assessment is done when the organization is applying for VBE membership based on the data filled on base trust (application forms) questionnaires. The collected data will also be stored in the VBE management system and will be updated periodically. Table 1 shows some base trust criteria identified with this study and validated by experts in ECOLEAD project and existing VBEs (VF in Germany, Virfebras in Brazil, and IECOS in Mexico). SPECIFIC trust criteria refer to those criteria that are generated and applied for a specific trust objective. Section 3.2 describes how to generated specific trust criteria.

3.3 Generating SPECIFIC trust criteria

Generating specific trust criteria needs to be achieved by trust experts knowledgeable about the VBE. At the highest level the process of establishing trust relationship is characterized by a set of trust objectives. Each of these trust objectives is characterized by a set of trust perspectives. Trust perspectives for FA1 are shown in Fig 1. Based on the trust objective and preferred trust perspective, trust requirements are then identified (Fig. 2). Also, for each requirement, the specific criteria are identified. Metrics and constraints for each criterion are then specified.

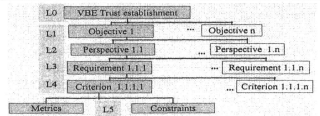

Figure 2: Abstraction hierarchy for the trust establishment in VBEs.

To further describe our approach, consider the case where the *partner selection process* at the VBE has made a list of suggestive VBE members that can fulfill VO requirements. Then, the planner of that VO needs to measure the trustworthiness of the suggested VBE members for invitation decision. Suppose that VO is focused on online selling of movies and therefore, trusting the capacity of the ICT infrastructure for each VBE member that may be invited to VO is important requirements and specifically, its download supporting capacity must be totally trusted. Figure 3 shows an example on how trust criteria are generated.

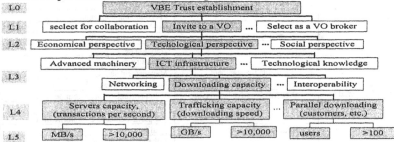

Figure 3: Generating specific trust criteria for assessing ICT-I based trustworthiness.

3.4 Analysis of relations among criteria

In order to perform the trustworthiness assessment efficiently, inter-relations among the criteria must be studied and well understood. While the inter-relations among the pre-defined "base" trust criteria can be developed a-prior to the VBE establishment, and suggested to the trustor in the VBE, the trustor may also require to dynamically defining "specific" criteria for which their inter-relations with other criteria must be dynamically defined. In our approach we use causal relations among the criteria to represent their inter-relations. To present this approach, consider the example in figure 3. Figure 4 shows a causal diagram including both the "specific criteria and selected base criteria". Factors that also influence the behavior of criteria must be identified and represented in the causal diagram. Factors (e.g. request rate, queuing time, etc.) must also be measurable, but they cannot stand alone or become criteria themselves. In the causal diagram, the plus sign (+) indicate that the increase or decrease of the first factor/criteria causes the increase or decrease of the second factor/criteria, and the minus sign (-) indicate that the increase or decrease of the first factor/criterion causes the decrease or increase of the second factor/criterion.

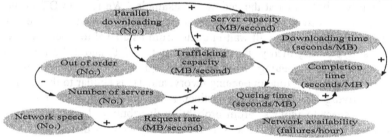

Figure 4: Qualitative analysis of relations among criteria using causal diagram.

3.5 Formal representation of relations among criteria/factors

We use the causal effect as in figure 5 to represent the relations among criteria in form of mathematical equations. Using the reasoning (approach as addressed in section 3.4), the plus sign (+) in the causal diagram represents either addition or multiplication, and the minus sign (-) represents subtraction or division depending on the metrics that scale the criteria. The selection of the correct arithmetic operator depends on the balance of dimensions (when complex relations are involved, dimension analysis[1] can be applied). In developing equations, arrows that are directed to the respective factor/criterion are considered for the equation. For illustration purposes (short forms in table 1), we provide three examples.

Example 1: Formulating equation for trafficking capacity (TC)

We refer to TC as the number of movies (expressed in Megabyte MB or Gigabyte GB) that can be downloaded in a specified amount of time. Three factors influence the TC: number of server (**NS**), server capacity (**SC**), and parallel downloading (**PD**). Assuming that each server can support a certain number of requests, and each request has certain size, the product of these factors balances the dimensions of the equation as shown in equation 1. The derivative of equation (1)

---

[1] Checking the correctness of an equation which you have derived after some algebraic manipulation:
http://www.physics.uoguelph.ca/tutorials/dimanaly/

represents the rate of change of each of the factor with respect to time and the relations among the changes (equation 2). The integration of equation 2 provides the accumulation of TC, which represents the total number of movies that can be downloaded for a period of time t1 to t2 (equation 3).

$$TC = NS * PD * SC \tag{1}$$

$$\frac{d}{dt}TC = (PD * SC)\frac{d}{dt}NS + (PD * NS)\frac{d}{dt}SC + (SC * NS)\frac{d}{dt}PD \tag{2}$$

$$\int_{t1}^{t2}\left(\frac{d}{dt}TC\right) = \int_{t1}^{t2}\left((PD * SC)\frac{d}{dt}NS\right) + \int_{t1}^{t2}\left((PD * NS)\frac{d}{dt}SC\right) + \int_{t1}^{t2}\left((SC * NS)\frac{d}{dt}PD\right) \tag{3}$$

Example 2: Formulating equation for completion time (CT)

Similar to example one, the respective three equations for CT are as below:

$$CT = QT + DT \quad (4), \quad \frac{d}{dt}CT = \frac{d}{dt}QT + \frac{d}{dt}DT \quad (5), \text{ and } \quad \int_{t1}^{t2}\left(\frac{d}{dt}CT\right) = \int_{t1}^{t2}\left(\frac{d}{dt}QT\right) + \int_{t1}^{t2}\left(\frac{d}{dt}DT\right) \tag{6}$$

Where **QT** is queuing time and **DT** is downloading time,

Example 3: Formulating equation for queuing time and processing time

For these criteria we applied queuing theory[2] to formulate their respective equations. However, it is also possible to formulate the equation using the approach applied earlier as it will be shown at the end of this example. We refer to DT as the time (can be average) needed to download a specified number of movies. We refer to QT as the period that a request will wait in queue from its arrival to when its download starts. Using queuing theory, the three factors: DT, QT, and TC are statistically related. Comparing to queuing theory terms, DT is similar to the service time, QT is the same as the queuing time in queuing theory, and TC is similar to the service rate. Requests arriving for download are distinct. Also, the downloading for movies is distinct in respect to movies. From probability distribution, both the RR and TC follow Poisson distribution[3]. The DT follows exponential distribution[4] since it measures the time required to process a single job. Based on queuing theory definitions, the equations for DT and QT are as shown in equations (7) and (8). For this case, request rate (**RR**) is similar to the arrival rate in queuing theory.

$$DT = \frac{1}{TC} \quad (7) \quad \text{and} \quad QT = \frac{RR}{(TC - RR)TC} \tag{8}$$

Consider the relations among these factors in the causal diagram (figure 3). TC is negatively related to DT and thus, proves the fact that a minus sign can be represented as a division in the mathematical equation as in equation (7). The same reason applies for TC to QT in equation (8). RR is positively related to QT but in the equation its representation is a special case. Although it is in the quotient part of equation (8), the RR in the quotient is negated to indicate that it is positively related to QT. Completion time (**CT**) in principle is the sum of DT and QT, which match the relations as indicated in the causal diagram and also from queuing theory. Therefore, equation (9) shows the CT. Thus CT equation is also written as follows:

$$CT = \frac{1}{PC - RR} \tag{9}$$

The rates of change and as well the accumulations equation for CT, QT and DT can be generated in same way as in equations (2), (3), (5) and (6).

---

[2] http://www.eventhelix.com/RealtimeMantra/CongestionControl/m_m_1_queue.htm
[3] http://www.itl.nist.gov/div898/handbook/eda/section3/eda366j.htm
[4] http://www.itl.nist.gov/div898/handbook/eda/section3/eda3667.htm

3.6 Quantitative trustworthiness assessment

Based on the selected *base trust criteria*, *specific trust criteria*, and the *collected data*, trustworthiness of an organization can be assessed. When, trustworthiness needs to be forecasted to enable long-term assessment, simulation can be applied, using the developed equations. Also, when a large amount of data must be analyzed fast and efficiently, simulation is suggested. For the purpose of this paper, a simulation model was developed in Powersim to study the behavior of CT, TC, and QT. Here, we assumed that we have data for a number of past years. In this example, we assume that the trustworthiness of this VBE member can be assessed (and forecasted) based on its capability to support short time downloading. For this experiment (figure 6), the following parameters were applied: RR follows Poisson distribution with mean 1000MB and seed 0GB, number of PD as 10 per server for the 5 servers each supporting 10MB/s.

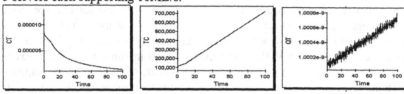

Figure 6: Simulation results for trustworthiness assessment based on TC, CT and QT

From the results presented in Figure 6, trustworthiness can be assessed and decisions can be made about when in future an organization reaches a level of time for downloading, in order to be technically trusted. Nevertheless, in real cases clearly this aspect provides only one among several criteria that are considered for useful trustworthiness assessment.

4. CREATING TRUST FOR VBE MEMBERS TO THE VBE

In this section we address the question on how VBE members can trust the VBE and the VBE administration. Thus, FA2, as described in section 2.2, is further addressed in this section.

4.1 Trust perspective square for FA2

There are four trust perspectives that a VBE member can assume as primary aspects when assessing trustworthiness of the VBE and the VBE administration (Fig 7). The VBE member must be supported by being provided the mechanisms to access the needed information on the preferred trust perspective stored in the VBE.

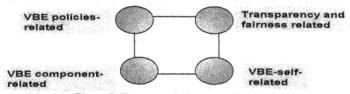

Figure 7: Trust perspective square for FA2

4.2 Trust criteria for assessing trustworthiness of VBE and its administration

A VBE member, in different cases, will need to be convinced to trust the VBE and the VBE administration. For example, the VBE member will compete to win a chance for participation in VOs within the VBEs. For any decision made, VBE members must be convinced on why the selected members qualify than others. We suggest providing information about the following basic criteria in each perspective:

VBE policy related perspective: Policy is plan of action to guide decisions and actions. Policies in short can be understood as political, management, financial, and administrative mechanisms arranged to reach explicit goals. In VBE aspects and related to trust, policies that must be accessible to members include the following:

- Cooperation rules
- Governance principles
- Bylaws

Transparency and fairness related perspective: The VBE administration must be transparent and fair to all VBE members. For this purpose the following information must therefore be accessible by all VBE members:

- Trustworthiness measures
- Performance measures
- Partner selection processes
- Incentives and rewards

VBE component related perspective: Refers the components that constitute the VBE. The main component of a VBE is its members. VOs in some cases, when existing, become components of the respective VBE. Another, component is the supporting institutions. A member that wants to assess trustworthiness of a VBE and its administration might possibly prefer information related to VBE structure and its components. We suggest that a member can be provided with information about:

- VBE members restricted profiles
- VBE supporting institution restricted profiles
- VO restricted profiles, etc.

VBE-self related perspective: When it comes to trusting a VBE as whole, VBE members must also be supported with information that can build a positive picture about the VBE. We suggest providing information about the following:

- Member restricted performance history
- VBE self restricted profile
- VBE performance history
- VO performance history

5. CREATING TRUST FOR CUSTOMER TO THE VBE

In this section we address the question on how an external organization can trust the VBE. Thus, FA3, as described in section 2.2, is further addressed in this section.

5.1 Trust perspective triangle for FA3

There are three trust perspectives that a customer can assume as primary aspects when assessing trustworthiness of the VBE (Fig 8). Customers (section 2.2) must be provided with relevant information based on their preferred trust perspectives.

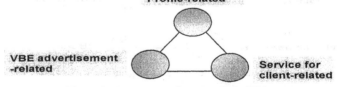

Figure 8: Trust perspective triangle for FA3

5.2 Trust criteria for assessing trustworthiness of a VBE

A customer, when selecting a VBE, (e.g. when a customer wants to provide a tender or need to recommend a VBE for an opportunity), will need to trust the VBE. In this paper, we recommend providing the customer with the following information:

Profile related perspective: This information will enable the customer to understand the constituents of the VBE and its related competences. This includes:

- VBE public profile including list of members and list of VOs,
- VO public profile including partners' information and VO performances,
- VBE members public profiles,
- Previous product/service recognitions or acknowledgements,
- Specific previous achievements.

VBE advertisement related perspective: As in normal business world, VBEs will also advertise their products and services (offered through VOs) to the market. Information on advertisements that are usually made can indicate the capability of the VBE to reach customers. Such information can include the following:

- News letters,
- Copy of advertisements in the media,
- Link of advertisements in various websites.

Service for client related perspective: A customer can be convinced to trust the VBE based on how it will be supported when acquiring the services. This includes:

- Customer portal,
- Customer registration functions.

6. REFLECTION ON THE TRUST CHALLENGES IN VBEs

In section 2.3, three trust challenges were identified namely: *causality, transparency and fairness, and complexity*. In this work causality was addressed with the use of causal analysis about past behavior of the member based on the causal relations among the criteria. The use of past performance of members, the VBE and its administration indicates how causally their today and future trust is influenced by the past. Transparency and fairness is addressed by enabling trustors, and trust experts to formally reason (based mathematical formulas) for the trustworthiness assessment (section 3). The use of transparency and fairness measure, governance rules, cooperation rules and bylaws, also enhance the transparency and fairness (section 4). The suggested approach also, addresses the trust complexity by use of multi- objective, perspective, and criteria in the trustworthiness assessment.

7. CONCLUSION AND FURTHER WORKS

VBEs have proved promising for enhancing survivability of organizations, especially SMEs, in the current market with highly volatile opportunities and requirements. VBE is a strategic alliance, providing a cooperative environment that aims at enhancing organizations' preparedness for getting involved in potential virtual organizations. Among the important preparedness aspects to be supported within the VBEs, are the creating, assessing, and managing trust [Camarinha-Matos, L. M.*, et al 2005].

In this paper, three main focus areas for trust in VBEs were identified. Approaches for assessing and creating trust, considering the identified challenges were introduced. The kinds of information that a trustor needs to use in order to assess the trustworthiness level of a trustee were also addressed. Thus, this paper has contributed to the subject of assessing and creating trust in VBEs, which can also be applicable to the VO environments.

The paper has addressed the challenging tasks of assessing and creating trust in VBEs. Other important areas of trust (trust management) studies such as trust relationship establishment and trust modeling are not addressed in this paper, but it is an important subject in our trust studies in the ECOLEAD project, and the topics of forthcoming papers. Furthermore, some other collaborative environments that their memberships involve individuals, such as the Professional Virtual Community (PVC) and Virtual team (VT), are not addressed in this paper. The trust assessment and creation approaches are in fact very different for organizations than for individuals.

Acknowledgement: This work was supported in part by the ECOLEAD project funded by the European Commission. The authors thank the valuable contributions of their partners in the ECOLEAD consortium.

8. REFERENCES

1.   Afsarmanesh H., Camarinha-Matos L., A framework for management of virtual organization breeding environments, in Collaorative Networks and their Breeding Environments, Springer, 2005, pp. 35-49.
2.   Camarinha-Matos, L. M*., Silveri, I., Afsarmanesh, H., & Oliveira, A. I., Towards a Framework for Creation of Dynamic Virtual Organizations, in Collaborative Networks and their Breeding Environments, Springer, 2005, pp. 69-81.
3.   Camarinha-Matos, L., Afsarmanesh, H. Collaborative networks: A new scientific discipline. In the international journal of Intelligent Manufacturing. Springer, Volume 16, 2005
4.   Castelfranchi, C., Falcone, R. Trust Is Much More than Subjective Probability: Mental Components and Sources of Trust. In proceedings of the 33rd Hawaii International Conference on System Sciences – 2000
5.   Dasgupta, P. Trust as a Commodity. In Trust:. Making and Breaking Cooperative Relations, 1988.
6.   Deutsch, M. Cooperation and Trust: Some Theoretical Notes. In proceedings of Nebraska Symposium on Motivation. Nebraska University Press, 1962.
7.   Dillon, T. S., Chang, E., Hussain, F. Framework for a trusted Environment for virtual collaboration. In Proceedings of the 5th International Conference on Advances in Web-Age Information Management, Dalian, China, 2004.
8.   Good, D. Individuals, Interpersonal Relations, and Trust. In Trust: Making and Breaking Cooperative Relations, 1988.
9.   Josang, A., Lo Presti, S. Analysing the relationship between risk and trust. In the proceedings of trust management second international conference. Oxford, UK, 2004.
10. Marsh, S. "Formalising Trust as a Computational Concept", 1994.
11. Morgan, R. M, Hunt, A. D. The commitment-trust theory of relationship marketing. In the journal of marketing, Vol 58, No. 3, 1994.
12. Ratnasingam, P. Trust in inter-organizational exchanges: a case study in business to business electronic commerce. In the journal of Decision Support System, Vol. 39 , 2005.
13. Seigneur, J.M. & Jensen, C.D. (2004). Trading Privacy for Trust. In proceedings of second Trust Management International Conference, UK, 2004,
14. Shao, J., Gray, W. A., Fiddian, N. J., Deora, V., Shercliff, V., Stockreisser, P. J. Supporting Formation and Operation of Virtual Organizations in a Grid Environment. In proceedings of the UK e-Science All Hands Meeting 2004, Nottingham UK.
15. Sztompka, P. Trust: A Sociological Theory. Cambridge, UK: Cambridge University Press, 1999.
16. Williamson, O. E. The Economic Institutions of Capitalism. The Free Press. New York, 1985.

18

TRUST BUILDING FOR ENHANCING COLLABORATION IN VIRTUAL ORGANIZATIONS

István Mezgár
Computer and Automation Research Institute
Hungarian Academy of Science
Budapest, HUNGARY
(E-mail): mezgar@sztaki.hu
and
Department of Production Informatics, Management and Control
Budapest University of Technology and Economics

Virtual organizations play an important role in today's economy, as they are able to adapt themselves to the turbulent market environments. Team work and collaboration are main characteristics of virtual organizations, so the contacts among human beings have outstanding importance. A very important element of this human contact is trust. Trust building in virtual organizations has special characteristics, it is influenced among others by the type of media and communication device, and also by the duration of cooperation. The paper discusses the role of trust and trust building in the operation of virtual organizations from these aspects.

1. INTODUCTION

Based on the results of the information and communications technologies (ICTs), a new "digital" economy is arising. This new economy needs a new set of rules and values, which determine the behavior of its actors. In this dynamic and turbulent environment that requires flexible and fast responses to changing business needs organizations have to respond by adopting decentralized, team-based, and distributed structures variously described in the literature as virtual-, networked-, cluster- and resilient virtual organizations. One main aspect of this approach is that organizations in this environment are networked, i.e. inter-linked on various levels through the use of different networking technologies. Today besides the Internet new solutions are offered, the different types of mobile/wireless networks.

In this new organizational environment new methods and techniques of trust building has to be developed, as the conventional rules cannot be applied. The paper introduces the ways of building trust, the most effective approaches using different media, and also outlines the trends of this field.

Please use the following format when citing this chapter:

Mezgár, I., 2006, in IFIP International Federation for Information Processing, Volume 224, Network-Centric Collaboration and Supporting Fireworks, eds. Camarinha-Matos, L., Afsarmanesh, H., Ollus, M., (Boston: Springer), pp. 173–180.

2. VIRTUAL ORGANIZATIONS AND COLLABORATION

2.1 Main Characteristics of VO

A virtual organization (VO) refers to a temporary or permanent collection of geographically dispersed individuals, groups, organizational units or entire organizations that depend on electronic linking in order to complete the production process. They are usually working by computer e-mail and groupware while appearing to others to be a single, unified organization with a real physical location. A VO can be considered as a temporary, culturally diverse, geographically dispersed, electronically communicating group of organizations, people. The virtual corporation, virtual-, real time -, enterprise cover mainly the same term as VO.

A networked organization has multiple leaders, lots of informal links and interacting levels. Mutual links and reciprocity across the links are what makes networks work. Because of a lack of formal rules, procedures, clear reporting relationships, and norms, more extensive informal communication is required, so a key feature of virtual organizations is a high degree of this informal communication.

As the base of virtual organizations are the interdependent, separate production teams/units, the cooperation and collaboration has of vital importance. The structure, the communication systems and the collaborating people/teams/organizations that define today's organizations characteristics must be harmonized to accomplish complex, demanding tasks. The collaboration is done through different media according to the actual demands of the tasks. The conventional tools are the telephone, fax, writing letters. On the next level are the computer network-based solutions e.g. e-mail, ftp, telnet. A higher quality of communication media is the WEB-based communication solutions. Through WEB pages a secure, easy and fast communication can be realized.

A new way of connection is the application of different mobile wireless technologies for communication. Mobile wireless technology means mobility, namely individuals are available independently from location and time (24/7/365 availability). This mobility is an important attribute of today's organizations and people.

2.2. Collaboration in Virtual Organization

Collaboration is basic factor of VO operation so it is important to define the differences among the different types of techniques and approaches applied in team work. Himmelman developed a hierarchy of partnerships (Himmelman, 1997). One level of the hierarchy is distinguished from the next level by the amount of trust, time, and personal/group interests needed to establish and maintain the partnership. In Himmelman's framework, networking, coordinating, cooperating, and collaborating mean different things and build on each other. While closely related to networking, collaboration can be understood as a process that exploits a networked environment.

The qualitative difference between collaboration and cooperation is based upon the willingness of organizations/individuals to enhance each other's capacity for mutual benefit and to achieve a common purpose. Collaboration is a relationship in which each organization wants to help its partners become better at what they do.

In order to realize these goals different practical control/organizational concepts, models and techniques are implemented. Swarm Intelligence (SI) is the property of a system whereby the collective behaviours of (unsophisticated) agents interacting locally with their environment cause coherent functional global patterns to emerge. SI provides a basis with which it is possible to explore collective (or distributed) problem solving without centralized control or the provision of a global model.

3. TRUST BUILDING IN VIRTUAL ORGANIZATIONS

3.1 Definition and Forms of Trust

Collaboration is main characteristics of the virtual organizations, so the contacts among the users, the human beings have outstanding importance. A very important element of this human contact is trust. In a networked organization, trust is the atmosphere, the medium in which actors are moving, so it is a basic building block of the communication among people and systems too. Trust is the base of cooperation, the normal behavior of the human being in the society. The ability of enterprises to form networked systems depends on the existing level of trust in the society and on the capital of society (Fukuyama, 1995). As the rate of cooperation is increasing in all fields of life, the importance of trust is evolving even faster.

Trust can be defined as a psychological condition comprising the trustor's intention to accept vulnerability based upon positive expectations of the trustee's intentions or behaviour (Rousseau et al., 1998). Those positive expectations are based upon the trustor's cognitive and affective evaluations of the trustee and the system/world as well as of the disposition of the trustor to trust. Trust is a psychological condition (interpreted in terms of expectation, attitude, willingness, perceived probability). Trust can cause or result from trusting behaviour (e.g., co-operation, taking a risk) but is not behaviour itself.

The following components are included into most definitions of trust (Harrison, McKnight and Chervany, 1996)::

- willingness to be vulnerable / to rely,
- confident, positive expectation / positive attitude towards others,
- risk and interdependence as necessary conditions.

Trust appears in different forms. According to different authors (e.g. Luhman, 1979) trust has forms such as

1. Intrapersonal trust - trust in one's own abilities; self-confidence basic trust (in others).
2. Interpersonal trust - expectation based on cognitive and affective evaluation of the partners; in primary relationships (e.g., family) and non-primary relationships (e.g., business partners).
3. System trust - trust in depersonalised systems/world that function independently (e.g., economic system, regulations, legal system, technology); requires voluntary abandonment of control and knowledge (Luhman 1979).
4. Object trust - trust in non-social objects; trust in its correct functioning (e.g. in an electronic device).

3.2 Approches and Factors of Trust-Building

In building trust there are two approaches; information technology approach and human centered approach, based on culture, and morality. Information technology approach means that security has to increase by different architectures, protocols, certifications, cryptography, authentication procedures and standards and this increased security generates the trust of users. The feeling of security experienced by a user of an interactive system does not depend on technical security measures alone. Other (psychological) factors can play a determining role; the user's feeling of control can be one of these factors. From this aspect user interface has the main role, i.e. the menu structure, the messages send for the user by the system.

3.2.1 Technical side of Trust

Approaching security from the side of trust, security is the set of different services, mechanism and software and hardware tools for generating trust with pure technology. More generally security is a condition that results from the establishment and maintenance of protective measures that ensure a state of inviolability from hostile acts or influences. Approaching the term security from from human side a computer is secure if a user can trust it.

At different levels different security solutions have to be applied, and these separate parts have to cover the entire system consistently. The building blocks, elements of security are the security services and the security mechanisms. The following services form together the sense of "trust" for a human being who uses a service, or a given equipment (Menezes, 1996):

- Confidentiality: Protects against disclosure to unauthorised identities.
- Integrity: Protects from unauthorised data alteration.
- Authentication: Provides assurance of someone's identity.
- Access control: Protects against unauthorised use.
- Non-repudiation: Protects against originator of communications later denying it.

The means for achieving these properties depends on the collection of security mechanisms that supply security services, on the correct implementation of these mechanisms, and how these mechanisms are used.

3.2.2 Human side of trust-building process

Trust is a dynamic process and it alters based on experience. Trusting process begins when an individual perceives indications that suggest a person/organization may be worthy of trust. These indications can include behaviors such as manners, professionalism and sensitivity and these forms are designed to represent trustworthiness. These formal claims to trustworthiness become strengthened over time and are eventually transformed into "character traits," such as dependability, reliability and honesty.

It has to be analyzed why people feel safe and secure, what causes these feelings. The hypothesis of D'Hertefelt (D'Hertefelt, 2000) was that "The feeling of security experienced by a user of an interactive system is determined by the user's feeling of control of the interactive system". The more a user feels in control of an interactive program, the more the user will trust the site, the program.

3.2.3 Important factors of trust building

Today the different types of networked organizations need new types of cooperation as the members of the working teams are geographically (physically) separated, they use shared documents, communicate through e-mail, and high quality audio and video channels. These teams are called as "virtual teams" as they never meat personally, they have no face-to-face (FTF) contact. The work of teams without FTF contact is less effective and reliable based on the observation stated by Handy "trust needs touch" (Handy, 1995). According to case studies, it is evidence that trust of virtual team members is significantly lower than trust in conventional teams (Rocco, Finholt, Hofer, and Herbsleb, 2001). In other experiments where interaction was primarily via email, very similar results have gained as in geographically distributed teams (Jarvenpaa and Leidner, 1999)

In an experiment introduced in (Bos, 2002) four media types were compared: chat (text), phone conference, videoconference and face-to- face. Chat was significantly worse than each of the other three conditions, but audio and video did as well as face-to-face in overall cooperation, and were a definite improvement over text-chat only CMC. However, these two channels still showed evidence of delayed trust, in that they took longer to reach high levels of co-operation.

The process of building trust is slow; trust is formed gradually, it takes quite a lot of time and repeated positive experiences (Cheskin, 1999). On-line trust can be described as a kind of human relationship. The initial stage is that of interest and distrust; there has to be a motivation, a need, to get interested in the service, or co-working. In subsequent phases the trust will evolve or in case of negative experiences the cooperation will terminate.

Trust is depending on the time span of cooperation and the type of connection as well. It can be stated that there are differences in trust building process in short-term and long-term relationships. In case of short-term relationships trust must be achieved quickly, and then maintain with no, or rare face-to-face interaction. The members of these teams must assume that other remote team members are trustworthy, and then later on modify their assumptions according their positive or negative experiences.

In long-term relationships there are four factors that are influencing trust building (Rocco, Finholt, Hofer, and Herbsleb, 2001):

- greater investment in building trustworthy relationships,
- more time to establish trustworthiness through routines and culture,
- more communication channels,
- trust formation may assume a higher priority.

Latest researches show if people meet before using computer-mediated communication (CMC), they trust each other, as trust is being established through touch. In case participants do not meet formerly but they initiate various getting-acquainted activities over a network, trust is much higher than if they do nothing before, nearly as good as a prior meeting. Using chat rooms and forums to get acquainted is nearly as good as meeting, and "even just seeing a picture is better than nothing" (Zheng, et. al, 2002).

4. TECHNOLOGIES AND TOOLS OF TRUST BUILDING

4.1 Generating Trust by Human-Computer Interfaces

As a communication/information system term an interface is the point of communication between two or more processes, persons, or other physical entities. Interfaces are the key points for gaining the trust of the user/customer. They are the first connection point between the user and the system, identification of the users take place at this point (e.g. password input, fingerprint reader, smart card reader), so they have to be designed very carefully.

Different new types of interfaces are in research phase. Interaction has to be extended with more senses (touch, smell, and taste) and parallel make better use of the senses used today (hearing and vision) by exploring peripheral vision and ambient listening. All Senses Communication would be a way to enhance the communication with other entities (humans or machines) using a combination of several present or future senses of humans. Multimodal systems (Oviatt, 2002) process two or more combined user input modes— such as speech, pen, touch, manual gestures, gaze, and head and body movements— in a coordinated manner with multimedia system output. This class of systems represents a new direction for computing, and a paradigm shift away from conventional interfaces to the collaborative multimodal interfaces.

4.2 Generating Trust by Security Servicies

The security mechanisms provide with their correct implementation and usage the proper operation of security services. Security mechanisms are e.g. encryption, digital signatures and checksums/hash algorithms:

- Encryption is used to provide confidentiality, and also can provide authentication and integrity protection.
- Digital signatures are used to provide authentication, integrity protection, and non-repudiation.
- Checksums/hash algorithms are used to provide integrity protection and can provide authentication.

In the followings some solutions will be introduced how these mechanisms are applied in the practice to achieve the proper level of trust.

4.2.1 Confidentiality

The main factor of trust is confidentiality that can be achieved by technologies that convert/hide the data, text into a form that cannot be interpreted by unauthorized persons. Encryption is the major technique in generating confidentiality. Encryption is transforming the message to a ciphertext such that an enemy who monitors the ciphertext can not determine the message sent (Schneier, 1996).

Public key infrastructure (PKI) is the most widely applied technology on public networks such as the Internet. PKI is a framework encompassing the laws, policies, standards, hardware, and software to provide and manage the use of public key cryptography. This is a method of encryption that uses a pair of mathematically related keys: a public key and a corresponding private key. Either key can be used to encrypt data, but the corresponding key must be used to decrypt it. This method is also called assymmetric encryption.

4.2.2 Integrity

A message integrity check ensures that information has not been altered message in transit by unauthorized persons in a way that is not detectable by authorized users. In combination with a key, a message integrity check (or checksum, or keyed hash) insures that only the holders of the proper key is able to modify a message in transit without detection.

Digital signature is a data that binds a sender's identity to the information being sent. Digital signature may be tied with any message, file, or other digitally encoded information, or transmitted separately. Digital signatures are used in public key environments and provide non-repudiation and integrity services.

4.2.3 Authentication

Authentication is the process of identifying an individual. The typical computer based methods involve user ID/password, biometric templates or digitally signing a set of bytes using a keyed hash. Authentication usually relies on either direct knowledge of the other entity (shared symmetric key or possession of the other person's public key), or third party schemes. Authorization is the process of giving permission for a user to access to network resources after the user has been authenticated through e.g. username and password. The type of information and services the user can access depends on the user's authorization level.

4.2.4 Identification - Smart cards

There is a strong need for a tool that can fulfil the functions connected to trustworthy services. Smart card (SC) technology can offer a solution for current problems of secure communication by fulfilling simultaneously the main demands of identification (e.g. using biometric templates), security (including cryptographic features) and authenticity besides the functions of the actual application. Smart cards are bankcard size plastic plates that contain a chip. This chip can be programmed, can store different data and has all the basic functions of a computer.

5. CONCLUSIONS

Virtual organizations are main elements of the Information and Knowledge Society. These organizations apply ICT very intensive both for internal and external cooperation in order to react flexible to the changing business environment. Collaboration and communication are two basic building blocks of virtual organizations and collaboration relies on trust among working teams and organizations, so the importance of trust is increasing very fast. As it is pointed out by different analysis based on real-life statistics, when users do not trust a system/service they do not use it.

Those methods, technologies and tools that raise the level of trust among the collaborating partners or among the infocom systems and human beings (e.g. multimodal interfaces, all senses communication, encryption) have to be developed systematically. It is vital to introduce these technologies into the operation of virtual organizations, even by slightly changing their culture or organizational structures.

6. REFERENCES

Bos, N.D., Olson, J.S., Gergle, D., Olson, G.M., & Wright, Z. (2002). Effects of four computer-mediated channels on trust development. In *Proceedings of CHI 2002*. New York: ACM Press.

Cheskin, (1999), eCommerce Trust, A joint research study with Studio Archetype/Sapient and Cheskin, January, http://www.cheskin.com/p/ar.asp?mlid=7&arid=10&art=0

D'Hertefelt, S. (2000). Trust and the perception of security, http://www.interactionarchitect.com/research/report20000103shd.htm

Fukuyama, Francis, (1995). Trust – The social virtues and the creation of prosperity, The Free Press, New York,.

Handy, C. (1995). Trust and the virtual organization, *Harvard Business Review*. 73(3), 40-50.

Harrison, D., McKnight N. and L. Chervany. (1996), "The Meanings of Trust" *University of Minnesota Management Information Systems Research Center (MISRC)*, Working Paper. 96-04.

Himmelman, A. T. (1997). *Devolution as an experiment in citizen governancy: Multi-organizational partnerships and democratic revolutions*, Working Paper for the Fourth International Conference on Multi-Organizational Partnerships and Cooperative Strategy Oxford University, 8-10 July 1997, Retrieved October 16, 2004, from Community Building Resource Exchange Web site: http://www.commbuild.org/documents/himmdevo.html.

Jarvenpaa, S. L. and D. E. Leidner. (1999). Communication and Trust in Global Virtual Teams, Organization Science, 10(6), 791-815.

Luhman, N. (1979). *Trust and power*. Chichester: Wiley.

McAllister, D. J. (1995). Affect- and cognition-based trust as foundations for interpersonal cooperation in organizations, *Academy of Management Journal*, 38, 1, 24-59.

Menezes, A.P. van Oorschot, and S. Vanstone, (1996). *Handbook of Applied Cryptography*, CRC Press.

Oviatt, S., (2002) Multimodal Interfaces, in Handbook of Human-Computer Interaction, (ed. J. Jacko & A. Sears), Chapter 14, Lawrence Erlbaum: New Jersey, 2002.

Rocco, E., Finholt, T.A., Hofer, E.C., & Herbsleb, J.D. (2001, April). Out of sight, short of trust, Presentation at the Founding Conference of the European Academy of Management. Barcelona, Spain.

Rousseau, D. M., Sitkin, S. B., Burt, R., and Camerer, C. (1998), Not so different after all: A cross-disciplinary view of trust. Academy of Management Review, , 23, 1-12.

Schneier, B. (1996). *Applied Cryptography*. John Wiley & Sons, Inc.

Zheng, J., Veinott, E, Bos, N., Olson, J. S., Gary, Olson, G. M. (2002). Trust without touch: jumpstarting long-distance trust with initial social activities, Proceedings of the SIGCHI conference on Human factors in computing systems, Minneapolis, Minnesota, USA, Pages: 141 – 146, ISBN:1-58113-453-3.

19

IT IS NOT ALL ABOUT TRUST –
THE ROLE OF DISTRUST IN INTER-
ORGANIZATIONAL RELATIONSHIPS

Risto Seppänen and Kirsimarja Blomqvist
Department of Business Administration and Technology Business Research Center,
Lappeenranta University of Technology, FINLAND
risto.seppanen@lut.fi, kirsimarja.blomqvist@lut.fi

It has been consistently argued in prior research that mutual trust is essential for maintaining inter-organizational relationship quality and performance. The mirror side of trust – distrust – has received only scant attention, however. This empirical and qualitative study focuses on the roles of and relationships between trust and distrust in inter-organizational relationships. The results reveal that the two concepts are not merely the opposite ends of a continuum, and these phenomena may exist simultaneously. Moreover, they could both be understood as an essential means of managing uncertainty and risks in relationships.

1. INTRODUCTION

Interest in collaborative arrangements such as partnerships has increased significantly during the last two decades (Contractor and Lorange, 1998). The focus has changed from the transactional and short-term to closely integrated collaborative and longer-term relationships (e.g., Kwong and Suh, 1999; Sahay, 2003; Wong, 1999) as they are seen as a means of improving relationship flexibility and agility, and value creation. Trust is acknowledged to have a crucial role in such relationships (e.g., Dyer and Chu, 2000; Sako, 1998; Miyamoto and Rexha, 2004; Whipple and Frankel, 2000; Johnston et al., 2004; Handfield and Bechtel, 2002). The information age has challenged traditional business logic with the introduction of virtual and networked ways of organizing and managing transactions both within and between organizations (e.g., Bijlsma and Koopman 2003; Venkatraman and Henderson 1998).

Some scholars (e.g., Rotter, 1971; Arrow, 1974; Axelrod, 1984; Lewis and Weigert, 1985; Tardy, 1988) maintain that trust and distrust are the opposite ends of one continuum. According to this approach, inter-organizational trust and distrust are dimensions that are mutually exclusive, i.e. there cannot be high trust and high distrust in a relationship at the same time. On the other hand, others (e.g., Luhmann, 1979; Priester and Petty, 1996; Lewicki, McAllister and Bies, 1998) argue quite the opposite, i.e. that trust and distrust are separate yet linked concepts, which would suggest that both may exist side by side in relationships.

Obviously, the relationship between trust and distrust in inter-organizational relationships is not clear, as there are controversial findings and analysis (e.g., Sitkin

Please use the following format when citing this chapter:

Seppänen, S., Blomqvist, K., 2006, in IFIP International Federation for Information Processing, Volume 224, Network-Centric Collaboration and Supporting Fireworks, eds. Camarinha-Matos, L., Afsarmanesh, H., Ollus, M., (Boston: Springer), pp. 181–188.

and Roth 1996). This paper contributes to the discussion by reporting on an empirical study on trust and distrust in this context. We begin with a very brief review of the relevant extant literature. Our empirical research was based on short accounts of the role of trust in buyer-supplier relationships. The following research questions were addressed: *What are the roles of and the relationship between trust and distrust in inter-organizational relationships? What kinds of factors enhance buyer distrust?* Our analysis of the role of distrust is based on Luhmanian's (1979) approach: we emphasize its different function and nature, and acknowledge the fact that it exists simultaneously with trust in inter-organizational relationships.

2. LITERATURE REVIEW

In order to understand the concept and role of distrust, it is useful to assess the ways in which trust affects inter-organizational relationships. Previous research has acknowledged that trust is an essential factor in relationship quality and performance (Anderson and Narus, 1990; Zaheer, McEvily, and Perrone, 1998; Ford et al., 1998; Parkhe, 1998; Barney and Hansen, 1994; Arrow, 1974; Blois, 1999; Ganesan, 1994; Kwon and Suh, 2004). It is seen to facilitate information sharing, open communication, commitment, long-term orientation and conflict management (Blomqvist, 2002; Creed and Miles, 1996), and to increase predictability (Sako, 1994), adaptability (Lorenz, 1988) and strategic flexibility (Young-Ybarra and Wiersema, 1999). It is seen to have a crucial role in managing virtual organizations and in virtual organizing (Venkatraman and Henderson 1998; Kraut, Steinfield, Chan, Butler and Hoag 1999), since the traditional means of monitoring and controlling the other party are lacking (Handy 1995; Bijlsma and Koopman 2003)[i],[ii].

The role of distrust has mostly been examined within organizations, i.e. between employees, and between employees and management (e.g., Kramer, 1994 and 1999). Despite its increasing prominence, however, there is a lack of empirical studies on the critical incidents leading to increased or decreased trust in inter-organizational relationships, although there are a few exceptions, such as Robinson, Shaver and Wrightsman (1991) and Mancini (1993). A lack of trust – or low trust – is not usually defined in any specific way (see e.g., Bigley and Pearce, 1998) in these studies: it is rather seen as a situation in which the factors mentioned in various definitions of trust are absent.

As pointed out in the previous section, some researchers (e.g., Priester and Petty, 1996; Lewicki et al., 1998) argue that trust and distrust are separate dimensions, and thus not opposite ends of one single dimension or continuum. Moreover, they are seen as concepts that may appear simultaneously in a relationship (Priester and Petty, 1996). These views rely heavily on Luhmann's (1979) work, in which trust and distrust are considered coexistent mechanisms for managing relationship complexity. The basic point is that low trust and high distrust – and on the other hand high trust and low distrust – are not the same phenomenon.

The main justification supporting the argument for the simultaneous existence of trust and distrust lies in the notion that relationships are multifaceted and multiplex[iii] rather than unidimensional constructs, and moreover that the parties involved are inconsistent and in a state of imbalance[iv] (Lewicki et al., 1998). Parties in multiplex relationships are interdependent – even if they do not want to be – and consequently they have to interact and coordinate their actions, even against their will (for more on this reasoning, see Lewicki et al., 1998). The multiplex nature of relationships leads us to a state in which one party has different opinions and views about the other – in terms of capability and goodwill, for example[v]. Ultimately, this reasoning leads to the presupposition that trust is a multi-dimensional phenomenon – one person can trust another on certain issues but not necessarily on others or in different contexts (Blomqvist, 2002). In other words, the target of trust may vary in a relationship (Misztal, 1996). Since trust – and therefore also distrust - is a multidimensional phenomenon, the obvious argument is that they may both exist in these multiplex relations.

The fundamental assumption in these views suggesting that distrust is not the other end of the trust continuum, but is essentially a distinct (although naturally related) dimension, is that "trust is good, distrust is bad". This thinking is far too black-and-white, and neglects "the other half" of containing and managing uncertainty and complexity. Luhmann, (1979, 72) stresses this by referring to distrust as a "positive expectation of injurious action". In so far as it is an expectation of injurious action from the other party, distrust simplifies the social world, "allowing an individual to move traditionally to take protective action based on these expectations" (Lewicki et al., 1998). In other words, it is also an essential component of rational acting, especially in effective (economic) organizations.

All in all, it is proposed here that trust and distrust are distinct phenomena, and that they may exist at the same time in inter-organizational business relationships. Moreover, both are considered fundamental conditions in terms of managing uncertainty and complexity.

3. DATA ANALYSIS AND RESULTS

The empirical study was qualitative in nature and was based on large corporate industrial buyers' short accounts of well-functioning and poorly-functioning buyer-supplier relationships. The buyer company has several thousands of suppliers. Many of these supplier relationships are collaborative and partnership-type, rather than traditional arms-length buyer-supplier relationships. An industrial buyer needs to handle several hundreds of supplier contacts. Key suppliers act as system suppliers with their sub-suppliers, and therefore the large corporate production is truly networked. Broadly defined, an organization is virtual to the extent that it outsources key components of its production (Gallivan 2001) by means of ICT-enabled infrastructure (see e.g., Kraut et al., 1999). The case company collaborates mainly virtually with its supplier networks. The end product in question is a physical good, the manufacture of which involves major information flows (Rayport and Sviokla 1995) between hundreds of parties. Much of the information flow in ICT-enabled information networks, such as in EDI and CAD/CAM applications, supports inter-organizational information exchange. Consequently, the majority of the stories described collaborative relationships rather than traditional arms-length-type buyer-supplier relationships.

The accounts were collected during two internal seminars for industrial buyers held in a global metal manufacturer in 2003 and 2004. The buyers were asked to write short stories in which they should analyze the role of trust in well-functioning and poorly-functioning buyer-seller relationships. The assignment to write stories did not refer specifically to trust and distrust. The respondents were asked to write about their experiences of well- and badly-functioning collaborative relationships in relation to trust, but they were not specifically asked to describe or analyze the connection, or the difference, between the concepts of trust, lack of trust, and distrust. They produced 25 accounts of well-functioning relationships and 27 of poorly-functioning relationships. We chose qualitative content analysis (see e.g., Berg, 2004, 265-298) as our analytical tool. In broad terms, content analysis includes any kind of technique for "making inferences by systemically and objectively identifying special characteristics of messages" (Holsti, 1968, 608). We first organized and grouped the manifest content of the data into common categories, and then we condensed and summed the incidents into categories built up from earlier research. Finally, we re-examined the data for more latent content (Berg, 2004, 269).

Network relationships were referred to in several stories. This was not considered purely positive, however: if the supplier cannot handle deliveries as agreed it inevitably causes delays and problems for all parties in the supply chain.

"One bad thing is that our supplier also has its suppliers - and if the supplier's supplier's supplier turns its customer down, it will be reflected in the whole supply chain..." (a poorly functioning relationship)

In the great majority of the stories, trust was seen to be an essential and critical success factor in the relationship between organizations, and open information sharing and communication were considered prerequisites for the development and maintenance of trust. Similarly, factors and incidents related to lack of trust (e.g., lack of communication, inadequate information, promising too much, and hiding problems) were among the most cited in accounts of relationships in which trust did not develop, or was lost. Keeping promises – in terms of delivery dates, prices and quality, for example – was also seen as a critical factor enhancing trust.

On the other hand, if the supplier did not keep its promises it had a clear negative effect on perceived trust. The majority of the buyers also mentioned the important role of personal relationships in developing trust, but somewhat unexpectedly, poor personal relationships were not as clearly seen as a factor hampering trust in the other organization. This applied especially to distrust[vi], as poor personal relationships were not mentioned as causing distrust in the seller party. This suggests the presence of organizational trust in addition to personal-level trust. Furthermore, unidimensional dependence was seen as a critical factor hampering trust, even leading to distrust in the buyer-seller relationship.

Five of the 25 accounts of poorly-functioning relationships mentioned cases in which the supplier had either suddenly increased prices quite a lot, or had made smaller increases gradually. Some of them also recalled situations in which the supplier tried to charge for more goods than were actually delivered. Unreliable deliveries (delays, quality problems, delivering the wrong products) were the most frequently mentioned trust-hampering factors and incidents in the stories.

The buyers were not asked to differentiate or analyze the concepts of trust and distrust as such. Nevertheless, there were some interesting notions about the role of distrust embedded in the stories, as illustrated in the following quotation:

"...A certain amount of distrust keeps you sharp, though, and this way you will question things, and not take everything for granted. This forces you to check everything, and the possibility of making mistakes is smaller." (a well-functioning relationship).

Another account of a well-functioning relationship (about a transport company that had always responded remarkably well to all demands and changes) ended with the comment:

"It makes me wonder whether we are paying them much too much for their transport services!" (a well-functioning relationship).

In both of these stories, trust was considered essential for the functioning of the relationship. They thus supported both of our propositions - that distrust is not a phenomenon that affects the relationship only negatively, and that trust and distrust exist simultaneously.

We then proceeded to examine the data more in-depth in terms of its latent content in order to find out whether trust and distrust indeed were considered to exist simultaneously, thereby supporting the assumption that they indeed are distinct concepts. In this we relied on Luhmann's (1979, 72) reference to distrust as the "positive expectation of injurious action" to separate it from lack of trust. The latent content analysis revealed the simultaneous presence of trust and distrust in inter-organizational relationships. This came out in two ways: firstly, there were relationships in which the buyer did trust in the supplier's competence, but not in its goodwill, for example, and in some relationships there was trust in the supplier, yet the buyer felt distrust at some level (which s/he considered to be a sign of rationality).

Thus, our data gives indications of the simultaneous existence of trust and distrust in inter-organizational relationships and in buyers' perceptions of their suppliers. It also suggests that the role of trust may be more direct and more easily described and understood. Moreover, it is clear that the role of high trust in well-functioning relationships is acknowledged to be fundamental in relationship performance. It seems that the quality of communication and information sharing, i.e. timely and honest informing about expected problems in keeping promises concerning delivery dates, for example, are particularly strong factors enhancing perceived trust in the other party. The absence of these factors was seen to hamper trust - in other words it lead to a lack of trust in the relationship.

Again, distrust could be seen as a phenomenon largely resulting from unmet expectations. It quite clearly often led to a weakening in the quality of the buyer-seller relationship, and ultimately to its dissolution. Moreover, as noted earlier, unidimensional dependence was also seen as a factor causing distrust. In some cases, the above-mentioned factors leading to a lack of trust eventually also resulted in perceived distrust of the other party to the relationship.

The positive side of distrust as a complementary means of managing uncertainty in the inter-organizational relationship was directly mentioned in only two stories. This also came out in the latent content of the accounts, however. Furthermore, the simultaneous existence of trust and distrust was mentioned several times, thus supporting our assumption that they may indeed exist side by side. Their relationship is evidently quite complex and ambiguous, yet it clearly exists and is therefore worth studying more deeply.

4. DISCUSSION

The objective of this empirical study was, first, to investigate the roles of and the relationship between trust and distrust in inter-organizational relationships, and secondly to identify factors that enhance buyer distrust. Even though the empirical part of the study was conducted in only one industrial branch and context, it could be assumed that the results will hold in wider contexts. The findings support the argument that trust and distrust can be conceptualized as separate – although related – concepts, and thus not merely as opposite extremes of a single concept. What is even more important is that they may exist at the same time, and both are effective – in different ways – in terms of reducing complexity and uncertainty in inter-organizational relationships. We therefore propose that they should both be understood as a means of managing social complexity and inherent uncertainty in this context.

On the basis of our empirical findings, we argue that *distrust* in inter-organizational relationships could be seen as active belief in one party's willingness to engage in behavior that is aimed at exploiting the other party's vulnerabilities. Again, *lack of trust* is perceived as being more passive, yet not so reasoned and rational: it is more an evaluation of the other party's trustworthiness. Moreover, lack of trust was generally not believed to cause the dissolution of the relationship, although it may have made its development more difficult and slow. Whereas the absence of or shortcomings in communication, and inadequate information sharing, were acknowledged as factors causing lack of trust, the effect of unmet expectations was evident in causing distrust, thereby accentuating its active nature . On the other hand, in some cases the separation between lack of trust and distrust was not made quite clear, suggesting that there is still a certain amount of conceptual haziness surrounding these two concepts.

Limitations and suggestions for further research
Taking a one-sided approach to a dyadic collaborative relationship limits the value of any study, and we could have gained a more holistic picture by gathering data from both parties. Moreover, by using in-depth interviews instead of short and quite open accounts we might have obtained more in-depth information.

The limitations of the present study lead us to suggest some approaches for further research: the use of in-depth interviews and quantitative surveys, and the gathering of data from both sides of the relationship, could be fruitful in terms of gaining a deeper understanding of the roles of trust and distrust and the connection between them.

Moreover, as the conceptual clarification and separation between lack of trust and distrust remains somewhat blurred, there is a clear need for more theoretical and empirical research. Finally, as trust is argued to be a highly context-specific phenomenon, the same is presumably true of distrust, its antecedents and consequences. Therefore, conducting empirical research in other inter-organizational contexts, settings, and levels would be useful in order to increase the generalizability of the results of this study.

Acknowledgements. An earlier draft of this article was presented at the 3rd Workshop on Trust within and between Organizations in Amsterdam, the Netherlands, 2005. We thank FINT group members for their helpful comments on the paper.

i Handy (1995, 41) acknowledges this, noting the managerial dilemma taking shape in the question, "How do you manage people whom you do not see?" He goes on to state that virtual organizations are based more on trust than on control.

ii On the other hand – and quite on the contrary to the common argumentation – Gallivan (2001) claims that effective performance may be achieved in a virtual organization in the absence of trust, and that it may rather be a matter of ensuring control over the other party. Although we strongly disagree with Gallivan's argumentation about trust being unnecessary in relationships within and between virtual organizations, we acknowledge the connection between the need for a reasonable amount of control and monitoring, and distrust as a means of managing uncertainty in all kinds of relationships.

iii In all relationships, there are several ways in which the parties relate to each other. Moreover, they may have different experiences of various aspects of the relationship. In the inter-organizational context, there are several actors in each party, all with different capabilities, intentions, and ways of interacting with others. One party might trust another on a certain matter, but not necessarily on others. Consequently, there cannot be one, unidimensional and all-encompassing characterization of the other party in the relationship: it involves several and often complex constructs.

iv We do not normally have complete and adequate information about the other party: bounded rationality causes uncertainty and a lack of balance. As we face a continuous flow of information that we need to process and absorb, we are able reach a state of balance only transitionally, and not consistently.

v Trust is commonly acknowledged in existing research as a multi-dimensional phenomenon, usually comprising rational, (e.g., capability/competence/ability/expertise and predictability) and attitudinal (e.g., goodwill, benevolence, reciprocity) components (for more on this, see e.g., Blomqvist 2002; Seppänen, Blomqvist and Sundqvist (forthcoming)).

vi Situations of distrust are different from those of low trust, as there is - reasoned and rational – fear, skepticism, and wariness. On the other hand, when there is a lack of trust – or low trust – there is a more passive characterization of the absence of hope, faith, and confidence.

REFERENCES

1. Anderson, J.C. and Narus, J.A. "A model of distributor firm and manufacturer firm working partnerships", *Journal of Marketing*, vol. 54, iss. 1, 42-58, 1990.
2. Arrow K. J. *Limits of Economic Organization*, New York: Norton, 1974.
3. Axelrod, R. *"The evolution of cooperation"*, Norton, New York, US, 1984.
4. Barney, J. B. and Hansen, M.H. "Trustworthiness as a Source of Competitive Advantage," *Strategic Management Journal*, 15, 175-191, 1994.
5. Berg, B.L. *"Qualitative research methods"*, Pearson Education, Boston, 2004.
6. Bigley, G. A. & Pearce, J. L. "Straining for shared meaning in organization science: Problems of trust and distrust", *Academy of Management Review*, Vol. 23, no. 3, 405-421, 1998.
7. Bijlsma, K. and Koopman, P. "Introduction: trust within organizations", *Personnel Review*, vol. 32, no. 5, 543-555, 2003.
8. Blomqvist, K. "Partnering in the dynamic environment: The role of trust in asymmetric technology partnership formation", a doctoral thesis, Acta Universitatis Lappeenrantaensis, 2002.
9. Brown, P.G. *"Restoring the public trust"*, Beacon, Boston, 1994.
10. Contractor, F.J. and Lorange, P. "Competition vs. cooperation: A benefit/cost framework for choosing between fully-owned investments and cooperative relationships", *Management International Review*, vol. special issue, 28, 5-8, 1988.
11. Creed, W.E. & Miles, R.E. *"Trust in organizations: A conceptual framework linking organizational forms, managerial philosophies, and the opportunity costs of control"*, in Kramer, R.M. Kramer & Tyler, T.R. (eds.). *"Trust in organizations: Frontiers of theory and research"*, Sage Publications, London, 1996.
12. Dyer, J. H. and Chu, W. "The determinants of trust in supplier-automaker relationships in the US, Japan, and Korea," *Journal of International Business Studies*, 31 (2), 259-285, 2000.
13. Ford, D.; McDowell, R. & Tomkins, C. *"Exploring relationship strategy"*, in Naudé, P. & Turnbull, P.W. (eds.), *Network dynamics in international marketing*, Pergamon, Oxford, 1998.
14. Ganesan, S. "Determinant of Long-Term Orientation in Buyer-Seller Relationships," *Journal of Marketing*, 58 (April), 1-19, 1994.
15. Handfield, R.B. & Bechtel, C. "The role of trust and relationship structure in improving supply chain responsiveness", *Industrial Marketing Management*, 31, 367-382, 2002.
16. Handy, C. "Trust and virtual organization", *Harward Business Review*, May-June 1995.

17. Holsti, O.R. *"Content analysis for the social sciences and humanities"*, Addison-Wesley, Reading (MA), 1969.
18. Johnston, D.A.; McCutcheon, D.M.; Stuart, F.I. & Kerwood, H. "Effects of supplier trust on performance of cooperative supplier networks", *Journal of Operations Management*, 22, 23-38, 2004.
19. Kramer, R.M. "Trust and distrust in organizations: Emerging perspectives, enduring questions", *Annu. Rev. Psychol.* 50, 569-598, 1999.
20. Kramer, R.M. "The sinister attribution error, *Motiv. Emot.* 18, 199-231, 1994.
21. Kraut, R.; Steinfield, C.; Chan, A.P.; Butler, B. and Hoag, A. "Corrdination and virtualization: the role of electronic networks and personal relationships", *Organization Science*, vol. 10, no. 6, 722-740, 1999.
22. Kwon, I-W G. & Suh, T. "Factors affecting the level of trust and commitment in supply chain relationships", *Journal of Supply Chain Management*, 40; 2, 4-14, 1999.
23. Lewicki, R.J.; McAllister, D.J. & Bies, R.J. "Trust and distrust: New relationships and realities", *Academy of Management Review*, vol. 23, no. 3, 438-458, 1998.
24. Lewis, J.D. & Weigert, A. Trust as a social reality", *Social Forces*, 63, 967-985, 1985.
25. Lorenz, E.H. *"Neither friends nor strangers: Informal networks of subcontracting in French industry"*, in Gambetta, D. (ed.) *"Trust: Making and breaking cooperative relations"*, Blackwell, Oxford, 1988.
26. Luhmann, N. *"Trust and power"*, John Wiley & Sons, Chichester, England, 1979.
27. Mancini, P. "Between trust and suspicion: How political journalists solve the dilemma", *European Journal of Communication*, 8, 33-51, 1993.
28. Misztal, A. *"Trust in modern societies"*, Polity Press, Cambridge, 1996.
29. Miyamoto, T. & Rexha, N. "Determinants of three facets of customer trust: A marketing model of Japanese buyer-supplier relationship", *Journal of Business Research*, 57, 312-319, 2004.
30. Parkhe, A. "Understanding trust in international alliances", *Journal of World Business*, 33:3, 219-240, 1998.
31. Priester, J.R. & Petty, R.E. "The gradual threshold model of ambivalence: Relating the positive and negative bases of attitudes to subjective ambivalence", *Journal of Personality and Social Psychology*, 71, 431-449, 1996.
32. Rayport, J.F. and Sviokla, J.J. "Exploiting the virtual value chain", *Harvard Business Review*, November-December 1995, 75-85.
33. Robinson, J.P.; Shaver, P.R. and Wrightsman, L.S. *"Measures of personality and social psychological attitudes"*, Academic Press, San Diedo, US, 1991.
34. Rotter, J.B. "Generalized expectancies for interpersonal trust", *American Psychologist*, 35, 1-7, 1971.
35. Sahay, B.S. "Understanding trust in supply chain relationships", *Industrial Management + Data Systems*, 103: 8/9, 553-563, 2003.
36. Sako, M. "Does trust improve business performance?" In: Lane, C. & Bachmann, R. "Trust within and between organizations". Oxford University Press, Oxford, 1998.
37. Sako, M. *"Supplier relationship and innovation"*, in Dodgson, M. & Rothwell, R. (eds.), *"The handbook of industrial innovation"*, Edward Elgar Publishing, Aldershot, 1994.
38. Seppänen, R; Blomqvist, K. and Sundqvist, S. "Measuring inter-organizational trust – a critical review of the empirical research in 1990-2003", *Industrial Marketing Management*, (forthcoming).
39. Sitkin, S.B. & Roth, N.L. *"The road to hell: The dynamics of distrust in an era of quality"*. In Kramer, R.M. & Tyler, T.R. (eds.), *"Trust in organizations: Frontiers of theory and research"*, Sage, Thousand Oaks, CA, 1996.
40. Tardy, C.H. *"Interpersonal evaluations: Measuring attraction and trust"*, in Tady, C.H. (ed.), *"A handbook for the study of human communication*, Ablex Publishing, Norwood (NJ), US, 1988.
41. Venkatraman, N. and Henderson, J.C. "Real strategies for virtual organizing", *Sloan Management Review*, fall 1998.
42. Whipple, J.M. & Frankel, R. "Strategic alliance success factors", *Journal of Supply Chain Management*, vol. 36: 3, 21-28, 2000.
43. Wong, A. "Partnering through cooperative goals in supply chain relationships", *Total Quality Management*, 10: 4/5, 786-792, 1999.
44. Young-Ybarra, C. and Wiersema, M.F. "Strategic flexibility in information technology alliances: The influence of transaction cost economics and social exchange theory," *Organization Science*, 10 (4), 439-459, 1999.
45. Zaheer, A.; McEvily, B. & Perrone, V. "Does trust matter? Exploring the effects of interorganizational and interpersonal trust on performance," *Organization Science*, 9 (2), 141-159, 1998.

PART 7

TRUST AND RISK

20

COORDINATING SUPPLIER RELATIONS: THE ROLE OF INTERORGANIZATIONAL TRUST AND INTERDEPENDENCE

Toni Laaksonen
VTT Technical Research Centre of Finland, toni.laaksonen@vtt.fi
Harri I. Kulmala
VTT Technical Research Centre of Finland, harri.kulmala@vtt.fi
FINLAND

Various supplier networks consist of many different types of interorganizational relationships. The coordination and evaluation of these kinds of networks is becoming more challenging as the importance and relative power of a single supplier increases due to the centralization of purchases. The main objective of this study is to measure mutual interorganizational trust in the supplier relations of Finnish paper industry. The second objective is to classify suppliers by the type of the relationship into different categories and to illustrate the development of these relationships in order to use these methods to assist main contractor's supplier coordination.

The case network consists of seven companies operating in the fields of maintenance, engineering and consulting. During the study, the representatives of both the suppliers and the customers were interviewed using a questionnaire made in advance based on earlier literature. The results of the study show that mutual interorganizational trust along with interdependence is a central factor when main contractors choose and coordinate their suppliers in the network economy.

1. INTRODUCTION

Earlier studies concerning relationship, alliance and partnership formation have focused mainly on success factors, formation processes and rationales of interorganizational relationships (see e.g. Das & Teng, 2000; Hoffmann & Schlosser, 2001). However, the importance of identifying the characteristics of the relationship and classifying suppliers into different categories for the purpose of supplier coordination has been noticed (Cousins, 2002). Despite, there have been only a few studies concerning this research topic so far. This study tries to bridge the partial gap in the literature focusing on the supplier coordination and classification by the means of mutual trust and interdependence.

Networked organizations show often extensive dependence on interorganizational relationships. The challenge is to find ways to coordinate these relationships as many of them seem to fail as a consequence of opportunistic

Please use the following format when citing this chapter:

Laaksonen, T., Kulmala, H. I., 2006, in IFIP International Federation for Information Processing, Volume 224, Network-Centric Collaboration and Supporting Fireworks, eds. Camarinha-Matos, L., Afsarmanesh, H., Ollus, M., (Boston: Springer), pp. 191–198.

behavior, difficulties in partnership coordination, and/or mismatching expectations (Park & Ungson, 2001). In most cases, the coordination leans mainly on structural arrangements like regulations and rules which are the heart of formal control (Das & Teng, 1998). These arrangements are usually expensive and their extensive use may damage the quality of the relationship by indicating a lack of belief in one's goodwill or competence (Dekker, 2004). However, trust has been found to substitute formal controls as it reduces goal conflict and increases the predictability of partner's behavior (Gulati, 1995). In addition, using trust to coordinate interorganizational relationship may make coordination less expensive and allow greater flexibility in changing conditions (Nooteboom, 1996). The underlying problem with trust is that if it is not already in place, it has to be built which tends to be very slow and long-lasting process (Johanson & Mattsson, 1987). This is why trust can be mainly used for coordinating long-term oriented relationships.

According to Sako (1992) we may distinguish three types of trust: contractual trust, competence trust, and goodwill trust. Contractual trust rests on an assumption that the other party will carry out its oral and written agreements. Competence trust concerns partner's ability to perform according to these agreements and goodwill trust focuses on partner's intentions to perform in accordance with those agreements. All these forms of trust are present in an interorganizational relationship to some extent and usually they develop further over time.

In order to use trust for coordination purposes organization has to recognize the amount of trust and characteristics of the relationship. The following model (Fig. 1) is suggested as a way to classify suppliers by the type of relationship and to assist the coordination of the supplier base. The model is based on the ideas of Wicks et al. (1999) and Cousins (2002) about matching trust and interdependence levels and classifying relationships into categories. The type of the relationship adopted depends on the level of output desired and the nature of the asset specificity (Cox, 1996). If the outputs of the relationship for example will be realized in long-term and they are strategically important along with high asset specificity, the relationship should be developed towards the area of strategic collaboration.

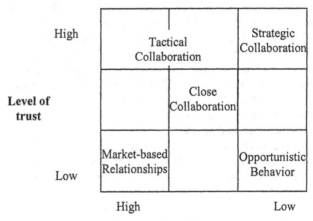

The number of alternative suppliers

Figure 1 – Categories of the interorganizational relationships

In the model, the main means for deepening relationships are mutual trust building and reducing the number of alternative suppliers by transaction specific investments or centralizing purchases. Transaction specific investments lock both supplier and buyer into the transaction because the value of this capital in other uses is much smaller and without these investments alternative supplier can not produce the item as cost effectively as current supplier can (Williamson, 1979). Decreasing the number of suppliers leads to higher switching costs which increase the interdependence of the relationship. Hence, if the organization cannot match the level of trust to the number of alternative suppliers, the relationship may fall to the dangerous area of opportunistic behavior. In the area of opportunistic behavior relationships are focused mainly on short-term price reduction instead of medium to long-term competitive advantage creation or cost reduction (Cousins & Spekman, 2003).

Along with high switching costs the interdependence of a relationship can be created through valuable resources and monetary value of deliveries (Barney, 1991; Matikainen, 1998). The resource-based view suggests that interorganizational relationships are used to gain access to other firms' resources, for the purpose of garnering otherwise unavailable competitive advantage to the firm (Das & Teng, 2000). Achieving competitive advantage through interorganizational relationship creates tight resource-dependency between partners (Das & Teng, 2003). Monetary dependence between the buyer and the suppliers can be analyzed by measuring the value of the deliveries and the share of the deliveries in proportion to the supplier's turnover (Matikainen, 1998). If the value of deliveries is high along with the share of the deliveries in proportion to supplier's turnover partners are strongly tied together. As the interdependence between partners and uncertainty of the relationship increase the coordination of the relationship by formal controls becomes difficult and expensive due to the extensive monitoring (Das & Teng, 1998). Especially in this situation other coordination device is needed and the most suitable seems to be building of mutual trust.

The first step when building trust is to select conditions that are conducive to the emergence of trust (Nooteboom 1996). In the beginning of a new supplier relationship the supplier selection should be based on good reputation which enhances the competence trust (Barney & Hansen, 1994). During a relationship the main ability to increase the mutual level of competence trust is to consistently deliver high quality products in a timely accurate manner (Cooper & Slagmulder, 2004). As the trust to the competence of the supplier is high enough the relationship can be developed further by other interorganizational trust building methods (Sako, 1992). These are for example transaction specific investments, repeated interaction, information sharing, long-term commitment and mutually fair risk and benefit sharing mechanisms (Jarillo, 1988; Sako, 1992; Tomkins, 2001; Suh & Kwon, 2006).

2. RESEARCH DESIGN

The empirical research was carried out as a multiple case study because it provided the opportunity to combine effectively qualitative and quantitative data from the customer-supplier relationships (see Eisenhardt, 1989). The study contains one supplier network and two customers of the network in Finnish paper industry covering in total 12 dyadic interorganizational relationships. The supplier network consists of seven small and medium sized enterprises operating in the fields of maintenance, engineering and consulting. These suppliers are organized as an equal network where any of the firms can operate in the position of a main supplier if necessary. The customers are international companies, one pulp and paper producer and another focusing on paper machine production.

The data for evaluating the levels of trust in case-relationships was collected through structured interviews. The interviews consisted of eighteen quantitative questions which measured both the level of trust and the number of alternative suppliers. Some of the questions provided also further information to evaluate the reasons for possible reduction of the number of suppliers as they measured the mutual transaction specific investments of the relationship. Trust was measured by evaluating levels of certain characters of the relationships by 3 point scale similar to Sako's (1992) ACR-OCR scale. These characters were, for instance, openness between partners, risk sharing agreements, intense of supplier competition, the asset specificity of the relationship and projected length of trading. The more relationship had these characteristics conducive to the emergence of trust the higher was the evaluated level of mutual trust.

The representatives of the suppliers were interviewed first and on the basis of these interviews suitable customers for the research were selected. The selection was based on the size of the customer and the number of supplier relationships towards customer. Two suitable customers were found and personnel of these customers were interviewed using the same but slightly revised questionnaire.

3. EMPIRICAL RESULTS

Suppliers were classified into different categories based on the results of the conducted interviews (Fig. 2). The size of the supplier's figure indicates the dispersion of the answers. The wider the figure is the more there is differences in the evaluation of the number of alternative suppliers. The height of the figure reflects the dispersion of the calculated average levels of trust. In order to match trust and interdependence supplier should be situated on the diagonal of the figure or near of it (Fig. 2). In the case of Customer 1, the levels of interorganizational trust have increased properly as the number of alternative suppliers has decreased. Instead, Customer 2 has slightly failed to match trust and interdependence. Most of the suppliers are positioned below the diagonal and so they are quite near to the dangerous area of opportunistic behavior. Luckily, the monetary value of deliveries is relatively low so the possible opportunistic behavior of the suppliers is not very damaging to the Customer 2.

During last few years Customer 2 has forcefully centralized purchases which can be seen as a low number of alternative suppliers (Fig. 2). The centralization of the purchases has increased the switching costs of suppliers while the dependency of the suppliers has stayed low due to a relatively small share of the deliveries of Customer 2 compared with the suppliers' turnover. This has led to one-sided dependency which is characteristic to the opportunistic behavior (see e.g. Cousins, 2002). In the case of Customer 1 the delivery volumes has stayed continuously high. Hence, the dependency has become mutual in most of the case relationships. Higher purchasing volumes than in the case of Customer 2 have also ensured the proper development of mutual trust in relation to the interdependency of the relationships.

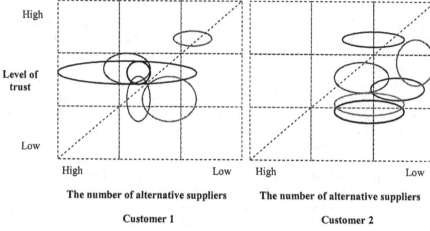

Figure 2 - Classification of the supplier relationships

Both valuable resources and transaction specific investments increase the supplier dependence of Customer 2 along with the one-sided monetary dependence. Customer 2 has outsourced nearly all maintenance and engineering know-how. Therefore Customer 2 needs the resources controlled by suppliers to maintain high production's utilization rate. In the cases of both customers the asset specificity arises mainly as a consequence of learning-by-doing and transfer of skills specific to a particular relationship. For example, the respondents of the both customers argued that it takes several years after a new supplier is as effective as the current suppliers are. Hence, the human asset specificity is high in both cases due to the transaction specific investments (see e.g. Joskow, 1985). This has also led to high switching costs which have especially locked Customer 2 to its suppliers because of the small supplier base. In the case of Customer 1 the dependency arises from the supplementary and complementary resource alignment in the relationships. The resources of the suppliers complete the resource base of Customer 1 creating valuable combinations which may enhance competitive advantage.

None of the case relationships has drifted fully to the area of opportunistic behavior. The main reason for this has probably been the supplier selection criteria. Both customers viewed that the most important factors affecting the supplier selection and the centralization of purchases are supplier's good reputation and valuable know-how along with competence trust. All the representatives of the customers said that in the long-run competent supplier is more cost effective than supplier offering low price products or services at the expense of quality. But they also stated that along with good quality competitive price is important. Therefore, suppliers having the best price-quality ratio probably get most of the purchases.

As the supplier relationships deepened, mutual trust was build up mainly by transaction specific investments, increased information exchange and long-term commitment. Especially customers built up trust by sharing information about their predicted demand on the maintenance and engineering services and increasing the projected length of trading. Long-term commitment was realized through annual contracts with the suppliers. These annual contracts were related to minor service piecework of maintenance and engineering. Most of the transaction specific investments were made by the suppliers as a result of learning-by-doing and transfer of skills. Better know-how of the processes, machinery and working methods of the customer increased suppliers' effectiveness in a particular relationship. As a whole, the trust in nearly all of the relationships was enhanced mutually after a few years of joint interaction.

In the case of three supplier relationships the mutual trust was enhanced furthermore. Increased openness between these partners and additional transaction specific investments created conditions that were conducive to the addition of trust. In these cases customers had courage to give even strategically important information to the suppliers which increased notably the level of mutual trust. Once again most of the transaction specific investments were made by suppliers. All the three suppliers had employees who provided services full-time to these close customers. In addition, some of these employees worked physically in the office spaces of the customers. This transaction specific know-how deepened these relationships even more. Due to the high mutual trust and interdependence, two of these relationships ended up clearly to the area of strategic collaboration (Fig. 2).

4. DISCUSSION

Based on the empirical findings of this case study and earlier literature a cyclical development model of an interorganizational relationship is proposed (Fig. 3). The proposed model consists of four phases which cause the gradual deepening of an interorganizational relationship. The phases formulate a circle and as the relationship deepens it can go through the circle several times. Central elements of the model are trust and mutual dependency which are also potential key factors within a successful partnership relationship (see e.g. Das & Teng, 2003). The development of the relationship begins when the customer recognizes that his/her resource base lacks valuable resources which can be combined effectively with the existing resources or when there is a need to have related supplementary resources. In the first phase, customer seeks reliable suppliers controlling valuable resources to the customer. So far, the interaction between customer and supplier has been minimal, the uncertainty of the relationship is high and dependency low. This is why supplier selection is based on supplier's good reputation and competence trust which enhance the overall interorganizational trust of the relationship. After the choice of the supplier the actual relationship begins. As the amount of purchases increases, transaction specific investments are made as a consequence of mutual adaptation and learning-by-doing (phase 2). This increases also the monetary dependence between the customer and the supplier.

The transaction specific investments affect many dimensions of the relationship. They increase the amount of trust and valuable resources along with reducing the number of alternative suppliers (see e.g. Peteraf, 1993) (phase 3). The last phase of the circle includes the growth of the interorganizational trust. The addition of mutual trust is gained through increased information exchange and long-term commitment to the relationship. Finally the higher level of interorganizational trust increases the amount of valuable resources of the relationship as trust is a rare and imperfectly imitable resource due to its significant degree of social complexity (Barney & Hansen, 1994). As a result of this development the relationship has moved from the field of market-based relationships to the area of close collaboration (Fig.1).

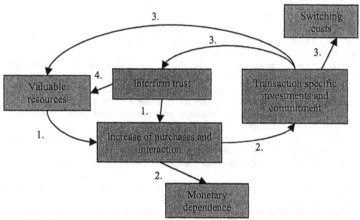

Figure 3 - Proposed cyclical development of an inter-organizational relationship

After the first development circle, the deepening of the relationship can continue as happened in three case supplier relationships. During the second development circle the additional transaction specific investments increased the human asset specificity of the relationships. Mutual trust was also developed further by the means of increasing the openness of the relationships. As a result of the second development circle two of these relationships deepened to the area of strategic collaboration.

The findings of the study can be summarized in two important aspects. A method of classifying interorganizational relationships was proposed to assist main contractor's supplier coordination mainly in the situations of supplier selection and centralization of purchases. Secondly, the classification was supported by the conceptual model for the purposes of deepening the supplier relationships. The major limitation of these findings is the extent of the study. The empirical part of the study covered only 12 dyadic inter-organizational relationships in Finnish paper industry. The results can not be generalized directly to other geographical areas. In addition, the empirical data was quite narrow and further research should be carried out before the proposed supplier classification and the development model can be used as a managerial tool. However, the observations can be a fertile basis for further research, for example statistical analysis on the proposed development model of inter-organizational relationships would be needed.

5. REFERENCES

1. Barney, J. Firm resources and sustained competitive advantage. Journal of Management 1991; 17: 99-120.
2. Barney J, Hansen M. Trustworthiness as a source of competitive advantage. Strategic Management Journal 1994; 15: 175-190.
3. Cooper R, Slagmulder R. Interorganizational cost management and relational context. Accounting, Organizations and Society 2004; 29: 1-26.
4. Cousins, P. A conceptual model for managing long-term inter-organizational relationships. European Journal of Purchasing & Supply Management 2002; 8: 71-82.
5. Cousins P, Spekman, R. Strategic supply and the management of inter- and intra-organisational relationships. Journal of Purchasing & Supply Management 2003; 9: 19-29.
6. Cox, A. Relational competence and strategic procurement management. European Journal of Purchasing & Supply Management 1996; 2: 57-70.
7. Das T, Teng B-S. Between trust and control: developing confidence in partner cooperation in alliances. The Academy of Management Review 1998; 23: 491-512.
8. Das T, Teng B-S. A resource-based theory of strategic alliances. Journal of Management 2000; 26: 31-61.
9. Das T, Teng B-S. Partner analysis and alliance performance. Scandinavian Journal of Management 2003; 19: 279-308.
10. Dekker, H. Control of inter-organizational relationships: evidence on appropriation concerns and coordination requirements. Accounting, Organizations and Society 2004; 29: 27-49.
11. Eisenhardt, K. Building theories from case study research. The Academy of Management Review 1989; 14: 532-550.
12. Gulati, R. Does familiarity breed trust? The implications of repeated ties for contractual choice in alliances. The Academy of Management Journal 1995; 19: 85-112.
13. Hoffmann W, Schlosser R. Success factors of strategic alliances in small and medium-sized enterprises-an empirical survey. Long Range Planning 2001; 34: 357-381.
14. Jarillo, C. On strategic networks. Strategic Management Journal 1988; 9: 31-41.
15. Johanson J, & Mattsson L-G. Interorganizational relations in industrial systems: a network approach compared with the transaction-cost approach. International Studies of Management & Organization 1987; 17: 34-48.
16. Joskow, P. Vertical integration and long-term contracts: the case of coalburning electric generating plants. Journal of Law, Economics, and Organization 1985; 1: 33-80.
17. Matikainen, E. Efficient governance of interorganizational business relationships. Helsinki: Helsinki school of economics and business administration, 1998.
18. Nooteboom, B. Trust, opportunism and governance: a process and control model. Organization Studies 1996; 17: 985-1010.
19. Park S, Ungson G. Interfirm rivalry and managerial complexity: a conceptual framework of alliance failure. Organization Science 2001; 1: 37-53.
20. Peteraf, M. The cornerstones of competitive advantage: A resource-based view. Strategic Management Journal 1993; 14: 179-191.
21. Sako, M. Prices, quality and trust: inter-firm relations in Britain and Japan. Cambridge: Cambridge University Press, 1992.
22. Suh T, Kwon I-W. Matter over mind: when specific asset investment affects calculative trust in supply chain partnership. Industrial Marketing Management 2006; 35: 191-201.
23. Tomkins, C. Interdependencies, trust and information in relationships, alliances and networks. Accounting, Organizations and Society 2001; 26: 161-191.
24. Wicks A, Berman S, Jones T. The structure of optimal trust: moral and strategic implications. The Academy of Management Review 1999; 24: 99-116.
25. Wernerfelt, B. A Resource-based view of the firm. Strategic Management Journal 1984; 5: 171-180.
26. Williamson, O. E. Transaction-cost economics: the governance of contractual relations. The Journal of Law and Economics 1979: 233-261.

21

INDUSTRIAL NETWORKS TRUST BONDS: A SOCIOLOGICAL PERSPECTIVE

Paula Urze

Faculty of Sciences and Technology, New University of Lisbon, PORTUGAL

pcu@fct.unl.pt

The core question that supports this paper aims to identify the role of trust bonds in a subcontracting/cooperation network. The empirical research relies on a case study of an industrial network, developed in the north of Portugal (Águeda and nearby), within the bicycles' subsector, covering about 25 enterprises. We identified patterns of relationships amongst the subcontracting and subcontracted companies. Once the relationships amongst the companies in the network were understood, it became important to place trust in business relationships. Afterwards how, and to what extent, trust interferes in these business relationships was examined.

1. INTRODUCTION

The terms networks, virtual enterprises, collaborative networked organisations and clusters have become the fashionable terms to describe contemporary organisations. In fact, the theme of cooperation among enterprises has inspired the literature and generated an extended debate in the social sciences. The eighties and nineties were characterised by apparently contradictory tendencies in industrial organisation. One of those refers to the dimension of the entrepreneurial structure, indicating that the majority of new jobs are created by small enterprises. On the other hand, one reads almost every day about a new merger between two or more giant corporations. The number of divisions and acquisitions in the industrialised world has taken place at an unprecedented rhythm over the last few years. Some authors (for example, Sengenberger *et al.*, 1990) identified the tendency of the crisis of the large enterprises and the flexibility of the small and medium enterprises as innovation agents and sources of job creation. But there is no agreement on this subject. For Harrison (1994), according to his analysis based on data obtained in the USA, Western Europe and Japan, large enterprises still concentrate a growing proportion of their capital and markets on the main economies: "production decentralisation does not lead to a corresponding power decentralisation – whereas large enterprises reorganise their various productive activities, the control of those units remains centralised." (Harrison, 1994 Cf. Powell and Smith-Doerr, 1994: 382).

The fast industrial development in Japan and in Italy in the seventies and eighties supported the idea that economic development is made easier when inter organisational relationships are based on trust. The trust game is played in network. The core question that supports this paper[1] aims to identify the role of trust bonds in a subcontracting/cooperation network.

---

[1] This paper is based on the work developed for the author's PhD thesis in Economic Sociology and Sociology of Organisations, in the Institute of Economics and Business Administration, Technical University of Lisbon, 2005.

Please use the following format when citing this chapter:

Urze, P., 2006, in IFIP International Federation for Information Processing, Volume 224, Network-Centric Collaboration and Supporting Fireworks, eds. Camarinha-Matos, L., Afsarmanesh, H., Ollus, M., (Boston: Springer), pp. 199–210.

2. THEORETICAL VIEWS ON TRUST

The study of trust was the target of special attention in the nineties (Sako, 1991, 1992; Dyer, 1996) and, emerging particularly strongly in literature about business relationships, it became a study theme within the framework of horizontal relationships amongst enterprises (*joint ventures*, forms of cooperation) and of vertical relationships between suppliers and clients (Humphrey, 1998). Therefore, in understanding trust within the restrict framework of inter organisational relationships, several different categories are identified (Cousins, 2001). Trust can be taken: (a) as an isolated concept (trust and power, trust and risk), (b) within an interactive model (focusing on relationship model) or (c) within an industrial context, which is the one that most interests us in this case. With regards to this, the concept of the three attributes developed by Sako (1992) has been particularly mentioned by scholars, because it was thought of within the specific context of the relationship producer – supplier and also because it deconstructs the notion of its various attributes: contractual, skills and "good will".

Dyer and Chun (1997) declare that there are several authors that consider that trust in the relationship supplier – client (a) reduces transaction costs and allows greater flexibility to respond to market changes (Dore, 1983; Sako, 1991; Barney and Hansen, 1994; Dyer, 1996), (b) leads to the optimisation of information sharing routines, which improve coordination in the sense that they minimise inefficiency (Clark and Fujimoto, 1991; Nishiguchi, 1994) and (c) makes it easier to invest in the transaction and in technologies that increase productivity (Asanuma, 1989; Lorenz, 1988; Dyer, 1996).

Even though trust appears as a critical theme in various social science fields, it is the economic perspective that appears to have considerably more weight in this case. In any case, this is clearly stated in the synthesis elaborated by Sako (1992), an author of reference on this subject. Sako (1992) turned some of the possible approaches to the problem into a system as follows: 1) Trust can be seen from the point of view of a preference (perceptible in behaviour) or as a meta-preference (based on beliefs or values) (Hirschman, 1984). Trust will be more meta-preference than a simple preference, meaning that there is a motivational force, a commitment to the normative value content (Etzioni, 1988). Trust, particularly the "good will" type, as a cultural predisposition, fits into this interpretation. 2) Trust can alternatively be treated as a scarce source, but present to different degrees, depending on the country. Therefore, in a country such as England where there is less trust than in Japan, businesses tend to lean on institutional motivation environments and standards, where very little relevance is given to trust. In the absence of trust, institutional controls are available to control abundant opportunistic behaviour. 3) As opposed to this, trust can be seen as a renewable resource (Hirschman, 1984; Gambetta, 1988). The prevailing idea is that trust grows with use; it has to be used in order to thrive. When it is not used, it has a tendency to waste away. This explains why relationships of trust are usually long lasting. 4) Trust building may be bilateral and specific of a particular relationship. Within this context, trust is an intangible capital, an asset held jointly by both sides. What is peculiar as far as trust is concerned, when compared to other assets, is the fact that it can be built upon slowly and quickly destroyed. 5) Trust in bilateral relationships can also be taken into account in the reputation game. To damage reputation means the loss of future business opportunities. This assumes that the "reputation effects" are effective to impose sanctions on opportunists. An efficient way to show the market that one is worthy of trust is to perform a set of reputable behavioural principles, even if those may not be in one's own interest in the short term. 6) Finally, trust can be dealt with as an input, for which there are no markets. According to this point of view, trust cannot be immediately bought or sold, in as much as the direction of the instrumental exchange destroys the foundation of trust (of good will in particular). It is this non instrumental aspect that, in part, motivates people to perform over and above the minimal level of necessary effort. In short, in terms of the concept of trust, there remains a complex commitment between an asset in which somebody invests for their own interest, and a social standard.

Sako has dedicated her work to the study of trust in the context of the relationship between assemblers and suppliers in Japan. In her work *Price, Quality and Trust: inter-firm relations in Britain and Japan*, the author makes a comparative analysis between Japan and England. "What is it that has weight in the competitiveness of the Japanese industry?" Is the basic query that accompanies the study (which includes three assembling companies and 36 suppliers in the electronics industry). Research clearly shows that the relationships between suppliers and clients have a strong effect on industrial results in terms of price, quantity and quality. And there seems to be a good reason to think that the model "obligation contractual relation" (OCR) can contribute to a better performance as opposed to the "arm's-length contractual relation" (ACR), where a contract is set up before the business, and if unpredictable problems arise, they are sorted out according to legal directives. OCR, on the other hand, presumes an economic contract which fits into specific social relationships between commercial partners who develop a sort of mutual trust. Even if each partner's tasks are negotiated, agreed and clearly stated in contracts before the business relationship starts, there is some incentive to do more than is expected by the business partner. Such an incentive is the result of expectations that the act of good will leads to a similar response by the partner and that in times of unexpected crisis, the good nature of the partner can be called upon in order to allow the non fulfillment of some previous agreements within the terms of the contract.

The essential normative values that give shape to ACR and OCR behaviours are based on the presence or absence of trust in the three types conceptualised by Sako. Contractual trust (mutual anticipation that promises made are kept) and trusting capability (trust in the capability of a partner to develop a certain activity) exist to a larger or smaller extent both in ACR and in OCR. It is good will that is found in OCR but not in ACR. Sako (1992) concludes that the Japanese electronics industry seems to have more OCR characteristics than the equivalent English industry (even though the latter has been carrying out changes towards OCR). Amongst suppliers, there are large variations between companies. But the range of relationships in the Japanese industry seems to be more OCR than the range of English relationships. The author adds that trust relationships can be necessary but not enough to reach competitiveness. High quality and competitive costs are achieved in Japan, by cultivating OCR type trust, but also rivalry amongst the known core of Japanese suppliers who are placed to compete according to their capabilities.

This work also makes it clear that ACR and OCR are fundamentally based on different business values and attitudes. The desire to enter into dependent relationships, or to invest in building trust by means of face-to-face communication, both leading to OCR, is present to different degrees both in Japan and in England.

Dore (1983, Cf. Gerlach and Lincoln, 1995: 495) mentions that "it is tangible relationship rather than impersonal market processes that explains the Japanese industrial organization."

3. CASE STUDY ON A PORTUGUESE INDUSTRIAL NETWORK

3.1 Methodological note

As far as methodology is concerned, we used the case study method, in its wider sense, to analyse the industrial network in the Municipality of Águeda (and surrounding districts), in the bicycle sub-sector. We identified patterns of relationships amongst the subcontracting and subcontracted companies. Once the relationships amongst the companies in the network were understood, it became important to place trust in business relationships. In order to understand broadly this web of relationships, we decided that a qualitative, in depth research strategy would be appropriate to the nature of the subject being studied, also taking into account the dimension of the circumscribed network. Therefore, it is important to underline that we are referring to a case that includes 25 companies, 21 within the network and four outside - company A^2 and 11 suppliers (A1 to A11) and company B and 8 suppliers (B1 to B8) – but collecting information also included interviews to Associations and privileged informants, namely entrepreneurs in the region with a vast knowledge of the sector (OE1 to OE4).

3.2. Trust

From rhetoric...

Trust is, as predicted, a concept full of variations that refers to practical aspects linked to business relationships. In other words, the idea of trust is gaining shape in association to price, quality, delivery times and the duration of the business relationship. *"Usually, trust is fundamental. People slowly gain trust."* (financial director of company A4) Entrepreneur B1 declares that *"there are several factors [that interfere with choice], one of those is price. Even though price is not everything. There is also the problem of quality."* When a supplier is selected, we can talk of objective criteria: the capability of responding in terms of quality, price and delivery times. These are the factors that are more related to trust.

From what interviewees say, it is clear that this value needs to be recalled as a fundamental reference of their business relationships, and is often introduced into the interview by the entrepreneurs themselves. But it is also clear from their declarations that the feeling of mistrust has been gaining ground in the field of entrepreneurial negotiations. This feeling of loss seems to lead the interviewees to

---

[2] Core companies (designated here as A and B).

reinforce the idea that this principle is still an element of differentiation in business practices. *"When we don't know what we are buying we say, 'I'll buy from that guy, I know he is a person who won't cheat on me'. It is fundamental to work with a regular supplier who you trust."* (entrepreneur A6)

The entrepreneurs reveal their concern in explaining that in their business there is no space for mistrust and mistakes. These words are mentioned but almost always by reference to others, they do not include themselves in that context, giving the idea that less transparent business practices exist, but are promoted by other entrepreneurs.

One of the entrepreneurs remembers that: *"It has to be a supplier who we trust completely because our clients analyse the parts and we cannot run the risk of selling them one thing for another."* (...) *Trusting is the same thing as having a signed contract. I trust as much a sale to company B without a contract as I would selling to some others with whom there should be a contract."* (Entrepreneur B1) This sentence explains well that trust, even though subjective, emerges here as an equivalent to the written contract that usually establishes the agreements of negotiation. The informal relationship based on trust is thus reinforced. The entrepreneur also notes the difference between "trustworthy" companies and the other companies where the business relationship should be regulated by formal contracts that work as a guarantee in case of condemnable actions.

The feeling of mistrust is often associated to the more recent assemblers, since the majority of them do not own physical property. These companies do not generally have their own facilities and due to the work they carry out (only assembly) they do not invest a lot on technology. The provisional way they set up their installations means they are looked upon by suppliers as companies that do not offer any guarantees. It is also important to stress that these assembling companies have been functioning as an alternative for the components companies, as in lately they have witnessed the closure of their once important clients. But, as we have seen, there is a shared sense of mistrust in relation to most assemblers, including some reasonably large assemblers, but also some small assemblers designated as "basement" assemblers. Gambetta (1988) reminds us that trust means there is a strong probability that we are considering getting involved in some form of cooperation. In this case, the link with the assemblers raises many doubts, since it is not possible to predict anything. Even if the manufacturers maintain these relationships and feel they have to invest in them, that does not mean that a relationship of trust is being cultivated. On the contrary, the business is based on strong feelings of mistrust.

.... To the facts

Price
The idea of trust emerges very much linked to price. To the question *"What does it mean to trust a supplier?"* entrepreneur A6 answers *"it means that we are convinced that he is selling the product to us at the best price."* For another entrepreneur, trust in a supplier is linked to the fact that he explains price variations for a certain product, in order to avoid business losses.

When we asked another entrepreneur if the fact that they have been buying from one supplier for a long time and the product has always fulfilled expectations was an element that set it apart from other suppliers, he answered *"Price is price."* With regards to this, entrepreneur A3 explains, *"The fact that I know the manager of company B and the fact that I know the purchasing director of company A [does not mean] that if I do not have the right price they will buy from me."* This extract from the interview also shows that the value of trust is relative when faced with product price. *"All our clients would change supplier for a small price difference"*, reminds entrepreneur A6.

According to the initial talk with entrepreneur A10, the most important criteria to select a supplier are the following: *"Speed, good price and quality. Fast delivery, because, you see, we have a delivery on a certain day. (...) There is price, which is also important, but in many cases speed and product quality are the most important. Good presentation. We also cannot go for the cheapest."*

On reading the interviews, it becomes clear that proposals by other suppliers put pressure on the regular suppliers, which is a natural part of business relationships. The interviewees mention that the supplier almost always matches the prices presented by the competition. The entrepreneurs declare that if the prices given by the old suppliers do not come near those of the others, there is a strong probability that the business relationship will end, if not completely, at least, it will not be as regular as before.

There seems to be a preference for maintaining the regular supplier, but also to negotiate a lower price, as stated by entrepreneur A6: *"Because we warn them when there are suppliers that offer lower prices for similar products. We inform our supplier. If he can offer the same price for a similar product we prefer to keep them."* As mentioned by this entrepreneur, the regular supplier is preferred only in a situation where the prices are identical, otherwise the duration of the relationship becomes less important in relation to the price.

Negotiation implies a daily and strong pressure to reduce prices. The game is endless. In the end it has to stop, even running the risk of loosing the business. Sometimes, businesses are agreed with very small margins, and payment conditions and schedules seem to compensate very little for the concessions made.

Still on the subject of the pressure exerted in relation to the price (or payment conditions) the financial director of company A tells us *"that a client who applies pressure, does so because he has the capability to come here or go elsewhere."* In this case, client pressure could be positive, in as much as the strength shown during the negotiation process demonstrates that the company has a market reputation, which means it has access to several suppliers. Entrepreneurs try to perceive the financial situation of the client trying to read different signals, so that they can protect themselves from prolonged debts or even from non payment due to bankruptcy processes.

"If he can he makes, if he can't, he won't." (Entrepreneur A2) The entrepreneur states that, with the necessary precautions, price is a relevant factor in supplier selection. However, past experience leads him to evaluate the proposals by new suppliers in a more rigorous manner. Entrepreneur A2 mentions some negative experiences due to changes in suppliers: *"We've learnt some lessons. The first time, the product was wonderful, the second time, so, so... If it is from a credible company to another credible company, I do not abandon them, such as today I buy a lot and tomorrow I don't buy at all."*

There is a mistrust component that slowly disappears as the supplier proves his credibility, this way reducing the margin of uncertainly, and therefore, risk. Trust is built over several completed agreements. In other words, the history of the relationship means that predictions can be made which offer the entrepreneur security, meaning they, on the other hand, commit to other businesses. There is a chain reaction, so that it is essential that raw material or component suppliers fulfil their commitments so that the remainder of the business is not compromised.

The financial director of company B4 tells us: "*The competition tends to be not only in terms of price, but also in terms of better conditions.*" Payment conditions are mentioned again and again as a way to gain some business. "*We are not too demanding in terms of payment. Nowadays, people who buy want to pay as late as possible*" (entrepreneur A8) So, entrepreneurs play not only with the price, but also with the setting up of payment conditions. Payment difficulty is constantly mentioned in the interviews, as entrepreneurs use this factor, defining more favourable conditions that may give them an edge with regards to the suppliers. In other words, apart from the price itself, there are payment conditions that may not be frequently practiced by other companies.

When we compare the price factor with other factors, namely trust in the supplier, we realise that advantage is often preferred. Immediate gain is fundamental since the companies survive with great financial difficulties, which also pushes them to value the present in comparison to a future investment in relationships of trust. It is necessary to maintain the business, even if it means leaving behind other types of less immediate profit. Sako (1992) reminds us that to damage one's reputation means losing future business opportunities. To gain trust implies to fulfil a set of reputable behavioural principles even if they are not in our own interest in the short term. Now, the logic of trust does not invest in the short term, as opposed to the logic of many entrepreneurs.

In short, price is a factor that influences a lot the entrepreneur's decision to select the supplier. Even though in some cases the entrepreneurs give the same weight to other factors (especially quality), the price issue is always the most important. However, it is obvious that suppliers are increasingly evaluated more carefully, considering experiences where entrepreneurs felt they had been cheated, and businesses that seemed attractive but ended up in significant losses. It is worth noting that a lot of the stories about situations that reveal trust, refer to issues linked to the price or to payments in agreement with pre-established conditions. Trust in the price offered by the suppliers illustrates many of the examples in the interviews. But a qualitative difference is noticed in the talks, mainly when the strength of price comes up in relation to the other issues. In other words, the link between the words (ideas) trust and price, is broken, being substituted by declarations where price (immediate) wins over and trust (based on long lasting relationships) loses.

Quality

Quality is also a factor largely associated to trust. A supplier is considered trustworthy if over time he guarantees that he always manufactures products of the same quality. Entrepreneur A8 agrees with this point of view, reminding us that trusting the supplier ...

> ... "*means product quality. We work on imported products and are concerned that we should not change clients in order to guarantee the same quality. If we work for two or three years with one supplier who gives neither us nor our clients any problems, we try to always have the same supplier and deliver*

products of the same brand. And we've had clients who ask for products of that brand."

These words refer clearly to the idea that relationships of trust are reinforced by means of a continuous realisation of quality expectations. In the end, it is a matter of reiterating trust through the quality of the product, which is tested in the different consignments.

What the entrepreneurs say suggests that quality prevails over price, which only changed when the quality of the products is similar. In these cases, the price would work as a differentiating factor, but only when it is possible to guarantee the usual parameters of product quality. This idea means that the importance of price becomes secondary.

In the end, it is important to distinguish, in the interviews, a discourse that tries, from the tales about practices, to relate what actually happens in negotiations to what is considered more correct in business relationships. On the one hand, the words of the entrepreneurs include the idea of a desirable business in terms of the priorities given to criteria, and on the other, the idea that business pressures often do not combine with this ideal which favours the quality criterion. It is a pressure that emerges, in the words of the entrepreneurs, as an external force, uncontrollable, and in many cases inevitable, to maintain the business.

Some entrepreneurs distinguish the suppliers they buy in function of the price, from those where this is not a defining factor. The joint development of some parts means that some suppliers gain importance due to that technical investment. This type of relationship strengthens the position of the supplier, gaining strength, in as much as a break in the relationship implies added costs. Along these lines, entrepreneur A/B says: *"It means there is a bidirectional trust so that we are guaranteed that they fulfil our requirements. When we need to increase or decrease output, they understand, since we work together. The contacts mean much more than a purely commercial contact. There is even a joint product development."*

The entrepreneurs also distinguish the suppliers between those who are trustworthy and those who are not. They develop a relationship of complicity with the companies they trust, which means it is possible to maintain a guaranteed supply platform, especially for the most important business for the company. Once this trust base is guaranteed, less important suppliers emerge around the core supplier. In short, the companies try to guarantee a core that ensures regular supply of essential products. These suppliers (generally more than one for each product) are the supply base of the company. Substituting them is usually a process that requires more attention. Usually, they are relationships where there has been investment in terms of trust and where the substitute company will have to maintain the existing standards in order to satisfy the demands of the clients. With regards with other marginal suppliers, easier to substitute, relationships are not necessarily based on trust links but mainly on factors that imply immediate advantages, namely the price.

Competition from Asian countries strongly worries entrepreneurs in Portugal, because some of these countries compete on the basis of price and have been improving their quality, which makes the competition scenario worse for the Portuguese companies. *"China and India are cheaper. (...) But at the moment, there are international companies for whom not even China is good enough and they are moving to Vietnam. (...) [China] It is a product that has to have a certain quality, even though it is lower than Taiwan products. These companies have some of their technicians there. Products from Taiwan are good quality, and their price is already not too cheap."*

As a general rule, competition from Asian countries is quite strong. Even though some countries have made their mark through (lower) price, leaving some margin for manoeuvre in terms of product quality, now better quality is emerging which diminishes the distinction between companies. But these countries have been bringing their quality parameters in line with the Europeans. India is often mentioned as an example, as it has more qualified labour, meaning that important technical knowledge is also valued in terms of understanding the specifications of the work commissioned. Entrepreneur A8 says: *"In India, not only is it cheaper, but they make the parts according to our specifications. When it is a matter of specific products that we commission they make a commitment not to sell to anyone else in our country. In Taiwan we have a supplier, but we haven't bought anything from him. They are intermediaries. They buy and put the parts together in a container and send them here."*

In short, entrepreneurs distinguish between core suppliers and marginal suppliers. The former are those who cannot be substituted easily and, if it is necessary to do so, the break in the relationship is felt as a loss. There are investments and guarantees that will not be easy to replace. Marginal suppliers are those with whom there is a more superficial relationship, and, in some cases, who provide supplies more sporadically, in other cases, they manufacture more standard products, without great added value.

Delivery times

Another factor also linked to the trust concept is the fulfillment of delivery times. One of the entrepreneurs explains that *"[a trustworthy supplier] is a supplier who guarantees continuity and uninterrupted supplies. It is a supplier who, when we place an order with him for X date, he will not tell me 'I am missing such and such.'"* (Entrepreneur A/B). Another entrepreneur tells us that you lose trust when....

> ... *"The supplier does not deliver on the agreed date. I have to stop production and he did not deliver and in that case, I do not forgive. Nappa leather for example."* (Entrepreneur A2)

Still on this subject, entrepreneur A/B adds: *"If the supplier [is] trustworthy, he immediately warns us that he is going to have a problem, therefore we take action so that we do not have problems. That is almost a guarantee. A competent supplier does that because a supplier who is not competent is always hoping we don't notice that he is going to be missing something."*

In this case, they are dealing with guaranteed supplies in working time, or, in case that is impossible, with trust in the way they deal with supply problems. When asked what it means to have absolute trust in a supplier, entrepreneur A/B answers that he has to have a supplier who fits the bill and tells them *"yes, sir, it will be here within a week."* This factor gains importance when companies try to reduce stocks, especially within the framework of a *just-in-time* strategy.

Entrepreneurs try to reduce stocks as much as possible. Delivery speed gains importance as most orders are made giving little warning. Delivery times are reduced for all those who contribute to the chain and there is lower tolerance for non fulfilment. Naturally, the risk is greater, but advance investments are avoided.

The evidence provided by the entrepreneurs makes it very clear that it is necessary to avoid stocks, which naturally gives more importance to this criterion.

The products used in most parts are bought somewhat regularly, in as much as it is believed that there is no investment loss. More specific products used in fewer parts, are bought as needed, as there is no guarantee that they will be commissioned. The logic is to reduce risk and investment and obtain an almost immediate return. Once again, that logic is extended to the whole production chain, from the assemblers to the last suppliers. Usually, the more dependent suppliers, and those with least negotiating capability, are those who are the least capable of imposing rules.

The financial situation of the companies is also mentioned in relation to the trust given to the response capability of the suppliers. It is well known that some companies in the cycle industry (and two-wheel industry in general) have closed down (bankruptcy), which produces a generalised atmosphere of lack of trust. Entrepreneur A/B reminds us: "*I think that trust in the supplier is important: the supplier's trust in us and ours in him. May be we can explain our reasoning. If I buy an article from a company that I know is almost bankrupt, that supplier cannot give me any guarantees that he will supply me with the product on the date I want, so he will put my whole product manufacturing line in jeopardy. When we are dealing with products that have quite extensive technical lists, it is enough that a nut, or a screw, fail us, and the product cannot go out. The whole production chain is interrupted.*"

Concerns for the financial situation of the suppliers (and the clients) is constant in the talks, because the stories of bankrupt companies, some of them at one time important companies, leave great worries as to what might be their own future.

If reference to delivery times is a recurrent factor in talks with entrepreneurs, again, concerns for this are not as strong as those for price and quality. Delivery times are not the most important element in supplier selection, even though it is a factor that entrepreneurs try to safeguard in business relationships. Entrepreneur A/B's declaration shows us the priority usually given to these criteria: "*[After price and quality] there are always other criteria we value: response capability, and proximity. We always favour those who are nearer us, as long as they are on an equal footing.*"

APIFER's (Portuguese Association of Builders and Furniture Hardware Manufacturers) President concludes, generalising: "*Generally speaking, people subcontract from a company they already trust. Usually, the relationship between subcontractor and subcontracted is initially difficult as we have an entrepreneurial spirit that is not very clear. We promise everything for the next day and deliver a month later, which is not viable. People deal with somebody they trust in terms of delivery times.*"

In conclusion, entrepreneur A/B stresses here the fact that the companies can reject the supplier based on the non fulfilment of delivery times in relation to other companies. The fact that they do not fulfil their commitments on a relatively regular basis means there is a behavioural pattern which is not in favour of the company being chosen as a supplier. In a small network like this one, exchange of information between companies is fast. The companies that are part of this circuit know that their actions mean they will have a positive or a negative reputation. In this case, and, to a certain extent, similar to the Japanese model, the non fulfilment by suppliers may mean they will not be able to be incorporated into our networks. A negative reputation is quickly spread and the (re)integration of the supplier strongly compromised. "*If they systematically fail, word goes round: you know, those guys are not doing very well"*. (Entrepreneur A2). If business takes place as predicted, a good reputation is spread around (and then you gain the trust of third parties). On the other hand, if companies do not comply with what was established, they lose the trust of the community.

4. CONCLUDING REMARKS

The perception the entrepreneurs have of the meaning of trust in business refers precisely to the issues of price, quality and delivery times. In other words, to be able to trust a supplier, he has to prove himself in terms of those three factors. The designation "trust relationship" is favoured by long lasting links where there have been several opportunities to test that same trust. But what is peculiar to trust, when compared with other assets, is the fact that it is built slowly and that it can be quickly destroyed. (Sako, 1992).

The price (immediate advantage) superimposes all other factors, namely trust based on the history of a relationship, which stops being relevant when the companies have to choose between subcontracted companies with different prices. The usual supplier is then preferred only in a situation where the prices are similar. Taking this logic into the global scheme of things, the prices of local companies have to be advantageous in relation to the prices of Asian countries.

The background of the bicycle sub-sector also includes the more recent emergence of companies that are purely assemblers, many set up with Spanish capital. These companies acquire all the components from other local companies and some of them also import from Asian countries. In general, they do not possess property and are set up in rented facilities, as the equipment needed for assembling does not require large investments. These companies have been giving work to some component producers but do not seem to offer many guaranties, since their position in the market inspires strong feelings of mistrust. *"Today they are here. Tomorrow they are elsewhere."* In other words, a breakdown in personal relationships is linked to the disintegration of that industry. There is a feeling of lost sense of devotion connected to the loss of entrepreneurial heritage. These assemblers work as "oxygen tanks" for some companies. But the fact that they are "disposable" does not offer guarantees. But even then they are valued. Why? Because some component companies have high production levels, aimed almost exclusively at those companies.

Entrepreneurs often choose suppliers who they already know so that the results correspond to what they expect when they sign contracts with important clients/businesses. In these cases, it is important to guarantee that supplies are fulfilled according to agreements, minimizing risk. They play safe, as the demanding patterns of the client are well-known, selecting suppliers who are capable of fulfilling the requirements (even though sometimes it may mean a smaller profit margin). There seems to be a trust capital associated to certain suppliers. As this trust base is guaranteed, then other less important suppliers emerge around those. In the case of the more marginal suppliers, therefore more easily substituted, relationships are not necessarily based on trust but on factors that bring immediate advantage.

What we see nowadays is that this local productive system (Reis, 1992) has been extended to a global level. In other words, the group of industrial companies strongly linked to each other has slowly expanded their relationships to a global level, whereas once they were mainly local. According to Lazerson and Lorenzoni (1999) (reporting on industrial districts) locally defined production systems are anachronistic in a global economy. The local productive system starts to wear off, resulting in the disappearance of many companies and the search for alternatives by others.

5. REFERENCES

Asanuma, B. , Manufacturer Supplier Relations in Japan and the Concept of Relation Specific Skills in *Journal of the Japanese and International Economies, Mar., vol.3, 1989.*

Bachmann, R., Conclusion: Trust – Conceptual Aspects of a Complex Phenomenon, in Lane, C., Bachmann B. (eds.), *Trust within and between Organizations: conceptual issues and empirical applications,* Oxford, Oxford University Press, 1998, pp: 298-322.

Castells, M., *The rise of the Network Society,* Londres, Blakwell Plublishers, 1996.

Cousins, P. D. "It's only a matter of confidence! A comparison of relationship management between Japanese and UK non-Japanese owned vehicle manufacturers", *International Journal of Operations & Production Management,* Vol. 21, No 9, 2001, pp: 1160-1179.

De Laat, Paul, Research and Development Alliances: Ensuring Trust by Mutual Commitments, in Ebers, M. (ed.), *The Formation of Inter-Organizational Networks,* Oxford, Oxford University Press, 1997, pp: 146-173.

Dyer, J. H. , "Specialized Supplier Networks as a Source of Comparative Advantage: Evidence from the Auto Industry." *Strategic Management Journal,* 17, 1996, pp: 271-91.

Dyer, J.H., Chu, W., "The Determinants and Economics Outcomes of Trust in Supplier-Buyer Relations", *Working Paper,* MIT/IMVP, 1997.

Gambetta, D., Can We Trust Trust? in Gambetta, D (ed.), *Trust: Making and Breaking Cooperative Relations,* Oxford, Basil Blackwell, 1998, pp: 213-237.

Gerlach, M. L., Lincoln, J. R., The Organization of Business Networks in the United States and Japan, in Nohria, N., Eccles, R. G. (eds), *Networks and Organizations: structure, form and action,* Boston, Massachusetts, Harvard Business School Press, 1992, pp: 491-520.

Humphrey, J., Trust and the Transformation of Supplier Relations in Indian Industry, in Lane, C., Bachmann B. (eds.), *Trust within and between Organizations: conceptual issues and empirical applications,* Oxford, Oxford University Press, 1998, pp: 215-240.

Lazerson, M., Lorenzoni, G., "Resisting Organizational Inertia: The Evolution of Industrial Districts", *Journal of Management and Governance,* 3, 1999, pp: 361-377.

Luhmann, N., Familiarity, Confidence, Trust: Problems and Alternatives, in: Gambetta, D. (ed.), *Trust: Making and Breaking Cooperative Relations,* Oxford, Basil Blackwell, 1988, pp: 94-107.

Nooteboom, B., Trust as Governance Device, in Casson M. C., Godley, A. (eds.), *Cultural Factors in Economic Growth,* Berlin, Springer, 1999.

Moniz, A. B., Urze, P., Socio-Organizational Requirements for a VE, in Camarinha Matos, Afsarmanesh (eds.) *Infrastructures for Virtual Enterprises - Networking Industrial Enterprises,* Kluwer Academic Publishers, Boston, 1999.

Powell, W. W., Smith-Doerr, L., Networks and Economic Life, in Smelser, N. J., Swedberg, R. (eds.), *The Handbook of Economic Sociology,* New Jersey, Princeton University Press, 1994, pp: 368-402.

Reis, J., *Os Espaços da Indústria – a regulação económica e o Desenvolvimento Local em Portugal,* Edições Afrontamento, Porto, 1992.

Sako, M. , *Prices, Quality and Trust,* Cambridge, Cambridge University Press, 1992.

Sako, M., Does Trust Improve Business Performance?, in Lane C., Bachmann, R. (eds.), *Trust in and Between organizations,* Oxford, Oxford University Press, 1998, pp: 88-117.

Sengenberger, W. *et al., The Re-emergence of Small Enterprises: Industrial Restructuring in Industrialised Countries,* Genebra, OIT, 1990.

Urze, P., *Redes Industriais – Mecanismos de Relacionamento entre Empresas na Zona Industrial de Águeda,* Tese de Doutoramento, Lisboa, Instituto Superior de Economia e Gestão da Universidade Técnica de Lisboa – ISEG/UTL., 2004.

22

STABILITY ANALYSIS IN THE FRAMEWORK OF DECISION MAKING UNDER RISK AND UNCERTAINTY

Dmitry Ivanov[1], Alexander Arkhipov[2], Vera Tolkacheva[2], Boris Sokolov[3]

[1]*Chemnitz University of Technology, GERMANY*
dmitri.ivanov@mail.ru

[2]*Saint Petersburg State University of Technology and Design, RUSSIA*
A_arkhipov@sutd.ru
vera_tolkacheva@mail.ru

[3]*Russian Academy of Science,*
Saint Petersburg Institute of Informatics and Automation (SPIIRAS), RUSSIA
sokol@iias.spb.su

Efficient methods of collaborative networks (CN) configuration should provide models and algorithms of decision-making under risk and uncertainty. In this paper, we present a multi-disciplinary framework of decision making in CN. Particular feature of this framework is stability analysis. We analyse basics of stability analysis and its challenges in the CN settings. Then we present a conceptual model of CN stability analysis and its dynamical interpretation. The stability analysis can be considered as an efficient tool to improve the quality of CN planning and execution models.

1. INTRODUCTION

In this paper, problem of value chain configuration and multi-echelon planning in collaborative networks (CN) is addressed. One of the CN management challenges is a combined formation of the CN structural-functional-informational configuration and the programs of the CN execution. An important point of such simultaneous formation consists in ensuring of the business-processes continuity, information availability, and system stability.

A number of recent research papers (Camarihna-Matos, 2004, 2005) have dealt with forming of CN configuration methodology. The papers presented grounded models and algorithms of how to configure CN based on the known "normative" values of parameters. However, the CN execution is accomplished by permanent changes of internal network properties and external environment. So, the "normative" values of parameters can oscillate. As a consequence of this, (i) the analysis of CN stability and (ii) the embedding uncertainty factors into the planning models are needed. The second means that all the CN management phases (planning, monitor-

Please use the following format when citing this chapter:

Ivanov, D., Arkhipov, A., Tolkacheva, V., Sokolov, B., 2006, in IFIP International Federation for Information Processing, Volume 224, Network-Centric Collaboration and Supporting Fireworks, eds. Camarihna-Matos, L., Afsarmanesh, H., Ollus, M., (Boston: Springer), pp. 211–218.

ing, analysis, and adjustment) must be considered as a whole based on the unified methodological basis (Ivanov et al., 2006). The planning subjects must be not only original objects, but also *dynamics of their interactions, environment, and models.* Planning process is interpreted as *continuous control of system dynamics under the terms of uncertainty.* Results of planning are not only ideal operations model, but also a set of the *CN execution scenarios, models, algorithms,* intended for system functioning support in case of disturbances and deviations. The above-mentioned challenges of the planning and control models interconnection are implemented in the DIMA-methodology (Ivanov, 2006). In this paper, we deal with the analysis of CN stability.

2. A FRAMEWORK OF DECISION MAKING FOR THE CN CONFIGURATION

We propose a framework of decision making for the CN configuration, which makes it possible to consider static network configuration and dynamic network reconfiguration combined. This framework is based on the combination of classic system and control theory with modern evolution system theories. The process of decision making is constructed as a combination of agent-based techniques with techniques of control and systems theories. It allows taking into account activity of the system elements, systematically risk embedding into the CN configuration and execution models, multiple model network description, interconnecting of configuration and execution processes.

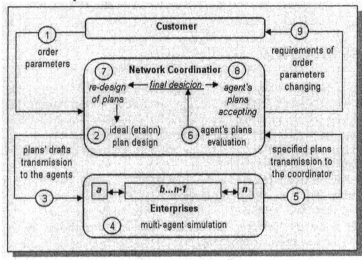

Figure 1. Decision making in the CN based on the combined using of multi-agent and control theory frameworks

This framework is based on the DIMA-methodology (Ivanov, 2006). In the DIMA-methodology, the conventional modelling approaches are not set off with each other, but considered as a united integrated modelling framework. The multi-agent ideology is considered as a basis for the *active elements modelling* at the conceptual, mathematical, and simulation levels. The control theory serves as a *theoretical background* of systems analysis and synthesis (Casti, 1979, Sokolov and Yusupov, 2004). Figure 1 presents the process of decision making in the CN based on the combined using of multi-agent and control theory frameworks.

Algorithms of the control theory and operation research are intended for the ideal (etalon) solutions finding, which can be taken as a basis for the evaluation of the solutions found by agents in regard to their quality, fullness, and reliability. The second advantage consists in balancing the global network criteria with the local agents' criteria. Ideal (etalon) plans generated by the network coordinator are adjusted and specified by agents' interactions. So such a combined procedure of decision-making allows implementing decentralized management concept.

3. BASICS AND CHALLENGES OF STABILITY ANALYSIS

The degree of deviation in a functioning complex system (including CN) from its planned states is related to the concepts of *stability and sensitivity* (Yusupov and Rozenwasser, 1999, Sterman, 2000). Sensitivity characterizes the rate of system's reaction in response to disturbances of different classes. *Sensitivity analysis* permits the determenation of potentially dangerous situations resulting from critical variations of system's functioning. Stability expresses the ability of a system to return to the initial (planned) state and (or) to remain within bounds of operation under the presence of perturbation factors. The stability analysis is performed regarding all of the states S_i that lie within the control horizon considered. This is an important part of the CN *operative diagnosis and forecasting*. The methodology of the CN comprehensive tactical decision making and operative diagnosis and forecasting taking into account decision stability is a subject of our research field.

The concept of 'stability' plays a fundamental role in the systems theory. The sense of this term in general is equal for different types and classes of systems. It consists in limited reaction of a system on scale-limited entering impacts (controlled and non-controlled). A special feature of the CN stability analysis consists in adjustment of actions elaborated by managers and combination of centralized and *decentralized* management. This means that in case a CN looses its balance state, a search of new balance state is executed with the decentralized coordination of all CN participants' interests in the framework of common global criteria.

The CN differs from a physical system. The latter is remarkable for its planning mechanisms, which have some elements of subjectivism. That is why it becomes necessary to broaden the sense of 'stability' term while CN considering. A CN is stable in its planned state, if i) it has a fixed variety of possible adjustment actions; ii) scale-limited and low-power influences occur; iii) these influences cause scale-limited and low-power oscillation of end parameters of the CN.

Let us examine some other aspects of the CN stability analysis. Stability characterizes a capability of a system to return to the initial (planned) state or to stay a certain period of time within admissible functioning area under the pressure of different disturbance factors. Moreover it is essential to understand, that the stability of a system is defined according to certain classes of disturbances. One of the aspects of stability analysis is the CN oscillation analysis. Usually three main classes of oscillations are introduced: damped oscillations, expanded oscillations, and chaotic oscillations (Sterman, 2000). The evaluation of *the CN stability* is meant for the final decision making about the network design, and is the last step in the network design process. The stability analysis is also necessary while CN functioning (in dynamics). The CN stability analysis is carried out within a certain period of time, because an influence of disturbance factors and their impact on the CN functioning have definite time delays.

4. CONCEPTUAL MODEL OF STABILITY ANALYSIS FOR THE CN CONFIGURATION

The stability analysis of the CN configuration is based on the conceptual model of CN design and control (Ivanov et al., 2006). After a set of non-dominated Pareto optimal alternative of admissible CN configurations is formed, the stability analysis takes place. In the CN settings, the stability analysis has two main particular features, namely (i) *decentralization* resulted in need of balancing global network criteria and local agents' criteria and (ii) existence of a number of *alternative CN configurations* resulted in need of advancing stability analysis because of possibilities of structural-functional CN reconfiguration in dynamics. The conceptual model of the stability analysis can be presented in graphical form (Figure 2).

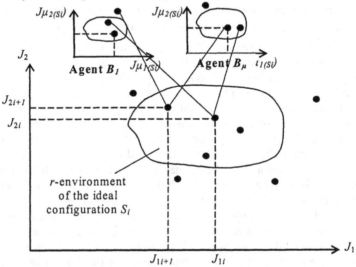

Figure 2. Conceptual model of the stability analysis

Figure 2 presents conceptual model of the stability analysis for a CN configuration S_i. To simplify the picture, we consider only two criteria J_1 and J_2 of CN configuration parameters

$$\boldsymbol{J}(\boldsymbol{x}(t), \boldsymbol{u}(t), \boldsymbol{\xi}(t), t) = \|J_1, J_2, J_3, J_4, J_5, J_6, J_7, J_8\|^{\mathrm{T}}, \tag{1}$$

where J is a set of CN configuration parameters, $x(t)$ is an initial state of the CN, $u(t)$ is a CN execution plan, and $\xi(t),t)$ are vector functions that defines the minimum and maximum values of perturbation impacts. The point (J_{2i}, J_{1i}) corresponds with the ideal CN execution plan. Then we introduce the r-environment of the ideal configuration S_i, which borders permissible oscillations of the criteria J_1 and J_2, so that the CN goal criteria can be achieved.

In accordance with the framework of decision making in CN (see paragraph 2) and due to decentralization and structure dynamics, balancing global network criteria and local agents' criteria and stability checking of alternative CN configurations are needed. Each agent builds its r-environment on the above-described principles. The CN configuration S_i can be selected and launched only if all agent plans are stable for each state of the given CN configuration within the CN r-environment. Figure 2 presents an example when agent plans are stable regarding point (J_{2i}, J_{1i}), but the plan of agent B_1 is instable regarding point (J_{2i+1}, J_{1i+1}). So the CN configuration S_i can not be selected and launched, and further decision making procedures are needed.

The stability analysis objective at the configuration stage consists in indicating of permissible CN execution parameter oscillations. Based on the stability analysis results, the decision maker can estimate the stability degree of the configured CN. As a rule, border extension of permissible CN execution parameter oscillations leads to worsened goal criteria values. The decision maker can simulate various CN configurations and execution scenarios trying to balance the goal criteria and the probability of their achieving. Additionally, other techniques of extended stability analysis such as CN *stability reserve analysis* and *perceptivity analysis* of CN execution parameters regarding various perturbation impacts can be applied.

The presented conceptual model is based on the forecasted information about the CN execution. However, the problem of including information update (Sethi et al., 2005) in CN decisions remains open. That is why the techniques of stability analysis in dynamics must be elaborated.

5. STABILITY ANALYSIS IN DYNAMICS

In dynamics, stability estimation can be performed on the basis of the attainability sets $D(t, T_0, X_0)$, where X_0 is a set of possible initial states of the system. To perform such analysis internal $D^-(t, T_0, X_0)$ and external $D^+(t, T_0, X_0)$ approximations of $D(t, T_0, X_0)$ should be constructed. Let us suppose that a set of admissible disturbances $\Xi(x(t),t)$ is defined as follows:

$$\xi_j^{(1)}(t) \leq \xi_j(t) \leq \xi_j^{(2)}(t), \; j = 1,\dots,m, \qquad (2)$$

where $\xi_j^{(1)}$, $\xi_j^{(2)}$ are vector functions for minimal and maximal disturbances consecutively. These disturbances may appear at the stage of each CN plan execution $(u_i(t), \; t \in (T_0, T_f], \; i = 1,\dots,n)$ within some particular scenario of external environment influences on the CN $(\xi_j(t), \; t \in (T_0, T_f], \; j = 1,\dots,m)$. Let the initial CN state be $x(T_0)$, hence examination of its functioning plan $u_i(t)$ is needed. So, the defined vectors and disturbances space (2) for the scenario $\xi_j(t)$ are corresponded to the area of possible variables of the CN configuration models, i.e. the set of different execution scenarios.

We propose this area to be named as the attainability set of the CN under disturbances. We define it as follows:

$$D_x^{(\xi)}(T_f, T_0, X_0, \Xi, u_i) \qquad (3)$$

The set $D_x^{(\xi)}(T_f, T_0, X_0, \Xi, u_i)$ is corresponded to the indicators values, which assess the CN efficiency and stability. The latter we define as follows:

$$D_J^{(\xi)}(T_f, T_0, X_0, \Xi, u_i) \qquad (4)$$

To make the further material more comprehensive we will examine two components of vector index only. These components correspond to the indicators of effectiveness (J_1) and resource-containing (J_2) of the CN functioning. In this case while geometrically describing the attainability area, it becomes possible to use Decart system of coordinates instead of polar system.

If for some fixed functioning plans $u_i(t)$, ($i = 1,...,n$) under disturbances $\xi_j(t)$ the requirements (5) are fulfilled

$$D_J^{(\xi)}(T_f, T_0, X_0, \Xi, u_i) \subset P_J, \qquad (5),$$

the $u_i(t)$ management program (the plan of the CN functioning) is considered to be stable under disturbances $\xi_j(t)$. In other words, feasible J_1, J_2 deviations of quality indices of the CN functioning are considered to be acceptable.

In this case, the final selection of most stable CN management programs (plans of the CN implementation) is reasonable to be carried out accordingly to the following condition:

$$S_i^*(u_i(t)) = \max_{1 \le i \le n} \min_{1 \le j \le m} S_i(u_i(t)), \qquad (6)$$

where $S_i(u_i(t))$ – is the area of sets $\overline{D}_J^{(\xi)}(T_f, T_0, X_0, \Xi, u_i)$ and P_J intersection; n – the total amount of analyzed CN implementation plans; m – the total amount of disturbance scenarios at the stage of CN plan realization.

It is possible to show that the search of the most stable CN functioning plan due to statement (6) is the realization of the multi-criteria selection under uncertainty, i.e. the principle of the guaranteed result.

Finally, we consider the decentralized stability analysis. Dynamic system of the CN execution can be described in the following way:

$$\dot{\vec{x}}_\mu = \vec{f}_\mu(\vec{x}_\mu, \vec{u}_\mu, t), \qquad (7)$$

$$\vec{u}_\mu(t) \in Q(\vec{x}_\mu, t), \qquad (8)$$

$$\vec{x}_\mu(T_0) = x_{\mu 0}; \quad \vec{x}_\mu(T_f) \in \mathsf{R}^{\tilde{n}'}, \qquad (9)$$

$$J_\mu^{ob} = J_\mu^{ob}(\vec{x}_1(T_f), \vec{x}_2(T_f),..., \vec{x}_{\tilde{m}'}(T_f)), \qquad (10)$$

where $\vec{x}$ is a general CN state vector; $\vec{u}$ is a general CN control vector. The known vector-functions $\vec{h}_0$ and $\vec{h}_1$ determine end conditions for $\vec{x}$ at time $t = T_0$ and at

$t = T_f$. The known vector-functions $\vec{q}^{(1)}(\vec{x}, \vec{u}) = \vec{O}$ and $\vec{q}^{(2)}(\vec{x}, \vec{u}) \leq \vec{O}$ set main constraints for the agent operation, $\mu = 1, ..., \widetilde{m}'$ is a number of agents (local decision makers) performing control functions.

Now the stable plan construction for full decentralization can be stated as search for equilibrium program controls of $B_1, B_2, ..., B_{\widetilde{m}'}$ agents in a differential game. First, the attainability sets $D\big(T_f, T_0, \vec{x}_\mu(T_0)\big)$ for each agent $B_1, B_2, ..., B_{\widetilde{m}'}$ at time $t = T_f$ is constructed. Then an equilibrium point for the system of functions $\big\{ J_\mu^{ob}\big(x_1(T_f), x_2(T_f), ..., x_{\widetilde{m}'}(T_f)\big)\big\}$ over $D\big(T_f, T_0, \vec{x}_1(T_0)\big) \times D\big(T_f, T_0, \vec{x}_2(T_0)\big) \times ...$ $\times D\big(T_f, T_0, \vec{x}_{\widetilde{m}'}(T_0)\big)$ can be determined. Here Brown-Robinson's method and its modifications can be used. After that management actions $\vec{u}_\mu(t)$, $t \in (T_0, T_f]$ for transition from the initial state $\vec{x}_\mu(T_0) = \vec{x}_{\mu 0}$ to the final state $\vec{x}_\mu(T_f) = \vec{x}_\mu^{(pc)}$ are constructed.

The set of agents B_μ, $\mu = 1, ..., \widetilde{m}'$ is split into the following subsets

$$\chi_\zeta, \zeta = 1, ..., P; \chi_\zeta \cap \chi_{\zeta'} = \varnothing, \zeta \neq \zeta', \bigcup_{\zeta=1}^{P} \chi_\zeta = \chi, \chi = \{\chi_1, ..., \chi_P\}, \chi \subseteq B(M), M = \{1, ..., \widetilde{m}'\}.$$

There is a subset for each coalition (a group of agents B_μ united into a competence structure). The set χ is called a *coalition structure*. We have examined three variants of coalition communication, namely (i) if agents of the coalition χ_ζ do not know coalition structure χ or functioning modes of other coalitions $\chi_{\zeta'}$ (where ζ, $\zeta' \in \{1, ..., P\}$) in coalition structure χ, (ii) if agents in coalition χ_ζ know the coalition structure χ, and (iii) if a finite set $\mathfrak{R}$ of coalition structures is known, rather than a particular structure χ.

6. CONCLUSIONS

Decision making techniques for the CN configuration must take into account risk and uncertainty as well as support decision making in decentralized way. In this paper, we presented a multi-disciplinary framework of decision making in CN, based on combination of control theory and multi-agent approach. Particular feature of this framework is stability analysis. We analysed basics of stability analysis and revealed its challenges in the CN settings. Then we presented a conceptual model of CN stability analysis and its dynamical interpretation. The stability analysis objective consists in indicating of permissible CN execution parameter oscillations. As a rule, border extension of permissible CN execution parameter oscillations leads to worsened goal criteria values. So, the stability analysis provides efficient tool how to balance the goal criteria and the probability of their achieving. The conceptual model of stability analysis is based on the forecasted information about the CN execution. The technique of stability analysis in dynamics includes information update in CN decisions and provides their adequacy to the current execution environment.

The presented stability analysis technique provides efficient tool how to embed risk and uncertainty factors into the CN configuration and execution models. Development of CN stability analysis methods has practical and theoretical importance. Generally, the efforts of CN configuration (scheduling) algorithms improving can be meaningful only in combination with appropriate CN stability analysis methods. Stability may be regarded as an additional indicator for the CN analysis, modeling, planning, operative management and forecasting. Its application in the CN design and control models not only supports theoretical basis of the CN, but has a practical importance also. It may be applied to improve quality and precision of planning and management, decision taking (at levels of the CN goal selection, scheduling, monitoring, forecasting and adjustment), as well as complex analysis of the CN activity, forecasting and strategic decisions elaboration.

7. ACKNOLEDMENTS

The research described in this paper is partially supported by grants from Russian Foundation for Basic Research (grant №05-07-90088), Institute for System Analysis RAS (Project 2.5), CRDF Project #: Rum2-1554-ST-05, and the Alexander von Humboldt Foundation.

8. REFERENCES

1. Camarinha-Matos, L. (ed.) (2004). *Virtual Enterprises and Collaborative Networks*, Kluwer Academic Publishers.
2. Camarinha-Matos, L., Afsarmanesh, H. and A. Ortiz (eds.) (2005). *Collaborative Networks and Their Breeding Environments*, Springer.
3. Casti JL. Connectivity, Complexity and Catastrophe in Large-Scale Systems. Wiley-Intersc., 1979.
4. Ivanov D., Arkhipov A., Sokolov B.: Intelligent Supply Chain Planning in Virtual Enterprises. In: Virtual Enterprises and Collaborative Networks, edited by L.Camarihna-Matos, Kluwer Academic Publishers, 2004: 215-223.
5. Ivanov, D., Käschel, J., Arkhipov, A., Sokolov, B., and Zschorn L. (2005): *Quantitative Models of Collaborative Networks*, In: Collaborative Networks and Their Breeding Environments, edited by L.Camarihna-Matos, H. Afsarmanesh, A. Ortiz, Springer, 2005, pp. 387-394.
6. Ivanov, D.A., Arkhipov, A.V., and Sokolov, B.V. (2006): *Intelligent planning and control of manufacturing supply chains in virtual enterprises*, in: International Journal of Manufacturing Technology and Management, in print.
7. Ivanov, D.A. (2006). DIMA - Decentralized Integrated Modeling Approach – Towards The Enterprise Network Theory, *Proceedings of the German-Russian Logistics Workshop*, 20.-21 April, Saint Petersburg, Russia, 2006, pp. 23-46.
8. Sethi, SP, Yan, H., Zhang, H. Inventory and Supply Chain Management with Forecast Updates. Springer, 2005.
9. Sokolov BV, Yusupov RM. Conceptual Foundations of Quality Estimation and Analysis for Models and Multiple-Model Systems. Int. Journal of Computer and System Sciences, 6(2004): 5-16.
10. Sterman JD. Business dynamics: systems thinking and modeling. McGraw-Hill, 2000.

PROCESS MANAGEMENT

| 23 | # DISSECTING INTER-ORGANIZATIONAL BUSINESS PROCESS MODELING: A LINGUISTIC AND CONCEPTUAL APPROACH |

Célia Talma Martins[1,2], António Lucas Soares[3,4]
[1]*LIACC-NIAD&R, Faculty of Engineering, University of Porto*
R. Dr. Roberto Frias, 4200-465 Porto, PORTUGAL
[2]*ISCAP, Rua Jaime Lopes Amorim, s/n, 4465-004 S. Mamede de Infesta*
[3]*Faculty of Engineering, University of Porto*
[4]*INESC Porto, PORTUGAL*
talma@fe.up.pt; als@fe.up.pt

The main objective of this paper is to contribute to the understanding of the of Business Process Modelling field focusing on the definition of the Inter-Organizational Business Processes from both a high-level modelling perspective and a technological one. We used a conceptual maps' approach in order to clarify all the fundamental concepts that surround these two fields. We will present the two conceptual maps we have achieved through the help of a web-based tool for corpus linguistics and knowledge engineering named Corpógrafo and using the IHMC Cmaps Tools for the design of the Conceptual maps.

1. INTRODUCTION

The fast and increasing development of networked business environments brings new ways of interaction among the enterprises, which eliminated the time and space gap between business partners. Enterprise Networks is a new organizational structure that accomplishes the requirements of dynamism and agility that electronic commerce entails. The automation of Enterprise Networks activities in dynamic environments, as it is the case, is still, in most business-to-business scenarios, an undergoing research topic. Business pure models and business process technologies research field for the design, definition and enactment of Inter-Organizational Business Processes (IOBP), focuses mainly on one of these features, failing when connecting the two. On our work we will try to fulfil this gap and attempt to combine both views, which is an actual and challenging research field.

In business networks, management information systems should be based on three fundamental ideas: networked collaboration support, networked decision support and networked knowledge management. The management of a network of enterprises can in fact be viewed as the management of relationships and interactions between the different actors, directly and indirectly involved in the activities. Relationships involve operations, processes, resources, knowledge, social interaction, trust, power, etc [16].

Business Process Modelling (BPM) is a well established research and practice

Please use the following format when citing this chapter:

Martins, C.T., Soares, A. L., 2006, in IFIP International Federation for Information Processing, Volume 224, Network-Centric Collaboration and Supporting Fireworks, eds. Camarinha-Matos, L., Afsarmanesh, H., Ollus, M., (Boston: Springer), pp. 221–228.

field (thought immersed in different research topics such as Enterprise Modelling or Information Systems Architectures, to name just two on opposite sides of the BPM spectrum), embraced in a first moment by the management and industrial communities and in a second moment by the computer science and information systems communities. Somewhere in between, we can identify the workflow management community. BPM is still an ongoing research topic. In fact, BPM is a research challenging issue, especially focusing on the expression of interdependencies among business processes, information systems components and the emerging web technologies. Recently, BPM has gained a new breath pushed by the technological development in the area of internet/web technologies: web processes, service oriented architectures (SOA), semantic web, among others. Although dealing with the same object of study - the inter-organizational business processes - the terminology used by both communities can sometimes be confusing. This happens due to the use of the same terms referring to different concepts (different here is a *continuum* from "slightly" to "completely" different), or the use of different terms referring to the same concepts.

This paper describes a research work encompassing a linguistic and conceptual analysis of the main fields dealing with BPM with the goal of conceptually clarifying the uses of BPM in the management (pure business perspective) and computer science fields (pure technological perspective). The main objective of this work is to contribute to the understanding of the BPM field focusing on a business architecture perspective and from a service oriented architecture one. Also an important goal (and the first aim of our work), is the setting up of a solid conceptual basis for interdisciplinary research in this area.

The paper is structured as follows: Section 2 presents the method for the linguistic and conceptual analysis of Business Process Modelling. In section 3 the two perspectives on Business Process Modelling presented are contrasted using a conceptual maps' approach. Section 4 synthesises some related work in the BPM field and section 5 presents some conclusions and points for further research.

2. A METHOD FOR A LINGUISTIC AND CONCEPTUAL ANALYSIS OF BUSINESS PROCESS MODELLING

Two corpora were defined as *a priori* analytical categories for business process modelling related papers: *business architectures* [5, 17] and *service oriented IT architectures*. The fundamental reason for choosing these two specific corpora was to make a deep analysis of these complementary domains of BPM research. Complementary because we cannot separate these two perspectives as they are intertwined. In fact, the second perspective is the technological implementation of the first one. So in order to automate an IOBP it is essential to understand the management perspective of BPM very clearly.

The method for the linguistic and conceptual analysis included the following steps:

1. selection of the papers to be included in the two corpora,
2. identification and selection of terms using a linguistic analysis tool,
3. elaboration of two conceptual maps using the terms selected in 2,
4. analysis of the conceptual maps regarding conceptual similarity,
5. disambiguation of similar terms in the two corpora.

In the first step, relevant papers of the two fields were selected, according to our purposes. Research in the BPM field exists for more than a decade, so several state-of-the-art and survey papers were selected (aprox. 65 papers). The same with the Business Architecture (BA) in SOA (aprox. 32 papers) [1, 9, 19]. Several papers where the link between BPM and SOA aspects was dealt with, were also selected [20, 8, 3].

The second step was undertaken with the help of *Corpógrafo*. *Corpógrafo* is an integrated web-based tool for corpus linguistics analysis and knowledge engineering. It is a computational environment on the web that allows users to build and research personal corpora without the need for specialized technical skills or additional software, apart from a web browser [13]. This tool helped to extract a set of candidate terms from each corpus, which formed the raw material for our analysis. From this set of candidate terms (about 65 for BAs and 30 for SOAs) a selection was made of those that stood for concepts more relevant to BPM.

The following step, and the most important one for the construction of the conceptual map, was to identify the relations between the selected concepts. This was also done using *Corpógrafo* but it was mostly based on the study of the selected papers covering these two research topics and on our knowledge of the domain. The result of steps 1 and 2 paved the way to build two conceptual maps for each of the areas which are described in the following section.

3. CONTRASTING THE BP MODELLING VIEWS USING CONCEPTUAL MAPS

To identify appropriate concepts shared in the business processes community there is the need to analyze and describe the business process (BP) itself. A *Business Process* is a set of ordered activities of an enterprise or of a network of enterprises that are executed according to some rules in order to achieve a goal. They are performed by one or more actors in a process. An actor can be an organization, a person, a software agent representing a person or an organization.

Different business process models are employed in the design and implementation phases of the Business Process Management life-cycle, where the business analyst perspective serves as input for the technical analysis for BP implementation. The translation between these two perspectives is prone to semantic ambiguities. First, because the two perspectives employ different business process modelling languages and secondly because there is an "identified gap" on the type of resources used by the activities in the two perspectives, namely the human resources which cannot be contemplated in the technological definition of the IOBP but definitely exists in the high-level IOBP definition we are trying to achieve. We used a conceptual maps approach in order to clarify all the fundamental concepts that surround these two perspectives: management and technological.

Conceptual maps are simple and practical representation tools that allow the representation of knowledge in the form of a graph and are an effective way of representing complex concepts and messages in a clear and understandable way [4]. The two conceptual maps, one for each corpus, were built using the IHMC Cmap Tools software [6].

3.1 A conceptual map for BPm from the BA point of view

The main objective of BPM is to provide a better understanding on how to express the business processes, their strategies and their behaviour. Business models provide ways of expressing business processes or strategies in terms of business activities and collaborative behaviour so we can better understand the business process and the participants in the process. Models are helpful for documenting, for understanding and communicating complexity. A *Business Process Model* is a representation that tries to capture the business processes which are essential to the organization function's understanding and performance, reflecting the business environment reality. BPM is not a recent research field; there are a lot of business processes modelling techniques that range from traditional data modelling (DFDs, Entity-Relationships Diagrams, IFEF-0, etc) to behaviour modelling techniques (State Transition Diagrams, Petri Nets, Role Interaction Nets, etc) [18]. A *Business Process* defines the behaviour of the process itself; it is a function that has *inputs*, *preconditions* that must be satisfied, *outputs* that result from the execution of the process and *results*. *Activities* in a business process can be business processes themselves, sub-processes or tasks - the basic part of a business process that cannot be divided. To model a business process we need to describe the BP itself in a detailed, reliable and unambiguous way which means we have to know *a priori* the activities involved in a BP. The BPM research community agreed that the three main views involved in BPM are *behavioural*, *organizational* and *informational* views. The behavioural perspective basically describes the order in which the different activities are executed. The organizational view describes the organization structure and, in particular, the resources and in which way these are involved in the BP. The informational point of view describes the information that is involved in a BP, how it is represented, and how it is propagated among the different activities. The conceptual modelling languages such as IDEF, Flow Charts, DFDs, Eriksson-Penker Business Modelling extension and UML are all graphical modelling languages but they only focuses on one of the views, e.g., the business view.

3.2 A conceptual map for BPm from the SOA perspective

The need to build complex business process, e.g. IOBP, in these highly competitive and dynamic business environments requires new methods and tools. Nevertheless, Web Services is an emerging technology that seems to meet this demand. Web Services technology is used for building complex distributed systems focusing on interoperability, which allows enterprises to describe the internal structure of their processes and explain how they can be invoked and composed. It also allows supported interactions between business partnerships based on the exchange of messages. This way, organizations can extend the business processes beyond the enterprise boundaries via this technology, thereby improving collaboration across partners and facilitating dynamic reconfiguration of business processes. A Web Service is like a unit of work which can complete a specific task [15]. Many businesses are adopting Web service technology to expose their business applications, allowing them to have business collaboration both within their organization and with business partners outside the organization. However, each enterprise has their processes described in different modelling languages, which increases the degree of complexity to exchange and share the knowledge between the enterprises involved in an IOBP. To fulfil this gap, some new approaches for

Business Process Modelling were developed; the most promising are BPEL4WS, WS-CDL, BPML, WSCI, WSFL, XLANG and WSDL which are XML (eXtensible Markup Language) based languages. WS-CDL and WSCI are languages appropriate to model abstract processes, e.g., they include every type of action executed between organizations and are accessible to the partners' organization [12]. The others are suitable for private processes, e.g., a process that describes the internal executable activities that support the activities of public processes [2]. A private process is private to the organization which means that the knowledge it possesses is restricted to the enterprise it belongs to. On the contrary, a public process has information that must and should be shared with other processes in order to obtain a composition of business processes that will form the IOBP. These concepts are also strongly connected with other two concepts: composition (or orchestration) and choreography of web services and we have adopted the following ones [9, 18]: *Composition* refers to the definition of the internal implementation of the executable business processes. *Web Services Composition* defines executable business processes that are built from a set of web services. *Orchestration* is usually private to the business party, since it contains reserved information (business strategies, business rules and business policies) on the specific way a given process is carried out. *Choreography* defines externally observable behaviour of a business process. Web Services *Choreography* refers to the correct content and order of messages that two parties exchange in a business process. *Choreography* is usually public, since it defines the common rules that make for a valid composition of the distributed business processes in the business domain; it describes collaboration among the needed enterprise services in order to achieve a common goal.

3.3 Connections and disambiguating of BPm concepts in the BA and SOA areas

We will now identify some near concepts through the analysis of the presented conceptual maps, e.g., to disambiguate different concepts with the same name and near concepts with different names referring to the two conceptual maps.

Form the pure business point of view, the central key element of this conceptual map is the term Business Process, through the use of diverse conceptual and formal languages. Business Processes have pre-conditions, inputs, outputs and goals; they execute a set of activities that consume resources. Whilst in the SOA approach, although we mention the BP concept, the BP is represented by a Web Service. The web service has inputs, outputs, a transforming function and its description is made through a specific language (WSDL-Web Service Definition Language).

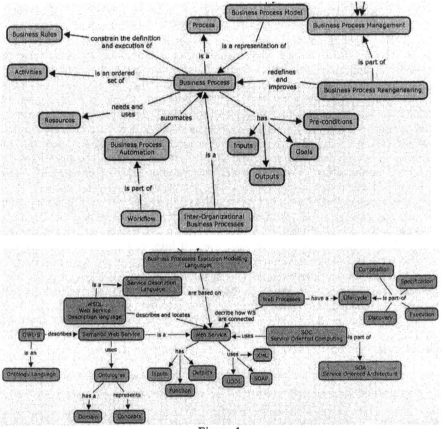

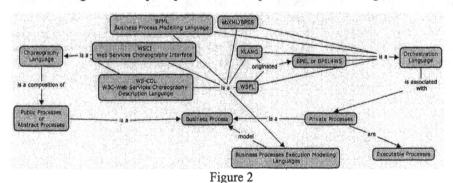

Figure 1

The concept of IOBP from the high level management perspective has the correspondent SOA approach, as choreography of web services. Much like what we can see through the concepts represented in the previous and following scheme.

Figure 2

4. RELATED WORK

There is a lot of work done on the definition of BP modelling languages, but it clearly misses some research clearly addressing the gap between the referred two complementary fields. [8] This paper aims at the realization gap between business and technical processes, discussing the differences between the processes modelled from the pure business perspective and those modelled with consideration of technical aspects. Designing a BP from the business point of view needs the message exchange between, activities and roles that are part of a process. However, when designing executable processes, attention must be paid to the business requirements and also to the technical context where the process should be executed. It also presents the design requirements that must be followed in order to create a lossless realization of a BP; their approach, based on a process description framework, defines the possible transformation needed when constructing a technical process from a business process.

According to [14] "There clearly exists a gap between the high-level process models used in the early stages of the process management life cycle and the detailed execution models of the implementation and enactment stages. This gap manifests itself in the following points: lack of an appropriate language that covers both high-level process design and low-level process execution; lack of appropriate conversion between languages of different stages of the process management life cycle; and lack of guidance for the conversion of high-level process models into low-level executable models".

The goal of BPMN [7] is to provide a business process modelling notation that is readily usable by business analysts, technical developers and business people that manage and monitor these processes. As such BPMN positions itself as a bridge between modelling and execution and between people that run the business and implementers of systems that support the business.

5. CONCLUSIONS AND FURTHER WORK

Modelling the IOBP integrating both the approaches - business and technological - is still far from being achieved. Modelling IOBP requires specific constructs and methodologies, and requires a high-level model and the corresponding executable one for exchanging and merging behaviours, resources and activities. The definition of IOBP from the management perspective only deals with the describing in what order the activities should be performed by the involved organizations in order to achieve a business goal. Whilst in the technical perspective the technological limitations must also be considered. The activities in the technical process can differ from the activities in the management business process (e.g., human resource activities cannot be modelled in the technical approach), regarding the goals, the message exchanges, the business requirements, among others. The analysis of the obtained conceptual maps and the revision of literature undertaken points out that Web Services seem to be a very appropriate communication mechanism to perform distributed business processes among several organizations, mainly because they are invoked and delivered through the Internet and also because they provide a standard interface. In our work we will try to bridge the gap between high level BP models and the execution of the IOBP achieved through the composition of the IOBP. The main objective of our work is to contribute to the understanding of Business Process Modelling field focusing on the definition of the IOBP, and for that we will need to generate a high level model for the IOBP and we will implement a prototype based on a Multi-Agent System (MAS) technology. Defining a BP in a detailed and comprehensive way is a complex task because of the dynamic environment they are involved in, such as complex business rules and policies, abnormally action from the involved partners, among others. The focuses of research are the composition of IOBP, at the management level, through semantic matching of business process descriptions, including goals, operational requirements and business rules; and the application of learning approaches in MAS to manage the composition of IOBP, dealing with the evolution of the languages and vocabularies that underpin business rules, business models, and the regulatory framework.

6. REFERENCES

1. Aalst, A.H.M. Hofstede, A.H.M., and Weske, M., Business Process Management: A Survey in BPM 2003, W.V.A. van der Aalst et al (eds)LNCS 2678, pp 1-12, Springer-Verlag Berlin Heidelberg,2003.
2. Akram, M. S., Managing Changes to Service Oriented Enterprises, PhD Thesis, Virginia, USA, 2005.
3. Benatallah B., Dijkman R. M. Dumas M., Maamar Z., Service Composition: Concepts, Techniques, Tools and Trends, Idea Group Inc. Copyright © 2005.
4. Brian R. Gaines and Mildred L. G., Concept Maps as Hypermedia Components, Shaw Knowledge Science Institute University of Calgary, Alberta, Canada.
5. Eriksson, Hans Erik, Penker, Magnus, Business Modelling with UML: Business Patterns at work, OMG Press, 2000
6. http://cmap.ihmc.us/].
7. http://bpmn.org/
8. Henkel, M., Zdravkovic J., Johannesson, P., Service-based Processes – Design for Business and Technology, in I 2nd Int.l Conference on Service Oriented Computing, New York, USA, Nov. 2004
9. Kazhamiakin R., Pistore M., Roveri M., A Framework for Integrating Business Processes and Business Requirements in the 8th Int. IEEE Enterprise Distributed Object Computing Conf., California Sep 2004
10. Medjahed B, Benatallah B, Bouguettaya A., Ngu A., Elmagarmid A., Business-to-business interactions: issues and enabling technologies in The VLDB Journal (2003) 12: 59–85 / Digital Object Identifier (DOI) 10.1007/s00778-003-0087-z
11. Muehlen, Z., Rosemann, M., Multi-Paradigm Process Management. In: Proceedings of CAiSE'04 Workshops - 5th Workshop on Business Process Modelling, Development and Support (BPMDS 2004). Eds.: Janis Grundspenkis, Marite Kirikova, Riga, Latvia, 2004, pp. 169-175. 2004.
12. Pušnik, M., Jurič B.M., Heričko M., Šumak B., Rozman I., Business Process Orchestration and eBusiness, 16th Bled eCommerce Conference eTransformation Bled, Slovenia, June 9 – 11, 2003
13. Sarmento, L., Maia, B., Santos, D., Pinto A., Cabral, L., "Corpógrafo V3: From Terminological Aid to Semi-automatic Knowledge Engine", in Proceedings of the 5th International Conference on Language Resources and Evaluation (LREC'2006), Genoa, Italia, 22-28 May 2006
14. Schmidt R., Composite Applications for the Enactment of Dynamic Inter-Organizational Business Processes, in Proceedings of the 1st Int. Workshop "Component Based Business Information Systems Engineering" (Internal Conference on Object Oriented Information Systems). Genova Sep 2nd, 2003
15. Shen, J., Yang, Y., Zhu, C., Wan, C., From BPEL4WS to OWL-S: Integrating E-Business Process Descriptions, in Proceedings of the 2005 IEEE Int. Conference on Services Computing, 2005.
16. Soares, António L., Sousa, J., 2004, Modelling Social Aspects of Collaborative Networks in Camarinha et al. (Eds.) Collaborative Networked Organizations. Kluwer Academic Press, Amsterdam.
17. Vernadat, F. B., Enterprise Modelling and Integration- principles and applications, Chapman and Hall, 1996
18. Weber I., Haller J., Mülle J.A., Automated Derivation of Executable Business Processes from Choreographies in Virtual Organizations in proceedings in eds.: Multikonferenz Wirtschaftsinformatik 2006, Band 2, XML4BPM Track, GITO-Verlag Berlin, 2006, ISBN 3-936771-62-6, pages 313-328.
19. Ying C., Hong L., Zhengchuan X., An Evaluation Framework for Inter-organizational Business Process Modelling Techniques in the 8th Pacific Asia Conference on Information Systems, Shangai-China, July 2004
20. Zhao J. Leon, Chengb H.K., Web services and process management: a union of convenience or a new area of research? (Editorial), Decision Support Systems: Special Issue on Web Services and Process Management, Volume 40, Issue 1, July 2005, Pages 1-8.

24
DYNAMIC PROCESS ORGANISATION

Sodki Chaari[1,2], Frédérique Binnier[1], Joël Favrel[1], Chokri Ben Amar[2]
(1) INSA de Lyon - Laboratoire PRISMa / IF502 - F69621 Villeurbanne Cédex, FRANCE
{Sodki.Chaari, Frederique.Biennier, Joel.Favrel}@insa-lyon.fr
(2) ENI de Sfax – Laboratoire REGIM / Route de Soukra, Sfax, TUNISIA
Chokri.benamar@enis.rnu.tn

Enterprises are evolving towards a more agile, dynamic and adaptive organisation that can make quick responses to the market and customer requirements. This carried out an increasing need for enterprises to get involved in collaboration strategies. Moreover, new IT organisation, namely Service Oriented Architectures (SOA), can be introduced to implement opened and agile information system. To align the enterprise strategy and the information support system organisation, we present a cooperation model based on SOA, called service oriented enterprise. Thanks to a multi-level process organisation, simple combination and filtering rules can be applied to build dynamically customised distributed processes on demand.

1. CONTEXT

Today, with the high competitive changing economy environment, lots of organisations have redesigned at least some of their systems and reviewed their process structures and strategies to take advantages of new business opportunities often leading to Collaborative Business. These collaborative organisations are set according to short term goal and implement dynamic and on-demand Virtual Enterprises (VE) (Kwon et al. 2003). To fit the required agility level required by such adaptive organisations, an efficient and agile information system must be set to support common process enactment and execution. This leads to take into account both the organisational constraints to establish efficient common processes and the technical inter-operability constraints.

While focusing on enterprise organisation, one can use enterprise modelling approaches. Due to these different levels of collaboration, a virtual enterprise organisation leads to two different strategies: either the VE is considered as a standard enterprise (in this case modelling methods must be adapted to fit the planned duration and respect enterprise autonomy) or the VE is seen as a set of co-operating organisations (in this more agile case a particular attention is paid on shared business processes).

While focusing on the IT side of collaborative business, a particular attention must be paid on inter-operability constraints. This leads to adapt the traditional information system organisation to support the necessary openness. Emerging technologies such as the Service Oriented Architecture (SOA) (Baglietto et al., 2005), ontologies (Yang et al., 2005) are generally perceived as core technologies to successfully deal with these challenges.

Please use the following format when citing this chapter:

Chaari, S., Binnier, F., Favrel, J., Amar, C. B., 2006, in IFIP International Federation for Information Processing, Volume 224, Network-Centric Collaboration and Supporting Fireworks, eds. Camarinha-Matos, L., Afsarmanesh, H., Ollus, M., (Boston: Springer), pp. 229–236.

Introducing SOA for enterprises information system can reduce dramatically the funds required to start up a business. Services are readily available for integration and orchestration. Moreover, while each service has a machine understandable representation, discovering the convenient service could be achieved in a dynamic and automated way. Hence, enterprises will be able to form on-the-fly, project-driven and on demand alliances. As the number of services increase, a particular attention must be paid on an automated service combination.

Nevertheless, enterprises define differently the service's granularity level. It can be associated to a whole workflow with several tasks or a single elementary task. Consequently, enterprise must "re-think" their business process organisation to find the suitable relationships with these services. Using object oriented approach, enterprises can attain this goal by modelling and decomposing recursively their business processes. Resulting business objects are turned into appropriate services either by adding a convenient interface directly, or by associating them into composed services. Thus, the IT support and the associated services are "prepared" both for an internal and an external use.

Furthermore, the inter-operability level requirements involves taking into account semantic constraints. A key idea is to use ontology to empower services with semantic descriptions. (Hu and Du, 2004) defines ontology as an "explicit specification of a conceptualization". Ontologies allow an effective services discovery and ensure a good management and organisation of available services space.

This paper focuses on the major difficulties which arise when building the inter-enterprise process. We argue that enterprise must be re-organised according to collaborative basis to benefit of market opportunities. Consequently processes must be defined in an adaptive way. Next, we present a multi-level framework based on SOA that can be used to assist the dynamic combination of enterprises services resulting in a collaborative inter enterprise process which provide a value-added service to users leading to a Service Oriented Enterprise organisation (SOE).

2. INTER ENTERPRISE PROCESS ORGANISATION

VEs require a lean and evolving structure, able to protect the flexibility and reactivity of each partner. Moreover, enterprise-engineering projects are rather long and their cost can be a bar. This can be overcome by connecting engineering processes to more efficient diagnostic processes to guide the way standard solutions are chosen. Such a bottom-up modelling approach proposed in the GRECOPME framework (Biennier et al., 2002) relies both on an efficient "collaboration" diagnosis and on re-usable collaborative business processes. Of course, in order to preserve enterprise autonomy and to favour the emergence of the global synergy, collaborative business processes and their support systems have to be adapted to this multi-enterprises context. In order to support these collaborative business processes, inter-organisational workflow systems can be set. For this purpose, different points of view can be developed:

- Each enterprise protects its own autonomy and has its own workflow. In this case, workflow interactions must be defined to provide a global organisation (Casati and Di Scenza, 2001), tasks managers can be co-ordinated thanks to tasks dependency relationships as proposed in the METEOR2 system (Miller et al., 1997).

- A centralised common workflow is defined and is turned into activity charts so that a decentralised execution, split among the different partners, can be used. Such an analysis process is proposed by (Muth et al., 1998) and makes a heavy use of Transaction Processing systems to provide the shared information consistency.

- A B2B workflow based approach can be derived from traditional EDI or C-Business environment: For this purpose, (Van der Aalst, 2002) proposes multiple descriptions of shared business process: public and private workflows are defined concurrently and the global consistency is achieved thanks to well-defined information exchange format (Bussler, 2002).

Both of these process organisations rely also on the interconnection of the enterprises IT support. Turning the monolithic information system organisation to a more dynamic one may be achieved thanks to service oriented architecture. These component based architectures are mostly business process oriented: thanks to the orchestration level, elementary services can be combined so that rather customised processes can be built from standard elements. To fit the enterprise needs, this IT architecture can be worthy combined to enterprise process oriented modelling tools as ARIS (Sheer, 1993) so that the IS can be tuned efficiently.

While the Service Oriented Architecture principle can be worthy used to define customised IT support and to improve the IT inter-operability thanks to common interfaces, the IS complexity remains a brake to the openness. Consequently, a particular attention has to be paid on the global corporate information system organisation so that it can evolve without loosing its consistency. To fit this last requirement, one can use the urbanism paradigm (Longepe, 2003): the information system is split in rather independent units associated to different business areas, so that local changes should not impact the full system. Coupled to the SOA organisation, it means that the engineering phase is achieved in a hierarchical way: for each business areas, business processes are identified and split among activities, processes and lastly operations associated to services (figure 1). This leads to a multi-dimensional organisation, clustering processes and information parts according to "independent" business areas.

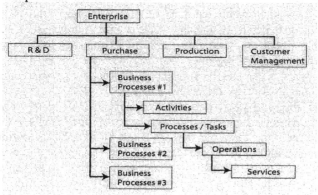

Figure 1 – Information system urbanism principle and its connection to services

Nevertheless, such an information system urbanism strategy leads to rather static organisations exhibiting poor collaborative abilities between the different business areas. In this case, organising shared processes consists in orchestrating independent process without taking into account the organisational consistency: for example juxtaposing different planning strategy in a supply chain when sub-processes do not share a common goal may be leading to a bull-whip effect.

Consequently, a technological inter-operability is not enough while building collaborative organisations: enterprises must be re-organised according to collaborative opportunities and processes must be defined in an adaptive way so that they can be re-orchestrated easily.

To support fast and efficient process organisation, one may use a dedicated orchestration process. This leads to service selection and assembly. After discovering the convenient services, consistency controls must be implemented while orchestrating these services. We found various approaches to service orchestration from academia and industry. (Medjahed et al., 2003) present a framework for orchestrating atomic services, which are semantically described using non-functional properties such as their function, their category and their QoS. Other approaches for service orchestration including model checking, modelling service composition as Mealy machines, and automatic composition of finite state machines (Fu et al., 2002). Automatic services composition is the "ultimate" goal of most composition efforts. Hence, (Berardi et al., 2005) presents a framework describing services' behaviour as an external execution tree and then translates it into finite state machines. In (Hamadi and Benatallah, 2003) Petri nets are used as tools to modelling service orchestration. Each service is associated to one Petri net describing service. They define a net for each service and composition operators that perform composition sequence to produce new services.

Nevertheless, these approaches focus on particular technical points. To support dynamic service binding, leading to dynamic virtual organisations, a more complex framework is required.

3. SERVICE ORIENTED ENTERPRISE ARCHITECTURE

Building dynamically a collaborative process involves taking into account both enterprises own organisation and dynamic service binding abilities. This leads to apply the urbanism paradigm globally on the enterprise organisation and not only on the IT system (Biennier and Mathieu, 2006). This approach leads to re-organise the enterprise according to activities that can be exposed to other partners and assembled dynamically and then to couple this enterprise organisation to the IT support, leading to a service oriented organisation.

To reach this goal we start from an organisational point of view, using basic elements to describe an enterprise i.e. activities, resources (including IT resources) and actors. Analysing these elements and their relationships according to several enterprise modelling approaches leads us to define basic properties attached to them and to re-organise them in a multi-level architecture, paying a particular attention to the inter-enterprise process combination requirements (see figure 2):

- **On the enterprise side,** we have to define a fragmentary organisation that can be used as elementary bricks to set a common process, and its links with the IT support system. To fit this requirement, we propose a 4-level organisation:
  - **Enterprise entities level:** contains the set of the basic enterprise entities: activities, resources, individuals, organisational units.
  - **Business object level:** this level is used to manage different business objects according to the business domain such as product, order, customer, payment and so on. This representation includes at least its business name and definition, attributes, behavior, relationships, rules, policies, and constraints. Business objects can be conceptual, i.e., analysis/design objects, as well as implementation objects, which are independent, language neutral and persistent objects that require a middleware infrastructure to run.
  - **Business component layer:** this layer is used to gather basic activities that exhibit common functional characteristics and goals into different business components. Business components are designed as packages encapsulating a well defined set of business objects. Each business component is made of two parts: first the interface that can be exposed and an internal part related to the own enterprise process organisation fitting the enterprise own business rules and defining precisely interaction between business objects. This involves that each business component are closely associated to resources and actors.
  - **Concrete services level:** This level consists of the real services implementing the information system. Each business component is related to an ordered set of "concrete services" orchestrating the related process. This level includes service-oriented design and development incorporate a broad range of capabilities, technologies, tools, and skill sets that include:
    - Managing services lifecycle: it includes identifying, designing, developing, deploying, finding, applying, evolving, and maintaining services.
    - Adopting best practices and tools for architecting services-oriented solutions in repeatable, predictable ways that fits changing business needs.
    - Delivering service oriented solutions fitting quality and QoS requirements.
- **On the collaborative process organisation side,** we define a 2-level organisation:
  - **Inter-enterprise common process:** this layer is used to describe the common process that must be built. The common process consists in orchestrating different virtual services, selected and bounded dynamically according the needs.
  - **Virtual services level:** This layer is used to describe in a generic way the services exposed by the different enterprises. These services are associated to basic functionalities that can be combined to set the common process (figure 3). As far as their implementation is concerned, these virtual services are associated to functions that business components can expose to be invoked and used by partner enterprises in cooperation scenarios. Differently, virtual service will act as exposed interfaces of the business components. Then

combination constraints are used to define the way concrete services should be assembled to be interfaced in the common process.

The dynamic binding process is organised as a selection followed by an assembly phase. To support an efficient selection process, we use the basic descriptors taken from the meta-model (figure 2) so that an efficient filtering process can be used.

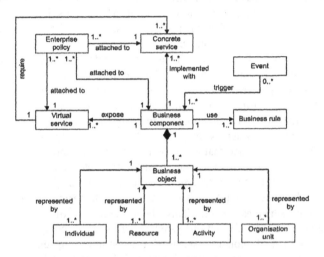

Figure 2 – Enterprise architecture's meta-model

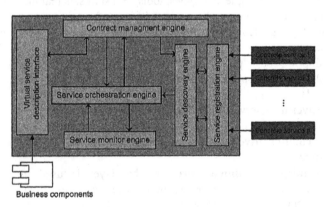

Figure 3 – Virtual service architecture

A simple ordering process example can be used to illustrate this service combination process. In such a case, the customer defines the product quantity and asks for the expected delivery date and product fees. As far as the manufacturer is concerned, creating the convenient process involves combining production and supply services. First, selecting the convenient partners involves defining competencies related to the ordered products. By this way, adapted partner selection can occur. Then, building the distributed ordering process mixes customer, manufacturer and its supplier production, supply and pricing processes. This involves that each partner exposes its virtual services namely ordering and production planning interface. As far as the ordering processes are concerned, the related business component gathers both the ordering process support system and the pricing algorithm. Then this business component is interfaced with the production business component so that delays can be adjusted. Despite of its simplicity, this example mixes different enterprise elements with standard interface:

- Entities/ Resources: estimate, request estimate.
- Activities: sending document, receive document, checking document.
- Individuals: customer, manufacturer, supplier.

Then the business component level includes associations between different businesses objects according to the different enterprises needs and business rules. In our case, we can define the following business component: (send document, customer, manufacturer), (send document, manufacturer, supplier), (receive document, manufacturer, customer), (receive document, supplier, manufacturer), (checking document, customer, manufacturer), (checking document, customer, manufacturer, supplier) that can be re-assembled to build dynamically the shared business process.

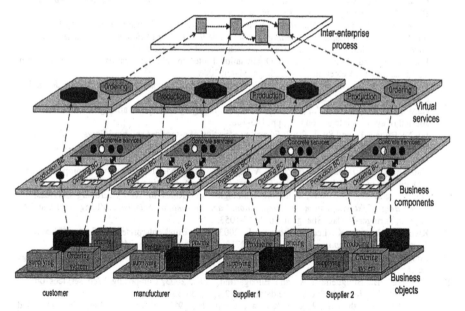

Figure 4 – Dynamic binding of virtual services

4. CONCLUSION

To support dynamic collaborative organisation, a dynamic process enactment service must be provided. This involves building both a common process and the dedicated IT support system. In this paper, we present how enterprise architecture can be re-organised to set a service oriented enterprise which can support inter-enterprise cooperation. This architecture, based on the IT SOA, is organised into different levels (business objects used to model enterprise process are associated to virtual services and finally to concrete services) so that the global infrastructure is closely related to the enterprise business strategy and exhibit convenient agility abilities. Several filtering processes are used to select the convenient services to bind and then an assembly process is set. Further works will deal with the automated integration of syntactic inter-operable services so that the combination scope can be extended.

Acknowledgements

This work is partly inspired by the GOSPI - INTERPROD project funded by the Rhône-Alpes area council.

5. REFERENCES

1. Baglietto, P., Maresca, M., Parodi, A. and Zingirian, N., 2005, Stepwise deployment methodology of a service oriented architecture for business communities, Journal of information and software technology (47), pp. 427-436.
2. Berardi, D., Calvanese, D., and Mecella, M., 2005, Composition of Services with Nondeterministic Observable Behavior, in: *Proceedings of the 3rd conference on Service Oriented Computing*, B. Benatallah, ed, Springer-Verlag, Amesterdam, pp, 43-85.
3. Biennier, F., Boucher, X., Hammami, A., and Vincent, L., 2002, Towards a modelling framework for networks of SMEs, in: *Proceedings of the 3rd IFIP Working conference on infrastructures for virtual enterprises*, L. Camarinha-Matos, ed., Kluwer, Algarve, pp. 11-18.
4. Biennier, F., and Mathieu, H., 2006, Organisational inter-operability: towards enterprise urbanism. To appear in I-ESA electronic proceedings. March 2006.
5. Bussler, C., 2002, The application of workflow technology in semantic B2B integration, Journal of distributed and parallel databases (12), pp. 163-191.
6. Casati, F., and Di scenza, A., 2001, Modeling and managing interactions among business processes, Journal of systems integration (10), pp. 145-168.
7. Fu, X., Bultan, T., and Su, J., 2002, Formal verification of e-services and workflows, in: *Proceeding of the workshop on Web Services, E-Business, and the Semantic*, C. Bussler, R. Hull, and S. McIlraith, eds, Springer-Verlag, Toronto, pp. 188-202.
8. Hamadi, R., and Benatallah, B., 2003, A Petri net-based model for web service composition, in: *Proceedings of the 14th Australasian Database Conference*, Adelaide, pp. 191-200.
9. Hu, H., and Du, X., 2004, Adopting Ontologies and Rules in Web Searching Services, in: *Proceeding of 1st symposium on Computational and Information Science*, J. Zhang, J. He, and Y. Fu, eds, Springer-Verlag, Shanghai, pp. 1047-1053.
10. Kwon, Y., Lee, H. K., Lee, S. and Lee, J., 2003, The virtual enterprise: redefining the concept, *Lecture Notes in Computer Science*, volume 2713, Springer-Verlag, pp. 249-258.
11. Longepe, C., 2003, The Enterprise Architecture It Project: The Urbanisation Paradigm, Kogan Page Science, ISBN:1903996384.
12. Medjahed, B., Bouguettaya A., and Elmagarmid, A.K., 2003, Composing Web services on the Semantic Web, Journal of very large database (12), pp, 333-351.
13. Miller, J.A., Sheth, A.P., Kochut K.J., and Singh, H., 1997, WebWork: Meteor2's Web-based workflow management system, Journal of intelligent information system (10), pp. 185-213.
14. Muth, P., Wodtke, D., Weissenfels, J., Dittrich, A., and Weikum G., 1998, From centralized workflow specification to distributed workflow execution, Journal of intelligent information system (10), pp. 159-184.
15. Sheer, A.W., 1993, Architecture of Integrated Information System (ARIS), in: *Proceedings* of the JSPE/IFIP TC5/WG5.3 workshop on the Design of Information Infrastructure Systems for Manufacturing, Tokyo, pp. 65-84.
16. Van der Aalst, W., 2002, Inheritance of inter-organizational workflows to enable business to business E-commerce, Journal of electronic commerce research (2), pp. 195-231.
17. Yang, H., Li, Z., Chen, J., and Xia, H., 2005, Web services composition based on ontology and workflow, in: *Proceedings of the 6th conference on Advances in Web-Age Information Management*, W. Fan, Z. Wu, and J. Yag, eds., Springer-Verlag, Hangzhou, pp. 297-307.

25

A COLLABORATIVE MODEL FOR LOGISTICS PROCESS MANAGEMENT

Giuseppe Confessore[1], Graziano Galiano[1,2], and Giuseppe Stecca[1]

[1] Istituto di Tecnologie Industriali e Automazione
Consiglio Nazionale delle Ricerche
Via del fosso del cavaliere 100, 00133 Rome, ITALY
{g.confessore, g.galiano, g.stecca}@itia.cnr.it

[2] Dipartimento di Informatica ed Applicazioni
Università degli Studi di Salerno
Via S. Allende, 84081 Baronissi (SA), ITALY

In this work we present a collaborative model for logistics process management addressing the problem of the integration of activities of a 3rd party logistics (3PL) operator. The scope of a 3PL operator is to achieve a balance between the warehouse and transportation costs and customer service level. In our model we define a collaborative network in which the 3PL operator interacts with subcontractors such as manpower suppliers and transporters, and the relationships are governed by contracts. The model supports a negotiation mechanism among partners and a cooperation system among macro modules in order to find optimal combined logistics and distribution plans. The architecture of the collaborative model is organized in operational modules and elements to support a chain's dynamic execution.

1. INTRODUCTION

Collaborative networks that connect customers and suppliers are creating value by making trading more efficient and possibly even more effective than traditional method. The term collaborative network (CN) was used in (Camarinha-Matos, and Afsarmanesh, 2004) to refer to the complex systems emerging in many forms in different application domains, and consisting of many facets whose proper understanding requires the contribution from multiple disciplines.

Companies focus on their core business and outsource secondary activities to other organizations. The coordination of processes by the customer's organization is difficult because part of the work is executed outside the company's boundaries. Indeed, the outsourced service can be considered as a sub-part of a process initiated in the customer's organization. Thus, the whole process spans the customer and the supplier of the service and could be considered as an inter-organizational workflow that should be defined and managed in order to ensure that it produces the desired level of quality (Stricker et al, 2000).

The traditional workflow approach to business process management involves describing the entire process from a centralised perspective (Jennings et al, 2000).

In order to co-ordinate the relationships among supply chain actors it is important to have integrating techniques at tactical level used in conjunction with

Please use the following format when citing this chapter:

Confessore, G., Galiano, G., Stecca, G., 2006, in IFIP International Federation for Information Processing, Volume 224, Network-Centric Collaboration and Supporting Fireworks, eds. Camarinha-Matos, L., Afsarmanesh, H., Ollus, M., (Boston: Springer), pp. 237–244.

integration tools at operation level (Perona and Saccani, 2004).

Supply Chain components can provide intelligence and flexibility to supply chain architectures. In (Verwijmeren, 2004) a software component architecture to provide intelligence and flexibility to supply chains is proposed. Supply chain engines are built on top of ERP, WMS and TMS to provide a global inventory management engine. For implementation issues Java Enterprise, CORBA and web service technologies are used.

(Mason et al, 2003) make use of a discrete event simulation model to examine the total cost benefits that can be achieved by suppliers and warehouses, through the increased global visibility provided by an integrated system. Global visibility can be considered as enabler for cost and service efficiency.

Our approach considers a set of agents to perform activities associated with logistics management providing more flexibility than the traditional methods. The agents provide an open system with loosely coupled components and perform common tasks of a 3rd party logistics (3PL) operator such as storage, replenishment, order picking, packing, shipment, etc. Some tasks are outsourced to the collaborative partners (i.e shipping to transporters) or scheduled on basis of availability of manpower supplied by the collaborative partners. The advantages of employing agents include the facilitation of inter and intra organizational cooperation and flexibility in controlling process parameters.

In some situations, it is not always possible to predict in advance all the parameters that may be important for the overall processes. This gives rise to the need of adaptive systems. (Piramuthu, 2005) presents a theoretical framework for dynamic formation and reconfiguration of supply chains.

In this work we present a collaborative model for logistics management addressing the problem of the integration of activities of a 3PL operator. The goal of a 3PL operator is to achieve a balance between the warehouse and transportation costs and customer service level.

In our model we define a collaborative network in which the 3PL operator interacts with manpower suppliers and transporters. The model supports cooperation between Warehouse Management System (WMS) and Transportation Management System (TMS) in order to find optimal combined logistics and distribution plans. The benefit of using this approach can be that better coordinated inter-organizational processes would cost less while decreasing inefficiencies and improve overall quality. The internal (flow of works among WMS and TMS) and external (flow of works with manpower suppliers and transporters) costs can be reduced and the quality of the services provided can be increased due a better planning.

The paper is organized as follows. In Section 2 we describe the logistics scenario, and the relationships among the existing partners. In Section 3 the proposed multiagent model is overviewed. In Section 4, we suggest how the actors should collaborate in order to reduce the logistics activities inefficiencies. Finally in Section 5 conclusions and future work is discussed.

2. THE LOGISTICS SCENARIO

The 3rd Party Logistics Operators (3PL) respond to the need of business operators (1st layer) and logistics operators (2nd layer operator – 2PL) to optimise the supply-chain performance by subcontracting operational tasks such as transport or warehousing to second-tier suppliers; screening, selecting and contracting the latter, and monitoring and evaluating their performance. A 3PL thus orchestrates supply chains.

To fulfil its role, the 3PL establish a business network driven by contracts and information systems. The most important information systems used by the 3PL are the Transportation Management System (TMS) and the Warehouse Management System (WMS). TMS is basically an Information System used to plan shipments. TMS solutions automate the entire shipping process of a company, from carrier selection to routing and scheduling. WMS is basically a software system to track and manage warehouse activities.

Once the logistics network is designed, the customer sends both shipping orders and storage orders to the 3PL. The 3PL forwards the orders to the *Warehouse Manager* and the *Transportation Manager* who build the operation plan outsourcing some activities to the 2PL operators (i.e. manpower and transportation suppliers). This step is fulfilled in two possible ways: by first solving the transportation problem, then by solving the warehousing operations problem or vice versa. Possible conflicts in the two plans are resolved mostly by phone.

We can now introduce the actors in our business model and explain their roles. Figure 1, illustrates the structure of the business model and the interactions among the actors. In particular, the 3PL operator can be represented as the *Contract Manager* (*CM*), the *Warehouse Manager* (*WM*), the *Transportation Manager* (*TM*), and the *Logistics Manager* (*LM*). The three decision makers interact with other partners of the logistics network and in particular with the *Transportation Suppliers*, the *Manpower Suppliers*, and the *Customer* (representing the 1st layer of the business model).

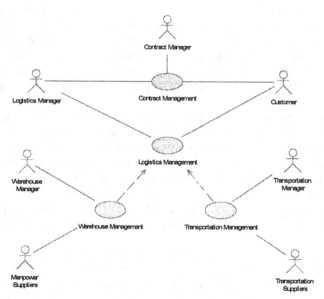

Figure 1 – The business model UML diagram

The actor interactions can be classified under three levels:

Strategic level. In this level the contract manager *CM* starts a contract with the customer, builds up the network and select the 2PL partners and internal resources to execute the business.

Planning level. At the planning level the actors interact defining their resources to fulfil orders. In this phase the WMS and the TMS are used in cascade. The interactions are mostly unidirectional. In this phase a planning flow can be individualised. At each step a subset of resources are booked and constraints are fixed for other resources.

Operation level. At operation level the interaction among actors is guided by process execution. The information and physical flows specify the sequence of interaction among partners.

3. THE MULTIAGENT COLLABORATIVE NETWORK

The mentioned interaction approach has some gaps. In particular one of the most important is the lack of flexibility in business planning and execution. The planning of resource allocation in cascade from WMS to TMS or from TMS to WMS in particular can result in inefficiency for the entire network. The research project PILOT-ICT (new integrated logistics framework based on ICT and distributed decision systems), partially founded by the Italian Ministry of Education University and Research - MIUR under the national law FAR n. 297/1999 - intends to undertake the development of a multiagent system for collaborative WMS and TMS integration.

Multiagent Systems have a successful application in supply chain integration (Nissen, 2001). In (Ito and Abadi, 2002), multiagent systems are used for warehouse system management. In this paper we present the multiagent model as a collaborative model for supply chain partners. Collaboration is the most important form of cooperation in multiagent systems. Collaboration means that a group of agents work together on a common project or task (Shen, Norrie, and Barthès, 2001). In the ongoing project the multiagent approach intends to achieve the following goals:

Flexibility: The whole system and each agent of the system are adaptive. By means of negotiation they can share information about resource allocations, times and costs. Through adaptive behaviour the agents are able to modify dynamically the behaviour in function of unforeseen situations. To assure predictable behaviour to agents a constraints system has to be defined (Spears, 2006). We use a mechanism of upper and lower bounds to key performance indicators (KPI) is considered. During strategic interactions, bounds to KPI are fixed whilst during planning KPI levels are allocated to agents by negotiation. The agents keep track of the history of KPI levels..

Modularity: One of the gaps of the classical systems is that they are build up around a problem instance; the solutions to the problems are indeed very difficulty to apply to other systems. Often the 3PL has to build up information systems for each customer. The considered model is designed to be implemented around decision modules on which the system's agents are built up. These modules (for strategic planning, warehouse optimisation, distribution scheduling, and performance evaluation) will have a high degree of modularity. The need for flexibility and adaptability implies an important trade-off between modularity and integration (Lakatta et al, 2004).

Effectiveness: Agents have the ability to share a set of alternative plans. A strategic plan agent (the *Logistics Manager* agent) will build a general plan over the received plans, resolving the plan constraints violations by means of negotiations. Each partner of the logistics network can indeed propose a set of plan alternatives and it is not forced anymore to build up its plan based on fixed plans of other partners. This will result in a higher degree of performance for the entire supply chain. The KPI are a measure of Service Level, cost of the activities, time, and productivity for each sub process.

The actor interactions under the three levels can be reformulated as following:

Strategic level. During the contract management phase the *Contract Manager* agent interacts with the *Logistics Manager* agent and fixes the bounds for the KPI; in this phase the *Contract Manager* and the *Logistics Manager* also establish the correspondence among sets of KPI intervals (or bounds) and collaborative sub networks of 2PL operators able to meet those intervals.

Planning level. As explained in detail in the next section, the planning level is performed through the following steps: once the order details (related to outbound logistics or incoming logistics, e.g shipment or storage orders) are received from customers the logistics manager starts a collaborative negotiation asking alternative plans to *Warehouse Manager* and *Transportation Manager* agents. Using their knowledge base the two agents can fix upper an lower bounds of KPI that are able to respect for different plan alternatives (also interacting with the 2PL operators *Transportation Suppliers* and *Manpower Suppliers*). An iteration to resolve conflicts and ask for extra resources may be needed. After the resource allocation the agents, using optimization algorithms embedded in the information systems modules, compute the detailed operation plan and update their knowledge of resource allocation and performances. We assume that an agreement is always found.

Operation level. At the operation level the interaction among actors is guided by process execution. During the execution, agents adapt their knowledge about KPI parameters and resource allocation confronting foreseen plans with real performances.

4. THE PLANNING SCHEMA

Once the order details are received from the customer, the Logistics Manager Agent (LMA) groups orders using a selection method based on a function of the features of the order such as type, constraints, priority, etc. Then, for each order batch it selects the needed resources to execute the required activities. The LMA communicates with Warehouse Manager and Transportation Manager Agents (WMA and TMA respectively) so that they may produce consistent and feasible plans with maximum profit. To do so, the LMA provides case-base and contextual information to the WMA and TMA. In particular, on the basis of historical data, the LMA defines a set of bounds BS (e.g. time constraints, level service bounds, priority, etc) that WMA and TMA have to follow for each order.

The LMA sends the order batch details with the relative BS to WMA and TMA.

These manager agents select the needed activities to order batch fulfillment and define which of them outsource.

In the first step, the outsourcer (WMA and TMA) prepares the requests for the execution of the activities that he wants to outsource and define the searching criteria that needed to be used to find the convenient suppliers (manpower suppliers and transporters respectively). Given a list of supplier candidates, a preliminary screening is carried out to determine which potential supplier appears to be qualified to execute the required activities and/or services. The decision maker should take into account the degree of successes in past executions operated by the bidding suppliers to ensure quality in the outsourcing operation.

After this step, the outsourcer broadcasts its requests to every selected supplier. To increase the rate of successful contracts, each supplier determines a set of offers that maximizes own profit and presents it to the outsourcer. Until the best offer is selected, whole offers are stored in a working memory of the outsourcer.

The WMA and TMA select the optimal set of offers covering all orders and compose and schedule the workflow of the required activities feasibly with the available resources. They initiate a simulation of this workflow with the appropriate details to evaluate the performance and then produce operation plans (WP and TP respectively).

The LMA receives the plans from WMA and TMA and check their feasibility. If the plans are inconsistent the LMA starts a negotiating process.

Here is the logic outline for the negotiating algorithm of the LMA:

> *Get the order batch OB to fulfill*
> *Set i = 0*
> *Calculate BS$_i$ related to OB*
> *Repeat*
> > *Broadcast OB and BS to the WMA and TMA*
> > *Receive the plans WP and TP from WMA and TMA respectively*
> > *Detect conflicts in WP and TP*
> > *Redefine the BS to resolve detected conflicts*
> > *i = i + 1*
> *Until BS$_i$ is equal to BS$_{i-1}$*
> *Inform WMA and TMA that equilibrium has been reached.*

After each iteration the BS is redefined and become more constricted allowing WMA and TMA to produce plans more convergent to reach an equilibrium.

Once the plans WP and TP are received, the LMA detects conflicts and ask new plans for a better convergence to WMA and TMA modifying the BS. Based on its own set of offers received by suppliers, WMA and TMA may send a new plan satisfying the new BS or not. If not WMA and TMA can restart the outsourcing phase. Once conflicts are resolved, the LMA closes the negotiation and validates the plans WP and TP.

4.1 Technological architecture

Architecturally, there are many styles and approaches to implement collaboration. The web has already become the communication infrastructure not only for people to people but also for application to application. The programmatic interfaces made available are referred to as Web services (Buhler, 2004). They are aimed at using XML to build distributed information processing systems that work across the Internet. Web services are now increasing in sophistication. Specifications for quality of service and service composition such as BPEL for Web Services (BPELWS) currently authored by IBM, Microsoft and BEA, WS-Coordination, WS-Transaction, WS-Security, WS-Reliable Messaging, and WS-Policy will allow for far richer, higher-level delivery of computing services via a web services management platform (WSMP).

While initial implementation of web services may be simple, over time business-to-business integrations will become complex. Business process integration may be aided by the increased adoption of BPEL or other standards such as business process management (BPM) for web services flow composition (Smith, et al, 2003).

We propose that the 3PL operator can make use of a composition of the Web Services. Each process to fulfilment of an order batch can be decomposed into a set of workflow managed by WMS and TMS. In the planning level required activities are defined and business objects are handled to compose the workflow. Then a workflow engine instantiates the workflow process specifications.

In this scenario also the outsourcing communication between WMA and TMA pass through Web Services. A two-level mechanism for selection of suppliers is used to configure a new business process that consists of a set of Web services. In order to narrow down the available suppliers list, at the first-level suppliers are selected by a Web Services discovery engine, whose search criteria are created automatically by the requirement document. In order to construct the best business process, at the second-level suppliers are selected in accordance with a global optimization algorithm.

Similarly for the negotiation phase it is possible to use the web service technology. In order to address these issues (Kim, 2003) proposed a framework for negotiation automation system. The framework leverages the scope of existing research on the negotiations and extends it to the level of complexity necessary for next generation eBusiness applications.

5. CONCLUSION

In this work we presented a multiagent model to undertake facilitation of inter and intra organizational cooperation, flexibility and effectiveness. In the proposed model the 3PL forwards orders received from customer to the Warehouse Manager and the Transportation Manager who build the operation plan outsourcing some activities to the 2PL operators. Furthermore we suggest how the actors should collaborate in order to reduce the logistics activities inefficiencies. Further developments will investigate the use of auction mechanisms to solve the planning problem. We have already implemented most of the optimisation modules and we are working on framework integration and on the simulation of the proposed collaborative multiagent model.

REFERENCES

1. Aertsa ATM, Goossenaertsb JBM, Hammera DK, Wortmann JC. Architectures in context: on the evolution of business,application software, and ICT platform architectures. Information & Management 2004; 41: 781–794.
2. Bernardi D, Confessore G, Stecca G. "A multiagent model integrating inventory and routing processes", in Virtual Enterprises and Collaborative Networks, L.M. Camarinha-Matos (eds.): Kluwer Academic publishers 2004.
3. Buhler P., Vidal J. M., Integrating agent services into BPEL4WS defined workflows. In Proceedings of the Fourth International Workshop on Web-Oriented Software Technologies, 2004.
4. Camarinha-Matos L. M., Afsarmanesh H. "The emerging discipline of collaborative networks". In Virtual Enterprises and Collaborative Networks, L.M. Camarinha-Matos (eds.): Kluwer Academic publishers 2004.
5. Ito T, and Mousavi Jahan Abadi SM. "Agent-based material handling and inventoy planning in warehouse". Journal of Intelligent Manufacturing 2002; 13: 201-210.
6. Mason SJ, Ribera PM, Farris JA, Kirk RG. Integrating the warehousing and transportation functions of the supply chainTransportation Research Part E 2003; 39: 141–159.
7. Jennings, NR, Faratin, P, Norman, TD and Odgers B. "Autonomous Agents for Business Process Management". Int. Journal of Applied Artificial Intelligence, 2000; 14 (2): 145-189.
8. Kim, J., Segev, A., Automated negotiation protocols conforming to eBusiness infrastructure, Working Paper, Haas School of Business, 2003.
9. Nissen ME. "Agent-Based Supply Chain Integration, Information Technology and Management" 2001; 2: 289–312.
10. Perona M, Saccani N. Integration techniques in customer–supplier relationships: An empirical research in the Italian industry of household appliances. International. Journal of Production Economics 2004; 89: 189–205.
11. Piramuthu S. Knowledge-based framework for automated dynamic supply chain configuration. European Journal of Operational Research 2005; 165: 219–230.
12. Shen W, Norrie DH, Barthès J-PA. Multi-Agent systems for concurrent intelligent design and manufacturing. London and New York: Taylor & Francis, 2001.
13. Spears DF. "Assuring the behaviour of adaptive agents", Book chapter in Agent Technology from a Formal Perspective, Kluwer Academic publishers 2006.
14. Stricker, C., Riboni, S., Kradolfer, M., and Taylor, J., 2000, Market-Based Workflow Management for Supply Chains of Services, IEEE Proceeding of the Hawaii, Int. Conf. On Systems Science, Jaunuary 4-7, Maui, Hawaii.
15. Verwijmeren M. Software component architecture in supply chain management. Computers in Industry 2004; 53: 165–178.

Karsten Menzel
University College Cork, IRELAND, k.menzel@ucc.ie
Martin Keller
Dresden University of Technology, GERMANY, martin.keller@cib.bau.tu-dresden.de

Projects in the building industry are extremely dynamic, driven by external conditions, modified user requirements and frequently changing business partners. Therefore, common principles should be established throughout the construction industry, which flexibly support the management of construction project information and processes. This paper presents an example of dynamic cross-enterprise process planning, execution and controlling on a conceptual and application level. It is based on a life-cycle oriented collaborative business process management model. The model supports collaborative business process modeling by using pre-defined process modules. The adaptation of the model to the specific requirements of the AEC&FM-domain is illustrated by the example of errors and omissions management in Architecture, Engineering, and Construction (AEC).

1. INTRODUCTION

This paper discusses novel methods and tools to support inter-organizational collaborations within the AEC-industry more efficiently. Firstly, the concept of local and global knowledge in construction projects is introduced. Secondly, a potential model for the description of inter-organizational construction project management information is briefly explained. Important parts of this model include pre-defined process modules. Process modules document local (in-house) knowledge of an individual participant, which are then contributed to a collaborative network. Specific parameters have been identified to adapt process modules to the context of a certain project. The newly developed *Process Module Chain* modeling approach supports the integration of local process modules into a virtual, project-centered process chain, representing a complete collaboration network. As a third step, an integrated IT-architecture for the management and controlling of collaborative business processes is briefly introduced.

Last but not least, the authors will explain a mobile computing system for Errors and Omissions Management in AEC. This E&O software system was developed to demonstrate the applicability of the methodological approach for distributed model management developed within the ArKoS research project (http://www.arkos.info).

Please use the following format when citing this chapter:

Menzel, K., Keller, M., 2006, in IFIP International Federation for Information Processing, Volume 224, Network-Centric Collaboration and Supporting Fireworks, eds. Camarinha-Matos, L., Afsarmanesh, H., Ollus, M., (Boston: Springer), pp. 245–252.

2. APPROACH

2.1 Project Centric versus Organization Centric Approaches

Construction projects are defined as complex one-of-a-kind projects. Thus, to derive a common model for collaborative construction project management, its complexity has to be reduced by subdividing it into integral/coherent sub-projects or project views. Therefore, the entire project has to be decomposed into its controlling elements and structured in a reasonable manner.

A requirement within collaborative networks is to clearly distinguish between publicly available "*global*" knowledge and specific technological knowledge, including business secrets of individual collaboration partners (so-called "*local*" knowledge). The Architecture for Integrated Information Systems (ARIS) (Scheer, 1999) supports the definition of different views in business process models. Global knowledge is represented on a vertical axis, including the organizational view and the output view, which are necessary to establish a goal-oriented collaboration. Local knowledge is represented on a horizontal axis. Local knowledge is bilaterally shared between partners (Zang et al., 2004).

Following the approach of global and local knowledge, an AEC-specific *Construction Network Schema* was developed (Keller et al. 2004&2005) to specify the global knowledge in a more detailed way. The *Construction Network Schema* consists of four major elements: *Project Organization, Project Structure, Project Information* and *Project Phase*. The dimension, *Project Organization,* is subdivided into the categories, *Organizational Structures* and *Roles,* characterizing the management aspects of a project (global knowledge). The decomposition of the project into technical and functional aspects is realized by means of the dimension, *Project Structure.* High-level tasks -necessary for the completion of a project- are defined by the category, *Function;* whereas, the category, *Building Object,* structures the project into spatial and/or physical sections. The dimension, *Project Information,* defines the *IT-Infrastructure* and systems for inter-enterprise information exchange. It also specifies the *Information Content* that is exchanged amongst project partners.

2.2 The Concept of Business Process Modules

Business Process Modules (BPM) store and preserve local knowledge in a reusable and coherent manner. The aim of introducing *Business Process Modules* is to support the integrated use of local and global knowledge within a project team in a secure way. Process modules are generally pre-defined for the performance of a certain bundle of activities and are adaptable to different project contexts. Each process module represents a logical element with distinct interfaces (Menzel, 2003). These process interfaces are developed for a seamless integration of instantiated process modules into the existing *Process Module Chain,* defining all relevant input and output parameters. Each process module will be identified by certain meta-information that describes the parameters needed for its selection, initialization and integration. A schematic representation of a process module for construction processes is given in *Figure 3.* The generic processes (modeled as an *Event-driven Process Chain*) will be identified by *Context* and *Initialization Parameters* as well as *Input* and *Output Information.*

3. COLLABORATIVE NETWORK INFORMATION TO SUPPORT ERRORS & OMISSIONS MANAGEMENT (E&O)

Currently, E&O management, in particular E&O documentation and inspection on the site, is little supported by software applications. Additionally, different inhomogeneous IT-formats are common practice. Therefore, it was decided to prototypically develop and implement an E&O management system, running on mobile wireless devices (such as PDA). The system architecture should support easy integration into already existing, desktop-based IT environments.

E&O management involves numerous organizations of different size and varying roles. It also comprises main as well as supporting functions. Furthermore, a precise specification of the building structure is required for E&O management.

The development of the showcase started with a project analysis, which led to a general specification of typical constraints and requirements for E&O management. Building sites of heterogeneous structure and different organizational types were examined. On the basis of the BPM developed, we demonstrated that seamless information exchange between different project participants can be organized more efficiently; especially, that existing global and local knowledge could be used as part of the mobile application.

To model global knowledge for E&O management, the following definition is introduced (cf. *Figure 1*): E&O management processes belong to the *"Construction-Phase"* of a building project. A common *Organizational Structure* in this phase is the *"General Contractor"* model. This model is composed of three major partners: a) the client, b) the general contractor, and c) subcontractors. The client contracts the general contractor for the installation of the complete building or major parts of it. The general contractor might be either one single company or a consortium of two or more companies. In each case, the general contractor usually assigns several subcontractors to distinct tasks. Each of these organizations has its own internal structure. However, for E&O-management, all companies have to establish the *Role "Quality Manager"*.

Each project is characterized by its individual *Building Objects* as output of the network. The availability and accessibility of that information is required if a so-called "context-sensitive" application is to be configured. In our showcase, additional SOAP-services were implemented supporting the information transfer from desktop-based project management applications to the mobile E&O management system. In this way, the existing global knowledge of the project can easily become an integrated part of the mobile E&O-system. The global project workflow was modeled by using the *Process Module Chain* approach, which is part of the ARIS-methodology.

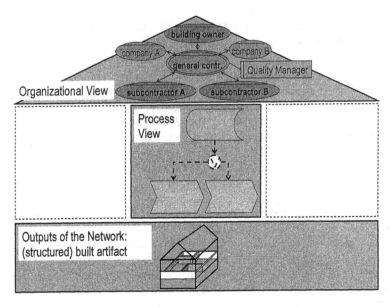

Figure 1 - Global knowledge of E&O management

However, additional local knowledge must complement global knowledge, describing the individual steps of how to fix detected errors and omissions appropriately. Therefore, the *Project Information* Structure indicated on the left of *Figure 2* has been developed and implemented. The developed service-oriented architecture allows mobile and office applications to access two servers: one storing the E&O documentation and the other managing all project-related information, such as *roles, participants, building product specifications*, etc.

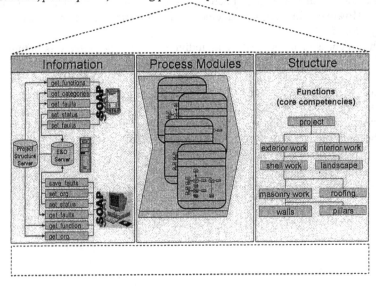

Figure 2 - Local knowledge of E&O management

The communication between the various applications and different servers is realized by web services. Information exchange is handled by XML based SOAP messages. The data structure for the exchange of E&O information and E&O categories was developed and is exchanged by WSDL-specifications. The usage of such an open, transparent, service-oriented architecture supports the integration of existing applications. Thus, each partner can participate in E&O management processes by using his own application(s) complemented by the mobile application.

This approach protects, on the one hand, the consistency of global collaborative network information and ensures, on the other hand, the extension of the project-specific knowledge space by homogeneously adding local knowledge.

3.3 Reference process models to support E&O management

At present, no standardized model for E&O management processes has been realized. Regulations are handled in a project-specific way. Therefore, we developed a general process model for E&O-management, synthesizing the findings of our intensive project studies. Subsequently, this detailed model was decomposed into coherent process modules based on the modeling methods introduced in chapter 2. Thus, the developed process modules can be applied to different construction project types. The various process modules are stored in the *Repository* of the *Architecture for Collaborative Scenarios* (Theling et al. 2005).

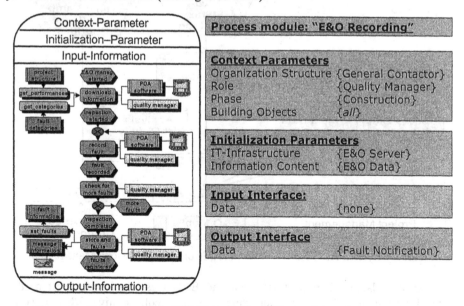

Figure 3 - Process module "E&O Recording" (Event-driven Process Chain)

For the identified process modules, the meta-information described in chapter 2.3 has been specified. An example of the "E&O Recording" process module is given in *Figure 3*. This module can be applied by the quality manager of the general contractor and is applicable for all major types of building objects. For the initialization of the process module, a server for E&O data management has to be established in the project. No input-data is required to start the process module. At the end of the process, a "fault notification" will be sent to the responsible partner.

4. APPLYING THE ARCHITECTURE

A general system architecture model developed in the ArKoS-project (Theling et al. 2005) was adjusted to our showcase as depicted in Figure 4. Firstly, a set of E&O reference processes was developed which supports the modelling of cross-company collaborative networks. Secondly, complementary project-specific process descriptions were made accessible by using the SOAP-services described above. The E&O-process modules and the project specific functions are both part of the process-data-pool.

Thirdly, diverse AEC-modeling tools, such as CAD-tools and their inherent standards (e.g. IFC, STEP AP 225), can be used to produce a complete model of the built artifact. The technical and structural information of the building are both combined in the project-data-pool. In addition, project documents can be attached to the process and project data by a document management application.

Furthermore, existing E&O-protocols were analyzed in depth in order to define a comprehensive but general catalogue of E&O descriptions. These descriptions were categorized, leading to a complete E&O classification.

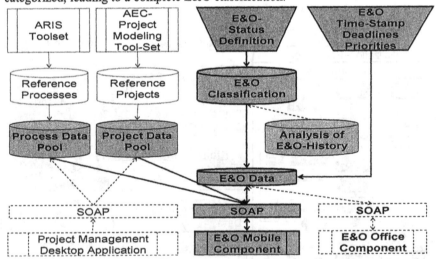

Figure 4 - System Architecture to support „Errors and Omissions Management"

The process-data-pool, project-data-pool and E&O classification are part of the global E&O-knowledge base, supporting a specific collaborative E&O-network. This knowledge-base delivers the input data for the mobile E&O system component. The accessibility of these knowledge components reduces data acquisition efforts, contributes to consistent data management and supports an effective, holistic project management for all participants of the E&O collaborative network.

The developed E&O system architecture also contains two management components. During build-time, nine different states were defined, describing the "life-cycle" of an error or omission. The precise definition of the different states allows at each time of the project the evaluation and analysis of the work progress with regard to E&O-management. The following states were defined: (1) E&O registered, (2) in progress by general contractor, (3) in progress by subcontractor, (4) rejected by subcontractor, (5) under negotiation with subcontractor, (6) completed by subcontractor, (7) completed by general contractor, (8) rejected by general contractor, (9) completed, (10) under negotiation with client.

Finally, for each error or omission a time-stamp is generated. Additionally, the user can define a priority and deadline for each detected error or omission. This data is generated during "build-time" and allows exact controlling of E&O management processes.

4.1 Errors and Omissions application

The mobile E&O-system component consists of three parts: (1) data acquisition, (2) data analysis, and (3) synchronization. Within this section, the first two parts are described in more detail.

The GUIs depicted in *Figure 5* illustrate the data acquisition sequence supported by the mobile system component. On the first screen, the user must localize the error. Most of the information is delivered from the project-data-pool (e.g. building, floor, room). The user only selects this information instead of needing to acquire this information redundantly. The second screen supports the error or omission specification. Again, the necessary information specifying the profession and the building part is delivered by the process-data-pool. The error category as well as a pre-defined error description is selected from the error catalogue.

Finally, the application automatically adds the current date and deadline. The user might wish to specify the cost necessary to fix the error in addition to specifying the original company responsible for fixing the error. The information of the responsible company (subcontractor) is already specified in the project-data-pool and can be selected according to the specified profession (e.g. electrician, plumber, painter, etc.).

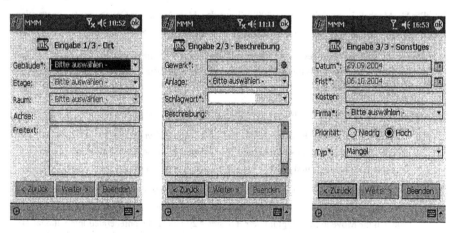

Figure 5 - Screen-shot Mobile Application for Error and Omission Management
(Ort=Localization, Beschreibung=Specification, Sonstiges=Costs & Deadlines)

The detailed and precise error & omission specifications are stored temporarily in a local database on the mobile device. The status of all new acquired errors is "1=registered". The local and the main "E&O-database" are synchronized by analyzing the E&O-states and using the SOAP-services, as described above.

All errors and omissions will be propagated without delay to the responsible partners of the collaborative network. The partners can act quickly and immediately to fix an error or omission. Short response times contribute to decreased costs of errors & omissions management and to a higher quality of the built artifact. Finally, the client is served in a better way, and the overall costs for delivering the built artifact are decreased.

5. CONCLUSION

A showcase, based on the example of errors and omissions management in Architecture, Engineering, and Construction, was developed and implemented. To achieve that, the required global and local knowledge was identified, and a general business process model was developed and decomposed into coherent process modules. Additionally, a mobile application was implemented to demonstrate the basic functionalities of the proposed system architecture. The application was successfully tested in demonstration projects of various sizes (€ 5Mill. to € 50Mill.).

The work has been conducted within the scope of the project 'Architecture for Collaborative Systems' (ArKoS – www.arkos.info) funded by the German Ministry for Education & Research since 2003. The design, realization and analysis of the E&O management showcase were supported by the Bilfinger und Berger AG. The mobile component will become a part of the company's software system in 2006.

6. REFERENCES

1. Keller M., Katranuschkov P. and Menzel K. (2004). Modeling collaborative processes for Virtual Organizations in the building industry, In proceedings of ECPPM, Balkema.

2. Keller M., Menzel K. and Scherer R.J. (2005). Towards a Meta-Model for Collaborative Construction Project Management. In proceedings of PRO-VE 05, Valencia, Spain.

3. Menzel K. (2003). Nachhaltiges Ressourcenmanagement mit mehrdimensionalen Informationssystemen. Habilitation (post-doctoral lecturer thesis), Dresden University of Technology, Germany.

4. Scheer A.-W. (1999). ARIS, Business Process Frameworks, Berlin et al., Springer.

5. Theling, T., Zwicker, J., Loos, P., Adam, O., Hofer, A.; „Enabling Dynamic Networks Uing an Architecture for Collaborative Scenarios"; in: Proceedings of the 22nd Conference on Information Technology in Construction (CIB-W78); TU Dresden, Germany (ISBN 3-86 005-478-3).

6. Zang S., Hofer A. and Adam O. (2004). Cross-Enterprise Business Process Management Architecture – Methods and Tools for Flexible Collaboration, In R. Meersman, Z. Tari & A. Corsaro (eds.) Proc. On the Move to Meaningful Internet Systems 2004: OTM Confederated International Workshops and Posters, GADA, JTRES, MIOS, WORM, WOSE, PhDS, and INTEROP 2004, October 25-29, Agia Napa, Cyprus.

PART **9**

PERFORMANCE AND NETWORK MANAGEMENT

PART 3

27

ENHANCEMENTS IN PERFORMANCE THROUGH VIRTUAL COLLABORATION AMONG SMEs
Potentials, Needs, and Research Challenges

Jannicke Baalsrud Hauge,
Bremen Institute of Industrial Engineering and Applied Work Science, GERMANY
baa@biba.uni-bremen.de

Ali Imtiaz,
Research Institute for Operations Management (FIR) at Aachen University of Technology,
GERMANY
Ali.Imtiaz@fir.rwth-aachen.de

Mirko Auerbach,
Research Institute for Operations Management (FIR) at Aachen University of Technology,
GERMANY
Mirko.Auerbach@fir.rwth-aachen.de

Jens Eschenbächer,
Bremen Institute of Industrial Engineering and Applied Work Science, GERMANY
esc@biba.uni-bremen.de

Marcus Seifert,
Bremen Institute of Industrial Engineering and Applied Work Science, GERMANY
sf@biba.uni-bremen.de

To compete and to thrive in the current global markets it is imperative for the regional businesses to form sustainable collaborative networks. Further, virtual inter-organisational collaboration not only requires changes in the organisational structure but also the increase the dependence on readily available information. The efficiency and effectiveness of this information depends on suitable collaboration tools; especially on the ICT infrastructure as well a trust and cultural understanding between collaborating partners. Especially for SMEs the ability for efficient networked collaboration is of key importance. At the moment, there are no affordable and customizable ERP tools for such a networked collaboration among SMEs.
This article presents a research approach focusing on the relevant challenges for the development and introduction of a collaboration tool based upon open source capabilities with industry specific ERP functionalities.

Please use the following format when citing this chapter:

Hauge, J. B., Imtiaz, A., Auerbach, M., Eschenbächer, J., Seifert, M., 2006, in IFIP International Federation for Information Processing, Volume 224, Network-Centric Collaboration and Supporting Fireworks, eds. Camarinha-Matos, L., Afsarmanesh, H., Ollus, M., (Boston: Springer), pp. 255–264.

1. INTRODUCTION

Globalisation has to led to fierce competition, customer driven markets and higher complexity in products, as a consequence there is a trend towards constantly changing partnerships characterises in the working environment of European manufacturing industry [Scheer, 2002, Sherman, 1996, Frederix, 2003]. This industry is vital to the European economy as it sustains 23.7 million jobs, an output of 1800 billion € (21% of EU GDP), and a positive contribution to the EU balance of payments (net of +120 billion € or 1.4% of GDP in 2001[Enterprise Europe, 2002]. Therefore, the ability to maintain and develop the competitiveness of European manufacturing industry is essential for the prosperity of the EU. Regarding the challenges of globalisation and the emerging networked economy, it has been recognised that significant improvements in the competitiveness can only emerge as a result of the combination of information and communication technologies with new managerial and organisational techniques [COM 2002] and with a shift from goods based to knowledge based products [Thoben, 2003]. The European manufacturing industry has dealt with these challenges for years and a clear trend toward concentrating on key competencies, which actually forced companies to outsource production steps to various other partners [Meyer, 2004] resulting in a collaborative production of highly complex, often knowledge intensive products has been observed.

The success of collaboration is not only a matter of finding a partner with the right key competencies, but more a question of having the right ICT tools for seamless information processing and the right people to perform the daily collaboration work as well as on the ability of the participating organisations to act in a dynamical environment. Typical ICT tools needed for fast and seamless information processing within large companies are ERP and CRM tools and for intra- organisational collaboration the newest SCM tools also provide some of the required functionalities. Up to recently, such tools have been quite expensive to buy and their implementation required a high degree of IT competencies within the company. Even though large industries enterprises play a more and more dominating role in the European manufacturing industry, the SMEs, mostly acting as suppliers to larger ones still remain the backbone of the economy, esp. in the Eastern European Countries. However, if the SMEs intend to survive and thrive, they need to stay competitive by higher efficiency and productivity; therefore there is a need of a fast, reliable integrating support system at an affordable price fostering collaboration between SMEs. In order to keep the cost and the access on a low level, such a collaboration tool should be open source based and offer just the needed functionalities.

2. THEORETICAL BACKGROUND

The European Charter for Small Enterprises, adopted by the General Affairs Council in Lisbon on 13th of June 2000 and endorsed at the Feira European Council on 19-20th of June the same year, recognizes that small businesses are the backbone of Europe's economy and the key to our competitiveness. Tool and die making workshops supply the European industry with customised mechanical components. Typically for these workshops is that they offer fairly knowledge intensive services and products to their customers and that these products and services are developed in close collaboration with other enterprises as well as the customer. The business is order-based, labour-intensive and most of the workshops are SMEs and typically they have one-of-a-kind production. Tool and die makers' customers are demanding industries from almost all branches where the manufacturing of goods is taking place: automotive industry, textile industry, IT & electrical industry, aerospace, etc.

2.1 Organisational aspects

In today's world, competition at every level of business activity is fierce; therefore only those enterprises that can minimise their costs will stay in the market and maybe as a winner. In the manufacturing business, costs are directly related to two ratios, productivity and efficiency. The related figures to these two characteristics show the worth of the money spent. This is where managers try to pull the lever. Several ways can be found to achieve higher productivity or better efficiency, but for the European manufacturing industry there has been a shift towards knowledge extensive products and services combined with a higher degree of collaborative production [Frederix, 2003], often based upon the concept of virtual organisations and extended products (compare **Figure 1**).

Looking at the supply chain of the manufacturing industry, it is obvious that the tool and die making workshops play a major role as suppliers of knowledge intensive services and products. Therefore, every change that large manufactures do to their supply strategies, leads to new requirement which a tool and die making workshop has to meet in order to stay as a supplier. Up to now, the tool and die making workshops have been able to meet these new requirements with high quality products and services as well as an excellent educated workforce but as the non-European competition from other SMEs as well from large enterprises growth, this isn't possible any more.

Furthermore, the one-of-a-kind production results in high costs and risks, since more complex products in terms of functionalities and high quality demands engage more complex and expensive manufacturing technologies. The range of needed manufacturing technologies comprises traditional as well as more innovative and expensive technologies. These are seldom all in-house, so there is need for sharing capacities (machines, materials, machine operator) and knowledge resources (technologies, competences).

The one- of a kind- product offered by the tooling industry fulfils the requirement of being an extended product. Complex extended products require various key competencies and hence it is often a collaborative product. The extended product includes a combination of a physical product (like the tool itself) and associated services/enhancements (like the engineering services offered) in order to improve the marketability [Baalsrud Hauge, 2004]. As shown in **Figure 1** an extended product consists of tangible and intangible assets. Consequently, tangible products can be intelligent, highly customised, and user-friendly and include embedded features like maintenance whereas intangible extended products are information and knowledge intensive and can consist of services, engineering, software, etc. [Thoben, 2003]. The co-operation includes both material and information flows in order to accelerate the co-operation within the value chain.[1]

Fitted into a typical manufacturing network, could mean that some suppliers delivers raw materials, some parts of the physical/tangible products, which builds the core of the extended product, whereas other either support with some specific manufacturing technology and engineering services depending on the specific customer's requirement.

However, looking at the layer model below it becomes obvious, that workshops producing the customised product in collaboration do have quite much in common with virtual organisations, for which general business models are available.

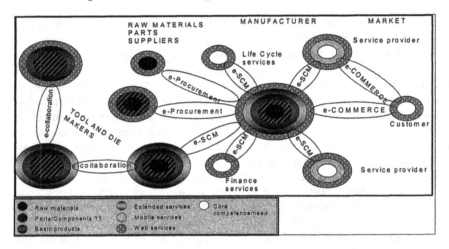

Figure 1: virtual organization, and extended product [based upon Oliveira 2000]

Toolmakers are operating in a highly dynamic market and are therefore forced to adapt their organisation and technologies to dynamic requirements as well as to constantly optimise their business processes in order to stay competitive. They have long experience with expertise, knowledge and competences-sharing as well as to mediate lessons learned throughout a cluster. So the basic premise for the collaborative work, the sharing culture is well developed and caused by the strong competition, a lot of workshops have organised themselves in tool-clusters or in associations. It is expected, that this trend will remain during the next decade.

2.2 Technical aspects

Additional to the challenges facing the organisational aspect of a virtual enterprise, the up coming and implementation of new IC Technologies among SMEs has opened new possibilities for collaboration but on the other side due to their limited financial and human resources they neither have a genuine need nor the possibility to implement the different ERP and SCM systems of their customers. However, in order to be able to process information in an efficient way and thereby stay in the market they need at least to be able to connect to such systems.

---

[1] Michael Porter Value chain model can be seen as appropriate

Collaboration platforms

Over the past years, a diversification has taken place regarding the categorisation of information systems. **Figure 2** below presents a systematic view of respective categories ordered by document management functions as well as communication and collaboration support. Furthermore, the figure shows an overview over the diverse categories of tools.

Setting boundaries between the mappings of individual collaboration tools to the categories is difficult, as individual tools can often be attributed to more than one category. Thus, the mapping is carried out according the most fitting category per tool. Further categories such as PIM, workflow, group work support and e-learning could also be added to the figure

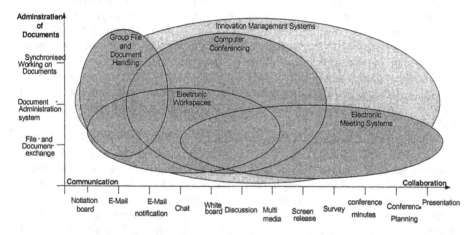

Figure 2:Categorisation of Tools [Based upon Bafoutsou/Mentzas 2002]

The combination of individual categories can contribute to the creation of new categories. Furthermore, group work support is increasingly being integrated into current OS, meaning the categories can be even further extended. For example, if one chooses to extend the above categories by their temporal and spatial dimensions a complete methodology can be created which is presented in Table 1 below.

Functional category	Temporal dimension		Spatial dimension	
	Synchronous	Asynchronous	Co-located	Remote
Group file & document handling	✓	✓		✓
Computer conferencing	✓	✓		✓
Electronic meeting Systems	✓	✓	✓	✓
Electronic workspace	✓	✓		✓

Table 1: Temporal and spatial differentiation of collaboration systems
[Bafoutsou/Mentzas 2002]

As has been shown, group work and document management are always distributed applications and can be synchronous or asynchronous. Similarly, conference systems can be co-located or remote. On the other hand, electronic workspaces generally represent synchronous or asynchronous communication and collaboration support.

The above mentioned collaboration tools are indeed usable for improving collaboration, but they do not solve the problem with getting the information automatically out of internal ERP systems neither do they offer the functionality of an ERP system inside the enterprise

ERP-systems
Many large companies have implemented ERP-Solutions but they are still restricted to internal and/or enterprise level. The solutions are more or less customised and even though much work has been carried out in the field of Enterprise application Integration(EAI) to solve problems with different data exchange formats and application which are not interoperable, most of this work is concentrated within an enterprise. In a dynamic business networks, the participating partners change, and with each change it is to expect that different ERP- systems needs to be connected to each other, either through defining specific interfaces or redundant data management has to be expected. This is one of the main obstacles networked businesses have to deal with.

According to various studies [Meyer, 2004]; only a few SMEs in Eastern Europe have implemented ERP-system. One reason is the lack of financial and human resources needed. Another reason is that the functionalities of these standardized applications do not fulfil the specific requirements of the tool and die making industry. Only about 30 percent of all ERP system's functionalities listed are common among all the industries. Therefore, based on preceding figures it is imperative to narrow the focus from all industries to individual industries and find out their core ERP functionalities that could supports collaborative network among companies

Even though it has been stated that the SMEs build the backbone of the European economy hardly any research have been carried out in order to establish information transfer and sharing among business networks for collaborative efforts supporting the competitiveness of SMEs. Some descriptions and procedures regarding the introduction of single tools and methods for network business in the tooling industry can be found in the literature, but a holistic approach is still missing. Appropriate models, methods and in particular a methodology of integrating is lacking for the tool and die making industry through open ERP solutions in distributed and globally dispersed entrepreneurial networks

3. MAIN RESEARCH CHALLENGES AND APPROACH

Even though there is a need of collaboration among enterprises, the past has shown that due to different goals among the partners and rapid changes of processes, collaboration are complex to handle. Additional, in dynamic and flexible networks, common experience is often lacking often resulting in the lack of trust. European collaboration networks also need to deal with the cultural aspect.

The above mentioned problems are relevant for almost all collaborations and mainly the identified problems can be classified into three categories:

- Interoperability, management and organizational models
- Sharing culture and technology transfer
- Cheap and effective software solutions based on open standards

Based upon this, it can be stated that for the tool and die workshop problems are mainly related to their production management and resource planning, as well as to e–collaboration but also with respect to management of customer relations and e-collaboration in carrying out their day-to-day business. Collaboration processes represent a key factor in the competitiveness of tool and die making clusters. By suitably improving these processes, clusters will be able to strengthen their position as suppliers. In order to effect such an improvement, we suggest the implementation of a collaboration platform utilizing emerging, innovative technologies made available to participating SMEs at the lowest possible cost.

In order to integrate the component into the overall supply chain, as well the SMEs' existing individual back-end enterprise systems, the solution will be augmented with (adaptive) service modules, allowing fast and flexible, standardised interfacing.

Based upon this, the idea of our research is to develop a collaboration tool with ERP functionalities for the tool and die making industry. Since this tool is supposed to be affordable for SMEs and interoperable, it will be based upon open source technologies. Not only the establishment of an IT infrastructure for supporting collaboration will a part of the research, but the SMEs will also be taught how the structured information sharing along complex and networked value chains can be accomplished. Therefore, our research project integrates both affordable open ERP-Solution and business interoperability driven approaches with information and communication technology (ICT) methodologies and instruments in order to develop and implement an innovative integration among SMEs of tool and die making industry.

For the networking of SMEs and other players in this sector it is imperative to have a collaborative development based on the open-source IT systems developed in the project as an internet based platform. To make the project results and particularly the open source ERP-application easily available for a wide range of users, a download service will be implemented on this platform. It will enable the partners to download relevant source-code, install it using the help from the online manuals or request support from the IT partners. In addition to that, all other project results will be disseminated via the platform.

Due to the nature of the project in which the tool clusters are involved, they still struggle to find the right organisational model for collaboration. The project will therefore emphasise on this aspect, since this a key to successful collaboration.

The project initiative is going to leverage the common goals with regard to different aspects identified so far. To harmonize the efforts of the different partners, it has been categorized into four main modules with each module achieving distinct goals and helping to achieve the final vision. The relation between the modules can be seen in Figure 3

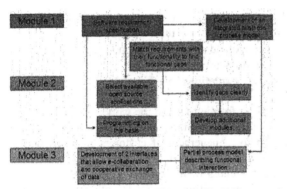

Module 1: Definition of a generic business model for tool and die making workshops

Module 2: Open source software architecture and application development

Module 3: Standard interfaces for open source applications

Module 4: Findings of training and education

Figure 3: Tool East modules

- Module I: Definition of a generic business process model for tool and die making workshops
  Modelling the business process is an essential part of any information based business networking development process. Deriving from the business model, the software requirement specification will be formulated as the basis for software development. It specifies the required behaviour of a system
  The performed survey of suitable process models shows that the Aachner PPC[Luczak,1999] model seems suitable for analysing the end user business processes and to collect the user requirements. How ever, this model is not very well known outside the German speaking area, therefore we found it necessary to also match this model with the SCOR[SCC2006]. At the moment it seems that the Aachner PPC model is more suitable, because it is more flexible and more detailed, but these results need to be verified and determined during the next couple of months. Additional, two main challenges were identified: First is that there is a large diversity in running processes within the tool and die making workshops (SMEs) – these differences were analysed using morphology and process landscapes. The second point focuses on one of a kind production that leads to some specific requirements for the CRM functionalities for the Tool-East software.
- Module II: Open source software architecture and application development (adaptation and improvement of one existing open source ERP solution; the development of another new open source ERP application is not the ambition)
  In order to develop software for SMEs as large group of companies which are not well served by the strong software suppliers the project will come up with an enlarged open source ERP-system with CRM-functionalities. The first objective of module-II is to evaluate and select the best open source solution available as basis for the intended specific development. The second objective is to develop additional modules to support processes described in the business process model. SMEs will be included in this work and to a very early stage a first prototype will be available in order to receive a first feedback.
  First results of a survey performed by the business process analysis have shown that the following functionalities are relevant: 'inter-operability and inter-communication', 'organisational structure and multi-site planning',

'production planning and control', project management', Engineering and master data management', material management/ requirement planning', 'purchase and procurement', 'outbound logistics and distributions' are core functionalities where as 'Financial accountant' and 'human resource' functionalities are not so relevant.

- Module III: Standard interfaces for open source applications
Competitive forces are driving technology efforts towards e-collaboration and cooperative exchange of data and applications within and across corporate boundaries. That means that intelligent interfaces have to support the exchange of data. Evolving new technologies provides an array of services to effectively design and develop integration and collaborative solutions that connect different systems like ERP, CRM, or other internal systems, as well as connectivity with partners, vendors, and other service providers. For SMEs not only the integration of large systems is problematic but also the possibility to import existing data stored e.g. in Microsoft Excel files or other individually programmed databases in order not to retype all information manually. The strategy is to provide additional functionality via interfaces, so the technical possibilities and latest development will be examined and evaluated.
- Module IV: Training and education
The findings of training and education module are critical to develop a methodology to carry out personnel training, establishing an appropriate relationship between classroom, on-site, and e-learning modules. It has to meet the different stakeholder groups' individual requirements and training needs.

This common structure facilitates the integration of different aspects. Different modules will be integrated to develop a synchronized open source ERP application in close relationship with each SME in the consortium.

4. CONCLUSIONS AND SUMMARY

The project Tool-East will provide a cost-efficient ERP application for tool and die making workshops on the basis of existing open source ERP applications. Within the project the open source application will be adapted and modified for the specific requirements of this branch. The new adapted and modified ERP application supports the efficient coordination of intra-enterprise order processing and strengthens competition and competitiveness of Eastern European SMEs. Primarily, orders management, work planning, resource allocation and CRM need to be optimised and linked together in a dynamic work environment. Moreover ERP applications are necessary for the electronic collaboration in dynamic business networks. To enable industrial cluster to e-collaboration the consisting process and data standards (for example ROSETTANET, ebXML etc.) will be considered for the Tool-East project.

This project focuses as a core on the use of open source technology for the development of an integrated business application for tool and die making enterprises with high performance regarding availability, safety and maintainability at the very onset. Further on this will be enriched by enabling coordination between the different players in this sector. Strengthening the open source initiative in general and particularly in this field of business opens an enormous potential for SMEs. A successful case study and dissemination platform in the specific branch addressed in this project will pave the way for future initiatives. Since demands for business software from other branches with specific SME structures are predominantly comparable, therefore results and concepts from this project can be transferred, so that a large impact can be assumed.

For the long term success it is essential for the tool and die making industry to continue to set on innovative business strategies long time in advanced. Such a strategy comprises participation in dynamic business networks. Two main challenges for a successful participation of tool and die making workshops in dynamic business network is to coordinate intra-enterprise order processing and that they bring their core capabilities into a flexible network.

Acknowledgements

This work has been partly funded by the European Commission through IST Project *Tool-East: Open Source Enterprise Resource Planning and Order Management System for Eastern European Tool and Die Making Workshops* (No. IST-FP6-027802). The authors wish to acknowledge the Commission for their support. We also wish to acknowledge our gratitude and appreciation to all the Tool-East project partners for their contribution during the development of various ideas and concepts presented in this paper

6. REFERENCES

[Bafoutsou/Mentzas 2002]: Bafoutsou, G., Mentzas, G.(2002): "Review and functional classification of collaborative systems", International Journal of Information Management , 22, 2002, S. 281-305.

[Baalsrud Hauge, 2004], Baalsrud Hauge et al.(2004): Enhancing e-commerce business models of selected SMEs by a multi-mode approach in International Journal of Internet and Enterprise Management, p.122, Vol.2, 2004

[COM 2002]: European Commission, COM 2002, 714, Industrial Policy in an Enlarged Europe, Communication from the Commission to the Council, the European Parliament, the Economic and Social Committee and the Committee of Regions

[Frederix, 2003]: Frederix, F.(2003): Cooperation in Dynamic Networked Organizations, p.221 In Gasòs,J. Thoben, K.-D. (Eds.): E-Business Applications – Technologies for Tomorrow's Solutions; Advanced Information Processing Series, Springer, 2003,

[Enterprise Europe 2002]: enterprise Europe (2002), No 8, July-September 2002

[Thoben, 2003]: Thoben, K.-D., Eschenbächer, J., Jagdev, H.S.:Emerging Concepts in E-Business and Extended Products; in: Gasos, J., Thoben, K.-D. (Eds.): E-Business Applications – Technologies for Tomorrow's Solutions; Advanced Information Processing Series, Springer, 2003, pp. 17 - 37

[Meyer, 2004]: Meyer, M et al(2004): Plug and do Business- ERP of the next generation for efficient order processing in dynamic business networks in: International Journal of Internet and Enterprise Management, pp.153 Vol.2, 2004

[Luczak, 1999]: Holger Luczak, Walter Eversheim: Produktionsplanung und -steuerung: Grundlagen, Gestaltung und Konzepte. 2. Auflage.: Springer-Verlag (1999), ISBN 3-540-65559-X

[Oliveira, 2000]: Oliveira et al. (2000) 'SMARTISAN-moving e-commerce to extended product', Helsinki Conference Proceedings.

[Scheer, 2002]: Scheer, A.-W., Grieble, O., Hans, S., Zang, S.(2002): Geschäftsprozessmanagement – The 2nd wave. In: Information Management & Consulting, 17, 2002 Sonderausgabe, pp. 9-14.

[Sherman, 1996]: Sherman, Heidemarie(1996): "Globalisierung: Transnationale Unternehmen auf dem Vormarsch", Ifo Schnelldienst, Nr. 23, 1996

[SCC2006]:Supply Chain Council: SCOR 7.0 overview booklet. More Information will be found on http://www.supply-chain.org/page.ww?section=SCOR+Model&name=SCOR+Model

28

CORRELATING PERFORMANCE WITH SOCIAL NETWORK STRUCTURE THROUGH TEACHING SOCIAL NETWORK ANALYSIS

Peter Gloor
MIT, pgloor@mit.edu, USA
Maria Paasivaara
Helsinki University of Technology, mpaasi@hut.fi, FINLAND
Detlef Schoder
University of Cologne, schoder@wim.uni-koeln.de, GERMANY
Paul Willems
University of Cologne, Paul_Willems@gmx.de, GERMANY

Teaching a course on optimizing online communication behavior and social network analysis permitted us to obtain preliminary results on correlating temporal online communication patterns with team performance. Students from Helsinki University of Technology and University of Cologne who had never met face to face formed virtual interdisciplinary teams collaborating on a common task. While collaborating over long distance, students kept track of their own communication activities by e-mail, chat, and conference calls with Skype. The contribution of this paper is twofold. First, we introduce an innovative course format creating an empirical base for team performance in a distributed online communication environment. Secondly, we provide basic analysis of correlations between SNA measures and team performance. Students used these insights to optimize their own communication behavior for future virtual collaboration.

1. INTRODUCTION

The advent of the Internet has provided new opportunities for collaboration thought impossible just a few years ago. Exchanging ideas and work by e-mail, chat, Internet telephony, blogs, and Wikis has opened up new avenues for spontaneous communication. Researchers have begun to study how these new communication channels influence productivity and creativity of virtual teams [Cro04, Cum03, Glo03, Kid05, Lee03, Lue03]. In our own work we studied Collaborative Innovation Networks, or COINs [Glo06]. COINs are virtual teams of self-motivated people with a collective vision, enabled by technology to collaborate in achieving a common goal – an innovation – by sharing ideas, information, and work.

This paper describes early results on how to improve online communication for better performance and creativity. These insights have been gained while teaching a graduate-level distributed course on online collaboration co-located at three universities. The main objective of this course had been to offer students an opportunity to improve their own communication behavior when collaborating in virtual teams to become better members of COINs. They did this by completing an innovation-centered distributed project as a virtual team, and then correlating their

Please use the following format when citing this chapter:

Gloor, P., Paasivarra, M., Schoder, D., Willems, P., 2006, in IFIP International Federation for Information Processing, Volume 224, Network-Centric Collaboration and Supporting Fireworks, eds. Camarinha-Matos, L., Afsarmanesh, H., Ollus, M., (Boston: Springer), pp. 265–272.

individual and team communication patterns with individual and team performance in the distributed project.

In fall 2006 we jointly taught a course to 13 students in Finland and 12 students in Germany on how to optimize their online communication behavior to become better net citizens and members of virtual teams, increasing their efficiency and creativity. Part of the course was taught from MIT, such that the course was distributed at three locations. Figure 1 illustrates the classroom teaching part of the course, where one virtual classroom was formed by participants from Helsinki, Cologne, and Boston.

Figure 1 – Snapshots from teaching the course

Our course was organized in three parts. In part one, students learned about principles of social network analysis (SNA) [Was94], Collaborative Innovation Networks (COINs), and Swarm Creativity [Glo06]. In the second part students formed seven interdisciplinary teams comprising three to four students from different institutions (University of Cologne, Helsinki University of Technology) and applied the tools framework taught in part one by analyzing a virtual online community. This permitted them to study rules of optimized online communication in other online communities. In part three the students analyzed the communication behavior of their own virtual team, based on their online communication record of e-mail, chat, and phone interaction. Communication records were collected by cc'ing all communication activities to seven dummy e-mail addresses.

The main goals of the course were to teach students how to be efficient online-communicators and collaborators in distributed virtual teams. Our objective was for students to become more effective communicators by becoming aware of their social position and their contribution pattern in the virtual team. In more general terms, course participants also learned to increase organizational innovation and effectiveness by converting organizations into "Collaborative Innovation Networks" (COINs). On a technical level, they learned how to apply social network analysis using the tool TeCFlow (Temporal Communication Flow Optimizer) developed at MIT and Dartmouth [Glo04].

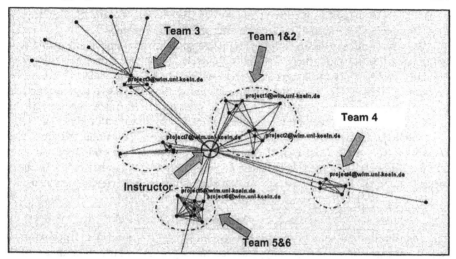

Figure 2 – Communication patterns of project teams in phase 2.

Figure 2 shows the social network during part two of the course, produced with TeCFlow. Ties between actors have been produced by mining the e-mail archive of the course communication. Note the central role of the instructor, with very little inter-team communication. Only teams 1 and 2, and teams 5 and 6 show inter-team communication.

2. CORRELATING PERFORMANCE WITH SOCIAL NETWORK STRUCTURE

The course participants formed seven separate project teams, each with team members from both Cologne and Helsinki. Each team analyzed an online community. They choose subjects such as communication among contributors to Wikinews, tracking of trends on RFID through using the ISIWeb literature database or analyzing e-mail communication among Enron employees. As the team members were geographically distributed, their communication was conducted online, mostly by e-mail.

Each student graded the quality of the work of the teams other than her or his own team on a scale from 1 to 4, with 1 being the best grade. The quality of the work of each team was ranked based on the quality of the final presentation of the team and the final report. Students also ranked the quality of the individual contribution of their own team members. This means that each student gave a grade to each of the other six teams, and to the two to three peers within the team. The best students and teams were rated 1, the worst a team was rated by a student was 3, the worst an individual was rated was a 4.

We tested three hypotheses based on the peer ratings. The three hypotheses are:

1. The internal (ingroup) team ratings are correlated to the communication balance of the teams.
2. The external team ratings are correlated to the communication balance of the teams.

3. There is a significant correlation between the external ranking of each team's output and the mutual internal ranking among team members.[1]

We also looked at more simple parameters such as the number of e-mails sent within each team. While there was indeed correlation between external rating and numbers of messages exchanged, it turned out not to be significant. This may be because of the small size of our sample. Applying typical SNA measures such as betweenness and degree centrality [Was94] did not make sense here, because of the small individual team size of three to four members, which were all fully connected.

The hypotheses were tested on the communication data collected from the course and the grades. All e-mail communication between the course participants was collected and was used as the basis for the communication analysis. The main measure to be used for this analysis was the contribution index, which is defined as:

$$contribution\_index = \frac{messages\_sent - messages\_received}{messages\_sent + messages\_received} \qquad [Glo03].$$

The contribution index takes on values between -1 and $+1$, it is $+1$ if a person only sends messages and -1 if it only receives messages. A contribution index of 0 indicates a totally balanced communication behavior. In the project most project related communication was communication within the team. Peripheral communication of team members with outside people, which would have had an impact on their contribution index and might have distorted its relation to the contribution index of the other team members, was almost non-existent.

Average weighted variance of the contribution index (awvci)

$$awvci^{ws}(team) = \frac{\sum_{i=1}^{T} m_i \cdot \text{var}(C_i^{ws})}{\sum_{i=1}^{T} m_i}$$

m_i = number of edges on day i

ws = window size

$C_i^{ws} = \left(ci_{i,n}^{ws}, \cdots, ci_{i,N}^{ws} \right)$ = vector of contribution indexes of all team members for day i

$ci_{i,n}^{ws}$ = contribution index of member n on day i

Figure 3 – Average weighted variance of contribution index to calculate the balanced'ness of a team's communication

To describe the balance of a team's communication the average weighted variance of the contribution index (figure 3) was defined. The window size denotes the sliding time window in number of days used to calculate the contribution index with TeCFlow. In order to reduce the impact of high variances of the ci caused by single messages by one member in phases of general low activity, which leads to distorting (weekend) peaks, the variances are weighted with the number of total edges on that particular day. This weighting increases the influence of patterns that appear in high activity phases like shortly before the deadlines. The resulting

---

[1] Tested by Lutz Tegethoff, Ilkka Lyytinen and Sebastian Schiefer during part three of the COIN course

average weighted variance of the contribution index (*awvci*) adopts values close to 0 if the communication is balanced.

2.1 Teams with high internal ratings have a 'balanced' internal communication behavior

The average internal ratings can be seen as a self assessment of a team. Teams in which information is shared fast and even among the members and where the response time on mails is short, should have more satisfied members, which give better ratings to the rest of the team. These teams are also expected to have a low *awvci*. Therefore the average internal rating should be correlated to the *awvci*.

As it turns out, there was no significant correlation between balanced internal communication behavior and internal rating[2] (see Table 1). We can speculate that team members differed in their willingness to give each other "harsh" grades, thus distorting the measurements in our small sample.

n=7 teams	*awvci*			
	Window Size 1		Window Size 5	
	Pearson Correlation	P-Value	Pearson Correlation	P-Value
External Rating	0.724	0.066	0.921	0.003
Average Internal Rating	0.187	0.688	0.494	0.260

Table 1 – Correlation between ratings and *awvci*

We calculated *awci* for window sizes of 1 and 5 days. With a time window of 1 day, contribution index values, which form the basis for *awci*, fluctuate too much. A Window size of 5 days gives better results, smoothing peaks of activity and inactivity periods. It corresponds to a 5-day work-week and fits well into the overall project period of one month.

2.2 A 'balanced' internal communication leads to a better external rating

In this case the correlation between the *awvci* and the ratings is high (see Table 1). The external ratings show a higher correlation with the balance of the team's communications than the internal ratings. It can be assumed that external ratings are more honest than the internal ones as students are not asked to rate team members they have been working with closely for a few weeks. They are more precise too, as they are based on a larger number of judgments.

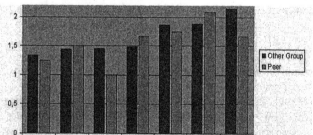

Figure 4 – Ingroup and external (other groups) ratings of 7 teams (low is better)

---

[2] There was no correlation between individual grade and contribution index neither.

2.3 Internal (ingroup) evaluation and external (by other group) ratings are correlated

The better the external team rating, the better the average internal rating of the team (Pearson Correlation=0.651; P-Value=0.113; n=7). A satisfied team gives good mutual ratings and provides work of good quality. This shows again that efficient teamwork has a positive impact on results (figure 4).

2.4 Limitations

While these early results are promising, they have to be taken with more than a grain of salt. The used dataset is small and somewhat incomplete. Communication was not completely recorded when it went through channels different from e-mail. Some teams sent messages to their team e-mail address to record these interactions, others did not. Ratings were done on a subjective basis with an underlying rigid structure. Also, our emphasis on temporal balance of contribution index only captures a subset of all communication activities.

3. CHALLENGES OF VIRTUAL COLLABORATION

The student groups faced several challenges during their virtual collaboration, which they reported at the end of the course. The students had not met each other face-to-face across countries, thus they did not know each other or their working styles, which caused some confusion and also getting a sense of "team work" was felt hard to achieve. The beginning was clearly the most difficult phase for many groups, it seemed to be quite hard to start an efficient work process and it took some time before a productive working mode was achieved.

The student groups were formed during a videoconference session: the students joined the groups according to their interest on suggested topics. The only rule for forming groups was that all the groups should have students from both countries. If a group had at least two students from the same country, this led to the formation of co-located sub-groups that at least partly communicated through other means than electronic (e.g., phone or face-to-face), thus this communication was not recorded and other group members could not follow it. Especially for groups having only a one-student sub-group in the other country, this caused difficulties for the isolated student to follow activities in the other country. Even though e-mail was the main communication medium, some groups started to use Skype (contains both chat and voice) or other chat programs especially for coordinating the work and making decisions. The synchronous communication was regarded as very efficient, but the problem was to find meeting dates suitable to all group members, since the students had many other courses at the same time. This problem often led to Skype or chat sessions between only two members at the time.

E-mail communication functioned quite well, but it was regarded as a less efficient communication medium than Skype or chat, since it was slow and thus not very interactive. Especially decision making was felt to be difficult through e-mail. Moreover, the asynchronicity of e-mail communication created uncertainty when others did not know how to interpret the silence of the non-responding team member. Interpreting the sent e-mail messages was not always easy, neither. Translating from "Finnish" English to "German" English and vice versa opened up room for wide interpretation!

Despite these challenges the student groups did very good work and gained interesting results from the analysis of both the on-line communities and their own communication. The student feedback was very positive – the students felt that despite of the problems they had learned a lot.

4. LESSONS LEARNED

By organizing this course we learned a lot both regarding the arrangements of a distributed course and regarding data collection for research purposes. In the beginning of the course we did not give the students much advice on how to communicate or how to record the communication. We just asked the students to send a copy of all e-mails to an e-mail-box where all the communication of each group would be archived to be used when analyzing communication during their second assignment. We also offered MediaWiki as a forum for discussions. We learned that in the future it might be beneficial to teach in the beginning of the course some rules about how to work and communicate efficiently in a distributed team. In this course the students had to figure it out by themselves and make all the mistakes first, which of course took time away from working on the projects.

Since the student groups found Skype and chat very useful, we will need to encourage use of this kind of communication channel in the future. Moreover, a way to systematically record this kind of communication should be designed and taught to the students. Even though there was active communication inside the groups, the communication across the groups was very limited and took mainly place in connection with class videoconference sessions. Encouraging communication across groups will be needed, e.g. for solving technical problems. For instance, a discussion forum for technical communication problems could be started. Questions to the teachers could be directed to this forum, allowing everybody to follow and participate in these discussions.

The country-specific sub-groups were the reason that not all communication was recorded, e.g. phone calls and face-to-face conversations. This communication was often invisible to other team members, causing problems especially to one-person country-specific sub-groups, when he or she was to a certain extent left outside of the team. This posed additional problems for our communication research setup. This problem could be solved either by forming more balanced groups (at least two persons from one country), advising the students to record the non-electronic communication and informing the others, or by choosing only one team member from each site and organizing the course across several sites. This later solution is what we plan for the next version of this course: to involve four universities, which means four participating sites. That kind of a course would be both more challenging to organize and more challenging for the students to work in, when the groups are highly distributed. However, it would also be more interesting both for the students and for studying the communication patterns. Moreover, all the communication across these sites would be electronic and thus easier to record and for other team members to follow.

5. CONCLUSIONS

In this paper we presented our experiences of organizing a novel course on optimizing online communication behavior. The distributed student teams applied social network analysis to analyze communication behavior both in a chosen online forum and afterwards inside their own group. We obtained preliminary results on correlating temporal online communication patterns with team performance. These results based on self-evaluation indicate that students in teams exhibiting balanced communication behavior performed best. Students used the insights they gained on the correlation of their own communication behavior with their group performance to improve their future communication behavior and collaboration style in COINs.

The presented communication analysis can only be considered indicative, as not all the communication was documented and as there were problems in the data recording. Despite these weaknesses, this experiment can be regarded as successful: the student feedback was very positive and we gained valuable ideas for both improving the course and better recording the communication data. Based on this experience we plan to teach this course again, this time among four universities, which will make the experiment both more insightful, but also more challenging! We would like to close with a quote from a student commenting on the course:

"This course was a great one. We learned a lot of things. The most valuable thing I learned was that the better communication is, the more successful you are (personally or as a team)."

6. ACKNLOWEDGEMENTS

The authors would like to thank the participants of this course from Cologne and Helsinki for being collaborative innovators themselves, coming up with many ideas for improvement of the course. Juha Itkonen and Kai Fischbach gave excellent suggestions on an earlier version of this paper.

7. REFERENCES

Cross, R, & Cummings, J.N. 2004, "Tie and network correlates of individual performance in knowledge-intensive work" *retrieved December 2004 at URL: http://ccs.mit.edu/fow/cross_cummings.pdf*

Cummings, J., & Cross, R, 2003 "Structural properties of work groups and their consequences for performance" *Social Networks, 25(3), 2003, 197-210*

Gloor, P. Laubacher, R. Dynes, S. Zhao, Y., 2003, "Visualization of Communication Patterns in Collaborative Innovation Networks: Analysis of some W3C working groups". *Proc. ACM CKIM International Conference on Information and Knowledge Management, New Orleans, Nov 3-8, 2003.*

Gloor, P. 2006,"Swarm Creativity, Competitive advantage through collaborative innovation networks" Oxford University Press, 2006

Gloor, P. Zhao, Y., 2004, "A Temporal Communication Flow Visualizer for Social Networks Analysis", *ACM CSCW Workshop on Social Networks. ACM CSCW Conference, Chicago, Nov. 6. 2004.*

Kidane, Y. Gloor, P. Correlating Temporal Communication Patterns of the Eclipse Open Source Community with Performance and Creativity , NAACSOS Conference, June 26 - 28, Notre Dame IN, North American Association for Computational Social and Organizational Science, 2005

Leenders, R.Th.A.J. Van Engelen, J.M.L. Kratzer, J., 2003 "Virtuality, Communication, and New Product Team Creativity: A Social Network Perspective", *Journal of Engineering and Technology Management, 20, 2003, pp. 69-92.*

Lueg, C. Fisher, D., 2003, "From Usenet to CoWebs, Interacting with Social Information Spaces", *Springer, 2003.*

Tyler, J,.Wilkinson, D. Huberman, B. A., 2003 "E-mail as Spectroscopy: Automated Discovery of Community Structure within Organizations" *HP Laboratories, 2003. Retrieved February 2005 at URL http://www.hpl.hp.com/shl/papers/e-mail/index.html*

Wasserman, S., Faust, K, 1994, "Social Network Analysis, Methods and Applications", *Cambridge University Press. 1994.*

29

ON THE ROLE OF VALUE SYSTEMS AND RECIPROCITY IN COLLABORATIVE ENVIRONMENTS

António Abreu, L.M. Camarinha-Matos
New University of Lisbon
Quinta da Torre – 2829 Monte Caparica, PORTUGAL
ajfa@fct.unl.pt, cam@uninova.pt

The establishment of a common value system is an important element for the sustainability of collaborative networks. This paper discusses the role of value systems in the VO breeding environment when the promotion of the cooperation is based on reciprocity mechanism. Some scenarios are included in the discussion and illustrations are given based on data from real networks.

1. INTRODUCTION

The behavior of an individual, society, or collaborative networked organization (CNO) is determined by the underlying value system. It is intuitively understood that the values considered in a business-oriented CNO (e.g. network of companies) are different from the ones in a non-profit context (e.g. disaster rescue network). Taking the simplified view that the goal of a CNO is the maximization of some "attribute" of its value system, in a business context the dominant value is the profit (in economic sense), while in the other case the objectives are altruist and the rewards expressed in terms of the amount of prestige or social recognition.

In general, the structure of a value system, and therefore the drivers of the CNO behavior, includes multiple variables / aspects. Complementarily there are other elements that strongly influence or determine the behavior of the CNO and its members, such as the schema of incentives, trust building and management, ethical code, the CNO culture, and the contracts and collaboration agreements.

On the other hand, it is commonly assumed the participation in a collaboration process brings benefits to the involved entities. These benefits include an increase of the "survival capability" in a context of market turbulence, but also the possibility to better achieve common goals. On the basis of these expectations are, among others, the following factors: sharing of risks and resources, joining of complementary skills and capacities, acquisition of a (virtual) higher dimension, access to new / wider markets and new knowledge, etc.

However, with the evolution of collaborative forms, the emergence of new roles, new actors and the continuous and repetitive interactions among partners make that the value generated by a collaboration process is no more determined only by its tangible assets (given by products/services supplied), but also by its intangible assets (e.g. relationship value, or "social capital"). Furthermore, in this new context the

Please use the following format when citing this chapter:

Abreu, A., Camarinha-Matos, L. M., 2006, in IFIP International Federation for Information Processing, Volume 224, Network-Centric Collaboration and Supporting Fireworks, eds. Camarinha-Matos, L., Afsarmanesh, H., Ollus, M., (Boston: Springer), pp. 273–284.

value system "borders" (or what characterizes the value system) are becoming less defined and its centre of gravity is changing place (Figure 1).

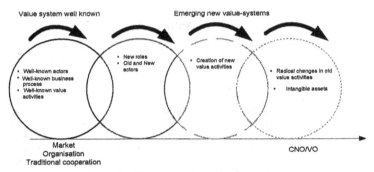

Figure 1 – Evolving nature of value systems

The purpose of this paper is to discuss the value system role in the VBE context when the promotion of the cooperation is based on reciprocity mechanism.

2. VALUE SYSTEMS

What is a value system? A value system frequently understood as *the ordering and prioritization of a set of values that an actor or a society of actors holds*. However, the values that a group or an actor holds may fall into several different categories since the concept of value is multifaceted. In literature we can find several definitions for the meaning of value, two main focuses for these definitions are referred to as economic values and ethical / ideological values:

Economic Value:
- An amount, as of goods, services, or money, considered to be a fair and suitable equivalent for something else; a fair price or return. What a customer gets in exchange for the price it pays.
- To make a judgment as to the worth of something, in the sense of appraise, assay, assess, calculate, estimate, evaluate, gauge, judge.

Socio- Ethical value:
- Ethical values are those values that serve to distinguish between good and bad, right and wrong, and moral and immoral. At a societal level, these values frequently form a basis for what is permitted and what is prohibited.
- Ideological values deal with the broader or more abstract areas of politics, religion, economics, and social morals.

A number of characteristics can be considered for the values in a value system:

◆ *Subjective* – For an identical context, distinct members may apply different values and might have different perceptions of a value.

◆ *Personal vs. social* – The personal values can be applied only to one member (e.g. assets, capacity, and price) and social values can be applied to a set of members (e.g. ethical code, cooperation agreements and contracts).

♦ **Normative vs. Exchange** - The purpose of normative values is to define a set of rules ("rights/duties") that contribute to assure the stability and the cohesion of the group since they transmit norms in a persuasive way and present an unquestionable form (e.g. trust, ethical code, and law). The purpose of exchange values is to "measure" the objects exchanged among partners in a certain context and moment.

♦ **Dynamic** - The values can change along the time. They can fade out, increase their worth or can appear for the first time.

♦ **Measurable** - The values can be measured using a quantitative or a quantitative scale.

The concept of a value system in a CNO context must be based on the notion that each product/service requires a set of value activities that are performed by a number of the network members forming a "value creation system" through a VO (this definition includes economic and ethical / ideological value as well). As a result, a value system is important in terms of providing a:

• Regulation role – for instance, regulation role can include assuring social cohesion, to understand members' behavior and to build performance indicator.

• Transactions mechanism between partners – such as, assuring an equality utility between objects exchanged.

3. MECHANISM FOR EVOLUTION OF COOPERATION

How to promote a cooperative behavior in a sustainable way? Several principles and mechanisms have been suggested in the literature, as illustrated in Table 1.

Table 1 – Cooperation mechanisms

Cooperation mechanism	Short description
Direct reciprocity	This mechanism suggests that actors should reciprocate help those that have intentionally helped them in the past. This model can explain social phenomena like for instance the live-and-let-live system in trench warfare in World War I, friendships, gratitude, sympathy, trustworthiness and in general all social dilemmas. In the biological field it can explain the symbioses mechanism. The mathematical model of cooperation via direct reciprocity is based on game theory and much of the work developed applies the prisoner's dilemma, stag hunt and chicken game metaphor [2][9][14].
Indirect reciprocity	This mechanism suggest that an actor should provide help if the recipient has helped others in the past. In this mechanism it is a common practice in human societies like for instance: social welfare principle, insurance principle, where the donor does not obtain a return from the recipient, but from a third party [1][13].
Kin selection	Kin selection leads to the concept that an individual should sacrifice itself in order to save "two siblings, four nephews or eight cousins". Kin selection has been used to explain the evolution of humanity's social structure, social insects such as ants and termites [11][12].

Group selection	This mechanism describes the process by which groups develop adaptive traits that improve their fitness in their environment compared to other groups. According to this approach the selection mechanism can operate not only at the individual level, but also at the group level where it is possible to explain the existence of altruistic behaviours. Altruists may be less fit than non-altruists within a single group, but groups of altruists are more fitted than groups of non-altruists. An approach similar to this process was the propaganda campaigns in the Great Depression "We're all in it together". According to social psychological, humans form coalitions on the basis of virtually any commonality of interest and all humans are in the "in-group" where the information "in-group" members is processed in more favourable ways than information about out-group members [10].
Social learning	According to this approach individuals learn the most dominant behaviours in their embedded social network. Based on this principle cooperation can evolve based on *cultural transmission.* The common metaphor, when a group of actors decide to solve problems that none of the actors alone could solve, leads to scenarios where cooperative behaviour is created among many individuals without conscious control are cooperation examples via social learning [4][15].

4. RECIPROCITY AS A MECHANISM FOR PROMOTING COLLABORATION IN A VBE CONTEXT

In the following discussion a VO breeding environment (VBE) is assumed as the target context [6][7]. A VBE represents an association or pool of organizations and their related supporting institutions that have both the potential and the will to cooperate with each other through the establishment of a "base" long-term cooperation agreement. When a business opportunity is identified by one member (acting as a broker), a subset of these organizations can be selected and thus forming a VO. A breeding environment, being a long-term networked structure, provide the basis to record data about past collaboration occurrences, presents the adequate base environment for the establishment of cooperation agreements, common infrastructures, common ontologies, and mutual trust, which are the necessary facilitating elements when building a new VO.

Let us consider Task Benefits (TB) as the benefits that result from the performance of a task in the context of a collaborative process. A collaborative process is understood as a set of tasks performed by the collaborative network members towards the achievement of a common goal (e.g. the business goal that motivates the creation of a Virtual Enterprise). For reasons of simplicity we consider a level of granularity of tasks such that each task is performed by a single member of the network (single actor).

In this discussion benefits are assumed as abstract quantifiable measurements with the same meaning as net profit.

Let t_{lj} be a task t_l performed by an actor a_j and $TB_{ji}(t_{lj})$ the benefits for another actor a_i as a result of the performance of this task.

When $i \neq j$ this represents a *received benefit* (RB) (perspective of actor a_i) or a *contributed benefit* (CB) (perspective of actor a_j) (Fig. 2); otherwise it is a *self-benefit*, case that will not be considered in this discussion.

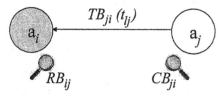

Figure 2 – Actor a_i receives benefits from the action of actor a_j

Based on this representation (see, [5] [6] for more details), a reciprocity mechanism can be implemented by analysing the balance between "social" benefits credit (the sum of benefits contributed by an actor a_j to all its partners) and "social" benefits debit (the sum of benefits received by an actor a_j as a result of the performance of all actors involved in the collaborative process). The reciprocity value (R_j) for an actor a_j is given by:

$$R_j = \sum_{i=1}^{N} CB_{ji} - \sum_{i=1}^{N} RB_{ij} \qquad i \neq j$$

Where: N – Number of actors involved in the collaborative process

CB_{ji} - Benefits contributed by a_j to a_i

RB_{ij} - Benefits received by a_j from a_i

When $R_j < 0$, the actor a_j may be seen, by its partners, as having a potentially "selfish" behaviour in the period of time in analyse, in the sense that it received more benefits than it contributed. If this balance remains negative in the long term, the actor would most likely be considered selfish and probably not an appreciated partner. On the other hand, when $R_j > 0$, the actor a_j might be seen, by its partners, as having a potentially "altruistic" behaviour and it would be considered altruist if it holds this behaviour in the long term.

In order to discuss the role of the value systems when the promotion of cooperation is based on a reciprocity mechanism, let us consider the following two scenarios.

Scenario 1 *– A VBE with a common value system*
Let us again suppose the actor a_j performs a task that benefits actor a_i. From the perspective of actor a_j, this action is perceived as an investment (contributed benefit

(CB)) in actor a_i. If the two actors share the same value system then they will have the same perception of the benefit value. Based on this premise actor a_i will valorise the benefits received (RB) (its satisfaction) to the same amount (RB=CB).

As result of actor's a_i satisfaction, actor a_i recognizes a "debt of gratitude" to actor a_j (kind of social debit) and actor a_j gets a "credit" from actor a_i. As both actors have the same perception of the benefit value then the total sum of benefits variations is null for a full cycle (Fig. 3).

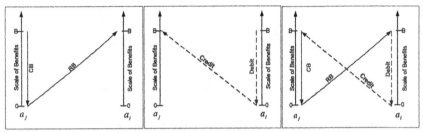

Figure 3 – Contribution of actor a_j to actor a_i

Later on, let us suppose actor a_j needs something done to him by others. As actor a_j has a social credit from a past exchange he can now expect, from the reciprocity principle, to get some service from the actor a_i (direct reciprocity) or from any other actor member of VBE (indirect reciprocity).

The assumption here is that sharing a common value system leads the two actors to perceive the value of a benefit in the same way. In this context the principle of reciprocity can be a good general governance rule for promoting collaboration. In order to illustrate this idea let us consider the following example.

Example 1 – Time Bank Case
The Time Bank concept induces mutually helping communities whose value system consists of only one variable that is the quantity of time exchanged among people. The cooperation benefit is measured as the number of hours that one person spends helping another. One key principle here is that one hour is equal to everybody. One hour of helping out with gardening is equal to an hour of baby-sitting. As an illustration, Fig. 4 shows some exchanges of services among members in a Portuguese Time Bank agency.

The reciprocity principle is applied in the Time Bank in the following way: people "deposit" time they when they contribute to the community by giving practical help and support to someone; in exchange they are able to "withdraw" time when they need something done to themselves by others.

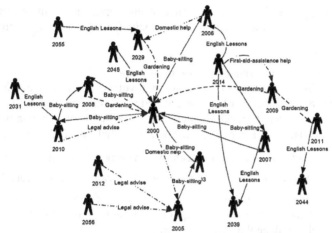

Figure 4 – Exchanges of services in a time bank agency

Based on real data from a Portuguese Time Bank agency, Fig. 5 (using UCINET [3]) shows the evolution of collaboration from the perspective of contributed benefits along two consecutive years. The nodes' size represents the level of contribution of each actor and the link's width represents the value of benefit supplied. Analysing the two graphs at the same time we can verify that in 2002 there are two nodes (2000 and 2014) that are the major contributors. When we look at 2003 the situation changed; in that year there are more big contributors and the number of links also increased, showing that a stronger cooperation level was achieved.

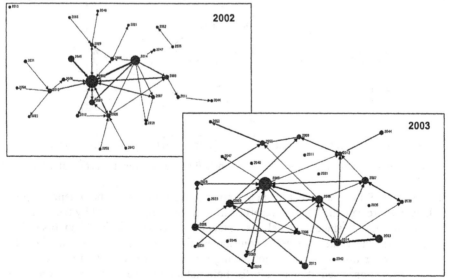

Figure 5 – CB over time

This increase in the level of cooperation, and the proliferation of time banks in many countries, depends in our opinion, among others factors (such as the leadership of the time bank promoter), on the existence of this simple and common value system and the application of the principle of reciprocity (mostly indirect reciprocity in this case).

Scenario 2 – *A VBE without a common value system*
Let us now discuss a scenario where actors involved in an exchange have distinct perceptions of the value of a benefit. Fig. 6 illustrates a case of benefits "depreciation", i.e. when an actor undervalues the benefits of an action performed by another. As illustrated, actor a_i performs a task that benefits actor a_j. From the perspective of actor a_i this action means an investment in (contributed benefit (CB) to) actor a_j. However, actor a_j gives it a lower value and therefore the "social" credit received by the performer is less than what it assumed to be its contribution (RB < CB). This difference in perception of a value is likely to create a sense of unfairness and to reduce the will to cooperate.

We could also consider the opposite situation (less common?), as illustrated by figure 8 that represents a case of additional gain to actor a_j. In this case, from the perspective of actor a_i, the outcome of this social interaction means an additional gain because for him the level of benefits contributed to actor a_j is lower than the level of satisfaction actor a_j got (RB > CB). Since actor's a_i contribution (CB) is lower than the "social" credit received from actor a_j (CB < Credit), it is likely that actor a_i will be motivated to keep cooperating with actor a_j.

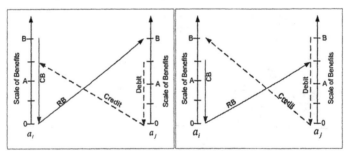

Figure 6 – Actor a_j depreciates benefits received from the action of actor a_i

Figure 7 – Actor a_j over appreciates the benefits received from the action of actor a_i

Figures 8 and 9 illustrate what happens between two actors when both depreciate or both over appreciate the benefits received from the action performed by the other. In the case of figure 8, since the level of satisfaction (perceived received benefits (RB)) is higher than the value of benefits contributed, the cooperation process is likely to stay stable over time in spite of not having a common value system as there is a mutual perception of additional gain for both actors. On the other hand, when the level of satisfaction (perceived received benefits (RB)) is lower than the value of benefits contributed, the willingness to cooperate is likely to be in danger, at least in the long term.

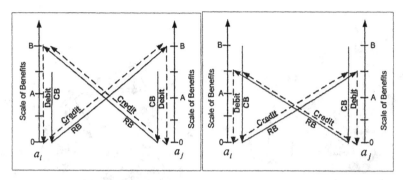

Figure 8 – Reciprocal over-appreciation of   Figure 9 – Reciprocal depreciation of
                received benefits   received benefits

As discussed above, the lack of a common value system, namely in case of depreciation of benefit value, is likely to be an obstacle for the sustainability of a collaborative network. One possible approach to remedy this situation is to elaborate a number of measurable indicators and making them explicitly "visible" to all partners. In this way transparency is promoted and hopefully will contribute to a convergence towards alignment of the different perceptions of value.

The development of graphical tools that allow the visualization of some indicators of collaboration [6] for all actors at the same time could be a good approach to increase the transparency among distinct partners and in that way contribute to building-up a common value system, thus assuring the network cohesion and simultaneously the feeling of fairness inside the VBE based on indicators that measure the quality and level of collaboration of each member in public way. As an illustration, let us consider the following example.

Example 2 – VBE of small and medium enterprises
This example uses input data based on Virtuelle Fabrik, a long term collaborative network (a VBE) in the metal-mechanic sector, located in Switzerland and Germany. For the purpose of the following discussion, let us consider the benefits are based only on one variable, the turnover of collaborative actions.

Based on the turnover data for 2004, the nodes' size in Fig. 10A represents the sum of benefits received, by each member, from the network and the link's width represents the value of the benefit supplied by one member to another. Hence, in this case who received more benefits were enterprises 10, 11 and 13.

On the other hand, the nodes' size in Fig. 10B represents the sum of benefits contributed by an actor to the network and the link's width represents the value of the benefit supplied to a specific actor. Hence, the major contributors are enterprises 16 and 58. If we look to the links between enterprises we can easily identify, for instance, a strong exchange of benefits between enterprises 16 and 13.

Analyzing the two graphs at the same time, we can conclude that for this period of time (one year) there are some enterprises, for instance enterprise 58, which might feel "uncomfortable" with its participation on this VBE. In fact, if the situation of enterprise 58 holds for a long time, its participation in this collaborative network could become unsustainable in the long term as it might consider that there is no reciprocity.

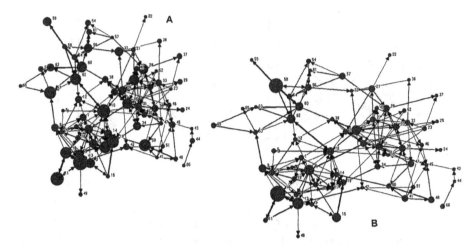

Figure 10 – Received benefits (A) and contributed benefits (B) for 2004

The graph in Fig. 11A shows the benefits credit balance $(R_j > 0)$ for all enterprises members of the VBE. Based on the period of time under consideration the enterprises 15, 16 and 58 exhibit a potential altruistic behavior in the sense that they contributed much more benefits than they received.

On the other hand, Fig. 11B shows the benefits debit balance $(R_j < 0)$ for all enterprises members of the VBE. For the considered period of time, enterprises 11, 50, 53 and 59 exhibit a potentially "selfish" behavior in the sense that they received much more benefits than they contributed, or at least this can be the perception got by the other partners looking at these indicators.

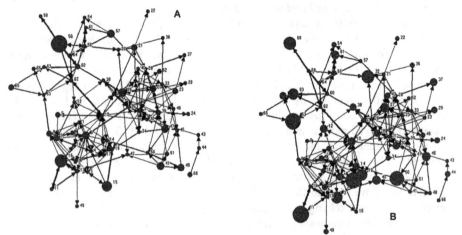

Figure 11 – Benefits credit (A) and debit (B) for 2004

In rational terms the motivation for a company to stay in the VBE should be based on a comparison of the benefits it gets versus what it could get if working alone out of this community. Nevertheless it is also important to consider the natural tendency of people to make comparisons with their partners and therefore it is very important to avoid the emergence of any feeling of unfairness.

In order to reduce the problems discussed above it is necessary to implement mechanisms that act as incentives for cooperation. For instance, honorific recognitions, higher chances to get access to business opportunities, more access to some assets and even punishment of "selfish" behaviors (e.g. less access to opportunities, higher cost in the access to common services/assets). Perhaps one challenge is to create, at the VBE level, a kind of indicator of the level of cooperation that lets members accumulate and use "credits" in a similar way as in the Time Bank.

For instance, in the social network analysis area there is an indicator of "prestige" of a member in a network. Applying this concept here, Fig. 12 relates actors' prestige to the sum of received benefits. Although in a broad sense it could make sense that the total of received benefits (RB) would grow with prestige, in the sense that actors that are more prestigious tend to receive more external benefits links, we can notice that for the same level of prestige different companies got quite different levels of benefits.

Different reasons can be considered for this situation, for instance: the amount of benefits an actor receives depends on several other factors belonging to the value system that were not taken into account in this example. Therefore, although explicit representations of the "status" of collaboration according to some indicators can increase the transparency of the network, it might also have a negative effect if the set of indicators is not properly defined and a good set of indicators is not introduced in the governance principles of the VBE.

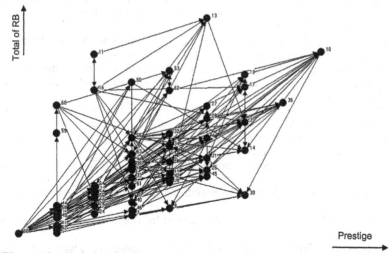

Figure 12 – Relationship between Prestige and Received benefits for 2004

5. CONCLUSIONS

The development of a common value system in a VBE context is an important step to support the sustainability of collaborative behavior over the time. When partners have different value systems, which typically leads to different perceptions of benefits, non-collaborative behaviors are likely to develop. In order to overcome this problem, some mechanisms to promote transparency and induce alignment of value systems might be implemented at the level of the governance rules of the VBE. A discussion of approaches in this direction, illustrated by a simple "value-set" case based on transactions values, was presented.

However, more work is necessary in order to identify a proper set of indicators of the collaboration level of each partner.

Acknowledgments – This work was supported in part by the ECOLEAD integrated project funded by the European Commission. The authors thank Stefan Bollhalter (Virtuelle Fabrik) for the help with example data.

6. REFERENCES

1. Alexander, R. D. (1987). *The Biology of Moral Systems*, Aldine.
2. Axelroad, R. (1984). The Evolution of Cooperation, Basic Books.
3. Borgatti, S.P., Everett, M.G. and Freeman, L.C. 2002. Ucinet for Windows: Software for Social Network Analysis. Harvard, MA: Analytic Technologies.
4. Boyd, R., and Richerson, P. J. (1982). Cultural transmission and the evolution of cooperative behaviour. *Human Ecology*, 10, 325-351.
5. Camarinha-Matos, L. M.; Abreu, António (2004). A contribution to understand collaborative benefits - Emerging solutions for future manufacturing systems, Springer, ISBN 0-387-22828-4.
6. Camarinha-Matos, L. M.; Abreu, António (2004). Performance indicators based on collaboration benefits- Collaborative Networks and their Breeding Environments, Springer, ISBN 0-387-28259-9.
7. Camarinha-Matos, L. M.; Afsarmanesh, H. (2003). Elements of a VE base infrastructure, J. Computers in Industry, Vol. 51, Issue 2, Jun 2003, pp. 139-163.
8. Camarinha-Matos, L. M.; Afsarmanesh, H. (Ed.s) (2004). Collaborative Networked Organizations – A research agenda for emerging business models, Kluwer Academic Publishers, ISBN 1-4020-7823-4.
9. Ernst, F., and Simon, G. (2000). Fairness and Retaliation: The Economics of Reciprocity. *Journal of Economic Perspectives*, 14, 159-181.
10. Eshel, I. (1972). On the neighbour effect and the evolution of altruistic traits. *Theoretical Population Biology*, 3, 258–77.
11. Hamilton, W. D. (1963). The evolution of altruistic behaviour. *The American Naturalist*, 97, 354-356.
12. Hamilton, W. D. (1964). The genetic evolution of social behaviour. *Journal Theoretical Biology*, 7, 1-52.
13. Nowak, M., and Sigmund, K. (1998). Evolution of Indirect Reciprocity by Image Scoring. *Nature*, 393, 573-577.
14. Roberts, G., and Sherratt, T. N. (1998). Development of cooperative relationships through increasing investment. *Nature*, 394, 175-179.
15. Simon, H. A. (1991). Organizations and markets. *Journal of Economic Perspectives*, 5, 25-44.

30

KNOWLEDGE MANAGEMENT BASED APPROACH FOR VIRTUAL ORGANIZATION INHERITANCE

Leandro Loss, Alexandra A. Pereira-Klen, Ricardo J. Rabelo
Federal University of Santa Catarina, Department of Automation and Systems
GSIGMA – Intelligent Manufacturing Systems Group
Florianópolis (SC), BRAZIL
{loss, klen}@gsigma.ufsc.br; rabelo@das.ufsc.br

This paper presents a framework for supporting virtual organization (VO) inheritance relying on knowledge management approach. It emphasizes that part of the problems to manage VOs is derived from the lack of information and lessons learned about the past businesses as well as that keeping the VOs' histories can be useful for augmenting and for given more agility in the decision-making process. The suggested framework presents VO inheritance as a horizontal activity that covers the entire VO life cycle, providing information for the several involved collaborative actors. An initial experiment using decision analysis is presented to show its use in VO inheritance. In the conclusions it is argued that VOs could be much more effective and the problems solved with more agility if a better use could be made out of the information inherited from VOs.

1. INTRODUCTION

Working collaboratively is becoming more and more important for enterprises as a strategic answer to respond to the increasing dynamics and competitiveness in the global market. Collaborative Networked Organizations (CNOs) has been considered the discipline in charge of studying all the manifestations of organizations when they work in an inter-linked and organized way (Camarinha-Matos et al., 2004a).

One of these manifestations is Virtual Organization (VO). A VO is a dynamic, temporary and logical aggregation of autonomous organizations that cooperate with each other as a strategic answer to attend a given business opportunity or to cope with a specific need, and whose operation is achieved by a coordinated sharing of skills, resources and information, totally enabled by computer networks (Rabelo et al., 2004). Its objective is to create and to deliver products or services to final customers and, at the same time, creating value for all entities engaged in the collaboration process (ECOLEAD, 2005a).

Managing the creation and the operation of VOs is, however, complex. Part of this complexity has been identified in several works, e.g. (McKenzie, 2001), (Afsarmanesh et al., 2005), (Karvonen et al., 2005). Another part of it is related to the lack of adequate support for VO managers to consider past experiences when dealing with problems along the VO life cycle. The inability to learn from a cumulative "project history" probably puts a new project's timetable in greater risk

Please use the following format when citing this chapter:

Loss, L., Pereira-Klen, A. A., Rabelo, R. J., 2006, in IFIP International Federation for Information Processing, Volume 224, Network-Centric Collaboration and Supporting Fireworks, eds. Camarinha-Matos, L., Afsarmanesh, H., Ollus, M., (Boston: Springer), pp. 285–294.

than all other factors combined (Reed, 2002). The same situation may occur for VOs. VOs operating without considering what have happened in past VOs will not necessarily fail, but accessing VOs' past information can require considerable – and unnecessary – effort from VO managers and from VO partners. This kind of information can be very much useful in several situations. For example, for speeding up the selection of partners for future VOs (reducing the search and negotiation processes) or for elucidating similar problems already solved in other VOs.

This work intends to exploit the part related to the difficulties originated by the fact that most of the information and knowledge generated along the VO life cycle use to be lost after the VO dissolution, i.e. the fact that VOs' history are not retained for future use.

VO inheritance (VO-I) has been emerging as the research area for dealing with the problems related to how generated information, knowledge, devised practices, products and services about VOs can be handled and managed (Camarinha-Matos et al., 2004b). In fact, this area is still in its infancy. Initial steps have been made in the ECOLEAD project (ECOLEAD, 2005c), comprising the VO creation phase, and calling *bag of assets* as the repository that contains common ontologies, basic software tools, and common information related to Virtual Organization Breeding Enviroments (VBE).

The proposed approach aims at presenting a framework based on knowledge management that extends the VO inheritance scope to the whole VO life cycle.

The paper is organized as follows: Section 2 introduces the concept related to VO inheritance and how it is placed in the VBE/VO context. Section 3 presents the knowledge management approach for VO inheritance. Section 4 depicts the basic concepts of decision support as well as of structuring decisions via decision analysis. Section 5 shows a practical example using decision trees and sensitivity analysis. Finally, Section 6 provides preliminary conclusions and future steps.

2. VIRTUAL ORGANIZATION INHERITANCE

VOs, by nature, have temporary and distributed behaviors and are logically and legally dismantled only after the contractual clauses have been all fulfilled. It means that the VO duration can vary from days to years. There are three basic difficulties that make the process of managing VO inheritance – VO inheritance management (VO-I-M) – complex:

- The amount of information of every VO uses to be naturally huge.
- It is difficult to elect which and how relevant information and lessons (successful and unsuccessful) are, as well as how they should be get, interpreted, analyzed, filtered, modeled, stored, organized, contextualized, systemized and showed to managers for more effective decision-making.
- The knowledge about VOs is usually spread among the VOs' members, i.e. each actor knows about what happened with a given VO inside his/her own company, but rarely or insufficiently knows what happened in other VO members.

Few significant results that face these difficulties can be found in the literature, meaning that there are several questions not well covered yet. Actually, it is a direct consequence of the fact that research in the VO-I area is still in its beginning.

Franke (Franke, 2000) describes a VO from an inter-organizational perspective where the concept of Virtual Web/Corporation as a partnership model is introduced. The basic idea is that virtual web members should make their resource base available to their partners. The knowledge-based perspective brings the potential to build core know-how and therefore to gain competitive advantage. Franke also states that one agent should act as a caretaker during the VO dissolution phase. The importance of the storage of acquired and generated knowledge was emphasized; however none guideline of how to proceed and/or store such knowledge was provided.

According to Blecker (2000), the knowledge management in VOs means designing, controlling, and developing a purpose-oriented knowledge together with the partners. It leads to the union of the knowledge among the VO's participants. Blecker argues that in short term forms of VOs, only the outcome of production process rather than knowledge is shared. This statement is not true when VOs emerge from VBEs that guarantee preparedness and long term partnership.

The approach presented in this paper aims at gathering the information and the knowledge throughout the CNO (for both short-term and long-term VOs) and organizing them in order to make this knowledge easily accessible.

The need related to the knowledge storage in VOs leads to a specific approach, namely VO-I. The authors define it as the set of information and knowledge accumulated from past and current VOs along their entire life cycle. VO-I-M corresponds to the VO activity that manages what has been inherited about given VOs, usually supported by computer systems[1].

VO inheritance is seen as a horizontal process with the aim of offering "services" to other "clients", like VBE and VO management (VOM) actors and related supporting systems. Figure 1 illustrates the VO-I process. In the bottom it is possible to visualize the whole CNO life-cycle comprising VBE and VO life-cycle. On the top of the figure it is represented the process of information gathering and its transformation into knowledge. The top-left side represents databases storing information from VBE partners, VO's performance metrics, clients, products, core competences, and whatever is important. Those databases are one of the sources of information for extracting knowledge (via data mining, for example). In a similar way, on the top-right side the unorganized information is represented by small circles. In an upper level the information is organized according to some rules or relevance; new knowledge – circles in bold – is also made available. For instance, the transformation of tacit knowledge into explicit knowledge via decision trees, questionnaires, and so on. The double-arrows in the middle of the figure represent the data/information flowing from CNO level to VO-I to be organized and processed, as well as its return to VBE/VOs. The overall process of gathering, storing, organizing, and extracting knowledge from information, related to CNOs, comprises the VOI process.

---

[1] VO-I-M is much more than Business Intelligence (BI). Although some works (e.g. Rabelo et al., 2002) have extended the traditional view of BI when also considering current/dynamic information of a company, BI tools work only with static and past information from just a given company, and not from (dynamic) VOs or supply chains, for instance.

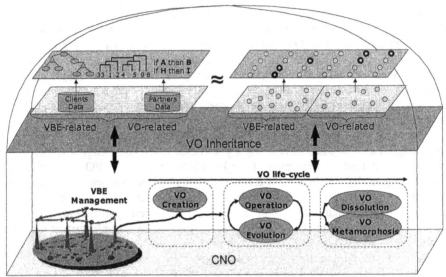

Figure 1 – Global framework for VO inheritance

Finally it is important to differentiate VO inheritance from VO life history. The VO life history is related to the time sequence of actions and their description in the stages during the VO life cycle (Tølle, 2002). As there is not a standard way in which activities can be performed over time, each VO has its own integrated activities describing its life history. Examples of life history can be found in Ollus (2002) and Tølle (2002). In VO-I knowledge and the expertise acquired can also be reused in VOs in execution. For example, comparing partner's performance in different VOs, or predicting cases when planned activities will have some delay. In its essence, VO inheritance aims at improving VO managers' decision making capability. One supporting approach for that is knowledge management.

3. PROPOSED KNOWLEDGE MANAGEMENT APPROACH

The definition for Knowledge Management presented by Malhotra (1998) states that *"knowledge management caters to the critical issues of organizational adaptation, survival and competence in face of increasingly discontinuous environmental change. Essentially, it embodies organizational processes that seek synergistic combination of data and information processing capacity of information technologies, and the creative and innovative capacity of human beings"*. Based on this, knowledge management applied to VO inheritance intends to create the synergy among pieces of information. In general, VO inheritance activity collects data and information by itself and it can discover new knowledge (e.g. Loss et al., 2005), whereas knowledge management organizes overall knowledge and makes it available to users in a structured and comprehensive way.

Some suggested tools/techniques for the task of knowledge discovery are: data mining algorithms (Fayyad, 1996) - for finding new patterns and/or models in data which can be useful; text and web mining (Mladenic, 2003) - for analyzing and discovering knowledge in unstructured data (e.g. documents in free text form); and decision analysis (Bohanec, 2003) - for deciding the best choice among a number of alternatives.

For the task of organizing and presenting knowledge, knowledge map is an interesting alternative because it corresponds to a visual representation of a knowledge domain in order to facilitate the location, comprehension or development of knowledge (Plumley, 2003). It deals with: i) explicit knowledge – core competencies, legacy systems, additional expertise, forms, documents, presentations, papers; ii) tacit knowledge – group dynamics, culture and social attributes; and iii) procedures (guidance, tips, checklists) – used by the CNO actors.

VO inheritance linked to knowledge management is more than a sum of parts of data and knowledge. It provides a framework with experiences and case studies for managers of both VBEs and VOs. Next section describes the general approach on how a decision support environment can be used as an integrated framework for handling the knowledge extracted in a VO inheritance scenario.

4. DECISION SUPPORT IN VO INHERITANCE

Decision Support is a broad term that comprehends all aspects related to supporting people in decision-making. Similarly to what happens in traditional companies, decision making problems are seen as the dilemma of choices also in VO where optimality rarely exist. That is why terms like "the best" or equivalent does not make sense anymore to be applied in real business regarding the so many variables and uncertainties usually presented in a decision. A VO manager is always confronted to situations like finding partners for a VO, evaluating current versus planned scheduling, analyzing financial effects of order replenishment or cancellation, comparing VOs´ historical data for performance analysis, planning actions for handling predicted problems, among others. All this aims to fulfill the VOs´ goals and contractual clauses regarding expected benefits and profits.

Therefore, in general, the relevant question is *"which alternative should be chosen when the VO manager has many variables involved to take a decision?"*, which reveals making a choice out of a number of alternatives (Bohanec, 2003).

Regarding the field of decision sciences (human decision making), some techniques are available to help in finding options to satisfy the decision maker's goals. The three main branches for decision support are (Bohanec, 2003): i) operation research; ii) decision support systems; and iii) decision analysis (Figure 2). Operation research structures real-life situations into mathematical models. Decision support systems deal with unstructured problems and uses data models to identify and to solve problems. Decision analysis breaks the problem in more manageable parts considering possible alternatives and available information. This paper exploits the use of decision analysis as it seems more suitable for dealing with the mentioned VO problems, which involve uncertainties and managers' preferences.

The process of making choices is more complex than just picking one option. It consists in assessing the current problem and understanding the objectives, and collecting as well as verifying available and pertinent information in order to identify possible alternatives (Clemen 1996). Alternatives are split into more manageable and understandable parts in order to model the problem and they are presented to the VO manager, who decides to apply one of them or not, also considering that different managers present different behaviors and adopt different management strategies for the same problem (Pereira-Klen et al., 2005).

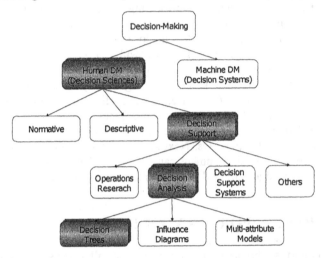

Figure 2 – Decision Making Areas (Source: Clemen, 1996)

Decision trees, a special technique in decision analysis was chosen since they are representations of decision problems and are used in the process of structuring decision elements like alternatives, uncertain events, and final outcomes (Clemen, 1996) which fits our case example. It utilizes a structure of three types of nodes: i) decision nodes: alternatives presented to the manager; ii) chance nodes: events with certain probability of occurrence; and iii) terminal nodes: the final outcome (*payoff*) for each leaf in the tree. It means that each problem can have two or more alternative solutions (which can be decomposed in several tree levels), and each alternative has decision nodes. At last, each alternative has a probability to happen (100% for all alternatives of a given problem) and an associated cost.

5. THE EXPERIMENT

In a CNO scenario a given enterprise is usually involved in several VOs, and decisions should be taken for each VO and for every problem related to. These decisions are different from each other because each situation is likely unique. The example below describe how a decision making process related to one problem in a given VO would be carried out.

This example is related to a case where one VO partner in a given VO is delayed in its planned delivery. In this case, VO-I aims to store information about the decisions taken and their reasons as well as the final outcome for future use by the VO manager. A hypothetic scenario for a VO producing special chairs – named as *chairs production* – has been devised and decision trees and sensitivity analysis were used to model and to base the final decision for facing such delay.

In this scenario it was assumed that the foreseen VO profit will be of 10K€ in the case no problems occur during its execution. However, as a partner is delayed, a decision should be taken about what to do, regarding other partners' capacities and scheduling, contract penalties, and know-how about the production. It will be also assumed that this problem is considered relevant to be solved (regarding the involved values), its solution should be found as soon as possible (as they affect the current schedule), it will be a one-stage solution (i.e. no further possibilities of refinements/renegotiations), and the VO manager will take the decision alone.

There would be four decisions to be taken:

- *Increase capacity* – the delayed partner should contract more employees in order to accomplish its deadline. But this will cost 4K€, i.e. the final outcome will be of 6K€ and this action has 65% of probability to overcome the delay. In the case this action does not solve the problem the VO should then pay for this. This means that the other 35% of probability is divided in other possible consequences. In this case, there would be two types of consequences: the worst one is a very drastic *image impact*, which is expressed as a zero € of profit; or *suffer penalties*. Three levels of penalties may be applied, which can vary from low, medium and high penalties, causing a loss of 6.5K€, 7.5K€ and 9K€, respectively, and with a probability of 20%, 35% and 45%, respectively, to happen. The probability numbers and, usually, the values associated with the consequences are provided according to the manager experience and managerial style.

- *Status quo* – it means to leave it as it is. *Status quo* is divided into two branches: *aware* and *unaware*. The former case represents the manager's knowledge about the overall VO schedule as well as the partners' capacity. The manager can decide to do nothing because he knows that one of the partners has been working with a loose schedule meaning that it is able to absorb the delay. This has 70% of probability to solve the problem and hence to keep with the original profit of 10K€. The latter case, the manager thinks that the problem will be "naturally" solved along the time by the involved partners. It has 30% of probability of success but he estimates a loss of 2.5K€ in the final outcome with the actions that would be taken by the partners.

- *More time* – the VO manager requires more time to the final client in order to adjust and to end the delayed production order, but this would be possible thanks a discount of 3K€. If the client accepts this alternative the final outcome will be 7K€ and this acceptance would happen with 65% of probability. However, there is 35% of probability that the client does not accept this. Then the manager should decide for analyzing the consequences *image damage* or *penalties*, described in the first decision type.

- *Sub-contracting* – the VO manager decides to go one step beyond and one or more partners will join the VO in order to fulfill the needs. The available options regarding time, costs, and quality of service are: i) *partner 1* will cost of 5K€; ii) *partner 2* 5.5K€; iii) *partner 3* 6K€; and iv) *partner 4* also 5K€. All these subcontracted partners have 90% of probability to succeed in this mission. In the case of failure (with 10% of probability), the profit is zero K€.

Rolling back the options of this decision tree and ranking them, the following sequence is found: *more time* with an outcome of € 5.258,75; *sub-contracting* with €

4.950,00; *status quo* with € 4.750,00; and *increase capacity* (work power) in the last place with an outcome of € 4.608,75.

Quantities incorporated into a tree are uncertain and many probabilities are just estimations. One option to validate the best alternative is to apply the *Sensitivity Analysis* technique. It is done ranging the values of some probabilities in order to assess how the decision is affected by the variation in one or more of the uncertain quantities in the model. It works like a *what-if* case. Figure 3 shows for example that the more the manager is aware about the status of the VO's partners the bigger the chances of taking the right decision tends to be. The probability of awareness, variable *p_awareness*, was ranged from 50% to 90%. The graphic shows a threshold in 73%, which means that only if the VO manager is more than 75% sure about his actions, "doing nothing" is a better choice than *more time*. Just to remember, *more time* was the best outcome before ranging the value of the probability *p-awareness*. The results sound obvious or too simple. However no one was aware of this conclusion before this analysis.

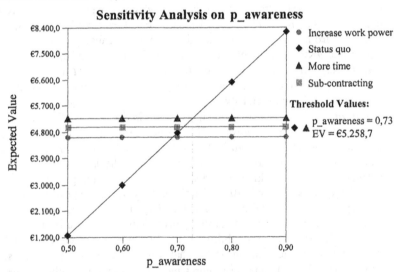

Figure 3 – Sensitivity Analysis on probability of awareness

Despite decision trees cannot be completely reusable regarding that each situation is usually unique, the case presented can be used as a model to be followed in similar situations. Surely different sets of alternatives will be made available in each situation. Sensitivity analysis can be used to study the deviation in some variables representing the probability in *chance nodes* in order to give more confidence to the decisions. In this context, knowledge management makes the knowledge obtained in decision analysis process explicit and hence easier to be modeled, systemized and available to VO managers for his further use. The content of this decision tree is hierarchically organized and classified in a taxonomy (represented by an ontology) so that short explanations can be provided about the elected decision option (*status-quo*).

6. CONCLUSIONS AND NEXT STEPS

This paper stressed the concept of Virtual Organization inheritance (VO-I), highlighting its increasing importance in the CNO discipline. An approach for supporting virtual organization inheritance was introduced, where knowledge management was used as the main guideline and decision support was the example chosen for the application presented. The rationale of the proposed approach is that the management of VOs could be much more effective and its problems solved with more agility and reliability if information and lessons learned from past VOs could be stored and properly retrieved by VO actors (e.g. VO managers and VO planners).

Regarding that problems and solutions can vary for every VO, the main goal of VO-I is not necessarily the reusability of decisions taken in the past but rather the possibility to consult what has happened in similar cases, the practices used and their effects, the adequacy of certain performance indicators to select partners to compose a VO as well as to monitor them along the VO operation, and so forth. Managing VO-I is therefore an important asset for organizations, specially if it is considered that this information is properly stored, processed, and organized. VO inheritance provides structure and guidance for thinking systematically about decisions even the ones that seem to be tricky to solve.

Despite its importance, the research about VO inheritance is still in its beginning and many open questions are present. Some of them were pointed out in the paper, showing an initial research path to this area. This paper did not intend to provide solutions for all the identified problems of decision-making in VOs, but rather to present an initial experiment that corresponds to a part of a wider framework.

In a former work developed the by the authors (Loss, 2005) the focus was put on how bunches of information can be collected and how new knowledge can be generated for decision-making purposes applying data mining. The present work adds another piece in the devised framework evaluating decision trees as a possible technique to support the modeling and costs of decision alternatives. However it is important to point out that the limitation of techniques such as decision tress (for instance the need of experts for both decision tree modeling and domain specific ones) has a direct influence on its application.

Next steps of this research will be devoted to analyze how VO-I can benefit from ontology in terms of better representation of knowledge, richer semantics to link the stored knowledge with problems, and a more sophisticated indexation mechanism to facilitate the search for knowledge by VO managers.

6.1 Acknowledgments

This work has been partially supported by the Brazilian councils of research and scientific development – CNPq (www.cnpq.br) and CAPES (www.capes.gov.br). It has been developed in the scope of the Brazilian IFM project (www.ifm.org.br) and the European IST FP-6 IP ECOLEAD project (www.ecolead.org). Special thanks to Mr. Marko Bohanec, from JSI – Slovenia, for his substantial support during the phase of the application of decision analysis techniques, and to Mr. Rui Jorge Tramontin Jr., from UFSC – Brazil, for his valuable comments about the paper.

7. REFERENCES

1. Afsarmanesh, H.; Camarinha-Matos, L.M.; 2005. A Framework for Management of Virtual Organization Breeding Environments. Proceedings PRO-VE'2005, pp 35-48.
2. Blecker, T.; Neumann, R.; 2000. Interorganizational Knowledge Management: Some Perspectives for Knowledge Oriented Strategic Management in Virtual Organizations. In: Malhotra, Y. (ed) Knowledge Management and Virtual Organizations. Idea Group Publishing.
3. Bohanec, M.; 2003. Decision Suppot. In: Mladenic, D.; Lavrac, N.; Bohanec, M.; Moyle, S.; (eds). Data Mining and Decision Support: Integration and Collaboration. Kluwer Academic Publishers – Boston/Dordrecht/London – ISBN 1-4020-7388-8. pp. 23-36.
4. Camarinha-Matos, L. M.; Afsarmanesh, H.; 2004a. Towards Next Business Models. In Collaborative Networked Organizations: a research agenda for emerging business models.
5. Camarinha-Matos, L. M.; Afsarmanesh, H.; 2004b. Support Infrastructures for New Collaborative Forms. In Collaborative Networked Organizations: a research agenda for emerging business models, Kluwer Academic Publishers, pp. 175-192.
6. Clemen, R.T.; 1996. Making Hard Decisions: An Introd. to Decision Analysis, Duxbury Press.
7. ECOLEAD, 2005a. ECOLEAD Project: European Collaborative Networked Organizations Leadership Initiative. Deliverable D23.1 ECOLEAD Project – Requirements and mechanisms for VO planning and launching.
8. ECOLEAD, 2005b. ECOLEAD Project: European Collaborative Networked Organizations Leadership Initiative. Deliverable D32.2 ECOLEAD Project – Report on Methodologies, Processes and Services for VO Management.
9. ECOLEAD, 2005c. ECOLEAD Project: European Collaborative Networked Organizations Leadership Initiative. Deliverable D21.1 ECOLEAD Project – Characterization of Key Components, Features, and Operating Principles of the VBE.
10. Fayyad, U.; Piatetski-Shapiro, G.; Smyth, P.; 1996. From Data Mining to Knowledge Discovery in Databases. AAAIMIT Press, p.37-54, 1996.
11. Franke, U.; 2000. The Knowledge-Based View of the Virtual Web, the Virtual Coportation, and the Net-Broker. In: Malhotra, Y. (ed) Knowledge Management and Virtual Organizations. Idea Group Publishing.
12. Karvonen, I.; Salkari, I.; Ollus, M. ; 2005. Characterizing Virtual Organizations and their Management. Proceedings PRO-VE'2005, pp 193-204.
13. Loss, L.; Rabelo, R. J.; Pereira-Klen, A. A.; 2005. A Generic Framework based on Machine Learning Techniques for Virtual Organization Management. Proc. PRO-VE'2005, pp.217-226.
14. Malhotra, Y.; 1998. Deciphering the Knowledge Management Hype. The Journal for Quality & Participation, July/August 1998 (Special issue on Knowledge Management), published by the Association for Quality & Participation.
15. McKenzie, J.; van Winkelen, C.; 2001. Exploring E-collaboration Space. In: The First Annual Knowledge Management Forum Conference. Proceedings. Henley Management College.
16. Mladenic,. D., Grobelnik, M.; 2003. Text and Web Mining. In: Mladenic, D.; Lavrac, N.; Bohanec, M.; Moyle, S.; (eds). Data Mining And Decision Support: Integration and Collaboration. Kluwer Academic Publishers – Boston/Dordrecht/London, pp. 23-36.
17. Ollus, M., Hartel, I., Tølle, M., Wubben, H., Hannus, M. (2002) Using scenarios for dissemination, Experiences from the IMS GLOBEMEN project, Proceedings of eBeW2002 conference, Prague, 16-18 October 2002.
18. Pereira-Klen, A. A.; Klen, E. R.; 2005. Human Supervised Virtual Organization Management. Proceedings PRO-VE'2005, pp 229-238.
19. Plumley, D.; 2003. Process-Based Knowledge Mapping: A practical approach to priorizing knowledge in terms of its relevance to a business or KM objective. Web page accessed in December 20th, 2005. URL: (http://www.destinationkm.com/).
20. Rabelo, R. J.; Pereira-Klen, A.; 2002. Business Intelligence Support for Supply Chain Management, Proceedings BASYS'2002 Conference, pp. 437-444.
21. Rabelo, R. J.; Pereira-Klen, A.; Klen, E. R., Effective Management of Dynamic Supply Chains, in International Journal of Networking and Virtual Organizations, 2004.
22. Reed Jr., P. R.; 2002. Reference Architecture: The best of best practices. http://www-128.ibm.com/developerworks/rational/library/ 2774.html.
23. Tølle, M.; Bernus, P.; Vesterager, J. 2002. Reference models for virtual enterprises. In. Camarinha-Matos, L. M.; Afsarmanesh, H. (Eds). Collaborative Business Ecosystems and Virtual Enterprises. Boston: Kluwer, pp. 3-10.

PART 10

DECISION MAKING

31

DECISIONAL INTEROPERABILITY: CONCEPTS AND FORMALISATION

Daclin N., Chen D., Vallespir B.

LAPS, University Bordeaux 1, ENSEIRB, UMR 3151,351 cours de la Libération, 33405 Talence cedex, FRANCE, nicolas.daclin@laps.u-bordeaux1.fr

This paper deals with interoperability of enterprises. Interoperability is a multi-form issue and can be studied at different levels. This research work focuses on the business level and particularly on the decisional aspect so called decisional interoperability. The objective of the paper is to present how to develop decisional interoperability using design principles with mathematical formalisation, in order to improve and to facilitate the decision-making activity in a collaborative context. Finally, an illustration example using the proposed principles is presented to show the interest of the decisional interoperability solution.

1. INTRODUCTION

Increasingly, competitiveness of an enterprise depends not only on its internal productivity and performance, but also its ability to collaborate with others. Enterprises need to collaborate with other partners in terms of communication and interaction, in order to reach their objectives including the ones that are common between partners. In this context the development of interoperability has become a key factor of success.

Interoperability can be studied at different levels, and one of the developments of interoperability is related to the decision-making activity (ATHENA, 2003). It is so-called decisional interoperability. The purpose of this paper is to present the basic concepts and principles of decisional interoperability.

However, this paper does not take into account the socio-psychological aspect of the decision-making but focuses on formal and quantitative aspects, in order to reduce the uncertainty in terms of the objectives that the partners have to reach during a collaborative decision-making process.

This work has been initiated within the frame of WP6 (Design principles for interoperability) of INTEROP NoE (INTEROP, 2003). It also aims at extending the GRAI decisional model concepts to the development of interoperability in the context of networked enterprises.

First, the definition and a mathematical formalisation related to the decision-making activity inside one enterprise are presented. Set theory is used to formalise the decision-making activity.

Then, the decision-making activity in a collaborative context is discussed. Based on these works, a definition of decisional interoperability is proposed. Some design principles to build a decisional interoperability solution are presented. Set theory

Please use the following format when citing this chapter:

Daclin, N., Chen, D. Vallespir, B., 2006, in IFIP International Federation for Information Processing, Volume 224, Network-Centric Collaboration and Supporting Fireworks, eds. Camarinha-Matos, L., Afsarmanesh, H., Ollus, M., (Boston: Springer), pp. 297–304.

notations are also used to formalise the basic concepts of the decisional interoperability.

A simple case study is proposed at the end of the paper in order to illustrate and show the applicability of the proposed approach.

2. DECISION-MAKING ACTIVITY: CONCEPTS AND DEFINITIONS

2.1 Definition

Decision-making is an activity that aims at making choice. The decision itself is the result of choosing between courses of action (CEN, 2000). The decision-maker disposes of a set of alternatives and has to choose the best one allowing reaching his objectives. According to (Doumeingts, 1998) and (Vallespir, 2002), in order to choose among possible solutions, several items may influence the decision-maker:

- One (or more) objective(s) that the decision must allow reaching;
- One (or more) decision variable(s) on which the decision-maker can act;
- Constraints that limit the use of the decision variables; and
- Sometimes, criteria that guide the choice to make during the decision-making process.

This set of items form a decision frame constraining the degree of freedom to make a decision. Therefore, the decision-making can be shown as the search of a solution reaching (or being near) the objectives in a space defined by the decision variables and delimited by the constraints (Vallespir, 2003). Figure 1 illustrates the principle of decision-making consistently with the decision frame.

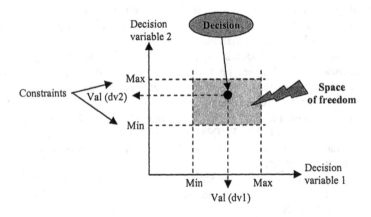

Figure 1 – Representation of the space of freedom for decision-making (two decision variables are considered)

2.2 Formalisation

Starting from the definitions given above, it is possible to propose a formalisation of the decision-making activity. Formalisation is necessary to understand and represent in a precise way the basic concepts relating to decision-making activity. Furthermore, it will allow giving general rules to make a decision that could be applicable in any situation including decisional interoperability.

Let us assume several **notations**:
Given *OB* the set of objectives that the decision must allow reaching,

$$OB = \{ob_1,..., ob_n\}, n \in N^*.$$

Given *VD* the set of decision variables,

$$VD = \{vd_1,..., vd_n\}, n \in N^*.$$

Given VD_{ct} the set of constrained decision variables,

$$VD_{ct} = \{vd \in VD | P(vd)\} = \{vd_{1ct1},...vd_{nctn}\}, n \in N^*,$$

with $P(vd)$ = the decision variables respect the constraints.

In order to make the decision through the formalisation of the decision frame and the definition given by (Vallespir, 2003), it is possible to write:

Given *D* the set of the possible decisions (given by the set of the values of the decision variables defined by the constraints),

$$D = \{\{vd_{1ct1},..., vd_{nctn}\}\}, d = \{vd_{1ct1},...vd_{nctn}\}, n \in N^*,$$
$$card(D) = card(vd_{1ct1}) \times ... \times card(vd_{nctn}), n \in N^*.$$

To each element of *D* – that is to say each combination of values of the decision variables – one possible objective can be associated.

Given *OB'* the set of objectives that can be reached by the elements of *D*,

$$OB' = \{ob' \in OB' | ob' = f(d)\}.$$

The function f defines a series of mathematical operation that allow the transformation of the decision variables values into the corresponding objectives.
An objective, belonging to *OB*, can be totally fulfilled if and only if it also belongs to *OB'*. In the case where there is no solution, the decision-maker will choose a solution belonging to *OB'* that will be the nearest to the desired objective.

Finally, the set D_r of the decisions researched *d* is:

$$Dr = \{d \in D | OB' \cap OB\}.$$

This formalisation can be now applied to decisional interoperability.

3. DECISIONAL INTEROPERABILITY

3.1 Collaborative decision-making

In the context of collaboration, partners work together in order to reach a common goal (Kvan, 2000). At the level of decision-making, it concerns the decision-makers to take a decision reaching the objective of the collaboration and also satisfying their own interests. Currently, the decision-making process is well defined (Mercier, 2003). However, several problems emerge from this process (Chen, 2005) (Wikipedia, 2006):

- The majority of collaborative decisions have to do with subjective issues (there is no formalisation and no rational manner to take a decision);
- Decisions are usually imposed by one party to another;
- The time length to achieve a common decision.

Therefore, decisional interoperability has to support the collaborative decision-making activity and to prevent the mentioned problems.

3.2 Decisional interoperability

According to (IEEE, 1990), (Oxford, 1999) and (Daclin, 2005), decisional interoperability can be defined as the ability for several decision-makers to exchange support-information for decision-making, and to use these support-information in order to make a decision that allows reaching the objective of the collaboration and at the same time that respects their own interests. The principle is to generate a common decision space taking their own support-information for decision-making into account as shown in figure 2.

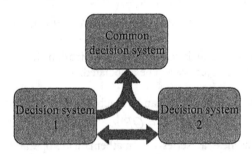

Figure 2 – Representation of the principle of decisional interoperability (Daclin, 2006)

The existing collaborative decision-making process is not designed for decisional interoperability. Consequently, it is important to define principles to design decisional interoperability solutions.

3.3 Design principles for decisional interoperability

A design principle is a rule to follow, that orients design decision-making. It can be defined as a fundamental truth which stands for evidence (Suh, 1990). Starting from the problems encountered in collaborative decision-making, three design principles for decisional interoperability have to be implemented according to the identified problems as summarised in figure 3.

In the case 1, decision-maker A makes a decision without knowing neither decision frame nor the possible decision which can be made by decision-maker B. In this case, the decision-maker A can make a decision which, on the one hand does not satisfy the decision-maker B and on the other hand does not satisfy the objective of the collaboration. This leads to some iterations and negotiations between both decision-makers to find a solution.

In the second case (case 2) the decision-makers A and B have clearly defined their decision frame including the possible decisions that can be engaged and make it known to the partner. In this case, the decision-makers can make a decision on the one hand without time loss and on the other hand which can satisfy both of them and the objective of the collaboration.

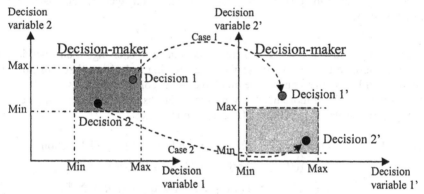

● Bad decision of A leading to a decision of B out of its frame
● Good decision taken by A knowing the decision frame and the capability of B

Figure 3 – Representation of the problems of collaborative decision-making in order to establish design principles

The three design principles for decisional interoperability that have to be implemented are:

Axiom 1: *"when designing a decision-making activity, make its decision frame explicit".*
The decision frame contains a set of items which limits the freedom of decision-making. It allows improving the decision-making transparency.

Axiom 2: *"Implement a mechanism to exchange the decision frame between all decision-makers".*
Building a decision frame known by your collaborative decision-maker improves decisional interoperability in terms of iterations between parties, and of the delay before reaching a decision.

Axiom 3: *"Establish capability for each decision-maker"*.
Decisional capability allows knowing admissible limits for the decision-makers, and improves the ability to make decisions that satisfy all decision-makers as far as possible.

3.4 Formalisation

Based on the conceptualisation of the decision-making activity previously proposed, a formalisation of the decisional interoperability is developed below.

Let us assume supplementary **notations:**
Given OB_c the set of the objectives of the collaboration,

$$OB_c = \{ob_{c1},..., ob_{cn}\}, n \in N^*.$$

Given P_c the set of the possible decisions that can be engaged by each partner in the collaboration,

$$P_c = \{p_{c1},..., p_{cn}\}, n \in N^*.$$

In order to obtain this set, the decision-makers have to exchange their own decision frame as defined above; otherwise they risk making a decision that will not allow satisfying other partners and/or the objective of the collaboration. As a consequence, the partners will have more negotiations and iterations to make a satisfying decision. This set represents the capability of the decisions-makers.

Given D_c the set of the possible decisions in the frame of the collaboration,

$$D_c = \{\{p_{c1},..., p_{cn}\}\}, d_c = \{p_{c1},..., p_{cn}\}, n \in N^*$$
$$card(D_c) = card(p_{c1}) \times ... \times card(p_{cn}), n \in N^*.$$

Given OB'_c the set of objectives that can be reached by the elements of D_c,

$$OB'_c = \{ob'_c \in OB'_c | ob'_c = g(d_c)\}.$$

The function g defines a series of mathematical operation that allow the transformation of the possible decisions that can be engaged by each partner into the corresponding objectives that can be reached in the frame of the collaboration.
An objective, belonging to OB_c, can be totally fulfilled if and only if it belongs to OB'_c.

Finally, the set D_{rc} of the decisions researched d_c is:

$$D_{rc} = \{d_c \in D_c | OB'_c \cap OB_c\}$$

This formalisation is applied to an illustration example presented in the section 4. This example is largely simplified to illustrate the decisional interoperability between two partners using a formal approach.

4. ILLUSTRATION EXAMPLE

Let us consider two partners (P_{c1} and P_{c2}), in a collaborative decision-making context.

The objective of the collaboration for the partners is: *"to produce n products for a maximum cost of 30 K€"*. This objective can be noted:

$$OB_c = \{0,1,...,30\}$$

The partners have selected the possible decisions (in this case in euro) that can be engaged in the frame of the collaboration. This selection of the possible decisions is performed and workable after that the decision-makers have clearly defined and exchanged their own decision frames. According to their own decision frame and the decision frame of the partner, these possible decisions can be noted:

$$P_{c1} = \{10,15,17\}$$
$$P_{c2} = \{13,16,24\}$$

The set of possible decisions of the collaboration is noted D_c.

$$card(Dc) = card(Pc1) \times card(Pc2)$$
$$card(Dc) = 3 \times 3 = 9$$

Thus, there are 9 elements in Dc. It is possible to write them on:

$$Dc = \begin{Bmatrix} \{10,13\}, \{10,16\}, \{10,24\} \\ \{15,13\}, \{15,16\}, \{15,24\} \\ \{17,13\}, \{17,16\}, \{17,24\} \end{Bmatrix}.$$

The set of objectives that can be reached by the elements of Dc is OB'_c.
It has been written above that $ob'c = g(dc)$. In this example, the objective is a cost and the cost supported by the partners must be summed. Therefore, in this case, the g function is defined by the sum of all elements of a given d_c set:

$$ob'c = \sum_{i=1}^{n} dci.$$

Thus, for the set of the objectives that can be reached by the elements of Dc, it gets:

$$OB'c = \{23,26,34,28,31,39,30,33,41\}.$$

Finally, the set of the decisions researched by the collaborative decision-makers can be noted:

$$cost \leq 30 \Rightarrow Drc = \{\{10,13\}, \{10,16\}, \{15,13\}, \{17,13\}\}.$$

Any of these four possibilities fulfils the given objective. Indeed, they meet the objective of the collaboration defined as *"to produce n products for a maximum cost of 30 K€"*. The decision-makers can make a decision among the D_{rc} set of solutions.

5. CONCLUDING REMARKS

This paper has presented a formalisation that aims at developing interoperability in the context of collaborative decision-making in order to solve and to prevent the problems identified (iterations, long delay...). This formalisation is independent from technological issues.

Some design principles to build decisional interoperability were proposed in order to allow the decision-makers to make right and appropriate decisions by clearly defining their decision frame, exchanging their decision frame and establishing a common decision space. This formalisation is simple to design and implement in enterprises and can apply in any kind of situations. The example is largely simplified to keep the presentation in a reasonable volume.

The proposed approach allows extending the GRAI decisional model concepts initially developed for intra enterprise integration to inter enterprise interoperability from the point of view of decision-making.

Future work is concerned with the development of functions – that allow obtaining the set of objectives that can be reached by the possible decisions of the partners of the collaboration - based on performance criteria of the enterprises. These functions represent the performances that are the most frequently targeted by the enterprises such as cost, quality and time. A real case study will also carried out in a SME.

6. REFERENCES

1. ATHENA. Advanced Technologies for Heterogeneous Enterprise Networks and their Applications, FP6-2002-IST-1, Integrated Project Proposal, 2003.
2. CEN TS 14818. Enterprise integration – Decisional Reference Model, CEN TC310/WG1, 2000.
3. Chen, David. "Practices, principles and patterns for interoperability". INTEROP deliverable D6.1, 2005.
4. Daclin N, Chen D, Vallespir B. "Design principles and pattern for decisional interoperability". In proceedings of IFIP 5.7 Advances in Production Management Systems, APMS, 2005.
5. Daclin N, Chen D, Vallespir B. "Towards a conceptualisation of decisional interoperability", Interoperability of Enterprises and Software Applications, I-ESA'06, 2006.
6. Doumeingts G, Vallespir B, Chen D. "Decisional modeling GRAI grid". In International handbook on information system, P. Bernus, K. Mertins & G. Schmidt ed, Berlin: Springer, 1998.
7. IEEE. "A compilation of IEEE standard computer glossaries", standard computer dictionary, 1990.
8. INTEROP. "Annex1-Description of work", Interoperability Research for Networked Enterprises Applications and Software. INTEROP NoE. Network of Excellence, n°508011, 2003.
9. Kvan, Thomas. "Collaborative design: what is it?". In Automation in Construction, vol.9, Elsevier Science BV, 2000.
10. Mercier N, Noyes D, Clermont P. "Modélisation des mécanismes de collaboration dans les processus décisionnels". 4ème congrès des doctorants, 2003.
11. Oxford dictionary. "Oxford dictionary", Oxford University Press, 1999.
12. Suh NP. "The principles of design", Oxford University Press, ed, 1990.
13. Vallespir B, Doumeingts G. "La méthode GRAI". Support de cours de l'école de printemps "modélisation d'entreprise", groupe de travail n°5 du groupement pour la recherche en productique, 2002.
14. Vallespir, Bruno. "Modélisation d'entreprise et architectures de conduite des systèmes de production". Mémoire d'Habilitation à Diriger des Recherches, 2003.
15. Wikipédia. "Les systèmes de prise de decision, www.wikipédia.fr, 2005.

32

TRAINING OF STRATEGIC DECISIONS IN COLLABORATIVE NETWORKS THROUGH SERIOUS GAMES

Reiner Kracke, Jannicke Baalsrud Hauge, Heiko Duin, Klaus-Dieter Thoben
BIBA at the University of Bremen, GERMANY
{krk,baa,du,tho}@biba.uni-bremen.de

Serious gaming is an upcoming approach for supporting training activities. Since games have been identified as an opportunity to increase familiarity of the player with any artifacts, they can also be used to mediate experience in management and strategic decision making. In combination with the current trend towards networked games, teaching of strategic decisions in collaborative network environments is the next step in the evolution of learning games. This paper presents such a gaming approach, supporting a virtual multi stakeholder environment, where trainees can experiment with new ideas without risk and effects on the real life.

1. INTRODUCTION

Collaborative Networks (CN) are emerging in many business areas. Thus planning and operating them is a skill that becomes more and more important for today's professionals. In order to mediate these skills and to enable them to assess the value creation through Collaborative Networks, new forms of training for the professionals are required. An upcoming approach of training in the business world is the serious gaming approach (Prensky, 2001; Thoben et al. 2000), which uses computer games as tools to let professionals gain experience as players in a "soft failure" environment.

This paper presents an overview on the general approach of using games to support professional trainings. Based on that, a specific gaming approach focusing on training strategic decisions in manufacturing is being introduced, explaining how to achieve the projected impact in terms of learning results. Therefore it will give an overview on strategic decisions, which should be supported by serious games, and how they can be integrated in a game by providing the player with events and information, to let him freely derive his corporate strategy and decide about necessary actions, instead of leading him through a storyline. The content of this paper is based on intermediate results of the EU-project PRIME (FP6-IST-016542), which has the objective to create a game, where professionals can experiment and learn how to handle a business in a multi-stakeholder Virtual Business Environment.

Please use the following format when citing this chapter:

Kracke, R., Hauge, J. B., Duin, H., Thoben, K.-D., 2006, in IFIP International Federation for Information Processing, Volume 224, Network-Centric Collaboration and Supporting Fireworks, eds. Camarinha-Matos, L., Afsarmanesh, H., Ollus, M., (Boston: Springer), pp. 305–312.

2. TRAINING OF STRATEGIC DECISIONS

Strategic decisions are far reaching and consequential for organizations. The importance of making the right decisions increases, when an organization is part of a collaborative network and the consequences of those decisions affect not only the own organization but also the connected partners in the network.

Strategic decisions must often be made under conditions, where parts of the environment are uncertain and assumptions about other involved parties may be incorrect or incomplete. In such situations, the decision maker has to rely on his experience to fill the gaps in the information foundation of the decision process. Additionally, decision effects are often indirect and might thus be unintended and unforeseen. At this point it's again the decision maker's experience that allows him to assess the long-term effects as well as the side-effects of his decision.

These circumstances underline the importance, that decision makers are aware of the difficulties and effects of the decision making process and in order to achieve this awareness and to provide accelerated experience, they require a special training. However, traditional vocational training methods are obviously not appropriate for this task, since experience cannot be taught in such a passive way. Instead, decision makers have to be exposed to environments and situations, where the required skills can be trained through practicing.

The real life and the real business environment would be a perfect playground to collect experience and train skills, but of course there is the problem, that the real life does not pardon failures and wrong decisions. Thus the trainees need a "soft failure" environment, where they can experiment without risking the reputation of their company or even of a whole networked organization.

3. SERIOUS GAMES

When coming to the point, where a model of the real world is required, computing technology usually provides solutions in form of simulation applications. Those simulations can help imitating and understanding the real world and with the ability to speed things up, long term effects can be analyzed in short time. However, simulations are not always a proper solution to support training, because their capabilities regarding interactivity are usually very limited.

A computing domain which provides extensive interactivity is the games domain. There are many genres in the computer games domain, and a special one of them is the serious game. The terminology "Serious Game" is quite new in the world of computer games and thus there's no universal definition for it, yet. However the term itself clearly states, what it is: a game with a grave background or content.

3.1 Evolution of Serious Games

The terminology "Serious Game" is mainly based in the computer games domain, which has experienced a rapid development in the last decades. With the introduction of personal and home computers in the 1980s, the computer games continuously gained importance in the recreational sector and with the advancing computer technology, new opportunities emerged, enabling the creation of even more sophisticated games (Herz, 2002). An ideal example for the development of games is the flight simulator genre. Whereas the first games of this type were very simple and just allowed the player to control an aircraft in a stylized environment with generic cockpit instruments and simple flight physics, modern flight simulators confront the player with a realistic environment including realistic cockpit instruments, realistic flight physics, a realistic world, where the landscape has been modeled using a topographic base and satellite images and even the airport towers use their real-life radio frequencies and allow in-game communication. This high degree of realism increases not only the attractiveness of the games, but it also allows the player to learn some basic about flying and thus this opportunity has been grasped by airlines and the military.

Whereas the steadily increasing computer technology can be seen as a major driver for the development of computer games, the internet and the networking capabilities in general enabled opportunities to create a new type of games: online games. The ability to play games online with other human players made games much more interesting, because a player's in-game fellows or opponents are not anymore as predictable as computer controlled ones are. Nowadays there are games, which are played by several 10.000 players at the same time – sharing a one virtual world (Ondrejka). The vast majority of online-games is still of entertaining character, but there are also some games, which have a serious and/or realistic background (Second Life). However the number of games, which address issues of learning for business life, is relative low.

3.2 Business Games

Business games are serious games by nature, because they're usually about managing a company, which clearly has a more serious than entertaining background. However, business games are often referred to as business simulations, where by definition a simulation is not the same as a game. A simulation's purpose is to imitate something, e.g. a flight simulator imitates the behavior of a real plane and the environment in terms of terrain and weather, but there are no elements in such a simulation that directly reflect an entertaining approach or a game's rules. In opposite to a simulation, a game always has rules and it defines a goal, which a player has to achieve in order to win the game. The reason why business games are often called business simulations might be that those games include an economic environment, which simulates the behavior of customers and competitors. But the majority of business games confront the player with a scenario and a goal, which must be achieve in order to win. This makes those games real games.

In business games the player usually has to deal with production, logistics, finance and marketing and the typical goal is to maximize the company's profit or to gain a vast market share. Even if those goals can also be found in a real company's business plan, it is a challenge for many people who like to play those types of games in their spare time. Since even the business games, which are intended for the entertainment market, have to be believable and the technical preliminaries nowadays allow a high grade of complexity in the economic system of a game, they confront the player with many terms, effects and details that can be found in the real business life.

3.3 Games as Training Tool

The circumstance that a game can reflect large parts of the real world can be exploited for training purpose. Besides, using games as tool for training has some positive effects on the trainees. Even if the object of serious games is not entertainment, they are still considered as games. Thus most trainees enjoy this form of training and their involvement is more intense than in other teaching methods. Additionally games are interactive, allowing active learning, which has been proven more effective than passive learning.

The usage of serious business games for training (see Serious Games Initiative) can already be observed in schools and universities, where students can play and learn the basics of business. However this kind of training has not yet been fully established in companies. Compared to the success of flight simulators which are an established training method, business games are far from being an inherent part of business training. There are several reasons that are responsible for that difference:

- Serious business games are not obviously saving costs, like the flight simulators do. Those flight simulators reduces the training costs by using virtual airplanes for training activities, thus saving fuel and additionally it reduces the risk of failure during a pilot's first flights, because a flight simulator does not crash physically. The training of business professionals usually doesn't require expensive equipment like airplanes, thus a game is not being regarded as a cost saver.
- It is more complicated to simulate a real world business environment than the environment in a flight simulator. In a flight simulator, the trainees in the cockpit have to deal with the status of the plane and react on the environmental influences in terms of the weather condition. In a virtual business world, the state of the plane is taken by the state of the company, but the interaction and interdependencies with the environment is more complex. The complexity increases especially when the trainee acts in a collaborative network, where there are usually many stakeholders involved, whose behavior depend on the trainee's actions.
- The third big difference regards the controls, which are available to the trainee. In a flight simulator, the trainee can use the cockpit instruments, which are more or less the same in each plane. In the business world, there is no common set of controls, which allows a professional to manage a company or department, thus the companies do not see a direct relationship between serious business games and their own business, if the game has not been developed for their specific training issues.

Because of these reasons, business games still reside on the entertainment level and haven't become an inherent part of training in the business world yet. Some games may have the potential, to mediate basic knowledge of economics and can thus be used to train students on a basic level, but those games usually lack the depth of detail to be sufficient for advanced corporate training.

4. TRAINING OF STRATEGIC DECISIONS THROUGH NETWORKED GAMING

4.1 The PRIME approach

The objective of the EU project PRIME is to create a serious business game, which can be used for advanced training of business professionals in the domain of strategic manufacturing. Thus the game is intended to be used in corporate training, the three issues of serious business games, which make the integration in professional training difficult, have to be addressed:

- To provide a set of controls, which are common to business professionals of different companies and different industries, the PRIME approach moves strategic decisions in the focus of the game. Those strategic decisions are supported in an indirect way, by providing the underlying information to the player and let him decide, what to do based on this input. This means, that there is no guide- or storyline, which leads the player through the game, querying his input at discrete turning points within the game. Instead each player has a game interface which allows him to assess the situation of his business unit and to freely decide about the necessary actions to improve his economic situation. (Decision Flows – Fig. 1)
- Even if games cannot help reducing costs in a direct way, they provide an environment, where trainees can experiment with new strategies and failures don't affect the company in the real world. PRIME aims to provide a virtual business environment (VBE) where the player can run his own business unit and gain experience through learning by doing. Especially the long term effects of strategic decisions are of interest, since a games capability to simulate those effects can provide a good feedback to the trainee, after he made a decision. (Business Units – Fig. 1)
- To provide a realistic multi-stakeholder environment, supporting collaborative networks, PRIME will be a multiplayer game, where many players share the same VBE. Whereas singleplayer games are usually based solely on simulation, the PRIME approach confronts the player not only with artificial stakeholders, but also with other human competitors and business partners. In the resulting networked gaming environment the players can communicate and interact with each other and are thus being confronted with unexpected scenarios which are influenced by the behavior and decisions of other players (Heide Smith, 2005). (Global Business Environment – Fig. 1)

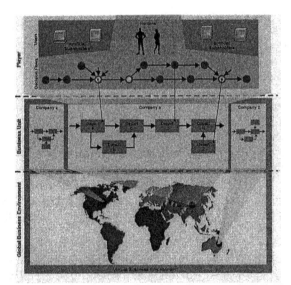

Figure 1: The Multi-Stakeholder Concept of PRIME

4.1 Strategic decisions in PRIME

To be of use for corporate training activities, a serious game has to provide support for the targeted training objectives. Since the PRIME approach focuses on strategic decisions, the game's qualification depends on the extent of the encompassed strategic decisions. Thus the first activity in the development of PRIME has been the compilation of a list of strategic decisions and issues, which are being regarded as important to be taught. This assessment has been done within the PRIME consortium, which not only includes developers but also end-users of the game. The following list is the result of the content related part of the user requirements analysis and shows an overview of the demanded training subjects. Additionally the training subjects have been rated by each end-user in the consortium with 1 being not important to 5, which indicates high importance for the end-users training plans.

In order to make these decisions a part of a game, it has to provide situations where the player can decide between various options. In games, where the player is guided along a predefined storyline, these decision making points are explicit present, letting the player choose between a set of possible options. This kind of decision making is not always realistic, since in real life, there are sometimes no discrete choices and even the timing of decision making is not always given. Thus the PRIME approach is based on free decision making, where the player is always asked to assess the current situation based and act or react, when he sees a need for action. This way, a player can be as active as he wants and he can even avoid making decisions, which most probably will not improve the situation of the player's business unit.

Table 1 – Importance of including training issues in PRIME

	Rating by End-Users					
Make or buy (outsourcing, off shoring)	5	4	5	5	5	1
Customer decoupling point position	4	3			4	
Supply/Delivery network level	5	2	4	5	4	1
Chase vs. stocking production plan	4	3	5	4	3	1
Stock levels; stock position (ex. bullwhip effect)	4	1		5	5	1
Integration of stakeholders (governments, NGO, etc)	1	2	5	5		3
Supplier integration (supplier vs. partners)	2	2	4	5	5	1
Plant localisation	5		2	3	4	1
R&D Product	1	4	5	2	4	1
Enterprise Integration	1	3	4	4	4	1
Manufacturing strategy	4	2	3	4		1
Modularity in products/processes	1	3	4	2	5	1
Labour skill level	1	3	4	4	3	1
Plant capacity	3	2	4	2	4	1
Maintenance approaches	1	4	3	2	2	2
Production planning strategies and methodology	3	3	1	2	2	1
Plant/shop-floor configuration	3	2	2		1	1

4.2 Example for Training of "Make or Buy"

The "Make or Buy" decision is the top rated strategic decision of the PRIME requirements list. Thus the following example is based on this type of decision, describing how the PRIME approach supports training.

As already mentioned, the player has to keep track of the current situation of his business unit. This is supported by the information, which the game provides in various ways. In case of the "Make or Buy" decision, there are information sheets, which inform the player about the costs for making a specific product. This information about costs can be either based on current costs, if the player is already producing this item, or can be estimated by the player by taking a look at the production cost of a similar product. On the other hand the player can issue an invitation to tender for the product, to get the information about costs when buying the product from a supplier. Those information sources can be regarded as direct input for the decision, but they are not being compiled for the player so he can simply choose between "make" or "buy". Besides the player has to consider other factors too, which are of an indirect nature and might not seem directly relevant for a player when making the decision. An example for this is the question, whether the item to be decided about represents a core or non-core product of the player's business unit. This question is not being asked by the game and thus must be assessed by the player. If the player runs a company, that produces cars, it might be of importance to retain the knowledge of constructing engines in the own company to remain competitive. If he decides to buy the engines from a supplier, he'll become dependant on the suppliers regarding a component of high importance. But those assessments are no explicit part of the game – by purpose. By not asking a player these questions, he is forced to consider all important inputs to a decision to prevent experiencing negative results as long term effects.

5. CONCLUSION

The presented approach of PRIME uses two important elements to support the training process of business professionals: The trainees act in a network, which is very important to create a sufficient complexity in the VBE especially since human players act not as predictable as simulation models or artificial stakeholders, which are only included to fill the VBE and guarantee a sufficient amount of active players. Besides, the fact that human players have to deal with each other makes negotiations more realistic and even the personal aspect of inter-organizational collaboration is automatically present. The second major element is the free decision making, which omits querying the player to react on discrete events. Instead the players have to be pro-active and maintain an overview over their virtual environment and assess the current situation.

Based on this concept, and combined with a good concept of integrating games into corporate trainings, the PRIME consortium is developing a game, which has high potential to address not only the grave background of a learning tool, but also to mediate fun while playing. This way the PRIME game will increase the motivation of the trainees, since they will be able to play a game, even if it's just a supportive training activity.

6. REFERENCES

1. Baalsrud Hauge, J., Schwesig, M., Thoben, K.-D., Eschenbächer, J.: Business games - an effective tool for experiencing collaboration in production networks. pp. 30-37. In: Proceedings of the 9.th Workshop of IFIP W.G 5.7 - Special Interest Group on Experimental Interactive Learning in Industrial Management. Esbo, 2005.
2. Heide Smith, J.: The Problem of Other Players: In-game Cooperation as Collective Action. In: Proceedings of the DiGRA Digital Games Research Association Conference 2005
3. Herz, J.C., Macedonia, Michael R.: Computer Games and the Military: Two Views. Defense Horizons, Center for Technology and National Security Policy, National Defense University, April 2002
4. Linden Lab: Second Life. http://secondlife.com, Accessed: 09.03.2006
5. McLean, Charles, Jain, Sanjay, Lee, Y. T., Riddick, Frank, A: A Simulation and Gaming Architecture for Manufacturing Research, Testing, and Training. Proceedings in the IFIP 5.7 Advances in Production Management System Conference, Rockville, MD, September 18-21, 2005
6. Ondrejka, Cory: Changing Realities - User Creation, Communication, and Innovation in Digital Worlds. http://lindenlab.com/whitepapers/Changing_Realities_Ondrejka.pdf, 07.03.2006
7. Prensky, Marc: Digital Game-Based Learning. McGraw-Hill Companies, 2001
8. Schwesig, M., Thoben, K-D., Eschenbächer, J.: A Simulation Game Approach to Support Learning and Collaboration in Virtual Organisations. In: Proceedings of the 6th IFIP Working Conference on Virtual Enterprises, PRO-VE'05, Valencia, 2005
9. Serious Gaming Initiative, http://www.seriousgames.org/, Accessed: 05.03.2006
10. Thoben et al.: Training through gaming - applying a simulation based business game to train people for collaboration in virtual enterprises. Online Educa Berlin 2005, 11. International Conference on Technology Supported Learning & Training. 2005

33

PRICING OF DELIVERY SERVICE
IN A LOGISTICS NETWORK

Giuseppe Confessore, Daniele Corini, Giuseppe Stecca

Istituto di Tecnologie Industriali e Automazione - Consiglio Nazionale delle Ricerche, Area della Ricerca di Roma Tor Vergata via Fosso del Cavaliere 100, 00133 Roma, ITALY
email: {g.confessore, g.stecca}@itia.cnr.it

In this paper the problem of finding a computational fast method for pricing of the delivery service in a logistics network has been analyzed. The objective is to develop a supporting method for effective interaction among logistics service providers and customers.
We make use of an analytical function to predict the final total cost of distribution and to develop an interaction protocol that, using the function, leads to a final win-win solution in which the most of the customers have agreed to accept a delivery time comporting a reduction of total distribution costs. We also validated the method by use of a simulation software, evaluating the results in terms of cost-efficiency and stability.

1. INTRODUCTION

Logistic activities represent the connection point between goods production and fruition locations, which are separated by time and space (Pareschi et al, 2002). Global competition and tremendous technological progresses, in information technologies and logistics, impose to logistics operators a substantial reduction of their costs, particularly of those originated by the delivery process, when goods must be delivered to customers at right time in the right amounts and positions. The costs sustained by the distributor can be decomposed in three drivers: the variable cost of traveled distance, the variable cost of the vehicles, and their fixed cost. The class of problems studying the minimization of the transportation costs is commonly known as Vehicle Routing Problem (VRP); when customers ask for delivery in a specified time window, the sub-class to which it is referred to is the Vehicle Routing Problem with Time Windows constraints (VRPTW). The presence of a large amount of tight time windows leads to the increase of the number of needed vehicles, and a consequent increase of the transportation cost. On the contrary, if a customer would accept the delivery in a large time window, this would mean an increase on his costs, which originated either by the extra work for unload of the shipment in a unforeseen time window or by the loss of money of a missed sale due to unavailability of goods.

(So and Song, 1998) analyze the interrelations among pricing, delivery time guarantee and capacity expansion decisions. (Basu et al, 2004) extend spatial pricing theory for delivery service to encompass multizone plans. In (Campbell and Salvelsbergh, 2005) an incentive scheme specialized for home delivery service is

Please use the following format when citing this chapter:

Confessore, G., Corini, D., Stecca, G., 2006, in IFIP International Federation for Information Processing, Volume 224, Network-Centric Collaboration and Supporting Fireworks, eds. Camarinha-Matos, L., Afsarmanesh, H., Ollus, M., (Boston: Springer), pp. 313–320.

proposed. In (Bianco et al, 2005) a formal decomposition of the vehicle routing problem and an interaction protocol is defined while in (Bernardi et al, 2004) a multiagent architecture is described. However, the high number of customers and the huge amount of possible solutions make difficult to resolve this problem to the optimum in a competitive interval of time, given that the problem belongs to the NP - hard in strong sense class of problems (Toth et al, 2002). In this paper we analyze the problem of finding a computational-fast method for the pricing of the delivery service in a logistics network, with the objective to develop a supporting method for effective interaction among logistics service providers and customers. The developed supporting method will help the implementation of an interaction protocol in which the logistics operator is able to price in a time-efficient manner the logistics service.

Given the opposite relationship between costs and windows widths, we have identified the trend of the costs as an analytical function, and then we have analyzed its ability to predict, with an adequately low error margin, the distribution costs using as the only input the measure of the time windows widths. Moreover, upon this analytical function we have built an algorithm for the solution of the delivery problem which leads to a final scenario where the most of the customers agree to broaden out their windows after an economical measurable saving on the transportation cost. On top of this algorithm, a multiagent system can be developed (Shen, and Norrie, 2001). Multiagent systems for supply chain integration and coordination (Durfee, Lesser, and Corkill, 1987; Gerber, Russ, and Klusch, 2003; Julka, Srinivasan, and Karimi, 2002; Karageorgos et al, 2003; Lee, and Whang 1999) can be thought as a building block for collaborative networks (Camarinha-Matos and Afsarmanesh, 2004). The remainder of this paper is structured as follows. In Section 2 problem and model definition are introduced. In Section 3 the proposed solving approach is presented. In Section 4 conclusions and future works are discussed.

2. PROBLEM AND MODEL DEFINITION

The problem consists in finding a computational fast method for the pricing of the delivery service in a logistics network, with the objective to develop a supporting method for effective interaction among logistics service providers and customers. The developed supporting method will help the implementation of an interaction protocol in which the logistics operator is able to price in a time-efficient manner the logistics service.

We model the problem as follows:

Given a set of n customers and an initial time window $W^0_i = [e^0_i, l^0_i]$ associated to each customer $i = 1, 2, ..., n$. Let $W_i = [e_i, l_i]$ be alternatives time windows associated to each customer $i = 1, 2, ..., n$ with $W_i \supseteq W^0_i$. Let $s^0_i = l^0_i - e^0_i$ and $s_i = l_i - e_i$ be the width of the time windows in hours with $s^0_i, s_i \in \{1, 2,..., l\}$ where l be the maximum time width. Let $\vec{w}^0 = (W^0_1, W^0_2, ..., W^0_n)$, and $\vec{w} = (W_1, W_2, ..., W_n)$ vectors of the time windows. Let Let n_j the number of customers having time windows width equal to j. Let moreover $S = (\sum_{j=1}^{l} n_j \cdot j)/n$. Given a market with a set of n customers and a given resources, network structure, and good requests for customers, we can define $c_i(s_i) \geq 0$ as the cost for the customer i for receiving delivery in a time window W_i and $tc(\vec{w})$ the total cost of transportation for the logistics operator. We introduce the integer variables $e_i, l_i \in \{1,2,...,l\}$. The problem is to find the combination of $\vec{w} = (W_1, W_2, ..., W_n)$ such that is

$$\min \quad tc(\vec{w}) + \sum_{i=1}^{n} c_i(s_i)$$

s.t.

$$W_i \supseteq W_i^0 \quad \forall i = 1,2,...,n$$
$$W_i = [e_i, l_i] \quad \forall i = 1,2,...,n$$
$$e_i < l_i \quad \forall i = 1,2,...,n$$
$$e_i, l_i \in \{1,2,...,l\}, where \; \vec{w} = (W_1, W_2,..., W_n) \; and \; W_i^0 = [e_i^0, l_i^0], \forall i = 1,2,...,n$$

We notice that for each instance of $\vec{w}$ the solving of a VRPTW problem is needed.

3. THE PROPOSED APPROACH

To solve this problem we apply to the model the following procedure:
1. Find the analytical relationship between tc and S/l;
2. Tune up of the function to prevent error margin;
3. Given an interaction protocol for the pricing of the delivery service, validate it;
4. Implement the interaction protocol in a multiagent based application.

3.1 The Analytical Function

The very first step of our research is made up by a set of tests, carried out with the goal of identifying an analytical function which is able to describe the distribution costs according to changes in customers' delivery time windows W_i.

We have considered 100 geographically-distributed customers (the position is defined by a couple of Cartesian reference points), with only 1 central depot, where the deliveries begin and end. Let p the percentage of customers requesting for a tight time windows p, with $0 \leq p \leq 1$, and the measure of such tight time windows be w hours, with $0 \leq w \leq l$; four scenarios have been considered:

Scenario 1: $p = 0.25$;
Scenario 2: $p = 0.50$;
Scenario 3: $p = 0.75$;
Scenario 4: $p = 1$.

Customers not demanding for a tight time window are supposed to have *l* hours wide windows, with $l = 9$.

For each scenario, 4 sub-scenarios have been considered:

Sub Scenario a): $w = 1$ hour;
Sub Scenario b): $w = 3$ hours;
Sub Scenario c): $w = 5$ hours;
Sub Scenario d): $w = 7$ hours;

Each sub-scenario has been resolved using a VRPTW "ad hoc" solver based on Solomon I1 heuristic (Solomon et al, 1987): particularly, 10 runs of the solver have been performed for each sub-scenario, randomly assigning the tight delivery windows to different customers, but not changing windows start-times and due-dates. A total of 160 runs have been resolved. The demand of each customer, based on Solomon "R" instances, has been kept constant in all the runs, as well as the service time equal to 90.

The outputs of the solver for each scenario are the total number of vehicles necessary to serve all the customers, and the total cost of distribution.

In Figure 1 a plot for each sub scenario ($w = 1, 3, 5, 7$) is drawn, showing the total cost in function of the percentage *p* of time window width. The total cost strongly increases with the increase of the percentage of customers, over the total, demanding for a tight delivery window: moreover, the differences in average total cost don't seem significant for requested delivery windows $w = \{3, 5, 7\}$ hours, while they are substantial between these 3 spans in which $w = 1$ hour

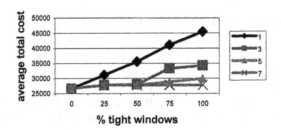

Figure 1 – Average total cost after percentages of tight windows

In order to find out the trend of the total cost in relationship with the *s/l* ratio, we used the minimum squares method. Using this method we have chosen as regression function the logarithmical expression:

$$\bar{t}c = a\, ln(S/l) + b$$

where *a* and *b* represent model constants with $a = -9395.7$ and $b = 24382$.

In the moment of choosing which function, out of the four produced by the software for each scenario, we will be using for our future experiments, we decided to select the one, shown in Figure 2, produced by the fourth scenario, for the two following reasons:

- the function has the highest r^2 index, equal to $r^2 = 0.9778$, of all the scenarios;
- the scenario represents the most difficult occurrence to solve, given that the totality of the customers ask for a tight window. The Figure 2 shows the plot of $\bar{t}c$ for the 4th scenario showing the variation of foreseen total costs in function of the S/l. Dots represent the computed cost tc.

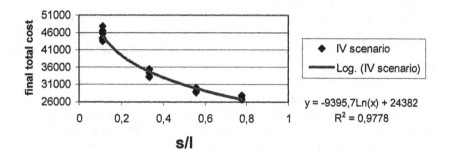

Figure 2 – scenario 4 output regression function

It is possible to see that the maximum distance between the regression function and the observed value corresponds to a S/l ratio equal to 0.1, then to a 1-hours-wide delivery window. In this point the function is approximately 6% lower from highest observed value (predictable, given that r^2 is very close but not equal to 1), so when we will be using it to predict the total cost of a particular market scenario, we must expect a 6% error on prediction accuracy.

Therefore, we are now able to predict, with a very low error margin, the total cost of a particular market scenario (the output), merely knowing the width of customers' delivery windows (the input), using the just found analytical function.

3.2 The function validation

In this section we explain how we assessed the goodness of the prediction made by the analytical function just found: to do this, we firstly resolve some market events with the function, supposing some percentages of tight-windows customers (the input of the function), and then we create solver instances which reflect these percentages, and resolve them, obtaining the exact results from the solver.

To validate the function, n_j are randomly selected and assigned to customers i. The average width $\bar{r}$, as:

$$\bar{r} = \frac{\displaystyle\sum_{j=1}^{l} n_j \cdot j}{n}$$

Now, putting this latest value inside the function equation, we finally obtain the predicted total cost $\bar{t}c$ for each group as:

$$\bar{t}c = a \, ln(\overline{r}/l) + b$$

Making use of the percentages and the widths decided in the previous phase, we build VRPTW instances, yet without any change in customers' service time, demand and position, still equal to Solomon's I1 ones.

We build 10 instances for each group of percentages, again assigning delivery windows to customers in a random way, and then we resolve them using VRPTW solver, which produces the total cost of transportation tc and the number of vehicles for each instance.

Each group $\bar{t}c$ and the 10 (exact) tc's are compared, and a correction rate that makes $\bar{t}c$ able to predict (merely, overtop) all tc's is evaluated

Looking at the results produced after the 4 groups of percentages, it is possible to observe that 70% of tc's are correctly predicted by the function. Thus, just carry a little correction to $\bar{t}c$ (the maximum needed is of 6%, what is more already expected), making our function able to predict 100% of results.

3.3 The interaction protocol

The developed cost function can be used as a tool for measuring the transportation cost based on received orders, and for computing price discounts during negotiation with customers. A basic interaction protocol exploiting these potentialities is structured as follows:

INIZIALIZATION:
-- $i = 1, j = 1; k = 1; \bar{t}c' = 0, \bar{t}c'' = 0;$
-- The n customers send orders to the Logistics Operator.
-- Computation of the number n_j of customers having time window width j
-- Computation of transportation cost tc' through the function and first assignment to customers as $tc'_i = tc'/n$.

STEP 1:
IF: $n_j - k > 0$
    -- $n_j = n_j - k,$
    -- $n_{j+1} = n_{j+1} + k$
    -- Computation of new total cost of transportation, tc'', and of the discount $\Delta = \bar{t}c' - \bar{t}c''$
    -- Send a propose to customers having time window width equal to j a discount of Δ/n_j
    IF: at least $m > 0$ customers exist for whom is valid $c_i(j) > c_i(j + 1) - \Delta$
        -- Enlarge time windows for such customers: $s_i = s_i + 1$
    ELSE:
        -- Set $k = k + 1$ and goto STEP 1
ELSE:
        -- goto STEP 2

STEP 2:

IF: $j < l$
-- Computation of new $n_j + 1$ and n_j,
-- Set $j = j + 1$; goto STEP 1
ELSE:
-- Computation of new n_{l-1} and n_l
-- Computation cost tc' related to final numbers $n_1, n_2, \ldots, n_l$

STOP

3.4 Simulation

With the aim of validating the interaction protocol, we implemented it on a simulation software, building a model which reproduces its steps in order to reach a market result where the final percentages of customers asking for tight delivery windows are much less than initial ones, having the customers negotiated to broaden up their windows after a consistent saving. A total of 40 runs have been resolved. In Table 1 we show results of two runs. If the customers' cost structure is feasible, the negotiation will always lead to a final decrease of total costs. In the table this results can be argued from the medium time window width S.

Table1 – Examples of negotiation results

j	Example 1		Example 2	
	Original n_j	Final n_j	Original n_j	Final n_j
1	50	49	12	11
2	0	0	11	8
3	20	16	11	8
4	0	0	11	8
5	20	13	11	5
6	0	0	11	2
7	10	2	11	6
8	0	9	11	4
9	0	11	11	48
S	2.8	3.47	4.96	6.26

Comparing the algorithm-made with the solver-made results, we can observe that our method has been able to reduce the number of customers asking for a tight, and troublesome, delivery window, carrying a real benefit to the whole system. Furthermore, the final total cost of distribution is always a little higher than the solver one, which means that the algorithm won't ever produce a lower cost than the real, needed one (produced by the solver), avoiding a loss to the distributor.

4. CONCLUSION

In this paper we have found a computational-fast method for the pricing of the delivery service in a logistics network, with the objective to develop a supporting method for effective interaction among logistics service providers and customers. We have developed and tested an analytical function which is able to predict transportation costs and we have shown an interaction protocol for customers and logistics operator to decrease total distribution costs. Future works will regard the ability of the analytical function to predict changes in quantity requests, the use of a better solving algorithm to find function parameters and the development of a multiagent system implementing the described interaction protocol.

5. REFERENCES

1. Basu A; Ingene CA, Mazumdar T. "The pricing of delivery services". Journal Of Regional Science, vol. 44, no. 4, 743–772, 2004.
2. Bianco L, Confessore L, Stecca G. "A multi-agent Model for distribution problems in logistics systems", in Proceedings of 18th International Conference on Production Research ICPR18, Fisciano(Sa) Italy, July 31th – August 4th 2005.
3. Bernardi D, Confessore G, Stecca G. "A multiagent model integrating inventory and routing processes", in Virtual Enterprises and Collaborative Networks, L.M. Camarinha-Matos (eds.). Kluwer Academic publishers 2004; 107-114.
4. Camarinha-Matos L M, Afsarmanesh H. "The emerging discipline of collaborative networks". In Virtual Enterprises and Collaborative Networks, L.M. Camarinha-Matos (eds.): Kluwer Academic publishers 2004.
5. Campbell AM, Savelsbergh M. "Incentive Schemes for Attended Home Delivery Services". Accepted to Transportation Science, publication forthcoming, 2005.
6. Durfee, EH, Lesser VR, Corkill, DD. "Coherent cooperation among communicating problem solvers". In IEEE Trans. Computers, C-36, 1275, 1987.
7. Gerber A, Russ C, Klusch M. "supply web co-ordination by an agent-based trading network with integrated logistics services". In Electronic Commerce Research and Applications 2, Elsevier Science Ltd., 2003.
8. Julka N, Srinivasan R, Karimi I. Agent Based Supply Chain Management 1 & 2, Computers And Chemical Engineering 26, Elsevier Science Ltd., 2002.
9. Karageorgos A, Mehandjiev N, Weichhart G, Hämmerle A. "Agent-Based Optimisation Of Logistic And Production Planning". in Engineering Applications of Artificial Intelligence 16, Elsevier Science Ltd., 2003.
10. Lee H, Whang S. *Decentralized*. "Multi-Echelon Supply Chains: Incentives and Information". in Management Science Vol. 45, No.5, May 1999.
11. Pareschi A, Persona A, Ferrari, E, Regattieri, A. Logistica integrata e flessibile. Editrice Esculapio, 2002.
12. Shen W, Norrie DH, Barthès J-PA. Multi-Agent systems for concurrent intelligent design and manufacturing. London and New York: Taylor & Francis, 2001.
13. So KC, Song JS. "Price, delivery time guarantees and capacity selection". In European Journal of Operational Research 111, 28-49, 1998.
14. Solomon MM. "Algorithms for the Vehicle Routing and Scheduling Problems with Time Windows constraints". in Operations Research 35, 254-265, 1987.
15. Toth P, Vigo D. The Vehicle Routing Problem. Siam, 2002.

PART 11

PLATFORMS FOR PROFESSIONAL VIRTUAL COMMUNITIES

34 | AREITO: A DEVELOPMENT PLATFORM FOR VIRTUAL LEARNING COMMUNITIES

César Garita, Ulises Agüero
Costa Rican Institute of Technology, COSTA RICA {cgarita, uaguero}@ic-itcr.ac.cr
Lorenzo Guadamuz
Innova Technology, lguadamuz@innovatechnology.net
DOMINICAN REPUBLIC

Areito is the name of a Virtual Learning Environment (VLE) that is being set up and used by multiple educational organizations in the Dominican Republic. Through Areito, it is possible to simultaneously create, manage and deploy a large number of Virtual Learning Communities (VLCs) oriented towards diverse aspects of learning processes in education, science and technology. The nature and specific contents of each VLC are defined by authorized end-users by selecting and configuring collaborative IT tools that best support the social interaction and knowledge exchange between members of a given VLC. This papers provides a general description of Areito and the development of pilot VLCs at educational organizations in the Dominican Republic.

1. INTRODUCTION

Although there is no formally standardized definition of the Virtual Community (VC) concept, the following description provided by Rheingold is widely cited in many related publications: *"Virtual communities are social aggregations that emerge from the Net when enough people carry on public discussions long enough, with sufficient human feeling, to form webs of personal relationships in cyberspace"* [1]. Currently, VC environments have become extremely popular and have expanded to many areas including professional, social, educational and entertainment domains. Nevertheless, independently of the main interest or purpose of a given VC, it is important to bear in mind that any VC is ultimately based on social networks of people that use the VC environment to maintain and strengthen their interaction through the web. This implies that the success of a VC heavily depends on the extent to which it allows effective sharing and exchange of information to support an underlying social interaction process among people with a specific interest or common goal.

One of the most important application domains of VCs is learning and education. Here, Virtual Learning Communities (VLCs - also referred to as On-line Learning Communities) can be defined as follows: *"learning atmospheres, a context providing a supportive system from which sustainable learning processes are gained through a dialogue and collaborative construction of knowledge by acquiring, generating, analyzing and structuring information"* [2].

Please use the following format when citing this chapter:

Garita, C., Agüero, Guadamuz, L., 2006, in IFIP International Federation for Information Processing, Volume 224, Network-Centric Collaboration and Supporting Fireworks, eds. Camarinha-Matos, L., Afsarmanesh, H., Ollus, M., (Boston: Springer), pp. 323–332.

According to this approach, the main foundation of VLCs communities lies on the proper exchange of knowledge among their members. In general, knowledge can be either explicit (e.g. organizational documents) or implicit (e.g. tacit experiences and knowledge of people). Normally, members build together the contents of the community instead of just using pre-existing materials. Furthermore, members have as common goal to mutually support each other during the accomplishment of learning activities. In general, the concept of VLC is rather complex since it involves aspects from multidisciplinary areas such as pedagogy, philosophy, sociology, communication and computer science.

In this context, this paper focuses on Areito[1] - A Virtual Learning Community Environment in the Dominican Republic [3]. Areito is the main component of the Digital Services Platform project of the State Ministry of Higher Education, Science and Technology (SEESCYT) of the Dominican Republic. Areito, by design, is a web portal to create portals with multiple tools available for online information, interaction and collaboration. Areito's portals represent Virtual Learning Environments (VLE) called Virtual Learning Communities (VLC). Here, a VLC is defined as a community of persons and organizations that come together through a web environment with the main purpose of improving learning processes in higher education and research in the Dominican Republic. Thus, a VLC represents a group of persons (e.g. students, teachers, researchers, professionals) and different educational organizations (e.g. universities, ministries, private companies, international organizations) in the Dominican Republic. The term *learning* is used here as the acquisition of knowledge through formal study and research experiences carried out at university level. Thus, a myriad of VLCs can simultaneously emerge around specific interest topics at universities such as for instance industrial engineering, manufacturing, chemistry, teachers training and nanotechnology, among many others.

The rest of this paper is organized as follows. Section 2 provides a brief introduction to Areito VLC reference model. Section 3 summarizes the analysis phase that led to the identification of the VLC interactive collaboration tools used in this platform. Section 4 includes several platform development and deployment issues regarding actual VLCs in the Dominican Republic. Finally, Section 5 outlines some related conclusions and future work activities.

2. AREITO VLC MODEL

In order to define the VLC model and functional requirements for Areito, many existing related projects, initiatives and resources were analyzed including virtual learning / academic communities ([4],[5],[6]), communities of practice ([7],[8],[9]) and specific virtual environments focusing on social, health-care and rural communities, among others [10],[11],[12]. Furthermore, relevant Collaborative Supported Cooperative Learning (CSCL) tools were studied as well as Learning Management Systems (LMSs) such as Blackboard, Angel and Moodle [13],[14], [15],[16]. After this extensive analysis, we concluded that although there is large number of virtual community initiatives on many different domains, there is still a

---

[1] This project has been developed with funds from the State Ministry of Higher Education, Science and Technology (SEESCYT) of the Dominican Republic through Innova Technology.

tangible need to develop environments focusing on collaborative learning with a strong sense of community.   Thus, one of the main distinctive features of Areito is its virtual community approach integrating aspects of VC, CSCL and LMS models. It can be clarified that although Areito is not a course management system, it allows for the creation of VLC with the purpose of supporting coursework.   In addition, state-of-the art CSCW reliable software technologies are the foundation of Areito's tools to develop VLC. These community-building tools are fully integrated through best web practices with high productivity and low technical support as design goals.

Furthermore, one of the novel features provided by Areito is the seamless integration of a wide variety of web-based interactive communication tools ranging from basic facilities typically found in VC environments (e.g. chat, mailing lists, instant messaging, discussion board, whiteboard, videoconference, application sharing) to higher-level collaboration tools that are rarely available within these environments, supporting for instance, organization of educational events (e.g. conferences, seminars, talks), digital publications (e.g. informative digital bulletin), knowledge base management, service centers (e.g. helpdesks) and digital markets to exchange services and products. Another major feature of Areito is the fact that VLC design and content management tasks are carried out by administrator users themselves in a flexible and configurable fashion using built-in VLC templates and drag-and-drop facilities for laying out web components on screen. Finally, Areito's end-user interface has been specially designed considering graphical elements closely related to Dominican art and culture in order to achieve an attractive personalized environment for target users.

The rest of this section describes the general reference model for VLCs used in Areito including its target audience, overall structure and typology.

2.1. Target Audience

According to the VLC definition given previously in Section 1, the general audience of virtual communities in Areito is composed of the following actors sharing an interest in improving learning processes in the Dominican Republic:

- Instructors and researchers.
- Students.
- Professionals in education.
- Universities and educational centers.
- State Ministry of Higher Education, Science and Technology.
- Public and private enterprises.
- International organizations.

The general audience members or actors were identified based on interviews and general meetings with potential end users from different educational organizations.

Subsets of this list of actors could join up dynamically and create different VLCs with specific goals and purposes. Clearly, the target audience of Areito is extremely large and varied in nature. Therefore, specific key aspects that are usually carefully identified when building a virtual community environment such as audience, purpose, kinds of interactions, duration, policies, IT tools, etc., will ultimately depend on each specific VLC created within Areito. As a result, the VLC environment must support a high degree of flexibility and configurability.

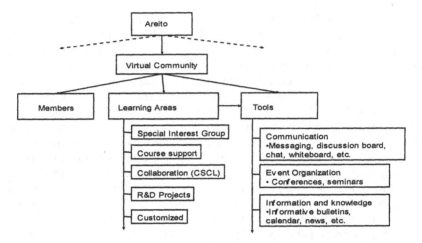

Figure 1 – Areito VLC reference model.

2.2. VLC Reference Model

Many related initiatives and projects have proposed reference models for virtual community design (see [17],[18]). In the case of Areito, the proposed VLC reference model is presented in Figure 1. As shown in this figure, Areito is in fact a portal of VLCs that can be applied in different learning scenarios. Each VLC is conceptually composed of a set of members (persons), learning areas and IT tools. Learning areas represent interaction spaces where members can collaboratively exchange and construct knowledge. Examples of learning areas include:

- Special Interest Groups (SIGs): SIGs represent (sub) virtual communities created by members with (more) specific interests within a given VLC.
- Course management: area where members can learn using an approach similar to Course Management Systems (CMS) like Moodle or Blackboard.
- Collaborative learning: area where members interact following a Computer Supported Cooperative Learning (CSCL) approach such as BSCW [13, 19].
- Research projects: areas devoted to support collaboration within R&D projects.
- Customized area: refers to spaces specially designed for other particular purposes depending on specific community needs.

Interactive and collaborative tools in this model can be associated to VLCs and learning areas. These tools will be described later in this paper.

Please notice that the proposed classification of learning areas reflects the fact that one of the main design goals of Areito is to apply an integral approach to support learning scenarios involving aspects from virtual communities, learning management systems and collaborative learning tools as mentioned previously.

2.3. Typology of VLCs

VLCs can be classified according to different criteria [2],[18],[20]. In Areito, the classification shown on Table 1 is used, based mainly on the type of activity carried out by members of the community.

Table 1 – Main types of VLCs in Areito.

Type	Description
Research, Development and Innovation (R+D+I) VLCs	VLCs allow members to focus on interest topics related to knowledge creation and novel application of existing technology. Members share a personal interest to contribute and participate in activities related to knowledge creation.
Educational VLCs	VLCs offer members a context oriented towards educational learning processes such as pedagogy, academic resources, instructors training, educational events and students support.
Professional VLCs	VLCs provide an environment in which members can share and exploit practical experiences and knowledge related with their profession, e.g. work culture, problem perception, professional values, best practices and novel trends.
Interest VLCs	VLCs gather people that share an interest in a particular subject or cause, e.g. handling of a certain disease, politics, culture, law, religion, environment, languages. Participants make an effort to understand and cooperate with other members.
Social VLCs	VLCs based on a network of contacts of individuals with an interest in social interaction and entertainment. Participants often sympathize with others very easily. Community contributes to a sense of group identity and membership

Please notice that in the above classification, VLC types show a very wide diversity of learning application domains (e.g. VLCs can focus on different areas of science, technology or engineering) and participant members (e.g. members of VLCs can be combinations of educators, students and professionals, among others). This reference typology is useful for end-users in order to better describe the purpose and context of a given VLC and it provides a standard way to classify and access entries of Areito's VLC directory. The proposed typology was validated and applied to actual VLCs suggested by end users.

3. ANALYSIS OF COLLABORATIVE VLC TOOLS

Different listings and classifications of ICT tools for VLC support can be found in [21],[22],[23],[24]. These classifications are based on characteristics such as: documentation vs. communication services; synchronous vs. asynchronous tools; interaction possibilities along time and space axes; and so forth.

As a first step to identify functional requirements in terms of communication and collaboration tools for Areito, an extensive survey of existing projects, initiatives and tools was carried out (see Section 2). After this survey, a list of commonly existing features was built and new advanced tools were proposed.

In order to assess the actual usefulness of the identified tools from the target-audience perspective, a workshop event was organized in which the general model approach of Areito was presented and a questionnaire was applied to more than 20 persons from 13 different universities in the Dominican Republic. The main objective of the questionnaire was to consult, identify and characterize the needs of universities in relation to Areito VLC environment. The questionnaire included items regarding the selection of adequate interactive / collaborative tools for VLCs proposed by end users themselves. As a result of this activity, several kinds of tools were identified for later specification and development, as summarized in Table 2.

Table 2 – Summary of Areito interactive and collaborative tools.

Basic information / communication tools	
Messaging	Email, SMS, instant messaging, presence indicator.
Communication	Video conference, chat, whiteboard, forum, blogs, wikis.
Special interest groups (SIGs)	Groups of people created within a VLC around a given subject.
Information management	Document library, calendar of events, search, news, informational multimedia elements, subscriptions, RSS feeds, SMS, WAP services, contextual help.
Advanced collaboration / interaction tools	
Group decision support	Voting, polls. These tools gather information about the opinion of persons about a particular statement of questions.
Event organization	Support for organization of educational events (conferences including participant registration, call for papers, paper evaluation).
Digital market	Website where offers and demands of services and products are placed by VLC members.
Course support	Website providing facilities for course management (e.g. projects, assignments, resources, course program, grades).
Digital bulletin	Allows creation of bulletin news templates, specification of bulletin sections and contents, web publishing and distribution.
Configuration and administration tools	
VLC management	Creation of VLCs based on templates, interface design (drag-and-drop of webparts), access rights definitions, VLC areas subscriptions, hosting facilities, members profile management, user roles, etc.

In later cycles of analysis and design, additional advanced tools were identified and developed such as knowledge base manager, service center (helpdesk), real-time forum and draft maker (real-time collaborative text editor).

Besides the identification of the above tools, other functional requirements were considered regarding the following aspects of VLC environments:

- Sociability: this issue involves people, purpose and policies associated with a VLC [25]. In particular, *netetiquette* policies (behavior) need to be clearly stated [26]. VLC administrators are encouraged to always include a section on community purpose and policies.
- Usability and accessibility: usability refers to user interface considerations including: consistent navigation, familiar language and icons and clear layout design. Accessibility is related to usability issues addressing special characteristics or disabilities of VLC members such as vision problems.
- Aliveness. A key for success in VLCs is "their ability to generate enough excitement, relevance, and value to attract and engage members" [27]. Therefore, the website must always look "alive" and continuously present new contents to users. This is supported in Areito through different ways. For instance, Areito, being organized as a hierarchy of portals, provides mechanisms to effectively make VLC and their activities visible in many levels of the hierarchy and in many ways. Areito's informational multimedia elements adapt to Areito's own interior aliveness to promote VLC's evolution. Namely, VLC

promotional mini-posters, automatically generated news, interactive informational multimedia elements with subscription modalities (e.g. email, RSS, podcast, SMS), list of on-line users and adaptive user interfaces are examples of means to ensure that VLC evolution is indeed noticeable for end users of Areito.
* Configurability and personalization. The environment should be able to adapt itself according to user preferences and profile information, instead of making users adapt to the environment. In addition, users should be able to easily select and configure tools that best suit their interaction needs.

4. DEVELOPMENT AND DEPLOYMENT ISSUES

The Areito portal has been developed using Microsoft SharePoint Services technology as support platform [28]. Through SharePoint, a set of basic collaboration and communication services are available in order to build organizational websites. Among the collaboration features of this product, we can mention: Microsoft Office integration, document collaboration and user presence indication. Other technical features include: ASP.NET extensibility, website templates (websites can be saved as templates for distribution and further instantiation), web parts (reusable components) and maintenance-free site development. Based on this platform, Areito communication and collaboration tools shown on Table 2 were developed or integrated.

Once the selected tools were developed and tested, specific VLC templates were designed in order to better assist end users with VLC creation and configuration tasks. Namely, VLC templates allow the creation of entire websites and associated tools using preexisting definition files. These templates represent "emerging use patterns" of Areito communication and collaboration tools. Moreover, any VLC website can in turn be saved as a template for future reutilization. Examples of developed VLC templates are: basic Areito VLC (VLC with main tools), Areito Portal (website with a VLC directory), and VLC for course support.

A snapshot of Areito portal (in Spanish) is shown on Figure 2 (see also [3]). The top section of the website includes the following elements: a banner specially designed with Dominican Republic art motifs and pictures, search toolbar, contextual help link, hot links (e.g. create VLC) and user identification. Below the top section, the three main layout areas are: configurable quick-access menu area (left), relevant information and knowledge exchange area (middle) and general information area (e.g. recent news, contact information, presence indicator) to the right. The middle area includes a welcome and introduction section to the portal, a directory of specific VLCs created within Areito, as well as general discussion section and on-line polls. Furthermore, the main menu on the leftmost area gives access to other relevant information components of the portal, such as calendar of events, document library, FAQs, digital bulletin and administration and configuration tools. Interface elements (web parts) on any area can be moved to any position on screen by a drag-and-drop facility available to administrators in page-design mode.

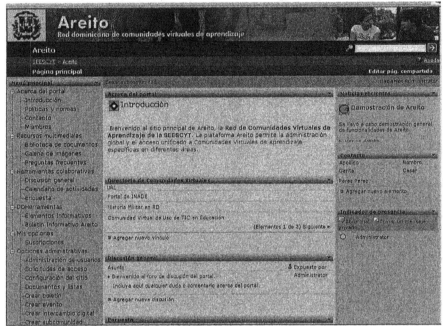

Figure 2 – Screenshot of Areito Virtual Learning Communities Portal.

The Areito VLC directory (central position on screen) contains entries with URLs to actual VLCs hosted for different universities and educational organizations in the Dominican Republic. Examples of current VLCs in this directory include specific communities on the following subjects: ICT Use in Education; Agroalimentary, Biotechnology and Business Sciences; National Defense Academy; Websites Visibility; English Teaching; Education on AIDS Issues; and Presidential Forum for Educational Excellence; among others. All these VLCs have been developed based on templates and make intensive use of collaboration tools such as digital bulletin, event organization and digital market, described earlier in this paper. It is expected that with adequate training and support, end-users will be able to actively create and cultivate many other VLCs themselves.

It is important to mention that since Areito was made available in January 2006, VLCs have recently been launched for end-user groups and are at an early "nurturing" stage. In this sense, they represent pilot VLCs that are starting up and that will soon provide valuable feedback for platform developers and managers. All VLCs were identified or proposed by end-users during workshop events or individual meetings. For each VLC a "route map" has been defined in collaboration with end users in order to have a customized VLC development and sustainability plan including training workshops, special VLC content uploading, VLC follow-up events, end-users group meetings and promotion of new VLCs. A route map can be seen as a graph containing information about activities, goals, deadlines, evaluation criteria, dependencies, required resources and responsible persons.

An example of a particular VLC is provided in Figure 3. *Becas Internacionales* is a VLC about international scholarship opportunities for students and professors of the Dominican Republic. This is a community where the Government publishes

Figure 3 – Screenshot of International Scholarships VLC.

available options and community members search for those options effectively. Additionally, the community serves as a training site for prospective scholarship recipients, and as a Service Center for real-time communication between students and professors and the people knowledgeable about scholarships.

Interested parties can apply online for scholarships, interactively query the scholarship system about the current status of their applications, use forum-like tools to ask questions and receive answers asynchronously, download relevant documents and application forms, review available scholarship options from international organizations and subscribe to receive electronic bulletins periodically. People can also query the international scholarship recipients database to find out about previous recipients and their universities.

For these tasks, Areito provides community administrators and users with a number of innovative tools to create bulletins, to organize relevant events, to create scholarships markets where options are published, interests are expressed and matches are automatically ranked, to maintain multimedia information elements such as news, to subscribe to SMS, PODCAST, e-mail and RSS information services, to organize interactive forums, to cooperate in the development of documents, to create and maintain contact lists, scholarship lists and much more. Imagination is the limit to the members of the *Becas Internacionales* VLC.

5. CONCLUSIONS AND FUTURE WORK

The Areito environment introduced in this paper represents an advanced platform for creation, development and management of Virtual Learning Communities in the Dominican Republic. Among the main distinctive features of Areito, we can summarize the following: i) use of an integral collaborative learning approach merging aspects of VCs, CSCL y LMS models; ii) wide variety of advanced interactive collaboration tools readily available; and iii) highly flexible and configurable management of VLCs and their contents.

Since launching of the platform has recently taken place, it is necessary to further assess and evaluate end-users perspective and feedback on daily usage and proper evolution of VLCs in Areito. In particular, more work is due regarding VLC design and cultivation guidelines, intensive training workshops and follow-up events. Future work also includes development of more tools to further assist course instruction activities. There are also plans to exploit Areito facilities to host VLCs for educational organizations from other Latin American countries besides the Dominican Republic. Development of an English version of Areito should also be considered.

5.1 Acknowledgments

The authors of this paper wish to acknowledge the work of Areito developers team as well as valuable inputs from educational organizations in the Dominican Republic.

6. REFERENCES

1. H. Rheingold, *The virtual community: homesteading on the electronic frontier*: Addison-Wesley, 1993.
2. U. Carlen, "Typology of Online Learning Communities", presented at First International Conference on NetLearning2002, Ronneby, Sweden, 2002.
3. Areito, "Areito - Dominican Network of Virtual Learning Communities", http://www.seescyt.net/areito, 2006.
4. TappedIn, "TappedIn Website", http://tappedin.org/, 2005.
5. RedIris, "RedIris Website", http://www.rediris.es/rediris/, 2005.
6. S. Barab, R. Kling, and J. Gray, "Designing for Virtual Communities in the Service of Learning": Cambridge University Press, 2004, pp. 16-52.
7. Tomoye, "Tomoye Website", http://www.tomoye.com, 2005.
8. VEForum, "VE Forum Website", http://www.ve-forum.org, 2005.
9. Knowledgeboard, "Knowledgeboard Website", http://www.knowledgeboard.com, 2005.
10. TeleCARE, "TeleCARE website", http://www.uninova.pt/~telecare/, 2005.
11. TARAhaat, "TARAhaat website", http://www.tarahaat.com/tara/home, 2005.
12. Orkut, "Google Orkut", http://www.orkut.com, 2005.
13. EuroCSCL, "Euro CSCL website", http://www.euro-cscl.org/, 2005.
14. Blackboard, "Blackboard website", http://www.blackboard.com, 2006.
15. Angel, "Angel Learning website", http://www.cyberlearninglabs.com/, 2005.
16. Moodle, "Moodle website", http://moodle.org/, 2005.
17. S. Seufert, U. Lechner, and K. Stanoevska, "A Reference Model for Online Learning Communities", presented at 11th Annual International Information Management Association Conference IIMA-2000, Seattle, Washington, 2000.
18. R. Luppicini, "Categories of Virtual Learning Communities for Educational design", *The Quarterly Review of Distance Education*, vol. 4, pp. 409-416, 2003.
19. Synergeia, "Synergeia website", http://bscl.fit.fraunhofer.de/, 2005.
20. M. Riel and L. Polin, "Virtual Learning Communities - Common Ground and Critical Differences in Designing Technical Environments", in *Designing for Virtual Communities in the Service of Learning*, S. Barab, R. Kling, and J. Gray, Eds.: Cambridge University Press, 2004, pp. 16-52.
21. Fullcirc, "Online Community Toolkit", http://fullcirc.com/community/communitymanual.htm, 2004.
22. M. Pazos, A. Pérez, and J. Salinas, "Comunidades Virtuales: de las listas de discusión a las comunidades de aprendizaje", 2002.
23. E. Wenger, N. White, J. Smith, and K. Rowe, "Technology for communities", in *CEFRIO Book Chapter*, 2005.
24. H. Afsarmanesh, V. Guevara, and L. O. Hertzberger, "Virtual Community Support in TeleCARE", presented at PRO-VE 03, 4th IFIP Working Conference on Virtual Enterprises, Lugano, Switzerland, 2003.
25. J. Preece, *Online Communities - Designing Usability, Supporting Sociability*: John Wiley & Sons, 2000.
26. J. Preece, C. Abras, and D. Maloney-Krichmar, "Designing and evaluating online communities: research speaks to emerging practice", *Int. J. Web Based Communities*, vol. 1, 2004.
27. E. Wenger, *Cultivating Communities of Practice*: Harvard Business School, 2002.
28. Microsoft, "SharePoint Technology", http://www.microsoft.com/sharepoint/default.mspx, 2003.

35	NETWORK OASIS: NEW PRACTICES FOR EMERGENT COLLABORATIVE WORKING ENVIRONMENTS

Ilkka Kakko, Mika Lavikainen, Tatiana Glotova
Joensuu Science Park Ltd., FINLAND
ilkka.kakko@carelian.fi, mika.lavikainen@flexlab.fi, tatiana.glotova@network-oasis.com

In this paper authors describe the development of an emergent collaborative working environment - netWork Oasis - and the practical findings discovered during the Oasis development process. The findings of the project indicate strongly that there is a need for further research and development of tools, practices and methods in the field of collaborative networked organisations (CNO). The main findings: Network Incubation and Serendipity Management, are described, while they are some of the missing elements in traditional theories of Virtual Organisation Breeding Environments and Professional Virtual Communities.

1. INTRODUCTION

In this paper we concentrate on the netWork Oasis as a practical example of emergent collaborative working environment. netWork Oasis is a development project of Joensuu Science Park, Finland. The objective is to design and construct a hybrid space into the premises of Joensuu Science Park in order to support and increase the productivity of modern knowledge worker.

The structures and hierarchies emerging within netWork Oasis are not controlled by any external force, but appear as a result of interactions between Oasis members. The behavior and characteristics of the emergent systems are complex and hardly predictable, but may give unexpected valuable results, which might be seen as demonstrations of serendipity concept. To support the value of serendipitous discoveries we develop network incubation and principles of serendipity management. Some of the most important, as facilitation, motivation and trust management, are described in this paper.

2. BUSINESS ECOSYSTEMS: OASIS CASE

The term "business ecosystem" refers to an environment, which functions like nature. In fact, the business field can be described trough actions and functions occurring in nature. Business and markets evolve and change all the time and companies have to keep up and cope with the changing environment. Like in nature,

Please use the following format when citing this chapter:

Kakko, I., Lavikainen, M., Glotova, T., 2006, in IFIP International Federation for Information Processing, Volume 224, Network-Centric Collaboration and Supporting Fireworks, eds. Camarinha-Matos, L., Afsarmanesh, H., Ollus, M., (Boston: Springer), pp. 333–342.

it requires clever moves and rapid adaptation. It means that the strongest may not survive, but the most adaptable will.

Business Ecosystem concept was introduced by James F. Moore in 1993 (Moore 1993): "organisms of the business world" – interacting organizations and individuals, who produce goods and services for the members of the ecosystem. The roles and capabilities of the members may change with the time. But the function of ecosystem leader is valued by the community members and enables to move towards shared visions.

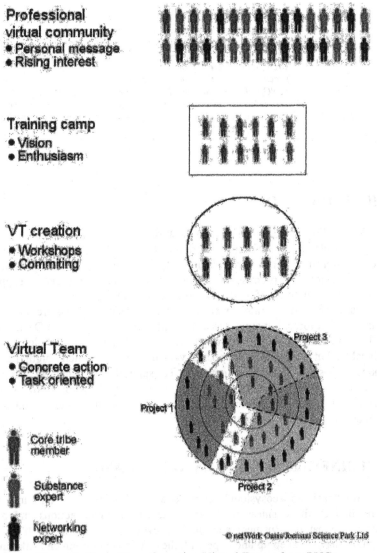

Figure 1. Oasis Way of creating Virtual Teams from PVCs

netWork Oasis project as a business ecosystem started to function from the Kick-off meeting on February 2004 (Figure 1). It was organized by inviting possibly interested people through the personal networks of core tribe members. More than 40 people were participating to the Kick-off meeting. The idea was to have professionals with their ideas, but CVs were not allowed. Instead of CVs members had to use mottos to describe themselves. The interactions during the Kick-off and Training Camp were facilitated: everyone had to have a conversation with a number of other members, whom s/he hasn't met before. For example, even the seats for the dinner were distributed through some kind of a lottery. The vision was given on the Kick-off meeting on the previous night and the number of ideas produced during the Training Camp was numerous. The goal was to collect those ideas and get the main directions for further development. Initially, all ideas were divided into three main categories: Interior, Instruments and Interactions.

During the following months several workshops were organized, where the whole netWork Oasis Concept was developed in details. New members were introduced through the invitations as it was from the very beginning. Term "Oasis Way of Working" was used already on the second Oasis workshop, thus the Oasis culture started to develop. On that step Oasis Way of Working included 24/7 availability of the environment; mixture of work, learn and play; then serendipity from nature and strangers was added. At some point the necessity of socially rich environment and diversity at all levels was clear, but at the same time the family friendliness was important for Oasis members. The concepts of Oasis Tribe and Oasis Warriors were born. The values proclaimed by Tribe members are: Sustainability, Diversity, Individuality, Trust & respect, Co-discovery, and Wellbeing.

As a testing environment for Oasis Way of Working, FlexLab was opened on Autumn 2004. Virtual environment (Oasis Garden) is used for collaboration between the workshops and functions as a knowledge database. Currently several projects are going on in the virtual environment: Interior design, FlexLab Concept, selling the Concept, GLOW and some others as well. GLOW-subproject is devoted to the development of hybrid space tools. It is based on personal user profiles and combines three dimensions: real, virtual and social.

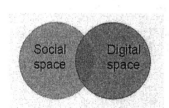
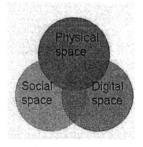

Traditional community tools   Hybrid-space community tools
Figure 2. Traditional and hybrid community tools

Traditional community tools like bullet-boards, e-mail, instant messaging programs and conference tools concentrate only on connecting people (social space) through digital media like the Internet. Some community members may work daily in the same premises or at least they meet face-to-face every now and then. Still, the physical element is missing in the community tools. We think that the physical space is essential part in modern communities and it has to be integrated and supported

(Figure 2). We call this combination of social-, digital- and physical space as hybrid space. To create and to support this kind of hybrid space in netWork Oasis we have created a tool called GLOW. We suppose that digital space (like Oasis Garden) provides means for asynchronous collaboration mostly, while hybrid space enables synchronous interaction.

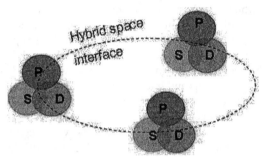

Figure 3. netWork Oasis hybrid space ecosystem (P - Physical, S – Social, D – Digital spaces)

netWork Oasis hybrid space ecosystem is represented by a number of places, each of which is a combination of physical, digital and social spaces, connected by the means of hybrid space interface (Figure 3). Each of these complex triple-space structures are netWork Oasis'es located in different places of Europe/World, or smaller centers – FlexLabs, where the presence of hybrid space might be weaker than in fully-functional netWork Oasis. Figure 4 demonstrates netWork Oasis infrastructure, where Oasis I is current netWork Oasis in Joensuu Science Park premises and will be opened on January 2007; blue circle stands for the current Joensuu FlexLab; other grey dashed circles represent possible future netWork Oasis centers and FlexLabs. netWork Oasis ecosystem is open for interaction with external networks.

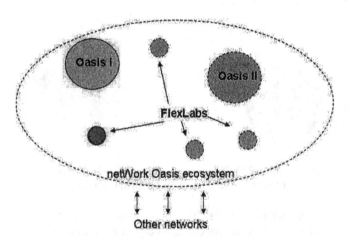

Figure 4. netWork Oasis infrastructure

The netWork Oasis is an example of business ecosystem, where future users of Oasis environment and current users of FlexLab are the developers of the environment themselves. Oasis Garden and, in the future, GLOW hybrid space function as Professional Virtual Community (PVC) tools, where one may find peers and experts from a number of organizations. Garden made it possible to develop several projects in virtual environment, which operate as Virtual Teams, employing members from different companies and physical locations. We'll describe the collaboration process and supportive techniques in more details in the next chapter.

3. NEW EMERGING COLLABORATIVE PLATFORMS

A PVC is an association of individual experts, who collaborate, share ideas and interact in order to create common value. The formation of PVC and distribution of the roles in it is usually not controlled or managed from top-bottom, it is rather spontaneous process. In this context term 'emergence' should be described, as the patterns of PVCs are the emergent structures. Those patterns are based on interactions between the parts of PVC. An emergent behavior appears when a number of simple entities operate together and form more complex behaviors as a system. The properties of emergent systems are hardly predictable, as the number of interactions between the entities increases combinatorially with the number of components. Serendipity is a key word in the behavior of emergent structures (see Chapter 3.2).

At the netWork Oasis we aim at developing Peer-to-Peer (P2P) networks. P2P networks are characterized by the equipotency of all members. They are dynamic and don't have a stable hierarchy. These networks are important from the value creation point of view, as well as they are interesting areas of research on themselves.

Oasis Tribe and Oasis Way of Working are the examples of emerging structure and behavior. Tribes, generally speaking, are characterized by fluid boundaries and heterogeneity, are not parochial, and are dynamic (Fried 1975). Oasis Tribe promotes diversity of its members and their equality in collaboration with each other and contribution to different sub-projects of netWork Oasis project or even new separate project establishment. New members are invited through the existing Oasis network, broadening the areas of expertise and possibilities of the whole Tribe.

Tribe is one of the examples of possible emergent structures from social and professional networks. The behavior developed during its formation is not common for the regular organization and not easily acceptable in the hierarchical structures, but is very beneficial in the networks context. Oasis Way of Working, as an example of emergent behavior, is a culture which was developed by the Tribe members during the conceptual planning. New members learn from other Tribe members and naturally follow. It gives support for networking, favoring serendipity and encouraging diverse and trustful interactions, love for potential, and co-discovery. Oasis Way of Working is a continuously evolving process. Network Incubation and Serendipity Management are two very important results created thanks to the Oasis Way of Working.

3.1. Network Incubation

Business Incubation is one of the key elements in science parks and other development organizations. The role and importance of business incubation has been widely accepted.

In the netWork Oasis project we have noticed that there is one very important link missing in the beginning of this innovation system – Network Incubation. In order to have good quality interactions between diverse people a new approach is needed. During the netWork Oasis conceptual planning the aim for diversity was very high and it was achieved in many levels: age, gender, social background, professional background, geographical background. Network Incubation can be defined as: *"Creating supportive environments and methods for high quality interactions between diverse people in order to create new combinations of competences"*.

In our project *we have created supportive environments* – netWork Oasis, FlexLab and GLOW- *and methods for high quality interactions* – Oasis Way of Working *between diverse people* – Oasis Tribe plus added members - *in order to create new combinations of competences* – in our case to create an innovative and productive collaborative environment netWork Oasis.

When FlexLab – the test bed for Oasis environment – was established in Autumn 2004 in Joensuu Science Park we were also able to experience the benefits for people from different organizations working in same physical space. Developing our own hybrid space - GLOW - and using our interaction tool Oasis Garden accelerated the serendipitous interactions and thus created a need for Serendipity Management.

3.2. Serendipity Management

Serendipity Management is something out of which we have not found any references in the modern business literature. There are certain elements of it, which are widely known, but again the whole concept of Serendipity Management is new and first time mentioned in our paper in eBRF (Glotova, Kakko, Marjomaa, 2005).

Serendipity Management will be one of the hot topics in near future and our definition for it is: *"Serendipity Management is a concept where you attract curious talent in order to find unexpected, emergent, tacit competence by using facilitation and trust management in very diverse environments."* When successfully implemented, Serendipity Management can improve the possibility to discover new and intersectional ideas which can be developed to breakthrough innovations.

3.2.1. Theory of Serendipity

There is actually not any clear theoretical definition of the theory of serendipity. One accepted definition of serendipity is: "Serendipity is the faculty for making desirable discoveries by accident, Horace Walpole so named a faculty possessed by the heroes of a tale called "Three Princes of Serendip"" (Webster's Dictionary 1994).

In the book "Serendipity - Accidental Discoveries in Science" by Royston M. Roberts is described that "In the fields of observation, chance favors only the prepared mind" (Louis Pasteur). The vital character of discovery in serendipitous findings must be underlined by Albert Szent-Gyorgyi "Discovery consists of seeing what everybody has seen and thinking what nobody has thought". So it all depends on "discoveries made by accident and sagacity of things which they were not actually in quest of" (Roberts 1989).

The list of these accidental discoveries in science is impressive from Archimedes to Columbus from Teflon to Viagra from Isaac Newton to finding the secrets of DNA.

3.2.2. Tacit Competence

Organizational knowledge creation, according to Nonaka (Nonaka et al. 2000), is a spiral process that starts from the tacit knowledge exchange, through externalization and conceptualization processes transforms to explicit, and through experiences in particular contexts to tacit knowledge of individuals again. Tacit knowledge in this spiral plays a role of starting point.

Knowledge, contrary to information, is always context-dependent. In a professionally and culturally diverse environment, such as netWork Oasis, it is a challenge to find a balance between the benefits of diversity and the necessity for common shared context in order to build trust. Trust in a network is especially important for sharing tacit knowledge, which can be discovered and exchanged only in face-to-face communications and common experiences.

Motivation is "a must" for creating shared context, knowledge exchange and finally, building competence network. Motivation can be seen as a sum of several factors: self-motivation of individuals, support from network, inspiration from results, and facilitation.

Self-motivation is hard to control or facilitate, it is personal factor though it can be developed. Motivation from network is one, which comes from the feeling of being a part of the network. In netWork Oasis we build "Oasis Tribe" and develop methods for collaboration, traditions and rituals for the Tribe members in order to increase their attitude and motivation.

Inspiration and motivation from results appears when celebrating success, which can be seen in a variety of events: not necessarily the foundation of a new company or development of a new product, but sometimes a good idea just found in a short-talk or catching up the inspiration from people or place can be much more important. Discovering serendipitous ideas might become the greatest motivator based on previous results.

Facilitation is a key element in increasing motivation on different levels. It is hard to overestimate the importance of facilitation in the complex organizations and networks of diverse people, where creativity and knowledge sharing are the corner stones for success.

Tacit competence has two main multipliers: tacit knowledge of individual experts and, which is more valuable, their motivation to share that knowledge, which can be personal or facilitated, and trust.

Availability of tacit competence in a particular network is one of the main elements of serendipity management.

3.2.3. Facilitation

Facilitation is the enabler to increase motivation to collaborate and share knowledge, as been told in previous chapter. Facilitation can be used in other cases: to increase the quality of interactions, to harness diversity, to improve the productivity of knowledge work, etc.

As interactions make ties between the nodes of the network, thus support, facilitation and motivation for interactions are the key elements for effective network functioning. Interactions can happen spontaneously or in a facilitated manner. Spontaneous interactions are supported by the environment: innovative interior and instruments. But facilitated interactions are also needed in the network of diverse and creative people.

Creative people are often skilled in individual processes, but may have more difficulties cooperating with others. We want to associate facilitation with border breaking, opening up for new potential, achieving results that could not be achieved spontaneously (netWork Oasis Concept Document 2004).

The key factor and vital enabler of motivation is a certain state of mind called Flow (Csikszentmihalyi 2003). Flow is an experience of feeling the deep enjoyment, which comes from doing some activity, and a feeling of being deeply involved in it. After the Flow one feels the increasing self-esteem. The possibility to experience Flow is a strong motivating factor for individuals, organizations and networks. The challenging job within the person's capabilities, including increasing capabilities to grow and learn, will be the most probable place where Flow can occur. To stimulate the interest in the particular job we can do three things:

1. Make the objective conditions of the workplace as attractive as it is possible.
2. Find ways to saturate the job with meaning and value.
3. Choose and reward individuals who find satisfaction in their work.

Creative people can experience Flow more often then others, but even they need to be facilitated to feel so. Creating the environment and developing the working culture, which supports Flow, is one of the main objectives in the netWork Oasis project.

3.2.4. Trust Management

Trust is the core element in working collaborative networks and VOs (Järvenpää, Shaw Thomas 1998). Thus, it is important part of business ecosystem. Trust can be established in several ways and the most important incentives in trust building are deliberate trust supporting leadership and commonly recognised and accepted group norms (Baron, 1992). The role of trust supporting leadership is to "guide" and enable trust building whereas group norms reduce uncertainty and bring security into the network or community.

Having well established trust in the network brings several advantages. Open communication and knowledge sharing improve reactivity and adaptability in the network. In addition trust and open communication help tacit competence to emerge from the network thus benefiting the whole network (Lavikainen, 2005). Trust also affects on serendipity. Although serendipity can occur without trust, it may not be exploited without the help of other network members. In this case, if there is no willingness to share the new idea, the opportunity induced from serendipity will be neglected and the potential innovation is lost.

This was just one viewpoint of how trust affects on networks, VOs and communities. We have to remember that trust affects strongly also in individual level for example in the workplaces, reflecting relationships also to the network. In fact trust is always established in individual level and the networks and communities are run by the very individuals.

In Oasis we concentrate specifically on the individuals and trust building is therefore aimed at personal networking. This means that individuals represent themselves and not the companies they work for. Our way to do this is to leave out the work titles and thus people are in equal level in the community. In addition we believe that trust is built socially so we try to support social interactions through physical and virtual community tools.

In traditional business contracts have played major role in building trust between the companies. Unquestionably contracts are still needed in today's business life but we think that the viewpoint should be very different. Our opinion is that trust is needed when we want something to succeed and the contracts are needed only when something goes wrong. That is why we want to lay more emphasis on trust building than in formulating watertight contracts.

4. CONCLUSION

In our view, recently business ecosystems are transforming to network ecosystems. Thus the question of how to make networks more effective and productive arises, meaning how to facilitate and support members of PVCs to interact, share, discover and establish new VTs.

At netWork Oasis Project we are driving to a new networking culture, which is based on equality, curiosity, and collaboration. According to our experiences some totally new practices are needed. In our paper we have described more in details Network Incubation and Serendipity Management, which we believe are going to be the vital elements when improving the productivity of PVCs and emerging VTs.

4.1 Acknowledgments

We want to thank Oasis Tribe for contributing to the development of netWork Oasis practices and thus inspiring us to create these new emerging theories.

5. REFERENCES:

1. Csikszentmihalyi, M. (2003). Good Business. Leadership, Flow, and the Making of Meaning. Viking Press.
2. Baron Robert S. Kerr, Norbert L. Miller Norman. 1992. Group Process, Group Decision, Group Action. Open University press, Great Britain, p.11-13
3. Glotova T., Kakko I., Marjomaa E. (2005) "New Approach to Innovative Milieus: How to Create Competence by Co-Discovering Tacit Knowledge", eBRF Conference, September 26-28, Tampere, Finland
4. Fried, Morton H. (1975) The Notion of Tribe. Cummings Publishing Company.

5. Järvenpää S.L., Shaw Thomas R. 1998, Global Virtual Teams: Integrating Models of Trust. eJOV –
    electronic Journal of Organizational Virtualness, Proceedings of the VoNet – Workshop, April
    27-28, 1998, p.35-51
6. Lavikainen Mika, 2005, Virtuaaliorganisaation toiminta innovaationäkökulmasta: kommunikaatio,
    tietojärjestelmät ja työkalut, Lappeenrannan Teknillinen Yliopisto, p.100-103.
7. netWork Oasis Concept Document (2004), Joensuu Science Park, Finland.
8. Nonaka, I., Toyama, R. and Konno, N. (2000) SECI, Ba and Leadership: a Unified Model of
    Dynamic Knowledge Creation. Long Range Planning 33, pp. 5-34.
9. Moore, James F. (1993) Predators and Prey: A New Ecology of Competition , Harvard Business
    Review
10. Roberts, Royston M. (1989) Serendipity: accidental discoveries in science, John Wiley & Sons, Inc.,
    USA
11. Webster's Encyclopedic Unabridged Dictionary of the English Language, New York, Gramercy
    Books, 1994, p.1302.

36

A PROCESS MODEL FOR COLLABORATIVE PROBLEM SOLVING IN VIRTUAL COMMUNITIES OF PRACTICE

María Clara Casalini, Tomasz Janowski, Elsa Estevez[1]

The United Nations University
International Software for Software Technology
(UNU-IIST), Macau
{mcc,tj,elsa}@iist.unu.edu

We present a model for collaborative problem solving in Virtual Communities of Practice. The model applies a repository, comprising resources, properties and statements, to underpin the process of problem-solving. The process allows for formulating, exploring, matching and gradually refining abstract problem descriptions (one kind of resource) into the corresponding concrete solutions (another kind of resource), expanding the underlying repository with new resources, properties and statements in the process. The model is defined formally, its usefulness is argued with a simple case study and a possible implementation is described using Semantic Web.

1. INTRODUCTION

Virtual Communities of Practice (VCPs) enable distributed knowledge workers to share experience and seek solutions to concrete problems in a given field of interest, all through computer-supported interaction and collaborative work. VCPs allow members to develop individual performance and establish best practices in the field.

The extent of computer support for VCPs differs depending on the nature, scope and field of interest, ranging from member registration, to collaborative review and version control. Both synchronous interactivity (chat rooms) and asynchronous (email forums) are supported. However, while technical functions are generally supported, supporting creative aspects of community work is difficult. One reason is the shortage of methods to carry out creative activities through computer-supported processes. This is not surprising - creativity is inherently hard to formalize!

This paper presents a process-oriented model for collaborative problem solving in Virtual Communities of Practice. The model describes a systematic process of solution-building for a given problem description. The model relies on a repository to keep the record of various kinds of web resources - publications, projects, case studies, problems, solutions, etc.; properties – data about or relations between resources; and statements. Statements are triples of a subject (resource), property and object (resource or data). Problem-solving is carried out in six stages:

---

[1] On leave of absence from Universidad Nacional del Sur, Bahía Blanca, Argentina.

Please use the following format when citing this chapter:

Casalini, M. C., Janowski, T., Estevez, E., 2006, in IFIP International Federation for Information Processing, Volume 224, Network-Centric Collaboration and Supporting Fireworks, eds. Camarinha-Matos, L., Afsarmanesh, H., Ollus, M., (Boston: Springer), pp. 343–350.

1) *problem description* – A member formulates a problem description from its own practice and adds this description to the repository as a resource.
2) *problem exploration* – Members explore the problem and gradually add to the repository the relevant resources, properties and statements.
3) *problem matching* – Members try to match the problem against similar problems described in the repository, including solved and unsolved problems.
4) *solution design* – Members decompose the problem into a number of sub-problems and add each to the repository as a problem description.
5) *solution refinement* – Members gradually add new resources, properties or statements relevant to the solution obtained so far, and link the solutions to sub-problems with the solution design, when available.
6) *solution deployment* – When all sub-problems are solved, the member adds a solution statement relating the abstract problem with the concrete solution.

The model is described conceptually then formalized using RSL (George, 1992). The repository and operations invoked by members as part of the problem-solving process are formalized. Thereafter, we discuss a possible implementation relying on Semantic Web. The usefulness of the model is argued through a case study – design an XML language and software to write and display presentation slides.

The rest of the paper is organized as follows. Section 2 provides background information in three areas related to the paper. Section 3 presents a process model including: concepts (Section 3.1), formalization (Section 3.2) and implementation (Section 3.3). Section 4 presents a case study and Section 5 draws some conclusions.

2. BACKGROUND

This section provides a brief account of the three areas related to this paper: Virtual Communities of Practice, Collaborative Problem Solving and Semantic Web.

Virtual Communities of Practice: A Virtual Community is an aggregation of individuals or businesses interacting around a shared interest, where interactions are supported by technology and guided by some norms (Porter, 2004). A Community of Practice (CoP) is a group of people sharing a concern for something they do and learning how to do it better by interacting regularly (Wenger, 2004). A Virtual Community of Practice is a CoP where interactions are supported by technology.

Following (Porter, 2004), five attributes characterize VCPs: purpose - the interest shared by members; place - the virtual space comprising the members' sense of presence; platform – the nature of interactions between members, whether synchronous, asynchronous or both; population - pattern of interaction according to the structure and social ties of the group; and profit - the economic value that a community may produce. Following (Cambridge, 2005), the lifecycle of a community comprises: (1) inquiry - identifying the audience, goals and vision of the community, (2) design – defining activities and roles to support community's goals, (3) prototype – piloting the community with selected stakeholders, (4) launch – rolling out the community to a broader audience, (5) growth - encouraging members and newcomers to participate and get engaged in the activities, and (6) sustain – cultivating and assessing the knowledge created by the community.

Collaborative Problem Solving: We defined a Problem as an intricate unsettled question. Problem-solving deals with the processes involved in finding solutions to problems. Collaborative problem-solving is problem-solving done by peers, performing the same actions, having a common goal and working together (Dillenbourg, 1999). Collaboration is the process of intertwined activities of two or more actors while solving a problem. Direct collaboration is realized by communications between actors. During indirect collaboration the actors apply the knowledge other actors made available in a repository (Conen, 1996).

Semantic Web: The Web is essentially a repository of documents aimed at human consumption. Semantic Web extends the Web by capturing formally the semantics of documents, thus automating the discovery, integration and reuse of documents (Berners-Lee, 2001). Semantic Web is implemented using several technologies and standards. For instance, Resource Description Framework (RDF) is used to specify resources (W3C, 2005). Another technology is the Web Ontology Language (OWL), used to describe relationships between resources (W3C, 2004).

RDF is a language for representing and exchanging metadata about the resources on the Web, with precise syntax and semantics. Syntactically, RDF applies an XML language called RDF/XML. Semantically, it describes web resources in terms of properties and their values. Resource descriptions are called statements and consist of a subject, predicate and object. The subject identifies the resource, the predicate determines a property of the resource, and the object defines the value of the property. Resources and properties are identified through URIs.

An ontology is a specification of a set of concepts and their relationships in a particular domain of knowledge (Gruber, 1993). Ontologies are usually expressed in a particular logic language enabling the definition of classes, properties and their relationships. For instance, OWL can be used to define ontologies. OWL is the language developed by W3C as a standard for the Semantic Web, with several tools existing to define, encode and develop ontologies.

3. COLLABORATIVE PROBLEM SOLVING FOR VCPs

This section presents the main contribution of this paper – the process for Collaborative Problem-Solving in Virtual Communities of Practice.

3.1 Conceptual Model

The process of Collaborative Problem Solving relies on a repository, with an underlying ontology, owned and developed by the community. The components in the repository are: *resources* – community assets categorized into classes, *properties* – relations between resources or data about resources; and *statements* – expressions about resources and their properties. Properties are binary relations between pairs of resources or between resources and simple values. Statements are triples of a subject (resource), property and object (resource or data), written [sub,prop,obj]. Figure 1 depicts the resources stored in the repository and how they are used to build solutions. Solutions can be composed by any type of resource, for instance a solution to a previous problem can be used to build a solution to a new problem.

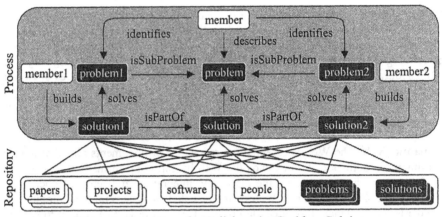

Figure 1: Repository for Collaborative Problem Solving

The process is carried out in six phases: *problem description* – adding a problem resource to the repository; *problem exploration* – analyzing the problem by adding statements linking it to existing or new resources; *problem matching* – identifying similarities between the problem and other problems in the repository by adding relevant statements; *solution design* – decomposing the problem into sub-problems and adding them as new resources to the repository; *solution refinement* – adding new statements, resources and properties related to the solution, and linking solutions to sub-problems with the solution design when they become available; and *solution deployment* – adding a solution statement when all sub-problems are solved.

Figure 2 depicts the process and how the number of statements about the problem increases during all phases. It also shows how the number of unsolved sub-problems increases during *solution design* and decreases during *solution refinement*. The process can be carried out fully collaboratively since sub-problems can be assigned to different members, who in turn apply the same process for solving them.

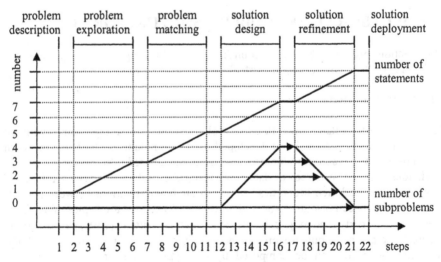

Figure 2: Process for Collaborative Problem Solving

3.2 Formal Model

The aim of this section is to show how it is possible to formalize the model described in Section 3.1. First, we introduce abstract types to represent data, resources, properties and statements. `Value` type is defined to comprise plain data or complex data (resource). In addition, three functions are defined to return a subject (`sub`), predicate (`pred`) and object (`obj`) parts of a statement.

```
type                  type
  Data,                 Value == plain(Data) | complex(Resource)
  Resource,           value
  Property,             sub: Statement -> Resource,
  Statement             pred: Statement -> Property,
                        obj: Statement -> Value
```

A repository is modeled using a type `Repos`, with functions defined to return sets of resources, properties and statements. The type is constrained to ensure that all statements in the repository only use the existing resources and properties.

```
type                                    value
  Repos',                                 iswf: Repos' -> Bool
  Repos = {| r: Repos' :- iswf(r) |}      iswf(r) is all s: Statement :-
value                                       s isin stat(r) =>
  res:  Repos' -> Resource-set,             sub(s) isin res(r) /\
  prop: Repos' -> Property-set,             pred(s) isin prop(r) /\
  stat: Repos' -> Statement-set             case obj(s) of
                                              plain(_) -> true,
                                              complex(o) -> o isin res(r)
                                            end
```

A number of functions are defined to modify the repository. Among them are the functions to add resources, properties and statements. All functions must ensure that the resulting repository is well-formed according to the constraint above.

```
value                                    value
  addRes: Resource >< Repos --~> Repos     canAddStat: Statement >< Repos -> Bool
  addRes(o, r) as r' post                  canAddStat(s, r) is
    res(r') = res(r) union {o} ...           s ~isin stat(r) /\
    pre o ~isin res(r),                      sub(s) isin res(r) /\
  addStat: Statement >< Repos --~> Repos     pred(s) isin prop(r) /\
  addStat(s, r) as r' post                   case obj(s) of
    stat(r') = stat(r) union {s} ...           plain(_) -> true,
    pre canAddStat(s, r),                       complex(o) -> o isin res(r)
  addProp: Property >< Repos --~> Repos      end
```

A problem is a particular kind of resource. We introduce the types representing resource and property types, along with functions `hasType` from values to types. `Problem` type is defined as a subtype of `Resource`. A function is also introduced to return a set of properties used in the statements about a given problem.

```
type                       type
  ResType,                   Problem = {| o: Resource :- hasType(o) = problem |}
  PropType                 value
value                        isProblem: Problem >< Repos -> Bool
  problem: ResType,          isProblem(p, r) is
  exactProp: PropType          p isin res(r),
value                        problemProp: Problem >< Repos --~> Property-set
  hasType:                   problemProp(p, r) is
    Resource -> ResType        { t | t: Property :- exists s: Statement :-
  hasType:                       s isin stat(r) /\ p = sub(s) /\ t = pred(s) }
    Property -> PropType       pre isProblem(p, r)
```

In the following, we introduce example functions supporting various phases of the problem-solving process. In problem description, we only add the problem resource.

```
value
  describe: Problem >< Repos ---> Repos
  describe(p, r) is addResource(p, r) pre ~isProblem(p, r)
```

During problem exploration, new statements about the problem are repeatedly added to the repository, along with new properties and resources as required. For instance, function explore is defined to add a single statement.

```
value
  explore: Problem >< Statement >< Repos ---> Repos
  explore(p, s, r) is
    let r' = if pred(s) isin prop(r) then r else addProp(pred(s), r) end in
      case obj(s) of
        plain(_) -> addStat(s, r'),
        complex(o) ->
          if o isin res(r') then addStat(s,r') else addStat(s, addRes(o,r')) end
      end
    end pre sub(s) = p /\ isProblem(p, r)
```

During problem matching, the problem is compared to existing problems and suitable statements are added to record the similarities. One measure of similarity is that the two problems use the same set of properties in the statements about them. A property type exactProp has been defined to express this. The following function matchExact adds the corresponding statement, if applicable.

```
value
  matchExact: Problem >< Problem >< Repos ---> Repos
  matchExact(p1, p2, r) is
    let s: Statement :-
      sub(s) = p1 /\ pred(s) = exactProp /\ obj(s) = complex(p2)
    in addStat(s, r) end
    pre isProblem(p1, r) /\ isProblem(p2, r) /\
        problemProp(p1, r) = problemProp(p2, r)
```

The remaining phases of problem-solving include solution design, refinement and deployment. Specific functions are defined to support these phases. For solution design, the functions add new problems as sub-problems of the original problem. For solution refinement, the functions add new statements, properties and resources related to the solution, as well as functions relating the solution to the solutions of sub-problems. For solution deployment, the function adds a statement relating the problem and the final solution, when all sub-problems are eventually solved.

3.3 Implementation

The process described above is currently implemented to support the community portal for the UNeGov.net initiative – Building a Community of Practice for Electronic Governance (UNeGov.net, 2006). The portal is developed in Java using the Jena Semantic Web Framework (Jena, 2006). The portal maintains the database of members and the repository relies on the ontology described in OWL. Jena API is used to manipulate the ontology, browse and search the repository, and maintain the knowledge created by the community. All resources are represented by URIs. For papers or software resources, the URIs link to their electronic versions. For member or organization resources the URIs link to their home pages.

4. CASE STUDY

Consider a Virtual Community of Practice focused on XML technology and software development. Suppose this VCP is presented with the following problem P: "Define an XML language and software to write and display presentation slides".

Suppose the repository contains the resources of the types language, tool, element and schema, problem P' with some statements, and its solution S':

P' : Define an XML Language for specifying contents of documents.
S' : XML4Doc specifies contents of documents.
[P',about,schemas], [P',includes,title], ...

The problem-solving process is depicted in Figure 3. The process begins by adding P as a problem resource to the repository (phase 1). During problem exploration (phase 2) we add statements [P,about,schemas] and [P,about,tools]. Similarities identified throughout problem matching (phase 3) are expressed by [P,subProp,P'] - P contains some but not all properties of P'. Three sub-problems are identified during solution design (phase 4):

P1 : Analyze existing presentation slides to identify typical elements.
P2 : Define an XML Schema to describe the contents of slides.
P3 : Select a tool for the presentation of slides.

Once the sub-problems are identified, similar problem-solving is carried out for each of them (see Figure 3). P1 is solved with S1 identifying presentation elements found in the analyzed slides. Several statements are added to relate P2 to these elements. As the same elements were found in documents, P2 is matching the properties and values of P', therefore its solution S' is also suitable for P2. P3 is further sub-divided into P4 – transform XML to HTML, and P5 – select a tool to display HTML. P4 is solved by the XSLT transformation for the schema obtained in S', while P5 is solved through browsers recorded as tools in the repository.

Phase	Problem	Sub-Problems		
1	P:define slides	P1:analyze slides	P2:define schema	P3:select tool
2	[P,about,schemas] [P,about,tools]	[P1,about,elements]	[P2,about,schemas] [P2,includes,title]	[P3,about,tools]
3	[P,subProp,P']	[P1,subProp,P'] [P1,exactProp,P]	[P2,exactProp,P'] [P2,exactValue,P']	[P3,exactProp,P] [P3,subProp,P2]
4	P1:analyze slides P2:define schema P3:select tool			P4:XML to HTML P5:HTML tools
5	S:XML4Doc/browser [Si,part,S] i=1..3	S1:slides analyzed		S3: HTML browser [Si,part,S3] i=4,5
6	[S,solves,P]	[S1,solves,P1]	[S',solves,P2]	[S3,solves,P3]

Figure 3: XML Case Study – Problem Solving and Sub-Problem Solving

During solution refinement (phase 5) for P, S: "XML4Doc is a schema for slides and any browser can display them." is added. Statements [Si,part,S] for i = 1..3 are added to relate sub-problem solutions with S. Finally, during solution deployment (phase 6), [S,solves,P] is added to link P with its solution S.

5. CONCLUSIONS

The main objective of this paper was to present a process-oriented model for cooperative problem solving in Virtual Communities of Practice, suitable for implementation as part of community portals. This was motivated by the shortage of computer-supported methods to support creative aspects of community work.

The process relies on a repository containing resources, properties and statements. Problems, solutions and partial solutions are all expressed as resources. Problem-solving is about connecting a problem description to the existing resources, creating new statements, properties and resources in the process. In particular, new sub-problems are identified and solved through the same six-phase processes. The paper formalized the model, indicated a possible implementation, and illustrated its usefulness through a case study in XML language/tool development.

The main benefit of the approach is the definition of a systematic process to carry out problem-solving in any domain of knowledge, enabling computer support to organize the process and maintain the repository. At the same time, the approach requires that problem-solving conforms to a particular formal structure, and the suitability of this structure for particular problem domains is yet to be investigated.

Future work includes expanding the model to cover community concepts, exploring opportunities for automation in different phases, implementing the model and assessing its effectiveness in various domains of knowledge.

ACKNOWLEDGEMENTS

We would like to thank Irshad Khan, Adegboyega Ojo and Gabriel Oteniya for useful discussions and comments about this work.

REFERENCES

1.   Berners-Lee Tim, Hendler James, Lassila Ora. The Semantic Web. Scientific American, May 2001.
2.   Cambridge Darren, Kaplan Soren and Suter Vicki. Community of Practice Design Guide, 2005. http://www.educause.edu/ir/library/pdf/NLI0531.pdf.
3.   Conen Wolfram, Neumann Gustaf. Prerequisites for Collaborative Problem Solving. Proceedings of WETICE 96, IEEE 5th Intl. Workshops on Enabling Technologies, Stanford, CA, June 1996.
4.   Dillenbourg Pierre. What Do You Mean By "Collaborative Learning". Collaborative-Learning: Cognitive and Computational Approaches, pp 1-19. Oxford: Elsevier, 1999.
5.   George Chris, et al. The RAISE Specification Language. Prentice Hall, 1992.
6.   Gruber Thomas. Toward Principles for the Design of Ontologies Used for Knowledge Sharing. Formal Ontology in Conceptual Analysis and Knowledge Representation. Kluwer, August 1993.
7.   Jena. Jena - A Semantic Web Framework for Java, 2006. http://jena.sourceforge.net/.
8.   Porter Constance Elise. A Typology of Virtual Communities: A Multi-Disciplinary Foundation for Future Research. Journal of Computer-Mediated Communication. Vol. 10 (1), 3, November 2004.
9.   UNeGov.net. Community of Practice for Electronic Governance, 2006. http://www.unegov.net.
10. Wenger Etienne. Communities of Practice - A Brief Introduction, June 2004. http://www.ewenger.com/theory/index.htm.
11. W3C. Technology and Society Domain, Semantic Web Activity. Resource Description Framework, October 2005. http://www.w3.org/RDF/.
12. W3C. OWL Web Ontology Language Overview. W3C Recommendation, February 2004. http://www.w3.org/TR/owl-features/.

PART **12**

FRAMEWORKS FOR PVC

37

ADAPTIVE COLLABORATION IN PROFESSIONAL VIRTUAL COMMUNITIES VIA NEGOTIATIONS OF SOCIAL PROTOCOLS

Willy Picard
Department of Information Technology
The Poznań University of Economics
ul. Mansfelda 4
60-854 Poznań, POLAND
<picard@kti.ae.poznan.pl>

Support for human-to-human interactions over a network is still insufficient, particularly for professional virtual communities (PVC). Among other limitations, adaptation capabilities of humans are not taken into account in existing models for collaboration processes in PVC. This paper presents a model for adaptive human collaboration. A key element of this model is the modeling of some social elements involved during the collaboration process. Processes are modeled as social protocols. A second contribution is the proposition of negotiation as a mean for adaptation of these protocols.

1. INTRODUCTION

Enterprises are increasing constantly their efforts in order to improve their business processes. A main reason for this may be the fact that enterprises are exposed to a highly competitive global market. As a consequence, enterprises improve their business processes to become more competitive and to increase their performances. Among the most visible actions associated with this effort towards better support for better business processes, one may distinguish the current research work concerning Web services and associated standards: high-level languages such as BPEL or WS-Coordination take the service concept one step further by providing a method of defining and supporting workflows and business processes.

However, it should be noticed that most of these actions are directed towards interoperable machine-to-machine interactions over a network. Support for *human-to-human interactions* over a network is still insufficient and more research has to been done to provide both theoretical and practical knowledge to this field.

Among various reasons for the weak support for human-to-human interactions, one may distinguish the following two reasons: first, many *social elements* are involved in the interaction among humans. An example of such a social element may be the roles played by humans during their interactions. Social elements are usually difficult to model, i.e. integrating non-verbal communication to collaboration models. Therefore, their integration to a model of interaction between

Please use the following format when citing this chapter:

Picard, W., 2006, in IFIP International Federation for Information Processing, Volume 224, Network-Centric Collaboration and Supporting Fireworks, eds. Camarinha-Matos, L., Afsarmanesh, H., Ollus, M., (Boston: Springer), pp. 353-360.

humans is not easy. A second reason is the *adaptation capabilities* of humans which are not only far more advanced than adaptation capabilities of software entities, but also not taken into account in existing models for collaboration processes.

The insufficient support for human-to-human interactions over a network is particularly important for *professional virtual communities*. As mentioned in [Camarinha-Matos 2005], "professional virtual community represents the combination of concepts of virtual community and professional community. Virtual communities are defined as social systems of networks of individuals, who use computer technologies to mediate their relationships. Professional communities provide environments for professionals to share the body of knowledge of their professions [...]". According to [Chituc 2005], little attention has been paid to the social perspective on Collaborative Networks (CN) business environment, including obviously professional virtual communities in which social aspects are of high importance.

This paper is an attempt to provide a model for human-to-human interactions within professional virtual communities. The proposed model addresses, at least to some extent, the two characteristics of the interactions between humans. It should however been kept in mind that the results presented here are a work in progress and therefore they are not claimed to be neither sufficient nor exhaustive.

The rest of this paper is organized as follows. In section 2, the concept of *social protocol*, used to model collaboration processes, is presented. Section 3 then expands on the use of *negotiation* as a mean for *adaptation* of social protocols. Next, related work is reviewed. Finally, section 5 concludes this paper.

2. SOCIAL PROTOCOLS

A social protocol aims at modeling a set of collaboration processes, in the same way as a class models a set of objects in object-oriented programming. In other words, a social protocol may be seen as a model which instances are collaboration processes.

Social protocols model collaboration at a group level. The interactions of collaborators are captured by social protocols. Interactions are strongly related with social aspects, such as the role played by collaborators. The proposed model integrates some of these social aspects, which may explain the choice of the term "social protocols". A formal definition of the proposed model has been already presented in [Picard 2006].

2.1. Modeling collaboration processes

A *social protocol* p is a finite state machine consisting of $\{ S_p, S_p^{start}, S_p^{end}, T_p, \varphi_p \}$ where S is the set of states, $S_p^{start} \subset S$ is the set of starting states, $S_p^{end} \subset S$ is the set of ending states, $S_p^{start} \cap S_p^{end} = \varnothing$, T_p is the set of transitions from states to states, and $\varphi_p : T_p \rightarrow [0,1]$.

In a social protocol, collaborators – as a group – are moving from state to state via the transitions. A transition may be triggered only by a collaborator labeled with the appropriate role. A transition is associated with the execution of an action.

Execution of an action means the execution of remote code. SOAP or CORBA are examples of technologies that may be used to such remote code executions.

The φ_p function puts an additional constraint on the execution of transitions. The φ_p function defines the "desirability" of a transition within the given protocol for the whole group. The highest the value of the φ_p function for a transition t is, the highest the desirability of this transition for the group will be. If the value of the φ_p function for a transition t is zero, then the group does not desire this transition to be executed. It allows collaborators for presenting various granularity levels of a given social protocol with regards to a *desirability threshold*. Desirability filtering is the transformation that causes all transitions with desirability value lowest than the desirability threshold to be suppressed.

The conditions that protocols have to fulfill to be valid, both structurally and semantically have already been presented in [Picard 2005a].

2.2. Social protocol example

The example of social protocol which is presented in this section is oversimplified for readability reasons. It is obvious that social protocols modeling real-world collaboration processes are usually much more complex.

The chosen collaboration process to be modeled as a social protocol may be described as follows: a set of users are collaborating on the establishment of a "FAQ" document. Some users only ask questions, while others, referred as "experts" may answer the questions. Other users, referred as "managers", are may interrupt the work on the FAQ document. The work on the document may terminate either by a success (the document has been written and the manager estimates that its quality is good enough to be published) or by a failure (the users did not find any way to collaborate and the manager has estimated that the work on the FAQ should be interrupted).

A possible model of this collaboration process as a social protocol is presented in Figure 1.

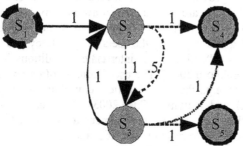

Figure 1. Example of social protocol

In Figure 1, five states s_1... $s5$ are represented as circles. State s_1, s is a starting state; states s_5 and s_5 are ending states. States are named as follows:

- state s_1: *waiting for first question*
- state s_2: *waiting for answer*
- state s_3: *waiting for next question*
- state s_4: *failed termination*
- state s_5: *successful termination*

Transitions are represented as arrows, and the line style is associated with the role of the users that may execute a given transition. Continuous line style is used to represent transitions that may be executed by "normal users", fine-dashed style for transitions that may be executed by "experts", and fine-dotted style for transitions that may be executed by "managers".

The figures closed to the arrows represented the value of the desirability function for the associated transition. As an illustration of desirability filtering, the "suppress question" transition would be suppressed by desirability filtering for the value of the desirability threshold 0.6. Transitions are summarized in Table 1.

Table 1 — Transitions for the example of social protocol and their associated desirability values

Source state	Destination state	Role	Action	φ
s1	s2	Normal	Ask question	1
s2	s3	Expert	Answer question	1
s2	s3	Expert	Suppress question	0.5
s2	s4	Manager	Failure ending	1
s3	s2	Normal	Ask question	1
s3	s4	Manager	Failure ending	1
s3	s5	Manager	Successful ending	1

3. ADAPTATION OF SOCIAL PROTOCOLS VIA NEGOTIATION

While social protocols support, at least to some extent, the integration of some social elements (such as roles) to models of interactions among humans, the adaptation capabilities of humans are not taken into account into social protocols. There is however the need to provide adaptation mechanisms to social protocols. Indeed, interactions among humans are often a context-aware activity. In this paper, context-awareness refers to the capabilities of applications to provide relevant services to their users by sensing and exploring the users' context [Dey 2001, Dockhorn 2005]. Context is defined as a "collection of interrelated conditions in which something exists or occurs" [Dockhorn 2005]. The users' context often consists of a collection of conditions, such as, e.g., the users' location, environmental aspects (temperature, light intensity, etc.) and activities [Chen 2003]. The users' context may change dynamically, and, therefore, a basic requirement for a context-aware system is its ability to sense context and to react to context changes.

Adaptive mechanisms are therefore required as complements to the formerly proposed model for human collaboration processes. The mechanism proposed in this paper is based the idea that social protocols may be negotiated. Two aspects of social protocols may be negotiated independently: first, the desirability function may be negotiated, second, states/transitions sets may be negotiated.

3.1. Desirability negotiation

The first element of social elements that could be the object of adaptation may be the desirability function. The values taken by desirability function for various transitions define the desirability of the whole group with regards to single transitions. By modifying the value of the desirability function, the whole group may adapt the social protocol to the situation in which the group is.

By increasing the desirability value of a given transition, a group may decide that a transition is "desirable" for a given desirability threshold, and therefore the transition associated with the modified value will become available. By decreasing the desirability value of a given transition, a group may decide that a transition is not "desirable" any more, and therefore the transition associated with the modified value will become unavailable for a given desirability threshold.

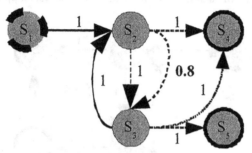

Figure 2 – Social protocol presented in section 2.2 after the desirability value of the transition "suppress question" has been increased by 0.3

Effects of a potential modification of the desirability function of social protocol presented in Section 2.2 are presented in Figure 2. In the presented example, the original social protocol presented in Section 2.2 has been adapted by the whole group via negotiations. The result of the negotiation is the group agreement stating that the desirability value for the transition "suppress question" has to be increased by 0.3. The modified desirability values associated with transitions are presented in Table 2.

Table 2 – Transitions for the example of social protocol and their associated desirability values

Source state	Destination state	Role	Action	φ
s_1	s_2	Normal	Ask question	1
s_2	s_3	Expert	Answer question	1
s_2	s_3	**Expert**	**Suppress question**	**0.8**
s_2	s_4	Manager	Failure ending	1
s_3	s_2	Normal	Ask question	1
s_3	s_4	Manager	Failure ending	1
s_3	s_5	Manager	Successful ending	1

3.2. Structural negotiation

The second element of social elements that could be the object of adaptation may be the set of states and/or the set of transitions. The set of states consists of the set of situations that may occur during the life of a collaboration process. The set of transitions consists of the set of interactions that collaborators may perform.

By adding/suppressing states, the whole group may adapt a social protocol by providing/suppressing situations to the collaboration process. It should be noticed that the addition/suppression of states is related with the addition/suppression of transitions leading and originating from the modified states.

By adding/suppressing transitions, the whole group may adapt a social protocol by providing/suppressing interactions to the collaboration process. It should be noticed that the addition/suppression of transitions is usually not related with the addition/suppression of states to/from which the added/suppressed transitions leads/originates.

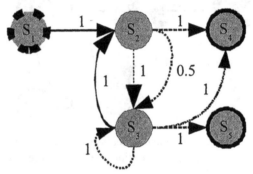

Figure 3 – Social protocol presented in section 2.2 after a transition related with the action "comment a question" has been added from s_3 to s_3.

Effects of the addition of a transition in the social protocol presented in Section 2.2 are presented in Figure 3. In the presented example, the original social protocol presented in Section 2.2 has been adapted by the whole group via negotiations. The result of the negotiation is the group agreement stating that a new transition is needed so that an expert may comment a question many times before answering it. The modified set of transitions is presented in Table 3.

Table 3 – Transitions for the example of social protocol and their associated desirability values

Source state	Destination state	Role	Action	φ
s_1	s_2	Normal	Ask question	1
s_2	s_2	**Expert**	**Comment question**	**1**
s_2	s_3	Expert	Answer question	1
s_2	s_3	Expert	Suppress question	0.5
s_2	s_4	Manager	Failure ending	1
s_3	s_2	Normal	Ask question	1
s_3	s_4	Manager	Failure ending	1
s_3	s_5	Manager	Successful ending	1

4. DISCUSSION

As process modeling is concerned, many works have already been conduced in the research field of workflow modelling and workflow management systems. Paul Buhler and Jose M. Vidal [Buhler 2005] proposed a mechanism allowing for enacting workflows in an adaptive way using multi-agent systems (MAS). Robert Müller and al. presented in [Müller 2004] various mechanisms for adaptation of workflows to deal with exception occurrences in running workflow instances, with an application to medical treatments. However, to our best knowledge, current works concerning workflow adaptation focus on interactions among software entities. Characteristics of interactions between humans, such as the importance of social aspects, are not or insufficiently taken into account by these works.

Still in the field of workflows, some works [Aalst 2000] have focused on formal models and conditions under which a modification of an existing – and potentially running – workflow retains workflow validity. However, in the case of human interactions, some of these conditions may be relaxed as adaptation of a social protocol may lead to a social protocol which is temporally invalid. Such a case appears when a new state is introduced. The state exists but transitions leading to it have to be defined. The same applies for transitions having the brand-new state as a source.

Some interesting works have been done in the field of electronic negotiations to model electronic negotiations with the help of negotiation protocols. In [Kersten 2004], it is stated in that, in the field of electronic negotiations, "the protocol is a formal model, often represented by a set of rules, which govern software processing, decision-making and communication tasks, and imposes restrictions on activities through the specification of permissible inputs and actions". One may noticed the similarity with the concept of social protocol. The reason for this fact is that the model presented in this paper was originally coming from a work on protocols for electronic negotiations [Picard 2005c]. However, to our knowledge, none of the works concerning negotiation protocols provides mechanisms for protocol adaptation. Moreover, these works are by nature limited to the field of electronic negotiations which is just a subset of the field of human collaboration.

5. CONCLUSIONS

While many works are currently done on modeling collaboration processes in which software entities (agents, web services) are involved, modeling collaboration processes in which mainly humans are involved is an area that still requires much attention from the research community. Some of the main issues to be addressed are the social aspects of collaboration and the adaptation capabilities of humans. In this paper both issues are addressed. The concept of social protocol aims at being a start of answer to the question of computer support for social collaboration. The idea of negotiation of social protocol is an attempt to weaken constraints usually limiting the interaction between collaborators, so that the adaptation capabilities of humans may be integrate in the life of a social protocol.

The main innovations presented in this paper are 1) the introduction of the desirability function as a way to provide filtering functions to social protocols, 2) the idea of negotiation of social protocols, based either on negotiation of the desirability function or on the negotiation of the structure of the protocol. The proposed concepts are currently under implementation as extensions to the *DynG* protocol [Huriaux 2005], a social protocol-based platform. The next steps will include a refinement of the concept of role, so that relationships between roles, e.g. specialization, compositions, may be integrate to the presented model. Automated support for social negotiation would be an interesting feature for a social adaptive protocol-based framework, but negotiation models supporting contextual and social elements are still to be built.

6. REFERENCES

[Aalst 2000] W.M.P. van der Aalst, T. Basten, H. M. W. Verbeek, P. A. C. Verkoulen, M. Voorhoeve, "Adaptive Workflow: On the Interplay between Flexibility and Support", Enterprise Information Systems, Kluwer Academic Publishers, Norwell, 2000, pp. 63-70.

[Buhler 2005] P. Buhler, J. M. Vidal, "Towards Adaptive Workflow Enactment Using Multiagent Systems", Information Technology and Management Journal, Special Issue on Universal Enterprise Integration, Vol. 6, (1), 2005; pp. 61-87.

[Camarinha-Matos 2005] L.M. Camarinha-Matos, H. Afsarmanesh, M. Ollus, "ECOLEAD: A Holistic Approach to Creation and Management of Dynamic Virtual Organizations", Proceedings of the 6th IFIP Working Conference on Virtual Enterprises (PRO-VE 2005), Valencia, Spain, September 26-28, 2005, Springer, in: Collaborative Networks and their Breeding Environments, pp. 3-16

[Chen 2003] H. Chen, T. Finin, A. Joshi, "An Ontology for Context-Aware Pervasive Computing Environments.", Knowledge Engineering Review, Special Issue on Ontologies for Distributed Systems, Vol. 18, No. 3. Cambridge University Press, 2003; pp. 197-207

[Chituc 2005] C.M. Chituc, A.L. Azevedo, "Multi-Perspective Challenges on Collaborative Networks Business Environments", , Proceedings of the 6th IFIP Working Conference on Virtual Enterprises (PRO-VE 2005), Valencia, Spain, September 26-28, 2005, Springer, in: Collaborative Networks and their Breeding Environments, pp. 25-32

[Dey 2001] A. K. Dey, D. Salber, G. D. Abowd, "A Conceptual Framework and a Toolkit for Supporting the Rapid Prototyping of Context-Aware Applications.", Human-Computer Interaction, 16(2-4), 2001; pp 97-166.

[Dockhorn 2005] P. Dockhorn Costa, L. Ferreira Pires, M. van Sinderen, "Designing a Configurable Services Platform for Mobile Context-Aware Applications", International Journal of Pervasive Computing and Communications (JPCC), Vol. 1, No. 1. Troubador Publishing (2005)

[Huriaux 2005] T. Huriaux, W. Picard, "DynG: a Multi-protocol Collaborative System", Proceedings of the 5th IFIP International Conference on e-Commerce, e-Business, and e-Government (I3E 2005), Poznan, Poland, October 26-28, 2005, Springer, in: Challenges of Expanding Internet: e-Commerce, e-Business and e-Government, pp. 591-605.

[Kersten 2004] G.E. Kersten, S.E. Strecker, K.P. Law, "Protocols for Electronic Negotiation Systems: Theoretical Foundations and Design Issue", in Proceedings of the 5th Conference on Electronic Commerce and Web Technologies (EC-Web04), Sarragoza, IEEE Computer Society, Spain, 2004.

[Müller 2004] R. Müller, U. Greiner, E. Rahm, "AGENTWORK: A Workflow-System Supporting Rule-Based Workflow Adaptation.". Data and Knowledge Engineering, Elsevier, 2004.

[Picard 2006] W. Picard, "Computer Support for Adaptive Human Collaboration with Negotiable Social Protocols", Proceedings of the 9th Int. Conference on Business Information Systems in cooperation with ACM SIGMIS, Klagenfurt, Austria, May 31 – June 2, 2006, LNCS, Springer, to appear.

[Picard 2005a] W. Picard, "Towards Support Systems for Non-Monolithic Electronic Negotiations. The Contract-Group-Message Model", Journal of Decision Systems, Electronic Negotiations - Models, Systems and Agents, Volume 13, No.4/2004; Hermes, Lavoisier (Paris); pp. 423-439

[Picard 2005b] W. Picard, "Modeling Structured Non-monolithic Collaboration Processes", Proceedings of the 6th IFIP Working Conference on Virtual Enterprises (PRO-VE 2005), Valencia, Spain, September 26-28, 2005, Springer, in: Collaborative Networks and their Breeding Environments, pp. 379-386

[Picard 2005c] W. Picard, T. Huriaux, "DynG: A Protocol-Based Prototype for Non-monolithic Electronic Collaboration", CSCW in Design 2005, LNCS 3865, 2006, pp. 41-50.

38

THE SOCIO-TECHNICAL DESIGN OF A SME KNOWLEDGE COMMUNITY IN THE CONSTRUCTION INDUSTRY

Dora Simões[1,3], António Lucas Soares[1,2]

INESC Porto[1], Faculty of Engineering Univ. Porto[2], ISCA Univ. Aveiro[3], PORTUGAL
dora.simoes@isca.ua.pt, asoares@inescporto.pt

This paper presents the socio-technical design of a knowledge community which is part of a system to support an industrial association based collaborative network in the sector of construction industry. There are many explanations around the virtual community concept. Here is presented a fundamental phase of the Know-Construct project which involved the design of the Construction Industry Knowledge (CIK) Community using three analytical approaches. The generic architecture of the supporting system (Knowledge Community Support - KCS) is described, highlighting information and knowledge management, community building facilities and semantic resources management.

1. INTRODUCTION

It is well known that organizations and the environment in which they operate have changed considerably in the last few decades. The particular case of the organizations in the construction sector is no exception to the rule. They too have to renew themselves rapidly in order to adapt to a more competitive and changing environment, be much more flexible than in the past and also need more sophisticated ways of managing their knowledge assets. Most of knowledge management systems have emerged from document-centric approaches and are able to efficiently support, although only a fraction, of the whole knowledge cycle (classifying, storing, and retrieving knowledge).

The Know-Construct project[1] intends to improve the effectiveness of the Construction Industry (CI) SME's by enhancing and extending the relationship with their customers through an innovative support regarding information and knowledge about products, processes and associated issues. This is achieved through specifically developed tools, supporting in particular the formation and operation of SME's knowledge communities in the context of Industry Association Groups (IAG). More concretely these objectives are to:

- Provide a platform to support the creation and management of a community of CI SME's, coordinated by an association, fostering collaboration and

[1] COLL-CT-2004-500276 KNOW-CONSTRUCT Internet Platform for Knowledge-based Customer Needs Management and Collaboration among SMEs in Construction Industry (2005-2007). Project co-funded by the European Community under the "Horizontal Research Activities Involving SMEs - Collective Research" Programme.

Please use the following format when citing this chapter:

Simões, D., Soares, A. L., 2006, in IFIP International Federation for Information Processing, Volume 224, Network-Centric Collaboration and Supporting Fireworks, eds. Camarinha-Matos, L., Afsarmanesh, H., Ollus, M., (Boston: Springer), pp. 361–370.

knowledge sharing among its members. Knowledge to be shared includes, besides product and services information; companies' experience (e.g. best practices). This will lead to a wider and deeper technical and professional competence shared by the SME's community, fundamental in its ability to satisfy customer needs, obtained through closer co-operation and knowledge exchange.

- Provide problem-solving support to the individual IAG member's customers regarding the selection of products, their applications and processes, as well as addressing other related problems such as legislative issues, safety issues etc. This will be materialized as an internet-based platform that will offer the possibility to establish a "one to one" communications medium. Manufacturers and wholesalers (SME) may interact with their customers, advising them on specific topics relying also on knowledge created and maintained by a community of SME's mentioned in the previous point.

KC system was then designed to provide comprehensive services to their users regarding a large scope of construction issues, although centred in the SME knowledge community.

This paper describes a fundamental phase of the project which was the characterization of the Construction Industry Knowledge (CIK) Community and the generic architecture of the supporting system (Knowledge Community Support - KCS).

2. CHARACTERIZATION OF THE CIK COMMUNITY

There are many explanations around the community concept. After thorough review of the literature on this subject, we characterize CIK community according three approaches that we agree to be of great importance to the success of creation and maintenance of this community. Accordingly the CIK Community is characterized based on: type of utility, participant's behavior and typology.

2.1 CIK Community as Hybrid Community

The classification of different types of utility (Cornejo, 2003) presents a basic predictive model of different types of communities, with particularly relevance for those that can generate some type of utility for someone. We therefore classify the CIK Community as a hybrid of a *Practice* and *Interest Community* (see Figure 1). On the one hand, company employees as individuals should see a direct utility to their particular jobs when participating in the CIK community. On the other hand this direct utility also comes into light when an employee (and consequently the company) realizes that, when solving a problem for an important customer, the information/knowledge used to reach the solution has been contributed by other community members. Nevertheless, not all the activities can be tracked to a causal benefit to the SME. For example, a chat session between two employees exchanging professional experiences or a report on a concern regarding the performance of a material in a news or blog item by another employee, are activities that make sense in a community but cannot be assigned a concrete and immediate value for the organization.

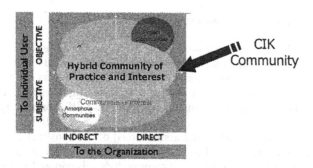

Figure 1 – CIK Community on Quadrant of Communities of Cornejo (2003)

2.2 CIK Community as Professional Community

Looking at professional development as the process of continually developing knowledge, skills and attitudes of professionals by means of formal and informal learning in the course of practice, the use of on-line knowledge communities for this, implies that an on-line knowledge community has to support this process. As a KC community member, professionals in the construction sector will have a place for continual professional development that gives: individualized, flexible and easy access to a coherent and current knowledge domain, a range of opportunities to interact with like-minded persons, and a range of opportunities to develop and exploit the knowledge domain. An example of this is: applying knowledge, learning from it, guiding others, disseminating ideas and results or doing research, embedded in a professional network. What do we expect from this use? Given the discussion so far, our premise is that the membership of professionals of an on-line knowledge community will have positive effects on their continuing development not only expressed in competences like knowledge, skills, experiences and attitude, but also, the development of organizational knowledge assets expressed in the growth and elaboration of the professional knowledge, applicability of knowledge and legitimacy of knowledge.

So, based on work of de Vries *et al.* (2004), we synthesize the following characteristics of CIK Community:

- The goal is to **develop and exploit knowledge** about civil construction sector.
- There are continuous interactions between participants in order to meet these goals.
- Information and communication processes are continuously made explicit.
- It **adds value to the participants** (professionals within the sector and customers alike).
- The on-line meeting place that is **usable**.
- The **culture focuses on the needs of the participants** as the route to high performance; involvement and participation create a sense of responsibility and ownership and, hence, greater commitment to the community.
- The context is highly complex and constantly evolving and the CIK Community will have to **continuously comply with the expectations** of its participants and their contextual of use of the system.

2.3 CIK Community as a Organization-Sponsored Community

Based on the typology of virtual communities proposed by Porter (2004) where the communities are classified under two levels: establishment and relationship orientation (see **Figure 2**), we classify the CIK Community as an organization-sponsored community relatively to **type of establishment** and as commercial community relatively to the **relationship orientation**. CIK Community will be a commercial organization-sponsored community because it will be sponsored by commercial organizations (SME's and associations) of the construction sector. This community will have key stakeholders and/or beneficiaries (ex. customers) that will play an important part in sponsoring the community's mission and goals. Being an organization-sponsored community, will foster relationships both among members (e.g. professionals belonging to the associations of the project partnership) and between individual members (e. g. customers) and the sponsoring organizations (associations of the project partnership).

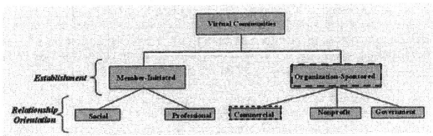

Figure 2 - Typology of virtual communities (Porter, 2004)

Based on the classification of the CIK Community under the virtual community concept and the attributes commonly suggested in the literature to characterize virtual communities (Mueller-Prothmann and Siedentopf, 2003; Blanchard, 2004; Burnett, G. and Buerkle, H., 2004), we now specify the key attributes of the CIK Community. The key attributes that will allow characterization of the CIK Community can be summarized as the Five Ps (Porter, 2004): Purpose (Content of Interaction), Place (Extent of Technology Mediation of Interaction), Platform (Design of Interaction), Population (Pattern of Interaction) and Profit Model (Return on Interaction).

Table 1 - Conceptualization of the CIK Community attributes

Purpose	To share professional knowledge aiming to provide a better individual service to company's customers.
Place	Virtual place where companies develop and maintain social and economic relationships, mostly virtual, but also physical (e.g., association meetings, customer contacts, etc.).
Platform	Synchronous and asynchronous communication (hybrid). Interactivity is multi-modal: co-presence based interaction through instant messaging; differed interaction through basic mechanisms such as forums or weblogs, and through complex tools such as content management tools, fostering coordination mechanisms (workflow).

Population	The Association is both the context of interaction and an actor in it. Companies and individual professionals are actors. Individual professionals can assume both an individual role (the professional) or organizational role (company's representative). Customers can assume also the role of actor in the community. The motivation of the interaction is due to both individual interests and company orientated goals. Companies also look for enhanced reputation and improved levels in efficacy and efficiency. Individual professions may also seek peer recognition and personal improvement. Such companies, associations and individual professionals are geographically and socially dispersed and focus on the functional benefits of the community such as information acquisition or problem solving. It is likely that the interaction patterns will be characterised by a mix of small group characteristics (where strong ties tend to dominate), and network characteristics (where weak ties are prominent and stressful ties are likely). Relationships are addressed by user needs, where small group and network attributes are blended.
Profit model	Revenue generation of individual companies in the construction sector. Although the CIK community will provide mainly intangible benefits, it is expected that by providing a better service to customers, individual companies will increase their revenues.

2.4 CIK Community Concept

To summarize we define the CIK Community as *an aggregation of professionals and customers who interact around a specific shared interest of construction sector, sharing information and knowledge about products, services, techniques, legal aspects, experiences, etc, and where the interaction is totally supported and/or mediated by web technology and guided by some agreed protocols or norms.*

3. THE GENERIC ARQUITECTURE OF KCS SYSTEM

As mentioned before, the KC project has a very specific goal: to enable individual SME's to better solve the problems of their customers. Therefore, KCS is focused on pursuing this goal in the first place. Although a knowledge community encompasses, as stated before, mechanisms that surpass this simple instrumental goal, the initial vision of the KCS system was specifically conceived with this in mind. This means that the KCS system supports CIK community building in a broad sense, though focused fundamentally in generating wide ranging and detailed knowledge to be used in managing the SME's customers' relationship, particularly in problem solving. The operationalization of the KCS system is made through the use of mechanisms (Nabeth et al., 2002; Hearn et al., 2002; Simões and Soares, 2004) that will allow:

1. For the support the social processes (trust building, group formation and coordination), i.e., conditions for tacit knowledge exchange;
2. For increased levels of interactivity and to stimulate the dynamic exchange of knowledge (collaborative content management systems);

3. To support the personalization of user interaction (via the selection and presentation of content), maximize the impact of distributed knowledge and also to facilitate the development of new relationships between the users).

3.1 The KCS system concept

Keeping in mind the basic idea that the KCS system should support the CIK Community building in a broad sense, but focused fundamentally in generating a knowledge base that is as comprehensive and detailed as possible to be used in managing the SME's customers' relationship, particularly in problem solving, the following general functions (see Figure 3) of this module were specified:

1. **Community building tools**: this part of the KCS system supports the processes of community building by providing the instruments to foster professional interaction and socialization. Forums and weblogs are two such instruments and are tailored in KCS to be tightly integrated with the semantic structure supporting knowledge management in KC.
2. **Semantic resources management**: this is the infrastructure and corresponding set of functionalities that support information and knowledge acquisition, organization and storage in KCS system. More specifically, they enable the (i) management of classifications, thesauri and vocabulary, (ii) the acquisition of knowledge from digital content (including forums and weblogs entries, web pages, etc.) both internal to the CIK and from external sources, (iii) the maintenance of an ontology which is the base of knowledge representation, access and storage.
3. **Knowledge resources access**: creating, searching and updating knowledge resources is a fundamental set of functionalities in KCS. Although much of the community's information/knowledge will be created in communication/interaction processes (forums, weblogs), there will be also the need to create/access knowledge in a more structured way. Digital content management and document management are the natural approaches regarding this issue.

3.2 The KCS system layers

This generic architecture can be decomposed in two layers: *KCS Core Services layer* and *Systems/Applications layer*. KCS Core Services layer provide a set of services centered in the semantic resources management of KC.

The basic architectural idea of KCS is to have a set of services to be used by specific, adaptable and, eventually, off-the-shelf systems/applications. The rationale is to take advantage of as great a number of open source systems/applications as possible that already provide the end user functionalities required in a knowledge community. For example, we can use a content management system (CMS) such as Zope/Plone[2] or OpenCMS[3] providing off-the-shelf functionalities to organize reports, data sheets, legal documents, and to publish web pages related with some community topic. The CMS is configured and extended to use content/document services, search services and semantic navigation services in order to provide value added knowledge management to the community.

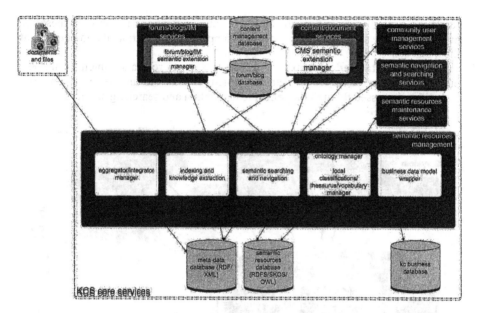

Figure 3 – KCS System Functional Architecture

The KCS core (see Figure 4) services are divided into a *Semantic Resource Management* layer and a set of functionalities that provide the systems/applications with access to the semantic resources as described below.

Ontology manager - this part of the semantic resources management deals first with all the aspects of maintaining the CIK community's ontology and allows users to: browse the entities, add/remove concepts/relations, create new attributes, deprecate a concept, import taxonomies, and configure system settings. It should also handle multilingual ontologies. Closely related with the ontology manager, is the *local classification/thesaurus manager*. Classifications, thesaurus, vocabularies are important semantic resources in the CI sector. This functionality is fundamental in managing the local aspects of the CIK community.

Indexing and knowledge extraction - a CIK Community is a dynamic social organization. It is obvious that the community knowledge will evolve and consequently, that the way in which the participants organize their knowledge will also change with time. This requires that KCS system be able to cope with these dynamics by enabling the CIK ontology to be (to some extent) automatically updated from the knowledge sources managed by the community (documents, web pages, etc.) and from content generated interactively such as weblogs and forums entries. This sub-system provides a set of functionalities that implement the before mentioned ontology updates, as well as functionalities to classify the digital content used by the community.

Semantic searching and navigation - this is a set of services provided to the upper layer systems/applications for searching and navigating the KC content using the ontology/thesaurus as the underlying structure. In order to support the KC system's sophisticated searching capabilities, this set of functionalities includes the capacity to search and reason about metadata.

Aggregator/integrator - specific external knowledge sources related with the CIK Community must be accessed by the KC user. This part of the semantic resources management will aggregate meta-data descriptions in the case these are available. If they are not, this manager will support the generation and integration of the metadata.

Business data model wrapper - provide access to relevant content in the KC business database through the metadata structure. The relevant content is indexed and will be accessed through the semantic navigation and searching services.

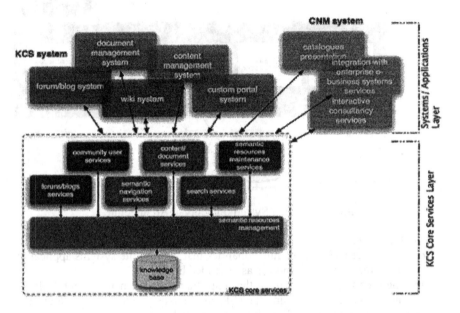

Figure 4 – KCS Core Services

Besides the semantic resources management functionalities, the KCS system core services will provide a set of functionalities to link the KCS semantic resources to the end-user systems applications. These include:

- **Content/document services** - these are the services that provide access to indexing, knowledge extraction, semantic navigation and searching for the content and document management functionalities.
- **Forums/weblogs/IM services** - these are the services that provide access to indexing, knowledge extraction, semantic navigation and searching for the forums, weblogs or instant messaging functionalities.
- **Semantic navigation and search services** - will provide access to semantic navigation and searching to upper layer applications that are not part of the two previous categories.
- **Community user management services** - these services encompass all that is necessary to create, maintain and access the profiles of the end-users from a community point of view. This includes the support to social relationships through sophisticated searching and matching of profiles and content.
- **Semantic resources maintenance services** - the maintenance of the CIK ontology and the local ontologies is accessed by the upper layer applications through these services.

3.3 The KCS system design

Semantic web technologies are a fundamental option if the KCS is to provide complex information retrieval, both internally and externally to the CIK community. We think that compliance with the semantic web is potentially one of the major success factors for Know-Construct. This concurs with the opinion expressed by the CEN Workshop Agreement on European eConstruction Ontology (EeO) (CWA 15142, 2004) stating that it is possible to rely on a standard "foundation" where complementary efforts can be combined in a harmonic and holistic way, especially regarding the developments related to the Semantic Web.

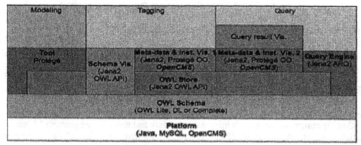

Figure 5 - KC high-level design and development tools

A strategic aspect then to be considered is the compliance with the Semantic Web in the sense that the European Ontology for the construction sector has to be aware of the recommendations and developments promoted, mostly, by the W3C. According to this view, a high-level design was developed which organizes KC functionalities in four main areas: modelling (ontology development and use), tagging, query, and visualization. As infrastructure and development tools, Jena2, Protégé, and OpenCMS were chosen (see Figure 5).

4. CONCLUSIONS AND FURTHER WORK

In this paper was presented the characterization of the Construct Industry Knowledge (CIK) Community according to three approaches in the context of the Know-Construct project. Summarizing, the CIK Community was conceptualized as *an aggregation of professionals and customers who interact around a specific shared interest of construction sector, sharing information and knowledge about products, services, techniques, legal aspects, experiences, etc, and where the interaction is totally supported and/or mediated by web technology and guided by some agreed protocols or norms.*

To present the generic architecture of the KCS (Knowledge Community Support) system that supports the CIK community, it was described the concept, layers and high-level design of KCS system. The high-level design organizes KC functionalities in four main areas: modelling (ontology development and use), tagging, query, and visualization. The future work will involve, obviously, the implementation and validation of the system. Further, one of the crucial development and validation tasks are related with the ontology implementation and the associated functionalities. Although the phase regarding the analysis and specification of the CIK ontology (high-level) and local ontologies integration process definition has been comprehensive, and involved the users (Soares *et al.*, 2006), it has been necessary to refine the requirements and design options through the use of an early prototype. This process is complex as we are dealing with virtual communities, thus there was the need of using innovative ways to establish a social test environment in order to achieve the goals of prototyping. This will be the subject of a forthcoming paper.

REFERENCES

1. Blanchard, A. (2004). Virtual behaviour settings: An application of behaviour setting theories to virtual communities. Journal of Computer Mediated Communication, 9(2).
2. Burnett, G., & Buerkle, H. (2004). Information exchange in virtual communities: A comparative study. Journal of Computer Mediated Communication, 9(2).
3. Cornejo, M. (2003). Utility, value and Knowledge Communities. Knowledge Communities. online: http://www.providersedge.com/docs/km_articles/Utility_Value_and_K-Communities.pdf (last accessed January 2006)
4. Gronau, N. and E.-M. Kern (2004). Collaborative Engineering Communities in Shipbuilding. Virtual Enterprises and Collaborative Networks (PROVE'04), Toulouse, France, Kluwer Academic Publishers.
5. Hearn, P., A. Bradier, et al. (2002). "Building communities: organizational knowledge management within the european comission's information society technologies programme." ITcon 7: 63-68.
6. Maedche, A., B. Motik, et al. 2003. "Ontologies for enterprise knowledge management." IEEE Intelligent Systems (Intelligent Information Processing): 2-9.
7. Mueller-Prothmann, T. and C. Siedentopf (2003). Designing online knowledge communities: developing a usability evaluation criteria catalogue. 3rd European Knowledge Management Summer School, San Sebastian, Spain.
8. Nabeth, T., A. A. Angehrn, et al. (2002). Towards Personalized, Socially Aware and Active Knowledge Management Systems. E-business and E-work - Challenges and Achievements in E-business and E-work, Amsterdam, Holland, IOS Press.
9. Porter, C. E. (2004). "A Typology of Virtual Communities: A Multi-Disciplinary Foundation for Future Research." Journal of Computer-Mediated Communication (JCMC) 10 (1), Article 3.
10. Simões, D. and A. L. Soares (2004). The Formation and Dissolution of Organizational Networks: A Knowledge Management Perspective. Virtual Enterprises and Collaborative Networks (PROVE'04), Toulouse, France, Kluwer Academic Publishers.
11. Soares, A.L., Silva, M. Simões, D., 2006, Selecting and structuring semantic resources to support SMEs, ICEIS 2006,
12. Staab, S., J. Angele, et al. (2000). AI for the Web: Ontology-based Community Web Portals. AAAI/IAAI Conferences.
13. Staab, S., R. Studer, et al. (2001). "Knowledge processes and ontologies" IEEE Intelligent Systems(Knowledge Management): 26-34.
14. Stojanovic, N., A. Maedche, et al. (2001). SEAL: A Framework for Developing SEmantic PortALs. K-Cap, Victoria, Canada.
15. Vries, S. d. and P. Kommers (2004). "Online knowledge communities: future trends and research issues." International Journal of Web Based Communities 1(1): 115 - 123.
16. Weib, P. and A. Maedche (2003). Towards adaptive ontology-based virtual business networks. PRO-VE'03, Lugano, Switzerland.

39

USING SOCIAL CAPITAL AS A CONCEPTUAL FRAMEWORK FOR PROFESSIONAL VIRTUAL COMMUNITIES FORMALIZATION

Servane Crave [1, 2], Thierry Bouron [1], Sylvie Ladame [1, 2]
[1] France Telecom R&D division,
{surname.name}@orange-ft.com
[2] University of Nice Sophia Antipolis
FRANCE

This paper presents the first step of a research work which aims at predicting the propensity of Professional Virtual Communities (PVC) to create temporary alliances of business. This work is starting from the observation that up to now these business oriented communities lack a conceptual framework for analyzing this issue in a theoretical way. Our approach consists in developing such a conceptual framework using Social Capital as a structuring element. This paper shows how to improve the formalization of PVC by revisiting and using Social Capital concept.

1. INTRODUCTION

It is often advanced that professional communities acting in industrial sectors could be a way to foster cooperation among firms. The interpersonal relationships developed inside the communities could enable SME to have access to competences for the life-time of a project, competences that they can not afford on a long-time basis. However until now there has been a lack of conceptualization and formalization of the professional communities to establish in theoretical ways in which context they can effectively create or reinforce temporary alliances of business inside clusters of SME called hereafter Virtual Organizations (VO).

Our first assumption is that Social Capital models are relevant for formalizing links between PVC and VO. A lot of similarities in the use of terms actually appear when studying Social Capital, PVC and VO. For instance, professional communities are usually addressed using dimensions such as social norms, social values (trust, and networks) which appear to be constituents of Social Capital; according to Fukuyama [9], "alliances (of business) operate on shared norms and values beyond those necessary for ordinary market transactions." Although Social Capital seems relevant to analyze the concepts of communities, the review of literature achieved so far shows a lack of research investigating professional communities with a Social Capital perspective that validates this assumption.

Please use the following format when citing this chapter:

Crave, S., Bouron, T., Ladame, S., 2006, in IFIP International Federation for Information Processing, Volume 224, Network-Centric Collaboration and Supporting Fireworks, eds. Camarinha-Matos, L., Afsarmanesh, H., Ollus, M., (Boston: Springer), pp. 371–378.

Our second assumption is that the communities developing efficient and productive cooperation have a higher propensity to develop VO. Since the Social Capital can be recognized as a stimulating factor for efficient cooperation, this question is still open.

In the long term, our aim is to enhance and use Social Capital theories to predict if certain kinds of PVC have more or less propensity to create VO. The objective of this paper is to improve the formalization of PVC from these theories. It describes the Social Capital conceptual framework that allows us to address this question in a more theoretical way that has been done until now. After this introduction of our fields of investigation, Section 2 of this paper presents the Social Capital conceptual framework that we have designed from a review of Social Capital theories. Section 3 introduces the Professional Virtual Communities baselines and details some key features useful to our perspective. Section 4 presents the summary of the links established between PVC and Social Capital and details the next steps of our research program.

2. SOCIAL CAPITAL CONCEPTUAL FRAMEWORK

When studying Social Capital over the last decades, one can notice a shift from developing theories around this concept from a societal perspective (civic commitment which is more or less synonymous with active citizenship, leisure, etc.) to the extension on professional issues, such as networks of professionals and firms. On this topic, **social relationships** appear to be the main concern of scholars. Therefore, it is commonly agreed that the extent to which an actor has access to resources through Social Capital will depend on three criteria: the actor's connections, the strength of these connections and all the resources available through these connections. This relates to the noun **connectivity** which can be defined as the degree to which someone has connections.[1]

Social relationships are mainly addressed by Social Capital theories and connectivity by social network theories. We use as a starting point for our conceptual framework the Nahapiet & Ghoshal model [16] that has constituted a real breakthrough over the last decades, since it first defines a structured environment of Social Capital with inputs from both Social Capital theories and social network theories. Their model is based on constitutive elements distributed in three key dimensions: Cognitive, Relational and Structural (i.e. network of connections). Their model being focused on the creation of intellectual capital, we will transpose it to the PVC context and enhance it when required with additional works.

The following review of literature on Social Capital enables us to envision our conceptual framework where Social Capital refers to elements of social organization summing up three interrelated dimensions whereas Nahapiet and Goshal [16] see them analytically as distinct dimensions and didn't achieve further developments on their interrelationships. Shared Cognitive dimension and Relational dimension relate to interpersonal relationships (intrinsic and extrinsic behaviours, specific to the

---

[1] *This is different from the definition of connectivity in Information and Communication Technologies (ICT) context, where connectivity is seen more on the propensity of being connected and interconnected than to the fact that exchanges and interactions have already occurred on this connection.*

individuals) whereas Structural dimension defines the configuration of the network in terms of connectivity (architecture of the network [20]). Both two first dimensions are going to impact the network's configuration through interactions and collective actions; in return, action feedback will impact them. Cooperation depends on action's efficiency partly determined by the Structural dimension. These interrelations are represented in fig.1.

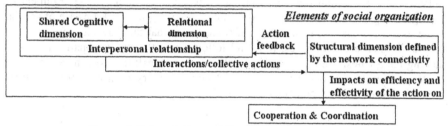

Figure 1: Interrelations of Social Capital dimensions

2.1 Inputs from Social Capital theories to Cognitive and Relational dimensions

Several characteristics can be found in the literature to provide a complete overview of Social Capital constituents. First defined by Jane Jacobs [11] as "the result of *interpersonal relationships* developed over time which create the basis for *trust, cooperation and collective actions* among *communities*", Social Capital has been enhanced by Bourdieu [1] with the subsequent features: *feelings of gratitude, respect and friendship*. Cohen [6] adds to these definitions the ideas of active connections among individuals, mutual understanding and shared values which tie individuals in social networks and communities, then enabling cooperative actions.

Putnam [18] has for his part taken into account "elements of a social organisation such as *networks, norms,* and *values* which facilitate *coordination* and trust for a mutual benefit". Social networks are represented by interconnected groups usually having at least one attribute in common. Social norms are informal rules which govern behaviours: the keystone element being reciprocity. Social values are strongly linked to the issue of trust and can be summed up under the subsequent questions: how can one actor be sure that others will act as they have promised or as they are supposed to, or how can one be sure that they are trustful? Putnam [19] has moreover defined two types of Social Capital: "*bridging* Social Capital" as bonds of connectedness that are formed across diverse social groups, and "*bonding* Social Capital" which only cements homogenous groups. This definition is a first step toward the introduction of a structural dimension detailed hereafter.

2.2 Inputs from Social Network theory to the Structural dimension

As Social Capital is a multi facet concept, inputs from Social Network Theory about connectivity are of interest for our research work. Social network theory represents networks in terms of nodes (individual actors within the networks) and ties (relationships between the actors). Scholars have divergent visions of the required network topology to create Social Capital: Coleman [7] establishes as sources of Social Capital very *dense networks* in which each individual is connected and seen by others. With this definition, he introduces the notion of a facilitated development of trust among these closed networks (*network closure*). Coleman argues that the success of a community is its closure and we can assume that this is certainly due to a strong *social proximity*. On the contrary, Burt [2, 3] argues that "the *structural hole* argument is that Social Capital is created by a network in which people can broker connections between otherwise disconnected segments." His theory advocates for an open and extended network generating creativity, closure of the network being then seen as reductive in terms of innovation.

The concept of *weak ties* developed by Granovetter [10] is to a large extent also linked to Social Capital development. According to this author, "the argument of Strengthening Weak Ties (SWT) implies that only *bridging* weak ties are of special value to individuals; the significance of weak ties is that they are far more likely to be bridges than are strong ties. It should follow, then, that the occupational groups making the greatest use of weak ties are those whose weak ties do connect to social circles different from one's own." Social Network theory reinforces the structural dimension as defined by Nahapiet and Goshal [16].

3. PVC BASELINES

This paper considers existing communities in a professional context interacting mainly in a virtual way that could develop businesses activities. The IST6 Ecolead Integrated Project[2] has explored what such communities could be and calls them Professional Virtual Communities (PVC). Ecolead PVC is defined "*as an association of "individuals" explicitly pursuing an economic objective identified by a specific knowledge scope. It aims at generating value through members' interaction, sharing and collaboration. This interaction is optimized by the synergic use of ICT-mediated.*" Until now, few cases studies have analysed the development of business under the form of VO by existing professional communities. The most known cases are in software developments and especially in the Open Source (OS) context. In this section we will characterize the PVC starting from the most widespread types of communities in the professional context and summarize the elements that define or characterize such a community, next we will capture the features that have enabled the development of business oriented activities from existing professional communities in OS context.

3.1 Professional communities' characteristics

Above all we need to clarify what kind of communities we are considering and which one we focus on. We are mainly concerned by communities where the virtual and remote coordination is the rule, the geographical regrouping being the exception. These communities are not necessarily restricted to a given firm. Communities established with a business goal, especially PVC, are still a future projection. However, various types of communities can be considered in this context: communities of practice (Cop), epistemic communities, learning communities, communities of interest. In professional context, Cops are probably the most widespread forms of communities and own some features overlapping the epistemic communities; the learning communities can be seen as a rather radical form of Cops whereas communities of interest are virtual places on the Internet where individuals can exchange ideas on a given subject and appear to be further

---

2 *Additional information on www.ecolead.org*

from a productive system than Cops and have less legitimacy in a professional context. Consequently we will focus on Cop.

A Cop can be defined as "a group of people who share a concern, a set of problems, or a passion about a topic, and who deepen their knowledge and expertise in this area by interacting on ongoing basis" [21]. It is characterized by the fact that community members have a *common purpose*, there is a real *member participation*, the *motivation* of individual participation is composed of an *interest in* (individual utility function), and an *interest for* the social (civic) dimension of a given community, there is a social *proximity* (geographical versus institutional in virtual Cops) between members, the *value of the person* is the key element in the system organization. *Common purpose* can be for instance relative to learning objective or best practices development. It could be seen as a specific case of *joint intention* that is related to the elaboration of knowledge useful for *distributed problems solving*. The joint intention has been described in an operational way as a *persistent shared goal*[3]. *Participation* covers in fact several concepts. On the one hand it refers to the effective implication of individuals, i.e. the *observation of individual actions* in collective activities and the evaluation of the cooperativeness and goodwill of the individuals; on the other hand it refers to the *network centric positioning* of individuals in a set of collective actions. The *degree of participation* is used as a structural element of the community. Three to four levels of participations linked to expertise levels are considered (kernels, experts, beginners, lurkers). The reference value in Cops is centered on the *individual value*. It is difficult to model this value as a whole (i.e. *not contextual.*) Participation and *reputation* criteria can be used to do it partially. In broad lines, the value of an individual can be perceived as a function of evaluation which has participation as input and reputation as output. *Interest in* can be seen as the utility function that will determine the interest for a person to invest a collaborative activity corresponding to some expectations: learning, *recognition, reciprocity. Interest for* refers to the need of an individual related to the collective identification. Let us recall that the prevalence of the individual process of identification to the collective one is rather recent. This identification gives in particular to individuals a set of social values and rules of actions which will make their possible sphere of activities more deterministic, and make the coordination inside the community easier. *Social proximity* defines a shared space of representations, rules of action and model of thought (ethics). The outline of a given virtual community is thus delimited by institutional proximity in contrast with geographic or organizational proximities.

3.2 Characteristics that enable Cops to be a system of production

From an economic point of view, there are two fundamental differences between Cops in a professional context and temporary alliances of business (VO):

- Business alliances are production systems whereas Cops are not -considering that classical understanding of production systems do not see the knowledge creation as a product-; Cops with their learning dimension are closer from consumption systems.

---

[3] *For a formalization of several concepts mentioned in this paragraph, in particular collective action, cooperativeness evaluation, joint intention, distributed problem solving, the reader can refer to research done in the Multi-Agents context [8].*

- The business temporary alliances are market based types of coordination mechanisms whereas the Cops are not. Let us note that they are not hierarchical based types of coordination any more and as a consequence do not lie within the scope of the usual economic approaches [5, 14].

These two points can be considered in order to determine on which conditions Cop can form VO. The OS context gives us an example of a community that is also a production system that delivers products and that has found a solution (free products) to be compatible with a market based type of coordination. We have identified in OS communities various conditions under which Cop would be able to shift towards a system of production.

- The products achieved (software sources) have a very high level of "standardization", by nature the programming codes are determinist and correspond to a very high level of *knowledge exchanges formalization*.
- The rules of the community with regard to the commercial spheres are formalized by a *social contract* (open source licenses).
- The products can be thought and achieved in the *distributed modular approach* and in addition, this distributed environment can be *virtual* (all exchanges are mediated by ICT tools). The software production is more and more based on a *component* approach where each component can be developed separately. The negotiation between the various contributors doesn't necessarily need face to face meetings because the semantic of exchanged knowledge (code programming) doesn't result from a negotiated process.

4. FINDINGS AND RESEARCH ISSUES

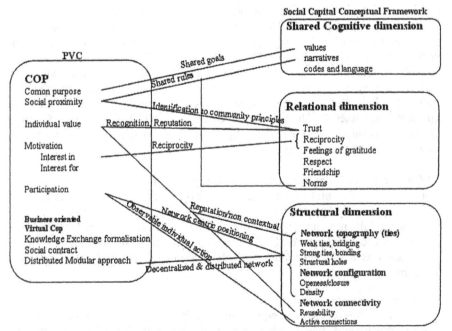

Figure 2: Links between PVC features and Social Capital conceptual framework

4.1 Links between PVC and Social Capital elements

This subsection shows the links between PVC features and the Social Capital conceptual framework elements. It underlines how these links can be used to achieve a questionnaire for an empirical cases based study of PVC in order to assess their Social Capital.

In fig.2, the links are labelled; they join the key features of PVC to the conceptual framework elements. This approach presents the advantages of addressing PVC characteristics in a more theoretical way and of enlarging the way to study them. For instance, "shared goals" links "common purpose" (PVC) to "values" (shared cognitive dimension). Consequently we reuse work developed on shared values by Fukuyama [9] who defines Social Capital "as the existence of a certain set of informal values or norms shared among members of a group that permit cooperation among them." for addressing common purpose issues in Cop and expressing relative questions. "Social proximity" is linked by "shared rules" to (shared) narratives. We will be able to steer our research towards authors such as Orr [17] who explained how shared narratives - soft knowledge that is tacit and difficult to codify - become artefacts (e.g., shared rules) since through them experience becomes reproducible and reusable. "Identification to community principles" links "social proximity" (PVC) and "trust" (Relational dimension) that refers partly to expected behaviours. Research works that we are also leading attempt to design a trust model will be there capitalized [15]. We can reuse, in PVC context, Lin's work [13] for the "recognition, Reputation" label, as his vision of Social Capital represents the "Investment in social relations with expected returns in the marketplace".

For the structural dimension, i.e. all issues in touch with the network, "participation" is one of the relevant PVC features that can be studied with the structural dimension via "Network Centric position" and "Observable individual action" links. [4] defines closeness of the two partners as key to the degree of tacit knowledge transfer. This analysis is a result based on Knowledge Management background.

4.2 Future works

We have identified elements which are missing in the Social Capital framework to improve and perfect the PVC characteristics modelling. Then, there is a need to add a distinction between individual and collective actions and a need to address the distributed dimensions. For these two points, Multi-agent formalization will be used to complete the conceptual framework [8].

With this framework, we explore to what point Social Capital allows us to differentiate more or less productive PVC especially in terms of innovative creations, efficient coordination and successful cooperation. This propensity to have productive cooperation is intrinsic to VO. We are currently addressing cooperation and coordination in VO context by combining three main dimensions: *Proximity* (geographical, technological and organisational), *Degree of formalization of Cooperation or Coordination* and frequency of *Interactions* [12]. The formalization of VO will be improved in using and completing, if necessary, the Social Capital conceptual framework presented in this paper. Once the set of formalizations is ended, we will be able to establish transitivity links between PVC and VO and be able to provide assumptions to the propensity of certain kinds of PVC to form a VO.

We will next validate the assumptions based on this theoretical work via an empirical study on different kinds of Professional Communities: intra/inter organisation communities such as (virtual) COP and inter firm communities such as PVC. Findings of this empirical study on real communities will give us accurate inputs on professional communities and their ability to form temporary alliances of firms or professionals. In a later step and depending on the results of this empirical validation, our research target is to work out a first set of functionalities for an ICT tool in the context of PVC creating VO.

4. REFERENCES

1. Bourdieu, P, " The Forms of Capital ", in J. G. Richardson (dir.), Handbook of Theory and Research for the Sociology of Education, New York, Greenwood Press. 1986
2. Burt R.S. "Structural Holes versus Network Closure as Social Capital" in Social Capital: Theory and Research edited by Nan Lin, Karen S.Cook, and R.S. Burt. A. de Gruyter, 2001
3. Burt R.S. "Structural holes and Good Ideas" pre-print of an article to appear in the American Journal of Sociology 2003
4. Cavusgil, S.T., Calantone, R.J., Zhao, Y. "Tacit knowledge transfer and firm innovation capability ", in Journal of Business & Industrial Marketing, 18 (1), 6-2 2003
5. Coase R "The nature of the firm" Economica 1937
6. Cohen, D., & Prusak, L. "In good company: How Social Capital makes organizations work." Massachusetts: Harvard Business School Press. 2001
7. Coleman, J. S. "Social Capital in the creation of human capital." American Journal of Sociology, 94, 95-120. 1988
8. Ferber J "Multi-Agent systems" Addison-Wesley 1999
9. Fukuyama, F. "The Great Disruption: Human nature and the reconstitution of social order", Profile Books, London 2000
10. Granovetter "The strength of weak ties: a network theory revisited" presented as a paper at the Conference on Contributions of Network Analysis to Structural Sociology, Albany, N.Y., April 4, 1981.
11. Jacobs, J. "The death and life of great American cities." NJ: Penguin Books. 1965
12. Ladame S, Crave S "Le concept de "Proximité" comme élément structurant et favorisant des coopérations des modes organisationnels réticulaires et modulaires." Cinquièmes journées de la proximité June 06 Bordeaux
13. Lin N "Building a network theory of Social Capital" Connections 22(1):28-51, INSNA 1999
14. Malone T W "Modeling coordination in organizations and markets" Management Science volume 33 n°10 1987
15. Melaye D, Demazeau Y, Bouron T, "Which Adequate Trust Model for Trust Networks?" 3rd IFIP Conference on Artificial Intelligence Applications and Innovations (AIAI), June 2006
16. Nahapiet J, S. Ghoshal "Social Capital, Intellectual Capital, and the Organizational Advantage" in The strategic Management of Intellectual capital and organizational knowledge – Oxford University Press
17. Orr J. "Sharing Knowledge Celebrating Identity: War Stories and Community Memory in a Service Culture." In Middleton D. S. and Edwards D. (Eds) Collective Remembering: Memory in Society. Beverley Hills CA: Sage Publication 1990
18. Putnam, R.D. "The prosperous Community", The American Prospect vol.4 n°13 1993
19. Putnam, R.D. "Bowling alone: America's declining Social Capital." journal of Democracy, 6, 65-78 1995
20. Thomas C, Barlatier P-J "Solution TIC et développement de capacités réseau : le rôle du processus de codification dans l'expérimentation KMP." AIMS, XVème Conférence Internationale de Management Stratégique juin 2006. 2006
21. E. Wenger, R. McDermott, and W. Snyder "Cultivating Communities of Practice." Harvard business School Press 2002

PART 13

VO CREATION

40 OPERATIONAL DESIGN IN VO SUPPLY NETWORKS CREATION

Cathal Heavey, PJ Byrne, Paul Liston, James Byrne
Enterprise Research Centre, University of Limerick, cathal.heavey@ul.ie
IRELAND

Outsourcing is a major driver in the growth of Virtual Organisations (VOs) in the manufacturing domain. These outsourcing networks can be classified as Virtual Organisations (VOs) as they are created from different organisational entities for a specific purpose and exist for a specified period of time. The electronics industry is in the vanguard with a projected 23% of electronics manufacturing forecasted to be outsourced in 2007. The process of establishing these VOs is known in the industry as the Request for X (RFx) process. This paper argues that in the creation of VO supply networks, supply network design support is required.

1. INTRODUCTION

It is estimated that in total 75% of the EU GDP and 70% of employment in Europe is related to manufacturing (Flegel, 2004). Outsourcing networks are a defining characteristic of modern manufacturing and uptake by companies of this manufacturing strategy is predicted for strong growth in the future. For example, in 2003, about 15% of all electronics manufacturing was outsourced. That percentage is predicted to grow steadily into the future with a projected 23% of electronics manufacturing outsourced by 2007 (Carbone, 2005). Growth in outsourcing is also predicted across several other sectors. For example, in the pharmaceutical industry the value of the drug discovery outsourcing market is reportedly set to increase at a rate of 15% from a 2005 figure of $4.1 billion to nearly $7.2 billion by 2009 (Kalorama Information, 2005). Clearly, this structural adjustment of industry will require manufacturing enterprises across Europe to adapt.

Outsourcing networks (or virtual networks) typically link highly innovative but deverticalized lead firms (OEMs) with sets of highly functional suppliers who provide a wide range of production-related services (Sturgeon, 2000). These networks are highly flexible systems characterized by fluid relationships with short-term contracts between participants within the network. The process of establishing a contact between two enterprises in a virtual network is known collectively as the Request for X (RFx) process, with RFx representing Request for Information (RFI), Request for Quotation (RFQ), etc. In this process a customer (i.e., Original Equipment Manufacturer (OEM), Contact Manufacturing (CM) or sub-supplier), also denoted as a buyer, will issue a RFQ to suppliers and typically request a response to the RFQ within weeks.

Current literature pertaining to VOs generally examines obstacles to the creation and execution of VOs and presents innovative methodologies for tackling these issues. For example, Bosch-Sijtsema (1997) studied possible communication difficulties faced by VOs and identified five boundaries which both create and

Please use the following format when citing this chapter:

Heavey, C., Byrne, P. J., Liston, P., Byrne, J., 2006, in IFIP International Federation for Information Processing, Volume 224, Network-Centric Collaboration and Supporting Fireworks, eds. Camarinha-Matos, L., Afsarmanesh, H., Ollus, M., (Boston: Springer), pp. 381–388.

inhibit learning and communication. These are time, space, diversity, structure and distribution and are all characteristics of a VO. Meanwhile, the CONOISE project (Norman et al., 2003) examined methodologies for the initial formation and continued management of VOs in dynamic, open and competitive environments. Due to the often dispersed nature of VOs they can be heavily reliant on communication technology. Consequently, VO related literature maintains a focus on new technologies which can support the continued operation of such organisations (Kamio et al., 2002). This paper examines the formation of VOs but emphasises the importance of streamlining this task into standard business practice plus the importance of including operational detail at the design phase. It is argued that supply network design support needs to be embedded into the RFx process and that this could act as a catalyst to increase VO creation and participation of SMEs in VOs.

The paper is structured as follows. Descriptions of three VO supply networks obtained from field work and the operational design issues faced at VO creation time are given in Section 2.0. Using one of these VOs, Section 3.0 illustrates how operational design can be supported using simulation. Finally, Section 4.0 gives requirements of a tool that would encompass operational design support for VO supply network creation.

2.0 EXAMPLE SUPPLY NETWORKS

Research has been carried out into the use of simulation to support contract costing for companies in the electronics outsourcing sector (Byrne et al., 2005; Liston et al., 2006). As part of this research, field research was conducted in companies operating in a variety of supply chain echelons in the electronics sector, more specifically: two Original Equipment Manufacturers (OEMs), two first tier Contract Manufacturers (CMs), one second tier CM, one Third Party Logistics Provider (3PL) and two Fourth Party Logistics Providers (4PLs). In this analysis, three instances of VO supply networks were identified and studied. These instances are only a sample of the many types of VO supply networks found in practice.

2.1 Contract Manufacturer

Bridgefield (2003) gives the following description of a Contract Manufacturer (CM): "A third party that performs one or more production operational for a manufacturer who will market the final item under their own name. They often charge on a per-piece or per-lot basis for the labour required for their services while using components or materials supplied and owned by the final item manufacturer." Contract manufacturers can be further categorised depending on their positioning within a supply chain. The phrases 'First Tier', 'Second Tier', etc. are used to denote these positions. When responding to a RFQ a CM will very often be required to develop a VO supply network. An example RFQ obtained in a field study was where an OEM decided to outsource all of its packaging activities and issued a RFQ to this effect. To respond to this RFQ the CM needed to develop and cost a solution where it would be responsible for managing all material, procurement, warehousing, inventory, IT, logistics and quality activities. This involved developing a VO supply network as illustrated in Figure 1. To develop such a solution the CM needed to address in short time frame (6 weeks was given to respond to the RFQ) a range of operational design issues typically encountered in developing a supply network. In this example qualifying RFQs went on to participate in a reverse auction.

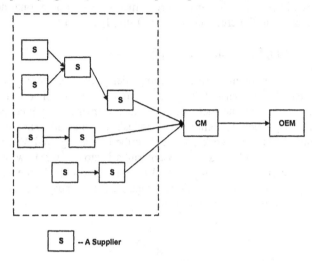

Figure 1 - CM VO supply network example

2.2 Supplier Sourcing Company

This example involves a company focused on sourcing suppliers in response to a RFQ. In a number of instances this involves developing a VO supply network in order to supply a product or component. One common reason why a VO supply network is needed is that a single company with all the technological capabilities required may not exist. Another probable reason may be that even if one company is capable of completing all tasks, there may be other companies who can complete certain tasks either more competently, more economically or both.

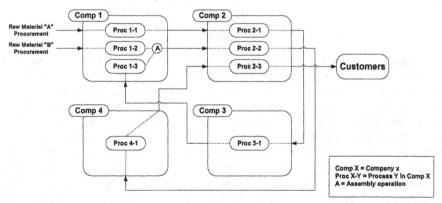

Figure 2 - Process steps for component supplied by Supplier Sourcing Company

An example encountered in the field study was a VO supply network designed to supply a component as illustrated in Figure 2. Figure 2 presents the process steps and their sequence for the manufacture of the component. Four different manufacturing companies were involved in two countries with significant transportation of the component. Note from Figure 2 that the component parts visit company 1 three times and company 2 three times. Again, operational design issues need to be addressed in the creation of this VO supply network.

2.3 Virtual Breeding Environment Supply Network

The third example is an open network of companies in the Shannon region of Ireland that was established in January 1999. The network was established to provide more business opportunities for the member companies primarily achieved through joint marketing initiatives such as exhibitions, tradeshows, and advertising and greater profile awareness. This network is best described as a regional Virtual Breeding Environment (VBE) (Afsarmanesh, Camarinha-Matos, 2005) with individual members currently creating supply networks, within and outside the network, on a global scale. A goal of the network is to increase the capability of the network members to collaborate in response to RFQs.

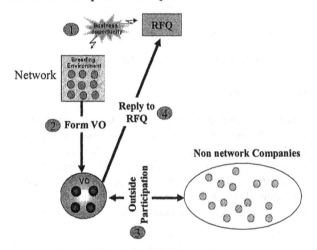

Figure 3 - VBE scenario

Figure 3 illustrates a "to-be-situation" with the network. A RFQ is received either by the network organization or a member of network (see label 1 Figure 3). A real example would be a RFQ for the design, manufacture and product life cycle management of a family of products. Members of the network will form a VO to bid for this work (see label 2 Figure 3). Capabilities in the network would allow a member to carry out product design, another member to carry out plastic moulding, test, de-bug and repair by another member and a 3PL member could coordinate logistics. As shown in label 3, participation of outside companies, who maybe located globally, will typically also be required. Past work by the open network identified many barriers to reach this "to-be-situation". One of these barriers is the lack of supply network design capabilities in developing, costing and selling a VO supply network solution to the customer.

3.0 OPERATIONAL DESIGN SUPPORT FOR VO CREATION

This section reports on work carried out to validate the use of simulation to support VO supply network development and costing for a Contract Manufacturer (CM) as described in sub-section 2.1 (Liston et al., 2006). The CM was selected from the three other VOs encountered, as it is widely found in industry. Also, VOs created by a CM will have a relatively stable structure compared to the two other VOs reviewed in Section 2, reducing the complexity of developing support tools. A model (see Figure 4) was built using eM-Plant on the scenario presented in Figure 1.

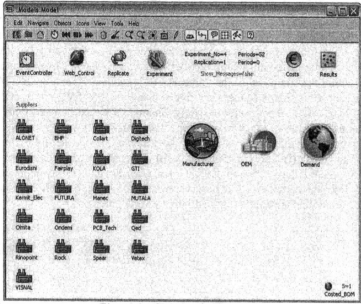

Figure 4 - CM simulation model

The model contains extensive operational details as indicated by Figure 5.

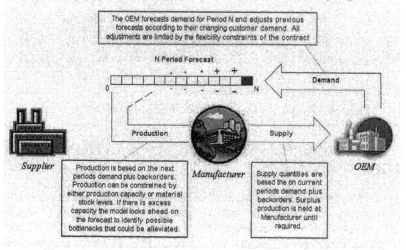

Figure 5 - Model interaction between Manufacturer and OEM

The simulation sequence begins with demand being communicated to the OEM frame where it is used to generate a continuous thirteen period forecast for the CM. Figure 5 shows how this demand is translated back to the CM and how the CM responds. The OEM frame also contains the information concerning flexibility constraints as stipulated in the RFQ. These flexibility constraints allow a customer (OEM) to increase or decrease the order quantity by a limited amount depending on the time left to the due date (a more comprehensive discussion on such contract terms can be found in the work of Tsay et al. (1999) or Bassok et al. (1997)).

To illustrate how simulation can assist in VO creation, some sample output from the above model is depicted in Figure 6. This graph shows the minimum, maximum and average values for unit cost of a component using eleven different VO scenarios. The range at each design point in Figure 6 is obtained by running each design point under different random number streams (15 in this case). This is done to mimic future uncertainties. If the unit cost of a component is set by the CM at the price level shown in Figure 6, there is a risk of losing money if VO configurations 6, 7, 10 and 11 are used. This example briefly illustrates the type of operational design issues that need to be addressed when responding to an RFQ.

The model together with extensive experimentation on the following were presented to CMs: **(i)** Supplier Selection; **(ii)** The pattern of sales demand; **(iii)** Flexibility constraints specified in the RFQ; **(iv)** Capacity and **(v)** Inventory policies. Feedback from the companies was positive; however, feedback highlighted the need to develop a tool that is better integrated into the RFQ process.

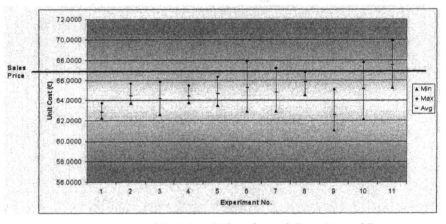

Figure 6 - Range of Unit Cost Values for each Experimental Run

4. TOWARDS SUPPLY NETWORK VO CREATION SUPPORT TOOLS

RFx-based procurement tools, a segment of the Supplier Relationship Management software sector, are used for the sourcing, qualification and choosing of suppliers. These tools have the features of: sending out a request for information, sending out a request for quotation, setting up an on-line auction, and scoring features to choose a supplier(s) for a particular product. These tools are controlled from the buyer side. Once the supplier has been chosen, contract management tools can be used to create the contract between the supplier and purchaser, and to manage the contract throughout its lifecycle until termination. Separate contract management tools can be used on both the buyer and seller sides. A sample of RFx-based procurement tools are listed in Table 1. Also, listed in Table 1 are the main features of these tools. These tools are all web-based facilitating communication with suppliers. None of the tools surveyed include operational design support for VO supply network creation. It is clear that any operational design support tools developed will need to integrate with RFx existing procurement tools or incorporate their capabilities to facilitate information gathering and communication with suppliers.

The requirements, ascertained so far, of a software application that will support operational design for VO supply network creation are as follows:

1. The application should provide the ability to evaluate different VO supply chain solutions and in these evaluations capture operational related costs.
2. The software must integrate with existing RFx procurement tools or incorporate their communication and information gathering capabilities.
3. For decentralised (or VBE) instances of VO creation the application should facilitate collaborative design. This feature may not be important in centralised instances of VO creation, such as the CM case.
4. The application would need to facilitate rapid analysis of VO scenarios, as the time to respond to a RFQ is typically short.
5. The application should require a low level of expertise to use. For example, resources required to develop the simulation models described in Section 3.0 would not be justifiable for a tool used on a continuous basis.

A prototype tool for the CM instance is being developed and evaluation of this tool by companies is planned.

Table 1: Sample RFX-based Procurement Tools: vendors/tools included and identified features

RFX-based Procurement Tools			
Vendors/Tools included in the Survey			
ASC Bids	PCBspecialist	FreeMarkets	EBreviate
Ariba	Procuri	Frictionless	Emptoris
B2emarkets	PurchasePro	Iasta	Silanta Technologies
Bellwether RFQ module	Tradestone	SAP RFQ and Auctions	XTO software
Commerce One Source	Upside RFX	Epiq	
Overall Features Identified	**Description of Features**		
RFx Creation	Questionnaires, templates, attachment of files, Tracking of Ammendments, automation (wizards)		
Collaboration/Communication	Online Message boards, email, negotiation window		
Reverse Auction	Multiple Attributes, Countdown Clock, Pricing Curves, Savings Charts		
Supplier Scoring	Weighted Questions, Optimisation Capabilities, Weighting of evaluators, side-by-side comparisons		
Architectural Features	Fully Web-based, Centralised Repository/Database		
Monitoring and Reporting	Online queries/reports, ability to export reports to other software tools		
Integration	Integration with other systems including legacy systems to import/export data		

5. CONCLUSIONS

Outsourcing is a major driver in the creation of VO supply networks. The process by which VO creation takes place is the RFx process. Three instances of VO supply networks were described in the paper, spanning from a highly centralized mode (i.e.,

CM example) of VO creation to a decentralized or network mode of VO creation. For all instances operational design support is lacking for VO creation. In relation to the CM it was illustrated how simulation can be used to assist VO creation. In regard to decentralized or network VO creation many barriers exist in increasing collaboration among network members. In relation to VO supply networks this paper argues that operational design support tools need to be developed and embedded into the RFx process. Current research is being undertaken in developing tools for the CM VO creation case.

Acknowledgments

This work was conducted as part of a collaborative project between the University of Limerick and the NITL, Dublin Institute of Technology, and is funded by Enterprise Ireland under project ref. no. TD/03/411 (SIMCT).

4. REFERENCES

1. Afsarmanesh, H; Camarinha-Matos, L. M.: A framework for management of virtual organizations breeding environments. In Proceedings of PRO-VE'05 – Collaborative Networks and their Breeding Environments, Springer, pp. 35-48, Valencia, Spain, 26-28 Sept 2005.
2. Bassok, Y., A. Bixby, R. Srinivasan and H. Z. Wiesel. "Design of component-supply contract with commitment revision flexibility." IBM J. Res. Dev., 1997, 41(6): 693-704.
3. Bosch-Sijtsema, P.M.: Crossing Learning Boundaries. The Utility related Virtual Organisation ISES. Newsletter of virtual-organization.net in VoNet 1, 1997, 5 (Dec.). Electronic journal: www.virtual-organization.net
4. Bridgefield. "Bridgefield Group ERP/Supply chain Glossary", 2003. http://www.bridgefieldgroup.com/glos2.htm, Accessed on 23th September, 2005.
5. Byrne, J., C. Heavey and P. Byrne. "Requirements for a Simulation-Based Tool to Aid in the Contract-Costing Process". In Proceeding of 18th International Conference on Production Research, University of Salerno, Italy, July 31 - Aug 4, 2005.
6. Carbone, J. "Worldwide Outsourcing Rises", 2005. http://www.purchasing.com/article/CA501253.html, Accessed on 12th December, 2005.
7. Flegel, H. "Manufacturing a Vision for 2020: Report of the High Level Group." 2004. http://europa.eu.int/comm/research/industrial_technologies/pdf/manufuture_vision_en.pdf, Accessed on March 20th, 2006.
8. Kalorama Information. "Outsourcing in Drug Discovery, 2nd Edition", 2005. http://www.prnewswire.com/cgi-bin/stories.pl?ACCT=109&STORY=/www/story/03-02-2006/0004312261&EDATE=, Accessed on March 24th, 2006.
9. Kamio, Y., F. Kasai, T. Kimura, Y. Fukuda, I. Hartel and M. Zhou. "Providing Remote Plant Maintenance Support through a Service Virtual Enterprise". In Proceeding of GLOBEMEN (Global Engineering and Manufacturing in Enterprise Networks), Helsinki, VTT, 2002, 195-205.
10. Liston, P., P. J. Byrne and C. Heavey. "An Evaluation of Simulation to Support Contract Costing." Computers & Operations Research, 2006 In Press, Corrected Proof, Available online 28 Feb 2006.
11. Norman, T. J., A. Preece, S. Chalmers, N. R. Jennings, M. M. Luck, V. D. Dang, T. D. Nguyen, V. Deora, J. Shao, W. A. Gray, and N. J. Fiddian, "CONOISE: Agent-based formation of virtual organisations," in Research and Development in Intelligent Systems XX: Proceedings of AI2003, the Twenty third International Conference on Innovative Techniques and Applications of Artificial Intelligence, 2003, 353-366.
12. Sturgeon, T. J. "How Do We Define Value Chains and Production Networks." MIT IPC Globalization Working Paper 00-010, 2000.
13. Tsay, A. A., S. Nahmias and N. Agrawal. "Modeling Supply Chain Contracts: A Review". Quantitative models for supply chain management. S. Tayur, R. Ganeshan and M. Magazine, Kluwer Academic Publishers, Norwell, MA.: 1999, 299-336.

41

PARTNER SELECTION WITH
NETWORK INTERDEPENDENCIES:
AN APPLICATION

Toni Jarimo and Iiro Salkari
VTT Technical Research Centre of Finland
toni.jarimo@vtt.fi, iiro.salkari@vtt.fi, FINLAND

Stefan Bollhalter
Virtuelle Fabrik AG
stefan.bollhalter@virtuelle-fabrik.com, SWITZERLAND

This paper describes a virtual organization (VO) partner-selection case of
Virtuelle Fabrik AG, which is an operating virtual organization breeding
environment (VBE). We approach the partner-selection problem through a
recently developed optimization framework; therefore we also study the
applicability of the framework. The results suggest that an optimization
framework is potentially useful for supporting VO creation.

1. INTRODUCTION

Collaborative networks are an increasing trend both in global and regional business. As individual companies seek efficiency by focusing on core competences and outsourcing other operations, the degree of inter-firm transactions grows. Simultaneously, the efficient management of network relations becomes a condition of survival. Therefore, models that support the management of network relations are called for. (E.g. Gulati et al. 2000, Camarinha-Matos and Afsarmanesh 2005)

A specific problem of collaborative networks is partner selection. On one hand, partner selection is a matching problem between the needs of the customer and the competences of partner candidates. On the other hand, it is a portfolio selection problem, where the consideration of the whole is relevant. The reason for this is that different network interdependencies between partner candidates may well affect the efficiency of the whole, which makes it insufficient to select partners one by one (e.g. Degraeve et al. 2000). Examples of such interdependencies are collaboration history, geographical locations, and ICT infrastructure (Camarinha-Matos and Afsarmanesh 2003). Accounting for network interdependencies has been empowered through the emergence virtual organization breeding environments (VBE, Camarinha-Matos and Afsarmanesh 2003), which consist of member-organizations that have developed a mutually agreed cooperation structure for the

Please use the following format when citing this chapter:

Jarimo, T., Salkari, I., Bollhalter, S., 2006, in IFIP International Federation for Information Processing, Volume 224, Network-Centric Collaboration and Supporting Fireworks, eds. Camarinha-Matos, L., Afsarmanesh, H., Ollus, M., (Boston: Springer), pp. 389–396.

creation of virtual organizations (see also Lau and Wong 2001, Tølle and Bernus 2003).

In this paper, we apply our recently developed partner selection framework (see, Jarimo and Pulkkinen 2005, Jarimo and Salo 2006) to a real-life case of an existing VBE, the Virtuelle Fabrik AG. The partner selection framework uses multi-criteria optimisation techniques to identify Pareto-efficient network configurations, which the decision-maker (DM) can manually compare.

The rest of this paper is structured as follows. Section 2 briefly reviews the partner selection framework. Section 3 analyses the case and Section 4 concludes.

2. OPTIMISATION FRAMEWORK FOR VO PARTNER SELECTION

This section briefly reviews the model used in the application this paper presents. The model is described in more detail in Jarimo and Pulkkinen (2005) and Jarimo and Salo (2006).

2.1 Purpose of the model

Our model finds and evaluates feasible VO configurations with respect to user-defined criteria. The problem is formulated as that of work-allocation, where the feasibility of a configuration is defined through its ability to perform a project. The project is described by tasks, each of which requires a specific competence. In addition, work-loads (e.g. person month) can be attached to the tasks.

The model accounts for a large variety of selection criteria. First, total costs include fixed and variable work costs and transportation costs. Second, stochastic risk measures are applied to model risks of failure, delays, or capacity shortfall. Third, network interdependencies, such as collaboration history or total number of partners can be taken into account.

Using the model, a decision-maker (DM) can identify a set of Pareto-optimal configurations, of which the DM can manually select the preferred one. In other words, the model suggests several alternatives that are "good" in respect of different preferences over the selection criteria. Hence, the DM does not need to explicitly weight the criteria, but instead can identify configurations that reflect different preferences.

2.2 Approach

The model formulates the VO partner selection as a work-allocation problem, which is approached by multi-objective mixed integer linear programming (MILP). The benefit of MILP models is that they can be readily solved using well known algorithms. Indeed, computational experiments suggest that our MILP models are tractable for problems of reasonable size and consequently potentially useful for VO decision making.

The multi-objectivity is captured by goal-programming techniques (e.g. Taha, 1997) or additive value functions (MAVT, Keeney and Raiffa, 1993). Heuristic algorithms are used to find Pareto-efficient solutions.

2.3 Inputs and Outputs

The inputs of the model are as follows. There are n tasks with a work-load (e.g. person month) attached to each of them. The tasks also have a relational work sequence, and information on possible transportation needs between tasks. For each task j, there are m_j partner candidates, the total number of candidates being $m = \Sigma_j$ m_j. Each candidate has a capacity, and fixed and variable cost for working on the tasks to which it is a candidate. This data is easily represented by matrices, where the rows and columns represent the candidates and the tasks. A candidate can have a probability distribution over its capacities, reflecting the uncertainty on true capacity. Moreover, each candidate can have a fixed cost for working on the project, a geographical location, collaboration history with other candidates, etc.

The DM needs to define the selection criteria for partner selection. The problem is to select a good VO configuration for the project, subject to the above information on the project and candidate partners. This problem is essentially that of allocating the task workloads to partners, in recognition of their capacities and the decision criteria that are relevant to the evaluation of alternative partner configurations.

The output of the model is a set of Pareto-efficient work allocations, i.e. VO configurations. The constituents of this set depends on how the DM has expressed his/her preferences over the selection criteria. If the DM provides with perfect information on the relative importance of the selection criteria, a unique Pareto-efficient configuration is suggested. Again, if the preference information is imperfect, possibly multiple configurations are identified. The DM can then manually select the most preferred configuration.

The scores of the identified configurations on the selection criteria are also given. Hence, in addition to the partners in Pareto-efficient configurations, the DM can compare the expected performance of the configurations.

3. APPLICATION: MAGNETIC CLUTCH PROTOTYPE FOR TRUCKS

We applied the model to a Virtuelle Fabrik partner selection case, which is described in this section. The results suggest that relevant criteria can be taken into account and reasonable configurations are identified.

3.1 Project Description

The aim of the project was to construct a prototype magnetic clutch to be used in trucks. The project was broken down into nine tasks, which were 1) Grinding, 2) Gear milling, 3) Metal sheet forming, 4) Milling and turning of bigger parts, 5) Welding, 6) Bending of pipes, 7) Engineering, 8) Milling and turning of smaller parts, and 9) Project management. For each task, there were two to five partner candidates, some of which were candidates for several tasks.

Three selection criteria were given with the following priority: 1) minimize delay risks, 2) maximize earlier collaboration, and 3) minimize costs. The project had a tight schedule, thus minimization of risks was most important. Moreover, it was assumed that a successful collaboration history contributes to finishing the project in time. Costs were in this case the least important criterion.

Each partner candidate was given a probability distribution for finishing the tasks in time. Moreover, data on the candidates' collaboration history was readily available (see Figure 1), and the candidates' costs were estimated.

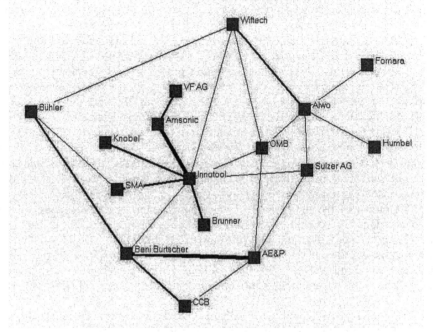

Figure 1 – Collaboration history of some members of Virtuelle Fabrik (line thickness corresponds to intensity)

3.2 Case Analysis

In the analysis of this case, fifteen Pareto-efficient configurations were identified using the optimization framework. Table 1 presents the performance of these configurations on the three selection criteria. The configurations have been sorted first by risk, second by collaboration, and third by cost, which was also the relative importance of the selection criteria. Moreover, Figure 2 illustrates this data in three dimensions.

The risk-measure used was the Expected Downside Risk (EDR, Eppen et al., 1989), where a smaller score is preferred to a greater one, zero being the theoretically best. The collaboration-score is calculated using a measure that accounts for earlier collaboration as well as for the total number of partners in a configuration. Also here a smaller score is preferred. Cost is the expected total cost in euros.

Table 1 – Performance of fifteen Pareto-efficient configurations on three selection criteria

Risk	Collaboration	Cost (EUR)
[1]0,25	58	131312
0,25	74	130795
[2]0,75	49	132116
[3]0,75	55	123215
0,75	62	122710
0,75	71	122698
1,00	69	122131
1,00	71	122119
[4]1,25	46	123215
1,25	62	122057
1,50	80	121702
1,75	53	122057
1,75	70	121640
2,25	62	121640
2,75	67	121628

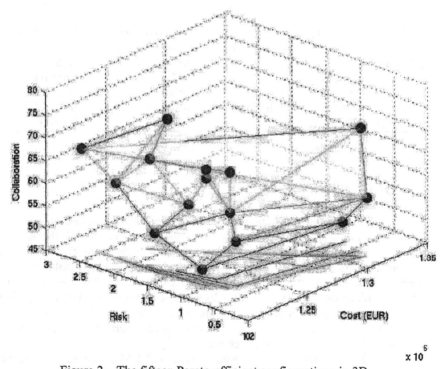

Figure 2 – The fifteen Pareto-efficient configurations in 3D

With a closer look at Table 1, one can identify at least four interesting configurations, labeled with superscripts 1-4. Configuration 1) has significantly better collaboration-score than the other configuration with a low risk, but only a slightly higher cost. Configurations 2) and 3) have a higher risk than Configuration 1), but a better collaboration-score, or lower cost, respectively. Configuration 4), in turn, has a medium risk, but the overall best collaboration-score and a low cost.

After identifying the interesting configurations from Table 1, the DM can check which partners would be selected in each case. For instance, Table 2 shows the partners for each task in Configuration 1) as well as the partners that were actually chosen to the Magnetic Clutch Prototype project. Configuration 1) is selected for illustration purposes because its performance is in line with the preferences of the DM, i.e. risk minimization is most important. The computer-suggested configuration differs from the truly selected configuration in two tasks (boldface). The reason for this is that in the computer-suggestion the total number of partners is seven, which is two partners less than in the true configuration. However, the final decision was made manually based on the DM's good experiences with Amsonic and Fornara. The DM stressed that these two partners would be very reliable when it comes to accuracy.

Table 2 – Partners selected in Configuration 1) and in reality

Tasks of Magnetic Clutch Prototype	Configuration 1)	Truly selected
Grinding	Brunner	Brunner
Gear milling	Okey	Okey
Metal sheet forming	Beni Burtscher	Beni Burtscher
Milling and turning of bigger parts	SMA	SMA
Welding	**Beni Burtscher**	**Amsonic**
Bending of pipes	**SMA**	**Fornara**
Engineering	Schuler	Schuler
Milling and turning of smaller parts	Innotool	Innotool
Project management	VF AG	VF AG

5. CONCLUSIONS

This paper presents an application of a recently developed optimization framework for partner selection. We model partner selection as a centralised decision-making problem. This is reasonable if one entity is fully responsible for selecting the network partners. However, there are situations where the decision-making is in fact decentralised. This is the case if the partner candidates themselves decide with whom to collaborate. An example of a decentralised partner selection process is the formation inter-organisational research projects. In this case, the formation of the final consortium is a multi-party negotiation process between research teams at universities, research institutes, and companies.

Our model is potentially useful in cases where one DM selects network partners. Such cases occur in a VBE that repeatedly creates VOs whenever there is potential for value creation through collaboration. Customers often wish that only a single partner – the broker – is responsible for the operations of the VO. It is therefore natural that the broker has the control over the VO and the partner selection.

The centralised decision-making may lead to the following paradox. Consolidation of organisational competences allows the companies to focus on niche core-competences, which enables VOs to construct more complex products and services than an individual company could possibly do. However, the growth in the complexity of niche competences make also marketing and project management processes more complicated, since the broker or the project manager needs to manage not only the expertise of one's own company but also the expertise of other companies. The training of such multi-professionals is costly, which limits the possibilities of collaborative networks. Therefore, networking calls for efficient models of inter-organisational knowledge management.

In partner selection, different option-contracts are a potential topic for further studies. A portfolio consisting of option-contracts together with traditional contracts could be used to hedge against the risk of capacity shortfall. Here, the theoretical foundations can be drawn from portfolio selection methodology and real-options theory. Moreover, robust models for identifying poorly-performing partner candidates would be useful. The elimination of some candidates reduces the total number of potential configurations, which helps the selection.

ACKNOWLEDGEMENTS

The work has been co-funded by the European Commission through the Sixth Framework Programme Integrated Project ECOLEAD, as well as by the National Technology Agency of Finland (Tekes) and the National Workplace Development Programme (Tykes) through the COBTEC project.

REFERENCES

1. Camarinha-Matos LM, Afsarmanesh H. Elements of a base VE infrastructure. Computers in Industry 2003; 51: 139–63.
2. Camarinha-Matos LM, Afsarmanesh H. Collaborative Networks: A New Scientific Discipline. Journal of Intelligent Manufacturing 2005; 16: 439-52.
3. Degraeve, Z., Labro, E., Roodhooft, F. An Evaluation of Vendor Selection Models from a Total Cost of Ownership Perspective, European Journal of Operational Research 2000;125:34–58.
4. Eppen GD, Martin RK, Schrage L. A Scenario Approach to Capacity Planning. Operations Research 1989; 37(4): 517–27.
5. Gulati, R., Nohria, N., Zaheer, A. Strategic Networks. Strategic Management Journal 2000;21:203–215.
6. Jarimo, T., Pulkkinen, U. A Multi-Criteria Mathematical Programming Model for Agile Virtual Organization Creation. Collaborative Networks and their Breeding Environments, PRO-VE'05 Sixth IFIP Working Conference on VIRTUAL ENTERPRISES, 26-28 September 2005, Valencia, Spain, editors L. M. Camarinha-Matos, H. Afsarmanesh, A. Ortiz, Springer, 2005:127–134.
7. Jarimo, T., Salo, A. Optimal Partner Selection in Virtual Organisations with Capacity Risk and Network Interdependencies. Submitted Manuscript. 2006.
8. Keeney, R. L., Raiffa, H. Decisions with Multiple Objectives: Preferences and Value Tradeoffs. Cambridge University Press, 1993.
9. Lau, H. C.W., Wong, E. T. T. Partner selection and information infrastructure of a virtual enterprise network. International Journal of Computer Integrated Manufacturing 2001;14(2):186–193.

10. Taha, H. A. Operations Research: An Introduction. Prentice-Hall International, 1997.
11. Tølle, M., Bernus, P. Reference models supporting enterprise networks and virtual enterprises. International Journal of Networking and Virtual Organisations 2003;2(1):2–15.

42

IDENTIFYING PARTNERS AND ORGANIZATIONAL LOGICAL STRUCTURES FOR COLLABORATIVE CONCEPTUAL DESIGN

Antonio P. Volpentesta, Maurizio Muzzupappa
Università della Calabria, volpentesta@deis.unical.it, muzzupappa@unical.it
ITALY

Recently much interest has been devoted to novel distributed approaches which lead to the formation of collaborative networked organizations, e.g. virtual organizations, specifically oriented to generate an innovative product concept . Making use of logical-formal structures based on concepts related to directed hypergraphs, we formally represent competitive inter-organization and collaborative intra-organization relationships. Thanks to these structures, models for distributed processes which lead to the emergence of both design chains and functional architectures of an innovative product are formally described and then illustrated through examples from an applicative scenario.

1. INTRODUCTION

The main contribution of this paper is aimed to give an answer to new decision problems that arise in managing early lifecycle phases of a Virtual Organization (VO) which is specifically oriented to generate an innovative product concept. In particular, we focalize our attention on conceptual design and VO formation phases (fig.1). Referring to the product lifecycle, conceptual design is the creative phase which is placed between the product planning and the embodiment design phases (Pahl, 1996). Main goals are generation of concepts (ideas) and specification of function structure (architecture) of a product. Referring to the VO lifecycle, formation phase of a VO includes partners and organizational logical structure identification. In a collaborative conceptual design, partner companies should be able not only to provide information about resources and equipment for their part of the business, but also to share appropriate knowledge and technologies for a VO formation (Camarinha,1999).

The study of formation process of a VO oriented to collaborative concept generation is relevant for the following reasons:

- the knowledge of a single design office (or enterprise) is often not sufficient to let emerge the conception of an innovative competitive product.
- in principle, a large number of design offices may exploit a wider range of competences and knowledge.

Please use the following format when citing this chapter:

Volpentesta, A. P., Muzzupappa, M., 2006, in IFIP International Federation for Information Processing, Volume 224, Network-Centric Collaboration and Supporting Fireworks, eds. Camarinha-Matos, L., Afsarmanesh, H., Ollus, M., (Boston: Springer), pp. 397–406.

- high levels of creativity may be achieved through effective collaboration of many distributed DOs.

-

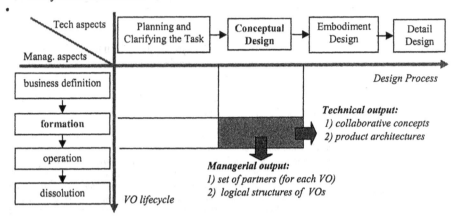

Figure 1 – Design Process and VO lifecycle

Due to interdependencies between managerial and technical problems, classical approaches (Frutos, 2004) for partners identification and VO formation are inadequate. As matter of fact, partners identification relies on the description of concept requirements but this knowledge is available only afterwards partners are already identified. Thus, knowledge and technologies cannot be well defined "a-priori". Moreover, VO partners rarely give away valuable concept design knowledge without expecting something in return. The formation process should utilize all and only information which is strictly necessary to define a VO architecture (members, their interactions and their roles in contributing toward the VO goal which is the generation of a new concept), but it could not rely on complete product part concepts description in order to not compromise enterprise private knowledge. In a previous paper (Volpentesta et al. 2005), we have outlined a combined approach where managerial and technical solutions are determined step by step in a circular way. In this paper, we introduce logical formal structures aimed to represent competitive inter-organization and collaborative intra-organization relationships in a Virtual Breeding Environment (VBE, for short) for conceptual design and we present formal process models for the formation of such structures.

2. RELATED WORK

Since the first appearance of the concept of VO much attention has been increasingly devoted to how to manage collaborative design in networked environment. Many researchers have tackled different aspects of this problem, from a technological and organizational point of view. In (Chiu, 2002), the authors provides a basic understanding of the role of organization in design collaboration and how it affects design communication and collaboration by empirical case studies.. An integrated environment for the coordination and management of worldwide-distributed multifunctional design teams (marketing analysts, engineering designers, suppliers, etc.) is proposed in (Tseng, 2004). A feature-based collaborative design system capable to support a distributed product development process in a virtual enterprise is presented in (Huifen, 2003). In (Baia, 2005), the authors introduce a Product Layout Feature model to resolve the problem of consistently maintaining a product scheme while collaborative activities among multi-teams from different disciplines are carried out. An approach to develop a knowledge repository as a basis for a domain ontology for conflicts is proposed in (Yesilbas, 2004). Specific studies are devoted to collaborative conceptual design. Haung and Mak propose a morphological chart analysis method to develop a set of Web-based design tools (Haung,1999). Extended reviews about methodologies and supporting technologies can be found in (Wang,2002;Roy,2000).

In order to study VO specifically oriented to the early stage of collaborative concept design, a key challenge is to determine how identify VO partners and product structure in a collaborative network environment. In (Haung, 2003) a prototype system embedding a Concept Base and a Solution Base is presented. Such a system is aimed to support synchronous/asynchronous collaboration in product concept definition. However, the authors don't face the problem of how to manage distributed knowledge to populate the system Bases. In (Chu, 2002), an integrated product design and partner synthesis process model is described. Such a model relies on the assumptions that "there is a master company which takes charge of selecting and managing its partner factories" and "the product development and production are distributed among the master company and all partner factories". This means that the product structure is always defined by a master company, so that it is impossible to achieve high levels of creativity by effectively taking advantage of distributed knowledge among many interacting design peers. Decentralized product design is considered in (Giannini, 2002), where "the emphasis is given to the product specification, and to the negotiation activity usually carried out to identify the right project partner and the final product configuration" in an enterprise network. The paper does not deal with the problem of which the network structure could be and how it can arise from a broader enterprise networked environment.

Our paper searches for answers to open issues related to the above-cited works. The main contribution consists in the introduction of a formal process model for the emergence of VO and product structures in a VBE oriented to collaborative conceptual design.

3. VBE FOR COLLABORATIVE CONCEPT DESIGN

Recently, the concept of VBE has emerged as the necessary context for effective creation of VOs. In (Camarinha-Matos, 2003) a VBE is defined as "an association of organizations and their related supporting institutions, adhering to a base long term cooperation agreement, and adoption of common operating principles and infrastructures, with the main goal of increasing both their chances and their preparedness towards collaboration in potential virtual enterprises". In our approach, VBE has the goal of blending collaboration contributions of a set of Design Offices (DOs) partners, in order to form a VE which is in principle capable of bringing new product concepts to life. In particular, a VBE for collaborative concept design consists of:

- a set of DOs which supply Requests for Concepts (RFCs), conditioned undertakings to respond to an RFC and RFC responses.
- a VO-planner that identifies a new collaboration opportunity and let it now to all DOs in the VBE (by launching an initial RFC). It selects necessary competencies and capacities for VOs capable in principle to seize the opportunity. Such a process may be carried out through managing RFCs, conditioned undertakings and RFC responses.

An RFC defines a set of requirements for a functional concept, by specifying characteristic parameters and their value range. These parameters generally refer to technical/functional requirements of a product element or part. However, they may also refer to requirements that a DO must satisfy when responding to the RFC, or to assessment criteria that may be used for ranking the concepts received from respondents to the RFC. Conditioned undertaking to respond to an RFC is an expression of interest to respond conditional on obtaining responses to other related RFCs. A response to an RFC consists of a functional concept description including, if necessary, other additional useful details. In the approach proposed in (Volpentesta et al., 2005), two main distributed processes (coordinated by VO-planner) take place in the VBE: *Conceptual Design Network Formation and Concepts Functionality and VOs Identification*. The first one defines a network consisting of all logical structures of VOs that rely on a collaborative minimal organization potentially capable of responding to the initial RFC coming from the VO-planner. The second one determines both concepts functionality and formal structures of VOs that are realistically able to generate the required product concept. In what follows, we give a formal representation of the two main processes necessary to identify partners and logical structures of VOs capable in principle to generate an innovative product concept in a VBE.

4. FORMAL STRUCTURES MODELS

In this section we introduce formal structures which are underneath concept design networks and VOs in a VBE. Such structures are based on concepts related to hyperpaths, hypernetworks and direct hypergraphs that are defined and studied in (Volpentesta, 2005; Nielsen, 2005).

In our context of reference, a Design Request Network is a triplet

$$\mathcal{R} = (\mathcal{H}, O, \alpha)$$

where:

1. $\mathcal{H} = (\mathcal{N}, \mathcal{E})$ is a directed hypergraph[1] in which
   - each node $n \in \mathcal{N}$ univocally identifies an *RFC* and where $s, d \in \mathcal{N}$ are two particular nodes: s is the "dummy" RFC for which no response is required, d is the initial RFC (say RFC_0) to which at least a response is required.
   - each hyperarc $e \in \mathcal{E}$ individuates an expression of interest to respond to the RFC identified by $h(e)$, conditional on obtaining responses to RFCs identified by nodes in $T(e)$;
2. O is a set of DOs in the VBE;
3. $\alpha: \mathcal{E} \rightarrow O$, is a function from $\mathcal{E}$ to O, $\alpha(\mathcal{E})$ individuates the DO that has given the conditioned undertaking individuated by e.

Let $\mathcal{H}_\pi = (\mathcal{N}_\pi, \mathcal{E}_\pi)$ be a sub-hypergraph of $\mathcal{H}$ and let $\alpha_\pi : \mathcal{E}_\pi \to O$ be the restriction of α on $\mathcal{E}_\pi$. It is reasonable to identify a VO architecture with a triplet $\mathcal{R}_\alpha = (\mathcal{H}_\pi, O, \alpha_\pi)$ where $\mathcal{H}_\pi$ is an hyperpath[2] from s to d, and we refer to it with the term *Design Chain* (DC). The fact that d is hyperconnected to s in $\mathcal{H}_\pi$ guarantees that initial RFC associated to d could receive a response by a means of recursive composition of responses to RFCs associated to nodes of $\mathcal{H}_\pi$. The fact that $\mathcal{H}_\pi$ is cycle free guarantees that stalemate situations in the *Concept Functionality Identification* phase do not happen. A stalemate situation occurs when some DOs are not able to respond to RFCs, even though they have expressed to interest to respond to it. A DC represents a formal model for a VO which, relying on a collaborative and minimal organizational structure in a Design Request Network, is potentially capable of responding to RFC_0 coming from the VBE. On the one hand it defines a decomposition of the RFC_0 in other less complex ones, on the other hand it identifies the DOs and information exchanges requirements necessary to respond to RFC_0. Of course, there exists a DC in $\mathcal{R}$ if and only if d is hyperconnected to s in $\mathcal{H}$. In such a case, we may consider the hypernetwork $\mathcal{H}_{\eta_{sd}} = (\mathcal{N}_{\eta_{sd}}, \mathcal{E}_{\eta_{sd}})$ on $\mathcal{H}$, i.e. the union of all hyperpaths from s to d in $\mathcal{H}$, and we refer to the triplet $\mathcal{R}_{sd} = (\mathcal{H}_{\eta_{sd}}, O, \alpha_{\eta_{sd}})$ with the term Conceptual Design Network. This network may be regarded as the union of all DCs in the Design Request Network. Within a DC its DOs collaborate to get a construction, in terms of functional elements, of the new product concept, required by the RFC_0, while, within the Conceptual Design Network, its DCs compete in order to be included among best VOs in developing a new product concept.

4.1 An applicative scenario

Let us consider a scenario in which VO-planner has forwarded an RFC_0 (i.e. $d=RFC_0$) for an innovative product concept of a jigsaw with lower cost and better easy-to-handle than the ones available on the market. The RFC_0 requires the design of an innovate jigsaw through an original and unusual re-combination of existing technologies and components. A Design Request Network may be represented by a set of tables and an hypergraph. All RFCs forwarded by DOs are described in table 1, where:

- columns are associated to RFCs,
- rows are associated to parameters considered in RFCs of jigsaw parts,
- the entry at place *(i,j)* contains the *j-th* parameter value ranges specified by RFC_i.

For sake of simplicity, we have simply restricted functional features exploration to the combination of a very limited number of parts, i.e. gear boxes, electric motors and crank mechanisms. The symbol x indicates that no specific constraints are required. The relation between RFCs and conditioned undertakings is represented by table 2, where:

- columns are associated to conditioned undertakings, denoted by $e_1, ..., e_{11}$;
- the entry in the first row at place *(1,j)* contains the index of the RFC for which e_j represent a conditioned undertaking to give a response,
- the entry in the first row at place *(2,j)* contains the indices of RFCs whose responses are declared in the conditioned undertaking e_j to be necessary.

Table.1. RFCs for a jigsaw

	Name of component	Electric Power	Stroke Length	Load Speed (stokes/min)	Rotation (rpm)	Gear Ratio	Process requir.
RFC$_0$	JigSaw						IGS format
RFC$_1$	Electric motor	300-500 (W)	x	x	2.500– 3.000	x	"
RFC$_2$	Crank Mechanism	x	20-30 (mm)	2.000-3.000	x	x	"
RFC$_3$	Electric motor	500-750 (W)	x	x	5.000- 7.500	x	"
RFC$_4$	Gear Box	x	x	x	x	0.5 - 1	"
RFC$_5$	Gearing	x	x	x	x	0.5 - 1	"
RFC$_6$	Eccentric	x	10-15 (mm)	2.000-2.500	x	x	"
RFC$_{dummy}$	x	x	x	x	x	x	x

For example, e_8 represents a conditioned undertaking to respond to RFC$_4$ (request for a gear box) provided that responses to RFC$_3$ (request for an electric motor) and to RFC$_5$ (request for a gearing) are available. Table 3 associates any conditioned undertaking to a DO.

Table.2. Conditioned undertakings/RFCs

e_1	e_2	e_3	e_4	e_5	e_6	e_7	e_8	e_9	e_{10}	e_{11}
0	0	0	1	2	2	3	4	5	0	3
1	1,2	3,4	dummy	dummy	dummy	dummy	3,5	dummy	1	4

Table.3 Conditioned undertakings /DOs.

conditioned undertakings	Design Office
e_1, e_3, e_6	DO$_1$
e_2, e_8, e_{10}	DO$_2$
e_4, e_{11}	DO$_3$
e_5	DO$_4$
e_7	DO$_5$
e_9	DO$_6$

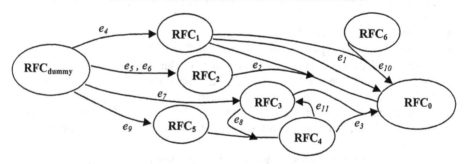

Figure 2 – The hypergraph $\mathcal{H}$ of the DRN

The three tables define a Design Request Network for a jigsaw concept. In particular, a graphical representation of the hypergraph $\mathcal{H}$ of such a Design Request Network is shown in figure 2. One may easily notice that RFC$_6$ is the only node which is not s-hyperconnected to s in $\mathcal{H}$. And that e_{10} and e_{11} are the only hyperarcs which do not belong to any hyperpath from s to d in $\mathcal{H}$. Their elimination determines the hypernetwork $\mathcal{H}_{\eta_{sd}}$ on $\mathcal{H}$. Such hypernetwork consists of the union of four hyperpaths corresponding to four DCs. Table 4 indicates the DOs involved in each DC.

Table.4 The Design Chains/DOs correspondance.

Design Chain	Design Offices
1	DO_1, DO_3
2	DO_2, DO_3, DO_4
3	DO_1, DO_2, DO_3
4	DO_1, DO_2, DO_5, DO_6

5. IDENTIFYING VO PARTNERS AND STRUCTURES

5.1. Conceptual Design Network formation

A request of a new product concept is represented by RFC_0 which is forwarded to the DOs in the VBE by the VO-planner. The problem we consider is how to individuate all DOs aggregations potentially capable of getting a collaborative construction of the product concept required by the RFC. In this section we describe a distributed process which leads to the emergence of a Design Request Network and, after that, lets the VO-planner determine the Conceptual Design Network. The process takes place in an established lapse of time during which each DO is able to:

- select an RFC, say r, amongst the ones which have been forwarded by the VO-planner,
- carry out a preliminary functional feature exploration to decide if it may respond to r and, in that case, let the VO-planner know the set $\mathcal{T}$ of all RFCs whose responses are considered sufficient and necessary to respond to r,
- send to the VO-planner an expression of interest to respond to r, conditional on obtaining responses to the RFCs in $\mathcal{T}$.

As DOs express their interest to respond to RFCs, a Design Request Network emerges. At the VO-planner side, its representation is obtained by adding RFCs and instances of both relations between RFCs/conditioned undertakings and conditioned undertakings/DOs, from time to time, until the time deadline is reached. In what follows the process, aimed to generate a Design Request Network, is formally described. Let:

d: the initial RFC forwarded by the VO-planner,
t_0: the moment in which d has been forwarded to the DOs in the VBE,
$t^\wedge$: the deadline by which the Design Request Network should be generated,
s: the "dummy" RFC whose response is not required,
O: the set of DOs in the VBE,

$t_1, t_2, \ldots, t_m$ (with $t_0 < t_1 < \ldots < t_m \leq t^\wedge$): the moments in which a DO (say o_i) sends to the VO-planner an expression of interest to respond to an RFC (say n_i), conditional on obtaining responses to RFCs, each of which is represented by a node in the set $\mathcal{T}_i$.
The process consists of the following steps :

➤ (inizialization at time t_0)   set $\mathcal{N}^0=\{s,d\}$, $\mathcal{E}^0=\varnothing$, $\alpha^0=\varnothing$;

➤ (iterative updating at time t_i)   for $i=1, \ldots, m$,

    $\mathcal{T}_\mathcal{V}= \mathcal{T}_i \, W \mathcal{N}^{i-1}$; $\mathcal{T}_\mathcal{V}$ represents the set of RFCs forwarded before time t_i and whose responses are necessary to o_i to respond to n_i;

    $\mathcal{T}_\mathcal{N}= \mathcal{T}_i\text{-}\mathcal{T}_\mathcal{V}$; $\mathcal{T}_\mathcal{N}$ represents the set of new RFCs forwarded at time t_i and whose responses are necessary to o_i to respond to n_i;

    $\mathcal{N}^i= \mathcal{N}^{i-1} \cup \mathcal{T}_\mathcal{N}$; $\mathcal{N}^i$ represents the set of all RFCs forwarded in the interval $[t_0, t_i]$;

    e_i: the hyperarc defined by setting $\mathcal{T}(e_i)=\mathcal{T}_i$, $h(e_i)= n_i$. It represents the conditioned undertaking given by o_i at time t_i

    $\mathcal{E}^i= \mathcal{E}^{i-1} \cup \{e_i\}$; $\mathcal{E}^i$ represents the set of all conditioned undertakings given by some DO in the VBE;

    $\alpha^i=\alpha^{i-1}$ on $\mathcal{E}^{i-1}$, $\alpha^i(e_i) = o_i$; it represents the functional relation between conditioned undertakings and DOs.

➤ (process end at time $t^\wedge$)   set $\mathcal{R}=(\mathcal{H},O,\alpha)$, with $\mathcal{H} = (\mathcal{N},\mathcal{E})$,
                                    $\mathcal{N}=\mathcal{N}^m$, $\mathcal{E}=\mathcal{E}^m$, $\alpha=\alpha^m$.

Once the Design Request Network, denoted by $\mathcal{R}=(\mathcal{H},O,\alpha)$, has been generated, the VO-planner may verify the hyperconnection of d to s in $\mathcal{H}$, by means of a hypergraph traversal algorithm that runs in polynomial time on the size of $\mathcal{H}$ (Nielsen, 2005; Volpentesta, 2005). Thus, the VO-planner is able to know if there exists at least one VO potentially capable of generating a product concept required by the RFC_0. Moreover, under some reasonable assumptions that reflect the reality of collaborative concept design, the hypernetwork $\mathcal{H}_{\eta_{sd}}$ on $\mathcal{H}$ may be found in polynomial time on the size of $\mathcal{H}$ and all the hyperpaths $\mathcal{H}_\pi$, $\pi \in \Pi(s,d)$ may be found in polynomial time on the cardinality of $\Pi(s,d)$, (Volpentesta, 2005). Thus, the VO-planner is able to determine $\mathcal{R}_{sd}=(\mathcal{H}_{\eta_{sd}},O,d_{\eta_{sd}})$ and $\mathcal{R}_\pi=(\mathcal{H}_\pi,O,\alpha_\pi)$, with $\pi \in \Pi(s,d)$, i.e. the Conceptual Design Network and all its DCs, respectively.

5.2. Concepts functionality and VOs identification

In what follows, we assume that there exists at least one DC in $\mathcal{R}=(\mathcal{H},O,\alpha)$, i.e. d is hyperconnected to s in $\mathcal{H}$. The process is divided in two phases: a) functional description phase; b) functional concept and DC evaluation.

a) In this phase, a recursive composition of Functional Description Tasks (FDTs), carried out by DOs along the Conceptual Design Network, takes place. The aim is to obtain functionality descriptions of the concept required by the RFC_0. Any FDT is associated to an hyperarc e in $\mathcal{E}_{\eta_{sd}}$, i.e. a conditioned undertaking in the Conceptual Design Network; the responses to RFCs identified by nodes in $\mathcal{T}(e)$ are the input of such FDT, while the response (eventually, a "null" response) to the RFC identified by $h(e)$ is the output. The FDT consists of a more or less detailed description (functional schemes, CAD models, delivery time, ...) of a new product part concept in accordance with requirements established by the RFC. A FDT is executed as many times as the number of DCs where the conditioned undertaking associated to the FDT occurs. This is due to the fact that FDT could be carried out according to some distinctive organizational, economical and technical criteria depending on the particular DC. Hence, executions of a FDT may take place only after the Conceptual Design Network has been individuated, since they depend on information which are available only after DCs have been individuated. Let $\mathcal{R}_{sd}=(\mathcal{H}_{\eta_{sd}},O,\alpha_{\eta_{sd}})$ and $\mathcal{R}_{\alpha}=(\mathcal{H}_{\pi},O,\alpha_{\pi})$, with $\pi\in\Pi(s,d)$, be, respectively, the Conceptual Design Network and all its DCs. Set:

$$\Pi(e)=\{\pi\in\Pi(s,d): e\in\mathcal{E}_{\pi}\}, \text{ for any } e\in\mathcal{E}_{\eta_{sd}}$$

and, for any $\pi\in\Pi(e)$, denote by $q_{\pi,e}$ the response to the RFC associated with $h(e)$ and given by $\alpha_{\pi}(e)$ when participating to the DC represented by $\mathcal{R}_{\alpha}$. Of course, such a response may be a "null response" (say $q_{\oslash}$), i.e. a message attesting no response will be given. For any $e\in\mathcal{E}_{\eta_{sd}}$, set:

$$Q(e)=(q_{\pi,e}), \pi\in\Pi(e)$$
and let $$Q=(Q(e)), e\in\mathcal{E}_{\eta_{sd}}$$

This phase is aimed to determine Q and, in what follows, we will see how it can be carried out. Since $e\in\mathcal{E}_{\eta_{sd}}$ and $\pi\in\Pi(e)$ if and only if $\pi\in\Pi(s,d)$ and $e\in\mathcal{E}_{\pi}$, we have

$$Q=(q_{\pi,e}), \pi\in\Pi(s,d), e\in\mathcal{E}_{\pi}$$

Therefore the phase may be divided into sub-phases $\mathcal{P}_{\pi}$, $\pi\in\Pi(s,d)$, each of which leads to the determination of

$$Q_{\pi}=(q_{\pi,e}), e\in\mathcal{E}_{\pi}$$

As it is shown in (Volpentesta, 2005) we have that $\forall~n\in\mathcal{N}_{\pi}$, with $n\neq s$, $1_!~e\in\mathcal{E}_{\pi}$ such that $h(e)=n$; hence, by setting $q_{\pi,n}=q_{\pi,e(n)}$, where $e(n)$ is the element of $\mathcal{E}_{\pi}$ such that $h(e)=n$, we have

$$Q_{\pi}=(q_{\pi,n}), n\in\mathcal{N}_{\pi}-\{s\}$$

This means that a response to any RFC, different from s, in $\mathcal{N}_{\pi}$, may be determined by recursively composing executions of FDTs along the DC represented by $\mathcal{R}_{\alpha}$. As matter of fact, the FDT associated with $e(n)$ in $\mathcal{R}_{\alpha}$ may be modelled as a computation of a function $f_{\pi,e(n)}$ which depends on the RFC individuated by n and on the responses $(q_{\pi,m})_{m\in\mathcal{T}(e(n))}$. Thus we have:

$$q_{\pi,n}=f_{\pi,e(n)}(n,(q_{\pi,m})_{m\in\mathcal{T}(e(n))}), \forall~n\in\mathcal{N}_{\pi}-\{s\}$$

where $q_{\pi,n}=q_{\oslash}$, if $q_{\pi,m}=q_{\oslash}$ for some $m\in\mathcal{T}(e(n))$.

Now, let $q_{\pi,s}$ be the "dummy" response to the "dummy" RFC associated with s and let $k=|\mathcal{E}_{\pi}|$. It follows that $|\mathcal{N}_{\pi}|=k+1$, (see footnote 2); the values in Q_{π} may be computed according to any sequence $s=n_0,n_1,...,n_k=d$ such that $\mathcal{T}(e(n_i))\subseteq\{n_0,n_1,...,n_{i-1}\}$, for $i=1,...,k$. The existence of at least one of these sequences is proved in (Volpentesta, 2005), and therefore the sub-process $\mathcal{P}_{\pi}$ can be actually carried out.

b) Once all responses in Q_{π}, $\pi\in\Pi(s,d)$ have been determined, the pairs $(\mathcal{R}_{\alpha},Q_{\pi})$, $\pi\in\Pi(s,d)$, may be ranked according to an evaluation function $v(\mathcal{R}_{\alpha},Q_{\pi})$ which is based on assessment criteria previously established by the VO-planner of the VBE. A model of such a function may take into account various organization factors (costs and time for the concept generation, relationship trust, coherence and cohesion, ...) with respect to a DC, as well as technical aspects (innovation level, consistency, feasibility, ...) with respect to concept functionality. Such an evaluation allows the VO-planner to identify those DCs that may constitute into VOs.

6. CONCLUSIONS

The shifting of the companies' attention from the necessity of "what to design" to the idea of "how to design", has led to the rising of new organizational models which can support innovative design paradigms such as co-design and concurrent engineering. In keeping with the viewpoint above, we have formalized an approach by which new concept function architectures and VO structures take shape in a circular way in a VBE for collaborative concept design. Hypernetworks and hyperpaths have been proposed as meaningful tools to represent logical structures underlying Conceptual Design Networks and Design Chains, respectively. This has allowed us to present a formal model of a process which identifies DO partners and their knowledge exchanges in a VO devoted to generate an innovative concept.

7. REFERENCES

1. Baia Y.W., et al. Collaborative design in product development based on product layout model. Robotics and Computer-Integrated Manufacturing, 2005; 21: 55–65.
2. Camarinha-Mathos LM, Afsarmanesh H. The Virtual Enterprise Concept, Infrastructures for Virtual Enterprises. Boston: Kluwer Academic Publisher; 1999.
3. Camarinha-Matos, L.M., Afsarmanesh, H. Elements of a base VE infrastructure. Computers in Industry, 2003; 51:139-163.
4. Chiu M. An organizational view of design communication in design collaboration. Design Studies, 2002; 23: 187–210.
5. Chu X.N., et al. Partnership Synthesis for Virtual Enterprises. Int. J.Ad. Man. Tech., 2002;19:384-391.
6. Frutos J. D., Borenstein D. A framework to support customer–company interaction in mass customization environments. Computers in Industry, 2004; 54: 115-135.
7. Giannini F., et al. A modeling tool for the management of product data in a co-design environment. Computer-aided Design, 2002; 34:1063-1073.
8. Huang G.Q., et al. Collaborative product definition on the Internet: a case study. J. of Mat. Processing Technology, 2003; 139:51-57.
9. Huang G.Q., Mak K.L.Web-based morphological charts for concept design in collaborative product development. J. of Intelligent manufacturing, 1999; 19:267-278.
10. Huifen W, et al. Feature-based collaborative design. J. of Mat. Proc. Technology, 2003;139:613–618
11. Nielsen L.R., Andersen K.A., Pretolani D., "Finding the K Shortest Hyperpaths", Computers & Operations Research, 2005; 32: 1477-1497.
12. Pahl G, Beitz W. Engineering Design. Springer, London; 1996.
13. Roy U., Kodkani S.S. Collaborative product conceptualization tool using web technology. Computers in Industry, 2000; 41:195-209.
14. Tseng C.-J., Abdalla H. A human–computer system for collaborative design. Journal of Materials Processing Technology, 2004; 155–156: 1964–1971.
15. Volpentesta A. Hyperpaths, Hypernetworks and Hypergraphs. Int. Rep. GiudaLab-DEIS Unical 2005
16. Volpentesta A., Muzzupappa M. The Formation of Collaborative Chains for Conceptual Design. In Collaborative Networks and Breeding Environments, ed. Kluwer Academic Publishers, 2005.
17. Wang L., et al.Collaborative conceptual design-state of the art and future trends.CAD, 2002;34:81-96
18. Yesilbas L., Lombard M. Towards a knowledge repository for collaborative design process: focus on conflict management. Computers in Industry, 2004; 55: 335-350.

---

[1] A *directed hypergraph* $\mathcal{H}$ is a pair $(\mathcal{N},\mathcal{E})$ where $\mathcal{N}$ is a non empty set of nodes and $\mathcal{E}$ is a set of hyperarcs; a hyperarc $e \in \mathcal{E}$ is defined as a pair $(T(e), h(e))$, where $T(e) \subseteq \mathcal{N}$, with $T(e) \neq \varnothing$, is its *tail*, and $h(e) \in \mathcal{N} - T(e)$ is its *head*.

[2] Let $\mathcal{H}=(\mathcal{N},\mathcal{E})$ be a directed hypergraph and let $s,d \in \mathcal{N}$. $\mathcal{N}' \subseteq \mathcal{N}$ is *s-hyperconnected* in $\mathcal{H}$ if $\mathcal{N}'=\{s\}$ or $\exists e \in \mathcal{E}$ such that $T(e) \subseteq \mathcal{N}'$ and $\mathcal{N}' - \{h(e)\}$ is *s-hyperconnected* in $\mathcal{H}$. We also say that n is *hyperconnected* to s in $\mathcal{H}$ if $\exists \mathcal{N}' \subseteq \mathcal{N}$ *s-hyperconnected* in $\mathcal{H}$ and $n \in \mathcal{N}'$. A *sub-hypergraph* $\mathcal{H}_\pi=(\mathcal{N}_\pi,\mathcal{E}_\pi)$ of $\mathcal{H}$, with $s,d \in \mathcal{N}_\pi$, is a hyperpath in $\mathcal{H}$ from s to d if $\mathcal{N}_\pi$ is *s-hyperconnected* in $\mathcal{H}_\pi$ and d is not *hyperconnected* to s in $(\mathcal{N}_\pi,\mathcal{E}_\pi-\{e\})$, $\forall\ e \in \mathcal{E}_\pi$. It's immediate to see that a hyperpath is cycle free and that one plus the number of its hyperarcs is equal to the number of its nodes.

43 | SOURCE NETWORKS FOR FORMATION OF VIRTUAL ENTERPRISES ACTIVE IN ELECTRONIC SYSTEMS DESIGN

Maciej Witczynski
Silesian University of Technology, Gliwice, Poland, witczynski@ciel.pl
POLAND

The paper proposes a model of a source network that can be applied for organizations active in different fields and especially in electronic systems design. In the second part of the article some implementation details are given concerning an IT system module to deal with dynamic virtual enterprise initiation. Search and selection of partners needed for collaborative design is performed with the use of web services technology. At the end we envisage a possible scenario of Virtual Enterprise creation for electronic design. Proposed model and methodology jointly with the applied technology make this procedure fast, simple and semi-automatic, thus very appropriate for an electronic design domain.

1. INTRODUCTION

The second half of 20th century was a time of fast growth of electronics. In the late 60-s Gordon E. Moore, one of the founders of Intel Company, predicted that the complexity of silicon integrated circuits (IC) would be regularly doubling about every 18 months. His predictions have been valid till nowadays and the trend still continues. Complexity of the IC can be measured by the number of single transistors located in a chip. Systems being developed within the last decade, like for instance: Field Programmable Gate Arrays (FPGA) and Application Specific Integrated Circuits (ASIC) include hundreds of millions of transistors. So complex systems are called Systems-on-Chip (SoC) as they incorporate on their one silicon structure the whole system including one or more microprocessors, large memory, analogue modules, input/output interfaces, connection buses, and peripheral elements.

Producers of electronic equipment are under a constant pressure to shorten the time between conceptualization of a new product and the time the product enters the market. In addition, producers aim at customization of the product in order to match requirements of a particular customer (or a group of customers) and bundle with it a set of additional services that span over the product lifecycle. These trends force electronic companies to seek for new design methods that improve design efficiency. On one hand a partial remedy can be a use of new types of hardware description languages, on the other one, a new "IP re-use design" paradigm can constitute a solution. Design re-use is based on previously designed electronic components, called Intellectual Property (IP) components that are used as pre-designed blocks of a newly designed system. This type of design can be especially fruitful when employed in collaborative environments of several

Please use the following format when citing this chapter:

Witczynski, M., 2006, in IFIP International Federation for Information Processing, Volume 224, Network-Centric Collaboration and Supporting Fireworks, eds. Camarinha-Matos, L., Afsarmanesh, H., Ollus, M., (Boston: Springer), pp. 407–416.

electronic companies that are IP component owners. Here comes the idea of a source network of electronic companies that can share among each other their IP components (Witczyński, 2005). Besides, members of the source network can share other resources, like design tools, competencies, etc. Creation of a dynamic virtual enterprise (VE) in response to market demands can additionally influence time-to-market decrease. Thus, collaborative electronic design performed by VE created within the source network can be the remedy to increasing requirements but it will work only when all cooperative processes both during a VE action but also during a source network operation are conducted in an agile and efficient way.

The rest of this paper is structured as follows. Section 2 shortly presents overviews of published relevant research results with stress on model and technology aspects. Section 3 describes basic models proposed for the source network. Section 4 addresses some issues related to the technology implemented in a context of a VE initiation module of an IT system. Section 5 depicts a scenario example of an electronic design initiation. Section 6 concludes the work and points out the innovations in the author's approach.

2. EXISTING SOLUTIONS

Many R&D projects addressed already the issue of computer supported source networks. Research based on a cluster of Virtual Organization (VO) related projects (Katzy, 2005) summarized VO modeling approaches. According to these studies a list of basic management roles in VO has been recognized. It includes: competence manager, project manager, auditor, network-coach, manager of in-/outsourcing, and broker. Prime actors in source networks named also Virtual Breeding Environments (VBE) have been identified in (ECOLEAD, 2005) as well.

These are:

- VBE Member – an organization registered at the VBE and ready to participate in the VBE activities
- VBE Administrator – an organization responsible for the VBE operation, evolution, and promotion
- Opportunity Broker – an organization that acquires new collaboration opportunities by marketing VBE competencies and negotiating with customers
- VO Planner (Integrator) – a player that identifies the necessary competencies and capacities, selects proper partners, and structures the new VO when a collaboration opportunity appears (often Broker and VO Planer can be the same organization)
- VO Coordinator – an organization that coordinates a VO during its life cycle
- Common model/information/tool Provider
- VBE Advisor
- Public Guest.

Proposed IT solutions in R&D projects were based on various technological approaches (Camarinha Matos, 2005). A computer assisted approach was proposed in the Prodnet project. VO creation and coordination functionalities were implemented in Borland C++ on the PRODNET platform (Camarinha Matos, 1997, 2001). The PRODNET platform included two main modules for each node-enterprise in the network: Internal Module and Cooperation Layer. The Internal Module included the complete structure of a specific company's information (data bases, information systems, etc.). The Cooperation Layer comprised coordination functionalities containing negotiation support system for facilitating partners search and the contractual processes during the formation of a VE, management of a contracts data base, and electronic catalogues (Camarinha Matos, 1997).

Agent based approaches were employed by different groups with various architectures. An example of such a solution is the VE Cockpit system described in (Rabelo, 2004), where multi agents were implemented with use of C++, Java, XML/Corba. The system was composed of local relational databases and a number of agents realizing system functionalities through three main tools (i.e. VE Configuration tool, VE Design tool, and VE Integration tool). The tools supported with different levels of automation following VE creation phases: the specification of the type of information exchanged among VE partners, the integration of VE partners' legacy systems with VE platform, the identification of VE topology, establishing access rights for VE partners.

A service based approach considers companies that are potential members of VE as "service providers". Collaboration among companies is based on sharing the services by the companies. There is one entity that keeps a catalog of services announced by various VE members. Three main functions are executed by the network members: service publishing, discovering and invoking. Web services (WS) are a proper technology for this approach. There is however no direct partners search in this case. Searched and selected are services offered by different VE members and then they are composed in more complex tasks (Camarinha Matos, 2005, dos Santos, 2004).

Another solution from the technology point of view is a mix of the two later mentioned. It includes both technologies: computer agents and web services. A proposed solution of this type is XESS (XML based Expert System Shell). The system contains three main components: the Business Rules Composer, the Agent Administrator, and the Business Rules Engine Agent. All these components together give the possibility to integrate data and plan common business processes in VE with a special attention to a virtual multi-organizational supply chain (Shields, 2004; Camarinha Matos, 2005).

3. INFRASTRUCTURE MODEL

This paper concentrates on the concept of a source network incorporating companies active in electronic systems design and its efficient operation. In this section its base model is depicted. By the base model we mean a management model that describes the structure of the network, main roles, and its functionalities. The source network is a group of companies that joined their forces and developed a common preparedness to quickly respond to specific market needs and customer demands. All companies in the network can play certain role according to the network architecture and specific situation at the moment. In the case of electronic design source network we can see four main characters of member companies. These are: Network Manager (NMG) – preferably one company for the whole network, Network Broker (NB) – one or few companies in the network, Project Manager

(PM) – potentially all members, in a particular moment the company that won the competition for the project coordination, Network Member (NMB) – all companies in the network – see Figure 1. The architecture and main roles are similar to those applied in the research cited above. Hence, our proposal can be also adopted in other disciplines. The difference is that we limited the number of key roles to only four in our solution. This results in a simplification of the source network model and consequently in a plain IT infrastructure. This could be achieved by fastening together VO Planner and VO Coordinator as one Project Manager. It is quite natural, especially in electronic design sector. Roles like Opportunity Broker and VO Planner should be kept separate in our opinion.

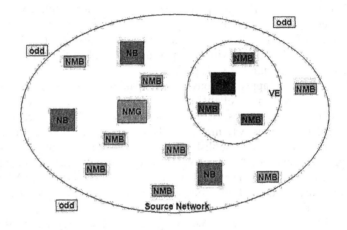

Figure 1 – Idea of a source network for electronic systems design

Main tasks related to each source network role are as follows.
  1) Network Manager (NMG):
- defining service range offered by the network to potential customers
- maintenance of network knowledge (technical standards, standard network procedures related to the services offered)
- data maintenance about members core competences
- search for new network members and their registration
- evaluation of potential network members
- network members common activities financial control.
  2) Network Broker (NB):
- search for customers and collecting external RFQ/orders
- marketing of network services and competences outside the network
- announcing possible projects inside the network (ad board, sending RFQ)
- organizing a competition for Project Managers concerning different projects
- passing details of the task and responsibility to the winning Project Managers
- participation in the customer - network contract negotiation together with PM.
  3) Project Manager (PM):

- preliminary detailed planning of a project (an electronic design task) – determination of all sub-tasks and processes
- VE initiation (confirmation of final plan of the project)
- VE contract negotiation basing on the action plan confirmed during VE initiation
- VE / design project coordination.
  4) Network Member (NMB):
- search for customers and collecting external RFQ/orders – passing them to NB
- data maintenance about its core competences, tools, available IP
- possibility of search in NB ad board
- possibility of receiving RFQ and making the offers for NB (applying for the PM position) and PM (applying for the project participant position)
- cooperation with PM and others NMB within VE – project participation.

Not all tasks and functionalities mentioned above can be accomplished as a part of our IT system. Some of them must be supported by a human activity (e.g. a financial control or contractual negotiations). To make clearer the view of the network another model can be applied. This is a management-oriented process model that shows data flow and distribution of activities related to core business processes of the network. This model is depicted on Figures 2, 3, and 4. Here we concentrate on functionalities to be carried out by the IT system.

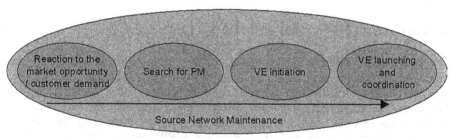

Figure 2 - Main functionalities (business processes) of the network.

Models illustrated above have a rather descriptive character. When the IT infrastructure of a source network is designed we have to apply more sophisticated models that cover in detail all small steps, exceptions, data entities, and possible scenarios. These models should be created by using a dedicated modeling language and tool. The choice of a proper modeling language depends highly on the technology provided. In our opinion the web services (WS) technology is the most suitable for source network implementation.

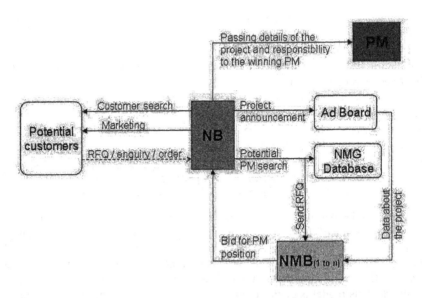

Figure 3 - Information flow and distribution of activities during PM search phase.

4. VE CREATION – IMPLEMENTATION ISSUES

The selection of the WS technology as a base technology for source network implementation is due to several factors. This technology provides the possibility for secure business processes execution and exposition in the Internet domain outside of firewalls. It gives a possibility for business processes publishing as services. Although the services can use internal data, they are separated from more stable company systems because they are located on WWW servers. WS are based on universally agreed specifications and standards (HTTP, XML, SOAP, WSDL), which do support their interoperability. Since WS are based on XML, they are proper for information exchange among heterogeneous systems, so the access to them is possible from any platform.

Management-oriented process modeling is a source for the IT system model which should be accomplished with use of a dedicated modeling language. There are many enterprise modeling languages (ATHENA, 2005) that could be used for a virtual distributed organization. If WS are to be applied, one can consider the following: UML (Unified Modeling Language), UEML (Unified Enterprise Modeling Language), UML for EAI (UML for Enterprise Application Integration), WSCDL (Web Services Choreography Description Language), WSCI (Web Service Choreography Interface), BPEL4WS (Business Process Execution Language for Web Services) shortly named BPEL. A proper modeling language can give the possibility for direct usage of the model during the implementation process. Thus the best choice seemed to be UML, WSCI, WSCDL, and BPEL. However the real value of the proposed languages can only be assessed during the implementation. It seems that our solution requires usage of a couple of them.

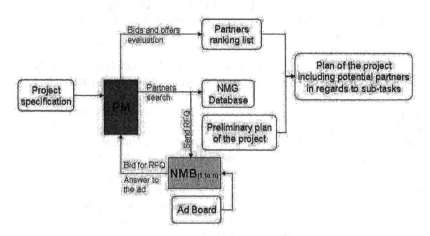

Figure 4. Information flow and distribution of activities during VE initiation phase.

An implementation endeavor has been focused on the VE initiation phase so far. This stage consists of the following steps (see Figure 4):

1) PM searches for partners within data stored on NMG servers (project requirements are taken into consideration).
2) PM sends RFQ to the several NMBs chosen (potential project participants).
3) NMBs answer RFQ sent by PM or answer to NB ad read on the ad board.
4) Offer evaluation by PM – building a ranking list of potential project participants for each design sub-task in the project (considering core competencies, available tools and IP catalogs, as well as trust and own past experiences).
5) PM creates preliminary plan of the project including all sub-tasks and potential partners (preliminary VE contract definition).

The VE initiation module that helps to complete these steps is a part of the whole IT system for the source network drafted above. The system realizes all necessary functionalities through flow of proper software applications. A part of these applications can be executed due to web services that are placed on WWW servers of different network members. Which services are located on the server depends on the role the company plays in the source network. In the following a list of applications and services needed for the VE initiation module is enumerated:

- WWW NMG server:
  - Access to data about different NMBs – PM fills in a form of required competencies / tools / IP data and database search is performed
  - Access to data about potential projects / NB ad board
- WWW PM server:
  - VE potential partners list creation based on the service and data from NMG
  - Sending RFQ to the potential partners from the list (taking into account required competencies, description of the task)
  - Receiving and evaluation of the offers given by NMBs– building a ranking list of potential project participants for each design sub-task in the project

- Based on the offers given by NMBs planning the projects (task flow, time schedule, responsible partners and their potential substitutes)
- WWW NMB server:
  - Reading NB ad board
  - Answering to RFQ from PM and to NB's ad (info about its own competencies and resources, evaluation of its own preparedness for the project participation, etc.).

As pointed out above, web services composition can be performed with aid of different languages. Each one has some advantages and disadvantages. We preferred to model the IT system with graphical UML. Then we can migrate to either BPEL or WSCI. This action can be already automatically made with proper tools like for instance: Emerging Technologies Toolkit version 1.1 (ETTK) released by IBM / Alphaworks, which takes process defined in the UML and generates the corresponding BPEL and WSDL files to implement that process (Mantell, 2003).

To model the complete functionality of a system more than one modeling language is necessary in order to organize WS execution. BPEL is appropriate for WS orchestration and WSCI is suitable for WS choreography (dos Santos, 2004). WS orchestration is a description of services behavior with applying workflow concepts. This description is interpreted and executed by an orchestration engine that is controlled by one of the services. Applying BPEL is useful when we have to coordinate complex processes that consist of many executable services. The choreography approach is less centralized. Each service only "knows" about its own interactions and behavior. There is no process that has a global control of the composition. Both discussed languages for WS composition description, depending on the functionality performed, should be adopted in the system. Currently the detailed IT model of the whole source network is under development. During this action the mentioned modeling languages will be investigated for their appropriateness for particular cases.

5. SoC DESIGN INITIATION – A SCENARIO EXAMPLE

In this section a scenario example of System-on-Chip (SoC) design initiation is presented. We assume that the source network received an enquiry concerning SoC design. The required system should be composed of a microprocessor part, memory, and I/O interfaces. Detailed requirements are included in the specification attached to the enquiry sent by a customer. We also assume that PM has been established and that PM prepared a preliminary plan of "IP re-use" design project including design sub-tasks: IP component search and selection, design creation, simulation, synthesis, verification. The scenario shows a possible project initiation phase (Figure 5).

The preliminary plan of a design project is an input data for further actions. This plan defines the main sub-tasks (the required core competencies related to them), required IP components (that should be available – in our example these are: microprocessor, memory, I/O interface), and tools (e.g. software to perform certain design sub-tasks). The service "Partners search" (1) checks data records stored on NMG server about all NMBs and as a result gives addresses of all NMBs that have required factors marked as positive (answer: The best partners(2)). Then PM sends detailed RFQ to all NMBs indicated (3). An answer to RFQ service is a bid received from each interested NMB. The bids (4) are of similar form to the answer about the best partners (2) – these are a kind of forms that include evaluation of all important factors mentioned above. The evaluation is more precise this time – not only positive or negative but each factor is assessed by a number of points. Since the evaluation is made by NMB itself, it is called a subjective evaluation. The form of a bid can include additional fields like e.g. availability in a specified time period, price for sub-tasks to be completed by the particular NMB. The bids can be filled in automatically by the service located on the NMB server or with human assistance. The same forms in regards to all offering NMBs are filled in by PM according to its previous knowledge and experience with specific NMB. After summing the "objective" evaluation made by PM with "subjective" evaluations of NMB, PM receives ranking lists of potential partners that gives the possibility to create the final plan of the project with potential partners given for each sub-tasks. The next step will be the contract negotiation that is assumed to be accomplished without an IT system help.

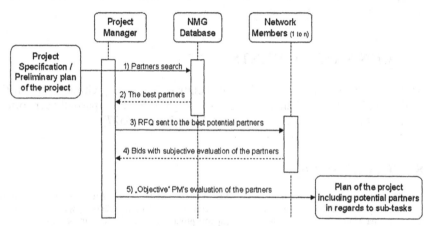

Figure 5 – An envisaged scenario of a project initiation

6. CONCLUSIONS

A contribution of the paper in relation to already published research results is mainly in the proposed model and methodology. Innovation is also in an application domain, namely in electronic systems design. The employed Web Services technology, although very popular nowadays, is still not mature enough, so dealing with it can bring new findings. Some of them have been envisaged in the paper.

The proposed model of the source network organizes the work of the whole network in such a way that the response to the customer's enquiry or market demand can be really fast. The model includes small number of key roles in the source network. The responsibilities are clearly shared. The main responsibility is taken by the PM that decides about project participants and a precise project plan. Some important activities, like negotiation or contracting need to be completed with a human assistance.

The methodology includes only two network internal competitions – for PM establishment and for a proper design partners selection. The whole VE creation procedure is quite simple and many of its steps are accomplished promptly and automatically with the use of WS. The value of the presented solution when compared to the competing ones is its simplicity. The methodology of partner selection could be improved in future by applying a more sophisticated multi-criteria mathematical support for building potential partners ranking list.

We expect that the technologies applied during the current system development will lead to an easy communication within the heterogeneous source networks. Due to the similarity of both internal competitions some of web services can be likely used in both of them exchangeable.

The proposed source network concept has been influenced strongly by the application domain. A VO dedicated for design projects should have centralized management, hence the role of PM is so strong. Consequently the fact that PM has to plan and coordinate the whole project affects relatively simple model and methodology. An idea of conducting electronic systems design by VE created on the source network base is also an original one.

7. ACKNOWLEDGMENTS

This work has been realized in the Collaborative Engineering Group of the Institute of Electronics, Silesian University of Technology. It has been partially supported by the EU MAPPER project (FP6-2004-IST-NMP-2 No 016527).

8. REFERENCES

1. ATHENA project's public deliverable, WD A1.1.2 - State of the Art in Enterprise Modeling Techniques and Technologies to Support Enterprise Interoperability, 2005, www.athena-ip.org;
2. Camarinha Matos, L. M. – A platform to support production planning and management in a virtual enterprise - Proceedings of CAPE'97- IFIP/SME Int. Conference on Computer Applications in Production and Engineering (Chapman & Hall), Detroit, USA, Nov 97;
3. Camarinha Matos, L. M.; Afsarmanesh, H.; Rabelo, R. J. - Infrastructure developments for agile virtual enterprises, International Journal on Computer Integrated Manufacturing, 2001;
4. Katzy, B.; Zhang, C.; Löh, H. – Reference Models for Virtual Organisations - in Virtual Organizations – Systems and Practices, Springer 2005, ISBN: 0-387-23755-0
5. Camarinha Matos, L. M.; Silveri, I; Afsarmanesh, H.; Oliveira, A. I. – Towards a Framework for Creation of Dynamic Virtual Organizations - in Collaborative Networks and their Breeding Environments, Springer 2005, ISBN: 0-387-28259-9
6. ECOLEAD public deliverable, D 21.1 – Characterization of Key Components, Features, and Operating Principles of the Virtual Breeding Environment, 2005, http://www.ecolead.org;
7. Mantell, K. - From UML to BPEL - Model Driven Architecture in a Web services world, 2003, http://www-128.ibm.com/developerworks/webservices/library/ws-uml2bpel/index.html;
8. Rabelo, R. J.; Baldo, F.; Tramontin, R.; Pereira-Klen, Jr., A.; Klen, E. R. - Smart Configuration of Dynamic Virtul Enterprises, IFIP 18th World Computer Congress, Toulouse, France, 2004;
9. dos Santos, I. J. G.; Madeira, E. R. M. – VM-FLOW: Using Web Services Orchestration and Choreography to Implement a Policy-based Virtual Marketplace, IFIP 18th World Computer Congress, Toulouse, France, 2004;
10. Shields, B.; Molloy, O. - Dynamic Configuration of Collaboration in Networked Organisations, IFIP 18th World Computer Congress, Toulouse, France, 2004;
11. Witczyński, M.; Pawlak, A. – Virtual Organizations in the Electronic Sector - in Virtual Organizations – Systems and Practices, Springer 2005, ISBN: 0-387-23755-0

PART 14

NEGOTIATION AND CONTRACTING

44

A CASE STUDY ON ELECTRONIC CONTRACTING IN ON-LINE ADVERTISING - STATUS AND PROSPECTS

Samuil Angelov, Paul Grefen
Technology Management Department
Technical University Eindhoven
THE NETHERLANDS
s.angelov@tm.tue.nl
p.w.p.j.grefen@tm.tue.nl

Business-to-business electronic contracting has gained attention in recent years as a way to improve traditional contracting practices as well as a paradigm that allows the support of new business models in an enterprise. This paper presents the business case of the Dutch news medium Telegraaf for contracting of advertising spots in its on-line edition. We discuss replacement of current contracting practices with advanced electronic contracting that will allow Telegraaf to highly automate its contract establishment, enactment, and management processes. This high level of automation presents an opportunity to Telegraaf for organizational restructuring and for the support of new business models that improve the competitiveness of the company.

1. INTRODUCTION

Since the very beginning of human history, people have been exchanging values. Contracts between value-exchanging sides have been adopted to specify the exchanged values and the rights and obligations of the participants. Nowadays, contracts are an indispensable tool in business exchanges. In business-to-business relationships "all economic production and exchange processes are organized through contracts. Contracts are the instruments and the means for the organization of exchange relations" (Wigand *et al.*, 1997).

Business-to-business e-contracting uses information technologies for improving the efficiency and effectiveness of contracting processes of companies (Griffel *et al.*, 1998; Koetsier *et al.*, 2000). One way to implement e-contracting is by simply digitizing existing paper contracts and using fast communication channels for contract establishment (e.g., e-mail). We call this type of e-contracting "shallow e-contracting" (Angelov and Grefen, 2004). Shallow e-contracting improves the efficiency of the contracting process by reducing the time and costs for communication. However, shallow e-contracting requires significant human involvement and does not change traditional business and organizational models in a company. Shallow e-contracting can be supported by existing and widely accepted information technology (e-mail clients, scanners, text editors, etc.). An alternative

Please use the following format when citing this chapter:

Angelov, S., Grefen, P., 2006, in IFIP International Federation for Information Processing, Volume 224, Network-Centric Collaboration and Supporting Fireworks, eds. Camarinha-Matos, L., Afsarmanesh, H., Ollus, M., (Boston: Springer), pp. 419–428.

way to support e-contracting is by implementing a dedicated e-contracting system that can fully (or to a great extent) automate the e-contract establishment, enactment, and management. We call this type of e-contracting "deep e-contracting" (Angelov and Grefen, 2004). Deep e-contracting eliminates human participation in contracting processes (or significantly decreases it). The high level of automation of contracting processes allows companies to realize new business and organizational models that lead to improved market competitiveness. We call these new models the "paradigms of e-contracting". In our previous work, we have identified five main paradigms of deep e-contracting (Angelov and Grefen, 2004), namely, the micro-contracting (μ-contracting), just-in-time-contracting (τ-contracting), precision-contracting (π-contracting), enactment-contracting (ε-contracting), and management-contracting (γ-contracting) paradigms. The micro-contracting paradigm represents the opportunity contracts to be customized on a mass scale. In the just-in-time-contracting paradigm, companies can establish contractual relationships in the most suitable for them moment, with the preferred contracting party and contracting conditions. In the precision-contracting paradigm, companies can automatically define and verify e-contracts. In the enactment-contracting paradigm, parties can automatically link contract establishment and contract enactment due to the use of electronic contracts and can subsequently automatically enact contracts. In the management-contracting paradigm, parties can automatically link the contract establishment process with the contract management process, and can subsequently automatically manage the contracting relations. In contrast to shallow e-contracting, deep e-contracting requires from an enterprise the implementation of an advanced information system that can support complex contracting processes in diverse business contexts.

Currently, the domain of advertising is based on relatively long lasting campaigns that are agreed upon significantly ahead of time (Angelov and Udo, 2005). Thus, advertising can be seen as a mainly static market. The reason for this status quo is the static space that was used until recently for advertising, e.g., newspapers, billboards, TV commercials, etc. Traditionally, the agreement between an advertiser and an advertising medium for an advertising campaign is stated in a written contract.

With the introduction of the Internet, a new advertising space that provides opportunities for dynamic advertising and precise audience targeting has appeared (The Economist, 2005). On-line advertisements are intangible products. Consequently, the delivery of the advertisement to the advertising medium and its publishing can be highly automated. However, traditional paper contracting requires many communications (which might require traveling) and legal and business expertise during the contract establishment and enactment. The slowness and the high costs of traditional, paper-based, written contracts make them unsuitable for the protection of the rights of parties in the dynamic, highly automated environment that is offered by on-line advertising. The possibility for dynamic and flexible agreement and execution of on-line advertising campaigns (already supported by a number of companies, e.g., Google and Yahoo!) and the need for legal protection of the trading parties in these highly automated settings (currently, marginally addressed by companies) were the incentive to select the domain of on-line advertising as a domain in which to discuss the application of deep e-contracting.

In this paper, we investigate the current level of automation of the contracting process for on-line advertising in the Dutch news medium Telegraaf. We describe the currently implemented paradigms of e-contracting and the technology used for it by Telegraaf. Based on these observations, we discuss the implementation of deep e-contracting with its full potential, allowing Telegraaf to support all five paradigms of deep e-contracting. The consequences from the support of these five paradigms for the future of the on-line advertising business are addressed.

The paper has three main contributions. First, the paper contributes to the popularization of deep e-contracting. Currently, the opportunities offered by e-contracting are underestimated by the industry. The paper provides an elaboration of a practical example for the new opportunities revealed by deep e-contracting to companies that operate in dynamic and highly automated business environments. Second, the paper paints a picture for the future development of on-line advertising and the legal protection of the companies involved in it. Conclusions are based on the description of the case of Telegraaf (which involves the usage of explicit business contracts but lacks dynamics) and on the dynamic and flexible advertising scheme supported by Google (which currently lacks advanced contracting support). Last but not least, the application of research results from the domain of e-contracting on a real business case allows us to validate existing, theoretical, research findings.

This paper is organized as follows. In Section 2, we provide a description of the case. The contracting process at Telegraaf and its level of automation are discussed. In Section 3, we analyze the case in terms of supported e-contracting paradigms and the possibility for their full support. In Section 4, validation of the conclusions from Section 3 is presented. The validation is based on the on-line advertising scheme of Google. The paper ends with conclusions.

2. CASE DESCRIPTION

The Dutch news medium Telegraaf offers advertising space on its network of electronic editions to potential clients. Its network includes the main news web site[i], as well as a number of specialized web sites (e.g. "Auto Telegraaf" is dedicated to trading of cars).

This section contains a description of the contracting practices for on-line advertising at Telegraaf. The usage of a contracting framework for the case description facilitates the elaboration of a well-structured discussion that focuses on the main contracting issues. That is why, in this section, we use the "4W framework for contracting" (Angelov and Grefen, 2003). The 4W framework defines and describes the main contracting concepts and the relations between them, and is thus a convenient tool for capturing the key elements of the case and for its structured presentation. The 4W framework is constructed on the basis of the four interrogatives (hence the name 4W), namely, "Who" (describing the *actors* involved in the business relationship), "Where" (describing the contracting *contexts*), "What" (describing the *values exchanged* and the *conditions* for their exchange), and "How" (describing the *means used* and *processes performed* during the contracting relationship). Next, using the 4W framework as a guiding tool, we discuss the main contracting concepts in the case of Telegraaf (shown in the text in italics).

2.1 Who

Four main *parties* can be involved in the on-line advertising scenario. Telegraaf plays the role of a *service provider*. The Advertiser (i.e., the *service consumer*) can create and plan its advertising campaign in-house (see Figure 1). If this scenario takes place, the Advertiser directly establishes a contract for its campaign with Telegraaf. Alternatively, an advertising agency can be used by the Advertiser as a *mediator* for planning and handling its advertising campaign. If an Advertiser makes use of an advertising agency, it signs a contract for its campaign with the agency that in turn signs a contract with the medium where it will advertise the products/services of its client (in this case Telegraaf). Additionally, a graphical media company can be used by the Advertiser as an *auxiliary implementor* for the creation of the advertising material. If an Advertiser makes use of a graphical media company, it signs a contract with it. In scenarios which involve a graphical media company and/or an advertising agency, the Advertiser forms a virtual enterprise (VE) with them. From the perspective of Telegraaf, the client may appear to be the Advertiser or the advertising agency. The case presented in this paper investigates both, the classical scenario of contracting between the Advertiser and Telegraaf, as well as the more complex scenario of contracting between the virtual enterprise and Telegraaf. In the case description, often, the general term "client" is used to denote the counter party of Telegraaf, abstracting from the type of the client. When the difference in the type of counter party introduces differences to the trading scenario, advertisers and advertising agencies are explicitly distinguished.

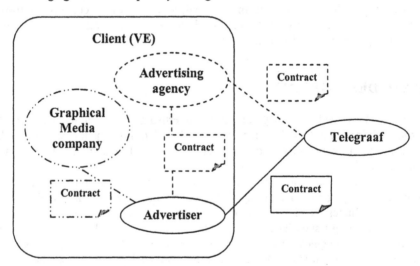

Figure 1 - Actors in the case

2.2 Where

A number of *business* and *legal* issues define the *context* in which contracting relations between Telegraaf and its clients take place.

Telegraaf plays the dominant role in the business relation. It controls the contracting process, provides the contract offers, etc. Clients are usually large or medium-sized companies that want to advertise their products or services. Clients that are recognized by the ROTA organization (Council for Control and Supervision of Advertising) are allowed to make their payments on fixed dates (regardless of the date of the invoice) and can be given discounts at the discretion of Telegraaf. Usually, ROTA recognized clients are advertising agencies.

A new contract is established for each advertising campaign and no contract dependencies exist. Each contract between Telegraaf and a client is bounded to the general provisions of Telegraaf.

2.3 What

Telegraaf offers the *service* of publishing digital advertisements in its on-line editions. In return, clients must provide a corresponding *financial reward* to Telegraaf, i.e., an agreed payment.

Telegraaf offers different advertising plans. An advertisement can be agreed to be published on the main news web site of Telegraaf, on one of the sites part of the network of Telegraaf, or on a sub-section of the news web site (international news, sport, weather, etc.). An advertising plan is assigned a fixed tariff ("BasicTariff"). For each advertising plan Telegraaf offers several types of advertisements, i.e., banners, large rectangles, pop-unders, screen-ads, textlinks. Each of these types of advertisements is assigned a factor ("Factor") that shows its "advertising power".

Telegraaf requires a minimum amount of 1000 euros for an advertising campaign. The price for a campaign is based on the number of desired impressions (an impression is the delivery of a single advertisement to a single viewer one time). The advertising tariff for one thousand impressions (also known as CPM - cost per thousand) is calculated through the formula: Adv.Tariff = "BasicTariff" x "Factor".

For advertising in Telegraaf, a number of general *provisions* apply. These provisions are contracting clauses that are valid for any contract of Telegraaf on on-line advertising and express general rights and obligations of the contracting parties. The complete set of general provisions is provided on-line[ii]. Examples of such provisions are:

- The client has to deliver its advertisement at least two days before the beginning of the campaign.
- Each of the parties can end the contract by means of a registered letter out of court, if the other party fails to fulfill its obligations.

The conditions that are specific for the business relation are specified in the contract in the form of *exchange value provisions*. A reference to the general provisions of Telegraaf is included in the contract.

2.4 How

Typically, during a *contracting process* a client will read the proposed advertising plans by Telegraaf and the general provisions imposed by Telegraaf. After consultation with representative of Telegraaf, it will inform the sales department of on-line advertising at Telegraaf for its decision on the preferred advertising plan and campaign. Telegraaf will send a signed contract to the client, which the client will sign and send back. As a last step the client will send the advertisement and after he receives an invoice will pay the required amount. Telegraaf will feed the established contract into its advertising system. It will check the advertisement for compliance with its requirements (optionally, it might make changes on the advertisement) and will publish the advertisement as agreed in the advertising plan. Depending on the level of trust in the client, Telegraaf will send an invoice to the client and expect payment prior to the start of the advertising campaign or after it.

Humans from both contracting parties are required for the negotiation of the advertising campaigns and the contract formation. Negotiations concentrate mainly on the duration of an advertising campaign, as well as on the values of advertising-related parameters (type of advertisement, network in which the campaign will take place). The possible sets of values for these parameters are pre-defined by Telegraaf. Constraints on selection of an advertising plan can be set by Telegraaf due to limited availability of spots and inventory. Negotiations for campaigns that include a single advertisement can be seen as multi-attribute negotiations. Negotiations for campaigns that involve a set of advertisements become of heterogeneous nature. However, Telegraaf has no special policies for negotiations on bundles of advertisements (negotiation on bundles of goods is an attractive form for exchanging values and has received a significant attention (Somefun *et al.*, 2004)). The time for contract establishment may vary from minutes to hours (or even days), depending on the need for verification of the client and the speed of decision making and contract confirmation from the client's side. The contract offer can be sent to the client by mail, fax, or e-mail. Telegraaf and its clients make use of popular applications like e-mail and text-processing tools, which lead to decreased costs and time for *communication* and contract establishment. In addition, Telegraaf uses two information systems for the *contract establishment* and *contract enactment*.

The "contract establishment system" supports the creation of contracts, as well as reservation of advertisement spots. For the contract *content*, predefined *templates* are used. The system provides an interface to human operators for selecting the proper template and filling it in. It supports *human-readable* representation, as well as *machine-readable representation* of contracts. The contract offer is sent to the client in a human-readable representation. The "contract establishment system" is based on an old legacy system that has recently been tailored by Telegraaf to support its needs for higher automation of the contracting process.

As soon as a contract offer is accepted by a client, a representative of the sales department of Telegraaf sends the machine-readable representation of the contract (provided by the "contract establishment system") to the "advertising system". The "advertising system" interprets contracts and starts the advertising campaigns. It automatically publishes the advertisements as agreed in the contract. Thus, the "advertising system" supports automation of the contract enactment and its *management* during the advertising stage. By the end of an advertising campaign, the system informs the sales department of Telegraaf.

3. CASE ANALYSIS - STATUS AND PROSPECTS

Next, we briefly evaluate the level of automation of the contracting process in the current business settings at Telegraaf and explain the benefits that full implementation of deep e-contracting may introduce to this case.

3.1 Status

The usage of information technology during contract establishment and contract enactment is a step towards deep e-contracting. From the case description, it can be concluded that Telegraaf with its contract establishment and advertising systems supports the enactment-contracting paradigm. The management-contracting paradigm is supported only partially in the contract enactment phase.

However, the involvement of humans required for contract establishment, does not allow Telegraaf to support micro-contracting, just-in-time-contracting, and precision-contracting. The lack of a dedicated information system for the automation of the contract management requires human involvement in the contract management during the contract establishment and enactment.

3.2 Prospects

In a possible future scenario, Telegraaf could implement deep e-contracting in its full potential. Telegraaf could employ all five paradigms of e-contracting, i.e., micro-, just-in-time-, precision-, management-, and enactment-contracting improving significantly its market competitiveness.

Micro-contracting will allow Telegraaf to support low-cost campaigns allowing small-size companies to use on-line advertising as well. For example, a campaign with a budget of 10 EUR will allow the publishing of about 500 advertisements. As on-line advertising allows precise targeting of advertisements to the proper audience, small campaigns may still bring benefits to an advertiser.

Just-in-time-contracting will allow Telegraaf to support contract establishment in the moment preferred by its clients. For example, clients might prefer to agree on an advertising campaign moments (minutes, seconds) before the actual start of the campaign. Incentives for clients to establish a contract at this late stage may be lower prices of advertising spots, publishing of news that will be of interest to the audience targeted by the client, occurrence of an event that will attract a huge amount of readers, etc.

The support of the micro- and just-in-time-contracting paradigms will lead to increased market dynamics in advertising. The high market dynamics will create an incentive for Telegraaf to support more flexible pricing policies, diverse bonus strategies (e.g., contracting of advertising bundles), and other complex business rules. For the dynamic establishments of such complex contracts, automatic contract verification is a prerequisite. Thus, precision-contracting will be required for the dynamic establishment of correct, complex contracts.

The employment of the contract-management paradigm in its full potential will allow Telegraaf automation of the management of contracting of advertising campaigns, further minimizing the requirements on human power at the department of on-line advertising sales.

By employing micro-, just-in-time-, and precision-contracting, and combining them with the already employed enactment-, and management-contracting paradigms, Telegraaf will achieve full automation of the contract establishment, enactment, and management processes. Only checking of advertisements for compliance with the company policies may still have to be performed manually. However, as estimated by Telegraaf, this step requires currently between 15 and 120 seconds and will not cause substantial delays. Furthermore, in the case of repeated campaigns, this step can be omitted. Another manual work that currently cannot be automated is the editing of advertising materials that do not comply with the requirements of Telegraaf. At this point this step requires at minimum 1 day (it can require up to 5 days). Thus, just-in-time- and micro-contracting will be applicable for clients with repeating campaigns and/or for clients that provide correct advertising material.

Exceptions that will require performance of certain activities by humans (e.g., the provision of a non-compliant advertisement will require its manual editing by Telegraaf) may occur in all scenarios. The future e-contracting system used by Telegraaf should support seamless transition from automated to human execution of activities. For the development of its e-contracting system, Telegraaf may use existing research results on design of e-contracting architectures (Angelov, 2006).

4. VALIDATION

Clearly, the management-, enactment- and precisions-contracting paradigms bring benefits to Telegraaf. A question that emerges after that discussion is whether advertisers and publishing media will be interested in providing higher dynamics in the on-line advertising domain by introducing micro- and just-in-time-contracting. Will it be beneficial to advertiser and publishers if advertisers can perform micro-advertising campaigns that last only a day or even less? Will companies be interested in having the opportunity of deciding on an advertising campaign at any moment, i.e., will they be interested in just-in-time-advertising? To answer these questions, we did two separate investigations. We presented these ideas to Telegraaf (Angelov and Udo, 2005), who found the new models highly intriguing and expressed intention for their support in the nearest future. Furthermore, we investigated the support for these new business models in one of the most advanced advertising schemes that currently exist, i.e., the advertising scheme offered by Google "AdWords". Next, we briefly discuss the AdWords advertising scheme.

4.1 The AdWords scheme

In the AdWords scheme, a company can publish a textual advertisement in the search result of a query submitted by a user (the popular term for this advertising scheme is "sponsored search" and was originally developed by Overture). To get its advertisement published, an advertiser participates in a fully-automated, multi-attribute, second-price auction performed at the time the query is sent. An auction on the relevant bids submitted by the advertisers is run every time a user submits a query. The duration of a "campaign" is dynamically defined by the client and can last from seconds to months. The registration process takes few minutes and after its completion the bid of the client is considered in auctions.

The AdWords advertising scheme is a significant success for Google (The Economist, 2005). Its global reach, precise audience targeting, fast and cheap campaign set-up, flexible payment schemes, etc. are attractive to small, medium, and large advertising clients (Pennock and Asdemir, 2005). The micro-advertising and just-in-time-advertising business models are supported in AdWords, allowing companies to initiate advertising campaigns in the moment preferred by them with either smaller or larger financial resources. The possibility to constantly adjust their campaigns gives companies enormous flexibility.

4.2 Discussion on the AdWords scheme

The example of the AdWords advertising scheme confirms that the opportunity for dynamic advertising offered by modern technologies is appealing to advertisers and profitable to publishers. The innovative advertising schemes have been discussed in the research community as well. The sponsored search as a special case of on-line advertising has been discussed in two workshops (Karnstedt *et al.*, 2004), (Pennock and Asdemir, 2005). The similarities and differences between the generalized second-price auctions supported in AdWords and the classical Vickerey auctions are discussed in (Edelman *et al.*, 2005). A formal model of sponsored search auctions is proposed in (Kitts *et al.*, 2005). A more general mechanism for dynamic advertising through auctions is presented in (Bohte *et al.*, 2004).

Currently, the rights and obligations of Google and its clients are specified in a general set of "Terms and conditions" that are defined unilaterally by Google. However, researchers already look into the implementation of more advanced and complex contract provisions between Google and its clients that will be personalized for each client (Parkes and Sandholm, 2005). This will bring forward the need of establishment of personalized contractual relationships that will require deep e-contracting support.

5. CONCLUSIONS

The domain of on-line advertising provides new opportunities to companies for more dynamic and flexible advertising plans. However, to provide legal protection to companies in the newly emerging dynamic business models in the domain of on-line advertising, a high level of automation of the contracting process is required. Deep e-contracting delivers the required automated support of the contract establishment, enactment, and management by using advanced information technologies.

It can be expected that having the example of sponsored search, Telegraaf and other on-line editions will implement a more flexible, dynamic, and highly automated advertising schemes, in which deep e-contracting is a necessity. Auction-based approaches for buying advertising space in on-line resources currently gain significant attention. In the context of advertising in on-line editions, such approaches may be applied as well. Similar to the current practice in sponsored search, media may use auctions for just-in-time-advertising. Combinatorial auctions may be used to support simultaneous selling of sets of advertising spots.

Acknowledgments

We thank Marcel Udo (sales manager of on-line advertising at Telegraaf) for his explanations and opinions expressed during our work on this case.

6. REFERENCES

1. Angelov S, Grefen P. The 4W Framework for B2B E-contracting. Int. J. of Networking and Virtual Organisations 2 (1), pp.78-97, 2003.
2. Angelov S, Grefen P. The business case for B2B e-contracting. Proceedings of the 6th International Conference on Electronic Commerce, Delft, The Netherlands, 25-27 October, 2004, pp. 31-40.
3. Angelov S, Udo M. Personal communication with Marcel Udo (sales manager of on-line advertising at Telegraaf). September, 2005.
4. Angelov, Samuil. Foundations of B2B Electronic Contracting. Ph.D. Thesis, Technical University Eindhoven, 2006.
5. Bohté SM, Gerding E, La Poutré JA. Market-based Recommendation: Agents that Compete for Consumer Attention. ACM Transactions on Internet Technology 4 (4), pp. 420-448, 2004.
6. Edelman B, Ostrovsky M, Schwarz M. Internet advertising and the generalized second price auction: selling billions of dollars worth of keywords. NBER Working Paper, No. 11765, November 2005.
7. Griffel F, Boger M, Weinreich H, Lamersdorf W, Merz M, Electronic contracting with COSMOS - how to establish, negotiate and execute electronic contracts on the Internet. Proceedings of the 2nd International Workshop on Enterprise Distributed Object Computing (EDOC '98), San Diego, USA, 3-5 November, 1998, pp. 46-55.
8. Karnstedt D, Boberg D, Frisbie A. Workshop on Using Search to Connect with Your Customers, San Francisco, CA, USA, 2004.
9. Kitts B, Laxminarayan P, LeBlanc B, Meech R. A formal analysis of search auctions including predictions on click fraud and bidding tactics. ACM Conference on E-Commerce – Workshop on Sponsored Search, Vancouver, Canada. June, 2005.
10. Koetsier M, Grefen P, Vonk J. Contracts for cross-organizational workflow management. Proceedings of the First International Conference on Electronic Commerce and Web Technologies, 4-6 September, 2000. Lecture Notes in Computer Science 1875, pp. 110-121, Springer-Verlag 2000.
11. Parkes D, Sandholm T. Optimize-and-dispatch architecture for expressive ad auctions. ACM Conference on E-Commerce – Workshop on Sponsored Search, Vancouver, Canada. June, 2005.
12. Pennock D, Asdemir K. ACM Conference on E-Commerce – Workshop on Sponsored Search, Vancouver, Canada. June, 2005.
13. Somefun K, Klos TB, H. La Poutré JA, Negotiating over bundles and prices using aggregate knowledge. Proceedings of the 5th International Conference on Electronic Commerce and Web Technologies (EC-Web), Springer Lecture Notes in Computer Science 3182, pp. 218 - 227, Springer-Verlag, 2004.
14. The Economist. The Online Ad Attack: Internet Advertising. The Economist .375 (8424), pp. 63, The Economist Newspaper Ltd., London, 2005.
15. Wigand R, Picot A, Reichwald R. Information, Organization and Management: Expanding Markets and Corporate Boundaries. John Wiley and Sons Ltd., 1997.

---

[i] http://www.telegraaf.nl/
[ii] http://service.telegraaf.nl/tarieven/website/index.php?39

45

ANALYSIS OF HUMAN NEGOTIATIONS FOR e-BUSINESS IMPROVEMENTS[*]

Beata Krawczyk-Brylka
Michal Piotrowski
Gdansk University of Technology
Faculty of Management and Economics
Faculty of Electronics, Telecommunications and Informatics
bkrawczy@zie.pg.gda.pl
bastian@eti.pg.gda.pl
POLAND

Nowadays, we can observe the transition of traditional business to electronic one, where negotiations still play very important role. In the paper we propose a general model of human negotiations and on the basis of which we have created a simplified model of quality analysis. The proposed quality model allows us to define various negotiation scenarios and to evaluate such negotiation metrics as completeness, effectiveness, performance and satisfaction. Two kinds of negotiations (f2f and chat) have been compared for buying/selling scenarios. More than 150 experiments have been carried out taking into account negotiation quality. Firstly, analysis has been made to examine the impact of negotiator personalities, experiences, roles and positions on that quality. Secondly, further studies have shown how negotiation quality is influenced by various types of negotiation strategies.

1. INTRODUCTION

In the time of transition of traditional to electronic business (e-business) companies should redesign their business processes in order to better satisfy customer needs (Patric, 2004). For this reason profound knowledge of such processes and market requirements should be acquired and deeply analysed (Peterson, 1997). Many researches based on specially defined questionnaires make a large-scale study to access e-business drivers facilitating achieving high levels of operational performance. These studies identify the critical links between e-business drivers, financial indicators and operational excellence measures (Barna, 2000). Besides, several descriptive theories and models try to describe selling/buying processes and improve negotiation procedures involved in such processes (Berenicke, 2003). In general, a buying/selling transaction comprises by the following six fundamental stages:

1. Identification of the user needs and recognition of the buyer motivations for buying a product.
2. Product brokering and information retrieval for consideration of different buying alternatives.

---

[*] This work was supported under national KBN grant No 4T11C00525

Please use the following format when citing this chapter:

Krawczyk-Brylka, B., Piotrowski, M., 2006, in IFIP International Federation for Information Processing, Volume 224, Network-Centric Collaboration and Supporting Fireworks, eds. Camarinha-Matos, L., Afsarmanesh, H., Ollus, M., (Boston: Springer), pp. 429–438.

3. Merchant brokering and first choice of the best alternatives using such buyer-provided criteria as prices, warranty periods, type of payments, delivery options, service availability, producer reputation, product quality.
4. Direct negotiation of different aspects including the above criteria to make selling/buying transaction accepted for both sides.
5. Contract definition for purchase, delivery and maintenance to finalise the negotiated transaction.
6. Past-purchase product life-phases and evaluation of user acceptation.

In practice, the above stages can overlap and migrate from one to another and can be implemented in different ways (Nguyen, 2004). One implementation technique is filtering (steps 1, 2, 3) the attractive products by their features described on the Web. Another one is collaborative filtering which tries to recommend products based on various user options and ranking of their alternatives. Besides, data mining techniques (Adamavicius, 2001) can be used to discover the best patterns in customer purchasing and to exploit these patterns to help in taking decisions by buyers (steps 4, 5, 6). In many cases agent based technologies can be used to support all stages of the buying process.

As it was shown in the stages given above, most business transactions involve negotiation procedures, which make use of different negotiation strategies and protocols (Maes, 1999). We distinguish two main kinds of negotiations: face to face (f2f) and computer mediated (cm) ones. The former occurs in natural communication environment, where people meet and make conversation, the latter takes place when different telecommunications means are used. The simplest example of cm negotiations is negotiations via e-mail or chat (Picard, 2002). In the case of more advanced technologies people can create agents, which seek out potential buyers or sellers and negotiate with them on behalf of their owners. In our opinion proper implementation of agent to agent (a2a) or cm negotiation strategies requires good understanding of f2f negotiations, which enables transforming traditional business into e-business more easily.

The paper focuses on f2f negotiations. The general model is formalised in Section 2. In Section 3, quality attributes of negotiations are proposed and the way of estimating completeness, effectiveness, efficiency and satisfaction of negotiations is discussed. These attributes are strictly related to negotiation outcomes and therefore play important role in improving of e-business activities. The main experiments are described in Section 4. They focus on the representative selling/buying negotiation tasks showing the importance of negotiators' personalities, experience, roles, positions and negotiation strategies when referred to negotiation quality attributes. In Section 5 general remarks about e-business improvements and new open problems are given.

2. MODEL OF NEGOTIATION

Negotiation is the process that occurs between at least two corresponding parties (negotiators) and involves a certain subject (buying goods/products, taking decisions, preparing solutions, executing services). In general, this process can be described by a sixth tuple, as follows:

$N = < S, P, G, D, C, E >$

where:

S is a subject of negotiation, as it was presented above;

P is a set of parties participating in negotiations; $P = \{P_1, P_2, .. , P_i..., P_I\}$

The cardinality of P is at least two i.e. $I \geq 2$, and each P_i $(i = 1, 2, ... , I)$ includes at least one negotiator. The parties first verbalise contradictionary demands and then move towards agreement by a search for new alternatives.

G is a set of goals describing attributes of the subject being under negotiation, i.e. $G = \{g_1, g_2, ..., g_j..., g_J\}$, where g_j $(j = 1, 2, ..., J)$ presents one attribute, for instance in the case of selling/buying negotiations: product cost, delivery time, warranty conditions and etc. can be considered. The concrete value of g_j is denoted by v_j.

D is a sequence of demands/replays formulated step by step by the parties during negotiation as modification of previous demands or presentation of new propositions, which should be discussed and modified later. $D = (D_1, D_2, ..., D_k...,$ $D_K)$, where: K means the number of negotiations steps and D_k is a value set of attributes: $D_k = \{v_1^k, v_2^k, ..., v_j^k..., v_J^k\}$. The set is a proposition of attribute values given by parties in k-th step of negotiation. D_k represents a point in J-multiple area and sequence D corresponds to the path of transitions from point D_1 to the point D_K. Such a graphical representation of negotiation steps in J-multiple area is called negotiation dance. For each party all values v_j^k should satisfy the following acceptation condition:

$$\min_j^k \leq v_j^k \leq \max_j^k \text{ for all } j, j = 1, 2, ..., J, k = 1, 2, ..., K.$$

C denotes the contract for the subject, when all parties make acceptation for the demand formulated in K-th step of negotiation. Then D_K is called the outcome of negotiation (contract values), i.e.:

$$O = D_K = \{v_1^K, v_2^K, ..., v_j^K..., v_J^K\} = \{c_1, c_2, ..., c_j..., c_J\}$$

E is an environment, where negotiation is being run. In the case of natural environment, f2f negotiation takes place. Using communication via Internet we have chat negotiation, and using agent technology we organise negotiation in more automatic way (i.e. a2a negotiation or e-negotiation). E may play an essential role in achieving the required level of negotiation quality and in implementation of e-business activities.

Parties can formulate demands in different order and all demands can be presented by all parties either at once or sequentially one by one. There are no rules in which order demands should be presented. Moreover, parties can remain either passive (when they only accept or reject the demands made by others) or active (when they can change the current proposals to make them more likely to be accepted). Each simple change of demands means a new step of negotiation. If current demands are not acceptable for the other parties, these parties can return to the previous proposition which seems more promising. Therefore, the track of some propositions $(D' \subset D)$ should be kept and recovery mechanisms should support such return operations. Taking into account a way of demand formulation and presentation, negotiation strategies can be competitive (the parties focus on the best outcomes for themselves), balanced (the parties are looking for a compromise following with the objective conditions) and collaborative (the parties try to understand reasoning of other sides). Negotiation strategies used by one party can vary over time according to the assumed tactics and current negotiator satisfactions and feelings. A graph of negotiation dance very well suggests types of negotiation strategies used for a contract completion.

3. NEGOTIATION QUALITY ATTRIBUTES

The assumed negotiation model allows us to define quality attributes of negotiation, as it is shown in Fig. 1a. Quality of negotiation (QoN) can be considered taking into account the main aspects: personal, process and technical ones. Correct description of subjects (QoS) and negotiation goals (QoG) and their proper understanding by the parties, as well as personality characteristics of the parties (QoP) are grouped as personal aspects of negotiation quality. On the other hand, processes of demands formulation (QoD) and contract preparation (QoC) belong to negotiation process (process aspects). Places and conditions of negotiations and technical means create negotiation environment (QoE), which is the other aspect of negotiation quality. In many papers, all these quality aspects are described and analysed separately. Moreover, the majority of the papers focus on the technical aspects only, primarily of how to improve communication channels for delivering the required information. Finally, the negotiation outcome (QoO) strictly depends on all aspects given above and directly determines a level of negotiation quality.

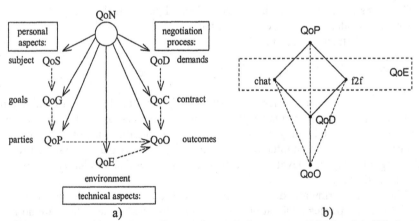

Figure 1 – a) The main attributes of negotiation strategy b) The simplified
negotiation model

The paper represents the combined approach which takes into account all the presented attributes. However, to avoid huge complexity some simplifications have been made. First, we focused on personality attributes, which in a way represent other personal aspects. Second, we chose QoO as representative attribute of the contract, and the negotiation dance as the base for calculating QoD. Third, we limited technical aspects to two communication channels: f2f and chat. As a result we obtained the quality model as it is shown in Fig. 1b.

It has been assumed that the quality of negotiations is higher when negotiators consider all required goals and obtain satisfactory outcomes in a shorter time. As it was shown in Section 1, negotiations are the essential part of e-business and make clients more content because of a shorter time of execution of business transactions and due to better outcome included in the final contract.

Table 1 shows the main quality attributes and metrics taken into consideration in this paper. To present quantitative metrics we consider selling/buying negotiations for I=2 with one negotiator in each party, and J=5. Let assume that b and s represent buyer and seller respectively.

Table 1 – Main quality attributes and metrics for model shown in Fig. 1 b)

Quality attributes	Quality metrics
Parties characteristics	personality (personal feature of the negotiator measured by sociology and psychology tests experience (low, medium and high in business activities) role of participants (seller, buyer) position in negotiation (measured by distance to alternatives)
Communication channels	f2f, chat
Negotiation strategies	competitive, competitive/balanced, balanced, balanced/collaborative, collaborative
Outcomes	effectiveness - the percentage of negotiations with complete contracts in the considered experiment performance - distribution of negotiation times for complete contract in the considered experiment completeness - the percentage of goals taken into consideration for each negotiation in the considered experiment satisfaction – the relative difference (in %) between the obtain outcome and the expected outcomes

Fig. 2 defines main parameters used for analysing quality of negotiations. Symbols of min(x) and max(x) denote boundary values of the considered attribute g for negotiator x, where x represents either a buyer (b) or a seller (s). These values allow to estimate the most expecting outcome area (dotted rectangular area in Fig. 2) and to estimate the mean values of demand g (i.e. $mv(x)$) for both negotiators, i.e.:

$$mv(x) = 0.5[\min(x) + \max(x)]$$

In similar way we can estimate the balance outcome (bv):

$$bv = 0.5[\min(s) + \max(b)]$$

The position of negotiator x before negotiation, denoted by $pos(x)$, can be defined as difference in values between two parameters: bv and $mv(x)$. Then $pos(x)$

can be evaluated in the following way:

$$pos(x) = \begin{cases} low & if \ \Delta x > \beta \cdot bv \\ medium & if \ \alpha \cdot bv < \Delta x < \beta \cdot bv \\ high & if \ \Delta x < \alpha \cdot bv \end{cases}$$

where $\Delta x = |bv - mv(x)|$, coefficients α, β describe the boundary levels of position and in experiments we assume that $\alpha = 0.1 \div 0.2$ and $\beta = 2\alpha$.

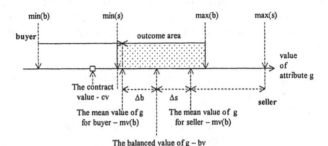

Figure 2 – Illustration of one of possible distribution of demands and outcomes for attribute *g* of negotiation

Completeness of negotiation can be evaluated in the following way:

completeness $[\%] = (J*/J) \cdot 100\%$,

where J^* is the number of the subject attributes taken into consideration during negotiation.

Satisfaction of negotiation related to the contract value (*cv*) is evaluated by each negotiator x separately. Let denote it by $sat_x(cv)$, then in general it can be expressed by the following formula:

$$sat_x(cv) = \begin{cases} 0\% & if \ cv \leq min(x) \\ w(x)\% & if \ min(x) < cv < max(x) \\ 100\% & if \ cv \geq max(x) \end{cases}$$

where: $w(x) = [cv - min(x)]/[max(x) - min(x)] \cdot 100$. However the above formula should be adjusted according to context of *g*.

Let note that in Fig. 2, for *g* = warranty period $25\% \leq sat_b(cv) \leq 50\%$ and $sat_s(cv) = 0\%$, but for *g* = price $50\% \leq sat_b(cv) \leq 75\%$, $sat_s(cv) = 0\%$.

We can normalise the result by restriction of satisfaction analysis to the existing outcome area, then $sat_b(cv) = 100\% - sat_s(cv)$.

All above formulas can be used for analysing different kinds of negotiations including f2f and cm ones. If our experiments consist of many tours of negotiations, the completeness and satisfaction can be expressed as either distribution of values of such metrics or as their mean values.

4. EXPERIMENTAL RESULTS

To analyse negotiation quality 156 selling/buying negotiation experiments have been done. Each experiment have been proceeding according to the scheme shown in Fig. 3. To implement this scheme, computer-based system GAJA was designed and implemented (Piotrowski, 2006). It is functional as it offers the possibilities to:
- monitor several kinds of negotiations (sell/buy, ranking, enterprise),
- define many versions (instances) of experiments for each kind of negotiations,
- support activities of different types of users (experts, negotiators, administrators),
- quality analysis of negotiators' behaviour, negotiation processes and negotiation outcomes.

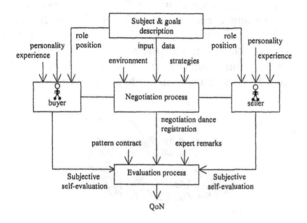

Figure 3 – Experiment schema for negotiation quality analysis

Table 2 shows the basic items of experiments. All negotiators were randomly divided into two groups: sellers and buyers. Then, their personality was tested, and pairs of negotiators (seller and buyer) were randomly assigned to one of two environments (f2f and chat). Next, each pair of negotiators received the same description of the negotiation task with some particular differences for seller and buyer. The same suitable initial conditions, admissible values of considered attributes were given for all participants.

After completion of a contract or after finishing negotiation without contract all negotiators made self-evaluation of both the processes and the obtained outcomes. Besides, the negotiation process was recorded as chat logs or video logs, which enables examining outcomes by experts. All collected data can be sent to *STATISTICA* application and analysed in many different ways.

Below we present only several experiment results strictly connected with negotiation quality analysis. Fig. 4 shows professional experiences of respondents. The biggest group (37%) has been working in business for 1-5 years. The next group (25%) has less than 1 year experience, which means that respondents were students or last year's graduates of our university.

Table 2 – Basic items of experiments

Items	Descriptions
Negotiators	156 pairs of negotiators, 50% female 50% male, I=2 30% for f2f negotiations, 70% for chat
Roles, positions	given in advance in description of negotiation task
Subjects	selling/buying negotiation of medical equipment having concrete functionality and quality
Attributes	price, warranty period, bank credit duration, delivery time, cost of maintenance course, J=5
Negotiation strategies	not suggested
Evaluations	Special questionnaires to fulfil by experts or negotiators

Other experimental results are shown in Fig. 5. It is easy to notice that chat negotiations take more time in comparison to f2f negotiations. Besides, performance depends also on the negotiator experience. Time of negotiation is shorter nearly twice for negotiators with 10-years experience in business compared to time of negotiation for negotiators with no or little experience. Results show that negotiators' personalities are also essential factors in this area.

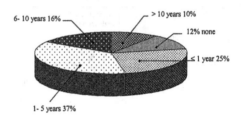

Figure 4 – Professional experience of respondents

General effectiveness of negotiations was 97,1%, but for f2f and chat negotiations 98,4% and 96,6% respectively, which means that also f2f negotiations are a bit more effective, but the difference is not really big. General completeness of negotiations was 89,1%, but for f2f and chat negotiations 98,1%, 84,5% respectively, which means that there is more opportunity to lose some attributes in chat negotiations. The reason for ending cm negotiation before reaching contract is the tendency to use the strategy of testing partner motivation and position by expressing lack of approval for his demands. In context of a few non-verbal signals (that are important for building positive negotiation climate and avoiding misunderstandings) it can lead to incompleteness of negotiation.

Factor analysis shows that personal features are the most important factors for chat negotiation effectiveness. The most important personal features are conscientiousness and extraversion, high level of them indicates high motivation and high negotiation position. It is especially important for women negotiating via Internet, because to be effective they need to be more conscientious and much less agreeable than in f2f meetings.

The most important factor for f2f negotiation is the subjective perception of negotiation process. The parties that estimate the negotiation climate as friendly are much more motivated to reach the compromise. The personal feature important for f2f negotiators is neuroticism – the lower level better negotiation results.

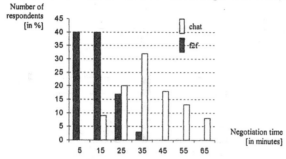

Figure 5 – Distribution of negotiation time (performance) for f2f and chat channels

Fig. 6 shows that negotiators working in natural environment gain the biggest satisfaction. However, in the case of chat negotiations more respondents get the mean satisfaction.

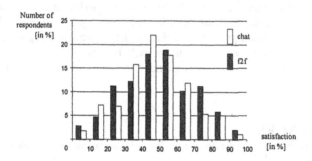

Figure 6 – Distribution of satisfaction for f2f and chat negotiations

Fig. 7 shows that, in general, negotiators communicating by chat use the competitive strategy (they use strategies of accusing and frightening interlocutors more frequently), inversely than negotiators working in natural environment. The latter prefer the co-operative strategy. However, the balanced strategy for both environments is the most preferable one.

5. FINAL CONCLUSIONS

The paper presents a quantitative model of negotiation. This model enables evaluating quality of negotiation in different environments and comparing these environments in order to point out the most important drawbacks. Four quality attributes are defined and analysed. It was shown that the effectiveness and completeness are strictly related to negotiators' personality and experience. The performance and satisfaction depend on personality of negotiators and their positions (evidently in chat negotiations). Negotiation strategies also impact on the performance and satisfaction.

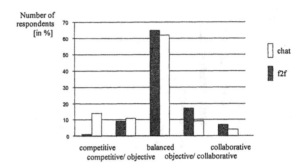

Figure 7 – Used negotiation strategies in f2f and chat channels

A very important conclusion is that technical aspects are not the main ones but they are still very important for chat negotiations. This means that application of modern communication technology needs further changes to increase negotiation quality. To improve the completeness, effectiveness, performance and satisfaction of negotiations more intelligent and flexible tools are required. Such tools should be able to check, control and predict behaviour of negotiators and register, analyse and predict the negotiation dances. Then we will be able to control an increase of negotiation quality and in consequence to improve quality of e-business transactions.

6. REFERENCES

1. Adamavicius Gediminas, Tuzhilin Alexander. Using data mining methods to build customer profiles. IEEE Computer, Feb. 2001.
2. Barna Anitesh, Konana Prabhudev, Whinston Andrew, Yin Fang. Making e-business pay: Eight key drivers for operational success. IT Professional Nov./Dec. , 2000.
3. Berenicke Morcel, Langendorfer Peter. Towards automatic negotiation of privacy contracts for Internet services. Proc. of the 11th Int. Conference on Networks, 2003.
4.. Maes Pattie, Guttman RH, Munkas AG. Agent that Buy and Sell. Communication of the ACH, March, 1999.
5. Nguyen TD, Jennings NR. Coordinating multiple concurrent negotiations. Pwc. of AAHAS'04, New York, USA.
6. Patric Charles, Sahai Akhil. Business processes on the Web. TEEE Internet Computing, Jan./Feb. , 2004.
7. Peterson Erika, Thompson Leigh. Negotiation Teamwork: The impact of information distribution and accountability on performance depends on the relationship among team members. Organizational, Behavior and Human Decision processes, No3, 1997.
8. Picard Willy. Multi-facet analysis of e-negotiations PhD Thesis. Ecole Nationale Superieure des Telecommunications, Paris, 2002.
9. Piotrowski Michał, Krawczyk-Bryłka Beata. The Web Based System for Recording and Analysing Different Kinds of Negotiations: WEBIST 2006, Proceedings of the Second International Conference on Web Information Systems and Technologies, Society, e-Business and e-Government/e-Learning, Portugal, 2006.

46

GAME THEORETIC NEGOTIATION STRATEGY FOR VIRTUAL ENTERPRISE WITH MULTIAGENT SYSTEMS

Toshiya Kaihara and Susumu Fujii
Kobe University, Department of Computer and Systems Engineering
kaihara@cs.kobe-u.ac.jp
JAPAN

Nowadays, Virtual Enterprise (VE) is an important paradigm of business management in agile manufacturing environment. Clearly, there is a need for a mechanism through which these different functions can be integrated together. In this paper, we focus on negotiation process in VE formation to clarify its effective management. Each enterprise in VE is defined as agent with multi-utilities, and a framework of multi-agent programming with marketing science and N-person game theoretic approach is newly proposed as negotiation algorithm amongst the agents. We develop a computer simulation model to form VE through multiple negotiations amongst several potential members in the negotiation domain, and finally clarify the formation dynamism with the negotiation process.

1. INTRODUCTION

Nowadays, Virtual Enterprise (VE) is an important paradigm of business management in agile manufacturing environment [1]. VE exists in both service and manufacturing organizations, although the complexity of the each enterprise may vary greatly from industry to industry. Traditionally, marketing, distribution, planning, manufacturing, and the purchasing organizations operated independently. These organizations have their own objectives and these are often conflicting. The result of these factors is that there is not a single, integrated plan for the organization - there were as many plans as businesses. Clearly, there is a need for a mechanism through which these different functions can be integrated together.

In this paper, we focus on negotiation process in VE formation to clarify its effective management. Each enterprise in VE is defined as agent, and a framework of multi-agent programming with marketing science and game theoretic approach is newly proposed as negotiation algorithm amongst the agents. Each unit is defined as agent in our VE model, and their decision makings are formulated as marketing science models [2] and N-person game theoretic methodology [3].

We firstly classify business model into three types, such as vertically integrated business model, horizontally specialised business model and hybrid business model. Then we propose CNP based negotiation protocol amongst enterprises with marketing science models, such as lexicographic model and Maximum Likelihood Hierarchical (MLH) model, and N-person game theoretic approach. CNP models

Please use the following format when citing this chapter:

Kaihara, T., Fuji, S., 2006, in IFIP International Federation for Information Processing, Volume 224, Network-Centric Collaboration and Supporting Fireworks, eds. Camarinha-Matos, L., Afsarmanesh, H., Ollus, M., (Boston: Springer), pp. 439–448.

transfer of control in a distributed system with the metaphor of negotiation among autonomous intelligent beings [4]. CNP consists of a set of nodes that negotiate with one another through a set of message. Nodes generally represent the distributed computing resources to be managed, correspond to "enterprises" in this paper. Marketing science based negotiation is applied into the vertically integrated business model considering a realistic enterprise management strategy. The horizontally specialised business model includes N-person game theoretic negotiations to realise the coordination amongst enterprises in the same business segment. We develop a computer simulation model to form VE through multiple negotiations amongst several potential members in the negotiation domain, and finally clarify the formation dynamism with the negotiation process.

2. BUSINESS MODEL IN VE

2.1 VE Concept

Virtual enterprises are defined as "agile" enterprises, i.e. as enterprises with integration and reconfiguration capability in useful time, integrated from independent enterprises, primitive or complex, with the aim of taking profit from a specific market opportunity. After the conclusion of that opportunity, the virtual enterprise dissolves and a new virtual enterprise is integrated in order to achieve the necessary competitiveness to respond to another market opportunity [2].

The knowledge and physical resources associated to the development and production of most of today's products often exceed what a single firm is able to accomplish. The new production enterprise is a network that shares experience, knowledge and capabilities – it is critical in this new environment for a manufacturing company to be able to efficiently tap these knowledge and information networks.

The organisational challenge of partitioning tasks amongst partners is of main concern, and can determine the success or failure of a project in the distributed manufacturing environment. They can fit and take advantage of the different competencies in VE, and that leads to their coordination and reconfigurability in order to keep alignment with the market requirements,

Faced to the requirements of competitiveness that the current environment is demanding, enterprises are expected to present at least the following characteristics:
- Fast reconfigurability or adaptability: the ability of fast change face to the unpredictable changes in the environment / market, implying substitution of resources (transition to a new A/V E instantiation)
- Evolutionary capability: the ability to learn with history.

Needless to say, it is very important and difficult activity in forming a virtual enterprise to select appropriate business partners, i.e. partnering, because each enterprise considers not only pursuing its profit but also sharing the risk to join the virtual enterprise. The partnering is described as coordination activity amongst the enterprises, and some sophisticated coordination mechanism is required to realise efficient interactions.

The development of coordination mechanism in computer science can be found in the area of workflow management system, computer supported cooperative work

(CSCW), and multi-agent systems. The area of multi-agent systems, especially when involving intelligent autonomous agents, has been discussing coordination issues and supporting mechanism [5][6][7]. The interaction capability, both amongst agents and between agents and their environment, is one of the basic characteristics of an agent. In this paper we focus on the contract net protocol (CNP), that is one of the mechanism coming from the early works on multi-agent systems [5], as the coordination and negotiation mechanism amongst business units in VE.

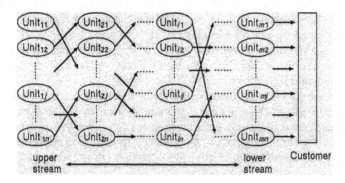

Figure 1 VE model

Figure 1 shows the assumed VE model in this paper. We call an enterprise as unit, and there exist m layers, which have m_n units in the VE model. The lowest level corresponds to consumers who can create original task requests to the VE. As the layer number, m, increases, we describe it 'lower' based on the product flow order in this paper.

At first, the customer dispatches new order to all the units in layer m, and then several units, which are satisfied with the order, responds and circulates the order toward upper units in the VE model. Finally a VE with single supply chain will be established for the order as a consequence of their negotiations through all the layers.

2.2 Business Model in VE

As described in the previous section, there exist many business models in VE environment. We classify three types of business models in this study, such as vertically integrated business model, horizontally specialised business model and hybrid business model.

Generally we can observe vertical business models in traditional industries. In this business model the manufacturing business processes top-down as well as bottom-up from the process requirements, resulting in an integrated approach to overall business requirements. We will call this business model, which is based on end-to-end proprietary solutions that lock a customer to a manufacturer, a "vertically integrated business models". Each unit at the same layer in figure 1 never tries to cooperate in our vertically integrated business model, because each unit is keen to find its appropriate partner just in vertical directions. For example, Unit$_{ij}$ tries to find an alliance unit at each neighbouring layer: layer $(i$-1$)$ and $(i$+1$)$ in figure 1. Consequently only one SC can be formed in this business model. We introduce consumer's behaviour in marketing science into unit behaviour, and that makes our VE model more practical.

On the other hand, enterprise relationships may represent a forerunning pattern of the learning alliance, whereby ongoing close interaction of horizontal alliance partners at single level or multiple hierarchical levels can be used to facilitate the mutual accumulation of superior organizational capabilities within the alliance firms. We will call this business model a "horizontally specialised business model". All the units at the same layer try to cooperate to maximise their profit in total in our horizontally specialised business model. They behave as if they are under joint management, and we can see a kind of this style of management in industrial cluster in Japan [8]. We apply N-persons game theory to formulate their behaviour in cooperation, because it describes a decision-making process to find their equilibrium solution in social manner.

Finally hybrid business model combines above-mentioned 2 business models. There exists a parent-child relationship amongst units in VE, and parent company has advantageous in their contract. Units in the child companies try to keep their harmony as a group sharing a common destiny in their management. We apply an alliance strategy based on cooperative game theory in this model.

3. AGENT DEFINITIONS

3.1 Unit Structure

Each unit (enterprise) is defined as agent in our VE model, and its structure is described in figure 2. We adopt CNP as the coordination and negotiation mechanism amongst the units. CNP models transfer of control in a distributed system with the metaphor of negotiation among autonomous intelligent beings. CNP consists of a set of nodes that negotiate with one another through a set of message. Nodes generally represent the distributed computing resources to be managed, correspond to "units" in this paper.

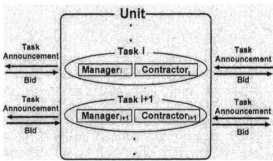

Figure 2 Unit structure

An agent (=unit) can act both as a manager and a contractor of a delivery sets. When a unit receives new order (= task announcement) i, it creates a contractor / manager set (Manager i / Contractor i) for the task inside. Manager i creates a new order towards the higher units to secure the contract with the lower layer.

3.2 Negotiation Algorithm

Negotiation steps according to agent roles are described as follows:
Manager (in layer *x*)
  Step M1: Create a new task based on the received bid information.
  Step M2: Task announcement (TA) to the lower units.
  Step M3: After the bidding period expired, check all the acquired bids according to its standard. If there exists no bid to select, go to M4. Otherwise go to M5.
  Step M4: Modify the task and go to M2.
  Step M5: Select the task and send reward (Reward) to the corresponding unit.
Contractor (in layer *x-1*)
  Step C1: Evaluate the received TA, and if satisfied, then create an estimated bid. Otherwise wait next TA.
  Step C2: Send the bid to the Manager.
  Step C3: If the contractor can get the contract, then request the manager in it to create TA to layer (*x-2*).
We prepare several parameters to define unit behaviours as follows:

P_{TA}^{ij} : TA price of Unit$_{ij}$ Q_{TA}^{ij} : TA quantity of Unit$_{ij}$

L_{TA}^{ij} : TA lead time of Unit$_{ij}$ $Q_{BID}^{(i+1)j}$: Bid quantity of Unit $_{(i+1)j}$

$L_{BID}^{(i+1)j}$: Bid lead time of Unit $_{(i+1)j}$ P_{BID}^{ij} : Bid price of Unit$_{ij}$

Q_{BID}^{ij} : Bid quantity of Unit$_{ij}$ L_{BID}^{ij} : Bid lead time of Unit$_{ij}$

$P_{TA}^{(i+1)j}$: TA price of Unit $_{(i+1)j}$ $Q_{TA}^{(i+1)j}$: TA quantity of Unit $_{(i+1)j}$

$L_{TA}^{(i+1)j}$: TA lead time of Unit $_{(i+1)j}$ $\cos t_{ij}$: process cost of Unit$_{ij}$ per product

$profit_{ij}$: profit rate of Unit$_{ij}$ $processingtime_{ij}$: process time of Unit$_{ij}$ per product

$procuretime_{ij}$: estimated procure time of Unit$_{ij}$ per product

Unit formulation in each business model is described in the following sections.

3.3 Vertically Integrated VE Model

CNP is just only the skeleton in the negotiation algorithm, and it is necessarily to define how to select the appropriate bid (Step M5) to establish profitable contract. Marketing science based negotiation is applied into the managers' decision makings to realise sophisticated bid selection based on consumers' behaviours in the vertically integrated business model.

First of all, each attribute of manager$_{ij}$ in TA producing process (Step M1) is as follows:

$$P_{TA}^{ij} = \cos t_{ij} \times (1 - profit_{ij}) \tag{1}$$

$$Q_{TA}^{ij} = Q_{BID}^{(i+1)j} \tag{2}$$

$$L_{TA}^{ij} = L_{BID}^{(i+1)j} - Q_{BID}^{(i+1)j} \times processingtime_{ij} \tag{3}$$

Then contractor$_{ij}$ tries to create its bid (Step C1) against TA from manager in layer (*i+1*) by the following equations:

$$P_{BID}^{ij} = \cos t_{ij} \times (1 + profit_{ij} / 2) \tag{4}$$

$$Q_{BID}^{ij} = Q_{TA}^{(i+1)j} \times (1 + plus_{ij}) \tag{5}$$

$$L_{BID}^{ij} = Q_{BID}^{ij} \times (\text{processing time}_{ij} + \text{procure time}_{ij}) \tag{6}$$

Marketing science approach is applied in the bid selection mechanism (Step M5) in the vertically integrated VE model. We consider 2 types of marketing science model, named lexicographic model and MLH model [3]. Bid selection mechanism is described in each model as follows:

Lexicographic model:

Step L1: Set priorities on all the attributes.

Step L2: Select a bid with the highest value in the attribute. In case of a tie, move to the next attribute and check the highest value. This routine is continued until only one bid is selected.

MLH model:

Step MLH1: Set priorities on all the attributes.

Step MLH2: Standardise the highest attribute with the following equations:

$$\tilde{z}_{ij} = \frac{(highest \quad z_{ij} \; amongst \quad unselected \quad j \quad) - z_{ij}}{highest \quad z_{ij} \; amongst \quad unselected \quad j} \tag{7}$$

where z_{ij} : evaluation value of task j on i th attribute

$\tilde{z}_{ij}$: standardised z_{ij}

Step MLH3: If $\tilde{z}_{ij}$ is within the tolerable amount (i.e. tolerance error: τ_i%), then keep this attributes for the calculation in the next step.

Step MLH4: After all the attributes are evaluated, then the preference index Vj of task j is calculated:

$$V_j = (\tau_1 - \tilde{z}_{1j}) \times (\tau_2 - \tilde{z}_{2j}) \times \cdots \times (\tau_i - \tilde{z}_{ij}) \tag{8}$$

Finally selection probability of task$_j$ is calculated by the following equation:

$$P_j = V_j / \sum_{k=1}^{n} V_k \tag{9}$$

3.4 Horizontally Specialised VE Model

The horizontally specialised business model includes N-person game theoretic negotiations to realise the coordination amongst enterprises in the same business segment. In this model we consider there is a coordinator to manage the negotiation process amongst all the enterprises (i.e. contractors) in each layer. The coordinator in layer i manages all the units in the layer. It receives all TAs form lower layer ($i+1$) on behalf of coordinators in the layer i, and replies the manager. N-person cooperative game approach is applied to share its profit amongst all the units in the layer based on their attributes. So it is regarded as a kind of joint order organisation.

Firstly, TA producing process (Step M1) is in common to the vertically integrated business model. Then the Bidding process is automatically replied based on the received TA, unless it yields no profit in any cooperation of contractor units (Step C2). So the attributes in the bid are defined as follows:

$$P_{BID}^{ij} = P_{TA}^{(i+1)j} \tag{10}$$

$$Q_{BID}^{ij} = Q_{TA}^{(i+1)j} \tag{11}$$

$$L_{BID}^{ij} = L_{TA}^{(i+1)j} \tag{12}$$

Finally the order sharing process is formulated with axioms called Sharpley value. We applied the Shapley value because our VE cooperation model doesn't always satisfy super-additivity condition. The Shapley value describes one approach to the fair allocation of gains obtained by cooperation among several actors even in non super-additivity condition. The setup is as follows: a coalition of actors cooperates, and obtains a certain overall gain from that cooperation. Since some actors may contribute more to the coalition than others, the question arises how to fairly distribute the gains among the actors, in other words, how important is each actor to the overall operation, and what payoff can they reasonably expect? The Shapley value is one way to distribute the total gains to the actors, assuming that they all collaborate.

At first we define characteristic function ($V(S)$) as follows:

$$V(S) = U_{profit}(S) \times U_{leadtime}(S) \tag{13}$$

where $U_{profit}(S)$: profit in cooperation S,　$U_{leadtime}(S)$: Boolean of lead time constraint (1: OK, 0: NG)

Then the task is divided under the cooperation S', which maximises $V(S)$. The contribution of unit i in cooperation S is calculated as follows:

$$\phi_i = \sum_{S:i \in S \subseteq N} \frac{(|S|-1)!(n-|S|)!}{n!}(v(S) - v(S \setminus \{i\})) \tag{14}$$

where N: a set of all units, v: all the profit in cooperation S, $|S|$: the number of members in cooperation S, $(S \setminus \{i\})$: cooperation without unit i

Then naturally the following equation is acquired:

$$\sum_{i \in N} \phi_i(v) = v(N) \tag{15}$$

So the profit, which gained in the coordinator, is divided into each unit in the layer according to the Sharpley value in (14).

3.5 Hybrid VE Model

Hybrid business model combines above-mentioned 2 business models. There exists a parent-child relationship amongst units in VE, and parent company has advantageous in their contract, such as in automobile or space industries. Units in the child companies try to keep their harmony as a group in their management.

TA producing process (Step M1) has also no difference in above-mentioned 2 business models. Then contractor$_{ij}$ creates its bid (Step C1) against TA from manager in layer (i+1) by the following equations:

$$P_{BID}^{ij} = \cos t_{ij}(1 + profit_{ij}) \tag{16}$$

$$Q_{BID}^{ij} = Q_{TA}^{(i+1)j} / N_i \tag{17}$$

$$L_{BID}^{ij} = Q_{TA}^{ij} \times (\text{processing time}_{ij} + \text{procuretim e}_{ij}) \tag{18}$$

where N: the number of cooperate units in layer i

Finally the bid selection process by manager (Step M5) is formulated by the cooperative game theory under super-additivity condition. We define characteristic function ($V(S)$) as follows:

$$V(S) = U'_{profit}(S) \times U_{leadtime}(S) \qquad\qquad (19)$$

where $U'_{profit}(S)$: manager's profit in cooperation S

Then the characteristic function values in all the received bids are calculated and the manager finally selects the bid with the highest value amongst them.

4. EXPERIMENTAL MODEL

We have developed a computer simulation model to analyse VE formation dynamism through multiple negotiations amongst several potential members in the negotiation domain. Although many experiments have done in this study, only a part of our analytic results is explained in this paper due to page limitation. The simulation parameters are shown in table 1.

Table 1 Experimental parameters

m	n	τ_i	$cost_{0j}$	$cost_{1j}$	$cost_{2j}$	$profit_{ij}$	$plus_{ij}$	Processing-time$_{ij}$	Procure-time$_{ij}$
3	3,10	0.4	15-25	45-55	85-95	0.17-0.23	0.08-0.12	0.08-0.12	0.10-0.20

The performances of finally acquired VE in three business models are compared in Table 2 (Model 1: vertically integrated business model), Table 3 (Model 2: horizontally specialised business model) and Table 4 (Model 3: hybrid model). We tried to analyse the VE robustness of each business model against "due date change" and "production volume change" in this experiment, and 500 trials are examined in each business model. The default due date and production volume are set to 30 and 100, respectively, and (0.5, 1.0), for example, means due date is shorten to 1/2 (0.5) and production volume is equivalent (1.0) to the default in these tables. Only the results of lexicographic model are described in Table 2.

The following points have been observed in those experiments:
- Any models don't satisfy lead time (15.00) in (0.5, 1.5), because the requirement change is too heavy to handle.
- Lead time is satisfied at Model 2 and 3 both in (0.5, 1.0) and (1.0, 1.5). These relatively slight changes are manageable in those business models except Model 1.
- Total profit is the highest at Model 1, because only the contributed units can take direct profit. Additionally stock is the least at this model.
- Model 3 attains the shortest lead time in most cases.

These results have been summarised as follows:
- It is difficult for vertically integrated business model to adapt due date change and production volume change, because it doesn't include any unit cooperation mechanisms. However, it performs best in profit, and this model is efficient in case there are enough margins in lead time (i.e. stable situations).
- Horizontally specialised business model is robust against due date change and production volume change, although the profit is less than vertically

integrated business model. This business model is suitable to agile manufacturing situations with autonomous cooperation alliance.
- Hybrid model takes a middle position between vertically integrated business model and horizontally specialised business model. Although it takes advantages of both models, it has been observed that the shared profit is inclined into lower layer units in SC.

Table 2 Experimental results of vertically integrated business model (Model 1)

	(1.0, 1.0)		(0.5, 1.0)	
	Ave.	Std. Dev.	Ave.	Std. Dev.
Profit	8076.05	947.00	8076.05	947.00
Stock(WIP)	21.14	2.50	21.14	2.50
Lead time	24.10	2.82	24.10	2.82
	(1.0, 1.5)		(0.5, 1.5)	
	Ave.	Std. Dev.	Ave.	Std. Dev.
Profit	12098.30	1413.53	12098.30	1413.53
Stock(WIP)	31.64	3.79	31.64	3.79
Lead time	36.10	4.21	36.10	4.21

Table 3 Experimental results of horizontally specialised business model (Model 2)

	(1.0, 1.0)		(0.5, 1.0)	
	Ave.	Std. Dev.	Ave.	Std. Dev.
Profit	6179.73	730.06	5919.06	708.20
Stock(WIP)	21.28	2.57	21.82	2.68
Lead time	16.44	2.14	13.47	1.81
	(1.0, 1.5)		(0.5, 1.5)	
	Ave.	Std. Dev.	Ave.	Std. Dev.
Profit	9263.05	1084.19	8889.12	1047.26
Stock(WIP)	32.12	3.82	33.04	3.81
Lead time	25.49	2.99	20.67	2.59

Table 4 Experimental results of hybrid model (Model 3)

	(1.0, 1.0)		(0.5, 1.0)	
	Ave.	Std. Dev.	Ave.	Std. Dev.
Profit	7928.55	930.86	7628.55	930.86
Stock(WIP)	22.32	2.70	22.32	2.70
Lead time	16.69	2.07	12.98	1.62
	(1.0, 1.5)		(0.5, 1.5)	
	Ave.	Std. Dev.	Ave.	Std. Dev.
Profit	11877.20	1390.56	11877.20	1390.56
Stock(WIP)	33.49	4.02	33.49	4.02
Lead time	24.95	2.99	19.41	2.31

5. CONCLUSIONS

In this paper, we focused on negotiation process in VE formation to clarify its effective management. We firstly classified business model into three types, such as vertically integrated business model, horizontally specialised business model and hybrid business model. Then we proposed CNP based negotiation protocol amongst enterprises with marketing science models, such as lexicographic model and MLH model, and N-person game theoretic approach. Marketing science based negotiation was applied into the vertically integrated business model considering a realistic enterprise management strategy. The horizontally specialised business model included N-person game theoretic negotiations to realise the coordination amongst enterprises in the same business segment. We developed a computer simulation model to form VE through multiple negotiations amongst several potential members in the negotiation domain, and finally clarified the formation dynamism with the negotiation process. It has been confirmed that the vertically integrated business model is profit-oriented and it is the best in relatively stable business situations. On the contrary, horizontally specialised business model is robust against the order change, and it suits agile manufacturing situations. Hybrid business model is moderate characteristic between them, and it seems useful practically as often shown in real situations.

6. REFERENCES

1. Camarinha-Matos, L. M. et al., The virtual enterprise concept, Infrastructures for virtual enterprises, Kluwer academic publishers, Boston, pp.3-14, 1999.
2. Katahira H., Marketing science (in Japanese), Tokyo university press, Tokyo, 1987.
3. Von Neumann, J. et al., Theory of Games and Economic Behavior, Princeton University Press, 1947.
4. Smith, R., The contract net protocol, IEEE Transaction on Computers, C-29, pp.1104-1113, 1980.
5. Kaihara, T. and S. Fujii, A study on virtual enterprise coalition with multi-agent technology in agile manufacturing environment, International Journal of Advanced Manufacturing Systems, Vol.1, No.2, pp.125-139, 2002.
6. Kaihara, T. and S. Fujii, IT based Virtual Enterprise Coalition Strategy for Agile Manufacturing Environment, Proc. of the 35th CIRP Int. Seminar on Manufacturing Systems, pp32-37, 2002.
7. Durfee, E. et al., Coherent cooperation among communication problem solvers, IEEE Transaction on Computers, N 36, pp.1275-1291, 1987.
8. Kansai Bureau of Economy, Trade and Industry, URL : http://www.kansai.meti.go.jp/3-2sanki/cluster-beam/english.html.

PART 15

ICT PLATFORMS FOR COLLABORATION

47

THE ECOLEAD ICT INFRASTRUCTURE FOR COLLABORATIVE NETWORKED ORGANIZATIONS

Ricardo J. Rabelo[1], Sergio Gusmeroli[2], Cristina Arana[3], Thierry Nagellen[4]

[1] *Federal University of Santa Catarina, BRAZIL, rabelo@das.ufsc.br*
[2] *TXT Company,ITALY, sergio.gusmeroli@txtgroup.com*
[3] *Software AG Spain,SPAIN, carana@softwareag.es*
[4] *France Telecom, FRANCE, thierry.nagellen@francetelecom.com*

This paper presents a distributed and open ICT infrastructure that is being developed in the ECOLEAD IST IP project to help members of Collaborative Networks in doing businesses and collaborations more efficiently. ICT-I design relies on the service oriented architecture paradigm, and it is implemented with web-services. ICT-I services are to be used on demand and pay-per-use models. It is flexible to support an easy entrance of new services and the withdrawn of others. So far the type of organizations envisaged by the proposed ICT-I are the ones members of virtual breeding environments, virtual organizations and professional virtual communities. This paper details the ICT-I requirements, its architecture and services. A small description of a first ICT-I prototype is given in the end.

1. INTRODUCTION

Reinforcing the effectiveness of collaborative networks and creating the necessary conditions for making them an endogenous reality in the industrial landscape, mostly based on SMEs, is a key survival factor. Collaborative Networked Organizations (CNOs) has been considered the discipline in charge of studying all the manifestations of organizations when they work in an inter-linked and organized way (Camarinha-Matos et al., 2004a). One of these manifestations is Virtual Organization (VO). A VO is a dynamic, temporary and logical aggregation of autonomous organizations that cooperate with each other as a strategic answer to attend a given business opportunity or to cope with a specific need, and whose operation is achieved by a coordinated sharing of skills, resources and information, totally enabled by computer networks (Rabelo et al., 2004).

The implantation of any form of collaborative network depends on the existence of an ICT infrastructure/middleware that allows different distributed/heterogeneous applications/actors to communicate with other transparently and seamlessly.

The fast evolution of ICT technologies with reduced life cycles and the need to cope with technologies with different life cycles and at different stages of the corresponding life cycle have represented a major difficulty for developing advanced collaborative tools. Therefore, in order to leverage the potential benefits of collaborative networks, more flexible and generic infrastructures need to be designed and implemented enabling networked organizations to agilely define and set-up relations with other organizations (Camarinha-Matos et al., 2004b).

Please use the following format when citing this chapter:

Rabelo, R. J., Gusmeroli, S., Arana, C., Nagellen, T., 2006, in IFIP International Federation for Information Processing, Volume 224, Network-Centric Collaboration and Supporting Fireworks, eds. Camarinha-Matos, L., Afsarmanesh, H., Ollus, M., (Boston: Springer), pp. 451–460.

This paper presents the ongoing work for developing an ICT infrastructure (*ICT-I*) that deals with such requirements. It is being developed within the ECOLEAD Project (www.ecolead.org), which aims to create strong foundations and mechanisms needed to establish the most advanced collaborative and network-based industry society in Europe.

The paper is organized as follows: Section 2 stresses the requirements of an ICT-I for CNOs. Section 3 introduces the proposed ICT-I rationale and architecture. Section 4 depicts the ICT-I services. Section 5 gives an overview of a first implementation. Section 6 provides preliminary conclusions and future steps.

2. REQUIREMENTS OF AN ICT-I FOR CNO

When dealing with ICT infrastructures for CNOs it is also important to consider the different nature and size of the companies. In Europe, more than 98% of the companies are SMEs (Europe-EU, 05). As such, most of them have difficulties to have access to the main products of the market as they are very complex, costly and requires a high investment on software and hardware (and people to maintain this). Actually, available solutions and business frameworks offer some support for collaboration. They support quite well traditional business processes transactions (purchasing, selling, manufacturing, shipping, etc.) and their integration at the intra-organizational level. More recently they have been also investing on the support of these transactions at inter-organizational level. These transactions represent means to support effective collaboration, i.e. they can be seen as collaborative services.

However, the kind of collaboration required by CNOs is rather different. In the envisaged scenario of the ECOLEAD project, primary sources of requirements are *VBE – Virtual Organizational Breeding Environment* (Afsarmanesh et al., 2005), *VOM – Virtual Organization Management* (Karvonen et al., 2005) and *PVC – Professional Virtual Communities* (Bifulco et al, 2005) types of CNOs. Roughly, this means the need for building an ICT infrastructure that allows well established groups of enterprises and of professionals to collaborate between each other as well as to manage this collaboration. Each of these areas has different needs, dependent on the nature of a CNO and of its actors. For example, both VBEs and PVCs need: ways to exchange information between their members in a secure way; services for VO creation support (e.g. partners search and selection, negotiation); CSCW tools to augment the efficiency of a collaboration as well as to manage involved IPR; means to monitor and to assist decisions upon current VOs; information historical should be generated and managed; business processes should be modeled and further supervised; among many other needs. These requirements cover part of the problem and can be seen as "vertical" and specific requirements.

Other requirements are technological, i.e. more "horizontal", independent on the nature of a CNO and of its actors. Some relevant requirements are: open, scalar and technology-independent infrastructure; federated information and resources management; flexible control mechanisms supporting a large variety of behaviors; full e-transaction security; privacy guarantee; and infrastructure reliability.

There are many B2B frameworks and collaborative platforms developed as products and in research projects that could be used to support those collaborative requirements. However, they present several relevant restrictions for their fast and easy adoption by (CNOs of) professionals and SMEs. Most of them, at several and variable levels, are not open at all, are not free, requires huge infrastructures, are very expensive and complex to deploy and difficult to use, and they don't support at all the CNO requirements. That is the niche ECOLEAD ICT-I intends to embrace. Actually, it doesn't aim to compete with existing platforms. Instead, some of them will be used to support specific issues (e.g. fault tolerance, services persistence), some of them will be complemented and/or adapted to ICT-I needs (e.g. CSCW and ontology tools) and there are issues for which specific CNO-related solutions will be developed. Therefore, ECOLEAD ICT-I will act as a comprehensive, integrated, seamless and transparent platform to better support CNO needs.

3. PROPOSED ICT-I

ECOLEAD ICT-I intends to cover part of this gap based on the vision of a *plug & play* infrastructure. This means that any VBE/VO/PVC member will be provided with adequate tools to be easily *plugged* into the ICT-I / CNO community and to *play* (i.e. to collaborate with other organizations) in secure, on-demand and pay-per-use way. In resume, ICT-I enables people to collaborate, systems to interoperate, knowledge to be shared, and processes to be synchronized. The authors advocate that, as such, ICT-I represents a step towards reaching the requirements of the *service oriented economy* of the future and *sustainable business networks*[1].

In order to cope with this need, ECOLEAD ICT-I has been fully developed based on open platform-independent specifications and ICT standards.

There is a number of conceptual approaches that can be applied to support these features. ICT-I applies the SOA (*Service-Oriented Architecture*) approach. SOA can be generally defined as an architectural paradigm for components of a system and interactions or patterns between them (Singh et al., 05). In other words, it can be seen as an application architecture in which all functions – or *services* – are defined using a description language and have invocable interfaces that are called to perform business processes. A service is seen as a software element that can both call for another service and be called by another service or, in other terms, a software system designed to support interoperable machine-to-machine interaction over a network (www.w3C.org). A service has an interface described in a machine-processable format that is usually platform-independent, meaning that a client from any device using any operating system in any language can use the service.

Web-services (WS) is the core technology that has been used to implement the SOA approach in the ECOLEAD ICT-I.

An important feature for the desired flexibility and scalability is that ICT-I is not a monolithic piece of software that follows the traditional notion of middleware as a "close world bus" that allows integration of distributed / heterogeneous parts. Instead, ICT-I is seen as a "pulverized" open bus composed of many distributed services. That is why it has been called ICT *infrastructure* and not ICT *middleware*.

3.1 Services Federation

A *Federation* corresponds to groups of devices and software components into a single, dynamic distributed system. The resulting federation provides the simplicity of access, ease of administration, and support for sharing that are provided by a large monolithic system while retaining the flexibility, uniform response, and control provided by a personal computer or workstation. Members of the federation are assumed to agree on basic notions of trust, administration, identification, and policy. The dynamic nature of a federation of services enables services to be added or withdrawn from a federation at any time according to demand, need, or the changing requirements of the workgroup using it (Sun, 99).

Adapting this concept to the envisaged ICT-I environment means to see all the involved services as members of a community, the *Services Federation*. This federation comprises the set of distributed services related to: i) the own ICT-I lifecycle and to the supporting services for high-level applications; ii) the CNO life cycle (comprising VBE, PVC and VOM vertical services); and iii) legacy / (intra-organization) systems services. The goal is that all existing services can coexist in a virtual logical repository of services and that can be accessed transparently and seamlessly according to some rules. From the ICT-I point view, the users and applications do not need to know about which services are needed to support a collaborative transaction, where they are, how they should be executed, and which technologies have been used in their implementations. Services are invoked, searched, discovered and properly executed no matter where they are.

One of the ICT-I underlying goals is to act as a catalyzer of independent software providers that can provide their services through the ICT-I. Such community can therefore be seen as a "CNO of services providers", which in turn has to establish its own policies and rules.

3.2 ICT-I Scope

The use of the ICT-I can be illustrated in Figure 1. Each CNO organization/actor tends to have its own portal. Each portal represents the access to services that have user interfaces. Depending on the configuration done, wider integrated collaborative portals can be created. The services themselves are stored in distributed services repositories, forming the Services Federation. From a user-centric perspective, CNO actors can, under flexible but well defined security and on-demand usage policy models, communicate (C), access data and information repositories (D), search and retrieve distributed bodies of knowledge as well as ontologies (K), and monitor and control the execution of business processes among CNOs (P).

From another side, networked organizations have their legacy systems. They perform their business transactions making use of ERP systems / B2B platforms, generating information to corporate databases. In general, ICT-I assumes that this information can be accessed by enterprise's services that somehow wrap existing legacy functions as well as that ICT-I services can also be invoked from enterprises' environments. This extends the level of collaboration as all (wrapped) enterprises' services can be accessible by other enterprises, according to security configurations.

As stressed in section 4, ICT-I is composed of Horizontal ($C\ K\ P\ D$) and Basic services. In practice, its services can be invoked in three basic situations: *(a)* Client-Server, *(b)* Intra-Server, and *(c)* Server-Server. Diverse ICT-I services (see section 4) can be invoked in each of these three situations. *Client-Server* case is used when a CNO actor (e.g. a VBE member) wants to access services provided by other CNOs through a centralized portal server. For instance a VO Planner who wants to know the competencies of VBE members or to open collaboration sessions with human peers in the CNOs. In this case, ICT-I needs to support the security and messaging, for instance. *Intra-Server* is used whenever a CNO portal is designed under SOA concepts, aggregating several vertical services. Depending on the business rules that have driven the services' logic, ICT-I can support, for instance, the orchestration of the required services. *Server-Server* is used to support inter-CNO collaboration. For example, when a PVC portal needs to access a VBE for obtaining the list of companies that has some profile. In this situation semantic mediation service for dealing with the different ontologies can be used.

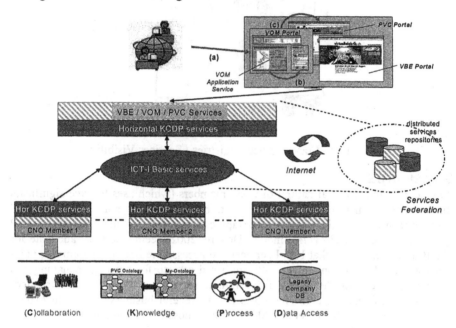

Figure 1 – Example of a scenario for the use of ICT-I

3.3 Interoperability and Security

Interoperability and security play an essential role in any infrastructure where CNO actors are distributed and heterogeneous. These two issues are covered in this paper in a very shallow way as it intends to focus on the ICT-I architecture. Detailed information about the ICT-I approach and strategy for interoperability and security can be found in (Arana et al., 2005) and (Sowa et al., 2006), respectively.

Interoperability is not the focus of the ECOLEAD ICT-I. It is seen as an *enabler* for collaboration. In this sense, attention has been put only on the essential aspects of interoperation required to support the planned collaborative services, also benefiting from outcomes of other initiatives in the area. The interoperability scope comprises the cases (a), (b) and (c) mentioned in the previous section.

Security in CNO is fundamental as a way to reinforce trust building. The security framework that is being incorporated in the ICT-I supports authentication, authorization and accounting along the collaborative transactions that are carried out among CNO partners, regarding the different roles and privileges each one has in a CNO. This framework is flexible, allowing responsibilities (and eventually delegations) to be dynamically assigned to actors and required security mechanisms settled accordingly. It means that the access to the services of the federation is filtered considering the CNO actors' privileges, as illustrated in figure 2.

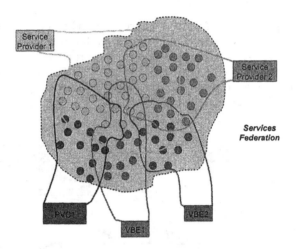

Figure 2 - Local Service Registries / Services Visibility

3.4 ASP Model

Considering the essential natural of CNO members (which uses to have significant financial and human resources restrictions to buy and to maintain sophisticated and huge infrastructures), their natural geographic distribution and mobility issues, ASP (*Application Service Provider*) model (Dewire, 2002) seems the most adequate for the ICT-I. This means that ICT-I services are accessed remotely, on demand, paid-per-use, based on a contractual software-based service for hosting, managing and providing access to the services federation, no matter where the (distributed) repositories of services are. This gives rise to several business models to exploit ICT-I, as stressed in (Borst et al., 2005), making possible to offer an affordable and "made to fit" ICT-I for companies.

3.5 ICT-I Reference Architecture

In order to provide an open and scalar model, ICT-I has a reference architecture from which instances-of it can be derived for different CNOs. Figure 3 presents the wider view of the ICT-I Reference Architecture. Its basic rationale is given below, and its services are generally explained in Section 4.

VBE, VOM and PVC have some very specific needs for each one. Thus, it can be said that they have *vertical* needs/services. As they have some common needs to help in the execution of their services, ICT-I provides *horizontal* services for them, i.e. services independent of any of those three specific application sub domains.

Horizontal services need in turn lower-level services to support their execution, transparently to the application services / CNO actor. These services are then seen as *basic* services. They are domain-independent and are basically used by other services. Basic services represent the very core of the ICT-I, comprising the discovery, selection and orchestration of services, security, basic interoperability services, etc.. They are called *Platform Independent Basic Services* (PIBS). The services intrinsically dependent on the PIBS's implementation are called *Platform Specific Basic Services* (PSBS).

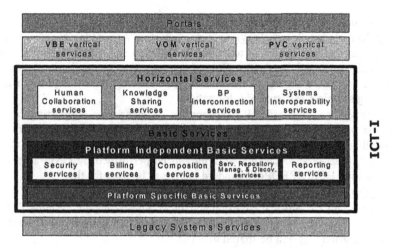

Figure 3 – ICT-I Reference Architecture

There are *legacy systems* services, which essentially provide information about activities inside a given company to satisfy vertical services needs. They use to be implemented in heterogeneous platforms and native front-ends.

Therefore, seen as a whole, vertical, horizontal, basic and legacy services compose the Services Federation.

A special and optional element of this architecture is *portals*. They act as an integrator front-end to the services themselves or even to other portals as a way to invoke services directly by the end-user. Portals are not seen as services.

Per definition, there is not a hierarchy among services. For example, the execution of vertical services requires the combination of services of different nature (considering security aspects, levels of visibility, context awareness, etc.) no matter the services type and layers they are placed. Anyway, the set of services to be involved and the sequence of their invocation / execution are configured by means of an orchestration / composition service.

Although not shown in the figure, there is another "class" of services called ICT-I management services. They are fundamentally used to manage the ICT-I life cycle, hence involving services associated to its deployment, plugging, use, maintenance, unplugging and undeployment.

4. ICT-I SERVICES

Actually the classes of services showed in the figure 3 (stressed below) correspond to the instance-of the ICT-I reference architecture that is being derived for the ECOLEAD project. New services can be added to and other can be withdrawn from the Federation according to a set of rules and policies, transparently to CNOs.

4.1 Horizontal Services

- CNO Actors On-Demand Collaboration Services. For supporting *human collaboration*, existing CSCW tools will be used to support the execution of the following services: mailing, chat, task list, file storage, notification, calendar, wiki, forum, voice and syndication.

- CNO Knowledge Search Services. For supporting *knowledge sharing*, existing engines are being empowered to manage distributed and heterogeneous bodies of knowledge exposed by CNOs. Proper ontology and reconciliation rules have been used for bridging the semantic gaps among knowledge repositories allowing seamless retrieval of information.
- Interactive, user-centered BP Management Services. For supporting *business process interconnection*, on top of an existing open-source BPM environment (modeling module and execution engine), ICT-I will provide support to task-oriented, interactive decisional activities to be performed by CNO actors. The forthcoming BPEL4PEOPLE standard intends to be used for that.
- CNO Data Access Services. For supporting *systems interoperability*, ICT-I is developing an easy-to-use environment for WS-based legacy systems RDBMS query. This service provides tools for defining and configuring the database and the information that will be shared to a VO.

4.2 Basic Services

- ICT-I Security Services. These services aim to support confidentiality, integrity, availability and authentication in the communications. This includes the log-in and user management service.
- ICT-I Billing Services. It will allow the implementation of different billing models to support the pay-per-use and on-demand service provision.
- ICT-I Services Composition. This service will provide facilities to define and execute composed services according with BPEL standard for services composition.
- ICT-I Reporting Services. For supporting the generation of reports to other services (e.g. "detailed billing usage", "services bill summary"), using pre-defined templates in well known formats (pdf, XML, HTML, etc.).
- ICT-I Services Registry and Discovery. For supporting the publishing of the web services in a UDDI repository as well as the search and browsing of services.

5. THE FIRST ICT-I PROTOTYPE

A first prototype has been developed with the aim to not only test some services in consonance with the ICT-I reference architecture, but also to act as an initial testbed for testing some open source tools, the integration of different containers for web-services, the deployment of services in distributed sites, the performance of mobile access, and the use of portlets to support user interfaces. *Orchestration, Billing, Logging, Log-In* and *UDDI Registry and Browsing* were the main services so far implemented. An ICT-I portal was also implemented, allowing *end-users* and *system administrator users* to access different services regarding *security* configurations.

Web-Services/WSDL/HTTP/SOAP/UDDI have been used as the standard technologies to implement ICT-I. *AXIS / Jonas* and *JBoss* have been the containers used and services were coded in Java. Portlets were implemented in *Liferay* and *Stringbeans*. Services were deployed both on a Windows XP and Unix platforms, in three different countries.

In order to test this prototype a fake vertical service for partners search and selection was implemented. Via a simple VBE portal, the user makes queries asking for potential partners that can provide a given product in a certain amount. ICT-I services were deployed in different countries but this was transparent to the callers. At the end of the process the results with the list of partners that fit the "business opportunity" are presented for user decision-making. This result can be visualized both in the web portal and in a mobile phone. More details about this prototype and its preliminary assessment can be found in (Rodrigo et al. 2005).

Concerning deployment, it should be analyzed under two perspectives: server and client. From the *server* point of view, services are built as components so they need component containers to deploy them. As servers usually have this kind of container, this task is easily made. In the case services are tightly connected to legacy systems, this can be complex. ICT-I doesn't provide means to make this type of integration but it provides guidelines to assist IT experts for doing this regarding the main existing different communication mechanisms. From the *client* point of view, there are two main ways to access ICT-I: through a normal web browser or by a vertical service. The former is typically already deployed with operating systems so the user doesn't need to install any additional software. The latter means that the user needs to install the client application itself. In order to simplify the deployment (although this is to some extent out of scope of ICT-I), client application should be self-contained, i.e., all the required components should be bundled with it.

6. CONCLUSIONS AND NEXT STEPS

This paper presented an ICT infrastructure (ICT-I) for supporting CNOs in doing businesses. It has been conceived based on the service oriented architecture paradigm / web-services technology, providing organizations with a transparent (mostly), platform-independent, easy deployable and configurable, secure-embedded, lean, distributed, scalar, on-demand and pay-per-use ICT-I. The presented features and approach of ICT-I seems to make it somehow unique.

It represents the ICT-I being developed in the IST IP ECOLEAD project, which comprises three main types of actors / "ICT-I clients": Virtual Breeding Environments (VBE), Virtual Organizations Management (VOM) and Professional Virtual Communities (PVC).

ECOLEAD ICT-I does not intend to compete with or replace existing / commercial B2B frameworks, but rather to complement them with the value-added of CNO-related supporting services.

One of the basic strategies being applied is to use existing open-source software as much as possible and then to make the required adaptations for the ICT-I purposes. These adaptations are both at "application-oriented" level (e.g. knowledge and ontology management systems) and at "infrastructure-oriented" level (e.g. fault tolerance and some aspects of security). The selection of these softwares is currently under analysis.

ICT-I is still under development. Although it has already been used in the project, a number of conceptual developments and implementations will be made in the next future. This includes the implementation of all remaining ICT-I services and the integration with vertical services that are also under development, besides a first set of test-cases close to real CNOs. In a posterior phase of the ICT-I development, attention will be put on evaluating and using existing frameworks in order to provide: i) supporting services for the management of the services federation life cycle, and ii) advanced searching mechanisms and semantic-driven services selection and composition over large-scale services repositories.

6.1 Acknowledgments

This work has been partially supported by the European Commission under the project IST FP-6 IP ECOLEAD project (www.ecolead.org) as well as by the Brazilian Council for Research and Scientific Development – CNPq (www.cnpq.br) under the project IFM (www.ifm.org.br). Special thanks to Mr. Rui Tramontin and Mr. Carlos Gesser (UFSC), Ms. Maria del Mar Rodrigo (Software AG Spain), Mr. Philippe Gibert (France Telecom), Mr. Roberto Ratti (TXT), and Mr. Walter Woelfel and Mr. Stanislav Mores (Siemens) for their collaboration in the conception and implementation of the ICT infrastructure. Also thanks to Mr. Luis Osorio (ISEL, Portugal) for his important insights and discussions about the ICT-I.

7. REFERENCES

1. Afsarmanesh, H.; Camarinha-Matos, L.M.; 2005. A Framework for Management of Virtual Organization Breeding Environments. Proceedings PRO-VE'2005, pp 35-48.
2. Arana, C.; Rodrigo, M.; Rabelo, R.; Tramontin, R.; Wangham, M.; Gibert, P.; Ratti, R.; Gusmeroli, S., Technical Report (Deliverable) D61.2 Global interoperability approach for a horizontal infrastructure architecture, October 2005.
3. Bifulco, A.; Santoro, R.; 2005. A Conceptual Framework for Professional Virtual Communities. Proceedings PRO-VE'2005, pp 417-424.
4. Borst, I.; Arana, C.; Crave, S.; Galeano, N., Technical Report (Deliverable) D62.2 ICT-I Business Models, October 2005.
5. Camarinha-Matos, L. M.; Afsarmanesh, H.; 2004a. Towards Next Business Models. In Collaborative Networked Organizations: a research agenda for emerging business models, Kluwer Academic Publishers, pp. 3-6.
6. Camarinha-Matos, L. M.; Afsarmanesh, H.; 2004b. Support Infrastructures for New Collaborative Forms. In Collaborative Networked Organizations: a research agenda for emerging business models, Kluwer Academic Publishers, pp. 175-192.
7. Dewire, D. T., Application Service Providers - Enterprise Systems Integration, 2nd Edition, pag.449-457. Auerbach Publications, 2002.
8. Karvonen, I.; Salkari, I.; Ollus, M. ; 2005. Characterizing Virtual Organizations and their Management. Proceedings PRO-VE'2005, pp 193-204.
9. Rabelo, R. J.; Pereira-Klen, A.; Klen, E. R., Effective Management of Dynamic Supply Chains, in International Journal of Networking and Virtual Organizations, 2004.
10. Rodrigo, M.; Arana, C.; Rabelo, R., Technical Report (Deliverable) D61.3a First Prototype ICT Infrastructure for Collaboration, November 2005.
11. Singh, M.; Huhns, M.; Service Oriented Computing -Semanics,Processes,Agents,Wiley, 2005.
12. Sowa, Grzegorz; Sniezynski, T.; Mulder, W.; Wangham, M.; Fraga, J.; Rodrigo, M.; Msanjilla, S., Technical Report (Deliverable) D64.1a – Configurable multi-level security architecture for CNOs, June 2006.
13. SUN - JINI Technology Architectural Overview, http://www.sun.com/jini/whitepapers/architecture.html, Jan 1999, in 30/08/2005.

[1] NESSI Strategic Research Agenda - Framing the future of the Service Oriented Economy. Version 2006-2-13 (http://www.nessi-europe.com/documents/NESSI_SRA_VOL_1_20060213.pdf); ICT for Enterprise Networking (http://cordis.europa.eu/ist/directorate_d/en_intro.htm).

48

DEVELOPMENT OF AN ICT INFRASTRUCTURE FOR INTERNET BASED INTEGRATION

John P.T. Mo
CSIRO, John.Mo@csiro.au
Ron C. Beckett
Reinvention Network, rcb@reinvent.net.au
Laszlo Nemes
CSIRO, Laszlo.Nemes@csiro.au
Stuart Woodman
CSIRO, Stuart Woodman@csiro.au
AUSTRALIA

Information Communication Technology (ICT) infrastructures supporting complex operations require collaborative effort to integrate a range of standalone software products into a coordinated system. However, the standalone products are normally developed with specific objectives and do not interoperate with each other. In a virtual enterprise environment, this imposes major challenges to ICT managers to manage a large variety of software products whereby each product only satisfies the unique requirements of a small portion of the user community. This paper discusses the development of the ICT infrastructure for a tooling virtual enterprise) using the open protocol standards as well as a new ICT infrastructure development tool known as Dynamic Network System (DNS). DNS models the operating characteristics of the ICT environment and generates the integrated internet web portal quickly from the system designer's view. It is built on standard JSP server capabilities using open source system that has the normal server security facilities.

1. INTRODUCTION

More than ever, global market conditions are characterised by frequent changes in products, services, processes, organisations, markets, supply and distribution networks (McNamara, 2003). Organisations need to be highly flexible in confronting this business environment (Nemes & Mo, 2004). They may form a temporary alliance to deliver a project or product which they dissolve when the job is completed. The teams work together as an entity for a goal but the relationships among themselves and the individual companies they come from often rely on trust and industry practices (Hao *et al*, 2005).

With the globalisation of manufacturing activities, it is inevitable that more and more companies adopt a new business model for managing the complete product life cycle of manufacturing from product design to after sales services (Van den Berg & Tolle, 2000). This type of temporary alliance is commonly known as a virtual

Please use the following format when citing this chapter:

Mo, J. P. T., Beckett, R. C., Nemes, L., Woodman, S., 2006, in IFIP International Federation for Information Processing, Volume 224, Network-Centric Collaboration and Supporting Fireworks, eds. Camarinha-Matos, L., Afsarmanesh, H., Ollus, M., (Boston: Springer), pp. 461–470.

enterprise (VE). Success for achieving the goal therefore demands well-coordinated agility in all internal and external aspects of the virtual enterprise. An effective ICT infrastructure can support the day-to-day operations of geographically separated partners (Shinonome *et al*, 1998).

Experience has shown that companies are willing to invest in improvements to their communication networks provided that there are clear benefits in return (Barrads & Pinto-Ferreira, 2004). Unfortunately, without proper understanding of the fundamentals in a digital virtual enterprise, company alliances seem to be trying to solve their problems in an ad hoc fashion. Custom tailored solutions are very costly, at the level of several million dollars, not only for the collaborative system, but also for resource management, training, team building, document management and constant modifications due to the ever-changing business process environment (Ortiz *et al*, 1999). The business world needs to have the capability to set up their collaborative system supporting the VE in a very short time frame without making costly mistakes.

Information Communication Technology (ICT) infrastructures supporting complex operations such as ship building, tool making, automobile manufacturing and utilities management require collaborative effort to integrate a range of standalone software products into a coordinated system (Jiang & Mo, 2001). However, the standalone products are designed with specific objectives and do not interoperate with other software products in an open computing environment in which many networks are interlinked. The challenge for many ICT managers is to manage a large variety of software products that each of them only satisfies the unique requirements of a small portion of the user community.

This paper discusses the development of an ICT infrastructure on which an internet based integration platform can be implemented. The platform, known as Dynamic Network System (DNS), uses a model driven concept which greatly reduces the need to re-program as the VE changes to different phases and entities in its life cycle.

2. COMMUNICATION FRAMEWORK FOR VE

In Australia, and in many other countries, large manufacturing firms are moving to countries with lower labour rates. Small contract manufacturing or tool making firms have traditionally been part of a vertically integrated supply chain where they were linked with product manufacturers and distributors. As these client companies move production offshore, or as they seek to reduce their internal costs by dealing with fewer suppliers, linkages with the small companies are broken.

An initiative called RELINK is investigating how small firms in the tooling and automotive industry can draw on innovations that are available to enable them to participate as part of a broader global supply chain. It is based on the establishment of large-scale virtual organizations of collaborating firms linked by a common vision and set of business practices that are supported by ICT tools.

RELINK is a joint initiative of two industry associations in Australia: FAPM (Federation of Automotive Products Manufacturers) and TIFA (Tooling Industry Forum of Australia). To understand how the formation of virtual enterprise relates to ICT infrastructure, a 5 layer model, RELINK Communication Framework (RCF), is used to describe the functionalities required to carry out the tasks of transmitting information from one end to another (Mo *et al*, 2005).

RCF is an open ICT infrastructure model that aims to support implementation of systems for the virtual enterprise at the appropriate level. The 5 layers are:

o   Application layer: describes the functions that a toolmaker needs to do their work.

o   Presentation layer: converts the information to a format suitable to be used by the application that the toolmaker wants to run.

o   Interpretation layer: performs the function of diverting information into relevant streams.

o   Verification layer: performs the function of ensuring the information transferred is actually the data that the sender wants to transmit.

o   Physical layer: represents the transmission media that will be used in the communication process.

By characterising the communication profiles in RCF, it is observed that the ICT requirements of a VE change over time at different stages of the virtual enterprise development. To understand this phenomenon, the Virtual Enterprise Reference Architecture (VERA) (Zwegers *et al*, 2003) was used to provide a framework for analysis. VERA conforms to the Generalised Enterprise Reference Architecture and Methodology (GERAM) (IFIP-IFAC Task Force, 1999). It provides a unified framework for knowledge integration in distributed environment. The high level modelling framework facilitates identification of processes but it does not address system implementation issues such as security or quality of service.

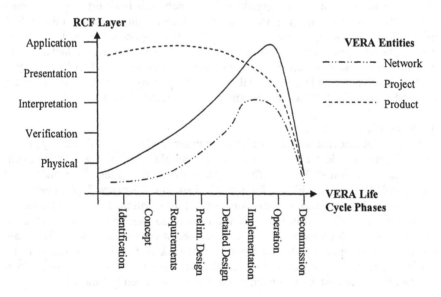

Figure 2   ICT profiles in VERA

The ability of the companies to quickly align their objectives and information systems with the amalgamated business processes can benefit the VE by supporting effective decision-making and informed actions. Without the right information at the right time, delays and more seriously costly mistakes can occur. VERA enables modelling of the relationship between the changes of ICT requirements to the maturity of the virtual enterprise, i.e. the life cycle phases in VERA.

In Figure 2, the Network entity represents the start of the virtual enterprise. There is very little demand for ICT support. Person to person relationships and trust are more important aspects towards the building of the entity. Hence, the ICT profile for the Network entity remains low until the point where the partners start to exchange documentation, which are the detailed design and implementation phases. Once the consortium is confirmed, the virtual enterprise changes to a Project entity.

The ICT profile for the Project entity increases quickly at lower RCF levels from the initial conceptual phases to highly sophisticated presentation and application levels as the entity progresses to the detailed design, implementation and operation phases. In these phases, large amount of data including design, production schedule, costing and legal documentations are exchanged.

The ICT profile remains at the high level as the Product (i.e. the tool) information is progressively refined during manufacturing. However, as described in the scenario in Figure 2, once production of the tool starts, the need to exchange complicated data sets reduces. The ICT levels become lower as the Product entity approaches completion.

3. EXPERIENCE ON APPLICATION SOFTWARE

There are many criteria for benchmarking ICT capabilities in an organisation (Shen *et al*, 2004). The ever-changing needs of the VE indicate that the criteria for an ICT infrastructure supporting complete VERA life cycle operation must be open to interoperate with pre-existing software as well as flexible with high adaptability to different levels of sophistication (Aerts *et al*, 2000). As part of the RELINK study, a range of relatively simple commercial ICT tools used by the tooling industry are evaluated against the criteria for supporting establishment of the VE.

3.1 Microsoft Project
It is highly sophisticated software with a large number of functions that many people have difficulty in understanding it. By way of example, a textbook available to help explain the operation of Project 2003 contains about 900 pages. The underlying principle of MS Project is PERT (Program Evaluation and Review Technique). The integration of different views of the same project information is the most important feature that it can offer. However, it is a standalone software and does not have the ability to share with partners without total transfer of the project model. There are also severe restrictions on the conceptual framework that makes it difficult to be used for managing VE activities, for example, the segmentation of tasks over a long period with intermittent operating requirement is not sufficiently handled.

3.2 Microsoft Project Server

It is marketed as an internet enabled version of MS Project. However, installation of MS Project Server is troublesome. It requires many software components that are not normally required in day to day computing. These include:

- o Microsoft Windows Server 2003
- o Microsoft SQL Server
- o Microsoft Sharepoint
- o IIS

These additional system components add another level of complexity and costs in the ICT infrastructure. As each of the above software components are expensive by themselves, the initialisation cost is almost 4 times more than MS Project itself. It was also noted that management of the infrastructure would require a full time IT staff, which many VEs are not prepared for when they are formed.

3.3 Outlook Express

It is common software that is available to everyone who has Windows based PCs. However, it is not interoperable with other operating systems such as Sun's Solaris, which is commonly used for professional CAD/CAM environments. Outlook has good network connectivity and can be used for email if the server it connects to supports Post-office protocol (POP3). In that regard, Outlook can be classified as supporting the Verification Level of the RCF.

3.4 Quickplace

It is a web-based software running on PC server to support web-based collaborative work. The interface is relatively easy to use but the functionality offered is rather limited. Significant enhancement in the form of specially written Java software modules is required to introduce abilities such as automatic message filing and directory changes.

3.5 KickStart

It is simple, low cost project management software that uses the MS Project concept but does not have all the sophistication. However, its capability is therefore limited on a PC based environment. Linkage to Outlook tasks can be enabled.

3.6 PHP Bulletin Board

The bulletin board is internet-based discussion software that captures the discussion of participants in a structural fashion. It runs on many platforms and can be accessed via an internet browser. The bulletin board is best used for idea exchange, knowledge search, and problem solving involving expert's interaction on a distributed environment. The problem of bulletin board is that although a data structure can be established easily, conformant to the data structure is highly dependent on the users.

4. DYNAMIC NETWORK SYSTEM

The software evaluation result shows that commercial ICT tools used by the toolmakers do not interoperate easily. This issue is well recognised and proved to be the bottleneck in fostering collaboration between companies (Kosanke, 2005). Solutions that are based on open distributed environment are of particular attraction to SMEs, which have limited ICT support resources to adopt full scale inter-enterprise collaboration systems (Davidsson *et al*, 2005). An added problem with ICT support for the RELINK type organisation is that at different states of the virtual enterprise, the requirements for ICT support change in time. Companies involved in the virtual enterprise find it difficult to optimise their ICT investments in the most cost effective fashion. A flexible approach that facilitates the detailed design of ICT systems and their rapid implementation and ongoing development is required. Systems that are component based and built on systems engineering approaches are more likely to meet the specification for large scale, change-capable enterprise systems (Weston, 1999).

The development of the Dynamic Network System (DNS) has the objectives of being highly flexible for adaptation to the VERA life cycle as well as integrating pre-existing ICT capabilities of the members of the VE into the collaborative environment with minimum cost requirements. DNS achieves these objectives by combining two conceptual designs. First, DNS models the operating characteristics of the ICT environment and can be used to generate the integrated internet web portal quickly from the system designer's view. Second, DNS is built on open source Java server pages (JSP) server capabilities and standard TCP/IP RMI technologies. The server security and management capabilities are interoperable with any other normal web servers. DNS does not provide specific enterprise functions by itself, but rather it is a concept capturing platform that incorporates third party software tools with those enterprise functions into an integrated information system. The underlying computing environment then manages the execution of the software tools which produce processed information passed on by the DNS model to the next software tool.

DNS software architecture can be depicted in Figure 3. An Apache server provides the web interface of the system to outside world. Enhanced by Tomcat, an open source server, development of DNS modules becomes a much easier project as most of the internal controls are already built in. Installation of Apache and Tomcat is easy and instructions can be found at http://tomcat.apache.org. DNS can be divided into two main parts: DNS Modeller and DNS RunTime.

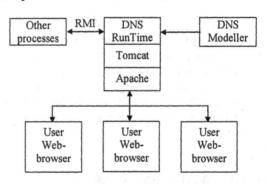

Figure 3   DNS software architecture

DNS performs its functions by calling operational components known as agents. An agent is a Java class that exhibits certain operational behaviour and so it is also known as behavioural class. Basic functionality such as displaying information and setting up user selection pages are included as built in agents in the system. Additional agents can be incorporated into the system easily by the user with his/her own Java classes. In essence, each agent must be "extended" from a class au.csiro.dns.behaviour.BehaviourClass, which is included in the DNS distribution jar file. When the user's agent is created, the user can call upon this behaviour in the DNS model after a simple registration procedure to DNS RunTime.

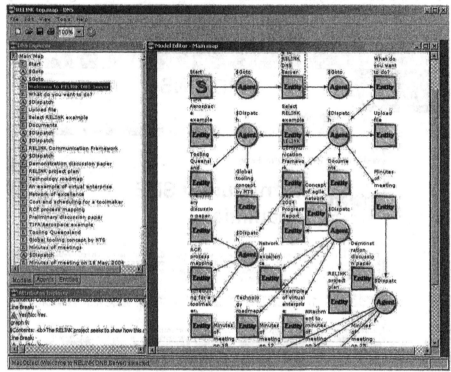

Figure 4   DNS Modeller user interface

DNS operates according to a defined DNS model, which is created by the DNS Modeller. The DNS Modeller is the user interface for modelling the functionality and behaviour of the collaborative system. The user interface is shown in Figure 4.

DNS modelling concept consists of two main components. The agent entity will deliver operational characteristics of the system when it is executed. An agent's behaviour will result in certain state of system known as entity. Hence, a DNS model captures the operational details of a remote user interacting with the system to achieve his/her goals. Since DNS can incorporate agents developed by any user supplied Java class, the system is highly flexible in exhibiting various desirable server capabilities through a wide variety of agents registered to it. The outcome of running the DNS Modeller is a DNS model that captures the anticipated interactive processes of the web-based collaborative system.

The DNS RunTime runs in conjunction with Tomcat and translates the DNS model into a governing framework. When the DNS model is activated through DNS RunTime, the information is translated into web server information and drives the Tomcat and Apache system to deliver the functionality to the web user (Figure 5). DNS uses standard internet server technologies with functionalities added on separately as needed. For example, knowledge is better managed by a structured directory that can be browsed by the users. Experience shows that a pre-agreed directory structure is necessary to gain acceptance by all VE partners. Since the agreed structure represents an alignment of the practices of individual companies to the VE, users of the system can find the mutually accepted knowledge repository easy to adapt.

Figure 5   DNS RunTime driven web server

Another example is the automatic processing of documents in the system. File downloading is an integral part of the server capability. Suitable links can be inserted easily in the text that can be activated to download files and data. File uploading is a separate feature that must be implemented using some server programming facilities. The JSP capability can be easily implemented from standard function library. Other functionalities such as bulletin board and email can also be incorporated in the open ICT infrastructure.

In addition to standard functionalities, DNS can integrate third party collaborative functionality using RMI. Interfacing agents that work with other systems such as invoking a third party software can be implemented allowing it to manage the interaction with third party processes that may need to be called upon during execution of the collaborative task. For example, information searching processes can be linked by DNS via a RMI enabled Java program that manages its own Java database connectivity (JDBC) with any SQL database. In DNS Modeller, the RMI behavioural class is defined in the same way as a normal agent.

5. CONCLUSION

This paper evaluated the usefulness of implementing and using a number of common server functionalities for supporting VERA life cycle. These functions are supported by capabilities that come as an integral part of the open source server. The development of DNS leads to a flexible and open platform for integrating pre-existing ICT infrastructures in VE partners.

Since the system requires open source server components and industry standard JSP technologies, the cost and development effort required for developing a collaborative server is low. Management of the system does not require substantial IT skills and is ideal for SMEs.

Recent developments in internet based technologies on open protocol standards such as SOAP have provided an opportunity to develop an integrated internet-based system while maintaining the autonomy of individual software products in their normal operating environments. Due to the complexity of the application, these open standards require highly skilled professionals who are well trained in the fundamental working principles of the standards as well as system diagnosis. To enable a more general use of the new internet based technologies, a simplified process and methodology is required. It is anticipated that by application of the latest distributed computing technologies, further development of DNS will be directed towards a multi-platform integrated environment.

6. REFERENCES

1. Aerts A.T.M., Szirbik N.B., Goossenaerts J.B.M., (2000), "Flexible Infrastructure for Virtual Enterprises", in *Global Engineering, Manufacturing and Enterprise Networks*, ed. Mo J.P.T., Nemes L., IFIP TC5 WG5.3/5.7/5.12 Fourth International Working Conference on the Design of Information Infrastructure Systems for Manufacturing (DIISM 2000), November 15-17, Melbourne, Australia, pp.26-37
2. Barradas L.C.S., Pinto-Ferreira J.J., "P2P Infrastructure for tourism electronic marketplace", Paper 49, 18th IFIP World Computer Congress, Toulouse, France, 22-27 August, 2004
3. Davidsson P., Ramstedt L., Tornquist J. (2005). "Inter-organisation Interoperability in Transport Chains Using Adapters Based on Open Source Freeware", Proceedings of the First International Conference on Interoperability of Enterprise Software and Applications, INTEROP-ESA'05, 22-25 February, Geneva, Switzerland
4. Hao Q., Shen W., Wang L., (2005). "Towards a cooperative distributed manufacturing management framework", *Computers in Industry*, 56 (2005) 71–84
5. IFIP-IFAC Task Force on Architectures on Enterprise Integration (1999). "Generalised Enterprise Reference Architecture and Methodology", Annex to ISO WD15704, Requirements for enterprise reference architectures and methodologies, GERAM v.1.6.3, March
6. Jiang H.C., Mo J.P.T., (2001). "Internet Based Design System for Globally Distributed Concurrent Engineering", *Journal of Cybernetics and Systems*, Vol.32, No.7, October-November, pp.737 754
7. Kosanke K. (2005). "ISO Standards for Interoperability: a comparison", Proceedings of the First International Conference on Interoperability of Enterprise Software and Applications, INTEROP-ESA'05, 22-25 February, Geneva, Switzerland

8.   McNamara, D.L (2003) "Scale, Space and Place – SME Flexibility in Cross-border Industrial Clusters" Asia-Pacific Researchers in Organisational Studies, Conference Proceedings, Oaxaca, Mexico, December 8-10

9.   Mo J.P.T., Beckett R., Nemes L., (2005). "Technology Infrastructure for Virtual Organisation of Tooling", Sixth IFIP Working Conference on Virtual Enterprises (PRO-VE'05), 26-28 September, 2005, Valencia, Spain

10.   Nemes L., Mo J.P.T., (2004), "Collaborative Networks in Australia – Challenges and Recommendations", in Collaborative Networked Organizations, ed. Camarinha-Matos L.M., Afsarmanesh H., pub. Kluwer Academic Publishers, ISBN 1-4020-7823-4, pp.97-102

11.   Ortiz A., Lario F., Ros L. (1999), "Enterprise Integration – Business Processes Integrated Management: a proposal for a methodology to develop Enterprise Integration Programs", Computers in Industry, 40, 155–171

12.   Shen H., Wall B., Zaremba M., Chen Y.L., Browne J., (2004), Integration of business modelling methods for enterprise information system analysis and user requirements gathering, Computers in Industry, 54 (2004), 307-323

13.   Shinonome M., Hashimoto H., Fuse A., Mo J.P.T., (1998). "Development of an information technology infrastructure for extended enterprise", IFIP TC5 WG5.3/5.7 Third International Conference on the Design of Information Infrastructure Systems for Manufacturing (DIISM '98), May 18-20, Fort Worth, Texas, U.S.A., pp.353-364

14.   Van den Berg R.J., Tolle M., (2000). "Assessing Ability to Execute in Virtual Enterprises", in Global Engineering, Manufacturing and Enterprise Networks, ed. Mo J.P.T., Nemes L., IFIP TC5 WG5.3/5.7/5.12 Fourth International Working Conference on the Design of Information Infrastructure Systems for Manufacturing (DIISM 2000), November 15-17, Melbourne, Australia, pp.38-45

15.   Weston R.H., (1999), "Reconfigurable, component-based systems and the role of enterprise engineering concepts", Computers in Industry, 40, pp.321-343

16.   Zwegers A., Tolle M., Vesterager J., (2003). "VERAM: Virtual Enterprise Reference Architecture and Methodology", in Global Engineering and Manufacturing in Enterprise Networks, ed. Karvonen I., van den Berg R., Bernus P., Fukuda Y., Hannus M., Hartel I., Vesterager J., VTT Symposium 224, Helsinki, Finland, 9-10 December, pp.17-38

49 | IT SUPPORT FOR PERIODS OF GROUP CREATIVITY IN VIRTUAL ENTERPRISES

Roger Tagg
University of South Australia; Roger.Tagg@unisa.edu.au
AUSTRALIA

Within the life cycles of Virtual Enterprises, there are usually periods where representatives of different organisations collaborate in creative ways to set guidelines for the operational stages of the VE. Examples of what has to be agreed or negotiated include legal contracts, financial terms, human responsibilities, joint processes to be followed, common terminology, data formats and common software. This collaboration may be a mixture of synchronous (physical or virtual meetings) and asynchronous activities. This position paper assesses the gap between what support is required and what is available in currently available tools, and suggests a number of key developments to the state of the art.

1. INTRODUCTION

This position paper addresses the issue of IT support for those periods within the operation of a Virtual Enterprise when groups of people have to develop ideas, designs and solutions, which are acceptable to all participants and which further both their joint and individual objectives.

The motivation for the work arises from a range of application needs. Some colleagues of this author are focussing on support for groups working in emergency situations, often involving the participation of different authorities such as Fire, Ambulance, Police and the Military. Others, including this author, are targeting requirements engineering, systems design and general administrative cooperative work. An additional goal has been to propose ways to overcome the epidemic of information overload.

The paper is organized as follows. First, the place of creative work in Virtual Enterprises is introduced. Then, the patterns of creativity in general are discussed. Next, the limitations and shortcomings of current facilities for supporting group creative activities are highlighted. A possible way forward is offered in two parts: a) an overall architecture; and b) specific software developments to support that architecture. A brief summary highlights some of the most critical success factors for these developments to become a reality.

Please use the following format when citing this chapter:

Tagg, R., 2006, in IFIP International Federation for Information Processing, Volume 224, Network-Centric Collaboration and Supporting Fireworks, eds. Camarinha-Matos, L., Afsarmanesh, H., Ollus, M., (Boston: Springer), pp. 471–480.

2. CREATIVITY IN VIRTUAL ENTERPRISES

2.1 Characteristics of a Virtual Enterprise

In this paper the term "Virtual Enterprise" (VE) includes a range of forms of cooperation that involve the participation of more than one legal entity or individual. The common feature of all VEs is that they present a single face to the outside world of customers, suppliers, the general public or the environment. They can vary from more formal arrangements like joint ventures, through loose confederations of small enterprises, to voluntary associations of individuals. In all cases, some level of "ground rules" has to be negotiated, as well as discussions of the goal and priorities.

2.2 Virtual Enterprise Life Cycles

(Tagg, 2001) proposed 4 stages in the life of a Virtual Enterprise, namely Establishment, Business Development, Business Execution and Winding Up. In each of these, some activities involve creative work, whereas others can follow processes agreed at earlier stages. Some examples are shown in Table 1.

Life Cycle Stage	Creative activities	Other activities
Establishment	- Identify broad market opportunities - Develop processes and protocols for the VE	- Apply joining procedures
Business Development	- Joint market research - Decide participants' responsibilities - Develop template business processes	- Bid in competitive tenders - Evaluate benefits, costs and risks - Project management
Business Execution	- Negotiate individual B2B business processes	- Customer Relationship Management - Accounting
Winding Up	Apportion assets and intellectual property	- Settle legal and financial issues

Table 1 – Examples of Creative and other Activities in
Virtual Enterprise Life Cycles

When a VE reaches the Business Execution stage, periods of creativity are less dominant. Processes that have been negotiated earlier on will often be followed. Indeed, the development of good processes, which participants can be expected to follow, is more important in a VE than a single organization, since it has to compensate for the fact that individuals primarily report to different managements. However as the table shows, creativity, in the form of negotiation of individual contracts and protocols, is still present; and it reappears more strongly when a VE is wound up.

3. PATTERNS OF CREATIVITY

3.1 The Nature of Creativity

The nature of creativity, and models to describe creative work, have been discussed recently by (Hoffmann, 2005), (Blackburn, 2005), and elsewhere. Creative work has been distinguished by its semi-structured or unstructured nature, in contrast to following pre-defined procedures.

Much IT support for creative work has up to now been targeted primarily at face-to-face or other synchronous meetings of participants, with the intention of "brainstorming". (Blackburn, 2005) proposes the monitoring of "cognitive dust" – the lowest level of recordable events in a high-tech meeting room, in order to provide a knowledge base for an electronic facilitator. This can be extended to include a number of "different place" – and even "different time" environments.

However creative work does not all happen within meetings. Much creativity takes place between meetings, often by individuals working alone, e.g. preparing ideas for discussion. Individuals often develop their ideas when totally off-line, such as when walking in the park or lying in bed.

Meetings are often the forum for debating proposals and individual ideas, rather than the place where the new ideas emerge. They also enforce a discipline, including convening the meeting (usually with an agenda) before, and recording decisions, allocated actions and other outcomes afterwards. This discipline still applies to "single meeting" creative work. Much of the information to do with meetings is in fact of a procedural nature.

As opportunities for creativity, meetings – especially face-to-face ones - have well-known problems. Regular meetings may become enslaved by their agendas and the creep of administrative overheads. All meetings, but especially recurring ones, may become bear-pits for egos and political agendas, and contributions of less pushy participants may be overlooked.

3.2 Cycles of Creativity

Creativity, especially in business, is often cyclic in character. There is almost always a goal that is to be achieved, but it may take several cycles to achieve the best result – or even an acceptable one. Creative work may also need to be broken down into smaller tasks and re-combined later.

The creative cycle often involves putting ideas to the test, or evaluating their worth by calculation, simulation or other models. Predicting risk, acceptability and ease of use of a proposed solution are more difficult in creative work than in operational work, where simple financial models are usually adequate.

One period of creativity may lead on into a subsequent one; for example developing requirements for a system typically leads into designing a technical solution.

In information work today, individuals are typically involved in multiple creativity cycles simultaneously. Some of these are related to the same area of creativity, while some are totally unrelated. Being involved in too many parallel activities is known to contribute to information overload, which in turn threatens creativity. Addressing this overload is one of the motivations for this paper.

4. CURRENT SUPPORT AND ITS LIMITATIONS

4.1 Current Support

Tools to support individual creativity are relatively plentiful in the software market. These range from the MS Word "outline view" to a graphical mind-mapping tool such as Mind Manager (www.mindjet.com). In specialist fields there are dedicated tools, e.g. CAD (Computer Aided Design) and music composition software.

Commercial Groupware such as Lotus Notes or Microsoft Exchange supports creativity, but only in an unstructured (and usually asynchronous) sharing and sending of messages and artefacts. Apart from version control, they do not generally offer any specific support for creativity. In a VE environment, there are also the problems that file formats may not be exchangeable, and there is no shared version control or access control, unless provided by one participant on behalf of the group.

For synchronous meetings, a number of commercial products and research prototypes are now available. Typically, several participants can view or manipulate an electronic version of the artefacts being discussed (e.g. text or diagrams). However once again, use of this technology in a VE requires all participants to support the same software.

4.2 Problems with Current Support

Heterogeneity of data formats, semantics and presentation is the first problem with any IT support for VEs. Different organizations in a VE may use different vendors' products, or different versions from the same vendor. IT tools that are currently used are usually the products of a competitive market place. Marketing considerations often result in the data formats for a vendor's proprietary software being non-standard and obscure. The vendor may provide support for importing foreign data into their format, but rarely for exporting. A good example of this is the MS Outlook .pst format for mailboxes.

Proliferation of user interfaces (UI) is a somewhat related problem. Whenever a user has to adopt a new tool – as someone involved in VE work is very likely to do – he or she has to learn yet another UI. Many individuals already suffer from having to use too many interfaces, and resent the waste of time when yet another one has to be learnt and remembered. This can result in a good tool not getting adopted.

Intra-enterprise bias is a problem because the cost of most computer infrastructure is almost always paid by real organizations (i.e. companies, or large public enterprises). Therefore, software that supports group work often favours groups that are entirely within that organization, and does not take account of the needs of VEs. The common use of the adjective "Enterprise" to describe future integrated systems, reveals this bias.

As discussed earlier, there is also a **synchronous meetings bias**. Products and prototypes have been developed to support synchronous meetings, but not so many are designed specifically to support what happens in between meetings. These periods are left to be supported by "ad-hoc" use of groupware tools, e.g. email or chat with attachments.

Another problem in supporting creativity is the **difficulty of capturing ideas when the human with the idea is not on-line.** Technology to support voice dictation and handwriting is improving, but to capture ideas expressed in hand-drawn diagrams is less simple.

Perhaps the hardest problem is **Context Recognition,** here defined as recognizing what a document or message is about and how it should be categorized within the structure of the group's (or individual's) area of concern. So far, even the best software has not yet matched the ability of a good secretary or filing clerk. Two approaches have been tried. One is **statistical text mining,** in which the frequency of words and phrases is mapped and candidate topic clusters are identified. An example of a tool using this approach is Leximancer (Smith, 2005). However this approach does not make use of any knowledge about the topic area already held by the groups or individuals. **Ontologies** (Noy, 2001) offer a complementary approach, by formalizing the structure of knowledge about a domain of discourse. However this also has drawbacks. In creative work, the focus of the knowledge often evolves rapidly. Also, significant effort is needed to build and maintain an ontology. In the VE environment there is the additional problem that no central ontology may exist unless all participants agree to follow the same one.

5. PROPOSED ARCHITECTURAL MODEL

5.1 Collaboration Architecture

Central to the work described in this paper is the observation that an increasing amount of collaborative work these days is "many-to-many". One human can participate in many groups, while collaborating groups can each involve several organizations or legal entities. Figure 1 illustrates this many-to-many concept.

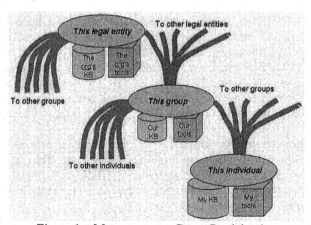

Figure 1 – Many-to-many Group Participation

Each group - and each individual - has a characteristic world view, represented in the diagram by the various levels of Knowledge Base (KB). There is also a set of tools that are used at each level. In a VE, there may be few group-level tools and everything has to be done by using individual tools and passing versions of artefacts. No distinction has been made between creative and non-creative work here; as discussed earlier, the two are interwoven within the cycles of creativity.

5.2 Software Architecture

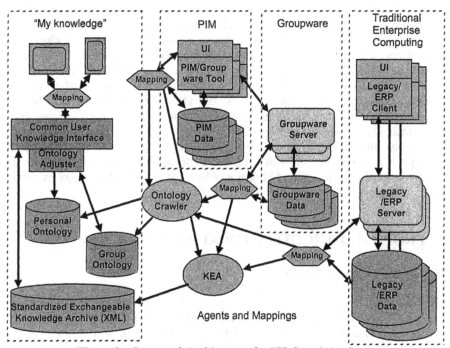

Figure 2 – Proposed Architecture for VE Creativity Support

Figure 2 shows one way in which the combined needs of a many-to-many model (Figure 1), a virtual enterprise and support for creative work can be addressed in terms of a set of software components. Two specific additions to normal software environments should be noted: **my knowledge** and **agents and mappings**.

My knowledge is essentially a single portal to a variety of information that is extracted or mapped from its original sources. The information is a combination of individual information and information from all the groups in which the individual participates.

Agents and mappings are a set of translators and transformation rules respectively, that deliver information in a consistent form. This might involve any combination of reformatting, indexing or linking. There may be agents operating for groups as well as individuals. The mappings depend on the meta-level definitions of the formats of the various source information types.

The diagram shows different user interfaces for the knowledge portal, traditional groupware and enterprise applications. The term PIM (Personal Information Management) has been introduced in this context by (Jones, 2005). These latter interfaces are typicaly access-restricted for each member organization in the VE.

6. PROPOSED DEVELOPMENTS

The four main new components in the architecture are the Knowledge Extraction Agent (KEA), the Ontology Crawler, The Ontology Adjuster and the Common User Knowledge Interface.

6.1 Knowledge Extraction Agent

Analogous to the work of a filing clerk, this architecture includes an autonomous agent known as the Knowledge Extraction Agent (KEA). It would operate in the background in a similar fashion to Google Desktop (Sullivan, 2004). The group would specify, through a Wizard, the sources of data and knowledge to be processed. This could include material reachable through networks as well as that stored on a specific computer.

The goal of a KEA is to make information available in a form that enables it to be read consistently by any collaborating participant. The output of KEA is an archive of marked up (in XML) records that either contain, or give links to, all information that the agent's "principal" (i.e. group or individual) deems relevant for further reference. It does not necessarily involve complete duplication – a set of keyword tags providing an indexing mechanism may be enough. Links would then point to the original content or service, assuming that a translator can be generated to at least render the source information readable.

In the VE scenario, multiple KEAs may operate on behalf of specific groups and individuals, each with their own objectives. The group coordinators or individuals can then determine who else can access the information by sharing or sending.

In order to categorize source knowledge, a KEA would need to be aware of the group's "knowledge structure", which could include ontologies, lists of relevant entities and rules derived from statistical text mining. For non-text sources such as pictures and multimedia, additional categorization rules would be required.

It is envisaged that the archive produced by a KEA would include standard formats for entities that appear frequently in knowledge bases. Examples are events, text messages, tasks, activities (i.e. task instances), rules, tables, diagrams, audio/video clips, annotations, processes, data structures and persistent business objects (e.g. Customers, Products).

For example, all data representing *tasks* would be accessible (either physically stored or realizable through mappings from data held in the original format) in a format such as PMXML (Curran, 2004). This would apply wherever those tasks originally come from, e.g. a Project Management System, a Workflow Management System that creates task instances from templates, or from a Groupware tool (e.g. MS Outlook) that supports tasks or "To Do" lists.

6.2 Ontology Crawler

As discussed earlier, ontologies have the disadvantage that they need to be created and maintained, especially where the creativity element is high. Without most of this work being automated however, the approach proposed in this paper will probably fail to gain acceptance.

At least an approximation to every human user's (or group's) knowledge structure can be deduced from an analysis of the files and applications he or she has access to. Valuable sources include:

- directory structures of local or networked data storage drives or places
- schemas of relational databases and fixed format files
- IDL (interface definition language) for remotely accessed programs (WSDL for web services)
- address books in an email client
- folder structures of web browser bookmark files

as well as registries, imported ontologies and the results of text mining.

Any automatic categorization also depends on recognizing (e.g. by name) instances of key entity types. Examples are persons (e.g. collaborators or correspondents), business partners, projects/subprojects, products (e.g. physical items and assemblies) and services. These must either be included in an ontology or linked as reference tables

This leads to the observation that any application using an ontology also needs access to a "lexicon" whereby strings (e.g. as they appear in documents) can be related to concepts in the knowledge structure. However this correspondence is non-deterministic; the same string could indicate more than one concept. For example, "Winter" could be a season or the name of a customer.

The ontology crawler represents the meta-level counterpart of the KEA. However changes to the structure of knowledge are not as frequent as changes to the body of knowledge itself. The biggest job would be the initial crawl; subsequent crawls might only need to take place occasionally (e.g. monthly).

6.3 Ontology Adjuster

The Ontology Crawler, however sophisticated, may not produce the knowledge structure that reflects the group's (or individual's) natural classification structure. There needs to be some means by which users can correct the structures detected.

(Einig, 2005) describes a prototype, built under the current author's supervision, for editing an ontology. This tool is targeted for use by non-specialist human users, rather than experts.

6.4 Common User Knowledge Interface

The final proposal is for a common interface - "My Knowledge" in Figure 2 (by analogy with the traditional "My Documents" of MS Windows).

To try and overcome the UI proliferation problem, it is desirable to have a standard set of logical interface patterns that supports users interacting with the standardized knowledge archive described in 5.2 above.

It is envisaged that this interface will also bridge to existing software and their associated file formats. One approach would be to repackage the existing software as "services" in the SOA (Service Oriented Architecture) sense. Also, mappings will be required that enable translations to be generated to convert the native formats to the KEA standard.

A further hurdle to be overcome here is the variety of user devices, such as PDAs, web-enabled mobile phones and wearable computers. (Javahery, 2003) proposed a system of patterns which can be modelled at a logical level between the server application and the different devices.

Figure 3 shows the structure of such a user interface architecture.

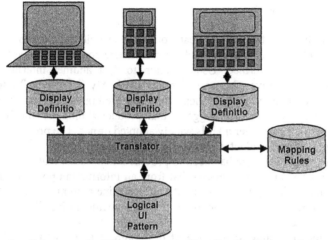

Figure 3 – Structure of a User Interface with a Device Independence Layer

7. SUMMARY

7.1 Work Done and Planned

In research projects supervised by the author, a number of test beds have been built and explored. We have built a simple ontology-based pre-processor for categorizing incoming email. Incoming email is one of the biggest irritants for many users. We searched message sender, subject and body text for strings that we could match with ontology concepts, then added keyword-style tags to create XML task records that represent the job of dealing the incoming request, enabling the tasks to be grouped by topic. We have also built a (hopefully!) end-user friendly tool for editing the knowledge structure stored in the RDF format commonly used for ontologies. However this prototype needs more serious testing with real users.

Our current work includes a combination of the above two techniques, development of a uniform model for tasks that derive from different applications such as workflow, enterprise applications, project management and PIM.

7.2 Related Work

The main vendors of groupware, including Microsoft and IBM, all have projects addressing some of these problems, but have not yet released much detail – see for example (Geyer, 2003) and the press release for IBM Lotus "Hannover" (IBM, 2005). University research seems more focussed on individual techniques such as text mining and categorization; one attempt to combine the statistical and ontology approaches is (Dittenbach, 2004). For details of a current project addressing this area, see (Ananiadou, 2005). The topic of Model Driven Architecture (Object Management Group, 2006) is also relevant, since MDA addresses the generation of mappings between different representations of information – something that is needed to provide the mappings in the architecture proposed.

7.3 Critical Success Factors

Apart from the immaturity in text categorization techniques, the most critical factor affecting whether or not the approach described here could ever be widely adopted is probably the user interface. User reaction to "yet another interface" would be understandably negative. To accept the proposed "My Knowledge" interface, users would need to be able to drop at least one, and preferably several, of their existing interfaces. However, history suggests that product timing, as much as technical design, determines whether a UI is widely adopted or not. The precedent of Visicalc, the first spreadsheet product, is perhaps a good example.

Although the challenge has been to provide an approach that addresses the need of creative work, analysis suggests that from an information point of view, creative work is usually closely interleaved with more routine administration. The following of processes may not be so important, but there seems no justification for a totally separate approach.

This paper has suggested a line of development that might lift IT support for groups, for both creative and other work, to a new level of effectiveness. Realization is perhaps a few years off, but research and development is starting to happen.

8. REFERENCES

1. Ananiadou, S., Chruszcz, J., Keane, J., McNaught, J., Watry, P., (2005): The National Centre for Text Mining: Aims and Objectives, http://www.ariadne.ac.uk/issue42/ananiadou/ , 2005
2. Blackburn, T., Swatman, P.A., and Vernik, R. Extending CSCW theories to Model and Support Creative Group Processes, submitted for publication, http://www.insyl.unisa.edu.au/publications/working-papers/2005-23.pdf , 2005
3. Curran, K., Flanagan, L. and Callan, M. PMXML: An XML vocabulary intended for the exchange of task planning and tracking information, http://www.xmlmania.com/documents.php?x=month&m=04&y=2004 , 2004
4. Dittenbach, M., Berger, H. and Merkl, D., Improving Domain Ontologies by Mining Semantics from Text, Proc. 1st Asia-Pacific Conference on Conceptual Modelling, Dunedin, New Zealand, http://www.crpit.com/confpapers/CRPITV31Dittenbach.pdf 2004
5. Einig, M., Tagg, R. and Peters, G. "Managing the knowledge needed to support an electronic personal assistant", In Proc Int'l Conf on Enterprise Information Systems (ICEIS), 2006
6. Geyer, M., Vogel, J., Cheng, L., and Muller, M. Supporting Activity-centric Collaboration Through Peer-to-Peer Shared Objects, http://domino.research.ibm.com/cambridge/research.nsf/0/ec360aeb7a39b10485256da9006506e2/$FILE/TR2003-09.pdf, 2003
7. Hoffmann, O., Cropley, D., Cropley, A., Nguyen, L. and Swatman, P.A. Creativity, Requirements, and World Views, Aust J of Info Systems, Vol 13, 2005; 1: 159-175
8. IBM, With the unveiling of the next release of Lotus Notes, code-named Hannover, press release, http://www-306.ibm.com/software/swnews/swnews.nsf/n/nhan6dbjwg , 2005
9. Javahery, H., Seffah, A., Engelberg, D. and Sinnig, D. Multiple User Interfaces: Multiple-Devices, Cross-Platform and Context-Awareness, chapter 12 "Migrating User Interfaces between Platforms Using HCI Patterns". Wiley, 2003
10. Jones, W. et al. Proceedings of the PIM (Personal Information Management) Workshop, Seattle, WA, http://pim.ischool.washington.edu/tools.htm , 2005
11. Noy, N. and McGuinness, D.L. Ontology Development 101. Technical Report SMI-2001-0880, Stanford Medical Informatics, 2001
12. Object Management Group, MDA – the architecture of choice for a changing world, http://www.omg.org/mda
13. Smith, A. Leximancer home page, http://www.leximancer.com/, 2005
14. Sullivan, D. Google Desktop Search Launched, http://searchenginewatch.com/searchday/article.php/3421651 , 2004
15. Tagg, R. Workflow in Different Styles of Virtual Enterprise, Proc of Workshop on IT in Virtual Enterprises, Aust. Computer Science Week, 2001

ADDRESSING AUTONOMY AND INTEROPERABILITY IN BREEDING ENVIRONMENTS

Toni Ruokolainen and Lea Kutvonen

Department of Computer Science
P.O. Box 68 (Gustaf Hällströmin katu 2 b)
FI-00014 UNIVERSITY OF HELSINKI
FINLAND

Toni.Ruokolainen@cs.Helsinki.FI, Lea.Kutvonen@cs.Helsinki.FI

Modern networked enterprises can preserve their competitive edge only by adopting a modern architecture for their computing systems, and thus, become agile with respect to changes in computing technologies, for pressures for modifications in external business processes, and for management of simultaneous and changing memberships in various business networks. Establishment of virtual enterprises is an essential trend and in progress of merging into research results of agent technologies and Service-oriented Computing. This paper describes the meta-information and agents needed for verifying interoperability during the breeding process for virtual enterprises. Taken together with operational time monitoring, the facilities provide type-safety across the bindings between members of the community. Behind the discussion is a set of prototype implementations of middleware facilities.

1. INTRODUCTION

Modern networked enterprises can preserve their competitive edge only by adopting a modern architecture for their computing systems, and thus, become agile for changes in computing technologies, for pressures for modifications in external business processes, and for management of simultaneous and changing memberships in various business networks. Establishment of virtual enterprises, i.e., loosely-coupled communities of autonomic business services is an essential trend and in progress of merging into research results of agent technologies and Service-oriented Computing.

The contribution of our research on this large field includes a contract-driven architecture (with supporting platform service implementations) where each business service is provided an enterprise level agent for a) managing virtual enterprise memberships, b) ensuring that interoperability requirements are met, c)

Please use the following format when citing this chapter:

Ruokolainen, T., Kutvonen, L., 2006, in IFIP International Federation for Information Processing, Volume 224, Network-Centric Collaboration and Supporting Fireworks, eds. Camarinha-Matos, L., Afsarmanesh, H., Ollus, M., (Boston: Springer), pp. 481–488.

detecting and managing breaches, and d) negotiating (refining) the contract with other community members.

The contract is formed by the breeding environment facilities including potential member discovery and selection based on interoperability requirements. The contract itself is designed to cover a range of aspects from business considerations to technical accessibility. The emphasis has been on ensuring continuous interoperability while preserving autonomy of business services. In this paper we do not address the trustworthiness of the selection process; extensions on trust management between enterprise agents and business services are discussed separately (Ruohomaa et al., 2006; Kutvonen et al., 2006).

For us, interoperability means effective capability of mutual communication of information, request of processing and results, suggestions, and commitments. It covers various aspects: technical interoperability concerns with ability to transport messages between computational services; semantic interoperability concerns with shared understanding of message contents by the senders and the receivers both in terms of information representation and messaging sequences; pragmatic interoperability concerns with the willingness of partners for the actions committed for the collaboration. The technical and partially the semantic interoperability levels have been covered by many solutions; the pragmatic dimensions are still under work and of specific interest to us.

The requirement of using autonomic business services for the communities raises a need for global infrastructure that provides facilities for comparing service types while matching service offers (Ruokolainen and Kutvonen, 2006). The business services (or the computational counterparts) are developed independently, and the meta-information describing the collaborations (business network models) and the members (service offers) need common ontologies for making the breeding process and the operational time monitoring of interoperability possible (Kutvonen et al., 2005).

Especially related to the pragmatic interoperability, preservation of the business service autonomy raises new challenges. First, the business service must be supported by a computational implementation providing capability of performing requested services. However, it is often the case that not all of this capability is given out into all kinds of business networks. The computational services must be guarded by enterprise policies for use. In addition, the business service comes partially defined by its role (commitments, responsibilities, rights) in the community it participates. This aspect is governed by the contract. The local policies and the community wide contract may contradict at operational time, causing breaches that need to be managed. The breaches may be caused by the natural mismatch between the key issues for the enterprise and the community, and there is no need to try to remove this feature. The breaches may also be raised by operational time changes of enterprise policies — as part of their autonomy.

This paper describes the meta-information and agents needed for verifying interoperability during the breeding process for virtual enterprises. Taken together with operational time monitoring, the facilities provide type-safety across the bindings between members of the community. Behind the discussion is a set of prototype implementations of middleware facilities. Section 2 introduces our framework for automated business network management. Section 3 introduces our concepts and mechanisms for overcoming autonomy-related problems in inter-enterprise collaboration.

2. A BUSINESS NETWORK MANAGEMENT FRAMEWORK

The web-Pilarcos framework proposes a federated model of inter-enterprise collaboration networks, or virtual enterprises, comprised of autonomic business services. The inter-enterprise business collaboration networks are called eCommunities and they are established dynamically to serve a certain business scenario or opportunity. A business service denotes a set of functionalities provided by an enterprise to its clientele and co-operators, and is governed by the enterprise's own business rules and policies, as well as by business contracts and regulatory systems controlling the business area.

The properties of an eCommunity are described in a Business Network Model (BNM). (Kutvonen et al, 2005). The structure of an eCommunity is defined as a set of business roles and their inter-connections. Responsibilities for the participants in terms of descriptions for expected behaviours are declared on the one hand by the behavioural descriptions included in the role descriptions, and on the other hand by policies and business rules declared in the BNM. Non-functional properties, which declare quality-of-service, communication security, and trust-related requirements for the eCommunity, are also provided by the BNM.

A business role is described as a set of service types, a set of role composition rules, and role assignment rules. A service type (Ruokolainen and Kutvonen, 2006) is an abstract definition of service capabilities and behaviour which enables efficient interoperability validation for business services. Service type describes the service's externally visible behaviour in terms of an interface protocol (a bilateral process description), structures for the exchanged documents in terms of XML-Schema definitions and optionally semantic annotations embedded in document structures as references to common business ontologies. The services types are composed to with a set of intra-role coordination rules form business role functionality. The coordination rules relate communication actions in distinct service types with causal and temporal inter-dependencies. An optional set of role-specific assignment rules, that is, additional constraints for service attributes and service providers can also be given in the business role definition.

The eCommunities are established by utilising a breeding environment which comprises of service trading and community population services, and multilateral negotiations between the participants (Kutvonen et al., 2005). The breeding environment services, such as populators and type repositories, are not required from all sites, but can be provided as infrastructure services as a business on its own right. Negotiations are executed between business network management agents (NMA) of each enterprise to refine the contract-templates provided by the breeding environment. The NMAs act as representatives for the autonomous business services during the breeding process and operation of collaboration networks. The elements of the business network management environment are illustrated in Figure 1.

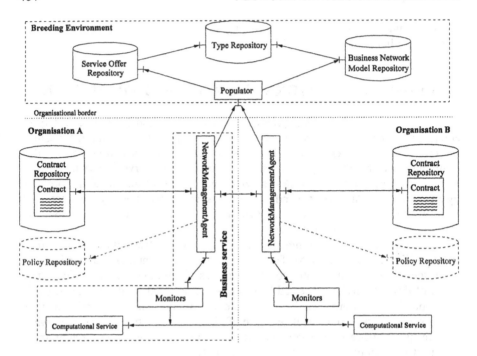

Figure 1 – An overview of the web-Pilarcos architecture. Arrows represent communication relationships, solid boxes are active agents and cylinders are information repositories.

The service trading mechanisms is provided by the service offer and type repositories which provide functionality similarly to the ODP trading and type repository functions (ODP, 1997; ODP, 1999). The type repositories are persistent storages of service typing information which are used as the primary means for achieving interoperation between business-services (Ruokolainen and Kutvonen, 2006). The service offer repositories are required to accept offers only from identifiable, tractable service providers. During publication of a service offer a conformance validation against the corresponding service type is initiated by the service offer repository; this is a necessary operation, in addition to runtime monitoring, for upholding type safety and interoperation in the system. Although the service offer repository itself thus becomes trustworthy, the service offers or service providers do not. A separate mechanism is designed for potential partners to collect experience information about provided services and pass around reputation information (Ruohomaa et al., 2006; Kutvonen et al., 2006)

The populator represents a breeding process phase where appropriate business service providers are selected for eCommunity roles. The populator function takes a Business Network Model and utilises service type and service offer repositories for fetching compatible business service providers for each eCommunity role. The populator selects the business services to an eCommunity on a basis of a constraint satisfaction process which considers the compatibility of the business service attribute values. When a set of compatible service offers have been found, populator returns the description of a populated eCommunity to the initiator of the population process. Population processes are initiated by enterprises willing to establish business collaborations. Publicly available Business Network Model repositories are used to publish and discover appropriate Business Network Models (Kutvonen et al., 2005).

For the negotiation phase, the web-Pilarcos framework provides generic negotiation interfaces and meta-level protocols. The negotiations and eCommunity management during the operation of the community are handled by the NMAs (Kutvonen et al., 2005; Metso and Kutvonen, 2005).The collaboration management interfaces of NMAs provide functionality for example for renegotiating part of the collaboration contract, to query the status of the contract, and to control transitions between eCommunity epochs, that is, distinct phases of the collaboration (Metso and Kutvonen, 2005). NMAs utilise local contract and policy repositories which store information concerning the electronic contracts, business rules and policies effective in the corresponding virtual enterprise.

3. ADDRESSING AUTONOMY IN VE ENVIRONMENTS

Autonomy of business network participants manifests itself as degrees of freedom given to them during the virtual enterprise life-time. A modern VE support environment should allow freedom of: 1) design and implementation of services, 2) decisions concerning the operation of services, and 3) willingness to collaborate. Nonetheless, interoperability and autonomy are inter-dependent aspects of collaboration: autonomy allowed for VE participants must be compensated with mechanisms to guarantee interoperation in presence of the corresponding freedom. In the following we describe the mechanisms that are used to support autonomy in the web-Pilarcos framework during eCommunity breeding, negotiation and operation and provide mechanisms for solving interoperability problems induced by the corresponding aspects.

3.1 Autonomy during eCommunity breeding process

The freedom of implementation of computational services leads to technological heterogeneity. Most of the implementation technology-related barriers for inter-enterprise collaboration can be solved with use of appropriate middleware, such as Web Services (W3C-WS, 2006) as a technological unification layer. Provided with technical compatibility between the computational services, more challenging aspects of autonomy and interoperability between business services can be addressed.

The freedom of design, of both existing legacy systems and newly developed services, induces semantic interoperability problems which must be solved during the VE breeding process. In the web-Pilarcos framework semantics are considered with respect to the meaning of individual messages exchanged between business services as well as the behavioural aspects of the business services. Interoperability, that is behavioural compatibility and substitutability, of business services is validated between service types (Ruokolainen and Kutvonen, 2006; Kutvonen et al., 2005). Interoperability is propagated to the level of business services via utilising service type checking during service offer publication. Thus service offer and service type repositories provide in concert the required functionality for validating semantic interoperability during community breeding.

Freedom of design and decisions concerning the operation of business services inflict both technical and pragmatic interoperability issues during selection and configuration of business services. Depending on the visibility and accessibility of service offer properties, business service attributes contribute to different phases of the breeding process. The information type (syntax and semantics) of an attribute is used as part of the service discovery criterion during the population process for finding compatible service offers. Values of publicly available service attributes affect service selection during the population of an eCommunity. Some business service attributes can be announced as private and their values are available only after prior commitments, i.e., during or after eCommunity negotiations. Private attributes express pragmatic aspects of interoperability related to local policies and business rules and provide service providers for context specific evaluation and expression of business service properties.

Table 1 provides a characterisation of the different business service attribute kinds that can be attached to service offers. Attributes are classified by visibility (public or private), type of the value (static or dynamic), and accessibility (how the actual attribute value can be obtained). An example of a typical usage of such attribute kind is also given. The "must negotiate"-kind of private attributes are used in situations where the service provider does not want to expose the attribute value before the client has at least identified himself (we presume that negotiations are held between identified partners). The service provider does not reveal a "must commit"-attribute value before a commitment to join the collaboration has been made by the client

Table 1 – Characterization of business service attribute kinds.

Visibility	Value type	Accessibility	Example
Public	Static	Published in the service offer	Service provider name
Public	Dynamic	Obtainable dynamically from service provider	Simple pricing information
Private	Dynamic	Must negotiate with the provider	Quality of service
Private	Dynamic	Must commit to contract before the value is exposed	Discount on the price of services

3.2 Negotiating the aspects of autonomy

Enterprises may express their willingness to collaborate during the negotiation phase of the breeding process. Negotiations are used primarily to come into conclusion about shared properties among autonomic agents; however, negotiation is also a mechanism to introduce autonomic decision procedures into the breeding process. An enterprise can keep its decision procedures and preferences private, since a negotiation about joining the collaboration leaves an option to decline the invitation to join the community. During the negotiations, partners agree about the private attribute values of business services discussed above, as well as granularity and permanence of collaboration commitments.

The participants of an eCommunity may commit to provide their business service functionality using three different time spans: the whole eCommunity lifetime, epochs, and business service sessions. Individual actions or business transactions are considered too fine-grained to be used as objects of commitments. An epoch is a block of collaboration defined in the BNM where the set of roles and services is stable; an epoch change captures a major reorganisation of the collaboration structure, membership, and commitments (Kutvonen et al., 2005). Service sessions are the smallest behavioural structures that can be committed to in the web-Pilarcos framework. The session boundaries are prescribed by the service types and they are used to define "natural" modular units of business service behaviour. Each of these commitment types can be in turn pre-negotiable or re-negotiable. A pre-negotiated commitment can not be changed between the commitments points, whereas re-negotiable commitments allow enterprises to express changes in their willingness to collaborate and decisions concerning business service provision during operation of the eCommunity.

3.3 Addressing autonomy during operation of an eCommunity

Autonomy of participants during the operation of an eCommunity manifests itself as 1) local policy conflicts, which usually lead to, 2) contract breaches. Local policies, that is, organizational policies and business rules are declarative rules that allow enterprises to control how, when and in which context their business services can be used. Local policies modify behaviour of business services by requiring certain actions to be taken instead of the others, by prohibiting actions, or influence the way an action is taken.

Local policy conflicts occur typically when an enterprise has previously committed to deliver a certain business functionality after which the local policies have changed due to changes for example in business strategies, or alliances. If local policies are expressed in the corresponding service offers, conflicts between the local policies and eCommunity requirements can be identified during the breeding process. However, organisational policies and business rules are inherently dynamic entities subject to organizations' autonomic intentions and not even necessarily published outside the organisations. Contract breaches occur either due to conscious decisions made by participants (e.g. changes in local policies) or due to involuntary failures to deliver the required business functionality. Runtime monitoring of business service behaviour against local policies and eCommunity contract can be utilised to identify and deal with both local policy conflicts and contract breaches.

4. CONCLUSION

The B2B-middleware developed in web-Pilarcos project provides support for autonomously administered business services that collaborate in a loosely coupled eCommunities. The eCommunity establishment and maintenance does not need facilities for distributed enactment of business processes, but instead focuses on ensuring semantic and pragmatic interoperability.

In many projects (see survey for example in (Camarinha-Matos, 2003)), the breeding environment provides facilities for negotiating and modelling the collaboration processes; the operational environment controls the enactment of the processes. Many of these virtual enterprise support environments use a shared abstract model to which all enterprises have to adapt their local services. In addition, the negotiations lean on an amount of human intervention for building the required trust relationships. In contrast to this, the approach in the web-Pilarcos project is a federated one and automation-oriented. Enterprises seek out partners that have services with which they are able to interoperate. The federated model provides the necessary flexibility and mechanisms to address pragmatic interoperability issues and autonomy. The automation is limited to routine decisions: strategic choices are left to humans while routine decisions concerning technical and semantic interoperability during eCommunity establishment or policy enforcement are provided with automated infrastructure facilities.

4. REFERENCES

1. Camarinha-Matos, L. M. (2003). Infrastructure for virtual organizations: where we are. In *Proceedings of ETFA'03 - 9th international conference on Emerging Technologies and Factory Automation,* Lisboan, Portugal.
2. Curbera, F., Goland, Y., Klein, J., Leyman, F., Roller, D., Thatte, S., and Weerawarana, S. (2002). *Business Process Execution Language for Web Services (BPEL4WS) 1.0.*
3. Kutvonen, L., Metso, J., and Ruokolainen, T. (2005). Inter-enterprise collaboration management in dynamic business networks. In *OTM Confederated International Conferences,* volume 3760 of *LNCS.* Springer-Verlag.
4. Kutvonen, L, Metso, J and Ruohomaa, S. (2006). From trading to eCommunity population: Responding to social and contractual challenges. Submitted manuscript.
5. Metso, J. and Kutvonen, L. (2005). Managing Virtual Organizations with Contracts. In *Workshop on Contract Architectures and Languages (CoALa2005),* Enschede, The Netherlands.
6. ODP (1997). *ISO/IEC 13235: Information Technology. Open Distributed Processing - ODP Trading function.* ISO/IEC JTC1.
7. ODP (1999). *ISO/IEC 14769: Information technology - Open Distributed Processing - Type repository function.* ISO/IEC JTC1/SC7.
8. Ruohomaa, S, Viljanen, L and Kutvonen, L. (2006). Guarding enterprise collaborations with trust decisions – the TuBE approach. *The 1st International workshop on Interoperability Solutions to Trust, Security, Policies and QoS for Enhanced Enterprise Systems). In the frame of I-ESA 2006 conference.* Hermes-Science Publishers.
9. Ruokolainen, T. and Kutvonen, L. (2006). Service Typing in Collaborative Systems. To appear in proceedings of INTEROP-ESA 2006.
10. W3C-WS (2006).*Web Services Activity.* W3C. http://www.w3.org/2002/ws/.

PART 16

DISTRIBUTED INFORMATION SYSTEMS

51	# DISTRIBUTED INFORMATION SERVICES SUPPORTING COLLABORATIVE NETWORK MANAGEMENT

W. Mulder,
LogicaCMG Netherlands, University of Amsterdam, wico.mulder@logicacmg.com
G. R. Meijer,
University of Amsterdam, LogicaCMG NETHERLANDS, geleyn@science.uva.nl

Information retrieval is one of the key processes in the management of collaborative networks (CNs). For large and complex networks manual processes need to be supported by automated retrieval systems.
We study the characteristics of information retrieval systems and discuss their applicability in distributed, dynamical, heterogeneous environments, such as CNs. We developed a model of a distributed information retrieval system, and implemented a prototype of distributed information services in the domain of collaborative organizations.

1. INTRODUCTION

A collaborative network (CN) is a network consisting of autonomous, geographically distributed, heterogeneous entities (e.g. organizations and people) that collaborate to better achieve common or compatible goals [1].

Typical examples of CNs are Virtual Enterprises (VEs), Virtual Organizations (VOs), Virtual Labs (VLs) and Professional Virtual Communities (PVCs).

While today the concepts of CNs are well known [8], aspects around their management are still subject to research. Karvonen et. all [5] focus on VOs and define VO-management as the organization, allocation and co-ordination of resources and their activities as well as their inter-organizational dependencies to achieve the objectives of the VO within the required time, cost and quality frame. We can broaden this definition applying it to CNs. CN management applies knowledge, skills and tools in order to achieve the CN goals.

One of the key elements of CN management is the acquisition of information about the status and operation of the network and its entities. In case the number of entities is large, the selection and retrieval of information needs to be supported by an information system. Such a system might relieve a CN-manager from the unnecessary complexity of specifying, searching and obtaining the information that is relevant for getting overviews and taking decisions.

We emphasize that many companies (amongst others SAP, IBM, HP, Microsoft, Tibco, Cisco and Oracle) have developed monitoring and control tools that support organizational management. Their solutions have evolved from monolithic systems towards centralized, homogenous network systems. However, most of these solutions are focused on processes and procedures within single organizational boundaries. Applying them in the area of CNs is not a trivial task due to the concepts and characteristics of a CN. A significant, generic characteristic of a CN is

Please use the following format when citing this chapter:

Mulder, W., Meijer, G. R., 2006, in IFIP International Federation for Information Processing, Volume 224, Network-Centric Collaboration and Supporting Fireworks, eds. Camarinha-Matos, L., Afsarmanesh, H., Ollus, M., (Boston: Springer), pp. 491–498.

that its entities are self-contained and work together only for a particular amount of time. Other characteristics are geographical spread and local influences.

As an example we take a collaborative network of organizations (CNO), which is a heterogeneous, distributed network of organizations in which each organization (member) acts within its own local environment to deliver a product or service to the network. Together they achieve a common goal, often in the form of a service to the outside world. The members can physically be located around the globe, introducing globalization management issues [4]. The issues go further than locality problems like date-time, units of measures or language; Culture [10] has significant influences on their operation and contributions to the CNO. The location and social habits of the country where a member is situated, combined with the fact that each member has to deal with particular local rules, laws and legislations has significant influences on its operation in the network. Furthermore, each member has its own internal procedures and mechanisms in order to produce its results or fulfill its services. This has impact on the frequency, amount and kind of information that a member is able to provide. Information that touches the member's core-business cannot or will not always be shared. The latter has to do with strategic goals and aspects of thrust.

Another characteristic of a CNO is called 'local control'. A CNO operates in a so-called shared, collaborative environment. Such an environment is characterized by shared processes which are controlled by multiple local domains. For a CNO this means that each participating member has the control of its own part of the environment, while it shares its services with other members in collaborative processes. The aspects of local control and local influences are typical for CNs in general: It holds for networks of organizations where business services are shared, as well as for networks of technical components such as large, shared computer infrastructures (collaborative infrastructures, grids).

The research in our group focuses on information retrieval in dynamic collaborative environments. We study the mechanisms of data acquisition and architectures for information gathering in such environments. We use the concept of Information Services, defined as entities that operate in large, distributed networks that provide information about that network and its components. As part of ongoing research in our group we study the use of information services to support the maintenance of grid environments [3].

Information services can also be applied to crisis management in the field of logistics and transport[6]. This holds preventive measurements such as early warning systems in order avoid accidents, as well as support for handling emergency situations when a traffic accident has occurred. In [7] we describe the concepts of adaptive information services that help mobile ICT teams, called Squads, in doing their work. It is here where we are working in the field of hybrid networks, studying man-machine interfaces and collaborative multi-agent learning.

In this paper we focus on the information retrieval in CNOs. We work out a model of a distributed information retrieval mechanism and discuss a prototype that supports the information retrieval in CNOs by means of Distributed Information Services.

2. DISTRIBUTED INFORMATION SERVICES

Distributed Information Services (DIS), are piece of software in a network environment that provide information about the state or usage of one or more components of that network environment.

This section gives an overview of the properties that characterize a DIS. We look in particular at those properties that are interesting with respect to the environments of CNOs

Local scope and control
A DIS is designed to operate in a particular part of the network, known as the local domain. In case of a CNO, a local domain is considered to be an environment that belongs to a particular member-organization. A DIS retrieves information from such a particular member environment.

Located inside that domain, a DIS has access to local systems and can be configured and controlled locally by system operators belonging to the member organization.

A particular member domain may use its own language, or specific technical interfaces to particular subsystems or components. Having access, a DIS fetches data from a particular hardware or software component. A DIS is designed to generalizations and translations between the local domain and the rest of the network.

Local scope and control also enables a DIS to react on events that are not allowed to be visible outside the borders of a particular organization. An example of this is the measurement of intermediate production progress details; although a DIS can be configured to inform a local manager about these figures, it may shield the details towards the CNO-manager.

Autonomous behavior
A DIS is an active component that fulfills measurement and provisioning tasks autonomously by means of rules. An example of such a rule is to measure each hour production details, and compare this with previous values and report when necessary. Rules may also define actions in case a certain pattern in the measured data is found. This enables local problem solving by reacting on events that are only visible inside the borders of a particular local environment. The definition and configuration of the rules can be given via one of its communication interfaces.

Communication interfaces
The communicative properties of a DIS can be divided into three groups:
-    Communication with a controller outside the local environment
-    Communication with its local environment
-    Communication with other DISes.

The first kind refers to configuration and control by a human or a system that consumes the provided information. This can be an individual who configures the rules about what and how often a DIS should measure. Such an individual might be a CNO manager who is interested in information about the operational status of the

CNO, or a system operator (squad team) who is interested in the operational status of the supporting ICT infrastructure.

The second kind of communication allows the local environment to interact with the DIS and vice versa. A DIS can respond to events broadcasted by components inside a local domain. A DIS can retrieve properties of the environment enabling operation in heterogeneous, dynamic networks.

The third kind of communication is the communication with other DISes. The possibility to exchange information between multiple DISses enables collaborative information provisioning and notifications of events that happen in other domains. Another reason for inter-DIS communication is the ability to react immediately to local events, without the involvement of central, hierarchical (broker) components. Communication between DISes involves the exchange of information over multiple local domains, security aspects have to be taken into account. Therefore, authentication rules describing what is allowed to communicate must be defined and shared between the various DISes.

For all three kinds of communication, protocols need to be defined. These protocols are not specified by the model, because they depend on the implementation, goals and purposes of the application area.

Adaptive behavior

Combining the two previous characteristics, i.e. having autonomous behavior and communication interfaces, a DIS is able to learn and show adaptive behavior. It may use its communication facilities in combination with its internal state and rules, to change its way of measuring data.

In general, adapting does mean 'changing behavior'. In case behavior is based on a set of rules, defined by means of parameters and metrics, changes can be provoked by altering a rule or one of its parameters. In case adaptation leads to improvement of results, we call it 'learning'. The ability to learn strengthens the autonomous capabilities; a DIS may e.g. take the initiative measure pro-actively, without intervention of its controller.

Collaborative goals

Communication between each other enables DISes to compete or collaborate with each other in order to provide better information. Combined with the aspect of adaptation, a DIS is designed to adopt mechanisms of collaborative learning.

Summarizing, our model of a DIS is has a set of properties that enable it to operate in dynamic, heterogeneous environments. These characteristics are reflected by a set of interacting DIS-components, shown in Figure 1.

The model allows an extensible and flexible configuration of these architectural parts. Still, the basic functionality is to provide information (output) based on configurations given by the controller (input) and autonomous data fetching.

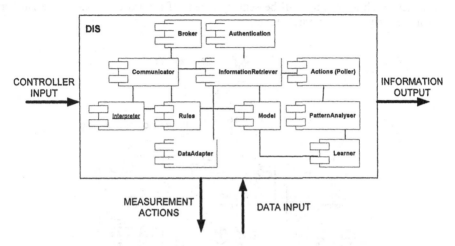

Figure 1 - architectural design of a Distributed Information Service

3. RESULTS

We apply our model in domain of CNOs. As part of our work in the Ecolead project[1] we work on a set of generic e-services supporting the management of collaborative organizations.

Here, management information is characterized by indicators like 'delivery due date', 'product quality' and other quantitative measurements. Also information about the collaboration between the partners and the planned activities, are indicators that are used to measure the performance of the network. In general, using the concept of Service Level Agreements, an indicator can represent any type of information that has to be fetched from each member location.

The prototype is named DI³ (pronounced dee-triple-eye) which stands for Distributed Indicator Information Integrator. The current version supports a basic information retrieval mechanism, and basic communication facilities.

Figure 2 shows the experimental setup of the prototype. DI³ consists of a set of collaborating components. At the location of each member-organization, an 'Information Retriever'-component measures the value of a pre-configured information indicator at a certain, pre-defined frequency.

At each heartbeat, a fetching request is send to an intermediate component, called a DataAdapter. This component fetches by means of a query on a local member system or, in case a member does not have a system that can be queried, it

[1] www.ecolead.org

may fetch the value by means of an email or browser screen, requesting a human individual to enter the value manually.

The Information Retriever stores the value returned by the DataAdapter in its local memory, and verifies whether it should inform its controller, i.e. the CN-manager. Such a briefing will be sent by means of a third component, the Broker having merely an intermediate function.

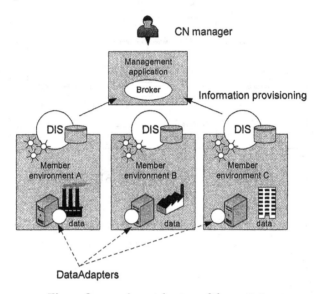

Figure 2, experimental setup of the prototype

In the current version (Figure 2) we deal with three different kinds of information:

- Performance information by means of progress indicators.
  An example is the measurement of the amount of the work that is done. In case the measured value is below a certain level, the Information Retriever launches an event message.
- Contract management information, such as 'due date' and 'expected production figures'. An event is launched in case it is suddenly changed.
- Collaboration information. For example a satisfaction indicator. This is measured by means of a list with satisfaction-figures filled in weekly by the members indicating the level of collaboration with other partners. Events may be launched in case of negative marks.

Currently, we are testing the feasibility of retrieving this kind of information. Furthermore, we use the prototype to work on the aspects of collaborative information provisioning, by studying implementation of ad-hoc communication algorithms in combination with learning algorithms.

The implementation of the prototype is based on Web-Services, and developed in Java. The technology of Web-services is common for implementations on a Service Oriented Architecture. It also uses the advantages of platform independency and message based communication.

5. DISCUSSION AND FUTURE WORK

The characteristics mentioned in section 2 show similarities with aspects of (at least) three other interesting fields of research. Our goal is to adopt results algorithms and technology achieved in these fields. Figure 3 shows the overlap of three fields of research. The central area reflects the domain of DIS.

A DIS has characteristics of Peer-2-Peer (P2P) systems [9]. The properties of P2P networks enable a high scalability and the ability to deal with heterogeneous systems. Information sharing is one of the main design goals of P2P systems. P2P communication mechanisms allow individual nodes to share data and work in a collaborative way.

Autonomous behavior is widely used in the field of Agent Technology. Communication and autonomous adaptive are used the area of Multi Agent Systems (MAS). An overview of learning in multi agent systems is given by Weiss [11].

A third field that has a significant influence on our design and model of DIS is Machine Learning. This field studies learning algorithms and mechanisms to model complex environments.

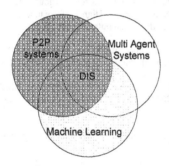

Figure 3, relationships with three overlapping fields of research

The implementation of the prototype is based on a modular approach; It is extensible and allows for replacements of individual parts our model.

We want to use the prototype also in other fields, such as emergency rescue teams and computer network maintenance. In general, distributed information services might be applicable in any kind of heterogeneous distributed networked environments, were situations are characterized by unstructured, unpredictable ways of information sharing.

Our prototype is used to study an adaptive frequency mechanism. We use the degree of deviation from expected values to decide about the need of increased frequency, in order to foster closer monitoring when needed. It is planned to add and study more adaptation capabilities to the information services. We plan to work on collaborative learning algorithms in order to improve the information provisioning in large, complex, dynamic networks. We want to include aspects of Epidemic information dissemination [2] and combine this with machine learning and theories of reinforcement learning.

6. CONCLUSION

In this paper we described our research on information retrieval mechanisms in collaborative networks. As being one of the applied areas, we discussed the aspects collaborative networks of organizations (CNOs) and the necessary management support. We described a model of a distributed information retrieval mechanism and worked out the characteristics of distributed information services. We also described a prototype that is being developed in the domain of CNOs.

7. REFERENCES

1. Camarinha-Matos, L.M., Afsarmanesh, H, Collaborative networks: A new scientific discipline, J. Intelligent Manufacturing, vol. 16, N° 4-5, pp439-452, ISSN: 0956-5515 , 2005.2.

2. Eugster P., Guerraoui R, Kermarrec A-M., and Massoulie L., Epidemic Information Dissemination in Distributed Systems, IEEE Computer, 37, 60--67, 2004.

3. Fitzgerald, S. 2001. Grid Information Services for Distributed Resource Sharing. In Proceedings of the 10th IEEE international Symposium on High Performance Distributed Computing (Hpdc-10'01) (August 07 - 09, 2001). HPDC. IEEE Computer Society, Washington, DC, 181.

4. Freeman, Craig. 1998. "The Influence of Culture on Corporate Structure." Macquarie University, School of Economics and Financial Studies, New South Wales, Australia.

5. Karvonen, I.; Salkari, I.; Ollus, M.; Characterizing Virtual Organization and Their Management. In: PRO-VE'05. (Sep. 26-28. 2005: Valencia, Spain). Proceedings. Ed. Springer, ISBN 0-387-28259-9, p. 193-204.

6. Konijn, M., Crises Management, using eCall principles in the Netherlands, Research proposal ICIS, internal report.

7. Mulder W., Meijer G.R., SQUADS: Software Development and Maintenance on the Grid by means of Mobile Virtual Organizations using Adaptive Information Services, Virtual Enterprise and Collaborative Networks, Proceedings PROVE04, WCC 2004, ISBN 1-4020-8138-3, p. 379-386

8. Proceedings PROVE04, WCC 2004, ISBN 1-4020-8138-3, Proceedings PROVE05, Springer, ISBN 0-387-28259-9

9. Ripeanu, M., A. Iamnitchi, and I. Foster. Mapping the Gnutella network: 'Properties of Large-Scale Peer-to-Peer Systems and Implications for System Design' IEEE Internet Computing, 6(1):50--57, Aug. 2002

10. Schein, E.H., Organizational Culture and Leadership, 3rd ed., Jossey-Bass,2004, ISBN 1-55542-487-2

11. Sen and Weiss G. (1999). Learning in Multiagent Systems. In Gerhard Weiss (ed.) Multiagent systems, A modern approach to Distributed Arti cial Intelligence, 259-298, Cambridge MA: MIT Press.

H. Mathieu, F. Biennier[1]

(1) INSA de Lyon - Laboratoire PRISMa / IF502 - F69621 Villeurbanne Cedex, FRANCE
{Herve.Mathieu, Frederique.Biennier}@insa-lyon.fr

Economical constraints impose to enterprises to regroup themselves into virtual enterprises to be more reactive. This association will create interdependencies between virtual enterprise processes, which can be a problem in case of a process failure, because such an issue can jeopardize the whole activity of the virtual enterprise. Thus, it seems relevant to set « survival » mechanisms enabling to improve processes reliability. First, we propose a method to determine how the information system resources supporting the processes are used. Then, we define the architecture of a system in charge of managing process survival. We designed the architecture so that it is adapted to a large scale, heterogeneous and dynamic context, which characterizes virtual enterprises. We validate our approach with a prototype giving its first results.

1. INTRODUCTION

In the actual economical context, which is more and more complex and changing, it is necessary to form virtual enterprises (VE) to cope quickly and efficiently to the market constraints. Despite of the intrinsic interest of collaboration, setting collaborative business is not obvious (Bremer et al. 1999; Wildeman et al. 1996). A real collaboration is more than just exposing manufacturing processes and services to an outside partner. It must integrate also cross-enterprise collaboration so that partners integrate their resources for mutual gain. However, the cooperation between the different VE entities is also the source of important problems. It is important to take into account that federating the different Information Systems (IS) of the entities composing the VE causes interoperability issues between the IS components, and can deeply impact on the quality of offered services.

IS Infrastructures availability will completely determine the quality of offered services. Thus, infrastructures availability is fundamental because one IS component dysfunction can jeopardize the whole VE's activity, which is not acceptable. To reach a good quality of the global IS, it is first necessary for the infrastructure to be

Please use the following format when citing this chapter:

Mathieu, H., Binnier, F., 2006, in IFIP International Federation for Information Processing, Volume 224, Network-Centric Collaboration and Supporting Fireworks, eds. Camarinha-Matos, L., Afsarmanesh, H., Ollus, M., (Boston: Springer), pp. 499–506.

« available » to support VE's business processes, even if some IS resources are corrupted or not operational. Therefore, it is important to set redundancy mechanisms inside the IS. Thus, in case of resource corruption, tasks performed on the corrupted resource can migrate to a « safe » resource, so that it becomes possible not to interrupt the processes, even in case of failure. Because of the growing IS complexity, of their instability and constant evolution, it is not possible to secure completely an IS to cope with both internal and external threats. Considering this problem, risk management and "survival" capabilities are interesting, because they enable to define and to set mechanisms to assure service continuity, even in case of attack or failure of some IS resources. The problem of these methods is that they are not implemented for now in unstable connectivity, great scale, and heterogeneous environments, which are properties characterizing modern IS. We propose in this paper a method to establish the sequence of tasks implied in business process execution, which enables to establish a chart of the IS resources use. Then, we describe the architecture of a survival system based on the mobile agent paradigm. We present our first results on a virtual enterprise prototype, whose entities share a common research and development process.

2. CONTEXT

In a virtual organization, some entities a priori independent form an association to perform a common project. This association impacts deeply on the IS of each entities because the different IS have to merge, at least partly, to support global collaborative processes. This « globalization » imposes constraints in terms of management of the services quality, in terms of interoperability, and in terms of processes safety. In this paper, we focuse mainly on this last point. During the collaboration, one of the collaborating entities can experience some problems and dysfunctions. Thus, its information system can be the target of attacks, or some services can fall due to technical issues. However, the virtual enterprise still must must support its activities, even if one of the entities does not work properly. This kind of problem is important in a conventional enterprise, but it is much more critical in enterprise networks, because a problem affecting one entity can block the activity of the whole organization. In such a context, it is important to settle mechanisms improving the reliability of the shared processes during their exploitation. This is a crucial issue to solve to improve the reliability of cooperating networks.

The interaction between business processes, tasks and resources can be represented as a model organizing sequentially the tasks being performed by processes as shown on figure 1. These tasks use some resources of the distributed IS. The resources implied by a task performance change in function of the task being performed.

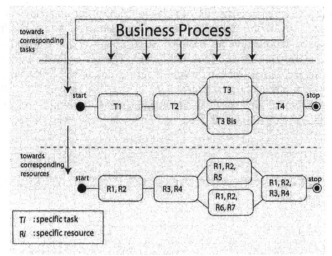

Figure 1 – Business Processes use different resources of the distributed IS system to execute themselves

To improve Business Processes reliability, we can try to settle rescue resources that are able to support services that are no more supported by a deficient resource. This simple idea arise numerous concerns. It is first necessary to be reactive to problems concerning the availability of resources used by the executing Business Process. This point is not obvious is a centralised architecture, but it can become very complex in a highly distributed architecture, such as Information Systems of virtual enterprises. Thus, this kind of architecture can be of large scale, of unstable connectivity, and heterogeneous.

Some workflow and business process management systems based on mobile agents have been proposed (Suh et al., 2001; Budimac et al., 1999, Loke and Zaslavsky, 2001). These models enable to negotiate tasks constraints (precedence, execution conditions…) thanks to mobile agents. This approach is very encouraging in a highly distributed environment. In fact, we can consider the distributed IS as a set of interconnected nodes which will evolve according to the alliances or separations between entities of the VE. In such a case, trying to give survival capabilities to the distributed IS can be considered as giving survival capabilities to a set of interconnected nodes, this set being dynamic, heterogeneous, and presenting unstable connectivity characteristics. In this context, which is highly distributed, it seems convenient to adopt a survival system based on an intrinsic distributed paradigm. Mobile agents enable to work around the limits imposed by centralized environments in terms of infrastructure management (Tomarchio and Puliafito, 2000). The use of mobile agents proved its efficiency to solve key problems bound to distributed infrastructure such as packet routing in dynamic network infrastructures (Kramer et al., 2000; Caro and Dorigo, 1998), or intrusion detection (Fenet, Serge, 2001). Even if the mobile agent use seems adapted to the context, it is necessary to structure the way they are exploited. As underlined in (Schulz et al., 2004), to make the best of the mobile agent paradigm, it is necessary to make them evolve in a well-defined frame. In our context, the specific survival services act independently from each other. Thus, it seems relevant for us to use several kinds of mobile agents, each one dedicated to the management of one of these specific services. These mobile agents perform all the data collection and modification related to the survival service they are bound. The servers are interconnected and watch themselves. In case of failure of one server, any other server can be elected to replace the corrupted server. Our prototype use the "aglet" platform (SourceForge, 2006) to implement the survivability management system: it is an operational platform, fairly extensive and free, which suits very well to our prototyping constraints.

3. ARCHITECTURE OF THE SURVIVAL MANAGEMENT SYSTEM

3.1 Architecture

We propose here an approach based on the mobile agent paradigm, to settle survival mechanisms inside the collaborative IS, so that it becomes possible to improve process reliability, even if some IS resources get corrupted. The functionalities of our « survivability » management architecture are implemented by the following mobile agents:

- inventory and planning agents: they are in charge of roaming the network to discover the equipments (nodes), their configuration, services and applications they are hosting. Besides, they determine the nodes which can potentially host applications and services located on other resources, to provide redundancy in case of failure.
- pre-migration agents: these agents are in charge of settle mechanisms to make easier the application or service migration working on a corrupted resource.
- detection agents: they are in charge of roaming the network to control that strategic configuration files have not been modified unexpectedly and to control that the nodes are operating properly, by performing elementary verifications, at the system level as well as at the application level. If a problem is detected, the central server is warned and will launch immediately migration agents enabling the applications and services executing on the corrupted node to migrate toward a safe node.
- migration agents: they are in charge of performing the migration of data and applications from a corrupted node to a safe node.

We developed a prototype implementing this architecture on a small virtual enterprise. To give applications the ability to migrate from one IS node to another is important, but it is also important to know the application transfer duration, to limit the time of service interruption. Knowing this transfer duration will impact significantly the IS services implantation. IS architects will try to implant those services to limit this time of service interruption. To determine this transfer duration, we simulated the corruption of an IS resource, triggering applications and services migration. The obtained results are interesting and show the potential of mobile agents to solve « survivability » problems related to IS management.

3.2 Impact of application transfer times on the IS implantation

We modelled the following virtual enterprise (figure 2). It is composed of 3 interconnected entities, (one in the USA, and 2 in France) which are collaborating on a common research and development project. The goal of this project is to develop an open source enterprise service bus (ObjectWeb, 2006), and some connectors specific to open source or proprietary ERP. This bus should enable clusters of enterprise to place common orders for buying, selling, or transporting goods. One of the strategic resource of the research and development project is the database containing all the data related to the development of applications (source code, documentation, compilation procedures). The difficulty is that this development project is an open source one, meaning that there are constantly actors coming and going out of the project. The environment is naturally dynamic and unstable. One key problem in such a context is to assure the conception project survival by assuring the survival of the resources supporting this process.

An important problem is to decide where to implant the DBMS (on which site, and on which node of that site), knowing that in case of problem appearing on this resource, or on the site hosting the resource, data must migrate easily towards a resource capable of relaying the defective resource, this rescue resource being located ideally on an other site. We implemented for this problem inventory agents and pre-migration mobile agents. Inventory agents are launched on each site by the « process survival server », and they detect the nodes which are able to host the database server, in terms of physical capacity (memory, CPU, disk space, bandwidth...). On each of those sites, a node is detected. The three potential candidates to host the DBMS are alpha, beta and gamma. They are said to be eligible to host the DBMS server. The next question is to locate where to implement the DBMS server. For this, pre-migration agents will install a « fake » database containing around 3Go of data on the eligible nodes. The corruption of the node hosting the DBMS is then simulated. The database (configuration + data) will migrate towards the closer eligible node. If the migration time is short enough, this means that in case of attack or failure the database is able to migrate fast enough, then the tested node is retained to host the database permanently.

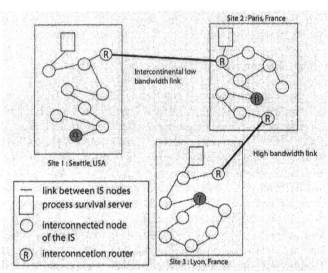

Figure 2 – Virtual enterprise organization for prototype implantation

In a first place alpha is chosen to host the database, and a problem is simulated on alpha. The problem simulation on alpha involves data migration towards beta, which is the closest eligible node. Because of the low throughput of the link binding the US site to the Paris site, the database migration lasts around 9000 seconds (2 hours and 30 minutes, figure 3). This important migration duration is not acceptable, because during this time, the database can be seriously damaged or completely destroyed.

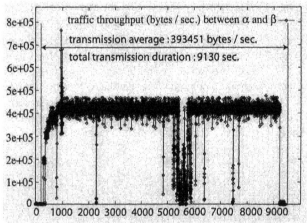

Figure 3 – Traffic generated by the database migration from the alpha node to the beta node

Consequently, the alpha node is not chosen to host permanently the database server. The same scenario is followed for the beta node. A problem simulation performed by the simulation agents causes the database migration towards the gamma node. The bandwidth being more important between Paris and Lyon than in Seattle and Paris, the duration of the database migration is 8 minutes and 30 seconds (figure 4), which is much more acceptable. Consequently, the beta node is retained to host the main database.

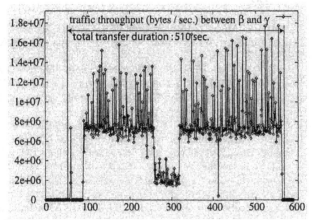

Figure 4 – Traffic generated by the database migration from the beta node to the gamma node

Thus, these first results show that it is possible to use mobile agents to implement survival policies to make stronger the shared processes in a virtual organization.

4. CONCLUSION

We showed in this paper how to improve to reliability of collaborative processes during their exploitation. We defined for this a method to sequence tasks performed by collaborative processes, and also indirectly the resources that are used by these tasks. A mobile-agent based architecture for improving process survival is then described. We prototyped this architecture and we tested it on a simple collaborative process of information sharing to validate our approach. An interesting project about this platform would be to generate automatically the mobile agents depending on the needs and on the context, to come closer to a reactive and adaptive management of the Information System. In this paper we try to improve process survivability but only during their exploitation phase. An interesting perspective would be to try to anticipate the needs of survivability. For that purpose, it would be interesting to integrate risk management concerns in the mobile agent generation process. The risks are different during the steps of execution of the BP, and it would be appropriate to generate specific agents (tagging, monitoring...) according to the risks. This would enable to refine the agent generation and to better define the survival management tasks that have to be done. We could start from the risk management methods existing for the Information System such as EBIOS (DCSSI, 2004) or OCTAVE (Reedy, 2003). We could use these methods from a process point of view, which could enable us to identify the critical phases of a process. These critical phases would be particularly watched by the survival management system.

5. REFERENCES

1. Bremer CF, Mundim APF, Michilini FVS, Siqueira JEM, Ortega LM. A Brazilian case of VE coordination. Infrastructures for Virtual Enterprises, Boston, Kluwer Academic Publishers 1999; pp. 377-386.
2. Budimac Z, Ivanovic M and Popovic A, Workflow management systems using mobile agents, In : Advances in Databases and Information Systems : Third East European Conference, ADBIS'99, 13-16 sept. 1999, Maribor, Slovenia, Springer, 1999, pp. 168–178.
3. Caro GD and Dorigo M, AntNet: Distributed Stimergetic Control for Communications Network, Journal of Artificial Intelligence Research, 1998;9:317-365.
4. DCSSI, Expression des Besoins et Identification des Objectifs de Sécurité: EBIOS, Direction centrale de la sécurité des systèmes d'information (french governmental organization), Technical Report, 2004, (http://www.ssi.gouv.fr/fr/confiance/ebios.html)
5. Fenet Serge, Toward a paradigm for programming distributed applications based on social insects behavior: application to network security, PhD Thesis (Claude Bernard University, Lyon), 2001.
6. Kramer KJ, Minar N, Maes P, Mobile Software Agents for Dynamic Routing, Mobile computing and Communications Review, 3(2):12-16, 2000.
7. Loke SW and Zaslavsky A, Towards distributed workflow enactment with itineraries and mobile agent management, Lecture Notes in Computer Science : E-Commerce Agents, 2001, vol. 2033.
8. ObjectWeb, Open Source Middleware, (http://www.objectweb.org), 2006
10. Reedy R., Healthcare Information Risks Assessment : Empowering Executives to Manage Information Risk, Master Thesis, School of Business Administration, Kennedy-Western University, 2003, 192p.
11. Tomarchio O and Puliafito A, Using mobile agents to implement flexible network management strategies, Computer Communications, 23(8):708-719, 2000.
12. Schulz S, Schulz M, Tanner A., Frame of Interest Approach on Quality of Prediction for Agent-based Network Monitoring, Proceedings of the International Conference on Architecture of Computing Systems 2004 (ARCS'04), Augsburg, Germany: Springer; p. 246-259, 2004.
13. SourceForge, Aglets framework, (http://aglets.sourceforge.net/), 2006
14. Suh Y, Namgoong H, Yoo J and Lee D, Design of a mobile agent-based workflow management system, Mobile Agents for Telecommunication Applications : Third International Workshop, MATA'01, 14-16 August, 2001, Montreal, Canada, Springer, 2001.
15. Wildeman L. and Stoffelen R. Alliances and networks of the next generation. KPMG Alliances Networks & Virtual Organisations. K. report. Amsterdam, The Netherlands, 1996.

Vanderhaeghen, Dominik; Loos, Peter

Institute for Information Systems (IWi) at the
German Research Center for Artificial Intelligence (DFKI)
Stuhlsatzenhausweg 3, Build. D3 2
D-66123 Saarbrücken
GERMANY
{dominik.vanderhaeghen|peter.loos}@iwi.dfki.de

Virtual enterprise network planning and design lead to complex challenges. From a conceptual point of view, business processes have proven to be the ideal design items in conjunction with the use of graphical methods and tools. Especially for network design and implementation, information modelling serves as the fundamental starting point. In the article, the authors depict a modelling approach dedicated to a global and a local description of business processes and a distributed model management platform. The latter supports the collaborative creation and application of models in network environments.

1. INTRODUCTION

Virtual enterprise (VE) network planning and design lead to complex challenges. Enterprise networks consist of autonomous economic entities, usually with a common target definition (Leimeister, Weigle, & Krcmar, 2004). Additionally, due to numerous points of contact VEs are characterized by common resources and interfaces (Specht & Kahmann, 2000). In a VE, at least two different organizations collaborate in order to create a common added-value. To do so efficiently, an integration and collaboration of network participants becomes necessary.

From a conceptual point of view, business processes have proven to be ideal design items in conjunction with the use of graphical methods and tools (Hammer & Champy, 1993). However, with information gaps across the borders of an enterprise business process coordination turns out to be a highly complex task in the network.[1] Thus, adequate instruments have to be designed and supported by Information and Communication Technology (ICT). For the planning and design of a VE network, information modelling serves as the fundamental starting point. A model depicts attributes and parameters necessary for requirement definitions. They comprise knowledge about business logic, data interfaces, or organizational responsibilities within a network. The structured design and provision of information for business and IT specialists is essential for an efficient setting-up of a network. As traditional

---

[1] Cf. requirements e.g. described in (Zang, Hofer, & Adam, 2004).

Please use the following format when citing this chapter:

Vanderhaeghen, D., Loos, P., 2006, in IFIP International Federation for Information Processing, Volume 224, Network-Centric Collaboration and Supporting Fireworks, eds. Camarinha-Matos, L., Afsarmanesh, H., Ollus, M., (Boston: Springer), pp. 507–514.

Business Process Management (BPM) approaches and tools do not provide support sufficiently, existing approaches and tools have to be extended.

The article depicts an approach towards general information modelling and model management in networks. The authors distinguish two modelling levels due to abstraction and selection of process information and the need for information security in cross-organizational collaborations. To support modelling tasks efficiently, an integrative platform for modelling and model management in distributed environments is described. Due to requirement descriptions have already been depicted in e.g. (Adam et al., 2005a) and (Theling et al., 2005) this article focuses on the description of solutions disregarding general requirements already described in former work. The article ends with a conclusion and an outlook on future research in the cross-organizational modelling and model management area.

2. BUSINESS PROCESS MODELLING IN NETWORKS

The systematic planning and design of business processes in VE networks demands a set of integrated methods and tools from the business concept level up to the implementation into ICT-systems. Existing BPM methods and phase models have to be used as a foundation and have to be adapted to the specifications of VE networks. Especially because of its completeness of vision and its proven practicability, both in the scientific and the economic context, the "ARIS House" (Scheer, 1994) is accepted as a generic framework for BPM. Hence, it serves as a basis for further considerations. The ARIS House describes a business process, assigning equal importance to the questions of organisation, functionality and the required documentation. First, it isolates these views for separate treatment in order to reduce the complexity of the description field, but then all the relationships are restored using a control view introduced for this purpose. Within the different ARIS views, information modelling serves as the main instrument.

To meet the design and implementation requirements of networks, instruments to describe as-is states and to design to-be states are considered in the dimensions of the ARIS House. Business analysts and IT specialists have to consider product and service descriptions, business process models and organisational structures for network planning, design and implementation. The transition between as-is and to-be in collaborative product development or process engineering is achieved by a successive synchronisation of organizations. Planning, design and implementation of a network require increased communication efforts between business partners involved. Thus, information is exchanged in the form of models which depict e.g. partner input/output descriptions, interface requirements, or process information.

Due to the characteristics of networks, knowledge is a critical resource. It is only shared with partners under given circumstances. Thus, based on (Adam, Chikova, Hofer, Zang, & Vanderhaeghen, 2005a), knowledge is classified

- to be managed on a **global level** and such
- to be managed on a **local level**.

Both description levels form a knowledge classification which is represented in the ARIS House by a vertical axis (global knowledge) and a horizontal axis (local knowledge) (see Figure 1).

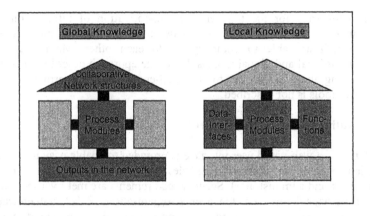

Figure 1 – Global and local knowledge in networks

Global knowledge comprises partner-spanning relevance on the one hand as e.g. a change of network structure due to partners leaving a network. This implies that products or services may be no longer available within the network. Thus, such information is *globally* important. Global models contain general conditions for e.g. application of ICT in a network. On the other hand, local knowledge as detailed processes or process interfaces is kept within the borders of an enterprise or bilaterally exchanged with direct business partners only. Consequently, models are required on a global and a local description and application level. While local information models are not made public to all business partners, global models intend a coordination of all partners.

To support local and global modelling in networks efficiently, the blueprint of a distributed model management platform is described in the following.

3. DISTRIBUTED MODEL MANAGEMENT PLATFORM

Networking enterprises implicates a close connection between discrete economic entities. However, the general design and implementation of internal business processes and ICT are usually managed without external exertion of influence. But at the same time internal organizational knowledge is shared selectively within enterprise networks in the form of models (Adam, Chikova, Hofer, Zang, & Vanderhaeghen, 2005a). The intended coordination of business partners requires information processes between decision makers and actors in order to harmonize network actions. Thus, we propose an approach towards a distributed model management platform. To plan, to design and to implement networked business processes, modelling is conducted in a **distributed** manner between two or more organizations. Integration of models becomes a critical task due to heterogeneous modelling frameworks and modelling tools being in use in a network (Theling, Zwicker, Loos, & Vanderhaeghen, 2005).

The authors describe a platform which is installed and applied in a VE network by every single participant organization. The platform mainly consists of a web-based front end, a model and model meta-data repository, interfaces to existing BPM tools and converters for the transfer and transformation of information models towards different syntactical representations. It is applied by multiple system instances which are able to communicate to each other. Main target is the management of local and global models due to the approach described in section 2. In the following, the authors revert to main challenges of the platform only. External integration of tools is not described.

3.1 User Authorization and User Interface

In the platform, a web-based user interface is provided to enable easy user access to information based on four different user roles (view user, modelling user, enhanced modelling user and administrator). Security requirements are met by a session-based module to manage login data. On a cross-organisational level, authentication is provided to external users by giving access on models which are stored in a single platform instance (c.f. also section 3.2). Single Sign-On (SSO) facilitates the work with different integrated modelling tools. The user interface provides a distinct navigation structure with multiple user information sets. Easy and quick access to basic functions is ensured by two navigation bars and links depending on the user role. Figure 2 illustrates the user interface with its basic functions (white boxes) and information sets (grey boxes).

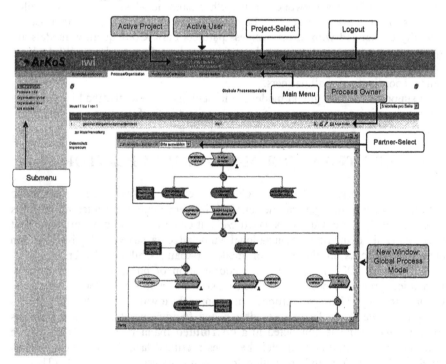

Figure 2 – Model Management User Interface

3.2 Information Access across multiple Platform Instances

Network participants are allocated in distributed environments. The coordination of collaboration partners requires communication efforts. In our approach, this communication is realized with a distributed information exchange of models. However, in a network the exchange of information requires measures building trust between business partners (Ratnasingam, 2003).

On a communication layer, necessary access authorization for model exchange can be designed on a global level (ensuring communication between all partners) and a local level (Adam et al., 2005b). On a local level, communication is negotiated bilaterally (e.g. for information exchange between exact two partners). Based on these two levels of spatial distribution, access authorities are realized in two steps.

Firstly, unique access information is given to all partners in a network (global partner user name and global partner password). Access information is associated to one running project. The project is named unique by every partner. Conciliated access information is achieved in combination with a first network exchange of global models. Information models depicting the overall organizational network structure are transmitted to all partners for network management purposes. Thereby, partners get information in two different dimensions: On the one hand global information for network planning and design is exchanged with organisational models. These models also contain knowledge about project partners and mutual business process dependencies. Partner addresses (Unified Resource Locators (URL) of corresponding platform instances) are added as attributes to global organisational models. On the other hand, the global access data is inserted to the global model. On a protocol layer information access is encrypted via Internet by Secure Hyper Text Transfer Protocol (HTTPS).

Thereby, every partner gets all necessary information for a bilateral exchange of data between direct business partners. With

- the knowledge which *partner combinations* require bilateral communication in the network,
- single *partner addresses* (URL) known to the network,
- global and unique *access information known to the network* and
- secure *communication channels* with encryption mechanisms

the first stage of cross-organisational access framework is achieved. It enables data exchange in distributed environments.

With global knowledge about business partners, detailed information can be transferred in a second step. Partners once identify the need for communication within a network project by organisational dependency descriptions (cf. step 1). Consequently, business processes of business partners have cross-organisational interfaces to be aligned. Synchronisation and communication are facilitated by models and their bilateral exchange. Models depict necessary information on a partner's public processes and interface descriptions. They offer a possibility to recognize mutual dependencies and to react by process reengineering or customization of application systems. To facilitate the exchange of detailed models on a local (bilateral) level, every partner requests individual access information (partner's local user name and password) to its direct business partner. Hereby, the unique project identification number and globally known username and password are transmitted in association to the request. Partners check if a request is valid (correct partner request URL, correct project ID, correct global access information) and accept or deny a request. If accepted, a partner creates access information for the business partner request. If it is not valid, the request is ignored. Successful access is valid for a whole project duration and must not exceed a given time limit. With the created local user name and password, business partners get access to the information another partner has directly made public to him. This information is managed in platform instances in the form of models as public business process models, public ICT interface descriptions or product and service trees.

A cross-organisational and distributed communication between business partners is accomplished.

3.3 Repository Storage and Distributed Information Exchange

In a network, models might occur in different syntactical representations. This is related to the use of heterogeneous modelling languages and supporting tools. Control instances might be missing as some forms of collaboration networks only imply equal participants being part of a network. Examples are VE networks without one or more central, steering management occurrences. Thus, it is not possible to enforce a common syntactical representation for models or the use of special languages and tools. However, an agreement has to be established either on a local level between collaboration partners or on a global level to get a collaboration-wide and standardized default. In the latter case, the default needs a partner-wide acceptance. In the first case, an agreement between at least two network partners is satisfactory.

Coordination efforts in modelling need to be reduced or even minimized. A standardized description of information with one storage format becomes necessary. The format needs independency from tool providers as it requires a common acceptance among all network partners. The Business Process Modeling Notation (BPMN) provides an appropriate modelling language. It helps to describe process information on a conceptual level. The BPMN addresses modelling experts as well as IT specialists (White, 2004). It is supported by various tool providers. However, a standardized BPMN XML description format does not yet exist. Thus, based on the BPMN meta-model, a XML-based description and storage format has been designed and implemented as well as first JAVA transformation converters based on respective meta model - mappings between different methodologies (Theling, Zwicker, Loos, & Vanderhaeghen, 2005; Vanderhaeghen, Zang, & Scheer, 2005). Hereby, local process models in heterogeneous representations are transformed to BPMN-compliant representations and syntactically stored as BPMN XML models in a platform repository. With transformation and standardized representations, process models become syntactically understandable for all network participants. BPMN acts as a common denominator for information description and information storage.

3.4 Model Synchronisation

To apply existing models of participants in a VE network, private models from BPM or software engineering are selected due to their relevance for network coordination. Hereby, a selection of models is copied and stored in the model management platform with a unique backtracking to their original model instances. The assumed repository of private process models are hidden to business partners and managed in separate tools not accessible to unauthorized, external people. Thereby, critical information models which must not be made public are protected. Participants of a network are able to manage their collaborative relationships with a pool of selected models being necessary for network and partner coordination.

Figure 3 depicts the proposed synchronization procedure which assures that model copies – selected for collaborative application and thus managed in the platform – enable retraceability to their local source pendants. A need for model alignment is identified by working with these copies of models. With new collaborative requirements, private models may be changed and updated for their collaborative application afterwards.

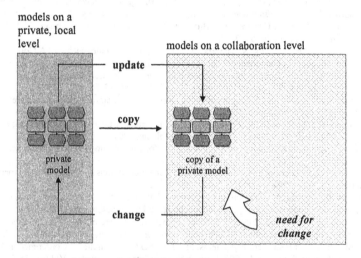

Figure 3 – Synchronization Procedure

4. CONCLUSIONS AND FUTURE WORK

With a vast variety of influencing factors, VE partner coordination becomes a highly complex task. This complexity needs to be reduced by appropriate methods and tools. The need for special coordination efforts and the development of enhanced methods and tools for modelling in networks has been derived from former research results. Information modelling could be identified as a well-established instrument for the design and implementation of enterprises and their role in VE networks. However, new requirements towards an enterprise-spanning modelling have to be considered due to existing approaches do not support modelling in VEs sufficiently.

The authors have presented an integrative approach towards the management of cross-organisational models in networks. Efficient modelling is supported by a platform for a distributed model management which has been partly described due to VE network requirements in this article. However, the platform approach has to be evaluated in future work. Hereby, case studies are currently being developed to be carried out in practice. New requirements towards information modelling in VE networks might arise which have to be taken into account for network model management.

The work, described in this paper, has been developed within the research project "ArKoS – Architecture for Collaborative Scenarios". The project is funded by the German Federal Ministry of Education and Research (BMBF). The authors want to thank Mr. Adam, Mrs. Hofer and Mr. Zang as well as Mr. Panfilenko and Mr. Woldert-Jokisz for their contribution within the project.

5. REFERENCES

1. Adam, O., Chikova, P., Hofer, A., Zang, S., Vanderhaeghen, D. "e-Collaboration architecture for customer-driven business processes in inter-organizational scenarios". In Challenges of Expanding Internet: E-Commerce, E-Business, And E-Government. M. Funabashi & A. Grzech, eds., Berlin: Springer, 2005; 63-77.
2. Adam, O., Hofer, A., Zang, S., Hammer, C., Jerrentrup, M., Leinenbach, S. "A Collaboration Framework for Cross-enterprise Business Process Management". In Preproceedings of the First International Conference on Interoperability of Enterprise Software and Applications INTEROP-ESA'2005 Geneva, Switzerland, February 23 - 25, 2005; 499-510.
3. Hammer, M., Champy, J. Reengineering the corporation : a manifesto for business revolution. New York: Harper Business, 1993.
4. Leimeister, J. M., Weigle, J., Krcmar, H. Effizienz virtueller Unternehmen: Ein Vergleich zweier Projekte bei AGI. Hohenheim: Universität Hohenheim, 2004.
5. Ratnasingam, P. 2003, Inter-Organizational Trust for Business-to-Business E-commerce. Hershey et al.: IRM Press.
6. Scheer, A.-W. Business Process Engineering : Reference Models for Industrial Enterprises. Berlin: Springer, 1994.
7. Specht, D., Kahmann, J. "Regelung kooperativer Tätigkeit im virtuellen Unternehmen". In Virtuelle Unternehmen, H. Albach, D. Specht, H. Wildemann, Gabler, 2000; 55-73.
8. Theling, Th., Zwicker, J., Loos, P., Vanderhaeghen, D. "An Architecture for Collaborative Scenarios applying a common BPMN-Repository". In Kutvonen, L; Alonistioti, N.: Distributed Applications and Interoperable Systems: 5th IFIP WG 6.1 International Conference, DAIS 2005, Athens, Greece, June 15-17, 2005. Lecture Notes in Computer Science, Volume 3543, Berlin: Springer-Verlag; 169-180.
9. Vanderhaeghen, D., Zang, S., Scheer, A.-W. Interorganisationales Geschäftsprozessmanagement durch Modelltransformation. Saarbrücken: Universität des Saarlandes, Saarbrücken, 2005; 182.
10. White, S. A. Business Process Modeling Notation (BPMN). BPMI.org. http://www.bpmi.org/bpmi-downloads/BPMN-V1.0.pdf . 2004.
11. Zang, S., Hofer, A., Adam, O. "Cross-Enterprise Business Process Management Architecture - Methods and Tools for Flexible Collaboration" In On the Move to Meaningful Internet Systems 2004: OTM 2004 Workshops, R. Meersmann, Z. Tari, & A. Corsaro, eds., Berlin: Springer Verlag, Berlin, 2004; 483-494.

54

INTEROPERABILITY IN COLLABORATIVE NETWORK OF BIODIVERSITY ORGANIZATIONS

Ozgul Unal and Hamideh Afsarmanesh
University of Amsterdam, THE NETHERLANDS
{ozgul, hamideh}@science.uva.nl

Schematic and semantic heterogeneity are two important types of heterogeneities that need to be resolved in order to enable interoperability and exchange of data among distributed and heterogeneous databases in a collaborative network of biodiversity nodes. This paper describes the SASMINT system, which performs schema matching and integration among databases. SASMINT identifies syntactic/semantic/structural similarities between two schemas as automatically as possible, resolving their heterogeneity and creating mappings among the pairs of matched components. Unlike other systems that are typically limited to specific algorithms, SASMINT combines a number of algorithms from the NLP and graph theory domains. After obtaining the user-input on validation/enhancement of matching results, SASMINT exploits the results of schema matching to automatically generate an integrated schema.

1. INTRODUCTION

The number of organizations willing and interested to collaborate with others is increasing at a high pace. As a result, different types of collaborative networks have been formed in the last years, such as the supply chains and virtual organizations (Camarinha-Matos and Afsarmanesh, 2005). Although the first examples of collaborative networks come from the manufacturing domain, the need for collaboration has been recently well understood in most areas of science and industry, including the biodiversity domain, which is the main focus of this paper.

Increasing biodiversity conservation activities bring about a variety of new needs for collaborative networks in this domain. For instance, they entail producing more accurate results by comparison and/or merging different biodiversity analysis activities, and making better predictions about the global distribution of species. This, in turn requires the collaboration and data / resource sharing among the biodiversity centers, organizations, and individual researchers. Although importance of collaboration in biodiversity has become clear to most involved scientists, most biodiversity related organizations hesitate to actively cooperate. This is mostly due to the sensitivity of some specific data categories, such as endangered species. Therefore, new mechanisms and infrastructures are needed, supporting collaboration among organizations, while taking these types of criteria into account. With the existence of such a mechanism, organizations can more easily decide to collaborate.

Please use the following format when citing this chapter:

Unal, O., Afsarmanesh, H., 2006, in IFIP International Federation for Information Processing, Volume 224, Network-Centric Collaboration and Supporting Fireworks, eds. Camarinha-Matos, L., Afsarmanesh, H., Ollus, M., (Boston: Springer), pp. 515–524.

Because of the growing number of heterogeneous databases, interoperability has become one most critical issue that such infrastructures for biodiversity, as well as for other domains, need to consider. Organizations typically design and use different structures for storage and processing of their data depending on their specific needs. Usually, even database schemas for identical concepts in two organizations have structural and naming differences. They might even use similar terms with completely different meanings. Since data sharing constitutes the main type of collaboration, the collaboration infrastructure has to consider such differences for providing effective mechanisms to integrate or inter-link and homogeneously access heterogeneous databases.

Semantic and schematic (structural) database schema heterogeneity are two main types of interoperability problems, where the former refers to differences in the meaning of data, and the latter is related to differences in the modeling and encoding of the concepts. In order to deal with these types of heterogeneity, schema matching and integration approaches have found considerable interest recently. However, most approaches typically require a large amount of manual work. Manual schema matching creates a major bottleneck due to the rapidly increasing number of heterogeneous data sources. As systems become able to handle more complex databases and applications, their schemas become larger, further increasing the number of matches needed to be performed. On the other hand, the suggested automatic resolution of semantic and schematic schema heterogeneity still remains challenging for provision of integrated data access/sharing among autonomous and distributed databases.

In order to address these problems concerning database interoperability in biodiversity domain, a Semi-Automatic Schema Matching and INTegration (SASMINT) system is proposed in the ENBI project (European Network for Biodiversity Information) (ENBI (2005)). The Collaborative Information Management System (CIMS) in ENBI aims at dealing with the information management related problems in biodiversity domain. Unlike other approaches to schema matching and integration, SASMINT requires minimal user input. It combines a number of linguistic and structure matching techniques from Natural Language Processing (NLP) and graph similarity research domains in a flexible way and (semi-) automatically matches the schemas. Then, after user validation/enhancement of matching results, SASMINT produces a new extended integrated schema. If there is an existing common schema in the collaborative network of nodes, it may not be needed to generate an integrated schema and the operation of SASMINT can be stopped after the identification of proper matches among the schema elements.

The rest of this paper is organized as follows. Section 2 provides an overview of related work. Section 3 describes the steps of the approach of SASMINT, addressing its syntactic and semantic similarity matching. Finally, Section 4 summarizes the main conclusions of this paper.

2. RELATED WORK

In this section, brief information about a number of related biodiversity projects is provided. Furthermore, as for the schema matching, an overview of main related work from database research domain is given.

There have already been a number of projects from the biodiversity domain that aim at providing data from distributed and heterogeneous databases through a common access system. These projects typically assume that existing biodiversity data standards can be used as the common schema, such as Darwin Core (Darwin Core (2006)) and ABCD Schema (ABCD Schema (2006)), and data from each provider has to comply with this schema when providing it to the outside world. The BioCASE (A Biodiversity Collection Access Service for Europe) project aims at establishing a web-based information service providing researchers with unified access to biological collections in Europe (BioCASE (2006)). In this project, users are expected to manually map the related fields between their local schema and the ABCD Schema, by using a simple user interface. The Global Biodiversity Information Facility (GBIF) (GBIF (2006)) is an international initiative that aims at providing biodiversity data globally and freely available to all users. Similar to the BioCASE, it is again the responsibility of the data provider to provide his data using Darwin Core or ABCD Schema by doing required mappings manually.

It is clear from the examples above that semi-automatic schema matching has not yet been considered in biodiversity projects providing access to distributed and heterogeneous databases. Furthermore, they usually use existing biodiversity data standards as the common schema to represent data from provider nodes. However, existing standards are not extensive enough to represent all types of biodiversity data and in some cases, it is required to generate an integrated schema from local schemas of participating nodes.

In database research domain, the challenge of schema matching to support interoperability has already been addressed by a number of projects. Cupid (Madhavan, Bernstein et al., 2001) normalizes the element names and then exploits a combination of name and structure matcher. However, the normalization step in Cupid is not as comprehensive as our pre-processing step. Moreover, name matching involves a syntactic matching, which employs only one string similarity metric. The COMA system (Do and Rahm, 2002) provides a library of matchers that utilize element and structural properties of schemas. However, it does not support the pre-processing of elements' names. Similarity Flooding (Melnik, Garcia-Molina et al., 2002) converts diverse models into directed labeled graphs and then identifies the initial maps between elements of two graphs using only a simple string matcher. These initial maps are then used by a structure matcher. However, Similarity Flooding has no knowledge of edge and node semantics. Similarly, (Wang, Goguen et al., 2004) borrows the string similarity implementation of Similarity Flooding and thus suffers from the same limitations. The ONION system (Mitra, Wiederhold et al., 2001) uses a number of heuristic matchers, but it does not employ any combination of string similarity metrics. Moreover, it is assumed that the relationships among concepts are defined using a set of relationships with pre-defined semantics, requiring a lot of manual effort. GLUE (Doan, Madhavan et al., 2002) provides a name matcher and several instance-level matchers. It is different from our system in that it uses machine-learning techniques. However, in order to train learners, ontologies need to be first mapped manually. Clio (Miller, Haas et al., 2000) generates alternative mappings as SQL view definitions based on the value correspondences defined by the user. For this reason, no linguistic matching techniques are used and a large amount manual work is required.

Although the importance of schema matching has been recognized in database interoperability research, previous approaches have some problems. They usually require substantial amounts of manual work and are limited in their solutions. Furthermore, these efforts mostly do not use linguistic techniques, which are needed to increase the overall accuracy of the schema matching system, when used effectively. Another problem is that none of these efforts considers how to use the result of schema matching for semi-automatic schema integration.

3. SEMI-AUTOMATIC SCHEMA MATCHING

Different organizations define their schemas differently. These definitions are frequently conflicting and thus making their matching and integration challenging. Among different types of heterogeneities, schematic (both syntactic and structural) and semantic heterogeneity are the most important obstacles to interoperability among databases.

As addressed in the Related Work section, most approaches in literature for resolving schematic and semantic heterogeneity require a large amount of user involvement. Furthermore, in related biodiversity projects aiming at interoperability, such as the BioCASE (BioCASE (2006)) and GBIF (GBIF (2006)), the idea of semi-automatic schema matching has not yet been considered and thus mappings between schemas remain to be identified manually. One key innovation of the approach suggested in SASMINT is that while it identifies the schematic and semantic heterogeneity and finds the "matches" between different schema elements, as automatically as possible, it also proposes to use the result of matching for schema integration. The SASMINT, can be used for two different cases of data sharing in a collaborative network of biodiversity nodes:

1. If a common schema such as ABCD Schema or Darwin Core is used in the network, SASMINT enables semi-automatic matching of the local schema of each node to the common schema.
2. If there is no common schema, SASMINT enables generation of a common integrated schema to represent data from participating biodiversity nodes. It helps to integrate local schemas of nodes by exploiting the result of schema matching.

In this section, the approach of the SASMINT system for semi-automatic schema matching and integration is described. The main processing steps of the SASMINT are shown in Figure 1. The comparison step of the schema matching is detailed, addressing its Structural and Linguistic matching that further involves different syntactic and semantic similarity matching. At the end of Section 3, it is briefly explained how to use the result of schema matching to generate integrated schema.

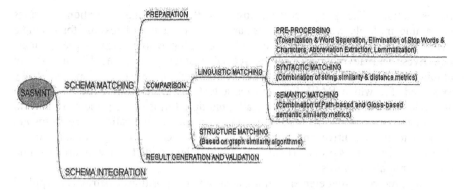

Figure 1- Processing Steps of SASMINT

3.1 Schema Matching

The Schema Matching itself consists of three steps: 1) Preparation, 2) Comparison, 3) Result Generation and Validation.

3.1.1 Preparation

In this step, SASMINT translates source schemas represented in different schema languages into a common Directed Acyclic Graph (DAG) format, which is necessary in order to compare two different types of schemas. The DAG has been chosen as the common format as we believe that it provides a balanced format among other alternatives supporting the representation of a relational schema, an object-oriented schema, etc., as a graph. Furthermore, existing graph theory concepts and algorithms can help us when comparing two graphs.

3.1.2 Comparison

After representing the schemas as DAGs, SASMINT automatically identifies correspondences between two schemas by resolving the structural as well as syntactic and semantic heterogeneities, referred to as *Comparison*. The comparison step consists of two kinds of matching: Linguistic and Structure Matching, as described below. Result of the Comparison Step is calculated as the weighted sum of Linguistic and Structure Matching. Formally, final similarity $Sim_F(a,b)$ for a pair of schema elements a and b is calculated by:

$$Sim_F(a,b) = ls_{a,b} * w_{ls} + ss_{a,b} * w_{ss}$$

where w_{ls} is the weight for the linguistic matching, while w_{ss} is the weight for structure matching. The sum of these values is equal to 1.0.

3.1.2.1 Linguistic Matching

Linguistic Matching involves both syntactic and semantic matching of element names from two schemas, which results in a linguistic similarity value (*ls*) between 0 and 1 for each possible name pairs. However, before any matching occurs, these names need to be pre-processed in order to bring them into a common representation. The pre-processing involves the following operations: Strings containing multiple words (or tokens) are split into a list of tokens, for example "First Name" is split into "First" and "Name". Stop words, such as prepositions, adjectives, and adverbs, as well as special characters, such as '/' and '-' are eliminated. Since the abbreviations are mostly used in the names, they need to be expanded, for which SASMINT utilizes a text file containing some well-known abbreviations and their extensions. Finally, multiple forms of the same word need to be brought into a common base form. By means of lemmatization, verb forms are reduced to the infinitive and plural nouns are converted to their singular forms. SASMINT exploits WordNet (Fellbaum, 1998), a lexical dictionary, in order to find out the lemma's of words.

After pre-processing element names, a variety of algorithms (metrics) are applied to identify syntactic and semantic similarities. Below are the details of these similarity algorithms.

I. *Syntactic Similarity*

There has been a lot of past research work in Natural Language Processing (NLP) on comparing two character strings syntactically. Unlike other schema matching approaches, which depend on only one metric, SASMINT uses a combination of several main syntactic similarity metrics. Since each of these metrics is best suited for a different type of strings, we find it more appropriate for SASMINT to use several of them together, to make SASMINT a more generic tool. The metrics used by SASMINT are explained below:

1. *Levenshtein Distance (Edit Distance):* Levenshtein Distance(Levenshtein, 1966), also known as Edit Distance, is based on the idea of minimum number of modifications required to change a string into another. The modification can be of type changing, deleting, or inserting a character. The costs of modifications are defined as 1 for each operation.

2. *Monge-Elkan Distance:* Monge and Elkan (Monge and Elkan, 1996) proposed another distance function using an affine gap model. Monge-Elkan Distance allows for gaps of unmatched characters. Affine gap costs are specified in two ways: one with a cost for starting a gap and secondly with a cost for continuation of a gap.

3. *Jaro (Jaro, 1995)*, a metric well known in the record linkage community, is intended for short strings and considers insertions, deletions, and transpositions. It also takes into account typical spelling deviations.

4. *TF*IDF (Term Frequency*Inverse Document Frequency)* (Salton and Yang, 1973) is a vector-based approach from the information retrieval literature that assigns weights to terms. For each of the document to be compared, first a weighted term vector is composed. Then, the similarity between the documents is computed as the cosine between their weighted term vectors.

5. *Jaccard Similarity* (Jaccard, 1912) between two strings A and B consisting of one or more words is defined as the ratio of the number of shared words of A and B to the number of words owned by A or B.

6. *Longest Common Substring (LCS)* is a special case of edit distance. The longest common substring of A and B is the longest run of characters that appear in order inside both A and B. Both A and B may have other extraneous characters along the way.

All the metrics described above are implemented within the Linguistic Matching component of SASMINT. Considering that schemas usually consist of mixed set of element names (strings) with different characteristics and each metric may be suitable for different types of strings, we propose to use a weighted sum of the metrics as defined below, which yields better final results.

$$sim_W(a,b) = w_{lv} * sm_{lv}(a,b) + w_{me} * sm_{me}(a,b) + w_{jr} * sm_{jr}(a,b) + w_{jc} * sm_{jc}(a,b) + w_{tf} * sm_{tf}(a,b) + w_{lc} * sm_{lc}(a,b)$$

where 'lv' stands for Levenshtein, 'me' for Monge-Elkan, 'jr' for Jaro, 'jc' for Jaccard, 'tf' for TF-IDF, and 'lc' for Longest Common Sub-string.

In addition to using a weighted sum of several metrics, another improvement of SASMINT over other schema matching systems is that it also utilizes the following new *recursive weighted* metric, which is a modified version of Monge-Elkan's hybrid metric (Monge and Elkan, 1996), to better support the matching of schema names when they contain more than one token. Therefore, the user can choose between the weighted sum metric and the recursive weighted metric based on his/her schema. Given two strings a and b that are tokenized into $a = s_1, s_2, ..s_l$ and $b = t_1, t_2, ...t_m$, the recursive weighted metric is as follows:

$$sim(a,b) = \frac{1}{2l} \sum_{i=1}^{l} \max_{j=1}^{m} sim_W(a_i, b_j) + \frac{1}{2m} \sum_{j=1}^{m} \max_{i=1}^{l} sim_W(a_i, b_j)$$

Identifying Weights Using the 'Sampler' Component
If the characteristics of the schema are known by the user in advance, he can modify the weights of metrics accordingly. However, it may not be always easy for the user to carry out this task. For this purpose, as another contribution of the system, a *Sampler* component is proposed in SASMINT, to help the user with identifying the most suitable weights. The sampler operates as follows: The user is asked to provide up to ten known "similar pairs" from his/her schema domain (e.g. "student_name" , "name_of_student"). The sampler *first* runs the six metrics individually over these pairs, and determines their calculated similarities (between 0 and 1) for each pair. *Second*, using the F-measure (Rijsbergen, 1979), which is a combination of the Precision and the Recall methods from the information retrieval field (Cleverdon and Keen, 1966), the sampler calculates the accuracy level (F-measure) for each metric, in relation to these pairs provided by the user. *Third* step of the sampler is that based on the F-measures, it calculates the weight for each metric, higher F-measure meaning higher weight. *Fourth*, after all "weights" for metrics are determined by the sampler component, they are presented to the user, who can accept or modify them. The sampler component can also be used for determining weights for semantic similarity metrics, for which the user needs to provide semantically similar pairs, such as "employee" and "worker".

II. *Semantic Similarity*
Similar to the syntactical similarity metrics, there are a number of semantic similarity algorithms from the NLP domain. The ones used in SASMINT can be categorized into two, using the names of groups mentioned in (Pedersen, Banerjee et al., 2005): 1) path based measures and 2) gloss-based measures, which are briefly explained below.

1. *Path-Based Measures:* These measures are based on the idea of calculating the
    shortest path between the concepts being compared in a IS-A hierarchy, such as
    the WordNet (Fellbaum, 1998). Among different alternatives in this category, we
    use the measure proposed by Wu and Palmer (Wu and Palmer, 1994). In addition
    to two concepts being compared in the IS-A hierarchy, this measure also takes
    into account the lowest common subsume of these concepts.
2. *Gloss-Based Measures:* Gloss refers to a brief description of a word. In this
    category of semantic similarity measure, gloss overlaps are used. In SASMINT,
    we convert the algorithm of Lesk (Lesk, 1986) to compute the semantic
    similarity of two concepts c_1 and c_2 as follows: for each of the senses of c_1, we
    compute the number of common words between its glosses and the glosses of
    each of the senses of c_2. A word can have different senses, depending on the
    context.

Both the measure of Wu and Palmer and the modified version of the measure of
Lesk are used in the SASMINT system for determining semantic similarity. These
measures utilize the WordNet. Similar to the case in the syntactical similarity,
semantic similarity is also calculated as the weighted sum of the algorithms
described above. Default value is 0.5 for each of them, but the user can run the
sampler functionality of the system to determine the weights.

3.1.2.2 Structure Matching

Unlike Linguistic matching, which considers only the element names, structure
matching takes into account the structural aspects of schemas also. Structure
matching uses the results of Linguistic Matching and applies a number of graph
similarity algorithms, which are based on the idea that if two elements have been
found to be similar, their adjacent elements (parent and children nodes) may also
match. Among different alternatives, following three algorithms were considered to
be relevant and chosen for the Structure Matching component of the SASMINT.

1. Graph similarity algorithm proposed in (Blondel, Gajardo et al., 2004) computes
    the similarity of two graphs G_A and G_B with the vertices n_A and n_B and edges
    E_A and E_B. For $i = 1,..,n_B$ and $j = 1,..,n_A$ the similarity scores are updated
    iteratively using the following equation:

    $$Z_{k+1} = \frac{BZ_kA^T + B^TZ_kA}{\left\| BZ_kA^T + B^TZ_kA \right\|_F} \quad k=0,1,....$$

    where Z_k is the n_B x n_A matrix of entries z_{ij} at iteration k, A and B are the
    adjacency matrices of G_A and G_B, and and A^T and B^T are the transpose of A and
    B. The matrix norm $\|.\|_F$ used here is known as the Euclidean or Frobenius norm
    and equals to the square root of the sum of all squared entries. The matrix
    subsequences Z_{2k} and Z_{2k+1} converge to Z_{even} and Z_{odd}.
2. Structure matching of Similarity Flooding (Melnik, Garcia-Molina et al., 2002)
    is based on a fix point computation. It does not use node or edge semantics and is
    based on the assumption that whenever any two elements are found to be similar,
    the similarity of their adjacent elements increases. Over a number of iterations,
    the initial similarity of any two nodes propagates through the graphs. The
    algorithm terminates after the similarities of all model elements stabilize.

3. Structure Matching in Cupid exploits a TreeMatch algorithm, which is based on the following perceptions (Madhavan, Bernstein et al., 2001): 1) Atomic elements in the two trees are similar if they are individually similar and if their ancestors and siblings are similar. 2) Two non-leaf elements are similar if they are linguistically similar and the subtrees rooted at the two elements are similar. 3) Two non-leaf schema elements are structurally similar if their leaf sets are highly similar, even if their immediate children are not.

All the above algorithms form the base for the structure matching component of SASMINT. Similar to the method followed in linguistic matching, structure matching uses the weighted sum of the three structural similarity algorithms introduced above resulting in a structural similarity value (ss) between 0 and 1 for each possible name pairs.

3.1.3 Final Result Generation and Validation

After the correspondences between the graph elements are determined, the resulting matches need to be displayed for the user, both because it is not possible to determine all possible matches automatically and also because not all the identified matches may be correct or desirable. The user can modify the matches and then save (or discard) the final results.

3.2 Schema Integration

After schema matching, user has the option to generate an integrated schema of the two schemas being compared. SASMINT aims to facilitate schema integration, by exploiting the validated results of semi-automatic schema matching.

The schema integration component is now under development and ultimately will enable iterative development of a common integrated schema for a collaborative network of nodes, two schemas at a time. This can be achieved as follows: First schemas S_1 and S_2 of two nodes are chosen and after the schema matching component identifies the mappings and the result is validated by the user, they are integrated by the schema integration component into S_{int1} and the result is saved. Then, the user selects S_{int1} and the schema of another node S_3 integrating them into S_{int2}. This process continues until the schemas of all nodes are integrated, resulting in a final integrated schema S_{int}. The result of schema integration is stored using a derivation language (Afsarmanesh, Wiedijk et al., 1994).

4. CONCLUSION

This paper addresses an important challenge to data sharing in collaborative network of biodiversity organizations: automatic resolution of syntactic/semantic/structural schema heterogeneity. In order to deal with this challenge, SASMINT system is proposed. SASMINT semi-automatically identifies the mappings between the local schemas of nodes and the common schema of the network. It simultaneously uses a number of NLP algorithms that together with the structure matching enable achievement of a more generic schema matching. Furthermore, a sampler tool is provided for users to influence the weights for these algorithms. If there is no common schema available in the collaborative network, SASMINT also supports the generation of an integrated schema from the schemas of participating nodes. The automatic use of the results produced by schema matching for generation of a new extended integrated schema is a part of the contribution of our work presented in this paper.

5. REFERENCES

ABCD Schema (2006). Access to Biological Collections Data (ABCD) Schema, http://bgbm3.bgbm.fu-berlin.de/TDWG/CODATA/Schema/default.htm.

BioCASE (2006). Biological Collection Access Services (BioCASE), http://www.biocase.org.

Darwin Core (2006). Darwin Core, http://darwincore.calacademy.org/.

ENBI (2005). European Network for Biodiversity Information (IST 2001-00618). http://www.enbi.info.

GBIF (2006). Global Biodiversity Information Facility (GBIF), http://www.gbif.org.

Afsarmanesh, H., M. Wiedijk, et al. (1994). The PEER Information Management Language User Manual. Amsterdam, Department of Computer Systems, University of Amsterdam.

Blondel, V., A. Gajardo, et al. (2004). "A measure of similarity between graph vertices: applications to synonym extraction and web searching." Journal of SIAM Review 46(4): 647-666.

Camarinha-Matos, L. M. and H. Afsarmanesh (2005). "Collaborative networks: A new scientific discipline." Journal of Intelligent Manufacturing 16(4-5): 439-452.

Cleverdon, C. W. and E. M. Keen (1966). Factors determining the performance of indexing systems, vol 2: Test results, Aslib Cranfield Research Project. Cranfield Institute of Technology.

Do, H. H. and E. Rahm (2002). COMA - A System for Flexible Combination of Schema Matching Approaches. In 28th International Conference on Very Large Databases (VLDB).

Doan, A., J. Madhavan, et al. (2002). Learning to Map between Ontologies on the Semantic Web. In World-Wide Web Conf. (WWW-2002).

Fellbaum, C. (1998). An Electronic Lexical Database, Cambridge: MIT press.

Jaccard, P. (1912). "The distribution of flora in the alpine zone." The New Phytologist 11(2): 37-50.

Jaro, M. A. (1995). "Probabilistic linkage of large public health." Statistics in Medicine: 14:491-498.

Lesk, M. (1986). Automatic sense disambiguation using machine readable dictionaries: How to tell a pine code from an ice cream cone. In 5th SIGDOC Conference.

Levenshtein, V. I. (1966). "Binary codes capable of correcting deletions, insertions, and reversals." Cybernetics and Control Theory 10(8): 707-710.

Madhavan, J., P. A. Bernstein, et al. (2001). Generic Schema Matching with Cupid. In 27th International Conference on Very Large Databases (VLDB).

Melnik, S., H. Garcia-Molina, et al. (2002). Similarity Flooding: A Versatile Graph Matching Algorithm and its Application to Schema Matching. In 18th International Conference on Data Engineering.

Miller, R. J., L. M. Haas, et al. (2000). Schema Mapping as Query Discovery. In 26th International Conference on Very Large Databases (VLDB).

Mitra, P., G. Wiederhold, et al. (2001). A Scalable Framework for the Interoperation of Information Sources. In International Semantic Web Working Symposium.

Monge, A. E. and C. Elkan (1996). The Field Matching Problem: Algorithms and Applications. In 2nd International Conference on Knowledge Discovery and Data Mining.

Pedersen, T., S. Banerjee, et al. (2005). "Maximizing Semantic Relatedness to Perform Word Sense Disambiguation". Supercomputing Institute, University of Minnesota.

Rijsbergen, C. J. v. (1979). Information Retrieval, Butterworths, London.

Salton, G. and C. S. Yang (1973). "On the specification of term values in automatic indexing." Journal of Documentation(29): 351-372.

Wang, G., J. Goguen, et al. (2004). Critical Points for Interactive Schema Matching. In 6th Asia Pacific Web Conference.

Wu, Z. and M. Palmer (1994). Verb Semantics and Lexical Selection. In 32nd Annual Meeting of the Association for Computational Linguistics.

PART 17

SERVICE ORIENTED APPROACHES

55

SERVICE DEVELOPMENT IN VIRTUAL ENTERPRISES

Günther Schuh[1], Heiko Dirlenbach[2], Laura Georgi[3]

Research Institute for Operations Management
at Aachen University of Technology
Pontdriesch 14/16
D-52062 Aachen, GERMANY
Tel: +49 (0241) 4 77 05-0
Fax: +49 (0241) 4 77 05-199
{1,2,3}@fir.rwth-aachen.de

In most European countries a structural change from a production dominated towards a service oriented society is progressing. Companies increasingly consider services as means to gain competitive advantages in a global competition. In order to provide holistic, value-adding solutions while simultaneously guaranteeing high quality standards, production companies increasingly join forces with external services' providers. Models, methods and tools for service development are rare and in most cases immature. In the context of virtual services' development this leads to a dual set of simultaneous challenges: an alignment of systematic services' and product development and the coordination of distributed R&D partners. The objective is to provide a meta-process that identifies all steps and decision points necessary to successfully develop innovative services. It is a result of combined service development and virtual enterprises'/ networks' research.

1. CHALLENGES IN COLLABORATIVE SERVICE DEVELOPMENT

On the macro-economic levels, most European countries realized a shift from agricultural to production and increasingly services' dominated economies (Ahlert, Evanschitzky 2003). On the micro-level individual companies – not only pure service providers but also production companies – use services as means to gain competitive advantages over a global competition. Innovative services are thus a prerequisite for economic success (Schuh et al. 2004; Luczak 2004).

A simple transfer of production oriented R&D models to the challenges of service innovation is not feasible. Holistic and repeatable approaches for developing and implementing new services are rare and on a low level (Scheer et al. 2003). Obstacles encountered can be deducted from services' characteristics of being intangible, of supply and consumption being simultaneously, of customers being directly involved in the production process, and of being perishable (Gill 2004;

Please use the following format when citing this chapter:

Schuh, G., Dirlenbach, H., Georgi, L., 2006, in IFIP International Federation for Information Processing, Volume 224, Network-Centric Collaboration and Supporting Fireworks, eds. Camarinha-Matos, L., Afsarmanesh, H., Ollus, M., (Boston: Springer), pp. 527–534.

Schuh et al. 2004). Services were and still are developed in unsystematic ways. The trigger for development is usually demand-driven. The company re-acts. As a consequence, the development results in complex service portfolios that are characterised by inefficient production, duplication of service development, cost-intensity and not meeting customers' demands (Luczak 2004; Scheer et al. 2003).

In the scope of this article service innovation is defined as results, procedures and processes that are of high quality and which are distinguishable from previous. The novelty has to be perceivable and marketable. An invention is not satisfactory, only sales or objective efficiency gains distinguish real innovations (Hauschild 1993). Based on this definition, service engineering is perceived as the systematic planning and development of technical services, making extensive use of engineering methods and tools as well as considering marketing issues at an early stage of the development process. A stepwise approach and the use of methods and models are the main characteristics, allowing for efficiency and efficacy as well as for high quality services (Schuh et al. 2004; Gill 2004). The company acts.

Hence, the intangible services are considered to be developable objects by using systematic methods and models in the creation process. Latest research shows several procedure models of varying details and foci (Bullinger, Schreiner 2006). In most models three phases are defined: Analysis, Concept, and Implementation.

An era characterized by re-organization, cost-cutting, shorter product life cycles and globalization demands companies for drastic re-orientation and focusing on core competencies. Yet, consumers request on one hand full-service solutions and on the other hand customization. As a consequence companies tend to set up breeding environments (BE) enabling cooperation in virtual enterprises (Afsarmanesh, Camarinha-Matos 2005). Thus, service providers and product suppliers joining forces in form of virtual enterprises (VE) lead to new ways of collaborative services' or extended products' development in order to satisfy customer requirements efficiently. This development is supported by the high-speed progress in information and communication technologies, allowing collaborative companies for specialization on core competencies, division of responsibility, reducing complexities but also for control and easy information exchange.

2. THE META-PROCESS FOR COLLABORATIVE SERVICES' DEVELOPMENT

To solve the dual and simultaneous challenges of developing services while maintaining good virtual enterprising, a meta-process has been defined. The process is deducted from the models of Jaschinski (1998) and Cooper, Edgett (1999); both focusing on service development in a single company. Moreover, findings of ongoing cooperative R&D projects on the development of innovative after-sales services are used to modify the existing approaches with regards to requirements arising from breeding environments in general and virtual enterprises in particular.

Based on the definition of service innovation, special emphasize has been put on business modelling as well as initiating marketing activities in early development stages. Thus, the meta-process shall support in generating not only inventions but real innovations by integrating the customer as early as possible in the analysis and design phases of new services; merging engineering disciplines with business administration. Thereby, a user-centric approach in virtual development environments is guaranteed.

The meta-process consists of four phases: Activation has been added prior to the three phases described above in order to cover the organizational set up. Individual activities per phase lead to a decision gate on continuation, repetition of single steps or complete termination of R&D activities. While setting up a project work plan, these can be considered as milestones. Each single step further consists of individual elements that are considered to be interim decision points. In the following, graphics visualise the process and further provide the envisaged process result per element on the right hand column. The individual elements are numbered as follows: Phase (0, I, II, III), Participants (N=Network, C=Company), Gate (0-5), Step (0-8).

Organisational Set up
Phase 0 Activation adds setting up a breeding environment to subsequent steps in service development. Central elements are decision of a strategy, definition of virtual enterprise goals, mutually accepted rules and procedures as well as a framework contract (Zahn, Stanik 2006; Afsarmanesh, Camarinha-Matos 2005). These could be set by one single company, by a task force initialized by some companies or all participants of a breeding environment. The individual constellation strongly depends on the general organisational set up. Based on this definition the further partner and team selection starts.

Service Requirement specification
The core service development process starts in the individual company with **Phase I Analysis**, where idea generation as well as the initial evaluation takes place and leads to the first decision gate. As innovations in distinction to inventions are sought the new service has to comply with the company's/ BE's strategy and shall fit into the existing products and services' portfolio (Cooper 2002). In case of generating several ideas in parallel, the first step leads to a prioritisation and is the starting point for subsequent activities.

Two scenarios concerning the described steps from idea creation to initial resources' planning are possible: one company conducts these steps or the BE partners perform all necessary steps collaboratively. The decision on an active cooperation – a virtual enterprise – is being taken after the initial resources' planning, see Figure 1 step I.C.24. By assumption, the subsequent description starts with idea generation in one company. Referencing to Figure 1, the process starts in the middle column (company) and after the decision on cooperation the further process is being described in the left hand column (virtual enterprise).

If the first and rough description of a service idea is satisfying and passes the first decision gate, it is used to conduct preliminary analysis of the target market, filtering out the basic user-requirements and leads to a first positioning strategy of the new service. Based on the latter, new requirements might emerge and shall be incorporated in the evolving concept. A technical feasibility study shall result in a rough process definition for the future service supply. This will be subsequently used for a preliminary resources estimate, i.e. human, financial resources as well as machines. The study might show that the single company will not be able to provide the service or an extended product, i.e. a product plus value-adding services, efficiently. In initializing a virtual enterprise the chance of opening up promising market opportunities by further developing and supplying the services collaboratively can be taken. After deciding on joint activities, the resource planning has to be further detailed with regards to the networked solution. The results will lead to a project work plan, reflecting costs, time, and resource allocation. The project work plan shall also be the starting point for a requirement description of plannable modules that are assigned to individual project partners.

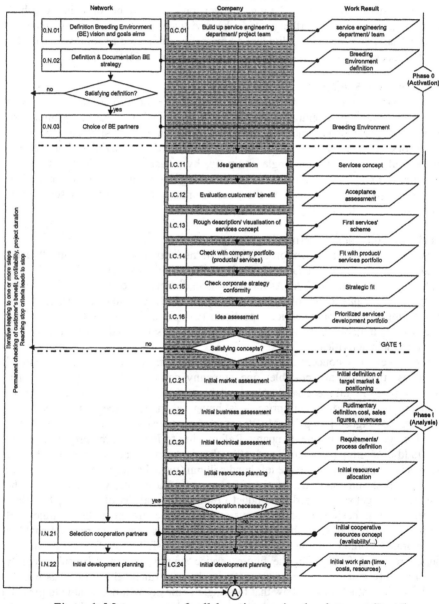

Figure 1: Meta-process of collaborative service development (Part I)

Service Concept definition

Phase II Concept induces the crossing from a breeding environment to a virtual enterprise, i.e. an active and goal oriented cooperation. Especially in case of extensive multi-player projects standards shall be defined, e.g. standardized status reports, work plans or data structures. A more detailed market assessment of the initial concept or prototype tests with customers allows for a better basis for further planning or refinement by repeating the last steps or could cause the termination.

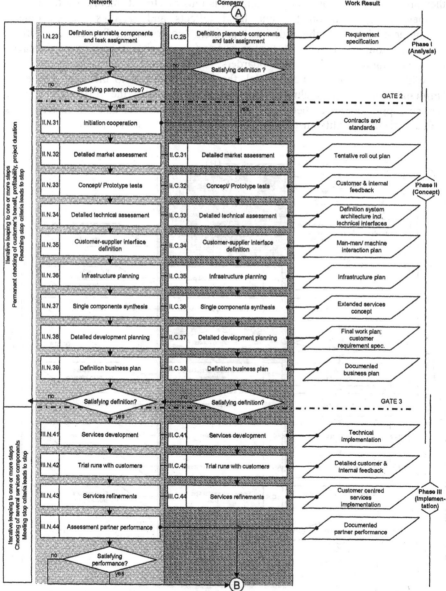

Figure 2: Meta-process of collaborative service development (Part II)

A system architecture defines all interfaces, i.e. technical, and customer-supplier interfaces in case of services, as well as infrastructure plans. The first service concept enables the VE to design a detailed project work plan as well as detailed and comprehensive requirement specifications, including specific activity allocation on partner level.

Customers generally prefer one face, i.e. one contact person they can address. Moreover, if services are being supplied by several partners, customers require uniform and stringent solutions that are being accounted for a single step, i.e. as if they are dealing with one supplier only. It is thus of utmost importance to define a business model that on the one hand reflects and satisfies the customers' requirements but also the individual partners' contribution. Process as well as documentation standards will further support a consistent service performance encompassing partner companies' boarders.

With a satisfying business model, the third gate leads to the final **Phase III Implementation**. The technical implementation includes the final definition of service supply processes between virtual enterprise partners and the customers as well as objective quality check criteria.

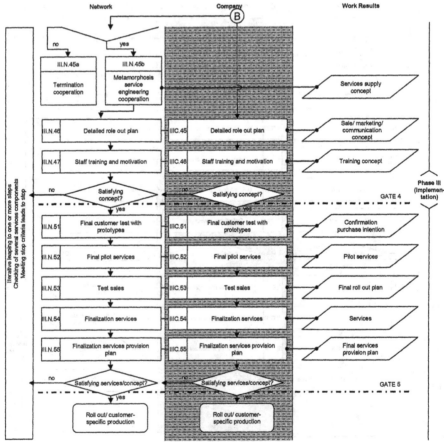

Figure 3: Meta-process of collaborative service development (Part III)

In test bed demonstrations detailed feedback of customers shall be acquired and mirrored with network internal testing procedures. These joint test results shall lead to a final and user-centred refinement of the services' concept.

As the final implementation of the newly developed service is at close hands, each partner's contribution during the development as well as – potentially – during the implementation is to be evaluated with regards to ability, capability and effectiveness. Based on this evaluation and well before actual market entry, it shall be decided which partners are part of the supply virtual enterprise and which shall move back to or out of the virtual breeding environment. Developing and supplying partners are not compulsively the same. A case is considered, in which a company jointly develops new services with non-profit research institutes. The service finally is only offered by the industrial partner. This is being depicted as metamorphosis of the development cooperation (Afsarmanesh, Camarinha-Matos 2005), the final stage that leads to sales, distribution, marketing and communiciation as well as training concepts. The latter not only evaluate qualification needs but shall also support motivation among virtual enterprise partners. The final gate before actual market entry shall be positively taken.

Final tests with specifically selected target customers, shall finally affirm the customers' willingness to buy. Based on a pilot service the decisive market entry plan will be the basis for the final top management decision on customer oriented production of the newly developed service.

3. CONCLUSION

A meta-process for the development of services in virtual enterprises has been introduced. The goal of this contribution is on the one hand to offer the practitioner guidelines for the collaborative development. On the other hand, it is envisaged to further contribute to the academically oriented discussions on holistic service engineering models and methods.

The results are based on several collaborative research projects. The validation will be conducted in the EC-funded integrated project MYCAREVENT (004202), in which 20 partners develop innovative IT-services and man-made services for the automotive after-sales market. Significant feedback from this project lead to further modification of the original meta-process and resulted in the described version. Most important conclusions with reference to discussions within the service engineering community are the more stringent combination of engineering and marketing activities.

Further research will be conducted on identifying the specific methods and tools needed to derive each element's results, see also Gill (2004). Moreover, critical success factors that allow for a competitive use of the proposed meta-process in daily business as well as to further refinements shall be empirically deducted. Finally, the success factors are basis for the definition of steering and control mechanisms that will be reflected in future versions.

4. REFERENCES

Afsarmanesh H.; Camarinha- Matos L. M.:	A Framework for Management of Virtual Organization Breeding Environments. In: Collaborative Networks and their Breeding Environments (PRO-VE05), Springer, Valencia, Spain, 2005, S. 26-28.
Ahlert, D.; Evanschitzky, H.:.	Dienstleistungsnetzwerke. Springer, Berlin, 2003
Bullinger, H.-J.; Scheer, A.-W.	Service Engineering: Entwicklung und Gestaltung innovativer Dienstleistungen. Springer, Berlin, 2003.
Bullinger, H-J.; Schreiner, P.:	Service Engineering: Ein Rahmenkonzept für die systematische Entwicklung von Dienstleistungen. In: Bullinger, H.-J.; Scheer, A.-W. [Hrsg.]: Service Engineering. Entwicklung und Gestaltung innovativer Dienstleistungen. 2. Auflage, Springer Berlin, Heidelberg, New York, 2006, S. 53-85.
Cooper, R. G.	Top oder Flop in der Produktentwicklung. Weinheim: Wiley- VCH Verlag GmbH, 2002.
Cooper, R.G.; Edgett, S.J.:	Product Development for the Service Sector. Lessons from Market Leaders, Perseus Books, 1999.
Gill, C.:	Architektur für das Service-Engineering zur Entwicklung von technischen Dienstleistungen. Schriftenreihe Rationalisierung und Humanisierung. Shaker, Aachen, 2004.
Hauschild, J.	Innovationsmanagement. München: Vahlen, 1993
Jaschinski, C.:	Qualitätsorientiertes Redesign von Dienstleistungen.. Schriftenreihe Rationalisierung und Humanisierung. Shaker, Aachen, Nr. 14, 1999.
Luczak, H.:	Service Engineering in Wissenschaft und Praxis. 1. Aufl., Gabler, Wiesbaden, 2004.
Scheer, A.-W.; Klein, R.; Schneider, K.:	Service Engineering. In Industrie Management, 19 (2003) 4, S. 15-18.
Schuh, G.; Friedli, T.; Gebauer, H.:	Fit for Service - Industrie als Dienstleister. Hanser, München, 2004.
Zahn, E.; Stanik, M.:	Integrierte Entwicklung von Dienstleistungen und Netzwerken - Dienstleistungskooperationen als strategischer Erfolgsfaktor. In: Bullinger, H.-J.; Scheer, A.-W. [Hrsg.]: Service Engineering. Entwicklung und Gestaltung innovativer Dienstleistungen. 2. Auflage, Springer Berlin, Heidelberg, New York, 2006, S. 299-320.

56

VIRTUAL ORGANIZATION MANAGEMENT USING WEB SERVICE CHOREOGRAPHY AND SOFTWARE AGENTS

Adomas Svirskas[1], Ioannis Ignatiadis[2], Bob Roberts[2], Michael Wilson[3]

[1]*Department of Computer Science*
Vilnius University, LITHUANIA
adomas@svirskas.com
[2]*Centre for Applied Research in Information Systems*
Kingston University, UK
{I.Ignatiadis, R.Roberts}@kingston.ac.uk
[3]*Business and Information Technology Department*
CCLRC Rutherford Appleton Laboratory, UK
m.d.wilson@rl.ac.uk

The purpose of this paper is to discuss an approach for the automated management of Virtual Organizations using Web Service Choreography and Software Agents. Web Service Choreography is important for the support and management of commonly agreed collaboration scenarios. In order for the scenarios to be understood and accepted by members of a VO, the scenarios need to be specified in a standard, machine-readable form and mapped to the implementation mechanisms of the VO participants. Software agents can then serve as the background support mechanism for the automation and management of the phases of identification, formation, operation and termination of a VO.

1. INTRODUCTION

A Virtual Organization (VO) is a temporary or permanent network of geographically dispersed entities (individuals, groups, organizational units or entire organizations). Virtual Organizations tend to be viewed as a radical approach to management, or a strategic approach that leads to dynamically reconfigurable enterprises (Sieber and Griese, 1999; Saabeel et al., 2002). The key enabler for Virtual Organizations is electronic business, with firms joining together to form short-term partnerships and/or long-term strategic alliances. Those partnerships are formed in response to more intensive competition, shorter product life-cycles, more specialized markets and faster technological change (Davidow and Malone, 1992; Hagel and Armstrong, 1997; Aldrich, 1999). In Virtual Organizations traditional external boundaries of organizations start to blur. However, the enablement of better exchange and sharing of information through inter-organizational systems can lead to greater efficiency, flexibility, and ability to respond to market requirements (Bovet and Martha, 2000; Timmers, 1999).

Please use the following format when citing this chapter:

Svirskas, A., Ignatiadis, I., Roberts, B., Wilson, M., 2006, in IFIP International Federation for Information Processing, Volume 224, Network-Centric Collaboration and Supporting Fireworks, eds. Camarinha-Matos, L., Afsarmanesh, H., Ollus, M., (Boston: Springer), pp. 535–542.

Virtual Organizations can be implemented using Service-Oriented Architecture (SOA) solutions, and Web Services in particular. Integration of those services requires standardized choreographies, which are definitions of the "conversations" between cooperating applications that allow them to work together correctly (Vinoski, 2001). Choreography is important to ensure that the sequence of states, operations and conditions that manage and control the interactions of the relevant services is carried out correctly (Web-Services-Architecture, 2004). In addition, enterprises involved in Virtual Organizations may utilize agent technology to simplify management and control of their operations, both internal and external. Agent technologies use principles of distributed decision-making, parallel and distributed computing, component-based software engineering, autonomous computing, and advanced methods of interoperability and software integration (Marik and McFarlane, 2005). Software agents can aid the formation of business alliances, planning short or long-term cooperation deals, and managing (including reconfiguration and dissolving) cooperation. This paper will therefore discuss the importance of Web Service Choreography and the use Agent technology for the operation and management of Virtual Organizations.

The rest of the paper is structured as follows: Section 2 presents the background on Web Service Choreography, and in particular Web-Service Choreography Description Language (WS-CDL). Section 3 presents the background on Multi-Agent Systems (MAS) and discusses interrelationship between the Web Service Choreographies and Agent Technologies. Section 4 discusses the importance of Web Service Choreographies and Agent Technologies for the management and operation of Virtual Organizations, while section 5 presents the conclusions of this paper.

2. WEB SERVICE CHOREOGRAPHY

Before discussing Web Service Choreography in more detail, it is useful to distinguish between choreography and orchestration, as there is sometimes confusion between the two. Orchestration specifies the behavior of a participant in choreography. This is achieved by defining a set of "active" rules whose execution decides what to do next. Once the rule is computed, the corresponding activities are then executed. Orchestration assumes the existence of a central point of control, which governs the overall workflow of activities, which effectively means the composition of a new service from existing services. Choreography, on the other hand, is meant to be enacted at runtime by peers in a Virtual Organization, without an intermediary. The choreography definition can be used to verify that everything is proceeding according to the plan (Ross-Talbot, 2005). Choreographies are defined in declarative description format, and are enacted by the collaboration participants at run-time.

Of course, it is important for collaborating parties to use the same language for choreography (business protocol) description. One of the service choreography description standardisation initiatives is W3C WS Choreography Working Group. It coordinates creation of the WS-CDL language (WS-CDL, 2005), which is the means to define a technical multi-party contract, primarily in Web Services domain. WS-CDL specification is aimed at being able to precisely describe collaborations between any types of participants regardless of the supporting platform or programming model used by the implementation of the hosting environment, thus addressing heterogeneity issues (WS-CDL, 2005). Choreographies must also completely hide component-level implementation details. Moreover, the same choreography definition (potentially involving any number of parties or processes) needs to be usable by different parties operating in different contexts (industry, locale, etc) with different software (e.g. application software) (WS-CDL, 2005).

Choreography definition using WS-CDL allows building of more robust services because they can be validated statically and at runtime against a choreography description, verification of absence of deadlocks and live-locks, etc. It also helps to ensure effective interoperability of services, which is guaranteed because services will have to conform to a common behavioural multi-party contract, mentioned earlier (Ross-Talbot and Brown, 2005).

There is a difference, between executable languages such as Java, C#, BPEL on one hand, and declarative description languages such as WS-CDL on the other hand. The latter capture a global view of messaging activity and are not designed to provide information about how participants implement their individual tasks. Therefore, there is a need for generating role-specific code skeletons from choreography description in order to facilitate faster and more convenient implementation of individual functionality. The choreography description language uses roles to differentiate between the participants in choreographies; this can be used efficiently for end-point code generating.

There are several ways to implement choreography support functionality, which involves both local and global tasks and relies on different types of information to perform them. For example, when a choreography description is first published or modified, it needs to be distributed to all the participants; the latter will negotiate the terms and quality of service, etc – this is global information. On the other hand, when analyzing an incoming message, sent by a peer in a choreographed exchange, the choreography support service relies on some local information – e.g. business rules, mapping definitions etc. The choreography support service, therefore, needs to interact intelligently with the corresponding services of the peers and those of the supporting and/or managing entities, for example reputation, policy decision, VO management services. One of the available implementation options is the Multi-Agent Systems (MAS) approach, which is discussed in the next section.

3. MULTI-AGENT SYSTEMS AND RELATIONSHIP WITH WEB SERVICE CHOREOGRAPHIES

Agent technologies are suitable mainly for domains of highly complex problems and systems with widely distributed information sources, domains with dynamically changing environment and problem specification, and for the integration of a high number of heterogeneous software systems (Jennings and Bussmann, 2003). Therefore, the agent technologies are suitable for usage in a Virtual Organization, where the participants are geographically distributed, usually with heterogeneous software systems, and where the environment is dynamically changing in response to market needs and requirements.

(Software) agents are autonomous, which is very desirable in unknown scenarios (which usually tend to appear in the real world), where it is difficult to control directly the behaviour of complex business collaborations. Even though it is possible to encapsulate some behaviour by specifying "private" methods, agents must decide by themselves whether to execute their methods according to their goals (agents must be proactive), preferences and beliefs. Agents are also flexible, they have to learn from, and adapt to, their environment. This is important, since when designing an agent system, it is impossible to foresee all the potential situations that a particular agent might encounter, and specify agent behaviour optimally in advance. This kind of situation is highly probable in the most of non-trivial VO interactions.

In a VO setting, a multi-agent system can be employed for supporting internal processes (intra-enterprise level) of the enterprise (e.g. planning and control, resource allocation, production process simulation - (Pechoucek et al., 2002)), and on the other hand, it can support cooperation and negotiation among enterprises (extra-enterprise level) across a value chain (e.g. customers, suppliers, material and service providers, etc). Both types of agents can coexist in an organization.

In addition to the external-internal dimension of agents' classification, there is another one, which is based on the *specific purpose* of the agent services. The reason for making this distinction explicit is the fact that the business services themselves can be considered as agents as they satisfy most of the agents' characteristics. (Maximilien and Singh, 2005a) in their work of cataloguing Web services interaction styles argue that viewing services as agents enables us to augment the interaction styles of Web services as interactions between and among service provider agents and service consumer agents. Therefore, it is important to denote the areas of responsibility of the business services and the supporting agents.

As we have explained above, Web services are characterized not only by an interface but also by the business protocols (choreographies) they follow. While business protocols are application specific, much of the software required to support such protocols can be implemented as generic infrastructure components (Alonso et al., 2004). For example, the infrastructure can a) maintain the state of the conversation between a client and a service, b) associate messages to the appropriate conversation, or c) verify that a message exchange occurs in accordance to the rules defined by the protocols (for example WS-CDL). Part of the task of the infrastructure is also the execution of meta-protocols, which are protocols whose purpose is to facilitate and coordinate the execution of business protocols. It is convenient to think of the agents as the meta-protocol enablers, paving the way for the business services.

For example, before the actual interaction can begin, clients and services need to agree on what protocol should be executed, who is coordinating the protocol execution, and how protocol execution identifiers are embedded into messages to denote that a certain message exchange is occurring in the context of a protocol. In the Web Services domain, WS-Coordination is a specification that tries to standardize these meta-protocols and the way WSDL and SOAP should be used for conveying information relevant to the execution of a protocol (Alonso et al., 2004). In the Multi-Agent System (MAS) domain, there are other protocols for agents' interaction, which can be useful for implementing the meta-protocols.

Having distinguished between the agents and the services, we need to make sure that these two types of entities coexist peacefully within a single architecture and interoperate properly. (Maximilien and Singh, 2005b) propose a framework that augments a typical Service-Oriented Architecture (SOA) with agents. Their principal idea is to install software agents between service consumers and each service that they consume. These consumer service agents expose the same interface as the service. However, they augment the service interface with agent-specific methods. The consumer communicates its needs via the augmented agent interface. Service method invocations are done via the service agent who, in turn, monitors and forwards all calls to the selected service. Both business and meta protocols can be modelled, validated and verified using the WS-CDL language and tools.

A good example of a consistent set of meta-protocols is the VO Management domain, where the business collaboration partners (peers) interact by the rules agreed by all the VO members and VO managers. These rules are enacted partly by direct interaction between the peers, and partly by the peers and the VO Management. We discuss Virtual Organization Management in the next section.

The concept of multiple agents can also be useful in general-purpose Web service composition. (Maamar et al., 2005) present an agent-based and context-oriented approach that supports the composition of Web services. To reduce the complexity featuring the composition of Web services two concepts are put forward in their work, namely, software agent and context. During the composition process, software agents engage in conversations with their peers to agree on the Web services that participate in this process. Conversations between agents take into account the execution context of the Web services. The security of the computing resources on which the Web services are executed constitutes another core component of the agent-based and context-oriented approach presented by (Maamar et al., 2005).

4. MANAGEMENT OF VIRTUAL ORGANIZATIONS

VOs follow a life cycle of four phases: (A) Identification (Opportunity Identification and Selection), (B) Formation (Partner Identification and Selection, and Partnership Formation), (C) Operation (Design, Marketing, Financial Management, Manufacturing, Distribution), and (D) Termination (Operation Termination and Asset Dispersal) (Strader et al., 1998). The management of a VO through those phases can be described just as a type of business process (or collaboration) that uses the same mechanisms as for "operational" business processes (or collaborations). The collaboration agreement of a VO then specifies the processes that are related to the administration of the VO itself, for example changes to the VO membership (Svirskas et al., 2005).

In some cases the management of a VO may take the form of a process carried out by an entity centrally located, so it might resemble an orchestration-type of management. This may be typical in vertically organized industries, e.g. aerospace, where a large vendor centrally controls a supply chain VO. However, in most cases a VO is amongst peers, those being either a VO member, or an enabling service (such as management, monitoring, security, etc). The interaction is usually binary, however in some cases (e.g. negotiation and need for consensus), the interaction may involve more than two parties (Svirskas et al., 2006). In addition, within a VO its members may belong to different organizations with different application and workflow implementation technologies, therefore resisting external control of their back-end applications (Papazoglou and Dubray, 2004). Also, the number of VO management collaborations (e.g. membership management, trust provisioning, monitoring) is limited. These considerations suggest that management of a VO centrally is not a suitable option, but that VO management interactions should be choreographed. The VO management protocol then comprises of the definition of the choreographies between the peers in the VO. As such, the previously described Web Services Choreography Description Language (WS-CDL) is well suited for this task. The VO management protocol exposes the common knowledge which the VO members need to share, while at the same time leaving the implementation of the protocol to the individual VO members (Svirskas et al., 2006).

With regards to agent technologies, those can bring various advantages to the domain of management of e-collaborations. The technological and integration aspect is covered by the Foundation for Intelligent Physical Agents (http://www.fipa.org), which tries to maximize interoperability across agent-based applications, services and equipment. Within a Virtual Organization, intelligent software multi-agents can take some of the load in each of the phases of identification, formation, operation and termination of a VO, by automating the relevant processes. Various agent technologies can also be used for the agents' private knowledge, maintenance, specification of various ontologies, and ensuring service interoperability across the value chain.

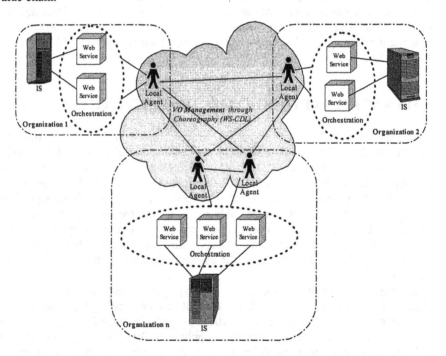

Figure 1 –Virtual Organization Management with Choreography and Agents

Figure 1 above illustrates our proposal for the management of Virtual Organizations using Web Service Choreography and Software Agents. The innovation lies in the fact that whereas Web Service Choreography can be used to coordinate the interactions between Web Services and their consumers, software agents can be inserted in front of those services, and their actions choreographed.

In Figure 1, the proposed solution is a generic one, in the sense that it does not distinguish between the number of agents or their type (e.g. per service, business process, or enterprise). It assumes however, that at least one local agent exists per each organization that participates in a VO. The interaction between the organizations in the VO is carried out with interactions between the respective agents. The latter communicate with the Information System (IS) of the organization via the appropriate Web Services. Whereas within a single organization those Web Services follow orchestration rules, as described in section 2, the whole VO is coordinated with choreography rules that are enacted by each of the local agents assigned to an organization. In that process, agents communicate and exchange information with local agents of other organizations. The use of agents adds flexibility to the operations of the VO, whereas at the same time the use of choreography rules ensures the efficient management of a VO without the need for a centralised service.

The process of the creation of a Virtual Organization has its counterpart in the cooperative team creation or coalition formation processes in the agent technologies domain. In this domain, a group of cooperating agents (coalition) is formed to fulfil a common goal. The individual agents are self-oriented and they don't share all information or their intentions. The agent technologies in this case classify the knowledge as public, private and semi-private. This has a high potential for the management of Virtual Organizations, where there is not a central point of control, but the e-collaborations are rather peer-to-peer, in which case it is important for each peer to have control over the availability of its own information to the other peers in the network and restricting access to the confidential data.

5. CONCLUSIONS

The purpose of this paper has been to present an approach for the automatic management of Virtual Organizations, using Web Service Choreography and (software) agents. Virtual Organization management in big conglomerates dominated by a large organization (e.g. in aerospace or automotive industries) can be implemented with a centralised approach, where the VO participants have to follow the mandates from the leading organization. However, most interactions in VOs are dynamic and among peers, which would make a centralised approach not viable. As such, this paper offers an important dimension in discussing the role of Web Service Choreographies and Multi-Agent systems for the (automatic) operation and management of a VO, without the need for a central hub of control.

Web Service Choreography, and particularly WS-CDL, need to be further developed and supported by the industry in order to successfully implement and support VO management. As was described in this paper, it is also important to link choreography descriptions to agent technologies, and this is an area of research worth pursuing in more detail. Some of the authors of this paper are currently engaged in designing the proposed architectural framework for an EU-funded FP6 IST project, entitled "Collaborative Process Automation Support using Service

Level Agreements and Intelligent dynamic Agents in SME clusters" (PANDA-Project, 2006). The results of this project will contribute towards that research.

6. REFERENCES

1. Aldrich DF. Mastering The Digital Marketplace. Chichester: John Wiley, 1999.
2. Alonso G, Casati F, Kuno H, Machiraju V. Web Services Concepts, Architectures and Applications. Springer-Verlag, 2004.
3. Bovet D, Martha J. Value Nets: Breaking the Supply Chain to Unlock Hidden Profits. Chichester: John Wiley, 2000.
4. Davidow WH, Malone SM. The Virtual Corporation - Structuring And Revitalizing The Corporation For The 21st Century. New York: Harper Collins, 1992.
5. Hagel J, Armstrong A. Net.Gain: Expanding Markets Through Virtual Communities. Harvard: Harvard Business School Press, 1997.
6. Jennings NR, Bussmann S. Agent-based control systems. IEEE Control Systems Magazine 2003; 23:3, 61-74.
7. Maamar Z, Mostefaoui SK, Yahyaoui H. Toward an Agent-Based and Context-Oriented Approach for Web Services Composition. IEEE Transactions on Knowledge and Data Engineering 2005; 17:5, 686 - 697.
8. Marik V, McFarlane D. Industrial Adoption of the Agent-based Technologies. IEEE Intelligent Systems 2005; 20:9, 27-35.
9. Maximilien EM, Singh MP, Multiagent System for Dynamic Web Services Selection. 2005a, http://www.csc.ncsu.edu/faculty/mpsingh/papers/mas/aamas-socabe-05.pdf.
10. Maximilien EM, Singh MP. "Toward web services interaction styles", In Proceedings of the 2005 IEEE International Conference on Services Computing (SCC'05), Orlando, Florida, USA, 11-15 July, 2005b, pp 147-154.
11. PANDA-Project, EU IST-027169, www.panda-project.com.
12. Papazoglou MP, Dubray JJ, A Survey of Web Service Technologies. Trento, Italy: University of Trento: #DIT 04-058; 2004, http://eprints.biblio.unitn.it/archive/00000586/01/mike.pdf.
13. Pechoucek M, Riha A, Vokrinek J, Marik V, Prazma V. ExPlanTech: applying multi-agent systems in production planning. International Journal of Production Research 2002; 40:15, 3681-3692.
14. Ross-Talbot S. "Orchestration and Choreography: Standards, Tools and Technologies for Distributed Workflows", In Proceedings of the NETTAB Workshop - Workflows management: new abilities for the biological information overflow, Naples, Italy, 2005, http://www.bioinformatics.org/NETTAB/2005/docs/NETTAB2005_Ross-TalbotOral.pdf.
15. Ross-Talbot S, Brown G. "Dancing in time with the services: WS-CDL", In Proceedings of the NY Java SIG, NYC, USA, 2005, http://www.javasig.com/Archive/lectures/JavaSIG-CDL-SRT.ppt.
16. Saabeel W, Verduijn TM, Hagdorn L, Kumar K. A Model Of Virtual Organization: A Structure And Process Perspective. Electronic Journal Of Organizational Virtualness 2002; 4:1.
17. Sieber P, Griese J. "Virtual Organizations As Power Asymmetrical Networks", In Proceedings of the 2nd International VoNet Workshop: Organizational Virtualness And E-Commerce, Zurich, 1999.
18. Strader TJ, Lin F, Shaw MJ. Information Structure for Electronic Virtual Organization Management. Decision Support Systems 1998; 23, 75-94.
19. Svirskas A, Wilson M, Roberts B. "Role and Applications of Pluggable Business Service Handlers in Web Services Choreography", In Proceedings of the WWW 2006, Edinburgh, UK, May 22-26, 2006.
20. Svirskas A, Wilson MD, Arenas AE, Lupu EC, Tuptuk N, Chadwick D, Giambiagi P, Dimitrakos T, Roberts B. "Aspects of Trusted and Secure Business-Oriented VO Management in Service Oriented Architectures", In Proceedings of the The First IEEE International Workshop on Service oriented Solutions for Cooperative Organizations (SoS4CO' 05), July 19, 2005.
21. Timmers P. Electronic Commerce: Strategies and Models for B2B Trading. Chichester: John Wiley, 1999.
22. Vinoski S. The Truth about Web Services. Web Services and Component Technologies 2001, http://www.proinfo.com.cn/chinese/menu2/3/102501.ppt.
23. Web-Services-Architecture, W3C Working Group Note, http://www.w3.org/TR/ws-arch/.
24. WS-CDL, Web Services Choreography Description Language Version 1.0, W3C Candidate Recommendation, http://www.w3.org/TR/2005/CR-ws-cdl-10-20051109/.

Iiro Salkari, Henri Hytönen
VTT Technical Research Centre of FINLAND
Iiro.Salkari@vtt.fi, Henri.Hytonen@vtt.fi

Many industrial Virtual Organisations (VOs) operate in manufacturing industry. Their business focus has been on investment product deliveries to industrial customers. Now the needs of their customers are changing. Besides a single delivery, their customers are increasingly interested in the lifecycle services related to their investments. It seems that in many cases, the ability to commit to the lifecycle services is becoming a prerequisite for getting the contract for the investment product delivery. This sets challenges for companies, who make these deliveries as VOs. A VO is a temporary collaboration for a specific task, but lifecycle services require long term commitment. This paper discusses and analyses the ongoing business focus shift from transaction and delivery centric towards lifecycle business centric in the context of industrial manufacturing VOs. The paper identifies challenges that this shift in focus set for VOs. It also analyses some prevailing approaches for VOs to provide lifecycle services. Still, many questions remain open, and thus this paper can be seen as setting some questions for the future research in the area of VOs and industrial lifecycle service business.

1. INTRODUCTION

Companies in manufacturing industry are facing hardening competition in their traditional line of business because the physical products that they manufacture have become commodities. The customers of the commodities are price sensitive and commodities can typically be produced effectively by challengers from the low labor cost countries. Simultaneously, the customers are starting to look at the lifecycle costs of their investments and the cost of a single transaction is in many cases becoming less important. In practice, this means that instead of a one-off delivery only, the customers are interested also in the services related to the delivery and to the operation (and also other lifecycle phases) of the investment [2] [10]. Previously, the lifecycle services were managed by the operator, but for the time being, operators do not necessarily consider e.g. maintenance as their core competence anymore. Especially this applies to capital-intense, long lifetime investments, like plants or systems in these plants. The need for lifecycle services opens up new business opportunities [5] because services are often knowledge intensive and hard to copy. Thus, the lifecycle services may be considered as one way to respond to the price competition from low labor cost countries.

Large investments in industry have typically been one-off projects, which however contain several systems and machines that are produced by some subcontractor networks repetitively. Virtual Organisations (VOs) are considered as one way to organize in this kind of business effectively. The VOs are dynamic (can

Please use the following format when citing this chapter:

Salkari, I., Hytönen, H., 2006, in IFIP International Federation for Information Processing, Volume 224, Network-Centric Collaboration and Supporting Fireworks, eds. Camarinha-Matos, L., Afsarmanesh, H., Ollus, M., (Boston: Springer), pp. 543–552.

be re-configured within one order), configured for a specific order, existing for the duration of one order only, and adherent to a specific life-cycle [3]. The changing business environment, with the emerging needs for lifecycle services set, however, challenges for the VOs in manufacturing industry. These VOs typically deliver long lifetime capital investments (like plants) or large systems to these. How a VO that delivers an investment product can offer lifecycle services in a similar way as a large company that self takes care of e.g. design, manufacturing and installation tasks, and the respective services during the different lifecycle phases of the investment? Regarding studies on services, which support products or their use, Mathieu [13] points out that the empirical studies on advanced product services are not too common and they take the customer rather than supplier viewpoint.

2. OBJECTIVES AND SCOPE

The main objective of this paper is to identify and analyze the challenges of business focus shift from manufacturing-oriented towards lifecycle service -oriented. The focus is on manufacturing industry VOs (supplier viewpoint) that have traditionally produced one-off investment products for their customers, but now their customers are indicating that they would like to purchase lifecycle services besides the investment. This paper also presents some potential ways how to respond to the challenge, but mainly it brings questions into discussion and for future research.

3. BUSINESS FOCUS SHIFT

3.1 Traditional business focus of manufacturing industry VOs

On the general level, it is defined that the added value that a VO produces is not restricted to physical products. For instance, an often used definition of VOs by Kürümlüoglu et al. [12] is as follows: "VO is a temporary consortium of partners from different organizations established to fulfill *a value adding task*, for example *a product* or *service* to a customer." This definition however, implies that the value add comes from a single product or service (.." *a* product or service.."). It must be noticed that the definition does not explicitly restrict to a single product or service only, but it is just the impression that the reader of the definition easily gets. Regarding the existing VOs in manufacturing industry this seems to hold also true in practice. As these VOs themselves put it often, they do "joint delivery projects", which often are single endeavors to fulfill customer's quite exact need – either a physical product or a service. The services may relate to a physical product delivery, e.g. process consultation, engineering, installation & startup, training services or they may be so called after-sales services, e.g. spare parts, repair, or upgrade projects [7]. The point is that the prevailing modus operandi is to consider these as single tasks. After the delivery (of the physical product or service), the VO has come to its dissolution, and the companies have moved to subsequent VOs (or to the VBE where they wait for the next VO and develop their preparedness).

Some of the subsequent VOs may have concerned upgrading or reparation of the investment (physical product) that they had previously delivered. Still, even in this case the starting point among the VOs in manufacturing industry has been that the customer (or the operator of the investment) has separately ordered the upgrade and reparation work for which the VO is created again. This kind of modus operandi seems in practice to fit e.g. Verkko A network, which was studied in Ecolead as one practical example of the existing VBEs in the manufacturing industry. The left end of the figure 1 represents the prevailing modus operandi: parts & machine, and maintenance suppliers.

In the figure, it can be seen that the current VOs concentrate on dealing with the customer purchasing process. They have limited understanding of customer's operational processes or business. As a consequence from dealing with the purchasing, the deal is often price-sensitive: The customer purchasing wants to buy the cheapest deal. The deal is often a single (project) transaction of a product or a single service, like repair, maintenance task or calibration. After the delivery, the business relationship ends. For the next delivery (either a new product delivery or delivery of service to the previous product) the VO is created again and in many cases the price continues to play a central role when the customer selects who will do the work.

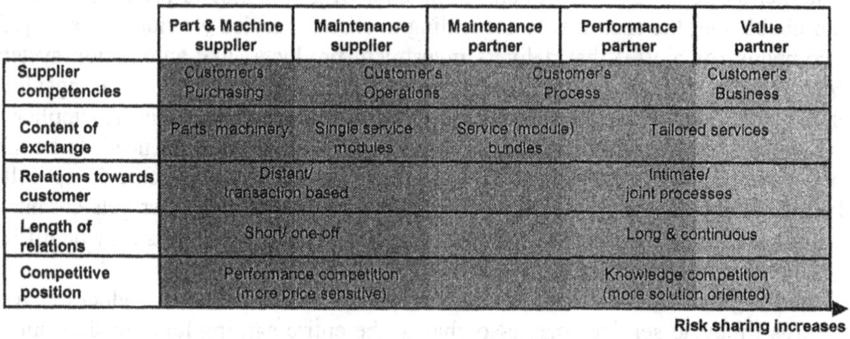

	Part & Machine supplier	Maintenance supplier	Maintenance partner	Performance partner	Value partner
Supplier competencies	Customer's Purchasing	Customer's Operations	Customer's Process		Customer's Business
Content of exchange	Parts, machinery	Single service modules	Service (module) bundles	Tailored services	
Relations towards customer	Distant/ transaction based			Intimate/ joint processes	
Length of relations	Short/ one-off			Long & continuous	
Competitive position	Performance competition (more price sensitive)			Knowledge competition (more solution oriented)	

Risk sharing increases ▶

Figure 1 – Business focus shift from delivery - oriented supplier to lifecycle service - oriented partner. (The figure is based on Kalliokoski et al. [7], Parrinello [15] and Docters [6]).

3.2 Lifecycle service -oriented business focus and its drivers

The trend in industry has been concentrating in core competencies. The same applies to many investment owners and operators who want to do less work with maintenance because they do not consider it as their core business. The systems have also become so complex that even the operators may not have the know-how that is required to maintain the systems properly.

The traditional approach has been buying services as one-off deals, which also fits in the above described traditional business focus of manufacturing industry VOs. The problem, however, is that the single one-off deliveries do not encourage the suppliers to develop solutions that would holistically support the customer. Rather, the one-off deals have lead to sub-optimums, where the ordered single service (e.g. maintenance task) is carried out efficiently, but as a whole there could be better and more efficient ways to plan and carry out the services (e.g. the maintenance as whole). The operators and owners are also becoming more and more interested in sharing the risks related to e.g. availability and usability of the investment. This takes the focus of service from supplied product towards maximising customer's all the different processes, actions and strategies that are associated with the supplier's product, as discussed by Mathieu [13].

Therefore, the customers have started to demand lifecycle services and related partnership, which are illustrated on the right half of the figure 1. Recently, the lifecycle costs have become even more important criteria for selecting some supplier than the price of the investment product alone. Thus, the investment product customers are increasingly demanding an offer for the whole lifecycle services already when buying the investment in the first place.

Offering lifecycle services sets new requirements to supplier competencies, content of the exchange, customer relations, supplier commitment and to the competitive position of the supplier. The fundamental difference compared to one-off product deliveries is the length of the commitment; after the delivery of the investment product, there are a lot of responsibilities left. All the lifecycle services, which need the same competencies as the delivery of the investment product need to be taken care of. The benefit for the supplier companies is that there is a secured income for the agreement period. After the period, the gained knowledge concerning customer's operative processes and business is of great value to the customer. So, it is probable that the customer is not willing to change service provider too easily. For a company (or a VO) that delivers investment products (like automation systems) there may be several customers who wish to buy lifecycle services alongside the physical product. Thus, there are several customers, towards which the supplier has to commit and with whom one has to develop joint processes. This needs to be taken into account when developing service business: the economics of scale do not follow the same logic as with products. So, on the other hand the supplier gets committed customers, but on the other hand the economics of scale in services may be difficult to gain over these customers.

Shifting the business focus from transaction based investment product deliveries towards lifecycle services may also change the entire earning logic of the supplier. Whereas the supplier previously earned mainly from the delivery of the investment product, in future, a great deal of the income may actually come from the lifecycle services related to the delivered investment. Well known examples of this kind of shift in earning logic are two Finnish companies, Wärtsilä and Kone. Wärtsilä produces diesel engines and related power plant and ship engine room solutions. Kone produces elevators and electric stairways. For both of these companies services play a major role. Wärtsilä's total sales in 2004 were 2 473 million € of which services comprised approximately 38% (936 million €) [16]. The share of services for Kone in 2005 was even higher, 60% of the total pro forma sales [11]. Mainly these services were lifecycle services (i.e. services that are provided after the delivery).

The transition from an investment product supplier to a lifecycle service partner is, however, not easy even for large companies. For instance, Metso corporation (paper machines, control systems etc.) tried with a service concept called "Future Care", which however needed to be refocused (see: [14]). The original Future Care was not fully accepted by the customers in the way it was planned in the beginning. After the refocusing, Metso has recently reported good success for its service business.

The transition towards lifecycle service business is even more challenging for companies that deliver investment products as VOs, because of the *temporally* restricted nature of these VOs. How can these companies commit to the long time collaboration with a customer who wishes to buy knowledge intensive services from the deliverer (a consortium of companies in the case of VO) of the investment product? It must be noted that these services are not only large maintenance projects, but also smaller tasks. Figure 2 illustrates this change of business focus. "One-off" deliveries represent the traditional transaction or single delivery -oriented business focus. The "Lifecycle service (&commitment)" represent the lifecycle service -oriented business focus. In the "one-off" deliveries each service in the middle-of-life -section is a single transaction. In the "lifecycle service (&commitment)" the services during the delivery and the middle-of-life (and even during the end-of-life) are lifecycle services, to which it is often necessary to commit already during the delivery of the physical investment project.

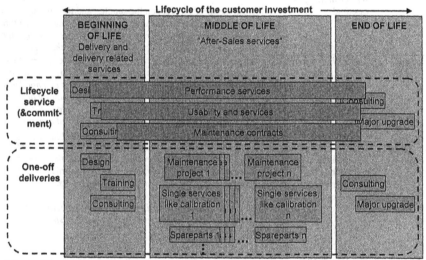

Figure 2 – Value to a customer regarding a single solution – from separate value adding transactions to lifecycle services. Modified by VTT from a summary of BestServ Industrial Service Business Forum discussions [1].

3.3 Challenges for VOs when business focus shifts towards lifecycle services

This chapter summarizes the challenges that the described business focus shift causes. The focus is on challenges that especially VOs will face due to their nature. Our overall focus of this study must also be kept in mind. We concentrate on manufacturing industry VOs that produce investment products and whose customers are now saying that the ability to provide lifecycle services is one central precondition for getting the deal at all. Table 3.1 summarizes the challenges that the business focus shift causes for these kind of VOs. The issues to the table 3.1 came from the figure 1.

Table 3.1 Summary of business focus shift needs and challenges for VOs.

Issue	What is emphasized in lifecycle service business?	Challenge for service supplier (network/VO)
Supplier competencies	Supplier needs to understand *customer processes and business.* Understanding of *customer business environment* is needed. Ability to *collaborate on daily basis in service delivery* is essential.	Long term customer relationships needed, because understanding of customer processes and business is challenging, and expensive and time consuming to gain: - The organization that coordinates the lifecycle service business must not change too often. - The companies that deliver the services on site must not change too often. ⇒ Solely inheritance from previous VOs is not enough to enable delivery of subsequent lifecycle services, *but it is probable that mainly the same companies must participate and commit to the service deliveries for a longer time.* Customer needs to trust on the supplier and that the supplier is not going to enter customer's core business, and thus is not a threat → *strategic (management) level collaboration between supplier (coordinator) and customer is needed besides the operative level.*
Content of exchange	*Service bundles and tailored services:* value-shop approach for configuring the service.	There is a need to manage several areas of expertise → there is a need to involve specialists from different companies (like during the delivery of an investment) → *one company can not deliver all the lifecycle services alone or take the responsibility of them alone. Already when the lifecycle service is sold to the customer, there must be an agreement among the required companies that they will commit to the delivering of the services.*
Commitment → Relations towards customer	*Intimate,* necessitates trust and collaborative approach (even development of joint processes). Partners locating near or *at the customer site* are often needed for lifecycle services.	*Companies that deliver the service may not change too often because seamless collaboration necessitates joint development work though which the trust evolves. This restricts, which companies can be involved in service deliveries.* *Coordination need towards the customer and between the companies that participate lifecycle service business increase.*
Length of relations	*Long and continuous. Necessitates commitment* (ability to commit).	Readiness to commit to a long time business relationship. This requires models and solutions for pricing, delivery practices, and the risks related to the length of the relationship. *The total lifecycle service can not be delivered as several subsequent VOs with no connection between them and with (partly) different companies every time.*
Competitive position	*Knowledge about the customer and solutions, which add value to the customer are important (price may be less so)*	Long term income if knowledge of customer and customer needs and solutions are kept on higher level than the competitors are able to do. The competitors are clearly in more week position, because their relations to the customer are more distant and therefore they may not be able to develop the same knowledge. Knowledge intensiveness may even change the earning logic: instead of single one-off deliveries, the income comes from lifecycle service agreements and the income is known quite a long time in advance. This is because it is easy to find a new supplier to a commodity, but more difficult to find a new supplier to a task, which requires in depth and wide knowledge of customer operations and business.
Risk sharing	*Shared risk with customer* concerning the investment.	*Sharing risk among the companies that offer the total lifecycle service. Long term risk sharing between companies.*

4. POTENTIAL WAYS FOR RISING TO THE CHALLENGE AND QUESTIONS FOR FUTURE RESEARCH

The problem related to service business around capital goods is already addressed by some studies, but the viewpoint has much been from customer viewpoint [13]. The supplier viewpoint seems to be less paid attention to, though some examples exist even in the field of VOs. For instance, in Karvonen et al. [9] there is a chapter dedicated to sales and services issues. However, in the VO context the challenge related to service business is often addressed from technological solution viewpoint or from the viewpoint that there is a problem that needs to be solved fast and a VO is created for that problem. These all are still very relevant, but they consider that the single (service) delivery - oriented VOs are solutions to this: the business and solution still comes from a single delivery. For instance, this can be seen in Kauer et al. [10], were the starting point for a VO creation is a complete problem description and a task list, and the VO ends on documented customer order (service report and invoice).

However, our approach concentrates more on taking the responsibility of some operations that the customer does not perceive as their core business. I.e. in our understanding the challenge related to the lifecycle service business is not the efficient creation of VOs to solve some well defined single problems. Rather the challenge is the long term commitment to whatever the customer finds valuable: the maintenance as a whole, the performance of the investment, or the availability of the investment. Further, in the business that we described as lifecycle service centric, also the earning logic changes. Whereas previously the income was transaction based, in the lifecycle service business it is based on long term agreements. Single transactions are not that valuable to the customer as the entities (lifecycle services) that are provided. Simultaneously, in the lifecycle service focused business the organizations that provide the services must commit to the long term collaboration with the customer - they can not be "freely" selected VO per VO (see table 3.1).

To achieve the commitment, the lifecycle service business necessitates creation of a specific Service Network or Breeding Environment. Its rules and practices may be somewhat different from those of Manufacturing Networks. On the other hand, in many cases the Service network and the Manufacturing network are overlapping: they have partly the same partners. [8] Also, the different lifecycle service tasks require different preparedness from the Breeding Environment: Preventive maintenance tasks may be foreseen and planned beforehand, but repair tasks come unexpectedly and require fast reaction time. In both cases one alternative is to view them as Service Virtual Organizations which are not dissolved after the task but only switch to a stand-by state, from where they can again be evoked when needed – the commitment differs in this modus operandi from the prevailing one.

One way to accumulate experiences over single VOs (and thus create long span view to business) is so called *inheritance*. Inheritance is considered to be systematically collected information of VO operational phase. This information is gathered during the VO lifecycle and it is used to facilitate the utilization of experiences and knowledge related to the object of the collaboration and to the collaboration practices, processes and partner combinations. The inheritance management is a way to record and learn systematically from experiences. Proper inheritance management includes e.g. following: Saving the VO experiences in utilizable format; sharing the experiences among partners; taking care that the experiences are utilizable in the next VO initialization, planning and execution; communicating the experiences towards the VBE in utilizable format in order to enable the use of experiences in the next VO. [4]

The previous research with its solutions together with a proper inheritance management seems to clearly support the lifecycle service-oriented business of collaborative organizations. Still many challenges, which relate to the different nature of the lifecycle service business, remain unsolved:

- How to be able to commit and offer the lifecycle services, which require risk sharing, already when preparing an offer for an investment product delivery? This commitment means in practice commitment to future service VOs with pre-agreed price and other principles. This involves the coordinating company (or organization) as well as the companies that actually deliver the services.
- What kind of organizing the lifecycle service business necessitates from the networked organizations:
  - What kind of role and responsibility can the VBE bear?
  - What kind of responsibilities and roles require that there is a single company (a single legal entity) that bears the responsibility?
  - What this coordinating company (or other form of organization) must require from those companies that commit to the actual future service deliveries?
  - How to define the responsibilities between the VBE and the customer and how to integrate to the customer processes?
  - How to serve different customers which potentially have different service needs? How to make one VBE able to take care of different customers?
- Modus operandi and business issues:
  - How the modus operandi of the lifecycle service -oriented VOs truly differs from the modus operandi of the delivery -oriented VOs?
  - What are the consequences to the VO business concept if the earnings come from long term commitment rather than from timely limited deliveries?

5. CONCLUSIONS

5.1 The lifecycle service business sets challenges for manufacturing industry VOs

The customer needs of manufacturing VOs are changing. Customers are increasingly interested in solutions, i.e. delivery of an investment product and the related services both during the delivery and during the operation of the investment. The deliverer of the investment (e.g. a VO) must already during the delivery be able to offer also lifecycle services and commit to them too. This sets challenges for the companies that collaborate as VOs when they focus their business on lifecycle services.

These companies need to develop their own competencies so that they match the customer processes and business environment. They also need to be able support the customer, and to do this, collaborate with other supplier companies, also in cases that are not explicitly specified in the service contract. All these activities and competencies necessitate readiness for long term commitment towards the customer and towards the other service suppliers, because developing these skills is costly and time spending. Risk sharing towards the customer is often related to the lifecycle services. Therefore, also the supplier companies need to have some capabilities to bear and share long term risks related to the lifecycle services that are not as rigorously defined as the work these companies are used to deal with – the one-off deliveries.

The lifecycle service business also opens up new opportunities. It often provides an opportunity for a longer term cash flow, which is also more predictable in advance. In lifecycle services also the competition is often knowledge centric and the price does not play that an important role. Gaining knowledge concerning the customer, customer's processes and solutions gives a competitive edge to the prevailing service provider(s). This competitive edge is hard to break.

The existing research has already addressed the challenge related to Virtual Organisations in service business. However, it seems that still more research work is needed. This is because the existing research has mainly concentrated on IT solutions and single services that need to be delivered. The lifecycle service – oriented business, however, necessitates longer term commitment and related long term risk sharing. As such, the VBE-VO concept seems to fit for the lifecycle service business too, because it enables combining knowledge of different companies in order to produce complex lifecycle services, which none of the companies could produce alone. Large enterprises in manufacturing industry can already show some success stories related to the lifecycle service business, but the VOs will still have to improve in order to be able to say that the lifecycle service business is good business for them.

5.2 Acknowledgements

This paper is based on work that is carried out in two research projects, ECOLEAD and BeSeL. ECOLEAD is a EU FP6 integrated project, which researches collaborative networked organizations. BeSeL is a national project funded by the Technology Agency of Finland (TEKES) and it studies industrial service business. Further, in terms of resources, this study was also supported by TEKES funded Cobtec - project. This research does not directly represent official results of the mentioned projects, but rather it must be considered as a modest attempt of the writers for cross-disciplinary analysis of the topics of the projects.

6. REFERENCES

[1] Airola, 2006. Summary of Views of Industry representatives in the BestServ Service Business Forum Meetings 6-12/05. The BestServ (www.bestserv.fi) forum is coordinated by the Techonology Industries of Finland.

[2] Burger, G., Hartel, I., Schnetzler, M:, Rüf, C., 2001. Company survey "Successful Service Management – Trends and Practices in the After-Sales". ETHZ-BWI, Zurich, Switzerland.

[3] Camarinha-Matos, L. and Afsarmanesh, H., 1999. The virtual enterprise concept In: L.M. Camarinha-Matos and H. Afsarmanesh, Editors, Infrastructures for Virtual Enterprises— Networking Industrial Enterprises, Kluwer Academic Publishers, pp. 3–14

[4] D322 public Ecolead deliverable. Available through Ecolead web page: www.ecolead.org (visited 24.2.2006)

[5] Deloitte, 2006. The Service Revolution in Global Manufacturing Industries.

[6] Docters R., et al (2004): "Capturing the Unique Value of Services: Why Pricing of Services Is Different", The Journal of Business Strategy, 25:2.

[7] Kalliokoski P., Andersson G., Salminen V., Hemilä J., 2003. BestServ Feasibility Study Final Report. Technology Industries of Finland, Kerava, Finland.

[8] Karvonen, I., Jansson, K., Ollus, M., Hartel, I., Burger, G., Anastasiou, M., Välikangas, P., Mori, K., 2002. Inter-enterprise eCollaboration in Sales and Service of one-of-a-kind products. In: Stanford-Smith, B. & Chiozza, E. & Edin, M. (Ed.). Challenges and Achievements in E-business and E-work, pp. 1388-1395. IOS Press / Ohmsha, Berlin, Germany, 1636 p.

[9] Karvonen, I., van den Berg, R., Bernus, P., Fukuda, Y., Hannus, M., Hartel, I., Vesterager, J., 2003. Global Engineering and Manufacturing in Enterprise Networks – GLOBEMEN. VTT Symposium 224. Espoo, Finland. 394p.

[10] Kauer, M., Burger, G., Hartel, I., 2003. An Internet-based Platform for Distributed After-Sales Services in the One-of-a-kind Production". In: Karvonen, I., van den Berg, R., Bernus, P., Fukuda, Y., Hannus, M., Hartel, I., Vesterager, J., 2003. Global Engineering and Manufacturing in Enterprise Networks – GLOBEMEN. VTT Symposium 224. Espoo, Finland. 394p.

[11] Kone, 2005. Annual Report2005. Available through Kone web page (www.kone.com). Direct address: http://www.kone.com/static/ImageBank/ GetFile_pdf/0,,fileID=268939,00.pdf (visited 24.2.2006).

[12] Kürümlüoglu M., Nøstdal R., Karvonen, I. Base concepts, in Camarinha-Matos, L., Afsarmanesh, H., Ollus, M. (eds.), Virtual organizations. Systems and Practices, Springer-Verlag (2005), pp.11-28.

[13] Mathieu V., 2001. Product services: from a service supporting the product to a service supporting the client. Journal of Business & Industrial Marketing, Vol. 16, No. 1, 2001. MCB University Press.

[14] Metso, 2003. Annual review 2003. Available through Metso corporation web page (www.metso.com). Direct address: http://www.metso.com/corporation/ir_eng.nsf/WebWID/WTB-041108-2256F-EC538/ $File/Metso_vsk03_en.pdf (visited 24.2.2006).

[15] Parrinello S. (2004): "The Service Economy Revisited", Structural Change and Economic Dynamics, 15:4.

[16] Wärtsilä, 2004. Annual Report – Busines Review. Available through Wärtsilä web page (www.wartsila.com). Direct address: http://www.wartsila.com/Wartsila/docs/en /press/pdf/Wartsila _AR_ Business_2004_GB_low.pdf (visited 24.2.2006).

58 SINGLE SIGN-ON AND AUTHORIZATION FOR DYNAMIC VIRTUAL ORGANIZATIONS

R.O. Sinnott[1], O. Ajayi[1], A.J. Stell[1], J. Watt[1], J. Jiang[1], J. Koetsier[2]

National e-Science Centre
[1]University of Glasgow, Glasgow, SCOTLAND
[2]University of Edinburgh, Edinburgh, SCOTLAND
r.sinnott@nesc.gla.ac.uk

The vision of the Grid is to support the dynamic establishment and subsequent management of virtual organizations (VO). To achieve this presents many challenges for the Grid community with perhaps the greatest one being security. Whilst Public Key Infrastructures (PKI) provide a form of single sign-on through recognition of trusted certification authorities, they have numerous limitations. The Internet2 Shibboleth architecture and protocols provide an enabling technology overcoming some of the issues with PKIs however Shibboleth too suffers from various limitations that make its application for dynamic VO establishment and management difficult. In this paper we explore the limitations of PKIs and Shibboleth and present an infrastructure that incorporates single sign-on with advanced authorization of federated security infrastructures and yet is seamless and targeted to the needs of end users. We explore this infrastructure through an educational case study at the National e-Science Centre (NeSC) at the University of Glasgow and Edinburgh.

1. INTRODUCTION

The vision of the Grid [7] is to support the *dynamic* establishment and subsequent management of virtual organizations (VOs). The term *dynamic* is italicized here as it could be argued that this is what distinguishes Grid infrastructures from other large scale distributed systems. With no prior detailed agreements in place, it should be possible to create a VO which will allow collections of individuals and/or institutions to *securely* share resources whether these resources are data sets, data archives, computational resources, services or more specialized equipment. A key element of this vision is the notion of *single sign-on* where a single set of user security credentials are sufficient to allow access to a multitude of federated resources across the VO.

Perhaps the greatest challenge in realizing this dynamic model is security. Sites wishing to potentially form a VO need to be aware of the consequences of establishing such collaborations. It is the case in computer security that the weakest link rule applies; this fact is magnified by Grid infrastructures due to their openness. Highly secure multi-million pound compute facilities can be compromised by inadequately secured remote laptops. Rigorous security procedures at one site can be made redundant through inadequate procedures at another collaborating site. This problem is exacerbated by the predominant Public Key Infrastructure (PKI) [11] authentication-only based security models prevalent across most high performance computing related Grid infrastructures today, where establishment of user identity is the primary security focus (and not on restricting what the user is allowed to do on

Please use the following format when citing this chapter:

Sinnott, R. O., Ajayi, O., Stell, A. J., Watt, J., Jiang, J., Koetsier, J., 2006, in IFIP International Federation for Information Processing, Volume 224, Network-Centric Collaboration and Supporting Fireworks, eds. Camarinha-Matos, L., Afsarmanesh, H., Ollus, M., (Boston: Springer), pp. 555–564.

the given resource). With the move of the Grid community to more security focused areas such as the health domain, this authentication-only security model is unrealistic and does not lend itself to the adoption of Grid technology. Considerable progress has been made in developing advanced security infrastructures that are well integrated into Grid middleware [8,20]. However the challenge remains how to establish a VO in a dynamic manner where sets of fine grained distributed security authorization policies defining what end users are allowed to access/use on local institutional resources can be supported across multiple independent institutions.

One common approach to solve this is through the establishment of *federations* which can be considered as groups of organizations which agree to adopt common policies and technical standards to provide a common infrastructure for managing access to resources and services in a uniform way. The Internet2 Shibboleth architecture and protocols [18,19] have been developed to support the establishment of federations where devolved authentication and security attribute release across multiple independent institutions is supported. Through Shibboleth, authentication at a home institution Identity Provider (IdP) by a user can in principle support single sign-on across a federated VO where security attributes and assertions are released which can subsequently be used by service providers (SP) to make authorization decisions. This model of single sign-on lends itself to advanced authorization in more security focused VOs, but requires detailed negotiation of security attributes to be defined *a priori*. This pre-agreed and potentially detailed negotiation and agreements goes somewhat against the true vision of the Grid where dynamic VOs can be established and managed "on-the-fly", and where new agreements and policies can be added as new institutions, new resources and users are brought together for potentially short time periods.

In this paper we outline a novel solution prototyped within the UK JISC Dynamic Virtual Organizations for e-Science Education (DyVOSE) project [5] that, using a basic institutional trust relationship between sites supports single-sign combined with advanced authorization of federated security infrastructures based upon delegation of authority. We explore this infrastructure in an educational setting through a programming assignment set as part of the Grid Computing module part of the advanced MSc at the University of Glasgow.

2. EXISTING GRID SECURITY LIMITATIONS

Grid security is still predominantly based around PKIs to support authentication, i.e. the validation of the identity of a given user requesting access to a given resource. The simplest PKI involves a single Certification Authority (CA) which is trusted by all users and resource providers. With this model, users only accept certificates (signed by the CA which associate the users private key with their public key) and certificate revocation lists issued by this CA. This model makes certificate path analysis easy since there is a single step from a certificate to the CA who issued it.

Other more complex PKI architectures also exist. For example, users may keep a host of trusted CAs. However, issues such as how to tell trustworthy one from untrustworthy one arise. Hierarchical PKIs where there are chains of trust between the CA, sub-ordinate CAs and users may also exist. This model allows limiting the damage caused by compromised subordinate CAs. Thus if a subordinate CA is compromised then only the certificates issued by them (or their subordinate CAs) need to be revoked. Other more complex architectures exist again, such as meshes of

PKIs where trust relationships (webs of trust) are established on a peer-peer basis. This model often requires bridging solutions [12,15] between CAs and results in certificate paths that are harder to establish – potentially containing loops.

The main benefit and reason for the widespread acceptance of PKIs within the Grid community is their support for *single sign-on*. Since all Grid sites in the UK trust the central CA at Rutherford Appleton Laboratories (RAL) [23], a user in possession of an X.509 certificate issued by this CA can send jobs to all sites, or rather to all sites where a user has requested and been granted access. Typically with Globus based solutions gatekeepers are used to ensure that signed Grid requests are valid, i.e. from known collaborators. This is manifest through the Distinguished Name (DN) of the requestor being in a locally managed access control list (ACL) grid *mapfile* which typically maps DNs to local user accounts. These ACLs are typically manually updated and managed based upon individual user requests. The dynamicity of this manual approach is not conducive to the Grid-idea for dynamically establishing new, potentially short term VOs. Instead users have to statically have their DNs registered at collaborating sites which have previously made available/allocated local accounts. Once the Grid scales to the wider research and academic communities (as opposed to the current focus on the "Grid" community) where many millions of users[1] exist this centralized model of certification is likely to have scalability issues.

The process of acquiring an X509 certificate itself is off-putting for many of the less-IT focused research community since it requires them to convert the certificate to appropriate formats understandable by Grid middleware, e.g. through running cryptic (in the confusing sense!) *openssl* commands [13]. This problem is further exacerbated since *openssl* is not commonly available on platforms such as Windows and requires separate software to be installed. Once in the appropriate Grid format, users are then obliged to remember necessarily strong 16-character passwords for their certificates with the recommendation to use upper and lower case alphanumeric characters. The temptation to write down such passwords is apparent and an immediate and obvious potential security weakness.

The fundamental issue with PKIs for Grid security however, is trust. Sites trust their users, the CA and other sites. If the trust between any of these is broken, then the impact can be severe, especially since users are currently free to compile and run arbitrary code. With the now global PKI and associated recognition of international CAs through efforts such as the International Global Trust Federation (www.gridpma.com), this basic trust model is naïve. For this reason, Grids have been seen as at best something to be considered separately from existing compute infrastructures or at worst as a potential threat to those infrastructures.

3. SINGLE SIGN ON AND ADVANCED GRID SECURITY FOR *STATIC* VOs

Numerous technological solutions have been put forward looking towards providing various enhanced Grid security models and solutions such as CAS [14], GSI [9], PERMIS [2] and VOMS [1]. Examples of how these compare to one another is

---

[1] There are currently over 3 million Athens accounts across UK academia from over 2,000 organizations. To put this into context there are approximately 3500 UK e-Science certificates issued by the UK e-Science CA that are currently valid across the UK.

described in [21]. Recent developments in Grid standardization [8] and associated implementations [3] have shown, however, how finer grained models of security can be achieved supporting authorization closely integrated with Grid solutions.

Role Based Access Control (RBAC) based solutions represent one of the more scalable solutions for advanced authorization infrastructures [permis]. Such systems allow for definition of roles which are typically associated with given privileges on a system and as such, are less susceptible to change than individual user identities. The roles themselves are assigned to subjects (users) by issuing them with an X.509 attribute certificate (AC) [2]. These roles and ACs can in turn be used to form the security policies for a given site. Systems such as PERMIS allow for the expression of digitally signed (and hence tamper proof) security policies based upon triplets comprised of *<Role, Target, Action>*. A local authority – the Source of Authority (SoA) will specify policies based upon institutional roles, institutional resources (targets) and actions that can be performed on those resources. Once defined, these policies can be used to ensure that only users with appropriate roles (privileges) can access certain services or data resources and perform certain actions. It has been shown [22] how such infrastructures can be defined and used as the basis for limiting access to Grid resources and data sets. Such systems predominantly work at the local authorization level, i.e. the policies apply to the local site only. With Grid based inter-institutional VOs this model of security is not the norm and collective understanding of inter-institutional security infrastructures is needed.

Supporting multiple attribute authorities is something that the Internet2 community has focused on explicitly in the Shibboleth architecture and protocols [18,19]. The UK academic community is currently in the process of deploying Shibboleth technologies (http://shibboleth.internet2.edu/) to support local (existing) methods of authentication for remote login to resources. Through this model, sites are expected to trust remote security infrastructures for example in establishing the identity of users (authentication) and their associated privileges (authorization). To support this, the Shibboleth architecture and associated protocols identify several key components that should be supported including federations, Identity Providers (aka origins), Service Providers (aka targets) and optionally Where Are You From (WAYF) services. Through these components, end users will have single usernames and passwords from their home institutions which will provide for seamless access to a range of resources at collaborating institutions and service providers. Local security policies at service provider sites can then be used to restrict (authorize) what resources authenticated users are allowed access to.

To understand the impact of Shibboleth technologies on Grid security it is first necessary to have an appreciation of the interactions that typically arise with Shibboleth. When a user attempts to access a Shibboleth protected service or Service Provider (SP) more generally, they are typically redirected to a WAYF server that asks the user to pick their home Identity Provider (IdP) from a list of known and trusted sites. The service provider site has a *pre-established trust relationship* with each home site, and trusts the home site to authenticate its users properly.

After the user has picked their home site, their browser is redirected to their site's authentication server, e.g. an LDAP repository, and the user is invited to log in. After successful authentication, the home site redirects the user back to the SP and the message carries a digitally signed SAML [17] authentication assertion message from the home site, asserting that the user has been successfully authenticated (or not!) by a particular means. The actual authentication mechanism used is specific to the IdP. If the digital signature on the SAML authentication assertion is verified and the user has successfully authenticated themselves at their home site, then the SP has a trusted message providing it with a temporary pseudonym for the user (the handle), the location of the attribute authority at the IdP site and the service provider URL that the user was previously trying to access. The resource site then returns the handle to the IdP's attribute authority in a SAML attribute query message and is returned a signed SAML attribute assertion message. The Shibboleth trust model is that the target site trusts the IdP to manage each user's attributes correctly, in whatever way it wishes. So the returned SAML attribute assertion message, digitally signed by the origin, provides proof to the target that the authenticated user does have these attributes. We note that later versions of the Shibboleth specification have introduced a performance improvement over the earlier versions, by allowing the initial digitally signed SAML message to contain the user's attributes as well as the authentication assertion. Thus the two stages of authentication and attribute retrieval can be combined.

This security model offers several direct benefits over PKIs for dynamic establishment of VOs in that users are no longer trusted to manage their X509 certificates and remember complex passwords. Instead institutions within a federation have a degree of trust with one another. Sites/IdPs and SPs are still autonomous and are able to decide for themselves whether the provided attributes are sufficient for access to the resources and which attributes they are prepared to release to which SP. Another key benefit of Shibboleth for VO establishment and management is that users are only required to remember their own usernames and passwords at their home institutions.

Provided a common understanding of the roles and security attributes across the sites comprising the federation exists, single sign on can be achieved. Thus if a SP trusts a given site for authenticating a user requesting access to its own resource, and also an agreement on the attributes which are to be exchanged between the sites exists, then the SP can authorize/restrict access to its resources from those sites that are within the correct federation and that provide the necessary attributes and their values needed to give access to the resource. Within the UK a single federation is being proposed (www.sdss.ac.uk) and a small set of security attributes based upon a subset of the eduPerson specification is being adopted [16]. These attributes include *eduPersonScopedAffiliation* which indicates the user's relationship (e.g., staff, student, etc.) within their home institution; *eduPersonTargetedID* which is needed when an SP is presented with an anonymous assertion only as provided by *eduPersonScopedAffiliation*; *eduPersonTargetedID* attribute which provides a persistent user pseudonym; *eduPersonPrincipalName* which is used where a persistent user identifier, consistent across different services is needed, and *eduPersonEntitlement* which enables an institution to assert that a user satisfies an additional set of specific conditions that apply for access to a particular resource. A user may possess different values of the *eduPersonEntitlement* attribute relevant to different resources.

One key aspect of the UK federation which helps to support single sign-on across numerous resources is the facility to maintain session information. Thus in accessing their IdP, the user is able to specify whether the WAYF should remember them for the duration of the session, for a week or not at all. In accessing subsequent

Shibboleth protected services, the WAYF will automatically recognize which IdP the users are from and redirect them accordingly.

Proof of concept systems demonstrating how Shibboleth based access to Grid resources has been achieved is described in [25]. However Shibboleth by its very nature is much more static than the true vision of the Grid, where VOs can be dynamically established linking disparate computational and data resources at run time. Instead Shibboleth requires agreed sets of attributes that have been negotiated between sites. What is needed instead is a more dynamic way in which security attributes associated with a VO can be established and accepted across a given federation.

4. SINGLE SIGN-ON AND ADVANCED GRID SECURITY FOR *DYNAMIC* VOs

The definition of detailed policies for access to and usage of multiple site resources will face scalability issues for large scale Grid infrastructures where many different users, services and resources exist. This is further compounded when new users join, leave, new resources are added and removed etc. Having a single SoA to manage a security infrastructure at a given site is not realistic for large scale, evolving Grid infrastructures. Ideally, it should be possible to *delegate* the privilege for others including potentially those at other trusted sites to issue ACs which will be recognized locally. This is especially the case when complex or short lived dynamic VOs are to be established and managed. To address this, the DyVOSE project has prototyped a delegation issuing service (DIS) [3] as shown in Figure 1.

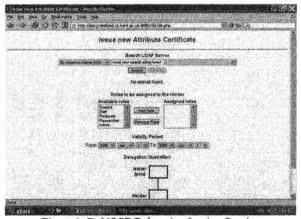

Figure 1: DyVOSE Delegation Issuing Service

The DIS is a web service that can issue ACs on behalf of a SoA. In a traditional PMI model a SoA that issues roles or privileges to users must have a PKI key pair. This restriction implies that the SoA is responsible for all privilege allocations within at its own site. Ideally a SoA, e.g. a systems-administrator, would like to be able to delegate the privilege to issue new roles to other trusted entities/people, e.g. to a local researcher wishing to establish a particular VO, or potentially to a remote but trusted entity. The DIS service itself does not require that delegated/trusted entities are required to hold a PKI key pair in order to issue ACs to their subordinates however the SoA will by definition restrict the roles that its subordinate authority will be able to issue. The DIS service also allows delegated entities to also delegate privileges to others. To minimize the potential security risks that might arise through this, subordinate authorities will always have lower privilege than their superiors.

Through the delegation of authority capabilities offered by the DIS service, sites wishing to establish VOs dynamically are able to create attribute certificates associated with the particular demands of the give VO. Once defined, users wishing to access resources across multiple institutions are able to use the single sign-on capabilities of Shibboleth to authenticate themselves at their home site, and have these attributes (which have been dynamically created) to be used by SPs to make subsequent authorization decisions. Through this, dynamic VOs can be established where fine grained authorization policies are created based upon attributes specific to the security of the VO and created by privileged members of the VO. Subsequent access to Grid resources across the VO can, through Shibboleth, be based upon the appropriate attributes being defined and subsequently delivered for authorization decisions to be made to VO resources.

To explore the capabilities of the DIS service for dynamic attribute creation and their usage for subsequent single sign-on through Shibboleth to access and use dynamically established VO resources, we have explored this technology within the advanced MSc Grid Computing module at the University of Glasgow.

4.1 Case Study

The Grid Computing module at the University of Glasgow required the advanced MSc students to undertake a large scale programming assignment. This assignment was focused on exploring latest developments in Grid middleware such as Globus and Condor [4], and exploring fine grained security infrastructures. Specifically, the students were required to implement a Globus-based bioinformatics application (BLAST) which was to run across a Condor pool. The application required them, in the first instance to develop a client to access a remote Grid service (*BlastData*) in Edinburgh University which was protected by the PERMIS authorization infrastructure and return the appropriate sequence data. This service and the associated security policy was developed and deployed in advance for the students. The students were split into two groups: *groupA* and *groupB*. These groupings (roles) were then used by the *BlastData* service and its security infrastructure to enforce/restrict access to the data accessible. The data itself was nucleotide or protein sequence data sets depending on the role (group) the students were in.

Once the data was returned the students were expected to use this as input to their own Globus based BLAST service which would run across the Condor pool. This service was also PERMIS protected with the policy such that only members of their team could invoke the service, i.e. people with their role. Diagrammatically the assignment and associated infrastructure is given in Figure 2.

In the infrastructure the *Glasgow SoA* used the Edinburgh DIS service to issue attributes within the Edinburgh PMI for roles needed across the VO, i.e. they were delegated the privilege by the *Edinburgh SoA* to create roles within the Edinburgh role hierarchy. Through creation of a VO specific role, e.g. *externalStudent* within the Edinburgh policy via DIS and mapping of the DNs of Glasgow students to this role, Glasgow students have subsequently been able to access and return the appropriate sequence data sets for input to the BLAST service. Through the hierarchy of the XML role policy at Edinburgh, any privileges that the external role holds will be inherited by the appropriate roles as deemed suitable by the local Edinburgh SoA, e.g. an *externalStudent* may have less privilege than an *EdinburghStudent* role which already exists within the Edinburgh PMI. This hierarchical management of roles allows distinct levels of trust to be implemented based on a user's function and location within the VO without surrendering local policy integrity. Thus for example, Glasgow students are able to access Edinburgh Grid compute resources but not allowed to print on local printers.

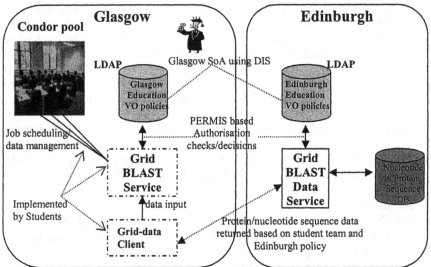

Figure 2: Grid Computing Assignment Utilizing Dynamic AC Creation and Authorization

4.2 Related Work

The Community Authorization Service (CAS) [14] implements a Role Based Access Control system using an authorization server. The central idea behind CAS is that while resource providers can specify a coarse-grained policy, the fine-grained policy decisions can be delegated to the administrator of the community that is served by CAS. Resource providers grant privileges to the community and establish a trust relationship with the representative of that community. That representative then uses CAS to manage the distribution of privileges within the community. When a user wants to access resources served by CAS, the user issues a request to the CAS server (using their own X509 certificate). If the CAS server decides that the user associated with this certificate has sufficient privileges, then it will issue a proxy credential with an embedded policy giving the user the right to perform the requested actions (assuming that the user has sufficient privilege). The user then uses these CAS credentials to access the resource. The local resource than applies its own local policy to determine the amount of access granted. Currently the only resource that can be accessed through CAS credentials is gridFTP. It is non-trivial to set up and use CAS (see www.nesc.ac.uk/hub/projects/etf). The centralized model of an authorization server is also likely to have scalability issues when dynamic VOs are to be established or very large VOs.

Virtual Organization Membership Service (VOMS) [1] is a system for managing authorization data within VOs. VOMS has been developed as part of the European DataGrid project and provides a database of user roles and capabilities and a set of tools for accessing and manipulating the database and using the database contents to generate Grid credentials for users when needed. The VOMS database contains authorisation data that defines specific capabilities and general roles for specific users. A suite of administrative tools allow administrators to assign roles to users and manipulate capability information. A command-line tool allows users to generate a local proxy credential based on the contents of the VOMS database. This credential includes the basic authentication information that standard Grid proxy credentials contain, as well as role and capability information from the VOMS server. One of the benefits of VOMS is that Grid applications can use the credential without using the VOMS data. Alternatively, VOMS-aware applications can use the VOMS data to make both authentication and authorization decisions regarding user requests.

VOMS represents the most common authorization mechanism on the Grid however it does not provide the dynamic establishment of VOs. Instead a VOMS server is statically identified and populated. The approach given here overcomes these limitations. We would also argue that the end user experience of advanced authorization infrastructures is improved through our system. For example, when submitting a Grid job in a VOMS-aware environment, the end user typically is required to include the VO that they are involved in at the command line. With the approach given here, this is implicit through the attributes that are dynamically defined and used with appropriate attribute request and attribute release policies.

5. CONCLUSIONS

The dynamic establishment and subsequent management of VOs represents a significant security challenge to the Grid community (if it is done correctly!), but a challenge that needs to be overcome in order for Grid technology to be taken up by the more security focused communities such as the medical domain, or industry more generally. The dynamic delegation of authority infrastructure supported within the DyVOSE project offers one possibility through which advanced authorization infrastructures can be linked dynamically. Through delegated creation of VO specific roles and attributes, VOs can be established in a dynamic manner without compromising the overall security. At the time of writing the students at Glasgow are in the final phases of their implementation work with the successful return of sequence data already completed based upon dynamically created security attributes – thus proving the proof of concept in using DIS for dynamic VO establishment and fine grained authorization.

To simplify the overall process in access to and usage of VO Grid resources, the Shibboleth technology offers direct benefits for single sign-on, but currently requires a more static view of the security attributes that are available. Through the DIS service, an SP may, subject to its having the appropriate privilege at IdPs be allowed to create attributes for those IdPs which will subsequently be needed for access to the resource. This model significantly changes the dynamics through which future VOs may be composed. Truly dynamic security oriented VOs where service providers not only offer services but the attributes needed for access to these services has hitherto not been addressed by the Grid community. This work is being explored in a variety of security oriented projects at the National e-Science Centre especially in the e-Health domain.

5.1 Acknowledgments

This work was funded from a grant from Joint Information Systems Committee (JISC) in the UK. The authors would like to thank their collaborators in this project in particular Professor David Chadwick and Dr Sassa Otenko at the University of Kent for their work on production of the DIS service.

6. REFERENCES

1. R. Alfieri,et al, Managing Dynamic User Communities in a Grid of Autonomous Resources, CHEP 2003, La Jolla, San Diego, March, 2003;
2. D.W.Chadwick, A. Otenko, The PERMIS X.509 Role Based Privilege Management Infrastructure, Future Generation Computer Systems, 936 (2002) 1–13, December 2002. Elsevier Science BV.
3. D.W. Chadwick, Delegation Issuing Service, NIST 4th Annual PKI Workshop, Gaithersberg, USA, April 2005.
4. Condor project, www.cs.wisc.edu/condor
5. Dynamic Virtual Organisations for e-Science Education, project www.nesc.ac.uk/hub/projects/dyvose
6. eduPerson Specification, http://www.educause.edu/eduperson/
7. I. Foster, C. Kesselman, S. Tuecke, The Anatomy of the Grid: Enabling Scalable Virtual Organizations, International Journal of Supercomputer Applications, 15(3), 2001.
8. Global Grid Forum, (V. Welch, F. Siebenlist, D. Chadwick, S. Meder, L. Pearlman), Use of SAML for OGSA Authorization, June 2004, https://forge.gridforum.org/projects/ogsa-authz
9. Globus Security Infrastructure (GSI), http://www.globus.org/security/
10. Globus toolkit, http://www.globus.org/toolkit/downloads/4.0.1/
11. R. Housley, T. Polk, Planning for PKI: Best Practices Guide for Deploying Public Key Infrastructures, Wiley Computer Publishing, 2001.
12. J. Jokl, J. Basney and M. Humphrey, Experiences using Bridge CAs for Grids, Proceedings of UK Workshop on Grid Security Practice - Oxford, July 2004.
13. OpenSSL, www.openssl.org
14. L Pearlman, et al., A Community Authorisation Service for Group Collaboration, in Proceedings of the IEEE 3rd International Workshop on Policies for Distributed Systems and Networks. 2002.
15. W. T. Polk and N. E. Hastings, Bridge Certification Authorities: Connecting B2B Public Key Infrastructures, http://csrc.nist.gov/pki/documents/B2B-article.doc
16. A. Robiette, T. Morrow, Blueprint for a JISC Production Federation, JISC Development Group, Version 1.1: issued 27 May 2005, http://www.jisc.ac.uk/index.cfm?name=middleware_documents
17. OASIS, Assertions and Protocol for the OASIS Security Assertion Markup Language (SAML) v1.1, 2 September 2003, http://www.oasis-open.org/committees/security/
18. Shibboleth Architecture Technical Overview, http://shibboleth.internet2.edu/docs/draft-mace-shibboleth-tech-overview-latest.pdf
19. Shibboleth Architecture Protocols and Profiles, http://shibboleth.internet2.edu/docs/draft-mace-shibboleth-arch-protocols-latest.pdf
20. R.O. Sinnott, D.W. Chadwick, Experiences of Using the GGF SAML AuthZ Interface, Proceedings of UK e-Science All Hands Meeting, September 2004, Nottingham, England.
21. A.J. Stell, R.O. Sinnott, J. Watt, Comparison of Advanced Authorisation Infrastructures for Grid Computing, Proceedings of International Conference on High Performance Computing Systems and Applications, May 2005, Guelph, Canada.
22. A.J. Stell, Grid Security: An Evaluation of Authorisation Infrastructures for Grid Computing, MSc Dissertation, University of Glasgow, 2004.
23. UK e-Science Certification Authority, www.grid-support.ac.uk/ca
24. J. Watt, R.O. Sinnott, A.J. Stell, Dynamic Privilege Management Infrastructures Utilising Secure Attribute Exchange, Proceedings of UK e-Science All Hands Meeting, Sept. 2005, Nott, England.
25. J. Watt, R.O. Sinnott, O. Ajayi, J. Jiang, J. Koetsier, A Shibboleth-Protected Privilege Management Infrastructure for e-Science Education, Proceedings of 6th IEEE International Symposium on Cluster Computing and the Grid, CCGrid2006, May 2006, Singapore.
26. ITU-T Recommendation X.509 (2001) | ISO/IEC 9594-8: 2001, Information technology – Open Systems Interconnection – Public-Key and Attribute Certificate Frameworks.

59

PRODUCT CENTRIC INTEGRATION: EXPLORING THE IMPACT OF RFID AND AGENT TECHNOLOGY ON SUPPLY CHAIN MANAGEMENT

Jan Holmström* and Kary Främling
Industrial Engineering and Management
Helsinki University of Technology
POB 5500, FI-02015 HUT, FINLAND
Corresponding author: jan.holmstrom@hut.fi

The paper describes innovation action research on discovering RFID and agent applications that enable a move to simpler integrating mechanisms in the supply chain. The potential solution designs uncovered in the study simplify the information chain and reduce the need for management interventions in the organization and operation of customized delivery of products and services. The paper also illustrates how the adoption of novel technological tools does not automatically translate to performance improvements but requires step-wise exploration to develop and introduce the novel technologies in practice.

1. INTRODUCTION

Recently, automatic identification (such as RFID) and Internet applications have started to change the premises that underpin how inventory is managed in business firms. Real-time tracking over the Internet can be used to keep track of inventory in locations managed by other firms (Kärkkäinen et al., 2005). In a specific location the control and the ownership of materials may be in the hands of a number of different firms, each running their own inventory management solutions. The most obvious example is Vendor Managed Inventory where several suppliers may share the responsibility for inventory control in the warehouse of a distributor (see e.g. Holmström, 1998).

The implication on supply chain management (SCM) theory of real-time tracking and distributed responsibility is the need to revise the view that managing flows is the core of SCM. Currently SCM is widely defined as the management of material and information flows between actors linked to locations (Lummus and Vokurka, 1999; Mentzer et al, 2001). Real-time tracking is the basis for developing innovative supply chain solutions that are different from the flow oriented solutions that we have become used to, and even take for granted. Instead of monitoring and controlling material movements and the flows of material and information between predefined locations, supply chain management may also be conceived as customizing the movement of product and control information, individual shipments, end-products, and composite parts in a network of service providers (see e.g. Kärkkäinen et al., 2003; Främling et al., 2005).

This paper reports on an innovation action research study (Kaplan, 1998) that explores the consequences of RFID and real-time tracking on supply chain

Please use the following format when citing this chapter:

Holmström, J., Främling, K., 2006, in IFIP International Federation for Information Processing, Volume 224, Network-Centric Collaboration and Supporting Fireworks, eds. Camarinha-Matos, L., Afsarmanesh, H., Ollus, M., (Boston: Springer), pp. 565–572.

management practice and theory and which resulted in the above re-conceptualization of supply chain management. The research contributes to the theoretical understanding of supply chain management, inter-organizational information systems, and extended enterprises, all of which are topics that Handfield and Melnyk (1998) considered to be in the early theory building stage, and in need of explorative and descriptive research. The research also attempts to relate a mature theory, inventory theory (Silver et al., 1998), to supply chain management and inter-organizational information systems in a novel way.

2. METHODOLOGY OF INNOVATION ACTION RESEARCH

This paper explores the significance of tracking and RFID on SCM theory. The concepts and solution designs underpinning the theoretical analysis have been actively developed since the beginning of the year 2000. The goal of the research was in the beginning to evaluate and understand the theoretical impact of RFID on SCM, and was later refocused on tracking.

The research reported in this paper uses the innovation action approach (Kaplan, 1998). In an innovation action study the emergent relationship between phenomena, models, and theory has to be described. This is necessary because we are dealing with emergent phenomena. First there may be nothing, then there is just an idea, and in the end there are a multitude of phenomena, models, and explaining theory. The entities are treated as independent artefacts, that each can be improved and developed based on observed problems and improvements in the other entities.

The emergent nature of innovation action research is described in figure 1. The first idea of a novel solution leads through implementation of the design to the creation of new artificial phenomena. These phenomena are both intended and unintended consequences of the design (Popper, 1963, p. 461).

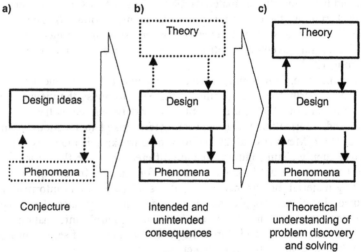

Figure 1 – Innovation action research studies phenomena that may not yet exist

The intended consequences are fulfilled design goals while the unintended often are new problems that need to be resolved. The last step is a theoretical understanding of the emergent phenomena, how they were created, and how to proceed in theory building as well as practical problem solving. This epistemology is consistent with McKelvey's semantic conception (2002), Popper's objective knowledge (1972), and Newell's knowledge levels (1981). It is also consistent with Handfield and Melnyk's (1998) description of theory building in operations management progressing from description and discovery to relationship building and theory refinement.

The first step in an innovation action study is difficult to describe and report. In order to make the base case development more transparent technical norms (Niiniluoto, 1993) are used in this paper. The technical norm is a statement describing what should or should not be done in a situation to achieve some specific goal, i.e. "If you want A, and you believe that you are in a situation B, then you ought to do X.". Account based inventory management that was discussed in the introduction can also be described as a technical norm. For example, it is the solution that should used to improve the accountability of material movements in situations where the material is kept in locations that can be clearly defined in advance and where responsibilities can be assigned per location.

3. THE CASE EXAMPLE: EXPLORING PRODUCT TRACKING WITH RFID AND SOFTWARE AGENTS

The case concerns the use of RFID and agent technology in logistics. The case is described by using a structure of three main-levels of analysis, with their respective sub-levels, these are:
- RFID and agent technology in logistics management (i.e. phenomena-level in figure 1)
- Problem discovery and solution design (i.e. design-level in figure 1)
- Evaluation and theoretical research (i.e. theory-level in figure 1)

3.1 RFID and agent technology in logistics management

RFID, or radio frequency identification, is a technology that makes it possible to identify physical objects by radio signal. There are two basic types of RFID tags, depending on how the tags transmit the identification information. In passive RFID a reading device activates by induction a radio circuit on the tag that is attached to the object. The activated tag then sends out a signal containing information about the object. In active RFID a transmitter that is attached to the object sends out the identification signal. The advantage with passive RFID is that the tag does not need to have an internal source of energy.

The identification of individual shipments and products is the major challenge that the application of RFID addresses in logistics. Any manual work involved in the identification and customized handling of shipments and individual products leads to a direct trade-off between efficiency and flexibility. In these situations reducing the manual work involved with identification and handling of individual products and parcels directly influences the performance frontier. In the parcel delivery industry companies such as UPS, DHL, and FedEx invest heavily in systems to identify and track parcels. Improvements in identification can be translated into improved handling efficiency and faster and better service. Partially due to better tracking and integrated information systems various expert couriers are able to deliver parcels within 24 hours in any place of the civilized world.

A software agent is an autonomous application in a distributed software architecture. Individual agent applications interact directly without centralized co-ordination. Such applications for logistics management have become feasible in practice with the arrival of the Internet. In logistics management software agents organized in peer-to-peer networks can potentially be used to establish secure, flexible and efficient communication of handling instructions and tracking information over the Internet.

Distributing handling and control information across a network of logistics service providers is the major challenge that agent technology addresses. In complex operational situations, such as production and project management, improvements in identification and peer-to-peer technology make it possible to develop innovative agent applications that reduce the need for management intervention. The performance frontier (Schmenner and Swink, 1998) is directly affected when these applications distribute control information more efficiently, reduce the need for manual integration, and make it easier to customize products and shipments.

3.2 Problem discovery and solution design

When starting the research the focus was on the application of RFID. Agent technology was not yet in the scope of interest. A focused review of industrial trials using RFID found that the potential impact on supply chain management, in addition to more efficient handling, and better integration of customization processes, is that it provides a new mechanism for information sharing and communication (Kärkkäinen and Holmström, 2002). This last point developed into a novel idea that would guide further research efforts by the research team. Product identification in combination with order information linked to the physical product was conceptualized as a tool for communicating important logistics and supply chain management information between companies. The term adopted to describe the idea was product centric supply chain management.

This conceptualization of product centric integration was on its own not a sufficient base case for starting work with industry. To find industrial partners interested to develop the concept a specific and relevant base case was needed. An interesting problem domain where product individuals already were controlled and monitored manually was found in the delivery of expensive equipment to project sites, for example the construction of new industrial plants.

In formulating the new base case the need to track the product individuals across many organisations surfaced and this prompted the researchers' interest in software agents and peer-to-peer systems. Identification and attaching instructions to the product individual was not sufficient in a project delivery environment. The location and movements of the product also needed to be recorded and monitored by project managers. To address this requirement the idea of linking a software agent to the individual product was introduced. It was proposed that the network of actors involved in the product delivery should access and update tracking and control information by referring to the product specific agent. This way a project manager, or other interested party, could follow the progress of a shipment at anytime over the Internet.

In the delivery of a project the project can be represented as an assembly of different services needed by a product individual. This product centric view of project delivery became the basis for formulating a concise base case in the form of a technical norm. Instead of looking at project delivery as a supply chain management problem, the goal for solution design was: "How can automated product identification and product specific software agents be used to improve the handling, customisation and other services needed by product individuals?" The answer is a technical norm (Niiniluoto, 1993) describing how a distributed information system (solution X) can be used to provide the logistics information management services (goal A) needed in project delivery and similar temporary supply networks (situation B).

A paper describing the base case (Kärkkäinen et al., 2003) was completed at the same time as a consortium of industrial companies in the project delivery business was searching for ways to implement material visibility and control in project networks. The product centric concept was this way introduced to the research plan of the industrial consortium. A simple product centric track and trace system was implemented and field tested for large project deliveries. After the first test was finished an open source community was established for the further development of the solution, and to facilitate the adoption of the approach in other application areas (http://dialog.hut.fi). The Dialog Open Source is currently developed further in an EU funded research project within the 6th framework. The objective of the TraSer project is to bring product centric integration within the scope of progressive small and medium sized companies.

The approach was then tested in a company managing a large number of projects. The challenge for the second pilot company was managing expensive inventory in a large number of temporary storage locations. The original simple tracking and tracing functionality was enhanced in the pilot application with better data collection and monitoring features. The researchers could in the pilot see first-hand how product centric tracking could provide inventory monitoring functionality and creating inventory visibility in a changing network of companies.

The base case for product centric integration in project delivery was simplified and generalised based on the pilots and a number of feasibility studies with other industrial partners. The result was a mid-range theory on how to achieve inventory and material visibility in changing logistics networks. The mid-range theory describes a material and inventory visibility solution that focuses on the product individual or shipment. The advantage of this solution is that it is forwarder, or handler independent. This Forwarder Independent Tracking (FIT) approach and descriptions of feasibility analyses and successful pilots in short-term multi-company networks are described in Kärkkäinen et al. (2004).

3.3 Evaluation and theoretical research

Product centric integration across a changing network of participants has so far only been implemented in pilots. Despite the ability to more efficiently collect and distribute logistics management information finding interested industrial partners has been difficult. Even though the basic advantage is becoming clear, i.e. material visibility and improved integration of operations in changing environments, which together provide a basis for innovative and performance enhancing supply chain practices, companies have found it difficult to introduce product centric integration in their operations.

The pilot implementations imply that existing systems and the existing architecture of enterprise systems limit the adoption of product centric integration. The problem is that product centric integration, instead of linking locations and focusing on accountability and transactions between locations, focuses integration efforts on value added operations that individual products in the value-adding network require. Figure 2 is an attempt to illustrate the difference between a conventional transaction driven chain and a product centric supply chain. A conventional chain is based on a a systems design that is focused on location specific material accounts and transactions between locations. This design underpins the familiar supply chain representation that emphasizes the integration of locations and the integrated control of transaction processes. A solution design that tracks and controls individual products independently of the location and the ownership of the product individual underpins product centric integration. This fundamental difference in how the systems are designed and how integration is represented makes it challenging to combine product centric systems with current enterprise systems.

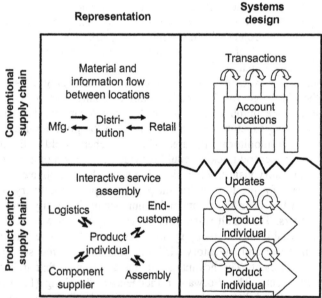

Figure 2 – centric and conventional supply chain management are underpinned by fundamentally different systems designs

The difference between material account and product individual focus requires further elaboration. The conventional supply chain is effective when well-defined standard goods are produced and can be delivered based on simple order and delivery transactions. For ordering and delivering more complex products advanced integrating mechanisms such as projects are needed. However, shifting to product centric integration makes explicit the role of the product as the co-ordinating entity in the delivery of customized products and many value added services (Callon et al, 2002). In a network of actors the recognition of the product as an integrating mechanism opens up opportunities to reduce the need for project management and a priori agreed handling and processing rules. In a product centric operation the service provider can refer to definitions linked to the product individual in many situations that before would have required human intervention and prior agreement. This way it is possible to move towards simpler integrating mechanisms and ad hoc integration (Galbraith, 1972).

Thus, the problem discovery and solution design described in the case can be understood as a finding a novel "virtual integration" mechanism and taking steps that potentially move the performance frontier for logistics operations in a changing environment.

4. DISCUSSION

Product centric integration across a changing network of participants has been implemented in two pilots. Despite a proven ability to more efficiently collect and distribute logistics management information finding industrial partners willing to invest in developing the pilots further is difficult. Even though the basic advantage is becoming clear, i.e. material visibility and improved integration of operations in changing environments, which together provide a basis for innovative and performance enhancing supply chain practices, companies find it difficult to introduce product centric integration in their operations.

The pilot implementations imply that existing systems and the existing architecture of enterprise systems limit the adoption of product centric integration. The problem is that product centric integration, instead of linking locations and focusing on accountability and transactions between locations, focuses integration efforts on the value added operations that individual products in the value-adding network require. A conventional chain is based on a systems design that is focused on location specific material accounts and transactions between locations. This design underpins the familiar supply chain representation that emphasizes the integration of locations and the integrated control of transaction processes. A solution design that tracks and controls individual products independently of the location and the ownership of the product individual underpins product centric integration. This fundamental difference in how the systems are designed and how integration is represented makes it challenging to combine product centric systems with current enterprise systems.

A fundamental theoretical benefit of the discovered alternative is that it is more loosely coupled (Gamma et al., 1995) to locations. Shifting to product centric solutions makes explicit the role of the product as the co-ordinating entity in a network of actors, and reduces the need for mutually agreed definitions of product states. It is a new alternative integrating mechanism that can be added to the list of already commonly used devices from the theory of organization design (Galbraith, 1972), and which links supply chain management to the economic theory of qualities (Callon et al., 2002).

Product centric integration should be considered in situations where the objective of the supply chain is project delivery, the value of items is high and have a complex lifecycle, or in general in situations where products and items require differentiated coordination. The implication of the research presented in this paper is that both operations managers and operations management scholars need to be aware of the product centric alternative, especially in demanding environments.

5. ACKNOWLEDGEMENTS

The authors wish to thank the Academy of Finland and TEKES (The Finnish Funding Agency for Technology and Innovation) for the grants that supported the explorative phase of our research and the European Commission for funding further development and exploitation in the TraSer project.

6. REFERENCES

1. Callon, M. , Méadel, C., and Rabeharisoa, V. ,2002. "The economy of qualities", Economy and Society, Vol 31, No 2, pp. 194-217.
2. Främling, K., Ala-Risku, T., Kärkkäinen, M., Holmström, J., 2005. "Design Patterns for Managing Product Lifecycle Information", forthcoming in Communications of the ACM
3. Galbraith, J. , 1972, Organization Design: An information processing view. In Jay W. Lorsch & Paul R. Lawrence (Eds.), Organization planning: Cases and concepts. Homewood, Ill.: Irwin, 1972, pp. 49-72
4. Gamma, E., Helm, R., Johnson, R., Vlissides, J., 1995, "Design Patterns", Addison-Wesley Professional Computing Series, Reading, Massachusetts, USA, pp.395.
5. Handfield, R., & Melnyk, S., 1998. "The Scientific theory-building process: a primer using the case of TQM", Journal of Operations Management, 16(4), p. 321-339.
6. Holmström, J., 1998. "Business Process Innovation in the Supply Chain - A Case Study of Implementing Vendor Managed Inventory", European Journal of Purchasing and Supply Management, Vol. 4. No. 2/3, pp. 127-131
7. Kaplan, R. S., 1998. "Innovation Action research: Creating New Management Theory and Practice." Journal of Management Accounting Research, vol 10, pp.89 –118
8. Kärkkäinen, M., Holmström, J., 2002. "Wireless product identification: Enabler for handling efficiency, customisation, and information sharing." Supply Chain Management: An International Journal, vol. 7, no. 4, pp. 242-252
9. Kärkkäinen, M., Ala-Risku, T., Främling, K., 2003. "The product centric approach: a solution to supply network information management problems?" Computers in Industry, vol. 52, no. 2, pp. 147-159.
10. Kärkkäinen, M., Ala-Risku, T., and Främling, K., 2004. "Efficient tracking in short-term multi-company networks", International Journal of Physical Distribution & Logistics Management, Vol. 34, No. 7., pp. 545 – 564
11. Kärkkäinen, M., Ala-Risku, T., Främling, K., and Collin, J., 2005. "Establishing inventory transparency to temporary storage locations – A case from the mobile telecommunications industry", IFIP 5.7 Advances in Production Management Systems – conference (APMS 2005), Rockville, Maryland, the USA, September 19-21, 2005
12. Lummus, R. and Vokurka R., 1999. "Defining supply chain management: a historical perspective and practical guidelines", Industrial Management & Data Systems, Vol. 99 Issue 1, pp11-18
13. McKelvey, B., 2002, Model-Centered Organization Science Epistemology. In J. Baum (Ed.), Companion to Organizations (pp. 752-780)
14. Mentzer, J., DeWitt, W., Keebler, J.; Soonhoong M.; Nix, N.; Smith, C., and Zacharia, Z., 2001. "Defining Supply Chain Management", Journal of Business Logistics, 2001, Vol. 22 Issue 2, pp 1-25.
15. Newell, A., 1982, "The knowledge level", Artificial Intelligence, vol. 18, pp. 87-127
16. Niiniluoto, I., 1993. "The Aim and Structure of Applied Research", Erkenntnis, Vol. 38, pp 1-21
17. Popper, K., 1963. "Conjectures and refutations – The Growth of Scientific Knowledge." First published by Routeldege & Kegan Paul in 1963, Routeledge Classics edition 2002, London, UK
18. Popper, Karl, 1972. "Objective Knowledge – An Evolutionary Approach", Clarendon Press, Oxford, UK, Revised edition, 1979
19. Schmenner R. W. ja M. L. Swink, 1998. "On Theory in Operations Management", Journal of Operations Management, vol. 17 no. 1, pp. 97–113.
20. Silver, E., Pyke, D., and Peterson, R., 1998. "Inventory Management and Production Planning and Scheduling", John Wiley & Sons, New York, 3rd edition.

60

GOVERNMENT-WIDE WORKFLOW INFRASTRUCTURE - ENABLING VIRTUAL GOVERNMENT ORGANIZATIONS[1]

Olumide Oteniya, Tomasz Janowski, Adegboyega Ojo[2]

The United Nations University
International Institute for Software Technology
(UNU-IIST), MACAU
{gab,tj,ao}@iist.unu.edu

Many governments worldwide are establishing one-stop portals to provide access to various public services based on the needs of citizens or businesses and not the internal structure of the government. A critical support for such one-stop portals is a workflow infrastructure, supporting the matching of the needs against provided services and coordination of the implementing processes, often spanning several government agencies. This paper describes a generic workflow infrastructure for one-stop government – GovWF. GovWF supports the operations of a Virtual Government Organization – a hierarchy of agencies providing collectively a set of public services, while offering a uniform one-agency view to its customers. Conceptual and formal models are provided to rigorously describe the operations of GovWF. We describe how GovWF is implemented and also present a case study for illustration.

1. INTRODUCTION

e-Government is one of defining features of modern public administration (PA). Traditionally, e-Government efforts are targeted at improving internal efficiency in the delivery of public services, with back-office integration as the holy-grail. Lately, there has been significant shift in focus from the supply-side of public service delivery to the demand-side. This is largely due to the poor take-up of online public services. Addressing this problem requires an organizational model which simplifies the highly fragmented view of the public sector consisting of delineated agencies and possibly some private organizations providing public services (Kubicek, 2000).

Government customers, like their private sector counterparts, are demanding better services. In response, governments are adopting new practices, policies and technologies. One-stop government is one of the dominant practices for integrating public services across agencies from stakeholders' viewpoint (Wimmer 2001). A one-stop government portal organizes public services into life events or business episodes targeted at specific customers at particular times in their life.

---

[1] This work is funded by Macao Foundation under the e-Macao project.

[2] On leave of absence from the University of Lagos, Nigeria.

Please use the following format when citing this chapter:

Oteniya, O., Janowski, T., Ojo, A., 2006, in IFIP International Federation for Information Processing, Volume 224, Network-Centric Collaboration and Supporting Fireworks, eds. Camarinha-Matos, L., Afsarmanesh, H., Ollus, M., (Boston: Springer), pp. 573–580.

We consider a one-stop government providing seamless services as a virtual government organization (VGO). Each instance of request by a customer leads to a dynamic selection of VGO members forming an alliance to collectively satisfy the business process associated with the request. Dynamic service composition is the enabling technology for service invocation and execution within the VGO.

This paper describes a workflow infrastructure (GovWF) which coordinates service provisioning within a VGO. It dynamically binds concrete services provided by agencies to business process schemas based on user requests and other constraints, e.g. government policies. GovWF also executes business processes and propagates service outcomes to the relevant agencies to ensure internal consistency.

The rest of the paper is as follows. The notion of a VGO is defined in Section 2. Section 3 presents the workflow infrastructure for VGOs - GovWF, from concepts (Section 3.1), to formalization (Section 3.2), to implementation (Section 3.3). A case study illustrating the working of GovWF - requesting a license to open a restaurant business is presented in Section 4. The final Section 5 presents some conclusions.

2. VIRTUAL GOVERNMENT ORGANISATION

A Virtual Organization (VO) is a network of independent organizations which collaborate based on some common goal and share some resources on the basis of some policies to accomplish their goal (Witczynski et 2000). Virtual organizations are goal-oriented and dynamic in nature. The key concept underpinning VOs is the separation of functional goals and the means of satisfying them. A VO is characterized by (Mowshowitz, 1997): (1) formulation of abstract requirements, (2) analysis of concrete satisfiers and (3) assignment of satisfiers to requirements.

While a number of successful models of VOs exist in the private sector, there are only a few such examples in the public sector. The notion of VO in the public sector or VGO (and same as Virtual Government) underpins seamless or integrated public service delivery (Zhiyuan Fang 2002). A VGO typically consists of a group of government agencies and possibly some private enterprises, cooperatively providing public services on behalf of the government. These agencies may themselves consist of several departments or units that could be seen as agencies on their own.

We assume that only service specifications and process handles are published by the agencies in the VGO. Service implementation details are always hidden. To request for a service from a VGO, a customer describes its need through a service specification, if a service to fulfill the need is unknown, or through a process handle, if known. In the former case, an intermediation infrastructure is required to match the specified needs against the services provided by the agencies (Legal 2002). In the latter case, the requested process is initiated within respective agencies. In both cases, coordination of the implementing processes is necessary. A workflow infrastructure is typically used for such coordination.

3. WORKFLOW INFRASTRUCTURE FOR VGOs

We describe here a workflow infrastructure for orchestrating and coordinating services across agency boundaries - GovWF. The concepts, model and implementation of this infrastructure is described.

3.1 Concepts

The one-stop-government is synonymous with our concept of a VGO. A government portal organizes services by different agencies in a user-oriented way, according to the life events or business episodes. Each service includes a specification describing what it has to offer and a sequence of execution steps - sub-services or sub-process. Both can refer to the agency's own services/processes or to the services/processes offered by other agencies. Given a service request, the selected agency's catalogue is searched for the process which matches the specification of the requested sub-service. In general, an agency may consist of several sub-agencies and be part of a super-agency. It may invoke functions of both sub- and super-agencies; see Figure 1.

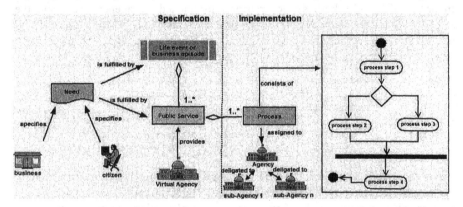

Figure 1: Workflow Infrastructure for VGOs - Conceptual Model

The workflow component GovWF connects the users and providers of services. It receives service/process requests, invokes processes at the agencies and coordinates cross-agency executions. Figure 2 depicts the sequence of interactions between a user, GovWF and agencies, taking place between requesting and receiving a service.

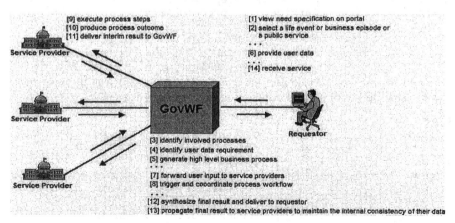

Figure 2: Workflow Infrastructure for VGOs - Usage Scenario

3.2 Formal Model

The aim of this section is to present a fragment of the formal model for GovWF, divided into Services, Agencies and Service Execution sub-sections.

3.2.1 Services

First, we introduce the abstract type to represent names in the model.

```
type              value
   Name              this, super, default: Name
```

In order to describe both service requests formulated by agency users and the services offered by individual agencies, and allow matching of the requested and offered services, we introduce the abstract type Service, function sat to compare services (reflexive, anti-symmetric and transitive) and the weakest service for sat.

```
type              value
   Service            sat: Service >< Service -> Bool
value             axiom all s, s', s'': Service :-
   weakest:           (sat(s, s)) /\
   Service            (sat(s, s') /\ sat(s', s) => s = s') /\
                      (sat(s, s') /\ sat(s', s'') => sat(s, s''))
```

A process is defined through the type Process and two functions: spec returning the service delivered by the process and impl returning the steps executed by the process. There are two kinds of steps: invocation of another process by name and invocation of a service by executing any process satisfying the service according to spec. In both cases, a provider is specified and can be: this – the current agency, super – the supervising agency, or sub – one of sub-agencies given by name.

```
type                            type
   Process                         Steps = Step-list,
value                              Step ==
   spec: Process -> Service,          process(Provider, Name) |
   impl: Process -> Steps             service(Provider, Service),
                                   Provider ==
                                      this | super | sub(Name)
```

For any process, we can calculate the execution context, which is the map from agency names to sets of process names executed within these agencies.

```
type                            value
   Context =                       context: Step -> Context
      Name -m-> Name-set           context(sp) is
value                                case sp of
   name: Provider -> Name               process(p,n) -> [name(p)+>{n}],
   name(p) is                           service(p,s) -> [name(p)+>{}]
      case p of                      end,
         this -> this,            context: Steps -> Context,
         super -> super,          context: Agency -> Context
         sub(n) -> n
      end
```

3.2.2 Agencies

Two more types introduced are Agency to represent the behavior and structure of agencies, and State to represent the agencies' internal state. For a given agency we can obtain its: state (function state), set of currently executing process instances (load), set of all offered processes with unique names (catalogue), state transitions for all atomic processes (operations), and all sub-agencies of the agency with unique names assigned to each of them.

```
type          value
  State,        state: Agency -> State,
  Agency        load: Agency -> (Name -m-> Steps-list),
              catalogue:  Agency -> (Name -m-> Process),
              operations: Agency -> (Name -m-> State -> State),
              structure:  Agency -> (Name -m-> Agency)
```

Several axioms are defined to constrain this definition. Among them are:

1) Every internal process invoked by an agency is defined in its catalogue.

```
axiom[internal_processes_exist] all a: Agency :-
   this isin dom context(a) =>
   context(a)(this) <<= dom catalogue(a),
```

2) Every process in the catalogue with empty implementation represents the agency's internal operation and has the associated state transition.

```
axiom[operations_have_transitions] all a:Agency, n:Name :-
   (n isin dom operations(a)) is
   (n isin dom catalogue(a) /\ impl(catalogue(a)(n)) = <..>)
```

3) Every sub-agency of an agency whose processes or services are invoked through its processes is recorded in the agency's internal structure.

```
axiom[agencies_invoked_exist] all a: Agency :-
   dom context(a) \ {this, super} <<= dom structure(a)
```

4) Every sub-agency process invoked directly through an agency process exists in the catalogue of this sub-agency.

```
axiom[sub_processes_exist] all a: Agency, n: Name :-
   n isin dom context(a) /\ n ~isin {this, super} =>
   context(a)(n) <<= dom catalogue(structure(a)(n))
```

5) Every super-agency process invoked directly through a sub-agency process exists in the catalogue of the agency.

```
axiom[sup_processes_exist] all a: Agency, n: Name :-
   n isin dom structure(a) /\
   super isin dom context(structure(a)(n)) =>
   context(structure(a)(n))(super) <<= dom catalogue(a)
```

3.2.3. Service Execution

After defining agencies, we turn to operations. Invoking an agency process means to insert the instance of the process into the agency's load, provided the process exists.

```
value
  invokeProcess: Name >< Agency -~-> Agency
  invokeProcess(n, a) as a' post
    load(a')(n) = load(a)(n) ^ <.impl(catalogue(a)(n)).> …
  pre n isin dom catalogue(a)
```

Invoking a service means: (i) selecting any process in the agency's catalogue satisfying the specification of this service using sat and (ii) invoking this process.

```
value
  selectProcess: Service >< Agency -> Name
  selectProcess(s, a) as n post
    n isin dom catalogue(a) /\ sat(spec(catalogue(a)(n)), s) …
  invokeService: Service >< Agency -> Agency
  invokeService(s, a) is
    let n = selectProcess(s, a) in invokeProcess(n, a) end
```

After the process is loaded, its execution is carried out. For internal operations, the corresponding state transition is invoked and the process is removed from the load.

```
value
  execOperation: Name >< Nat >< Agency -~-> Agency
  execOperation(n, i, a) as a' post
    state(a') = operations(a)(n)(state(a)) /\
    load(a') = load(a) !! [ n +> remove(load(a)(n), i)] …
  pre … load(a)(n)(i) = <..>
```

For the remaining steps, the nature of the first step of the process is examined. If the step is provided by the current agency, the process/service is invoked as described above. Otherwise, the invocation is carried out within a given sub-agency.

```
value
  execStep: Name >< Nat >< Agency -~-> Agency
  execStep(n, i, a) is
    let s = hd load(a)(n)(i), a' = removeStep(n, i, a) in
      case s of
        process(=this, m)    -> invokeProcess(m, a'),
        process(=sub(n), m)  -> execSubProcess(n, m, a'),
        service(=this, s)    -> invokeService(s, a')
        service(=sub(m), s)  -> execSubService(m, s, a')
      end
    end pre … load(a)(n)(i) ~= <..>
```

3.3 Implementation

The implementation of GovWF consists of five major components as follows:

1) *Client* - receives requests from the portal and hands them over to the Filter component for processing. Client also delivers responses back to the portal.
2) *Filter* – this component is responsible for message transformation and security. It performs specific functions such as validation, logging, encryption, decryption, authentication and others, upon receiving service requests.
3) *Processor* - identifies required processes and generates process steps required for coordination. It also forwards requests to the corresponding service providers through so-called Service Agents, and synthesizes the final outcome. It also triggers the delivery of the final outcome and propagates the necessary side effects to the relevant agencies to ensure internal consistency of the VGO.
4) *Global Service Repository* - provides online data related to service offerings by government to its stakeholders and describes how the services will be invoked.
5) *Local Service Repository* - located at individual agencies, it comprises online data describing the services provided by each agency or service provider.

Service descriptions and data exchange from the portal through GovWF to the various agencies participating in the VGO will be implemented using XML. This is to enable interoperability among government agencies which may store information in proprietary data formats and systems. Governmental Markup Language (GovML) is a potential framework for implementing this functionality (Kavadias, 2003).

4. CASE STUDY

We demonstrate how GovWF supports the operations of a VGO providing services relevant to establishing a restaurant business (see Figure 3). The VGO comprises four agencies: Legal Affairs (A1), Municipal Services (A2), Public Works (A3) and Health (A4). Each agency provides one or two services and the VGO itself offers five services. Each service includes an identifier (e.g. P1), specification (e.g. register) and implementation (e.g. register[A1]). An implementation is a sequence of steps carried out to produce the service. For instance, P2 P3 invokes sequentially the processes P2 and P3, register[A1] invokes any process to satisfy the register service within A1, and internal is done internally.

Suppose the VGO receives a request to open a restaurant business. The request is received as a business episode P1, implemented by a sequence of two processes: P2 (register business) and P3 (issue restaurant license). P2 is implemented by calling the register service of the agency A1, matching exactly the register service of A1. A1 implements this service internally. Process P3 of the VGO requests the restaurant service within the agency A2, which is matching the more general catering service of this agency. This service is implemented by requesting two sequential services inspect and P5 from the VGO itself, identified by "..". The former matches exactly the inspect service, which in turn requests the inspect service from the agency A3, while the latter is the sanitation service, which in turn requests the check service from the agency A4. Both A3 and A4 perform the requested services internally. GovWF supports all interactions in this scenario.

VGO	Business Support Services				VGO	Sub-Agencies
id	spec	impl	description		id	name
P1	-	P2 P3	open restaurant		A1	Legal Affairs
P2	register	register[A1]	register business		A2	Municipal Affairs
P3	issue	restaurant[A2]	issue restaurant license		A3	Public Works
P4	inspect	inspect[A3]	facility inspection		A4	Health
P5	sanitation	check[A4]	sanitation service			

Agency A1 - Legal Affairs				Agency A2 - Municipal Services		
id	spec	impl	desc	id	spec	impl	desc
P1	register	internal	registration	P1	catering	inspect[..]P5[..]	catering

Agency A3 - Public Works				Agency A4 - Health Bureau		
id	spec	impl	desc	id	spec	imp	desc
P1	inspect	internal	inspect	P1	check	internal	check

Figure 3: VGO Case Study – Opening a Restaurant Business

5. CONCLUSIONS

We described the concept of a Virtual Government Organization as a network of public agencies and private organizations involved in the delivery of government services. A VGO separates service specifications and implementations. To facilitate the dynamic matching of user needs against available services and the execution and coordination of cross-agency processes, we presented a workflow infrastructure to underpin VGOs - GovWF. The concepts and operations of GovWF were described informally and formally. A possible implementation was presented with a case study showing how a cross-agency request is handled within the GovWF-enabled VGO.

Following this work, we plan to detail the properties of GovWF and describe the protocols for coordination and monitoring. We are also working on building an implementation of GovWF within the context of an ongoing e-government project.

REFERENCES

1. Abbe Mowshowitz, Virtual Organization, Communications of ACM, Sept 1997, Vol. 40. No 9.
2. Herbert Kubicek, Martin Hagen, One-Stop-Government in Europe, http://www.e-gov.gr/local/ ism-egov/resources-egov/COST%20Project%20-%20One-Stop-Government%20in%20 Europe.pdf, 2000
3. Gregory Kavadias and Efthimios Tambouris, GovML: A Markup Language for Describing Public Services and Life Events, KMGov 2003, 106-115
4. Maciej Witczynski and Adam Pawlak, Virtual Organizations Enabling Net-based Engineering, [online], http://www.ecolleg.org/DISSEMINATION/VO-Dec2000-SUT.pps
5. Maria Legal, Gregoris Mentzas, Dimitris Gouscos and Panagiotis Georgiadis, CB-Business: Cross-Border Business Intermediation through Electronic Seamless Services, Rolland Traunmuller, Kluas Lenk (Eds.), Electronic Government 2002, LNCS 2456, pp. 338-343
6. Maria Wimmer and Johanna Krenner, An Integrated Online One-Stop Government Platform: The eGov Project, IDIMT-2001, Universitatsverlag Trauner, Linz, pp. 329-337, 2001.
7. Zhiyuan Fang, E-Government in Digital Era: Concept, Practice and Development, International Journal of the Computer, The Internet and Management, Vol. 10, No. 2, 2002, pp. 1-22

61

PAST, PRESENT AND FUTURE OF THE ANDALUSIAN AERONAUTICAL CLUSTER

Carmen M. Aguilera[1], Ana Castañeda[2], Fernando Guerrero[3]

[1]*Ingeniería y Soluciones Informáticas (ISOIN), Almirante Apodaca 13, E-41003, Seville, SPAIN, caguilera@isoin.net*
[2]*Ingeniería y Soluciones Informáticas (ISOIN), Almirante Apodaca 13, E-41003, Seville, SPAIN, acastaneda@isoin.net*
[3]*Escuela Superior de Ingenieros, University of Seville, Av. Descubrimientos, s/n E- 41092, Seville, SPAIN, fergue@esi.us.es*

Aeronautic industry in the Andalusian region (Southern Spain) is a highly developed and mature industrial sector. The cluster has established cooperation activities since its origin, evolving to the current Extended Enterprise structure. Activities are coordinated under stable long-term collaboration agreements in the supply chain, mainly under a subcontracting form. The business challenge is to exploit the key skills of the auxiliary companies by promoting joint offers to the main contractors to take on advanced engineering workpackages in the production chain which involve more risks in a more reliable environment.

This paper is focused on ongoing initiatives to drive the evolution of the cluster towards the advanced collaborative paradigm, and consolidate the Spanish aerospace sector on the European market of military transport aircraft.

1 INTRODUCTION

Aerospace production in Andalusia dates back to the 1930s and nowadays the cluster is composed of a few major factories (EADS-CASA, AIRBUS and GAMESA), together with 43 SMEs. Most of them are located in the provinces of Seville and Cadiz. It is being promoted by the Regional Government as a competitive instrument towards the consolidation of the aerospace Spanish sector on the European market of military transport aircraft.

The regional aeronautic industry boasts a splendorous situation with projects that strengthen the importance of Andalusia as one of the country's main aerospace production regions: design and production of 10% of the structural components of the A380 program, final assembly of the Eurofighter, Tiger helicopters assembly, production of the Boeing "737 Dreamliner" radder, together with proprietary aircrafts production. The cluster is focused on the production of components and engineering processes involved in the all-new A400M military aircraft. It will have its first flight from Seville's San Pablo Airport, after being assembled at EADS CASA's factory, the third largest Airbus production plant in the world with an investment of 340M€. Besides

Please use the following format when citing this chapter:

Aguilera, C. M., Castañedo, A., Guerrero, F., 2006, in IFIP International Federation for Information Processing, Volume 224, Network-Centric Collaboration and Supporting Fireworks, eds. Camarinha-Matos, L., Afsarmanesh, H., Ollus, M., (Boston: Springer), pp. 583–590.

the assembly line, the excellence centre in sheet metal production and composites are the key services provided to the aeronautic industry with outstanding potential impact in the global market.

The cluster coordinates their activities under stable long-term collaboration agreements, mainly under a subcontracting form, covering all the processes in the supply chain: engineering, planning, purchases, production, sales, and stock management. They currently operate under an Extended Enterprise model, with common supporting ICT infrastructure, together with methodologies, services, and tools for facilitating the cooperation. The market trends drive the dynamization of the local cluster, by providing attractive business opportunities. In this scenario, the business challenge is to exploit the key skills of the auxiliary companies by promoting joint activities and thus enable them to take on advanced engineering phases in the production chain which involve more risks in a more reliable environment.

This is a key strategy of the Regional Development Agency, which is the local motor of the cluster organisation and infrastructure, providing RTD instruments and funding resources to reinforce the cooperation initiative. This research provides an overview of ongoing projects and planned strategy within the cluster, in order to evolve towards the advanced collaborative paradigm, and thus to improve the competitiveness in the global aeronautic business market.

2   EXISTING THEORIES AND WORK

The factors which drive industry cluster development and growth are a subject of debate in the literature. Competition [Porter 1990] is a driving force behind cluster development, as happened in Silicon Valley. Clustering is a dynamic process, and as one competitive firm grows, it generates demand for other related industries. This, in turn, leads to new business spin-offs, stimulates R&D, and forces the introduction of new skills and services.

Face-to-face interaction is also cited in several of the sources as a critical factor in cluster development [Doeringer, Terkla 1995, Rosenfeld 1997]. Local proximity to firms in all aspects of the production process, such as the suppliers, machine builders, assemblers, distributors, and final customers allows the cooperating firms to adopt new technology and innovations rapidly, therefore increasing the overall efficiency of the production process.

The EC fifth and sixth framework programmes encourage cross-border co-operation. The AeroSME project, a joint activity of ASD (AeroSpace and Defence Industries Association of Europe) and the European Commission, was launched to support the participation of SMEs in the FP5th. It was also designed to facilitate co-operation among SMEs, between SMEs and large companies, and with other aeronautics related bodies in order to improve SMEs position in the supply chain and networking opportunities.

The development of collaborative working models and approaches is emerging as a strategic objective promoted by research programmes at national and European level. Some previous outstanding initiatives supported by the 5th and 6th EC Framework

Program are VOSTER, ALIVE, VIVE, CE-NET. Furthermore, ECOLEAD foresees that in ten years time most enterprises, specially SMEs, will be part of one or more sustainable collaborative networks and is aimed at developing technologies for such collaborative organisations.

In the specific domain of the aeronautical sector, VIVACE project defines methods and deliver processes, tools and systems recommendations which support the integrated operations in the Aeronautical supply chain. This project has produced VIBES (VIVACE Interactive Business Environment Simulator), a tool for investigating the future scenarios concepts that are most relevant to the key players in the industry. VIVACE has defined a Hub vision, specifying how a number of "services" provide collaborative and shared data functionality to a set of partners working together [Farr, 2005].

2.1 Previous cooperation experiences

The first cooperation initiative took place in 1990, when the main Andalusian subcontractors joint together in the "**ATESAER**" association with marketing purposes.

In the period 1994-2000, "**ANDALUCÍA AEROESPACIAL SA**" was constituted as a Virtual Enterprise bringing together public bodies and subcontractors, with the aim of sharing competences and resources in order to access to higher market opportunities in the aeronautical sector otherwise unavailable own due to their limited technical and financial capabilities. The contracts achieved by the built Virtual Organisations with Boeing and Dornier became the rate of 40% of the workload in the sector.

After the disclosure of the previous initiative, in 2002 **HELICE FOUNDATION** and **HELICE.NET** were launched by the Regional Development Agency in Andalusia, with the aim of fostering collaboration activities and improve their competitiveness in the European aeronautic market.

AEROPOLIS is a strategic project from the Regional Government, providing physical infrastructures in 580.000 m^2 to allocate the cluster members in the surrounding area of EADS-CASA in Sevilla.

The **Andalusian Aeronautical Forum** (promoted by the Aeronautic Engineering Association, Engineering University of Seville), brings together these professionals in a heterogeneous community sharing knowledge, experiences, and promoting discussions about the Aeronautic industry in the region.

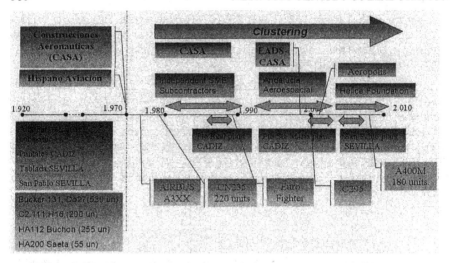

Figure 1. Cooperation history and experiences

2.2   Helice Foundation. Virtual Enterprise in the Andalusian aeronautical sector

The Virtual Breeding Environment (ECOLEAD project) in the Andalusian aeronautic cluster is built on the **Helice Foundation** legal form, a Non Making Profit Corporation owned by **39 entities**, linking aeronautic companies (EADS-CASA and subcontractors), supporting entities (Universities, Research Centres and Regional Government) and strategic partners with the aim to increase process efficiency and business opportunities while fostering innovation in a sustainable structure within the cluster. The motor and infrastructure for Helice Foundation stem from the Regional Development Agency in its initiative to reinforce the collaborative paradigm.

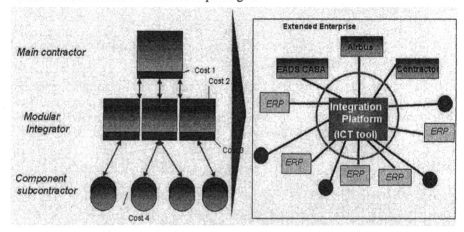

Figure 2: Helice Foundation Structure and challenges

The aim is to organize all the entities related to the aeronautic sector and conduct the activities in the Extended Enterprise under the guidance of the Foundation, providing methodologies, services, and tools for facilitating the cooperation. This structure is aimed at enabling the reduction of times and costs through the integration and synchronization of the processes by providing:

- Common exploitation of complementary resources and capacities.

- Systematic relationships with auxiliary companies

- Creation of a Knowledge Transfer Network

2.3 Helice.net: ICT collaboration infrastructure

HELICE.NET is the ICT infrastructure supporting the collaboration within the cluster and the delivery of supplied parts. The initiative has been launched Helice Foundation and promoted by the Regional Government and EADS-CASA. The solution is built by two main constituent blocks:

- SAPORTAL provides e-services for implementation and monitoring the collaborative operations in the network, from the order to the client delivery.
- SAPECMA is a resource planner enabling companies to integrate and synchronize internal and collaborative process management.

3 RESEARCH APPROACH

The design and implementation of the advanced cooperation scenario is being carried out with the support of European Initiatives (ECOLEAD) and national programs ('Programme for Innovation and Modernisation of Andalusia" (PIMA 2005-2010)0'. The plan is conceived in different conceptual phases, in order to introduce innovative processes and ICT platforms, with the goal of fostering the internationalisation of the regional industry

- **Feasibility study and dimensioning** in order to evaluate specific requirements collected at regional level for the consolidation of the cluster.

- **Cooperation readiness and effectiveness assessment methodologies** an internal pro-active assessment that a company can put itself through, in order to make its capabilities available for companies looking for suitable collaboration partners.

- **Design and implementation of the collaborative framework in the aeronautical cluster**, covering:

  - Legal & Governance Framework: defiinition of mutual responsibilities models between the different actors, to allocate relevant liabilities and to manage the various aspects of the collaborative actions.

- Cooperation management: best practices, methodologies and ICT tools to foster the interoperability within the network.

- Strategy, Business Architecture and Finance: Analysis of collaborative business opportunities and construction of specific models for the Virtual Enterprise. The aim is to enable the internationalization through connection and interoperability with analogue aeronautic clusters around Europe

- **IT & Technical Architecture**: ICT infrastructure enhancement: integration of complementary e-services in the existing platform to provide more integrated Supply Organisation, Product/Services and Processes to the customer (OEM) by improving the efficiency and effectiveness of coordinating the supply network.

- **Pilot case conduction** aimed at implementing the collaborative approach in an industrial context within the cluster, in order to validate the approach, evaluate the effectiveness and benefits of the collaborative paradigm. Feedback and best practice definition for further development and extension to other sectors.

- **Extension of the results** at regional level, by adapting the reference models, ICT solutions and best practices to the identified strategic industrial sectors.

4   FINDINGS

The exploitation strategy aims at overcoming the current demand oligopoly of the main contractors in the region, by promoting the connection and interoperability with analogue European clusters by building a full cooperative paradigm and thus assuming workload in the international market. The majority of auxiliary subcontractors run specific manufacturing activities, but has no organisational, technical and economic structure to assume further phases in the production phase.

The subcontracting strategy is driving towards the horizontal integration of auxiliary SMEs in collaborative networks to carry out process/product innovation to be competitive. Acting in this way, the companies reduce costs duplicity, and take advance of scale economies, in order to gain the needed capacity to face new excellence requirements and the previously identified business goals.

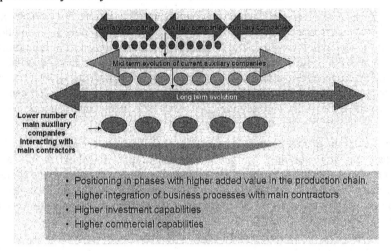

Figure 3. Horizontal SMEs integration

The evolution of existing associations towards a Virtual Enterprise, considered as a single business entity, compounded by companies that share capitals and competences, with dynamic and agile relationships is foreseen as a suitable form of linking companies to enhance the customer's value proposition and timely exploit the European market, otherwise not possible for the individual companies in a profitable manner.

The existing collaboration model and ICT infrastructure, which is already in use, were developed to fulfil the need of the main contractor EADS-CASA, and thus support cooperative processes in the upstream supply chain. At regional level, the adoption of ICT tools, complementary to the existing ERP derived ones, will support the collaboration among the SMEs in the cluster.

On the other hand, the advanced international collaborative scenario that is a reality in the global aerospace industry demands an evolution of this "Extended Enterprise" business case, where the main contractor demands technology and process compliance of the supply chain. When a consortium of distributed international partners (OEMs, integrators, SMEs) work together to produce a product, it will span the multiple participating extended enterprises. It is unlikely that all the partners use the same tools, even if that is the case these tools will be configured differently. The collaborative framework will therefore have to use a flexible collaboration platform to support collaborative practices with disparate tools and technologies.

5 CONCLUSIONS

An advanced collaborative network, providing the preparedness, methodological and ICT framework to foster the horizontal integration of SMEs is considered an effective instrument to consolidate the local industry in the global aerospace market.

Ongoing initiatives are focused on enhancing the cluster infrastructure, with preparedness/measures/enhancement oriented methodological and ICT solutions to support the dynamic management of Virtual Organisations to carry out joint projects at national and European level. This environment should support flexible collaboration between heterogeneous partners and suppliers (and different clusters), over compatible IT infrastructure and processes. The goal of SMEs is to gain the needed capacity to complement their skills and assume joint workload in the international aeronautic market.

The adoption of this cooperative paradigm will have an enormous impact on the regional economy, not only for the aeronautical cluster stakeholders, but also for different strategic industrial sectors. The multiplying effect will promote the adoption of the resulting "Best Practices" to set up clusters of companies, leveraging complementary technologies and capacities of their associates, considering the aeronautic sector as a starting reference.

Acknowledgements

The authors wish to acknowledge the Regional Development Agency of Andalusia and ECOLEAD project for their support.

References

AeroSME. Strategy Paper for Regional Associations. 2002. http://www.aerosme.com/

ALIVE: Advanced Legal Issues in Virtual Organisations. WWW page. http://www.vive-ig.net/projects/alive/

ARICON: Standardised Assessment of Readiness and Interoperability for Cooperation in New Product Development in Virtual Organisations. http://www.aricon.org.

ARIÑO, A. et. al.: Partner Selection and Trust Building in West European-Russian Joint Ventures. A Western Perspective. 1997. International Studies of Management and Organization, Vol. 27 (1): 19-37.

Bifulco, A; Santoro, R; Costanzo, F; Martinelli, M: First Application of a Developing Cooperation Readiness Assessment Methodology within the Aeronautical Value Creation Network. Proceedings of the 11th Internacional Conference on Concurrent Enterprising. June 2005

CE-NET : The Concurrent Enterprising Network of Excellence. WWW page. http://www.ce-net.org/

Das, T.K. Y Teng, B.: Resource and Risk Management in the Strategic Alliance Journal of Management. 1998. 24(1): 21-42.

Doeringer, P.B., and D.G. Terkla: Business strategy and cross-industry clusters. 1995. Economic Development Quarterly. 9: 225-37.

ECOLEAD: European Collaborative networked Organizations LEADership initiative. http://www.ecolead.org.

Farr, Richard; Bramham, Johanna; Er, Mahendrawathi; MacCarthy Bart: Scenario Planning in the Aerospace Business Environment-the VIBES Approach. 2005. Proceedings of the 11th ICE Conference.

Porter, Michael: The Competitive Advantage of Nations. New York: Basic Books, 1990.

Programme for Innovation and Modernisation of Andalusia" (PIMA 2005-2010).

Rosenfeld, Stuart A: Bringing Business Clusters into the Mainstream of Economic Development. 1997. European Planning Studies 5(1): 3-23.

62

KNOWLEDGE MANAGEMENT FOR DYNAMIC AUTOMOTIVE NETWORKS

Sven Thiebus, Ulrich Berger

ThyssenKrupp Presta AG
FL-9492 Eschen, Principality of Liechtenstein
sven.thiebus@thyssenkrupp.com
Chair of Automation Technology, Brandenburg University of Technology Cottbus
Siemens-Halske-Ring 14, 03046 Cottbus, GERMANY
ulrich.berger@tu-cottbus.de

The automotive industry is facing new challenges from increasing product diversification and complexity, decreasing product live cycle times and the permanent need for cost reduction. Car Manufacturers are assigning more and more development tasks and manufacturing orders to suppliers. Suppliers need to create temporary alliances of organizations to share skills, competences and resources. These dynamic automotive networks are facing similar challenges like Dynamic Virtual Organizations (DVO) do.
The ramp-up as linking phase between development phase and manufacturing phase has a crucial role for the success of the network. The whole system has to switch from a development network to a supply chain. The performance of a ramp-up depends on the maturity of the product and the manufacturing process. Knowledge management is an extraordinary driver for both.
Making the relevant knowledge of all enterprises accessible to the members of the network requires more than existing methods and tools in single enterprises could provide. The new approach considers methods and technologies to weave knowledge nets for entire dynamic automotive networks.

1. INTRODUCTION

The current situation in the automotive industry is characterized by increasing requirements from the customer side on quality and individualization of products and upcoming pressure on product prices at the same time. Car manufacturers create new product segments and enrich existing segments with more possibilities for individualization. The product diversification is combined with ongoing reduction of product life cycle times and an acceleration of innovation (Kuhn, Wiendahl, Eversheim, Schuh, 2002).

At the same time the competition between suppliers is turning increasingly to a competition among supplier networks. These networks consist of several independent enterprises, co-operating flexible with a common goal. Each member of this network concentrates on its core competencies in order to develop, manufacture and sell jointly products. They pursue the strategy of extensive outsourcing and act based on a common business comprehensive (Camarinha-Matos, Afsarmanesh,

Please use the following format when citing this chapter:

Thiebus, S., Berger, U., 2006, in IFIP International Federation for Information Processing, Volume 224, Network-Centric Collaboration and Supporting Fireworks, eds. Camarinha-Matos, L., Afsarmanesh, H., Ollus, M., (Boston: Springer), pp. 591–598.

2004). The described dynamic automotive networks have several characteristics of dynamic virtual organizations (DVO), however there is no unified definition for these kinds of organizations.

The dynamic automotive networks are facing new challenges from the increasing number of product launches. Especially the ramp-up is one of the most critical phases of the entire product life cycle in the automotive industry. Generally the product life cycle in the automotive industry comprises the development phase and the serial production phase. The development phase consists of several steps belonging to the main processes of product development and development of the manufacturing process (Wangenheim, 1998). The ramp-up is the linking process between development phase and the subsequent serial production phase. It is a transition phase for each enterprise and even for the entire dynamic automotive network. Before serial production starts only few products e.g. samples and prototypes exist. The ramp-up is characterized by the demand for an increasing production output from the customer side. The whole system has to change from a development network to a supply chain.

Therefore the ramp-up has a crucial role for the financial success of the entire project. Problems in the network could cause extraordinary additional efforts for trouble shooting. Delays in the network could lead to lost sales.

Several research activities pay attention to the importance of the ramp-up for financial success. German research institutes (Kuhn, Wiendahl, Eversheim, Schuh, 2002) identified five levers:

1. Planning, controlling and organization of ramp-up's
2. Robust manufacturing systems
3. Change management during ramp-up phase
4. Models for co-operation and reference
5. Knowledge management and training

Research activities in recent years covered the first four topics widely. Sophisticated project-management tools, reporting systems including escalation paths and early warning indicators provide solutions for planning, controlling, organization and change management. A lot of enterprises developed production systems similar to the Toyota Production System (TPS) with standardization guidelines to achieve robust manufacturing systems. Collaborative Engineering, Supply Chain Management (SCM) and Supplier Relationship Management (SRM) are examples for solutions to issue four. Nevertheless, needs for research concerning knowledge management and training still exist.

In this paper, the concept for knowledge management in a dynamic automotive network is described, in order to provide solutions for the improvement of ramp-up performance.

2. STATE OF THE ART

In order to support and improve the exchange of data and information among enterprises, several technologies and standards are available.

2.1 Data and Information Exchange among Enterprises

For the exchange of geometrical data (e.g. CAD) enterprises use tools based on the interface standards STEP (Standard for the Exchange of Product model data) or IGES (Initial Graphics Exchange Specification). The exchanged data comprises 3D models (solid models, surface models, wire frame models and combination models), drawings and assemblies. The exchange process includes the correction of conversion errors. (PROSTEP, 2006)

For the exchange of data concerning business processes among enterprises (e.g. customer and supplier), EDI (Electronic Data Interchange) or Web-IDE is established. The classical EDI uses protocol standards OFTP (Odette File Transfer Protocol) and EDIFACT (Electronic Data Interchange for Administration, Commerce and Transport) as message type. Typical cases for the use of Web-EDI are internet market places (e.g. SupplyOn).

Concerning quality data the new interface QDX (Quality Data eXchange) is available. QDX bases on XML (eXtensible Markup Language) and provides a neutral standard for data exchange among CAQ–Systems (Computer Aided Quality). QDX supports both preventive activities during product development and corrective activities during serial production (VDA-QMC, 2006).

2.2 Web-based Supplier Relationship Management (SRM)

Nowadays several enterprises of the automotive industry operate communication platforms. They use standards mentioned before for data and information exchange with their partners in the network. In most of the cases the enterprises on the customer site operate communication platforms and define the standards and rules of communication for their suppliers. Most of the communication platforms support one or more of the following processes: Project management, development and assurance, change management, prototype management and purchasing (Gottwald, 2005).

Some of these functions are also offered by neutral service providers such as the operator of internet market places mentioned.

2.3 Failure Mode and Effect Analysis (FMEA) as Knowledge Base

The Failure Mode and Effect Analysis (FMEA) belongs to the standard methods in the automotive sector. It has a certain role for gathering and sharing knowledge especially experience. The FMEA was originally developed for risk analysis but became more and more a knowledge base. In the automotive industry FMEA's usually refer to the guidelines of the German VDA 4.2 (Verband der Automobilindustrie, volume 4 part 2, 1996), the QS-9000 (Quality Systems Requirements) of the AIAG (Automotive Industry Action Group, 1998) or the ISO/TS 16949 (International Organization for Standardization, 2002).

The FMEA is a so-called living document, which goes along with the product and the manufacturing process from the first draft till the end of the product life cycle. All information about problems e.g. during ramp-up or serial production, complaints and revisions are added to the FMEA documents. The development of new product and manufacturing processes uses the FMEA documents of previous similar projects as basis. Suppliers normally provide an insight into the FMEA document for customers.

In practice many companies use special software tools to create and revise these documents. Different tools with different standards make data exchange difficult. The MSR (Manufacturer Supplier Relationship Consortium, 2005), a work group founded by leading German car manufacturers and suppliers, provides an attempt to solve the problem of data exchange. They are developing a Document Type Description (DTD) using the Standard Generalized Mark up Language (SGML) to simplify data exchange.

All concepts are characterized by customer-client-relations from one node of the network to another. There are several highly specialized standards available for the exchange of specific kinds of data and information. Regarding the challenges of distributed information and knowledge in dynamic automotive networks, there is no sufficient solution available. Dynamic automotive networks have to act like a single enterprise, using all the knowledge and experience of its members. Therefore a new approach covering the entire net of enterprises is needed.

3. SCIENTIFIC BASELINE

The theory concerning the cycle of organizational learning (Nonaka, Takeuchi, 1995) distinguishes two kinds of knowledge: Explicit knowledge is knowledge that easily can be formalized and visualized. It is easy to transfer that knowledge (e.g. specific "if-then-rules"). On the other hand tacit knowledge comprises all abilities and skills that are hardly or not at all describable by the knowledgeable person (Schulze, 2004). According to the theory there is an ongoing conversion from explicit to tacit and from tacit back to explicit knowledge in organizations running through four phases: socialization, externalization, combination and internalization (SECI).

During the first phase named socialization the employees start sharing their experiences, attitudes and perspectives. Based on common experiences from the past they begin to trust each other. In the second phase called externalization the employees begin to exchange their thoughts and ideas. Hidden tacit knowledge from their minds becomes explicit knowledge by dialogue. Ideas and thoughts are transformed into drafts and models. During phase three called combination employees combine the new explicit knowledge with existing explicit knowledge. The combination leads to so-called systemic knowledge, which has to be recorded in documentation e.g. drawings, specifications and procedures. The documentation supports the distribution of new knowledge through the entire organization. In the phase of internalization the new explicit knowledge is transformed into tacit knowledge. The new knowledge becomes part of the daily work and the employees embed the new knowledge into their routines.

The existence of the model is confirmed by long-term empirical investigation at a small car manufacturing enterprise (Dyck et al., 2005). Research on management of organizational knowledge creation in new product development process (Schulze, 2004) also reaffirms the existence of the cycle of organizational learning. The research model comprised a generic product development process and revealed several important interrelations between phases of the cycle and the results of product development.

The socialization has a positive influence on the efficiency of technical development. It contributes to finish the development within planned time and budget. The combination during the phase of technical development has positive influence on quality of development. Combination also has a positive impact on the quality of product launches, including ramp-up phase (Schulze, 2004).

According to further research, the performance of a ramp-up is positively influenced by the maturity of the product and of the manufacturing process at the end of the development phase (Weber, 1999). Both depend on the output of the two key processes of development phase in the automotive industry: product development and development of the manufacturing process. To achieve this high maturity the use of knowledge and experience during development phase is a crucial factor. It comprises a wide knowledge field covering technologies e.g. material science, physics, chemistry, electronics and software as well as methods for estimating feasibility and reliability, planning and project management. Even from that perspective, knowledge management has an extraordinary leverage for the improvement of ramp-up performance.

4. PREPARATION OF THEORY SET-UP

Information Technology (IT) embedded in an organizational frame could be regarded as enabler for knowledge management. In case of dynamic automotive networks an adequate organizational frame or model as meta-structure is needed.

The automotive pyramid is a well-known model which describes the basic structure of supplier-customer relations in the automotive industry. Enterprises typically can be categorized by their products. The car manufacturers or original equipment manufacturers (OEM) are at the top of the supply pyramid. The pyramid consists of three further levels:
— Supplier of modules and systems (1st Tier)
— Supplier of sub-assemblies (2nd Tier)
— Supplier of components (3rd Tier)

Examples for products of 1st tier suppliers are front-end module, braking-system, transmission-system and for the 2nd tier supplier shock-absorbers and electric motors. Development competences, manufacturing capabilities, knowledge and experience in particular refer to the basic structure of the automotive pyramid.

Regarding IT as enabler for knowledge management of dynamic automotive networks, two leverages on the described cycle of organizational learning could be identified: IT can simplify the identification of people with specific knowledge and connect them with communication functions. Both support socialization. IT can offer easy accesses to information and provide tools for efficient handling and effective distribution of information. These functions support the combination-phase of the cycle of organizational learning.

A model description comprising the meta-structure of dynamic automotive networks and the identified access points to leverage of improvement for ramp-up performance at the same time, offers ontology-based information sharing. Because of the differences in granularity of data belonging to enterprises of dynamic automotive networks, a hybrid model consisting of global and additional local ontologies would be the best choice in general (Stuckenschmidt, Harmelen, 2005).

The solution described in this paper focuses on global structures and do not pay attention to additional local ontologies which might be necessary in specific cases.

5. SOLUTION

In order to support the access to knowledge and experience for all members of the dynamic automotive network, a net of objects and relations is designed based on ontologies. The net consists of typical objects of the automotive business such as customers, materials or products, suppliers, employees, and production lines. These set of objects is linked with specific relations like "belongs to", "has part" and "is part of".

The ontology net or knowledge net covers all enterprises the dynamic automotive net consists of. Therefore the range of this net is limited by the module, system, sub-assembly or component the dynamic automotive net develops and manufactures. For example in case of a braking system, the net would cover the developer and producer of the whole system and its suppliers for components and electronic devices. The net could be operated by one of the enterprises, for example by the enterprise with the highest position in the automotive pyramid. Because trust among enterprises is limited, in some cases a neutral service provider could be involved.

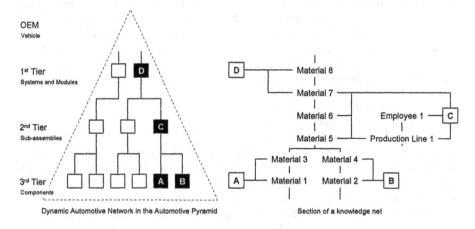

Figure 1 – Dynamic Automotive Network and Knowledge Net

The net itself offers basic objects and basic relations (see Figure 1). To weave a knowledge net master data from each enterprise involved in the dynamic automotive network is necessary. The master data is easily available from enterprise resource programs (ERP) and product data management (PDM) systems by export functions in usual data formats like CSV (Colon Separated Values). It is not intended to export large amounts of data from these databases. Only master data such as supplier name and ID, material name and ID, customer name and ID, production line etc. and their relations are necessary. To weave an extended net overlapping frontiers of the member enterprises, it is necessary to get match code data. These match code data links between different names and ID's used for one material, supplier or customer in different systems of the involved enterprises. In case of materials usual ERP-Systems store both ID's the customer specific and the internal ID of the material. The net is completed by data concerning employees with relevant experiences concerning customer and supplier complaints, problems and faults on the shop-floor and similar topics.

After the initial creation and configuration of the net, relevant sources and contents have to be identified and selected. There are two possibilities to utilize this process: Employees of each enterprise could manually select certain pieces of information and link them to objects and relations of the net. The manually processing is very time-consuming but leads to high quality results. The second possibility is to use search engines well-known from the internet. These applications could search for all objects and relations of the created net in the databases of the enterprises. The automatically processing is very fast but includes the risk of unintended selecting of sensitive data. In both cases the result is a mapping from a common knowledge net to the distributed sources of the member enterprises (see Figure 2; dotted lines symbolize the mapping).

Natural language documents like reports, analysis and minutes of meetings have a particular meaning. They comprise a lot of important experiences, because people tend to gather and share experiences in these special kinds of learning histories (Kleiner, Roth, 1998).

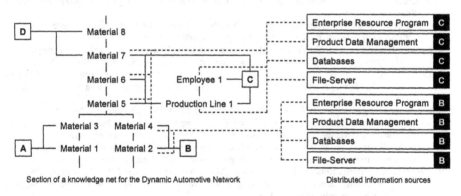

Section of a knowledge net for the Dynamic Automotive Network   Distributed information sources

Figure 2 – Knowledge Net and distributed information sources

Authorization plays a crucial role concerning access to the entire or parts of the knowledge net. The degree of trust among enterprises is limited. In dynamic virtual organizations, enterprises have common goals and therefore may tend to have higher degrees of trust than usual customers and suppliers have. For the authorization rules several scenarios could be imagined. A conservative scenario would contain a limited insight for each enterprise to the information's linked to the net-area covering its direct suppliers. This would be similar to the information exchange between suppliers and customers nowadays. An advanced scenario would allow access to the entire net for all members of the dynamic automotive network. This scenario would provide a maximum of access possibilities to knowledge and experience but requires even a maximum of trust between the involved enterprises. Probably the most realistic scenarios lay between those extremes.

The new approach enables enterprises in dynamic automotive networks to share their knowledge flexibly and effectively. It overcomes the limited exchange of knowledge in usual supplier-customer-relations. The solution enables to improve ramp-up performance for entire networks based on extensive knowledge management.

6. OUTLOOK

The described solution will be implemented step-by-step in cooperation with enterprises of the automotive industry. The effectiveness of the concept to the performance of ramp-ups will be part of future research studies. Especially the fields of rapid ontology creation for temporary and flexible organizations need further research.

7. REFERENCES

1. Afsarmanesh H, Garita C, Hertzberger LO. Virtual Enterprises and Federated Information Sharing. In proceedings of 9th IEEE International Conference on Database and Expert Systems Applications, DEXA'98, Vienna: 1998.
2. Automotive Industry Action Group (AIAG). Quality System Requirements QS 9000:1998, AIAG, Southfield, 1998.
3. Camarinha-Matos LM, Afsarmanesh H. Collaborative Networked Organizations – A research agenda for emerging business models. New York: Springer, 2004.
4. Dyck B, Starke FA, Mischke GA, Mauws M. Learning to Build a Car: An Empirical Investigation of Organizational Learning. In Journal of Management Studies. Oxford: Blackwell Publishing, 2005.
5. Gottwald A. Bis zu 20 Prozent outsourcen – Die BMW Group setzt auf webbasiertes Supplier Relationship Management. In Automobil-Produktion. Landsberg: mi verlag moderne indutrie, 2006.
6. International Organisation for Standardization (ISO). ISO/TS 16949:2002. Geneva, 2002.
7. Kleiner A, Roth G. How to Make Experience Your Company's Best Teacher. In Harvard Business Review on Knowledge Management. Boston: Harvard Business School Press, 1998.
8. Kuhn A, Wiendahl H, Eversheim W, Schuh G. Schneller Produktionsanlauf von Serienprodukten, Ergebnisbericht der Untersuchung 'fast ramp-up', Dortmund: Verlag Praxiswissen, 2002.
9. Manufacturer Supplier Relationship Consortium (MSR). MSR-Teilprojekt MEDOC, Failure Mode and Effect Analysis, Strukturelle Grundlagen der MSRFMEA DTD. Manufacturer Supplier Relationship Consortium (MSR), 2005.
10. Nonaka I, Takeuchi H. The Knowledge-Creating Company. New York: Oxford University Press, 1995.
11. PROSTEP. http://www.prostep.de/en/solutions/ (26/02/2006).
12. Schulze A. Management of organizational knowledge creation in new product development projects. Bamberg: Difo-Druck, 2004.
13. Stuckenschmidt H, Harmelen F. Information Sharing on the Semantic Web. Berlin/Heidelberg, New York: Springer-Verlag, 2005.
14. SupplyOn. http://www.supplyon.com (27/02/2006).
15. Verband der Automobilindustrie (VDA). Sicherung der Qualität vor Serieneinsatz. Oberursel: VDA, 1996.
16. VDA–QMC (Verband der Automobilindustrie - Qualitäts Management Center) http://www.vda-qmc.de/de/gelbdruck/QDX_V1_0_public_draft_online_de/index.htm (27/02/2006).
17. Wangeheim S. Planung und Steuerung des Serienanlaufs komplexer Produkte: dargestellt am Beispiel der Automobilindustrie. Frankfurt am Main: Europäische Hochschulschriften, 1998
18. Weber J. Schon früh an die Produktion denken. In Automobil-Entwicklung. Landsberg: mi verlag moderne indutrie, 1999

63

A FRAMEWORK TO CREATE A VIRTUAL ORGANISATION BREEDING ENVIRONMENT IN THE MOULD AND DIE SECTOR

Rolando Vargas Vallejos[1], Celson Lima[2], Gregório Varvakis[3]

[1] *University of Caxias do Sul, BRAZIL (rvvallej@ucs.br)*
[2] *Centre Scientifique et Technique du Bâtiment (CSTB), FRANCE (c.lima@cstb.fr)*
[3] *Federal University of Santa Catarina, BRAZIL (grego@deps.ufsc.br)*

The effective creation of Virtual Enterprises emerges of a previous work and environment called recently as Virtual Organisations Breeding Environment. The framework here proposed is one of the results of five years research project in the field of Collaborative Network Organisations. This paper describes a framework to create and support the Virtual Enterprises life cycle in the mould and die sector. The framework called AmbianCE was validated in a Brazilian Virtual Organisation Breeding Environment.

1. INTRODUCTION

The Virtual Enterprises (VEs) paradigm has been moved from the research domain to the business application, supported by the recent developments in the Information and Communication Technologies (ICT) and the new approaches in the management field. Dynamic collaborative networks provide intuitive approaches to face the challenges of turbulent markets. A key question is however how to guarantee the basic requirements to enable such collaboration. Afsarmanesh and Camarinha-Matos (2005) affirmed that the formation of any collaborative coalition depends on its members sharing some common goals, possessing some level of mutual trust, having established common (interoperable) infrastructures, and having agreed on some common (business) practices and values.

In order to support the VEs life cycle it is necessary that potential partners will be prepared to participate in such collaboration. It means that these enterprises need a common interoperable infrastructure, common operating rules and cooperation agreements, and principally 'trust' among other aspects. Therefore, the concept of **breeding environment** has emerged as the necessary context for the effective creation of VEs. Shortly, **Virtual organisation Breeding Environment (VBE)** is *an association of organisations and their related supporting institutions, adhering to a base long term cooperation agreement, and adoption of common operating principles and infrastructures, with the main goal of increasing both their chances*

Please use the following format when citing this chapter:

Vallejos, R. V., Lima, C., Varvakis, G., 2006, in IFIP International Federation for Information Processing, Volume 224, Network-Centric Collaboration and Supporting Fireworks, eds. Camarinha-Matos, L., Afsarmanesh, H., Ollus, M., (Boston: Springer), pp. 599–608.

and their preparedness towards collaboration in potential Virtual Organisations (Afsarmanesh & Camarinha-Matos, 2005).

This paper describes a framework to support the VE life cycle relying on a VBE. The framework proposed here has been validated in a Brazilian VBE called Virfebras. A peculiar characteristic of Virfebras is that the members are competitors operating in the mould and die sector. One important element in this framework was the application of the theory of Knowledge Management (KM) in order to maximise the capitalisation and dissemination of the knowledge created during a VE life cycle. In the mould and die sector, relevant knowledge is created, especially tacit knowledge. The idea is to transform it into explicit knowledge and store it in different but strongly related layers, which have to be managed properly.

2. THE VIRFEBRAS VBE

Virfebras is a VBE that resulted from the partnership involving the following organisations: (i) the University of Caxias do Sul (UCS); (ii) nine mould and die makers; (iii) the Brazilian agency supporting SMEs (SEBRAE-RS); and (iv) the government of the State of Rio Grande do Sul. These enterprises, which have common market interests, decided to take part in a research project coordinated by UCS aiming to learn how to build a cooperative environment supported by ICT.

Virfebras is located in the city of Caxias do Sul, south of Brazil. Whenever an order is submitted to the group, a VE is created. Companies belonging to this VE play two kinds of roles: coordinator (VE-C) and members (VE-M). The VE-C takes responsibility on both technical and legal aspects of the order. When the mould(s) and/or die(s) are delivered to the customer, and there are no more issues to be handled, the VE is dissolved (Vallejos, 2005).

It was necessary five years to create the Virfebras VBE. Only after having structured the VBE was possible to create VEs. Nowadays, within the VBE, several VEs may exist at the same time. It is worth noticing that every company keeps its identity, meaning its own capacity of make business individually.

The Virfebras VBE creation passed through several phases, which will be described in the next sections.

3. FRAMEWORK TO CREATE A VBE IN THE MOULD AND DIE SECTOR

Companies aiming at working collaboratively to create VEs should previously develop some competencies and create a favourable environment. For example, it is necessary to develop/deploy a common ICT-based infrastructure to allow the integration/interoperation of the companies among themselves and to develop some additional abilities to adapt the traditional culture of work of both entrepreneurs and employees towards the use of VE/VBE concepts.

The AmbianCE (*Ambiente de Criação de Empresas Virtuais*) is a framework to support the creation of a VBE tailored to the mould and die sector. It was also developed to face difficulties and barriers that appear when enterprises decided to create VEs. AmbianCE provides an environment where *trust, competence,* and *the use of ICT* are fundamental in order to support collaborative work.

The lack of trust is one of the problems found when creating VEs. It is overcome with the establishment of long-term relationships amongst mould and die makers. However, the creation of trust is a process built slowly along the time and is solely based on actions and results. The AmbianCE framework makes possible the VBE establishment that permits a long-term relationship among entrepreneurs and employees and creates opportunities for improvement.

The AmbianCE framework (figure 1) is composed of three steps, namely *Prepare AmbianCE, Structure AmbianCE,* and *Act.* In addition to that, its deployment is guided by the so-named *AmbianCE Strategy,* which is based on a *KM Program* and a *Benchmarking Methodology.* Such strategy also uses a 'vertical' element called *AmbianCE Evolution Vector* connecting steps two and three, creating a cyclical process that allows the constant improvement of the framework.

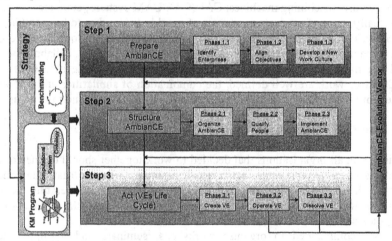

Figure 1 – General overview of the AmbianCE framework

3.1 Step 1 – Prepare AmbianCE

This step prepares the necessary environment to create a VBE. It is subdivided in three phases, namely *Identify Enterprises, Align Objectives,* and *Develop a New Work Culture.*

3.1.1 Phase 1.1 – Identify Enterprises

It aims at identifying the organisations that intend to work in a collaborative form creating VEs. Those organisations could belong to the same industrial districts, clusters, or can be geographically dispersed. If there is no initiative to work collaboratively, it will be necessary to look for industrial districts and clusters (already formed or on the way) where the candidate organisations are operating.

After detecting the organisations with the required potential to create a VBE, it is recommended to conduct interviews with the managers of those organizations, in order to understand their histories, culture of work, partnerships, the existing collaboration forms, as well as the willingness to work collaboratively through VEs. It is necessary to organise workshops about VEs and VBEs involving the participation of industrials, universities, technological centres, governmental agencies, and other organisations that support the referred sector.

It is recommended that neutral entities (e.g. universities, research institutes, associations, government, etc.) may coordinate the VBE creation. The authors argue that a VBE formed with competitors could be a good alternative to face the actual turbulent market. At first glance this seems to be a contradiction since a VE is formed with complementary enterprises. However, if well coordinated and created, a VE formed with competitors, with complementary competencies, can have more advantages than disadvantages. The organisations that work in the mould and die sector have similar types of products, same market interests, same problems to access new technologies, difficulties to find prepared employees, and sometimes even if they have similar processes they did not have the same *resources* (infrastructure, machining machines, CAD/CAE/CAM systems, etc.), etc..

Actually, a lot of products need a set of moulds and/or dies to be manufactured. Generally, one single enterprise cannot manufacture all these tools because of its work capacity. For that reason it is interesting to work in a collaborative way involving more enterprises, even if they are competitors. If the objectives of the collaborative work are well defined, the combination of similarities and differences create more opportunities for the organisations to find solutions and to work as VEs.

3.1.2 Phase 1.2 – Align Objectives

In this phase, all organisations that decided to work together should define common objectives to guide their future activities. They must define, at least, one common objective that is fundamental for the success of structuring and operating the VBE. A way to find those objectives is to offer bigger challenges to the members of the VBE, such as the existence of a more reachable market.

It is recommended to organise workshops, seminars and training courses, prepared by experts, in order to identify opportunities and strategies to attend the market. It is vital to emphasize that the union of enterprises will allow to: (i) access new and larger business opportunities; (ii) attend new customers and new markets; and (iii) access new technology and researches. It is suggested to organise visits to potentials customers and to organise trips (or business missions) to analyse new markets. In those trips it will also be possible to work behavioural aspects among entrepreneurs, mainly the aspect of 'trust'.

3.1.3 Phase 1.3 – Develop a New Work Culture

It aims to build a new culture of work amongst the entrepreneurs that have the intention to create VEs. The approach used for the construction of that new work culture considers three aspects, namely: *Culture of Trust, Competence Culture*, and *ICT Culture*.

The Culture of Trust is considered the most important for the success of VEs. The creation of a VBE is necessary to built trust among the entrepreneurs. In a VBE it is possible to organise courses and activities on organisational behavioural development. Another important and effective activity is to organise visits to each

VBE's member. Initially the entrepreneur to be visited may fear receiving competitors, but during the visit, he will likely notice that the information exchanged with other entrepreneurs can be very rich. Finally, it is important to organise business travels in order to visit national and international fairs and to visit research centres. In these trips, besides the establishment of contacts with potentials customers, the access to new technologies and the investigation of future markets, the entrepreneurs have the opportunity to develop trust knowing better each other.

The Competence Culture deals with the development, the investment and the consolidation of the organisation competencies. If one enterprise has the intention to participate in a VE, it is mandatory to have at least one competence that differentiates from the others. In a VBE is possible to identify, to develop and to evidence core competencies of each mould and die makers. Knowing the core competencies of the VBE enterprises, it is possible to create efficient VEs and to detect the absence of other core competencies necessary for the VBE.

The ICT Culture targets the correct use of ICT tools/technologies for communication and management of the information exchanged between enterprises. Some mould and die entrepreneurs have personal barriers to use ICT tools. For those entrepreneurs it is necessary to show the benefits and the need of using ICT to participate in VEs. It is necessary to establish patterns for the ICT among enterprises considering several application levels.

3.2 Step 2 – Structure AmbianCE

After the preparation of the AmbianCE it is necessary to structure the VBE promoting the establishment of a long-term relationship among mould and die makers. The step Structure AmbianCE is divided in three phases called: *Organise AmbianCE, Qualify People* and *Implement AmbianCE.*

3.2.1 Phase 2.1 – Organise AmbianCE

It aims to create an organisational and functional structure of the VBE. A hierarchical management structure will guarantee the good operation of the VBE. At least, it is necessary to have a *President* and a *Broker* to instantiate the VBE operation. Other actors and functions can appear according to the entrepreneurs' expectations and needs. The President has the responsibility to coordinate the creation of the statute, the ethics code, operational procedures, etc.. The Broker has the responsibility to detect business opportunities, to establish contacts with potential customers, to identify needs of core competencies, etc..

The VBE statute, the ethics code and the operational procedures should be created. The statute should cover, for instance, the admittance of new enterprises, the partners' responsibilities, etc.. The ethics code rules behavioural aspects, the entrepreneurs' bonuses, the entrepreneurs' punishments, etc.. The operational procedures rule the dynamics of the VEs life cycle. It is necessary be define clearly the functions and responsibilities of the VE Coordinator (VE-C) and VE Members (VE-Ms). For example, the VE-C should guarantee the execution of the Distributed Business Process (DBP) and to assume the technical and administrative responsibility of the order being executed. In a VBE, several VEs may exist simultaneously, and each organisation can play both roles in different EVs, at the same time. The operational procedures should consider the criteria to define who is who (i.e., who is the VE-C and who are the VE-Ms).

3.2.2 Phase 2.2 – Qualify People

In this phase the entrepreneurs that understood the importance to work collaboratively through VEs, have the challenge to involve their employees in that kind of collaborative work.

Some actions that the entrepreneurs should organise in their own enterprises are workshops and meetings with their employees to understand the benefits and the challenges of working creating VEs. It is recommended to form work groups to analyze and optimize different Business Processes (BPs). Those work groups should establish metrics to accomplish their performance along the time. It is recommended to organise meetings with the participation of several work groups of different enterprises. In those meetings each work group could present the improvements obtained. It is possible to organise visits of the work groups in different mould and die enterprises to show practically the improvements in that BPs. These actions are fundamental to develop a new work culture in employees involved in a VBE. The employees should feel that the new collaborative work brings benefits and opportunities, besides improving their work conditions.

3.2.3 Phase 2.3 – Implement AmbianCE

To implement AmbianCE is necessary to know all the core competencies of each enterprise and to identify the fundamental BPs to create and operate efficient VEs in mould and die sector. It is important to establish metrics for each fundamental BP.

To identify fundamental BPs and to accomplish their performance along the time it is suggested the application of a Benchmarking methodology. In the present work a Benchmarking methodology for mould and die enterprises was developed. The Benchmarking methodology is to be applied in a cyclical way and is being considered as a fundamental element to implement AmbianCE.

Other element that is fundamental to structure the VBE successfully is the KM application. This work proposes the implementation of a KM Program as a strategy of the AmbianCE framework aiming to reuse and disseminate knowledge. The implementation of a KM Program should be one of the primary actions of the VBE in formation. The effectiveness and the efficiency of future VEs depend on the good management of the knowledge created within the VBE.

In order to validate the operational procedures (ruling the VBE) to create, operate and dissolve VEs, it is suggested to look for 'pilot' business opportunities. It is necessary to evaluate these procedures, agreements, contracts, infrastructure and results. It is necessary to involve all VBE members to discuss these aspects. After having performed the 'pilot' experiences and solved (likely) technical, operational and behavioural problems the VBE is considered ready to attend new business opportunities.

3.3 Step 3 – Act

The Step 3 of the AmbianCE framework treats about the VEs life cycle and it is divided into three phases, namely *Create VE*, *Operate VE*, and *Dissolve VE*.

3.3.1 Phase 3.1 – Create VE

This phase targets the creation of the most efficient and competitive VE to attend a given business opportunity. When a business opportunity appears the VBE procedures to create a VE should be followed in order to select VE-C and VE-Ms. It should be defined precisely the DBP, considering their BPs delivered time. Important is to discuss the responsibilities and to establish clearly the profits and the risks that each company will assume.

Another issue to be discussed during the VE creation is the management of information (of the different enterprises) to be shared along the BPs. The efficiency of a VE depends on information sharing, including those considered as 'private' for a certain enterprise. How to treat this 'confidential' information and knowledge during the VE life cycle?

Once discussed the issues above mentioned, it is necessary to sign agreements and contracts between the enterprises that form the VE. Mould and die makers should create the habit of formalise their collaboration agreements in order to protect themselves from any problems that may occur in the future. After documenting these agreements and contracts the VE is considered created.

3.3.2 Phase 3.2 – Operate VE

In this phase the VE executes the customer order, performing the different BPs efficiently. It is important to monitor and to record the BPs, which could be done through a performance evaluation during the execution of BPs.

The information exchange is intensive, not only inside of each enterprise, but also among the VE partners. The information should be treated in several levels and should be separated in two groups: 'private' and 'public'.

Unexpected problems can appear along the BPs execution, which should be solved following the VBE norms and procedures. In extreme cases the VE can be reconfigured, to be treated in the *AmbianCE Evolution Vector*.

3.3.3 Phase 3.3 – Dissolve VE

Once concluded the DBP and having given the product to the customer, the VE should be dissolved. It is suggest to develop questionnaires to evaluate the customer, the VE-C and the VE-Ms satisfaction.

It should be capitalized the new information acquired along the BPs. The information to be reused should be stored and disseminated for the right people in the VBE. It should be evaluated if the VE will be created again in the future or not, the execution of the agreements and the contracts, as well as the VBE norms and the procedures.

3.4 AmbianCE Strategy

The base of the AmbianCE Strategy is the application of a *KM Program* supported by a *Benchmarking Methodology*. The AmbianCE Strategy has an integration vector called *AmbianCE Evolution Vector* and is supported by the *AmbianCE computational system* and a *Mould and die Ontology*.

3.4.1 KM Program

The implementation of a KM program should be one of the priority actions of the VBE. The effectiveness of a VE is risked when the information along the DBP is not managed appropriately. In addition to the information, knowledge is created and applied constantly during the VE life cycle. This knowledge should be stored and disseminated aiming to be reused in future BPs and in the future VEs creation. The effectiveness of future VEs depends on a good knowledge management.

This work adopted and adapted the KM model proposed by Nissen et al. (2000), which is composed by six phases, namely *Create, Organise, Formalize, Distribute, Apply, and Evolve*.

Create is the phase in which is necessary to invest to grow up (within the VBE) the conditions required to allow people to create new knowledge. In this phase the Nonaka and Takeuchi (1997) KM model and the Hutchins (2000) approach of Distributed Cognition are considered.

Organise deals with the knowledge organisation. The capture of knowledge can happen searching and finding existing knowledge or can start from the creation of new knowledge. To seek existing knowledge it can be used, for instance, 'knowledge map systems', 'semantic networks', 'knowledge-based systems', etc.. Once captured the desired knowledge it must be organised following some rules, previously defined to facilitate its classification, storage, dissemination and future capitalisation. The knowledge organisation can be appropriately driven with a specific ontology.

Formalise is the phase the knowledge should be validated monitoring its use from other experts. It should also guarantee that knowledge is rightly updated, through the creation of new knowledge and the exclusion of obsolete knowledge.

Distribute means to disseminate the knowledge for the right people considering previous criterion in an automatic way, which means that work groups should be created with common interests.

Apply is the phase in which the knowledge is capitalised meaning that it is applied in real situations into the DBP producing concrete benefits. To evaluate the results after the knowledge use it is suggested the establishment of metrics.

The *AmbianCE Evolution Vector* integrates the KM model with the AmbianCE Strategy in order to create a continuous life cycle.

3.4.2 Benchmarking Methodology

It was developed a Benchmarking methodology to implement the KM program in a mould and die VBE that was presented in (Vallejos & Gomes, 2004). Benchmarking is a continuous and systematic process used to evaluate enterprises' BPs in order to establish referential patterns. In addition, with the application of the Benchmarking methodology, a behavioural change occurs in the employees when they recognise the differences of BPs in other companies.

3.4.3 AmbianCE Evolution Vector

The AmbianCE Evolution Vector integrates Steps 2 and 3, Structure AmbianCE and Act (VEs life cycle) with the Benchmarking methodology and consequently with the KM program. The objective of this vector is to create a cyclical and continuous dynamics in the AmbianCE framework. In this phase it is possible to reconfigure a VE in process and to optimize the creation of future VEs using the KM approach. It can also identify the need of new enterprises with specific core competencies, or to decide for the VBE qualification contracting consultancies and research projects.

3.4.4 AmbianCE Computational System

The use of a KM computational system to support the AmbianCE Strategy is necessary. In the present work it was adopted the e-COGNOS project approach to support the KM in the Building and Construction industry (http//:www.e-cognos.org). The e-COGNOS approach is based on the development of the *e-COGNOS Knowledge Management Infrastructure* (e-CKMI). The AmbianCE Computational System used the e-CKMI methodology for their development. This system can be described differentiating its architecture, functionality and technical characteristics.

Architecture characteristics: Web-centred environment, ontology-based, push mechanisms, autonomous processes, and knowledge layer interdependence

Functional characteristics: human-centred, easy to use, appealing, adaptive, configurable, based on experiences and open.

Technical characteristics: interoperability, integration, flexibility, scalability, sustainability, heterogeneous inter-related knowledge sources, and large knowledge sources.

More details of the AmbianCE Computational System were published in (Lima & Vallejos, 2002).

3.4.5 Mould and Die Ontology

To support the AmbianCE Computational System was necessary to develop a mould and die ontology. According to Lima et al. (2002) the ontology allows the semantics process and communication of different sources of information between different people and computational systems. Ontology guarantees the no existence of semantic ambiguity on knowledge shared in a certain work domain. In the present work it was not intended to provide the ultimate and definitive ontology for the mould and die sector, but it can serve as a base for future developments.

4. CONCLUSION

This paper presented AmbianCE, a framework to create a VBE in the mould and die sector. The proposal is to develop a VBE before the VEs creation aiming to prepare mould and die makers for this kind of collaborative work. The VBE allows them to develop a new culture of work and to prepare an appropriate infrastructure for their operation.

The AmbianCE framework is constituted of three steps (*Prepare AmbianCE, Structure AmbianCE, Act*) and has a *Strategy* which is based on a *KM Program* and a *Benchmarking Methodology* for his implementation. The verification of the applicability of the present framework was realized in a VBE called Virfebras. The construction of the VBE was possible in five years of work, creating a basic infrastructure, an organizational structure, norms and operational procedures and, mainly, a new work culture. AmbianCE facilitates the development of a new work culture for the organizations considering aspects of trust, core competencies and the use of ICT.

As result it was possible to create a favorable environment to launch the VEs life cycle. It should be pointed out that even the Virfebras members are competitors; they create efficient and competitive VEs aiming at new customers and markets. In the beginning of the work it was common to observe that entrepreneurs and employees used to hide information from the partners. However, they realised that this behaviour should be replaced by a new one more suitable for a collaborative environment. They started sharing information and learned that they usually have very similar problems. If they started sharing solutions, every enterprise could benefit from this exchange process. The Virfebras enterprises have grew in infrastructure, contract more employees, developed new customers and suppliers and, mainly, adopted a new collaborative form of work.

Due the obtained results, the proposed framework shows to be efficient turning future VEs more competitive. If well implemented, the KM Program could be considered as a important facilitator factor for the VBE formation, motivating other enterprises to adopt that kind of collaboration work.

5. REFERENCES

1. Afsarmanesh, H.; Camarinha-Matos, L.M. A framework for management of Virtual Organization Breeding Environments. In: Camarinha-Matos, L. M.; Afsarmanesh, H.; Ortiz A. **Collaborative Networks and their Breeding Environments**. IFIP Vol. 186. Springer, 2005.
2. Camarinha-Matos, L. M.; Afsarmanesh H. The virtual enterprise concept. In: ____. **Infrastructures for Virtual Enterprises – Networking Industrial Enterprises**. Kluwer Academic Publishers, 1999.
3. Hutchins, E. Distributed cognition. **International Encyclopedia of the Social and Behavioral Science**. IESBS Distributed Cognition. <http://www.iesbs.com/pdf>. Accessed in: 18th may, 2000.
4. Lima, C. P.; Vallejos, R. V. Towards a Knowledge Management infrastructure to support Virtual Enterprises. In: **The European Conference on Information and Communication Technology Advances and Innovation in the Knowledge Society (eSM@ART 2002)**, Salford. Towards a European Knowledge Economy in the Construction and Related Sectors. Salford University, 2002.
5. Lima, C. P. et al. The e-CKMI: an Ontology-enabled platform to support KM in construction. In: **eWork 2002 Conference**. Prague: oct. 2002.
6. Nissen, M.; Kamel, M.; Sengupta, K. Integrated Analysis and Design of Knowledge Systems and Processes. In: Malhotra, Y. **Knowledge Management and Virtual Organizations**. UK: Idea Group Publishing, 2000.
7. Nonaka, I.; Takeuchi, H. **Criação de Conhecimento na Empresa**: Como as empresas japonesas geram a dinâmica da inovação. 6. ed. Rio de Janeiro: Campus, 1997.
8. Vallejos R.V. **Um modelo para formação de Empresas Virtuais no setor de moldes e matrizes**. Tese de doutorado. Universidade Federal de Santa Catarina, 2005.
9. Vallejos, R. V.; Gomes, J. O. Applying a Benchmarking methodology to empower a Virtual Organization. In: **6th International Conference on Information Technology for Balanced Automation Systems in Manufacturing and Services (BASYS 2004)**, Vienna. Emerging Solutions for Future Manufacturing Systems. Springer, 2004.

Luísa Faria[1], Américo Azevedo[2]

Universidade de Aveiro - DEGEI
[1]*Campus Universitário de Santiago,3810-193 Aveiro, PORTUGAL*
[2]*Faculdade de Engenharia da Universidade do Porto and Inesc Porto*
Rua Roberto Frias S/N, 4200-465 Porto, PORTUGAL
E-mail: luisaffaria@gmail.com, ala@fe.up.pt

In general, the aim of setting up collaborative networks is the reduction of uncertainty and the increase of competitiveness. One of the main goals is the exploitation of this collaboration networks guaranteeing the legal independence of partners on the basis of common and aligned strategic aims. Nevertheless, its practical implementation is not straightforward because of all the several dimensions it involves. This paper addresses some relevant issues in the domain of collaborative networks, in the scope of a research project based on a case study centered on a large industrial pole in Brazil and mainly established by SME.

1. INTRODUCTION

Nowadays, more and more enterprises become part of strategic enterprise networks in order to produce marketable products. In that context, companies generally recognize that tight interaction and coordination among all the participants of their business chain are a key requirement for their continued competitiveness. Therefore, the companies are in constant transforming, searching different alternatives to improve the critical business processes, in a way that these companies can meet the increasing demand, having more flexibility, greater delivery precision and lesser production times (Azevedo *et al.*, 2005).

The objective of this paper is to show the mainly advantages of cooperation, evidencing the difficulties, risks and opportunities of this strategy. We also underline the necessity to consider several critical aspects that have to be fulfilled for network success.

The reminder of the paper is organized as follows. After this introduction, the next section presents the main problems and difficulties for business networks success. The third section presents some successful experiences in the domain of collaborative networks of SME, showing that it is possible to get advantages from the cooperation and to conquer space in the market. The next section addresses the case study related to network cooperation in small textile enterprises of Nova Friburgo – Brazil. The last section contains the conclusions of this paper.

Please use the following format when citing this chapter:

Faria, L., Azevedo, A., 2006, in IFIP International Federation for Information Processing, Volume 224, Network-Centric Collabora-tion and Supporting Fireworks, eds. Camarinha-Matos, L., Afsarmanesh, H., Ollus, M., (Boston: Springer), pp. 609–616.

2. THE COOPERATION STRATEGY

2.1 Networking Advantages

In general, the aim of setting up strategic networks is the reduction of uncertainty and the increase of competitiveness. Today's leading edge companies try to focus and develop their core competencies in order to guarantee a sustainable competitive level in the market. However, the concentration on core competencies requires the establishment of business links with other companies that ensure the non core competencies involved. Therefore, we will establish a close relationship with partners that can deliver valuable contribution to the company's core competencies.

Inter-enterprise cooperation is important, not only in terms of the availability of resources, but also in terms of enterprise flexibility. Cooperative inter-enterprise relations help enterprises to be more flexible in terms of amount of production since firms may outsource more work when there is increased demand, and less when there is a decrease (capacity driven cooperation). Cooperation among enterprises also helps each entity to be more flexible in terms of type of production in that products can be made to order by grouping different contractors together according to the specialties required (technological driven cooperation).

Any of inter-enterprise cooperation requires coordination. In this context, the integration of their business processes, covering product development, the operations planning, the production, the distribution and the after sales services, should be careful managed. One of the main goals is the exploitation of this collaboration networks guaranteeing the legal independence of partners on the basis of common and aligned strategic aims. Alignment gives stakeholders at every level of business level the ability to rapidly deploy a coherent business strategy as well as to be totally market focused and, at the same time, continuously improve business processes.

In general, the topology and organization of strategy networks are technology or capacity driven. In particular, for technology driven strategic networks, the idea is that each member focuses on its core competencies, maximizing the value added contribution, while the whole network comprises the competencies necessary to produce a certain product.

In short, successful network enterprise can bring the following advantages: allows the definition of joint strategies; preserves the individuality and protects the information of the companies; values brands and enables shared marketing strategies; reduces production costs and investment risks; intensifies the communication and the access to the information; extends the productive scale and the market dimensions; facilitates the credit access to the management qualification.

2.2 Requirements for the networking success

Despite the fact that Business Networking and strategic cooperation networks are emerging as a valuable organizational instrument that can create considerable competitive advantage for small firms, unfortunately, its practical implementation is very complicated. Even if rational facts like the increase of market share, new business or cost reductions are key factors in evaluating the interest of a collaboration, "soft" factors like the exchange of experience and knowledge, human factor and sharing of common activities should not be underestimated (Pouly et al., 2005).

Very often, networking is considered a spontaneous phenomenon that is self-developed under certain environmental conditions. However, the complexity of Business Networking paradigm implies the use of a structured and professional management approach in all life cycle network phases: set-up, operation, evolution and dissolution. Some studies estimate that up to 60% of the alliances fail to meet their initial objectives (Ellis, 1996), in a clear indication that there is still a lot of work to be done regarding the creation and management of these networks (Caldeira, 2004).

From a strategic, business and organisational point of view, several critical success factors have to be fulfilled for network success, namely, the participants and their roles need a business model to describe their relationships and interaction as well as, how value is created and shared.

Other fundamental condition for network profitable survival is trust, identified by many authors as one of the main causes of networks failure (Casarotto Filho and Pires, 2001). Trust is so important because networks members have to share and make public confident information related to strategy, business processes, competencies that are often the source of competitive advantages.

From an operative point of view, beyond the suitable technological infrastructure support, the main difficulty that has to be faced for networks efficiency is the design of network business processes that cover the needs of specific business purposes on one side, and that reasonably fit with single business processes of network members.

The last crucial aspect to point out as a possible barrier for network consistency is the definition of the most appropriate legal structure that formally identifies responsibilities and liabilities of network members regarding stakeholders (Copani *et al.*, 2006).

3. SOME SUCCESSFUL EXPERIENCES IN THE WORLD

There are diverse known cases of network cooperation; however, each one has its particular characteristics that determine its success

To support the case study research project considered, some known networks experiences have been studied, here briefly reported: Italy's experience as pioneer country in the formation of network cooperation between companies, and Denmark's experience mainly due to its peculiarity by the fact that the cooperation between companies has been "imposed", as a consequence of the great need to increase the companies' competitiveness in the country when faced with the threat of an increment in the external competition.

The Italian and Denmark case studies have demonstrated that are many type of SME clusters, organized in different ways, namely, in small production networks, capacity or technological driven. Although, their characteristics vary in important ways, there are some common denominators that should be emphasized in the design and set-up phase of dynamic business network environment established mainly by SME. Moreover, in districts, there is often a strong presence of some form of intermediate governance structure (institutional organization of economic activity). The study of several case studies demonstrate that such intermediate governance structures play a key role in facilitating cooperative activities among firms and between firms and institutions.

3.1 Italy's Experience

In Italy, the cooperation is characterized by the relations between micro and small companies, having been the result of the existence of a sufficiently favourable scene for its development: a great number of companies who had accepted the culture of cooperation very easily. For the Italian economy, the formation of the enterprise networks, also involving unions and the local government, keeps contributing to the increase of the competitiveness and the flexibility of the companies.

In the known region of the Emilia-Romagna there are hundreds of networks that are constituted by about 25 thousand small companies and offer a great deal of services, such as the creation and the development of services centres where market research of technology benefits all constituent companies of the networks. This is one of the main characteristics of the region, which refers to the creation of the *"consortia"* between companies, and the most common refers to the financial provision and marketing services (Best, 1990).

One of the generating factors of success for the Italian nets was the fact that the companies provide chances for the executives to meet and to gain mutual confidence, which expedited the collaboration and allowed the companies to take advantage of the chances of the market together.

3.2 Denmark's Experience

In the late eighties, Denmark faced a period of an increasing commercial deficit, high taxes of unemployment and low capitation of investments. It was pointed that the generator of the problem was the fact that the Danish companies were very inefficient and small, while the changes in the business-oriented panorama favoured the wide scale operations of the multinationals companies.

For the fast development of the economy, the adopted solution was the prevalence of the small companies, but with flexible productive units. Therefore, these companies were joined in flexible nets, for which promoters were now needed.

The Commerce and Industry Ministry of Denmark established a general plan with the purpose of constructing a great number of companies' nets. For such, it started to promote the idea of cooperation by publishing information on the main concepts of cooperation and forming "brokers" for the enterprise network (private consulters who see in the cooperation networks a way of organizing the small companies in big groups), having in the mind the promotion of cooperative projects. This program was called "Strategy 92". Between 1989 and 1990, 3,000 of about the 7,300 Denmark's industrial companies had constituted network cooperation (Costa, 2001).

Therefore, the development of the Danish nets followed a different way than that of the Italian industrial districts. In Italy, the development of the flexible nets was the result of an evolution, with the support of the local governments. In Denmark's case, they developed a previous model just to create the cooperation.

4. CASE STUDY

The case study presented here is the result of a preliminary research study about the advantages and disadvantages of collaborative business networks for the increase of export levels in textile industry located in Nova Friburgo, state of Rio de Janeiro – Brazil.

Before making any study related with cooperation, it is important to perceive that the Brazilian culture is not come back toward the cooperation. Probably the main factors that make the cooperation so difficult are the great individualism of the entrepreneurs and the competition culture that diminishes the confidence. So, the companies see each other as "enemies".

The capital focus will be the identification of main characteristics, organizational structure, main tendencies, and future strategies. Furthermore, in the scope of the research work, we plan to quantify the main advantages the cooperation brought for the companies, as well as for the region where it is located.

4.1 Antecedents of the "Network" Development

With the increase of the international competition, the textile industry of Nova Friburgo entered a period of inevitable decline. The man power that was fired owned the know-how and so, it started to invest in machines and equipment opening its own business. For several identifiable reasons, the most viable alternative for these small companies was the confection of lingerie.

In 1998, the SEBRAE/RJ (Service for the Support to the Micron and Small Companies in Rio de Janeiro), together with the FIRJAN (Federation of the Industries of Rio de Janeiro), conducted a study that pointed the strong presence in the region of hundreds of small companies, very concentrated, and specialized in the sector of lingerie confection. The study recognized that most companies were rather disorganized concerning operational processes and most of them do not even have any formal organizational structure. As a result, the efficiency and effectiveness levels of these companies were very low. Thus, a regional project, encompassing all local companies, was initiated aiming to create the adequate conditions to foster export trade levels through production networks and with the mission to transform the region of Nova Friburgo into a recognized international pole specialized in lingerie domain. Therefore, the appearance of this specialized production network was not a natural development, having been induced, organized and fomented for diverse support institutions, with the prominence for the SEBRAE.

4.2 A Brief Analysis of the Confection Market

To analyze the Confection network in Nova Friburgo, it is important to know some economic characteristics of the international confection market.

The textile sector is one of segments that have bigger tradition of the industrial segment, with a position of prominence in the economy of more developed countries and of many countries called emergent. In Brazil, it has the same degree of importance, having played a role of great relevance in the development process of the country.

It can be verified that the global textile market is having a significant expansion, including even the sums produced and the commerce between the great producing and consuming countries. This growth was possible because of the expansion of the number of consumers in the whole world, for the income increase in the more developed countries and for the opening of the markets to the international trade. From 2004, with the ending of the quotas system and barriers for textile exportation, it is probable that the world-wide commerce can expand still more. Other important factors in this growth also must be considered, as the productive raw material use new and processes.

In accordance with Hammond (2001), an important obstacle for the Brazilian companies is the development of the Supply Chain Management in the more developed countries, being one strong trend in the textile productive chain. Brazil is still behind in terms of adoption of these techniques, basically because of its culture of low cooperation and low access to the technology.

4.3   Characterization of the Productive System

Currently, the industrial district of Nova Friburgo comprehends more than 4 thousands garment companies, and only about 600 are formally registered, corresponding to 25% of the Brazilian production of the segment, generating about 20 thousands ranks of work, with 8 thousands direct jobs and 12 thousands indirect ones. Most of the companies (68,5%) are very small (1 to 9 workers). In 2004, the turn-over of the pole was around 300 million USD (IntimaFriburgo , 2006).

Although the region hosts a significant concentration of very actively companies in same business domain, the existing pole cannot be characterized as a cluster yet, mainly due to the low degree of cooperation between the companies, as much in the production as in the constitution of national and international commercialization channels or even in the technological cooperation. One of the causes of the relatively low level of organization and cooperation is the lack of qualification and the low level of education of the entrepreneurs. The majority of the entrepreneurs is outdated and not interested in the qualification programs promoted by the operating entities in the pole.

An important factor that makes the relevant participation of the pole's companies in the market more difficult, is related to the fact that, for textile sector, in general, there is a lack of barriers concerning the entrance of new competitors and mainly because the available brands are identified with low price and insufficient quality.

The confection sector of Nova Friburgo is intensive in man power, with lack of qualified staff, rendering the work directed toward the operation very difficult, creating barriers to the entrance of new technologies.

Despite the small representation, the external market is the main focus of the development projects of the pole. The objective is to increase the exportation for the countries which are already experts in the region's potential, and also to expand to other markets. According to Prochnik (2002), the trusts are fundamental for the promotion of the exportations. The future strategy is that the consisting trusts launch a proper brand and a quality stamp to facilitate the products acceptance in the international market.

In accordance with the author, in 2002, there was little presence of business or services rendering between the companies. The ideal would be that, in the pole in question, there was the integration of the productive chain between producers and suppliers, inter-sector integration between the industrial and commercial areas, services and, still, solidarity and cooperation bonds between the companies. According to the study, in 2002, only 40% of the interviewed companies carried out some type of business.

The project implemented in the pole of Nova Friburgo is made of diverse programs that are part of the strategic development plan: the Strategic Program of Communication and Marketing; the Program for the Modernization of the Productive and Management Processes; the Program for Quality Increment and Design Improvement; incentives for better access to the markets; and simplified access to the credit.

4.3 Risks and Opportunities

The research study, developed so far, allows us to identify several main risks and difficulties for the Nova Friburgo's production network, namely: lack of information about the distribution channels and the final consumer, lack of politics of the product differentiation, technological difficulties of the small companies in improving its production and exporting, and the scarce participation of the entrepreneurs, workers and of the population in general in the project.

On the other hand, concerning the identified opportunities, we should underline the following ones: congruity and sharing of strategies and policy efforts for the institutions that support the network development, ample access to financial resources and great acceptance and future perspectives in the international market.

4.4 The Effects of the Pole for Nova Friburgo's Economy

It is important to point out that the proximity of lingerie's pole can represent important development opportunities for the other sectors of the region, as is the case of the metal-mechanic sector. However, Ferreira (Ferreira, 2002) evidenced that the interaction degree between the textile-confections sectors and the metal-mechanic one is still much reduced: only a very small number of the interviewed companies produces complementary accessories for the Lingerie's Pole. The enterprise leaderships considered this lack of complementation between the local activities to be one of the main problems for the development of the metal-mechanic sector. In special, the production of machines and components for the confection sector represents a great business chance for the local economy that must be explored.

In accordance with the author, one of the attitudes that are being taken to increase the generation of jobs is to look for new ways of diversifying the pole, creating new economic activities that can counterbalance the common cyclical variations of the region, as it is excessively specialized.

5. CONCLUSIONS

Although the research study is still running, the results achieved so far allow us to conclude that, despite the great expectations related to the development of the Nova Friburgo's Pole, it is essential for the project success that the sector entrepreneurs start to interact more between themselves and between the support institutions, so that the project can become self-sustainable. It is important to create the cooperation culture to allow the companies to obtain all the possible advantages of the Pole. If this happens, all regions will benefit from cooperation, mainly the ones that can be suppliers of the textile network.

An active participation of the institutions can be observed, mainly of the SEBRAE and the FIRJAN, in the implementation and coordination of the Pole. These institutions acted as mediators and brokers of the local development, inducing the most direct joint between the entrepreneurs, in benefit of the companies' modernization on the sector. But it cannot be like this forever. The companies have to learn how to walk alone and develop all the possibilities.

Finally, in spite of its initial development phase, this production network propitiates a development, not only for the companies of the confection sector, but also for the Nova Friburgo city as a whole. However, for this project to perpetuate and generate all its expected results, the companies must compulsorily change its individualistic culture and start to act in coordination with all members, or, with the predictable and planned retirement of the support institutions, it will not have any more "all" and it will be the end of the network.

6. REFERENCES

1. Azevedo A, Toscano C, Sousa JP. Cooperative Planning in Dynamic Supply Chains, International Journal of Computer Integrated Manufacturing, Vol. 18, No 5, 2005, p. 350-356
2. Best MH. Instituitions of Industrial reestructuring. U.K.: Polity Press, 1990
3. Caldeira JC. Joint Ventures for Innovation & Competitiveness, in E-Manufacturing: Business Paradigms and Supporting Technologies, Ed. J.J Pinto Ferreira, Kluwer Academic Publishers, 2004
4. Casarotto Filho, N, Pires, LH. Redes de pequenas e médias empresas e desenvolvimento local: estratégias para a conquista da competitividade global com base na experiência italiana. São Paulo: Atlas, 2001
5. Copani G, Bosani R, Tosatti LM, Azevedo A. A Structured methodology for business network design. Submitted to 12th international conference on Concurrent Enterprising. Milan-Italy, 2006
6. Costa, Carla C. P. C.. Redes de Cooperação entre Empresas: O caso da indústria de confecções de vestuário em Portugal. Tese de Mestrado em Finanças, Universidade Portucalense Infante D. Henrique, 2001
7. Ellis C. Making Strategic Alliances Suceed, Harvard Business Review, 1996
8. Ferreira, M. S.. A Formação de Redes de Conhecimento nas Indústrias Metal-Mecânica e de Confecções de Nova Friburgo. Rio de Janeiro: UFRJ/IE, 2002
9. Hammond, J.. Managing the Apparel Supply Chain in the Digital Economy. Sloan Industry Centers Meeting: Corporative Strategies for the Digital Economy. Cambridge, Massachussetts, 2001
10. IntimaFriburgo, www.intimafriburgo.com.br, accessed on 20.01.2006, 2006
11. Prochnik, V.. Perspectivas para a exportação de confecções: O caso do Pólo de Moda Íntima de Nova Friburgo. Rio de Janeiro: IE/UFRJ, 2002
12. Pouly M, Monnier F, Bertschi D. Success and Failure Factors of Collaborative networks of SME, in Collaborative Networks and Their Breeding Environments, Springer, 2005

PART 20

COLLABORATIVE NETWORKS IN SERVICES

65

THE NON-ACCIDENTAL TOURIST: USING AMBIENT INTELLIGENCE FOR ENHANCING TOURIST EXPERIENCES

Sobah Abbas Petersen and Anders Kofod-Petersen

Dept. of Computer & Information Science, Norwegian University of Science & Technology, Trondheim. NORWAY. E-mail: {sap, anderpe}@idi.ntnu.no

An Ambient Intelligent environment is aware of the presence of a person, perceives her needs and responds intelligently. Ambient intelligence can be used to guide a tourist through the city in such a way that is mutually beneficial for both the tourist and the city. The composite set of services delivered to a tourist can be personalized. This adaptive behaviour is best supported by Virtual Enterprises that are formed dynamically, at runtime. This paper considers an Ambient Intelligent scenario from the service providers' perspective and discusses how such scenarios can be realized through Virtual Enterprises.

1. INTRODUCTION

What might living with Ambient Intelligence (AmI) be like for ordinary people in 2010? The IST Advisory Group (ISTAG) has described a set of futuristic scenarios to address this question, (Ducatel et al. 2001). These scenarios outline the European vision of high-tech development in the field of AmI. One of these scenarios, "Maria", describes a busy business person travelling from Europe to an Asian country that has an AmI infrastructure. Maria's computer and personal communication device is her P-Com, which she wears on her wrist. She leaves the airport, checks in to her hotel and is able to go smoothly through her high-pressure world and concentrate on her work without negotiating each step of the way. The services that are required by Maria are available to her and she can make adjustments and selections as she desires. We are interested in the service providers' perspective of the scenario, in particular, how such scenarios can be realized easily and efficiently, and can be of mutual benefit for the individual as well as the community or the society.

AmI provides the seamless and intuitive support that Maria needs to obtain her services. Her personal communication device and the devices placed in her hotel room infer her needs at any point in time. We have considered the services that were available to her in order to analyse and understand how the scenario can be realized. For example, she has a rental car waiting for her at the airport. To have this service available at the time of her arrival requires the collaboration and coordination among

Please use the following format when citing this chapter:

Petersen, S. A., Kofod-Petersen, A., 2006, in IFIP International Federation for Information Processing, Volume 224, Network-Centric Collaboration and Supporting Fireworks, eds. Camarinha-Matos, L., Afsarmanesh, H., Ollus, M., (Boston: Springer), pp. 619–626.

several parties such as Maria or her personal agent, her travel agent, rental car company and credit card company. She is guided through the traffic which requires collaboration among the rental car company, traffic guidance authority and the credit card company. Similarly, the hotel booking requires a number of parties working together. All of these services are provided by a number of different parties, with different interests and business goals. They must collaborate, coordinate, exchange information and possibly negotiate to reach an agreement. The possibility of such collaboration is facilitated by the appropriate technical infrastructure and accessibility to the appropriate technologies.

In this paper, we consider a similar scenario where a tourist has a short stopover in the Norwegian city of Trondheim, a city with wireless coverage, and how the experiences of the tourist can be enhanced while supporting the business community and the city of Trondheim. The "Wireless Trondheim" initiative is a collaboration between the local council and the university. We see this as an opportunity for the ordinary person in the city and visitors to the city to enhance their experiences. Similarly, it is also an opportunity for the small and large businesses that are already in the city to enhance their services and increase their customer base.

We have chosen a scenario with tourists as they are likely to be one of the user groups where AmI is initially to be realized in the near future. Also a person travelling for any purpose may be a tourist and tourists are more likely to be open to new suggestions and explorations of what a city may have to offer. We consider the needs of the tourist along with the mutual needs of the city.

Virtual Enterprises (VE) are a promising business model for providing services as envisaged in the ISTAG scenario. We discuss the role and significance of VEs in this context and why VEs are a suitable means of realising AmI. The rest of the paper is organized as follows: Section 2 defines AmI, Section 3 describes our scenario, Section 4 analyses the scenario, Section 5 discusses the service providers in an AmI scenario as VEs and Section 6 proposes a functional system architecture for realising our scenario.

2. AMBIENT INTELLIGENCE

The concept of AmI has been described as human beings surrounded by intelligent interfaces supported by computing and networking technology that is embedded in everyday objects such as furniture, clothes and the environment (ISTAG 2005). The environment should be aware of the presence of a person (the user) and perceive the needs of the person and respond intelligently to these needs. It should be able to adapt to the needs of the user in a relaxed and unobtrusive manner.

The above description of AmI suggests some requirements for the success of it. There must be some technology that is accessible to the user or serves the user in a proactive yet unobtrusive manner (Weiser and Brown 1997), becomes aware of the user and her needs and responds intelligently to the context and needs of the user. We see AmI as an overlap of a number of paradigms; Ubiquitous Computing (Weiser 1991), Pervasive Computing (Satyanarayanan 2001) and Artificial Intelligence (Russel and Norvig 2002). The Ubiquitous Computing aspect addresses the notion of accessibility of the technology, where the technology and connectivity is available through everyday objects that are in the user's environment. Artificial Intelligence techniques provide the context awareness to establish the user's needs and the appropriate response and the Pervasive Computing aspect supports the architectural aspects to realize the situation.

AmI is often discussed from the perspective of the user, where the user is a human being. Obtaining the relevant information about the user's needs and establishing this constitutes a major part of this. Responding accordingly and the delivery of the appropriate services to meet the user's needs is a challenge that is gaining interest, e.g. (Myrhaug and Göker 2003). This requires an analysis of the user's needs from a service providers' perspective and addressing how two or more service providers can collaborate to do this.

3. TOURIST IN TRONDHEIM

Consider the scenario where a tourist arrives in Trondheim on a cruise ship. The cruise ship stops over in the Trondheim harbour for one day and the passengers have the opportunity to visit Trondheim, see some of the sights and museums and buy some souvenirs. Before leaving the cruise ship, the tourist signs on to the "Trondheim Experience", which provides her a mobile device such as a PDA or a smartphone. The harbour is 1 km from the city centre. The tourist leaves the cruise ship and walks towards the city centre. She is faced with some street signs, e.g. "sentrum", "pirbadet", and "solsiden". She accesses the glossary service using her device to get an explanation of these signs. She follows the signs that say sentrum to the city centre.

She passes Nidarosdomen, the cathedral in the city. She is presented a brief introduction to the landmark and is informed that there is a guided tour of the cathedral starting in 10 minutes. The cost of an entrance ticket and the directions for obtaining a ticket are provided. As she joins the guided tour of the cathedral, the Trondheim Experience service de-activates itself. She chooses to utilize a location-dependent guide installed in the cathedral, (Wang et al. 2005). As she leaves the cathedral, the Trondheim Experience service re-activates and she is informed that there is a concert in the cathedral at 16:00hrs, the ticket prices and how to obtain a ticket. She is prompted with two package offers; (i) to see the concert at the cathedral, visit the museum at the Archbishop's residence a few metres from the cathedral, a traditional Norwegian meal at a restaurant and transport back to her cruise ship after the concert, (ii) to walk to Skyssstasjon, which is a restaurant in one of the city's oldest buildings, a walk along Bakklandet, a trip to the island outside Trondheim, Munkholmen, and transport back to her cruise ship. She wonders if some of her fellow passengers who are also visiting the city would like these offers and forwards the offer to the other passengers that signed on for the Trondheim Experience service.

In order to utilize the limited time she has in Trondheim and enjoy the city rather than finding out what's on offer, she accepts the first offer and plans the rest of her day. She visits the museum at the Archbishop's residence and continues walking around the city centre until the time to go to the restaurant. As she passes various buildings and shops, she is informed about the architecture and history of the building and about sales and offers in the shops, depending on her interests. Also, she is able to find out who will be joining her for the concert and the traditional Norwegian meal.

4. ANALYSIS

The scenario described in the previous section establishes a tourist's needs and proposes some services. The tourist can ask for a specific service, for examples, the glossary service for explanations of street signs. However, the AmI component is mainly aimed at establishing the tourist's needs based on information available from the tourist, patterns of needs by previous users as well as what can be detected automatically, such as location and time (e.g. date, time of the day and season). The tourist is provided a set of services based on this. In addition to providing information that is directly relevant there and then, the tourist is also prompted with other potential services, e.g. the package including a museum and a meal. The tourist is also able to communicate with other tourists that use the same service. The services provided respond to a possible need as well as try to stimulate the user for possible needs in the near future.

Consider the **user's perspective**, in this case the tourist. The tourist would like to see and learn as much about the city as possible within the time that is available, i.e. one day. As the tourist walks around the city, she may wish to know about the architecture of the buildings, where to find specific items and souvenirs, listen to some local music and taste traditional food. Finding out these things is time consuming and joining a guided tour of the city can be constraining. The tourist who likes to walk around the city and see the sights and learn about the city would like a combination of the guided tour and a free walk, i.e. a personalized guided tour.

Consider the **service provider's perspective**, in this case the local businesses and the city of Trondheim. The city of Trondheim would like the tourist to have a good time, form a positive impression of the city and attract the tourist for a visit in the future. At the same time, it would like the tourist to visit the historical sights of the city, contribute to the maintenance of these by purchasing entrance tickets and souvenirs. The local businesses would like the tourist to visit their shops or restaurants and use their services, thus increasing their customer base and the volume of business they conduct. Rather than leaving the tourist to accidentally stumble upon what the city has to offer, the city could collectively be proactive in guiding the tourist through the parts of the city that suits the tourist's preferences. The number of parties that are interested in meeting the needs of the tourist and stimulate more needs from the tourist while enhancing their own business prospects is huge and varied. To achieve optimal benefit from this situation, the service providers need to collaborate and form alliances or VEs to provide a set of services to the tourist.

AmI establishes a user's needs while a VE can be used to meet the needs of the user. AmI focuses on the user's perspective of the situation while a VE is seen from a service provider's perspective.

5. SERVICES PROVIDERS AS VIRTUAL ENTERPRISES

We consider a VE as a set of entities, such as organizations, human beings or software agents that collaborate to achieve a specific goal (Petersen and Gruninger 2000). A VE can be characterised as a partnership of enterprises that collaborate as a temporary network, (Jagdev and Browne 1998), by sharing their skills, costs and risks. This network may consist of pre-existing enterprises that collaborate by means of specific Information Technology components (Garita and Afsarmanesh 2001). They align their goals and commit to achieving these goals through a process of negotiation. VEs are usually formed to exploit a market opportunity (Fischer et al. 1996), and their dynamic and flexible nature facilitates the quick and easy formation as well as adaptation to the market situation.

To provide the services in an AmI environment, a number of entities must collaborate behind the scenes. We believe that VEs are necessary for providing services that are seamless and cohesive in an AmI environment. The dynamic and flexible nature of VEs facilitates the adaptation to the user's needs. The relationship between AmI and VE is illustrated in **Figure 1**.

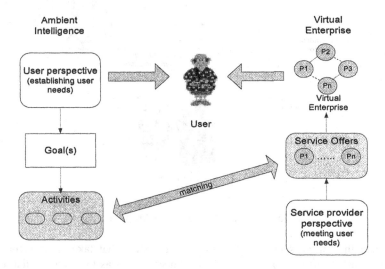

Figure 1: Relationship between Ambient Intelligence and Virtual Enterprises

A tourist's situation and desires, established by AmI, can be modelled as a set of goals that need to be fulfilled. Using ideas from Enterprise Modelling, goals can be achieved by performing a set of activities (Petersen and Gruninger 2000). The identification or the selection of the set of appropriate activities that best fulfils the goals can be done by reasoning.

Service providers in the city who are interested in serving the tourists are transmitting information about themselves as service offers. Some of these service providers, e.g. P1, P2, P3 and Pn as shown in **Figure 1**, could perform the set of activities that fulfil the goals. Thus, the response to the tourist's needs as a set of activities can be proposed by a group of partners that collaborate, i.e. a VE, to deliver a set of services. For example, the museum at the Archbishop's residence, the concert organizer, the restaurant and the taxi company form a VE to propose the first offer to the tourist. The tourist can pay for this package offer as a single product without negotiating with each service provider individually. Once this is accepted by the tourist, the VE needs to deliver the services and the mobile device guides her through the city to reach the goals that have been set, while continuing to dynamically assess possible changes in her needs.

In order for such VEs to form, each service provider must provide information about their offers, their interests, who they wish to collaborate with and other relevant information. This information can be used first to match against the requirements for performing the activities and second, to form an appropriate team of partners that constitute the VE. An example of such a VE formation model and supporting infrastructure are described in (Petersen et al. 2003).

6. SYSTEM DESIGN

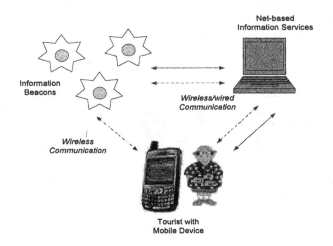

Figure 2: Functional System Architecture

To realize the tourist scenario, we envisage a system that takes into account the runtime context information for the tourist's needs, such as location, availability of services, as well as utilize information about past experiences and tourist's preferences. Reasoning capabilities can be used to establish the needs as well as to determine the services to offer. Based on the experiences from the AmbieSense project, (AmbieSense 2005) and (Kofod-Petersen and Mikalsen 2005(a)), a functional systems architecture for realising our scenario is shown in **Figure 2**. The tourist has a device that detects location. A net-based information service contains previous experiences and reasoning capabilities. Service providers submit their information to the information services using information beacons, e.g. (Kofod-Petersen and Mikalsen 2005(b)). The communication via the different entities can be wireless.

Establishing the tourist's needs/perception: the first step is to understand something about the tourist's interests. When she signs up for the Trondheim Experience service, she is asked to select some keywords that indicate her interests, e.g. medieval Trondheim, Norwegian food, shopping. In order to personalize the services offered to the tourist, a profile of the tourist must be established. A good candidate for constructing user models is through stereotypes as reported in (Jayaputera et al. 2003). This requires some form of reasoning. Why was the tourist prompted about the guided tour of the cathedral? One reason could be that she is currently in that location. Why was she offered the two specific packages for experiencing Trondheim? The selective offers can be based on what is known about the tourist, e.g. her interest in medieval Trondheim and Norwegian food and what tourists that have used the Trondheim Experience service in the past with similar interests have desired. Reasoning capabilities facilitate the personalization of the information and services offered to the tourist.

The net-based information services determine the information that should be presented to the tourist based on her needs. Since the tourist has signed on for the Trondheim Experience, we assume that she is interested in receiving some information and service offers. She can choose to receive personalized information or all information that is available (e.g. which may include some advertising information) and she can selectively turn the service on an off.

Service offers/personalized response: The services that are available for any context can be provided by a predefined model of the city. A more dynamic way of doing this is the use of information beacons in the city that provide runtime information to the system about the services that are currently available in and around any location, see **Figure 2**. Thus, the service providers transmit information about themselves using the information beacons. The use of information beacons by the service providers allow them to control the information that they publish about themselves and be selective about their audience. This allows the service providers the opportunity to submit their information and offers, if and when they desire, and to selected groups of users based on the user profile. For example, a shop selling scuba diving equipment may not desire to send information to a tourist that is interested in medieval Trondheim. Based on this information, reasoning capabilities in the system can be used to provide a response that is appropriate for the current situation, i.e. a personalized response.

Information services/reasoning: the information services that both the mobile device and the information beacons are connected to are capable of reasoning to establish the user's needs based on available information. The system establishes a profile of the tourist and determines the type of user she is. Then it will answer questions such as which offers shall we propose to the tourist? Once the tourist accepts a package, the goal of the system is to lead the tourist through the city to utilize the services that have been purchased. While traversing through this path, the system finds opportunities to propose other services to the tourist such as information about the architecture of a building and sales offers. Again, the tourist can choose to receive this information.

7. SUMMARY

VEs provide a promising business model for realising AmI scenarios. This paper describes the scenario of a tourist in a wireless city, who can be provided a personalized city guide via AmI. The tourist's needs are established using AmI and the needs are met by a group of service providers that collaborate as a VE. We have discussed the relevance of VEs for realising AmI scenarios and proposed the design of a system that facilitates such scenarios.

The ideas presented in this paper describe an innovative use of VEs to provide rich and personalized user experiences. Its main contribution is to propose means of realizing AmI where the business and societal perspectives are considered. As discussed, AmI is realized by the collaboration of several entities or service providers and VEs are a promising means of providing seamless and cohesive services in an AmI environment.

8. ACKNOWLEDGEMENT

The ideas presented in this paper are inspired by the work done in the projects MOTUS2, supported by the Norwegian Research Council, and AmbieSense, (EU project IST 2001-34244).

9. REFERENCES

1. AmbieSense 2005, Available from http://www.ambiesense.net/
2. Ducatel K, Bogdanowicz B, Scapolo F, Leijten J, Burgelman J-C. Scenarios for Ambient Intelligence in 2010, Final Report, IPTS-Seville, 2001.
3. Fischer K, Müller J, Hemmig I, Scheer AW. Intelligent Agents in Virtual Enterprises. In Proc. of 1st International Conference on the Practical Applications of Intelligent Agents and Multi-Agent Technology (PAAM-96), London, U.K.
4. Garita C, Afsarmanesh H. A Study of Information Management Approaches for Support Infrastructures. COVE Newsletter (1), 2001.
5. ISTAG, Ambient Intelligence: from Vision to Reality, in Ambient Intelligence, Lakatta Riva G, Vatalaro F, Davide F, Alcañiz M (Eds.), IOS Press, 2005.
6. Jagdev HS, Browne J. The Extended Enterprise - A Context for Manufacturing. International Journal of Production Planning and Control, 9(3), pp. 216-229.
7. Jayaputera G, Alahakoon O, Cruz LP, Loke SW, Zaslavsky AB. Assembling Agents On-Demand for Pervasive Wireless Services, Wireless Information Systems, Ed. Mahmoud QH, ICEIS Press, 2003.
8. Kofod-Petersen A, Mikalsen M. An Architecture Supporting implementation of Context-Aware Services. In Proc. of Workshop on Context Awareness for Proactive Systems (CAPS 2005), Eds. Florén P, Lindén G, Niklander T, Raatikainen K. Helsinki, Finland June 2005 (a).
9. Kofod-Petersen A, Mikalsen M. Context: Representation and Reasoning — Representing and Reasoning about Context in a Mobile Environment. Revue d'Intelligence Artificielle, 2005(b), 19(3):479-498.
10. Myrhaug HI, Göker A. AmbieSense — Interactive Information Channels in the Surroundings of the Mobile User. In Univeral Access in HCI, 10th International Conference on Human-Computer Interaction, Eds. Stephanidis C, Lawrence Erlbaum Associates, 2003, pp. 1158-1162.
11. Petersen SA, Gruninger M. An Agent-based Model to Support the Formation of Virtual Enterprises. International ICSC Symposium on Mobile Agents and Multi-agents in Virtual Organizations and E-Commerce (MAMA 2000), in Woolongong, Australia, 11-13 Dec. 2000.
12. Petersen SA, Rao J, Matskin M, Virtual Enterprise Formation with Agents - an Approach to Implementation, IEEE/WIC International Conference on Intelligent Agent Technology, IAT2003, Halifax, Canada, October 2003, pp. 527-530.
13. Russel SJ, Norvig P. Artificial Intelligence: A Modern Approach. Prentice Hall, 2nd Edition, 2002.
14. Satyanarayanan M. Pervasive Computing: Vision and Challenges. IEEE Personal Communications, 2001, 8(4), pp. 10-17.
15. Wang AI, Sørensen C, Brede S, Servold H, Gimre S.: The Nidaros Framework for Development of Location-aware Applications, In Proc. 2nd IFIP TC8 Working Conference on Mobile Information Systems - 2005 (MOBIS'2005), Leeds UK, 5-6 December 2005, pp. 171-186.
16. Weiser M. The computer for the 21st century. Scientific American, Sept. 1991, pp. 94-104.
17. Weiser M, Brown JS. The Coming Age of Calm Technology. In Beyond Calculation: The Next Fifty Years of Computing, Eds. Denning PJ, Metcalfe RM. Springer-Verlag, 1997, pp. 75-85.

66

CASE-STUDY: HOW TO IMPLEMENT COLLABORATIVE SOFTWARE SUPPLY- CHAINS – LESSONS LEARNED FROM THE TASK- INITIATIVE

Dieter Hertweck
Daniel Bouché

Heilbronn University
Faculty for Electronic Business, GERMANY
hertweck@hs-heilbronn.de
bouche@hs-heilbronn.de

This paper describes the evolution of organizational structures and collaborative behaviors of forty different software producing companies, in the state of Baden-Württemberg, with a common aim of developing component based business software. The case shows that the role and cultural experience of network facilitators has a major input on further organizational evolution. To analyze the forces for diverse structural evolution and the exploration of suitable implementation processes for regional catalyst are the central intentions of the paper.

1   INTRODUCTION

In July 2004 forty software companies in the state of Baden-Württemberg started a common initiative with the aim of producing standardized high quality component based business software and offering it to regional software-consuming SMEs, in different sectors under a common brand and certified trade mark. The initiative was coordinated by a state agency acting as the regional catalyst with the tasks of project and community management whilst controlling the success.

The idea to launch such an initiative came out of a final report considering the future of the IT industry that has been carried out by a work group of IT experts, leading entrepreneurs, government representatives and prime universities from Baden-Württemberg along with the first results of the just started Integrated EU Project Digital Business Ecosystem (DBE). Baden-Württemberg is known for its dense population of software producing and consuming SME, especially in the automotive and machine tool manufacturer sectors. Since their organizational "supply chain" was successful, a major aim of the project was to test the opportunities and boundaries of this approach by adapting it to software production.

Please use the following format when citing this chapter:

Hertweck, D., Bouché, D., 2006, in IFIP International Federation for Information Processing, Volume 224, Network-Centric Collaboration and Supporting Fireworks, eds. Camarinha-Matos, L., Afsarmanesh, H., Ollus, M., (Boston: Springer), pp. 627–634.

A major force in restructuring this scenario of the IT sector was forecast by Scheer (Scheer 2005) and Roland Berger. From their point of view future software and IT service production were based on the following further developments:

1. The coding of software to be developed into a commodity of the future, that could be outsourced to off shore regions like India or Eastern Europe
2. A continuous increase in the development of the value chain of selling hardware and software, towards selling IS solutions, or the execution of whole business processes (see fig. 1). The IS solutions to be customized by the orchestration of existing quality proofed software components
3. The business success of Baden-Württemberg, and of Germany, to be built on the knowledge of business processes, located in smart and medium sized automotive or machine tool companies

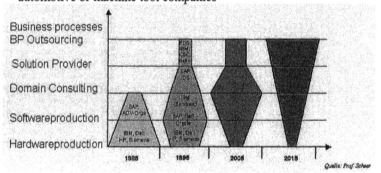

Figure 1 – future of the IT-Industry

These are the reasons why enterprises in Baden-Württemberg should be able to model and steer the value production in software supply chains, these consisting of: business process outsourcing, IS solution providers and software component suppliers at different levels. This paper shows how the experiences of the project TASK, along with the lessons learned for local governmental units in Europe

2   COLLABORATIVE FORMS IN COMPONENT BASED SOFTWARE PRODUCTION – AN OVERVIEW

Traditional software production is operated by one company with an internal development team with structured software processes, based on models like the Waterfall (Royce, 1970) or Rapid Prototyping (Pomberger, Blaschek 96). The advantage of this production process is the high level of internal quality control and knowledge keeping. The disadvantage is the high number of highly qualified human resources required, for the structured coding of new software releases or versions. To obtain such excellent resources is difficult in a dynamic market. To program software in a stronger object oriented process will help to save human resources. In sum software quality will be gained by the reuse of tested code fragments from the past.

2.1　Open Source (OS) Communities and component orientation

Starting with the disadvantages of traditional programming and the spirit to produce software in a slightly different way, there was a new production paradigm evolving in the late 80's - the open source development often linked with component orientation. The distributed production processes like requirements engineering, coding, versioning and testing were coordinated by the members of the OS community itself, supported by a shared development platform.

An interesting outcome of this production paradigm was the quality of the resulting software being considered as better and with the processes being faster than traditional software production. In the early period of OS, there hadn't been a business model behind the communities. They were often constituted by the engagement of their members and the code of the emerging solution being public, so participants could profit from the working results. With the saturation of good available OS components at the free market like: web-server, security or authorizing components; a new type of small system integration companies appeared. They took OS components as a base for their development of more complex systems like e.g. CRM or ERP. According to the GPL license they didn't charge the software to the end customer but services.

2.2　Component based Software supply chains

In comparison to these loose relationships of idealistic OS-programmers and communities, the supply chain paradigm has a strong division of labor and predefined roles, derived from the future development of the IT sector. The forecast industrial structure soon became reality and was supported by the component strategies introduced by players like IBM (Websphere) or SAP (Netweaver). The degree of flexibility and integration is optimized by implementing cross company business processes using predefined component frameworks. Therefore, software components are produced, integrated and consumed in a vertical supply chain, consisting of infrastructure, middleware and application component suppliers, system integrators and customers. (Vithrana, 2004, see fig. 2).

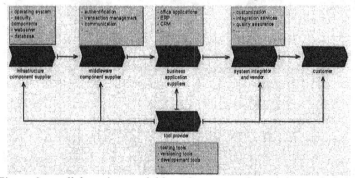

Figure 2 – collaboration model in software supply and demand chains

The system integrator delivers an individual IS derived from the customers' requirements and a fitting IS architecture. The architecture consists of high quality standardized components, offered by suppliers of different tiers (application, middleware and infrastructure) and tested by an independent expert of a quality assurance instance. A shared component development platform delivers helpful tools for orchestration, production, versioning and testing tasks.

2.3   Digital business Ecosystem (DBE)

A digital business ecosystem could be described as a systemic approach including parts of the OS-community and software-supply-chain approach. In difference to them the software and service component platform contains/includes an embedded intelligence, which supports the whole regional network with new business models and tools for self-organization. A DBE consists of:
- Research and education organizations and innovation centres
- Small and large enterprises with their associations
- Local government and public administration can be characterised *"by intelligent software components and services, knowledge transfer, interactive training frameworks and integration of business processes and egovernance models. The latter step in the adoption of Internet-based technologies for business, where the business services and the software components are supported by a pervasive software environment, which shows an evolutionary and self-organising behaviour, will be named digital business ecosystems". (Nachira et al. 2002)*

3   TASK-CASE: IMPLEMENTATION METHOD OF SUPPLY CHAINS IN BADEN-WÜRTTEMBERG

In 2004, when Baden-Württemberg started TASK to establish regional software supply chains, the initiative was embedded in several innovation and research projects, which were quite unique and risky. There was no experience in the transfer of the supply-chain-paradigm to the software sector available. The implementation strategy, chosen by the regional catalyst, was divided in 4 major steps (see fig 3):

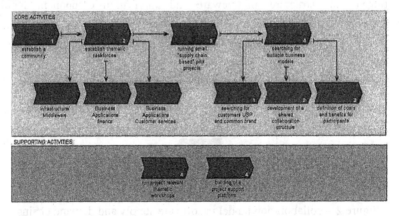

Figure 3 – planned implementation strategy

1. Establishing a powerful community of software producing companies
2. Foundation of three different task forces on an infrastructure/middleware and business application level, coordinated by three paid facilitators

3. Running small software-supply-chain pilot projects introduced by the facilitators, while developing a fitting project collaboration and information portal
4. Development of a common business model for all project partners including a common brand, a collaboration structure and a cost-/benefit model.

The establishment of a powerful community of interested software component and service providers was shown that 40 companies joined the TASK community. The strategy of grouping them into three different task forces, to produce component based information systems in a supply chain, was based on the assumption of their capabilities. To instigate the objective, the regional catalyst hired IT experts for each task force, to initiate and support the methodology of the supply chain pilot projects and to implement their management knowledge. In choosing well known moderators - two with long term open source development experience, and one with IT consultancy background - was based on the assumption that they could motivate further companies to participate and donate component solutions at different levels. Furthermore, local events with the topics of collaboration in software supply chains and communities were organized by the catalyst. The overall aim was to gain a critical mass of different reusable software components and the delivery of quality proved systems and services to a potential end customer.

4 RESULTS

Although there was a lot of strategic planning behind TASK, a real project success was the creation of a sustainable software production network; however this wasn't directly visible till the project's end. There was no implementation of a software supply chain in two of three of the pilot projects, because the moderators with an open source background couldn't see the sense behind fixing a collaboration structure as an added value on its own. They succeeded to produce their project results in an OS-community manner. In their opinion the project complexity was so low and the partners so equal to each other in size and power, that a hierarchical supply chain structure would have been a real overhead in comparison to the aimed IS solution.

This was different in the third pilot project that was moderated by an IT-consultant with a business background. He builds up a complete supply chain with a potent system integrator and IT-service provider, as well as different smaller component vendors, into the pilot project. The service providers were especially inspired by the idea of a component supply chain, and the opportunity to market a state own brand to regional medium sized enterprise customers. They forced the whole supply chain to instantiate the customer service solution out of existing software components and defined and developed an interface standard suitable for their project. When the moderator of this task force tried to get a commitment from component suppliers of other task forces and to define a common interface and data exchange standard, he failed. A main reason was that the standardization of a project would have created increased efforts by participants without them seeing the added benefits, by either the potential customer or by the state. This was due to a missing costs/benefit calculation, based on an estimated number of sold software licenses along with the supporting services required. Additionally there hadn't been a clear defined and communicated marketing concept, showing the benefits of supply chain produced component software to end customers and suppliers. Towards the project end, there was a lack of a serious future business model and marketing strategy or commitment to existing models e.g. to the economy of component reusability (Gill 2003).

At this moment the regional catalyst gave us the opportunity to do an independent review on the project to benefit from the lessons learned.

5   LESSONS LEARNED

One lesson learned from this case was the difficulty in implementing regional software supply chains, digital business ecosystem or the type of collaboration networks, without having a clear idea and concept of the future business model.

Traditionally, a business model consists of three elements (Timmers, 98): USP/market position, value chain design and cost/benefit structure. To cement the value chain design right at the start without knowing the product USP for the customer or the costs and benefits for the participants, is a questionable approach.

It would make sense to define the USP of a component based information system by doing a SWOT-analysis first. There would be strengths for the customer like high adaptability and flexibility of the product, as well as benefits for the system integrator, to reach these features by the recombination of existing components cheaply. A weakness of component based information systems is that they don't perform well when fast tracking is required. From this point of view it will be much easier to identify areas where component based information systems have a good USP, like the customer service domain. The next step would be to define the component architecture, with its fitting to the possible customer requirements. In this phase it is mandatory to define a common component interface and data exchange standard for all the participating component suppliers. Without standards, the benefits of reusability and easy integration couldn't be realized. The standardization and architecture definition at the beginning of the project would narrow the necessary variety of success critical components and ensure calculable adaptation efforts later on.

Apparently, if all components were compatible with each other, it would be a question of collaboration culture to establish a suitable organization of the value chain. In supply chains, component suppliers need a higher commitment and should be willing to pay a certain amount of money for services like quality assurance or marketing. Active OS communities are able to deliver continuous work instead of funds. So the question of choosing a supply chain or a community could be depends on the size and investment opportunities of the software companies. Furthermore the power of system integrators is quite immense in supply chains, because they are able to choose only one component supplier the whole time, so that other suppliers have costs for standardizing their components and paying for network services without getting a benefit. The cost and benefit questions are the last major step in successfully implementing virtual enterprise, that should be addressed after defining the value chain design. A component supplier should know how often his component must be sold, e.g. in CRM projects, to get a payback of their investments in the operation of the virtual enterprise.

Confronting the TASK participants with costs and benefits of the successful introduced supply-chain model, a few component suppliers mentioned that they don't need a cost/benefit structure, while others showed interest. It does make sense to structure the project implementation process and strategy differently (see fig. 3). Doing so, the collaboration structure appears as a system variable that will emerge in a self-organizing process similar to the DBE-approach.

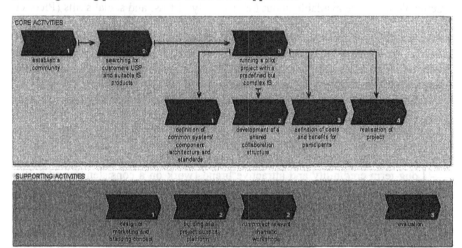

Figure 3 – target implementation reference process after review of the project

This work should be carried out by all component suppliers, rather than different task forces facilitated by an excellent IT consultant and software architect. The regional catalyst can support these works by increasing the size of the community, along with running marketing activities for a common brand, as well as compensating parts of the standardization efforts the suppliers have to get an easy lock-in (Shapiro, Varian, 1999). The value chain for system production should be co-developed and open to different collaboration scenarios, depending on the customers, integrators and suppliers' economic and cultural structure and their will to take risks or responsibility. Once an appointment made between system integrator/vendor and customer, the integrator can cooperate with his supplier contract or trust based – dependent on his knowledge about the quality of the components and the supplier performance. Acquiring new suppliers consequentially means discussing the issue of potential costs and benefits. Further, a higher number of system integrators in the community will hinder individual system integrators getting too dominant within the community.

6   FORECAST

The TASK case showed the difficulty in establishing a totally new structured virtual enterprise in the software sector. Major lessons learned were the questions of USP and branding, the component architecture, the value chain design, along with the cost and benefit structure, being closely linked to each other in reference to being addressed in the early phase of the project. To develop solely in software supply chains makes no sense if the resulting product, the customer, the authority of system integrators and suppliers are still insufficiently transparent. It was the aim of this case to show a capable method for a regional catalyst of implementing component based software and service production networks. But this was a single scenario. In the future more research needs to be done on business models for virtual enterprises, in the area of value chain design and cost/benefit analysis. There is plenty of practicable literature available about the necessity of trust and social skills (Picot et. Al. 2003) to participate in virtual enterprises or structural factors (Wagner et al., 2004), while less works show benefits and costs of collaborative scenarios in the IT industry. Nevertheless the first results from the DBE project showed (Dini, Rathbone, 2005, p.9), that there were similar experiences made. They identified the following success factors for implementation:

- Global solutions with a local input and sector approach (use of European wide solutions to adapt to regional conditions)
- No single point of failure and control in the virtual enterprise (no predetermination of a centralized organizational structure)
- Commitment to Open Source and Open Standards
- Long-term credibility and attractive brand (work on a consistent brand as the USP)
- Utilisation of proven technologies (reusable component technologies)
- Proven business cases and benefits for service providers and service users.

Bringing these experiences together in developing reference models and best practices, for the implementation of virtual enterprises around Europe, will be both an important and fruitful future issue.

7   REFERENCES

1. Dini, P., Rathbone, N., The Digital Ecosystem Research Vision: 2010 and beyond. http://www.digital-ecosystem.org/Members/aenglishx/linkstofiles/dbe_position_paper_vf.pdf/download, 2005
2. Gill, N. Reusability issues in component-based development, ACM Press, New York, NY, USA, 2003
3. Nachira, F. Towards a Network of Digital Business Ecosystem. Fostering the local development, http://www.digital-ecosystems.org/doc/discussionpaper.pdf, Bruxelles 2002
4. Picot, A. , Reichwald, R., Wiegand, R., Die Grenzenlose Unternehmung, Gabler-Verlag, Wiesbaden, 5. Auflage, p. 123 f., 2003
5. Pomberger, G., Blaschek, G., Software Engineering – Prototyping und objektorientierte Software-Entwicklung, Carl Hanser Verlag München Wien, 1996.
6. Royce, W. W., Managing the development of large software systems', Proc. WESTCON, Ca., USA, 1970
7. Scheer, A.-W., Ein Pionier blickt zurück in die Zukunft. Scheer magazin, IDS Scheer AG, Universität des Saarlands, 2/2005.
8. Shapiro, C., Varian, H. Information Rules, A strategic guide to the network economy, p. 222, Harvard Business School Press, 1998
9. Timmers, P.: Business Models for Electronic Markets. In: EM - Electronic Markets, Vol. 8, No. 2, 07/98
10. Vitharana, P., Risks and challenges of component-based software development. Commun. ACM 46, 8 (Aug. 2003), 67-72.
11. Wagner, C. Europe, Competing: Market Prospects, Business Needs and Technological Trends for Virtual, Smart Organisations in Europe. Report for the European Commission, Information Society 2004.

67

A COLLABORATIVE LEGAL FRAMEWORK FOR CERTIFIED ENFORCEMENT WITH ITSIbus ALPR

Jorge Silva[1], Arnaldo Abrantes[1], A. Luís Osório[2], Bruno Basílio[3], J. Sales Gomes[3]

[1]ISEL, Instituto Superior de Engenharia de Lisboa, M2A research group, PORTUGAL
{jgs, aja}@.isel.ipl.pt
[2]ISEL, Instituto Superior de Engenharia de Lisboa, GIATSI research group, PORTUGAL
aosorio@deetc.isel.ipl.pt
[3]BRISA, Auto-estradas de Portugal, DIT Innovation and Technology Department, PORTUGAL
{Jorge.Gomes, Bruno.Basilio}@brisa.pt

This paper discusses a collaborative framework for the legal certification of toll enforcement on motorways operated by Brisa Auto-Estradas de Portugal, based on the Advanced License Plate Recognition (ALPR) system/service. The developed ALPR service produces a composite JPEG picture documenting an irregular situation. An enforcement transaction is generated at Brisa's toll infrastructure and later delivered to the toll clearing company Via Verde Portugal (VVP). This company processes the generated composite picture, matching it with the client data base and, if necessary, pursuing legal action. The enforcement picture might also be delivered to other organizations, such as the official entity for car registration management, in Portugal the General Direction of Traffic (DGV). Certification is based on Public Key Infrastructure (PKI) and legal digital certificates. Its purpose is to guarantee the validation of an ALPR generated picture as genuine, at a court of law; any change will be detected by a validation service. The paper discusses the adopted strategy, considering not only technical but also organizational issues, since the trust required for the management of enforcement pictures along the involved networked organizations requires a set of procedures to be followed in order to ensure the required legal confidence (trust).

1. INTRODUCTION

Enforcement is an essential component of an automated toll system, and presents organizational as well as technological challenges. The success of an enforcement solution depends not only on its effectiveness but also on the trust that networked participants and actors involved in the enforcement process place in the solution. A key step in cementing such trust consists in the preemption of falsification claims regarding the evidence documenting any irregularity. This need is particularly acute when such evidence exists in electronic form and might have to be presented at a court of law. Furthermore, the number of involved networked organizations and

Please use the following format when citing this chapter:

Silva, J., Abrantes, A., Osório, A. L., Basilio, B., Gomes, J. S., 2006, in IFIP International Federation for Information Processing, Volume 224, Network-Centric Collaboration and Supporting Fireworks, eds. Camarinha-Matos, L., Afsarmanesh, H., Ollus, M., (Boston: Springer), pp. 635–642.

clients of the toll infrastructure configure a trusted collaborative network (Camarinha-Matos, 2004), where enforcement information is exchanged following the established legal framework.

This paper describes both a certification strategy and a collaborative model for the involved organizations, designed to address the above issue in the specific case of motorway toll enforcement for the Via Verde Portugal (VVP) toll clearing company, at motorways operated by Brisa Auto-Estradas de Portugal.

In regular conditions, electronic toll collection in the Via Verde is performed through Dedicated Short Range Communication (DSRC) at microwave frequencies (5.8 GHz) between an antenna in the toll plaza and an identifier device, also called an On-Board Unit (OBU), inside the vehicle. The identifier contains information about the owner's identity and the vehicle class, the latter being confirmed by the Automatic Vehicle Detection and Classification (AVDC) system.

Enforcement is based on the Advanced License Plate Recognition (ALPR) system/service, developed by Brisa and integrated in the ITSIbus architecture (Gomes, 2003), (Osório, 2004). In an irregular situation, such as a vehicle without an OBU, or when any other problem prevents the toll infrastructure from registering a valid transaction, the ALPR system generates a composite picture in Joint Photographic Experts Group (JPEG) format, showing a rear view of the vehicle, as well as sub-images of the front and rear license plates obtained from two separate IR cameras. Additionally, meta-information is appended so that other services may subsequently extract the license plate.

The certification technology is based on Public Key Infrastructure (PKI) (Schneier, 1996) and legal digital certificates. However, it is necessary to certify other processes beyond the service/system that appends the digital signature to the original picture. As an example, management of the private key, used to generate the digital signature associated with a certificate generated by a certification authority, needs to be maintained under rigorous collaborative guidelines. The overall certification strategy has been designed to comply with requirements expressed in national legislation for electronic documents to be used as evidence, while ensuring protection of the motorway users' privacy. The structure of this paper is the following: the logical and physical architecture of the enforcement data collection and transmission system, including the ALPR, integrated in the context of the overall toll management system, are described; next, the proposed security, collaborative framework and related organizational as well as legal issues are discussed, followed by concluding remarks.

2. ARCHITECTURE OF THE ENFORCEMENT SYSTEM

There are four levels in toll management, as illustrated in Figure 1, ranging from individual Via Verde lanes to the toll plaza and finally up to the central Toll Coordination System (TCS).

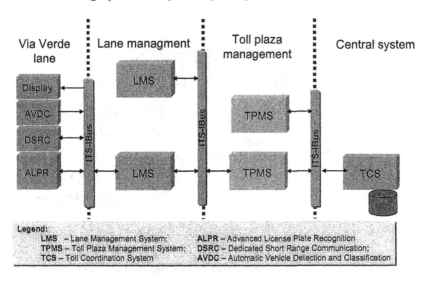

Figure 1 – Toll management levels.

Communication takes place between each level and the ones adjacent to it, using a service-based communication bus, the ITSIbus. The ITSIbus defines a set of basic services, such as security, configuration and administration, as well as "*plug-and-play*" mechanisms. Besides the basic services, an additional set of services is defined as standard for each class of systems, to be implemented by all developers.

The lane management level, implemented by LMS systems, controls the passage of vehicles and the generation of transactions according to each specific situation. Among the possible scenarios to be handled by an LMS, emphasis is given to the following: passage of a vehicle without an OBU; OBU with a low battery; mismatch between the automatically detected vehicle class and the class associated with the OBU.

In case such an irregularity occurs, the ALPR generates a proof of passage of the vehicle involved, at the request of the LMS. This proof of passage consists of a composite picture of the vehicle. The picture is forwarded by the LMS to the corresponding TPMS, where it is stored for later transmission to the TCS. Thus, pictures are generated by the ALPR system in response to events originating in lane-level equipment and systems like the DSRC and AVDC, resulting in a flow of information across the private and secure network infrastructure of the motorway operator, from the lane to the central TCS. The internal ITSIbus collaborative service infrastructure has no direct access from outside the organization, which removes the vulnerability from Internet-based attacks.

Under an enforcement scenario, should the authenticity of the picture need to be verified in court, a validation application (itself certified) can perform the necessary check, by confronting the digital signature in the JPEG header with the remaining data. A collaborative process models and manages the necessary information exchange, in this case between the motorway operator and the road authority and if necessary a court. The overall flow of information is illustrated in Figure 2.

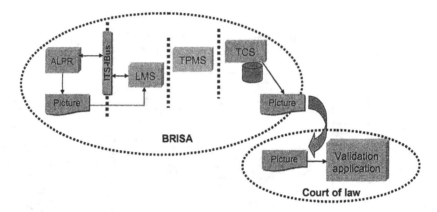

Figure 2 – Flow of an ALPR-generated picture across all involved systems.

The legal value of the ALPR-generated picture depends on other factors beyond the ALPR itself. In fact, the collaborative processes and procedures regarding physical equipment accessibility, as well as other involved systems, contribute towards maintaining the required information integrity and trust among the involved partners.

3. DESCRIPTION OF THE ALPR

The ALPR is one of the roadside systems on a Via Verde lane. Its purpose is to provide an electronic document (picture plus meta-information) allowing the identification of the vehicle, the place and date/time of passage, whenever the LMS, in response to a vehicle passage event, requires such a document. An example picture is depicted in Figure 3.

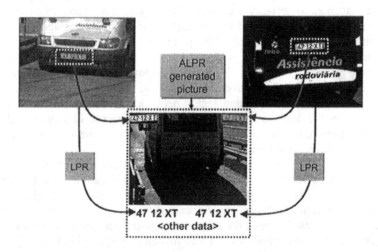

Figure 3 – Example of an ALPR picture.

The primary requirements of the ALPR are as follows:

- Acquisition of a panoramic rear view of the vehicle, allowing visual inspection
- Automatic recognition of the front and rear license plates
- Generation of a JPEG composite picture, with the cropped front and rear plate sub-images overlaid on the rear panoramic view
- Independence of the image quality on weather conditions, time of day, condition of the plate and other variables
- Regarding acquisition of the front image, only the license plate must be extracted and appended to the composite picture, while the remainder of the image must never even be written to disk

Figure 4 illustrates the logical architecture of the ALPR, including the optional certification module, which generates a digital signature included in the meta-information appended to the enforcement picture. The remaining meta-information includes a timestamp and also the vehicle class, as detected by the AVDC.

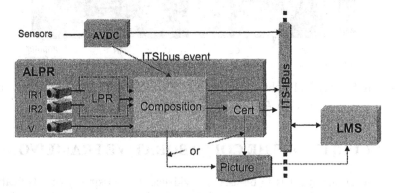

Figure 4 – Logical architecture of the ALPR system, including the optional certification module (Cert).

The ALPR was developed using artificial vision and Optical Character Recognition (OCR) technology (Rahman, 2003), (Duc Duan, 2005). The license plate recognition process has been decoupled from the visual inspection process by using different images, in different wavelengths: infra-red (IR) images for license plate recognition; visible images, in color, for human inspection.

One of the reasons for this decoupling is the fact that the recognition process benefits from high contrast images where the license plate is highlighted, unlike the visual inspection image, which should clearly show the vehicle and its surroundings. Also, the use of IR images for recognition is a common procedure for making the recognition process as independent from lighting conditions as possible.

The physical architecture of the ALPR can be seen in Figure 5. The system consists of two modules, one in front and another in the rear of a passing vehicle. The front module contains an IR camera and an IR illuminator, and it is connected to the rear module, which contains another IR camera and illuminator, together with a visible spectrum color camera and a computer equipped with a multi-channel frame grabber. The computer is connected to the LMS and the motorway operator's network.

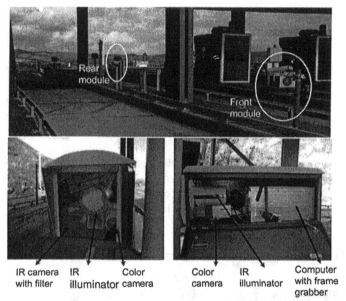

| IR camera with filter | IR illuminator | Color camera | Color camera | IR illuminator | Computer with frame grabber |

Figure 5 – Physical architecture of the ALPR system. Above: the front and rear modules. Below: detail of the rear module.

4. SECURITY OF THE COLLABORATIVE FRAMEWORK

Whenever a document is to be used as evidence, the possibility of falsification or forgery must be taken into account, whether or not the document exists in electronic format. The developed security collaborative framework takes into account the fact that several types of attack are possible (Coulouris, 2001), (Macgregor, 1996), namely:

- Replacement of a legitimate ALPR unit with a duplicate, built by a third party with knowledge of the technology
- Introduction of a "Trojan horse" into an ALPR unit, either during scheduled maintenance or by unauthorized access through the private network
- Eavesdropping into the messages exchanged through the private network, during transactions
- Tampering with the picture, for example editing the image to change license plate characters

Protection against these types of attack requires organizational as well as technological measures. Physical access to the units must be restricted, validated using, for instance, PINs or codes and smart-cards, and recorded for future traceability. Network security is also a concern. Sensitive information, such as PINs or passwords, should never be sent in clear text.

Encryption and digital signature are a key technological component of the security system, and so are the monitoring capabilities of the ITSIbus. For example, if an ALPR unit is removed, even temporarily, an exception is generated by the ITSIbus, either through sensors connected to the physical system or by detecting a loss of communication. Pictures from that particular unit will no longer be trusted until the source of the exception is investigated.

As for ensuring the integrity of the JPEG pictures, a digital signature scheme is used, as illustrated in Figure 6. The system uses the public key infrastructure (PKI), and the picture is digitally signed. This process may take place directly in the ALPR using the optional Certification module, as in Figure 4, or it may take place at a later point instead. Which option is used depends on whether or not the communication link with the central services is considered secure enough.

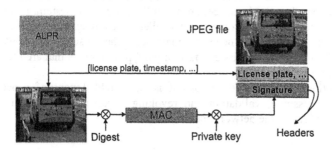

Figure 6 – Integrity control model.

The signature process is based on the concept of asymmetric cryptography (Schneier, 1996), where a private key encodes the message and a corresponding public key decodes it. The private key must be kept confidential within the organization that is responsible for the digital signature, while the public key may be issued to message readers. Both the private and the public key are associated with a certificate issued by a legally authorized entity. Access and use of the certificate is done securely.

For computational performance reasons, a Message Authentication Code (MAC) is signed instead of the entire message (in this case is a picture, which may have considerable size). A MAC is the output of a *digest function* which, given two distinct inputs, produces significantly smaller outputs that are almost certainly distinct as well (the probability of having the same output for different inputs is vanishingly small). Thus, the MAC is digitally signed and the resulting signature is placed in the JPEG file header, together with additional information such as the vehicle class, the recognized license plate number and a timestamp. If the picture is altered in any way, the change can be detected by recomputing the MAC and confronting it with the one present in the file header, after decoding the later with the public key. This operation can be performed by a validation application.

This security collaborative framework is compatible with the requirements expressed in Portuguese and European law, respectively Decreto-Lei 62/2003 and Directive 1999/93/CE, for electronic signatures. Certifying organizations are also members of the established collaborative network and are regulated by the

Portuguese Instituto das Tecnologias de Informação na Justiça, according to Decreto-Lei 234/2000.

5. CONCLUSIONS

The establishment of a collaborative network based on certification of electronic documents is still in a preliminary stage, the relevant legislation having been produced in 2003. Within this legal collaborative framework, a certification system has been developed for enforcement in motorway electronic toll collection, based on the ALPR system and a digital signature scheme.

Organizational as well as technical issues have been taken into account when developing the overall security collaborative framework. This certification is intended to contribute to the success of the toll enforcement system, by establishing trust between the partners involved in this collaborative network. Although complete invulnerability to attack can never be guaranteed, the presently afforded degree of protection is considered adequate in face of the types of attack that are foreseeable in the near future.

A direction for further development is the establishment of procedures for managing the issuing, validation and revoking of certificates, which should be agreed upon between the network members.

6. ACKNOWLEDGMENTS

This work was partially supported by BRISA group, through the research and development ITSIBus-Vision project. The research groups M2A and GIATSI from ISEL-DEETC in collaboration with DIT, the Innovation and Technology Department of BRISA, are developing the work. We also acknowledge the valuable contributions from Joaquim Pereira, Rui Gonçalves and Rui Lopes.

6. REFERENCES

(Camarinha-Matos, 2004) - Camarinha-Matos, L. M.; Afsarmanesh, H.; Supporting Infrastructures for New Collaborative Forms, in Collaborative Networked Organizations, pg. 175-192, Kluwer Academic Publishers 2004.

Coulouris, G., Dollimore, J.; Kindberg T. - Distributed Systems - Concepts and Design, 3rd edition, Addison-Wesley, 2001.

Duc Duan, T., Hong Du, T., Vinh Phuoc, T., Viet Hoang, N. - Building an Automatic Vehicle License-Plate Recognition System, Int. Conf. in Computer Science, RIVF'05, Vietnam, February 2005.

Gomes J. Sales, Jacquet G., Machado M, Osório A. Luís, Gonçalves C., Barata M. - An Open Integration Bus for EFC: The ITS IBus, in ASECAP2003, 18 - 21 May 2003 in Portoroz, Slovenia

Macgregor R. S., Aresi, A., Siegert A., WWW.Security, How to Build a Secure World Wide Web Connection, IBM, Prentice Hall PTR, 1996.

Osório A. L., Abrantes A. J., Gonçalves J. C., Araújo A.; Miguel J. M., Jacquet, G. C.; Gomes, J. S. - Flexible and Plugged Peer Systems Integration to ITS-IBUS: the case of EFC and LPR Systems, PROVE'03 – 4th IFIP Working Conference on Virtual Enterprises, published by Kluwer Academic Publishers, ISBN: 1-4020-7638-X, pages 221-230, 2003-b.

Osório, A. Luís; Osório; L., Barata, M.; Gonçalves, C.; Araújo, P.; Abrantes, A.; Jorge, P.; Gomes, J. Sales; Jacquet G.; Amador, A. - Interoperability among ITS Systems with ITS-IBus framework, BASYS 2004, Vienna, Austria 27-29 September 2004.

Rahman, A., Radmanesh, A. - A Real Time Vehicle's License Plate Recognition, Proceedings of the IEEE on Advanced Video and Signal Based Surveillance, 2003

Schneier B. - Applied Cryptography, 2nd Edition, John Wiley & Sons, 1996

e-HEALTH AND CARE SERVICE INTEGRATION: THE DEMOGRAPHIC CHALLENGE

Bryan.R.M. Manning and Mary.McKeon Stosuy

Centre for Business Information, Organisation, and Process Management, Westminster Business School, University of Westminster, UK

Bryan.Manning@btinternet.com
Mary.McKeon@doh.state.nj.us

The imbalance between demand and available resources, based on the forecast doubling of over 65s to about 40% of the populations of many nations will force radical changes in health and social care service delivery in the coming decades.

The creation of "Virtual Care Service Utilities" to coordinate and optimize use of scarce resources coupled with the extensive use of assistive technology systems is examined. The potential benefits are reviewed and weighed against the inherent loss of privacy involved, together with the trust building and change management implications of such a major rationalisation process.

1. INTRODUCTION – THE DEMOGRAPHIC IMPERATIVE

Governments across much of the developed world are faced with having to respond to growing impacts of an ageing population as forecasts all show a steep rise in the percentage of the population who are older than 65 years doubling to close to 40% by the middle of the century.

Even from these crude estimates it is evident that current models of care are wholly unsustainable on human resource grounds alone, since lowering birthrates will tend to reduce the available numbers of professionals, whilst demand for their services soar. Moreover expectations of evermore sophisticated, live-span extending treatments have taken hold and will undoubtedly increase this pressure for political action from the swelling numbers of voters concerned.

Whilst the most obvious response will of necessity be to try to get more out of the available system, there is an increased recognition that the traditional model based on multiple service providers operating mainly in informal collaboration with each other is hardly efficient. As a result the quality of care is far from optimal and all too easily results in repetitive and often unnecessary returns back into the care cycle, further increasing demand.

2. LOCUS OF CARE

This issue exemplifies the interlocking nature of effective care delivery, outlined in Figure 1, which the traditional 'silo' organisational approach to service provision misses. Over the past few years this interlinking dependency between medical and social care has begun to be recognised and responded to.

Please use the following format when citing this chapter:

Manning, B. R. M., Stosuy, M. M., 2006, in IFIP International Federation for Information Processing, Volume 224, Network-Centric Collaboration and Supporting Fireworks, eds. Camarinha-Matos, L., Afsarmanesh, H., Ollus, M., (Boston: Springer), pp. 643–650.

Figure.1 - Components in the Locus of Care

However the further dependencies on adequacy of housing in terms of cost, warmth, hygiene and security, together with that of personal logistics needed to obtain food and other basics necessities of life remain largely ignored and disconnected.

Similarly personal finance can be added to this list of disconnects, especially for the elderly who are frequently capital rich – through home ownership, yet revenue poor for many reasons, including lack of understanding of available benefits.

Finally whilst access to useful information across this spectrum of need is increasing, and its content of considerable potential use, its quality and coverage can be highly variable. Although Information and Communications Technology [ICT] has provided the enabling mechanism for all this, its ubiquitous nature has also logically expanded its boundaries to incorporate a wide range of diversified sensor based systems that are steadily becoming an unnoticed element in daily life.

Now recognized as Pervasive Computing, this plays a key role in the development of evermore sophisticated Assistive Technology designed to support the elderly at home.

3. OPTIONS FOR CHANGE

Whilst some further improvement can undoubtedly be wrung out of the existing multi-agency approach, the very scale of the problem indicates that a more radical solution will be required. In the circumstances the only really available option will be to restructure services by removing these boundaries and barriers and optimizing complete end-to-end care delivery processes within a 'virtual service utility'.

Although this has the potential to deliver considerable operational improvement, it is unlikely that this alone will stem the effect of spiraling demand and a diminishing resource pool. The best option to combat this will be to compensate for excessive workload imbalances by substituting Assistive Technology [AT] wherever practical and appropriate, as shown in Figure 2.

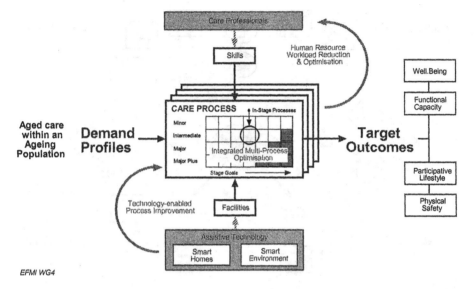

EFMI WG4

Figure 2 - Enabling Care Process Optimisation

Much of this can come from the deployment of systems to provide powerful proactive lifestyle support, as well as monitoring clinical conditions and behavioural patterns to identify and respond to any serious abnormal circumstances. These will preclude many an unnecessary home visit, whilst safeguarding and reassuring the individuals concerned that they have continuous cover with care readily at hand when needed.

This approach takes forward the concepts of the "Virtual Hospital" and combines them with a similar approach to providing more effective "Care in the Community". By providing a combination of medical and personal welfare monitoring through a "Care Watch" service, the level of care support will be similar to that available in a hospital high dependency unit. The obvious difference is that the response will need to be provided by existing paramedic services, extended to include additional "parawelfare" capabilities.

Its overall aim is to enable those suffering from increasing levels of impairment to continue to maintain an independent and participative lifestyle in the community for as long as possible.

4. OPTIONS FOR CHANGE

Whilst many ways to restructure and rationalize services will undoubtedly emerge to form an integrated service, the more likely model is that of a 'virtual service utility' rather than that of a monolithic entity. For optimum effectiveness it is likely to need to focus on fairly localized service provision to support communities rather than purely administrative convenience. However in the interests of good governance this will need to be set within an appropriate legislative and regulatory framework set to ensure maintenance of high quality services and standards, shown in Figure 3.

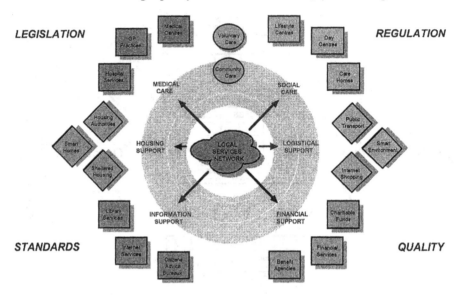

Figure 3 - Care Service Utility Elements

In essence the 'virtual service utility' will bring together the main strands identified within the locus of care and extend them out into the many individual units and specialist providers that deliver services across the complete spectrum of need. This will allow reconfiguration of local teams to maximum effect whilst still maintaining flexibility and relative autonomy.

The key to this will be the preparedness for all concerned to coordinate their efforts through one or more 'care watch' centers, which will be responsible for initiating appropriate responses to need of all types within the communities they serve. ·

5. e-CARE AND ASSISTED LIFESTYLES

The role of e-Care within the 'virtual service utility' is to combine coordination of human resources with those of semi or fully autonomous Assistive Technology [AT] systems to enable users to maintain their independence. As these AT systems can include physiological and behavioural monitoring they can be set to detect abnormal patterns and initiate appropriate care service responses.

All care cycles commence with a formal Assessment of Need. This is used to set up a Care Plan for planned and emergency professional support interventions. In this scenario this would also include Support System planning for the deployment of AT, as shown in Figure 4.

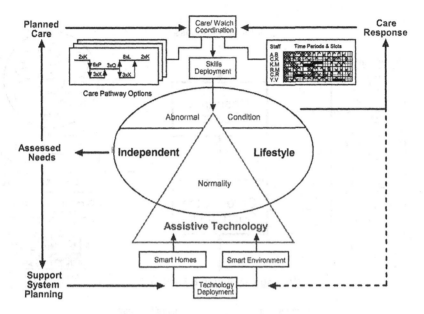

Figure 4 - Integrated e-Care Model Paradigm

Whilst professional care practice would broadly remain the same, the aim would be to use shared Integrated Care Pathway planning to eliminate the current wasteful tendency not to recognise key interdependencies between disciplines and/or agencies' procedures.

Service coordination and operational back-up would be provided via a shared Care Watch centre, which would be able to initiate action in response to any abnormal event/condition indications.

6. e-CARE WATCH COORDINATION

Although Care Watch coordination is essentially a back office function it can easily be combined with current "one-stop-shop" Resource Center practice as a single entity, since there is a considerable overlap in both functionality and skill requirements. Whilst the Resource Center approach is generally designed to cover matters across the complete locus of care service provision either through 'face-to-face' contact or by phone/e-mail, Care Watch extends the call centre component to include a monitoring and response function.

Rationalisation of multi-disciplinary multi-agency services into a "virtual utility service" operation does not require massive corporate restructuring, but does entail the merging of information resources within a mutually trusting environment. It also enables the pooling of administrative and management resources; the recognition of interdependencies between processes in the service supply chain and its resultant shortening; and more effective and appropriate deployment of resources, as shown in Figure 5.

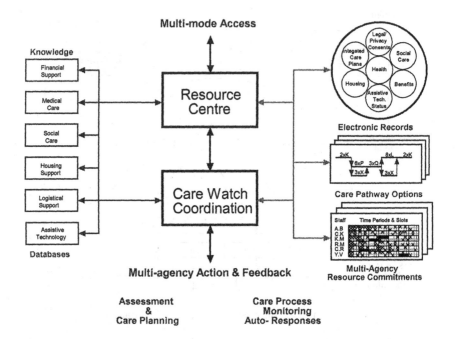

Figure 5 - An Integrated Care Service Model

Secure e-business information services within these 'hubs' would comprise shared:

- Multi-agency electronic client/patient records
- Multi-disciplinary Care Pathway Option maps
- Multi-agency, multi-disciplinary Resource Commitment schedules
- A library of knowledge databases spanning each of the elements of the overall the locus of care.
- A dedicated 24/7 manned Care Watch monitoring and response coordination unit

As currency and accuracy of information from all sources will be vital to ensuring that correct action is taken or right advice and guidance is given, the underlying information systems will need to be maintained and validated in real-time.

7. ASSISTIVE TECHNOLOGY

Assistive Technology has been evolving for several decades under a number of guises that have tended to be reserved for rehabilitation and disability. Indeed impairment and disability have long been somewhat of a clinical backwater and even an area that is almost alien to the rest of medicine. Disability thus sits uncomfortably between health and social care, impinging on both but set apart from each of them.

This apparent disadvantage has instead been turned to good effect through unfettered relationships across the whole range of professions involved with providing goods and services to the public. Considerable advances have been made in the development of the Smart Home and Smart Community concepts using sophisticated[5] wired and wireless communications and computing systems[5] in conjunction with innovative ergonomic product and built-environmental design

The Smart systems approach is based on an internet infrastructure communicating via an appropriate gateway either from individual devices or a local area network set within individual homes. These devices range in sophistication from alarms triggered by a range of safety and security condition monitoring sensors through to clinical vital signs monitoring arrays embedded with wearable vests.

With funding support from the European Commission COST 219 set of programmes, the Scandanavian and Benelux countries have led the way in proving these principles through a number of practical pilot projects spanning whole communities. These are not necessarily confined to features for the disabled but include improved ergonomic support for activities of daily living though a variety of interactive systems.

8. PRIVACY

Whilst there are undoubted benefits to be gained in terms of the independent, safe and secure lifestyle that Assistive Technology can help deliver, it carries with it disturbing overtones of unwarranted 'Big Brother' invasion of privacy. However despite these obvious and reasonable concerns, both a solution and a precedent already exist in medicine in terms of the Consent for Clinical Intervention procedures. These control the conditions and permissions under which medical staff are allowed to 'invade' their patients body to carry out investigative and therapeutic procedures.

In essence the same form control process could be applied to regulate invasion of the personal space and privacy of any individual.

As with all care decisions privacy rights like all others have to be weighed against the benefits that are likely to accrue, whilst protected against abuse by appropriate legal constraints. The ongoing concern of all parties engaged with the development and application of pervasive computing must be to build-in protection at all levels against unreasonable and unlawful misuse of unpredictable and largely invisible systems and their evolution.

9. CONCLUSIONS

The undoubted problems that the demographic challenge of the predicted growth in the numbers of elderly will present nations and their governments are already beginning to surface. However, whilst it has been argued here that technology has the potential to provide the means to deliver a solution, it is far from being the solution in itself.

Indeed this trap has been fallen into with monotonous regularity, particularly where Information Technology has been concerned. Sadly there have been innumerable, well documented failures, where high hopes and expectations have been dashed on the rocks of massive delays, cost overruns and fundamental failures to deliver systems that actually function effectively in the real world.

Unfortunately real tools, however well crafted, have to be used in an imperfect and ever changing human environment that has an infuriating tendency to reject what "ought" to be good or at least useful to, or for it. This is especially true where professions and professional judgement are central to service delivery and is particularly so in medicine.

In these circumstances it is vital to understand the nuances of the professional working cultures and work within them to help develop practical, pragmatic solutions to problems that regularly beset them and they would dearly like to have the time to solve. Framework models that map the gist of these problems in ways that these professionals can identify with and then help them find a solution that they own from the outset have proved far more likely to succeed, than force-feeding them a technically evaluated prescription for a complaint that they do not have.

9. REFERENCES

1. Acts of Parliament: The Human Rights Act 1998, Chapter 42, 1998
2. Benton S, Manning B.R.M. Assistive Technology – Behaviourally Assisted. Proceedings – 3rd International Council of Medical and Care Compunetics Conference. Den Haag, Netherlands. June 2006
3. Cameron J. The Information Society: Emerging Landscapes, Proceedings of the IFIP WG 9.2 Conference on Landscapes of ICT and Social Accountability. Turku, Finland, 27-29 June 2005. Springer Publishers, USA. 2005
4. Cas J. Privacy in Pervasive Computing Environments. IEEE Technology and Society Magazine Spring 2005. 24-33. 2005
5. Commission of the European Communities [COM(2001) 723 Final]: The future of healthcare and care for the elderly: guaranteeing accessibility, quality and financial viability. 5/12/2001
6. Commission of the European Communities [COM(2004) 356]: e-Health – making healthcare better for European citizens: An action plan for a European e-Health Area. 2004
7. Gill J. [Ed.]. Making Life Easier. COST 219. 2005.
8. Manning B.R.M, Stosuy M. McKeon, Layzell B.R, Madani K. e-Care: An Assistive Technology enabled Paradigm Shift. Proceedings – 4th International Conference On Smart Homes and Health
9. Office of the Deputy Prime Minister: A Sure Start to Later Life: Ending Inequalities for Older People - A Social Exclusion Unit Final Report. London, January 2006
10. Office of the Deputy Prime Minister: Inclusion Through Innovation Tackling Social Exclusion Through New Technologies - A Social Exclusion Unit Final Report
11. Roe P.R.W. (Ed.), Bridging the Gap? Access to telecommunciations for all people. Commission of European Communities. Presses Centrales Lausanne SA, November.2001
12. Parliamentary Office of Science and Technology. Inquiry Findings on Pervasive Computing, February 2006
13. Steg H, Strese H, Hull J, Schmidt S. Europe is facing a demographic challenge Ambient Assisted Living offers solutions, VDI/VDE/IT, September 2005
14. Stosuy G.A, Eaglin J.P. The Community Services Network: Creating an integrated Service Delivery Network – The Baltimore open systems laboratory model. New Technology in the Human Services Vol 12 1/2 87-98. NTHS 1999
15. Stosuy M.McKeon, Manning B.R.M. "Joining Up" e-Health & e-Care Services: Meeting the Demographic Challenge, Proceedings - 2nd International Council of Medical and Care Compunetics Conference. Den Haag, Netherlands. June 2005
16. Zetuny Y, Kecskemeti G, Terstyansky G, Madani K, "Service Management Architecture in ePerSpace", Eurescom Summit 2005, Heidelberg, 27/04/05.

AUTHOR INDEX